Achieve for *Modern Principles: Microeconomics*

Engaging Every Student. Supporting Every Instructor. Proven Success. Continued Enhancement.

Macmillan Learning's **Achieve for Economics** sets the standard for integrating **activities**, **assessments**, and **analytics** into your teaching. It brings together all of the features that instructors and students need—an e-book with interactive graphing, LearningCurve adaptive quizzing, and other instructional and application activities, assessments, and extensive instructor resources—in a powerful platform that offers:

- Deep platform integration with all LMS providers.
- Powerful assessment and adaptive quizzing.
- A fully integrated iClicker classroom response system.
- Exciting, enhanced, interactive graphing tools.

Our resources were **co-designed with instructors and students**, using a foundation of **learning research** and rigorous testing. The result is pedagogically superior content, organization, and functionality. Achieve's pre-built assignments engage students both *inside* and *outside* of class. And Achieve is effective for students of *all levels* of motivation and preparedness, whether they are high achievers or need extra support.

Macmillan Learning offers **deep platform integration** of Achieve with all LMS providers, including Blackboard, Brightspace, Canvas, and Moodle. With integration, students can access course content and their grades through one sign-in. And you can pair Achieve with course tools from your LMS, such as discussion boards and chat and Gradebook functionality. LMS integration is also available with Inclusive Access. For more information, visit MacmillanLearning.com/College/US/Solutions/LMS-Integration or talk to your local sales representative.

Achieve was built with **accessibility** in mind. Macmillan Learning strives to create products that are usable by all learners and meet universally applied accessibility standards. In addition to addressing product compatibility with assistive technologies such as screen reader software, alternative keyboard devices, and voice recognition products, we are working to ensure that the content and platforms we provide are fully accessible. For more information visit https://www.macmillanlearning.com/college/us/our-story/accessibility.

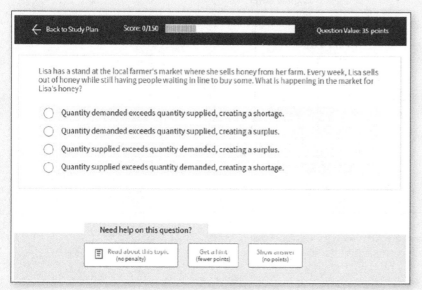

◀ **LearningCurve Adaptive Quizzing** With a game-like interface, this popular and effective quizzing engine offers students a low-stakes way to brush up on concepts and help identify knowledge gaps. Questions are linked to relevant e-book sections, providing both the incentive to read and a framework for an efficient reading experience.

▶ **Enhanced E-Book with Interactive Graphs and Integrated MRU Videos** The Achieve e-book offers highlighting, bookmarking, and note-taking. Students can download the e-book to read offline or to have it read aloud to them. Achieve allows instructors to assign chapter sections as homework.

The e-book also includes 112 embedded Marginal Revolution University (MRU) videos. Cowen and Tabarrok founded MRU as an extension of their world-renowned Marginal Revolution blog. MRU features perhaps some of the most extensive series of economics education videos available. They are deeply integrated into the text and pedagogy of *Modern Principles*, extending the authors' perspectives into the online learning space.

▼ The Achieve e-book now features interactive graphs. Students can now engage with economic models to see how components of the graph change as market dynamics change. Nearly every data graph in the text is now interactive, so students can explore live visualizations and improve their data literacy.

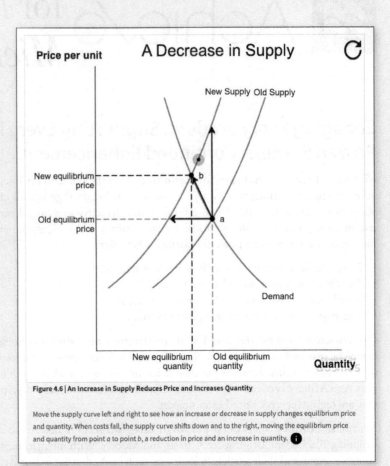

Figure 4.6 | An Increase in Supply Reduces Price and Increases Quantity

Move the supply curve left and right to see how an increase or decrease in supply changes equilibrium price and quantity. When costs fall, the supply curve shifts down and to the right, moving the equilibrium price and quantity from point *a* to point *b*, a reduction in price and an increase in quantity. ⓘ

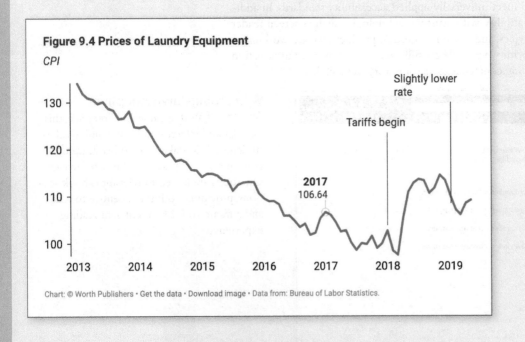

ACTIVITIES

▶ **MRU Video Activities** Short, fun, and engaging instructional videos are available for most chapters. Achieve provides assignable, automatically graded quizzes to accompany each MRU video.

◀ **Problem Video Walkthroughs** These skill-building activities pair sample end-of-chapter problems with targeted feedback and video explanations to help students solve problems step-by-step. This approach allows students to work independently, tests their comprehension of concepts, and prepares them for class and exams.

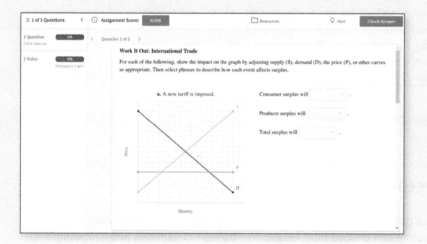

ASSESSMENTS

▶ **End-of-Chapter Questions** Developed by economists active in the classroom, these multistep problems are paired with rich feedback for incorrect and correct responses that guide students through the process of problem solving. These questions also feature our user-friendly graphing tool, designed so students focus entirely on economics and not on how to use the application.

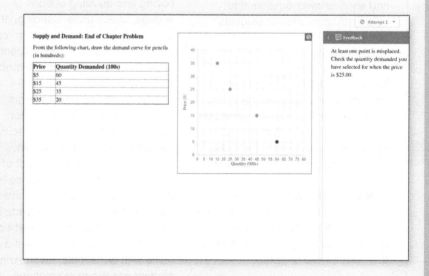

Homework Curated homework problems feature randomly sampled variables and our user-friendly graphing tool. These problems are multistep with a variety of answer inputs—each with detailed and targeted feedback specific to that answer.

Practice Quizzes Designed to be used as a study tool, these quizzes feature multiple-choice questions and allow for multiple attempts as students familiarize themselves with content.

ANALYTICS

▶ **Learning Objectives, Reports, and Insights** Every asset you can assign in Macmillan Learning's Achieve is tagged to specific Learning Objectives. Reporting within Achieve helps students see how they are performing against objectives, and it helps instructors determine if any student, group of students, or the class as a whole needs extra help in specific areas. This enables more efficient and effective instructor interventions.

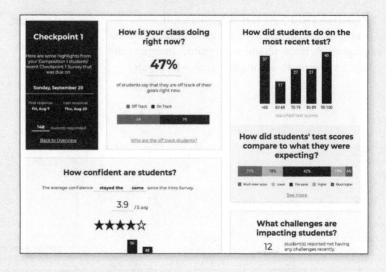

Achieve provides reports on student activities, assignments, and assessments at the course level, unit level, subunit level, and individual student level, so instructors can identify trouble spots and adjust their efforts accordingly. Within Reports, the Insights section offers snapshots with high-level data on student performance and behavior, to answer such questions as:

- What are the top Learning Objectives to review in this unit?
- What are the top assignments to review?
- What's the range of performance on a particular assignment?
- How many students aren't logging in?

Powerful Support for Instructors

Test Bank This comprehensive Test Bank contains multiple-choice and short-answer questions to help instructors assess students' comprehension, interpretation, and ability to synthesize.

Lecture Slides These brief, interactive, and visually interesting slides are designed to hold students' attention in class with graphics and animations demonstrating key concepts and real-world examples.

Clicker Slides These slides contain questions to incorporate active learning in the classroom. Students can participate by using the iClicker app on their smartphone or laptop.

iClicker Integration With Achieve's seamless integration with iClicker, you can help any student participate—in the classroom or virtually. iClicker's attendance feature gets students in class, then instructors can choose from flexible polling and quizzing options to engage, check understanding, and get feedback from students in real time. iClicker also allows students to participate using laptops, mobile devices, or iClicker remotes— whichever each student prefers. Additionally, we offer Instructor Activity Guides and book-specific iClicker question slides within Achieve to make the most out of your class time. It's no surprise that over a decade after being founded by educators, iClicker still leads the market. And thousands of instructors continue to give every student a voice with our simple, award-winning student engagement solutions.

Instructor's Resource Manual The Instructor's Resource Manual offers instructors teaching materials and tips to enhance the classroom experience, along with chapter objectives, outlines, and suggestions for further reading.

Gradebook Assignment scores are collected into a comprehensive Gradebook providing instructors reporting on individuals and overall course performance.

Customer Support Our Achieve Client Success Specialist Team—dedicated platform experts—provides collaboration, software expertise, and consulting to tailor each course to fit your instructional goals and student needs. Start with a demo at a time that works for you to learn more about how to set up your customized course. Talk to your sales representative or visit https://www.macmillanlearning.com/college/us/contact-us/training-and-demos for more information.

Powerful, Continued Input from the Faculty Advisory Board

We are delighted to partner with the following faculty members who provide us with feedback, insight, and ideas to continually improve Achieve for both students and instructors:

Annette Chamberlain, *Virginia Western Community College*

Christopher Clarke, *Washington State University*

Sherry Jensen, *Salt Lake Community College*

Erika Martinez, *University of South Florida*

Susan McCoy, *Des Moines Area Community College*

Eric Parsons, *University of Missouri*

Aisling Winston, *University of Buffalo*

Pricing and bundling options are available at the Macmillan student store: store.macmillanlearning.com/

WHAT'S NEW IN THE SIXTH EDITION?

Most instructors and students use Macmillan Learning's Achieve online courseware with *Modern Principles*. Thus, the new edition offers significant improvements to Achieve. New digital assets in every chapter include the following:

- New to the front matter, **Learning Economics from AI!** guides students on how to use resources such as ChatGPT or Bing Chat to get meaningful answers to economics questions. Fun fact: The cover for this edition was generated by author Alex Tabarrok's use of AI!
- **Interactive graphs.** To help students improve data literacy and understand economic models, Achieve now offers interactive graphs throughout the e-book. Students can manipulate graphs to simulate market dynamics and explore historical data, providing a more engaging reading and learning experience.
- **Updated end-of-chapter questions.**
- **More videos throughout the text!**

When it comes to new editions, the authors don't just add a box or two—they rewrite entire chapters with new examples and applications and cut older material to make way for the new.

The sixth edition also features new coverage and updates throughout:

- **Chapter 2** now highlights the economist Thomas Sowell, whose contributions to economics include how specialization and trade increase and deepen useful knowledge.
- **Chapter 3** includes a new video on demand curve shifts.
- **Chapter 5** includes a new figure on U.S. house prices.
- **Chapter 6** includes a new section, The Economics of Free Goods. This includes new figures on how the quantity of kidneys supplied makes it illegal to compensate donors and how subsidy drives the price down to zero to generate a deadweight loss.

- **Chapter 7** includes a new video on prediction markets.
- **Chapter 8** now includes an example of the reduction in product quality by exploring the impact of fixed rents in Mumbai, India. A new video on rent control in Mumbai now accompanies this new subsection.
- **Chapter 10** includes a new section on COVID-19 and the external benefits of vaccinations. This also includes a new video on the economics of COVID-19. A new section explores how the COVID-19 pandemic affects command and control. Another new section highlights

how economists study the impact of air pollution on health and wealth.

- **Chapter 11** includes a new example with photos of Dalton Carpet Factory, Hollywood, and Aalsmeer flower market to demonstrate economies of agglomeration.
- **Chapter 14** includes a new section on quality discrimination or versioning that uses FedEx deliveries as an example.
- **Chapter 19** includes new examples throughout, from cable TV to video streaming services. There is a new photo to support an example of planetary defense against asteroids.

- **Chapter 20** includes new videos on public choice, rational ignorance, concentrated benefits and dispersed costs, and short-sightedness in government.
- **Chapter 23** has updated coverage in Bubble, Bubble, Toil, and Trouble, which features apps that have made trading cheaper.
- **Chapter 24** includes an updated chapter opener. There is now updated information related to the Affordable Care Act (ACA).

LEARNING ECONOMICS FROM AI!

AI generated the cover for this edition, illustrating one of the many creative ways to use AI.

Another great resource to learn economics is from artificial intelligence (AI), such as ChatGPT, Bing Chat, or Claude. AIs can give you more information about a topic. For example, we asked ChatGPT-4:

"A price is a signal wrapped up in an incentive." Can you explain more?

And it responded:

Yes, Cowen and Tabarrok's statement "a price is a signal wrapped up in an incentive" suggests that prices in a market economy serve two primary functions simultaneously: they convey information about the relative scarcity of goods or services, and they also incentivize individuals to behave in certain ways.

To understand this idea better, let's break it down into two parts:

1. Prices as Signals: In a market economy, prices convey important information about the relative scarcity of goods or services. Higher prices typically indicate that the good or service is relatively scarce, while lower prices suggest that it is more abundant. This information helps guide producers and consumers in making decisions about what to produce, how much to produce, and what to consume.

2. Prices as Incentives: At the same time, prices also provide incentives for individuals to behave in certain ways. For example, if the price of a particular good is high, producers are incentivized to produce more of that good, while consumers are incentivized to purchase less of it. Conversely, if the price of a good is low, producers may be incentivized to produce less of it, while consumers may be incentivized to purchase more.

Taken together, prices serve as a kind of "language" of the market, communicating information about relative scarcity and incentivizing behaviors that help to allocate resources efficiently. Cowen and Tabarrok's statement captures this dual role of prices in market economies.

That's a great answer! You can ask ChatGPT about economic ideas, and it can often give you examples or present the material in ways different than your textbook. Ask ChatGPT what the elasticity of demand is, and it will give you a good answer, albeit one very similar to the answer you can find in this textbook. So try something different:

I forget the formula for the elasticity of demand. Write a limerick to help me remember it.

ChatGPT responded:

When price change makes you wonder,

And quantity changes asunder,

Just remember this little rhyme,

And calculate the elasticity in no time!

Elasticity of Demand is the key,

To measure how much quantity will flee,

It's % change in demand, over % change in price,

And you'll always remember it, that's rather nice!

Not bad! Here's a few tips to help you make the most of chatting with an AI.

Ask for answers in the voice of various experts. For example, if you are interested in the causes of inflation, don't just ask "What are the causes of inflation?" Instead ask:

What are the causes of inflation as it might be explained by Nobel Laureate Milton Friedman?

In essence, by mentioning Friedman, you are directing ChatGPT to look at a more intelligent segment of the potential answer space.

But don't stop there. **Ask what other experts think.** You will learn more, for example, by asking:

> Compare and contrast the views of Milton Friedman and Paul Samuelson on the causes of inflation.

Ask an AI to summarize doctrines. It's great at generating new ideas and hypotheses. Maybe you have to write a paper. Ask an AI for some ideas! For example, we asked Claude 1:

> Generate three ideas for how urban planning can be improved by the use of economic incentives.

And Claude responded:

> Here are three ideas for using economic incentives to improve urban planning:
>
> Congestion pricing: Charge fees for driving in city centers or on busy roads during rush hour. This discourages unnecessary driving and reduces traffic congestion while raising money to invest in public transit.
>
> Land value taxation: Tax the value of land itself rather than improvements on the land. This incentivizes efficient use of land and discourages vacant lots or underutilization. The tax revenue can be used to fund city services and infrastructure.
>
> Density bonuses: Provide developers with increased density allowances or other bonuses if they include public benefits like affordable housing, parks, or transit infrastructure. This incentivizes developers to address social goals and can help cities add amenities at a lower cost.

Three good ideas!

Of course, we emphasize that AIs are a tool that should be used to improve and deepen your ideas and research. Finally, beware! AIs might not always give you perfectly accurate answers on data, numbers, quotes, and references. It's better to ask an AI where to find data on inflation, for example, than to ask it what the inflation rate was in Germany in 1974. AI is still improving in this regard, but always do check their work.

One final tip, you can read more from us:

Marginal Revolution: http://www.marginalrevolution.com. Your textbook authors write this blog. It is quirkier and more opinionated than this book and more focused on current affairs, but nonetheless it offers economic content every day. Our "blogroll," on the left-hand side of the blog, offers links to other important economics blogs.

 And follow us on Twitter at @tylercowen and @ATabarrok.

ABOUT THE AUTHORS

ALEX TABARROK

Tyler Cowen (left, in North Korea) is Holbert C. Harris Professor of Economics at George Mason University. His latest book is *Big Business*. With Alex Tabarrok, he writes an economics blog at MarginalRevolution.com. He has published in the *American Economic Review, Journal of Political Economy,* and many other economics journals. He also writes regularly for the popular press, including the *New York Times,* the *Washington Post, Forbes,* the *Wilson Quarterly, Money Magazine,* and many other outlets.

Alex Tabarrok (right, in South Korea) is Bartley J. Madden Chair in Economics at the Mercatus Center at George Mason University. His latest book is *Launching the Innovation Renaissance.* His research looks at bounty hunters, judicial incentives and elections, crime control, patent reform, methods to increase the supply of human organs for transplant, and the regulation of pharmaceuticals. He was an advisor to the U.S. government on using incentives to speed up the production of vaccines. He is the editor of the books *Entrepreneurial Economics: Bright Ideas from the Dismal Science* and *The Voluntary City: Choice, Community, and Civil Society,* among others. His papers have appeared in *Science,* the *Journal of Law and Economics, Public Choice, Economic Inquiry,* the *Journal of Health Economics,* the *Journal of Theoretical Politics,* the *American Law and Economics Review,* and many others. Popular articles have appeared in the *New York Times,* the *Wall Street Journal, Forbes,* and many other magazines and newspapers.

PREFACE: TO THE INSTRUCTOR

> The prisoners were dying of scurvy, typhoid fever, and smallpox, but nothing was killing them more than bad incentives.

That is the opening from Chapter 1 of *Modern Principles*, and only an economist could write such a sentence. Only an economist could see that incentives are operating just about everywhere, shaping every aspect of our lives, whether it be how good a job you get, how much wealth an economy produces, and, yes, how a jail is run and how well the prisoners are treated. We are excited about this universal and powerful applicability of economics, and we have written this book to get you excited too.

In the first five editions, we wanted to accomplish several things. We wanted to show the power of economics for understanding our world. We wanted to create a book full of vivid writing and powerful stories. We wanted to present modern economics, not the musty doctrines or repetitive examples of a generation ago. We wanted to show—again and again—that incentives matter, whether discussing the tragedy of the commons, political economy, or what economics has to say about wise investing. Most generally, we wanted to make the invisible hand visible, namely to show that there is a hidden order behind the world that can be illuminated by economics.

Guiding Principles and Innovations: In a Nutshell

Modern Principles offers the following features and benefits:

1. We teach the economic way of thinking.

2. Less is more. This is a textbook of *principles*, not a survey or an encyclopedia. We use fewer yet more consistent and more comprehensive models.

3. No tools without applications. Real-world vivid applications are used to develop theory. Applications are not pushed aside into distracting boxes that students do not read.

4. Today's students live in a globalized economy. Events in China, India, Europe, and the Middle East affect their lives. *Modern Principles* features international examples and applications throughout, rather than just segregating all of the international topics in a single chapter.

5. *Modern Principles* has a more intuitive development of markets and their interconnectedness than does any other textbook. More than any other textbook, we teach students how the *price system* works.

6. *Modern Principles* helps students to see the invisible hand. We offer an intuitive proof of several "invisible hand theorems." See, for example, the unique material in Chapter 12 on competition and the invisible hand.

7. We offer an entire chapter (Chapter 22) on incentives and how they apply to business decisions, sports, and incentive design. When, for instance, should you reward your employees with a tournament form of compensation, and when a straight salary?

8. We offer an entire chapter (Chapter 23) on the stock market, a topic of concern to many students. We teach the basic trade-off between risk and return and explain why it is a good idea to diversify investments. We also explain the microeconomics of bubbles.

9. We cover network goods and platform markets like Uber, eBay, and OkCupid in Chapter 16.

Make the Invisible Hand Visible

One of the most remarkable discoveries of economic science is that under the right conditions the pursuit of self-interest can promote the social good. Nobel laureate Vernon Smith put it this way:

> At the heart of economics is a scientific mystery . . . a scientific mystery as deep, fundamental and inspiring as that of the expanding universe or the forces that bind matter. . . . How is order produced from freedom of choice?

We want students to be inspired by this mystery and by how economists have begun to solve it. Thus, we will explain how markets generate cooperation from people across the world, how prices act as signals and coordinate appropriate responses to changes in economic conditions, and how profit maximization leads to the minimization of industry costs (even though no one intends such an end).

Alternative Paths Through the Book

Modern Principles has been written with trade-offs in mind and it's easy to pick and choose from among the chapters when time constrains. We offer a few quick suggestions. Chapter 7 is fun to teach but more difficult to test than some of the other chapters. But don't worry, you will find plenty of testable material in other chapters, and for your best students the introduction to the price system in Chapters 7 and 8 will be an eye-opener!

We spend more time on price controls than do other books because we don't confine ourselves to the usual shortage diagram. We illustrate the general equilibrium effects of price controls. We have also included a section of advanced material on the losses from random allocation that may be skipped in larger classes or if time constrains.

We have greatly simplified the presentation on cost curves and removed most of production theory, so do take the time to cover monopoly and the chapter on price discrimination. Students love the material on price discrimination because once they understand the concepts, they see the applications all around them. Chapter 16, Networks, Platforms, and the Economics of "Free Goods," is a very appealing chapter for students, and we recommend it for its applications, but if you don't have time, it can be skipped.

Asteroid deflection and the decline of the tuna fisheries are a must, so do cover Chapter 19 on public goods and the tragedy of the commons. Once again, students appreciate the focus on important, real-world applications of the economic way of thinking.

Chapters 20 and 21 on political economy and ethics are optional. If you can teach only one chapter, we think Chapter 20 on political economy has crucial material for avoiding the nirvana fallacy: We should always compare real-world markets with real-world governments when doing political economy. Chapter 21 on ethics works very well in smaller classes with lots of student interaction—we think it important that the philosophy professors are not the ones who get the only say on questions of ethics!

Chapter 22, Managing Incentives, is fun to teach but it goes beyond the core and can be skipped. We believe this chapter will be especially appropriate for management, MBA, and prelaw students.

We encourage everyone to teach Chapter 23 on stock markets, time permitting.

Chapter 25, Consumer Choice, is for those instructors who wish to cover indifference curves in considerable detail.

Most of all, we hope that *Modern Principles* helps you, the teacher, to have fun! We love economics and we have fun teaching economics. We have written this text for people not afraid to say the same. Don't hesitate to e-mail us with your questions, thoughts, and experiences, or just to say hello!

ACKNOWLEDGMENTS

We are most grateful to the following reviewers, both users and nonusers, for their careful chapter reviews used in the development of the sixth edition of *Modern Principles*.

Mishal Ahmed
Western Michigan University

Rania Al-Bawwab
Middle Tennessee State University

Basil Al-Hashimi
Mesa Community College–Red Mountain Campus

William Baca Mejia
St. Charles Community College

Carter Braxton
University of Wisconsin Colleges

Jennifer Elias-Sobotka
Radford University

Jose Fernandez
University of Louisville

Gerald Fox
High Point University

Mark Gibson
Washington State University

Jeff Glover
Pitt Community College

Zachary Gochenour
James Madison University

Joseph Guider
Caldwell University

Jihan Hamzany
Lindenwood University

William Hankins
Jacksonville State University

Rolf Hemmerling
Embry-Riddle Aeronautical University

Rebecca Johannsen
Pasadena City College

Marilyn Markel
Illinois College

Damian Park
Santa Clara University

Brian Rosario
California State University Sacramento

Amanda Ross
University of Alabama

Eric Taylor
Central Piedmont Community College

Meg Tuszynski
Southern Methodist University

Madeline Zavodny
University of North Florida

We thank Eric Parsons for many excellent suggestions and pointing out where we could update facts in light of new events. We also want to thank Joe Nowakowski for his eagle eyes checking proofs of the text during the production process. The Mercatus Center supplied an essential work environment. Teresa Hartnett has done a great job as our agent.

Most of all we are grateful to the team at Worth. Paul Shensa and Bruce Kaplan were critical contributors to earlier editions, and Lukia Kliossis has brought fresh eyes to the project and has pushed us to keep improving and innovating. Marita Bley kept us on track in revisions and pushed us where we needed pushing! We are thrilled by the amazing interactive graphs that Joshua Hill and Kristyn Brown have created for the new edition. Thanks as well to the dynamic Carolyn Merrill, whose energy and ideas have been an inspiration!

We are fortunate to have had such a talented production and design group for our book. Ryan Sullivan managed the entire production process and patiently helped us! Natasha Wolfe and John Callahan managed the creation of the beautiful interior design and the cover. Robin Fadool went beyond the call of duty in tracking down sometimes obscure photos. It has been a delight to work with all of them.

Scott Guile stands out in the marketing of this book. He has been energetic and relentless.

Most of all, we want to thank our families for their support and understanding. Tyler wishes to offer his personal thanks to Natasha and Yana. It is Alex's great fortune to be able to thank Monique, Connor, and Maxwell and his parents for years of support and encouragement.

Tyler Cowen
Alex Tabarrok

BRIEF CONTENTS

CONTENTS

VIDEOS IN *Modern Principles: Microeconomics*

1

The Big Ideas

The prisoners were dying of scurvy, typhoid fever, and smallpox, but nothing was killing them more than bad incentives. In 1787, the British government had hired sea captains to ship convicted felons to Australia. Conditions on board the ships were monstrous; some even said the conditions were worse than on slave ships. On one voyage, more than one-third of the men died, and the rest arrived beaten, starved, and sick. A first mate remarked cruelly of the convicts, "Let them die and be damned, the owners have [already] been paid for their passage."[1]

The British public had no love for the convicts, but it wasn't prepared to give them a death sentence either. Newspapers editorialized in favor of better conditions; clergy appealed to the captains' sense of humanity; and legislators passed regulations requiring better food and water, light and air, and proper medical care. Yet the death rate remained shockingly high. Nothing appeared to be working until an economist suggested something new. Can you guess what the economist suggested?

Instead of paying the captains for each prisoner placed on board the ship in Great Britain, the economist suggested paying for each prisoner that walked off the ship in Australia. In 1793, the new system was implemented and immediately the survival rate shot up to 99%. One astute observer explained what had happened: "Economy beat sentiment and benevolence."[2]

The story of the convict ships illustrates the first big lesson that runs throughout this book and throughout economics: *incentives matter.*

By **incentives**, we mean rewards and penalties that motivate behavior. Let's take a closer look at incentives and some of the other big ideas in economics. On first reading, some of these ideas may seem surprising or difficult to understand. Don't worry: We will be explaining everything in more detail.

We see the following list as the most important and fundamental contributions of economics to human understanding; we call these contributions *Big Ideas.* Some economists might arrange this list in a different manner or order, but these are generally accepted principles among good economists everywhere.

Incentives are rewards and penalties that motivate behavior.

1

mru.org/intro-econ

Meet Your Authors

Big Idea One: Incentives Matter

When the captains were paid for every prisoner who they took on board, they had little incentive to treat the prisoners well. In fact, the incentives were to treat the prisoners badly. Instead of feeding the prisoners, for example, some of the captains hoarded the prisoners' food, selling it in Australia for a tidy profit.

When the captains were paid for prisoners who survived the journey, however, their incentives changed. Whereas before the captains had benefited from a prisoner's death, now the incentive system "secured to every poor man who died at least one sincere mourner."[3] The sincere mourner? The captain, who was at least sincere about mourning the money he would have earned had the poor man survived.

Incentives are everywhere. In the United States, we take it for granted that when we go to the supermarket, the shelves will be stocked with kiwi fruit from New Zealand, rice from India, and wine from Chile. Every day we rely on the work of millions of other people to provide us with food, clothing, and shelter. Why do so many people work for our benefit? In his 1776 classic, *The Wealth of Nations*, Adam Smith explained:

> It is not from the benevolence of the butcher, the brewer, or the baker, that we expect our dinner, but from their regard to their own interest.

Do economists think that everyone is self-interested all the time? Of course not. We love our spouses and children just like everyone else! But economists do think that people respond in predictable ways to incentives of all kinds. Fame, power, reputation, sex, and love are all important incentives. Economists even think that benevolence responds to incentives. It's not surprising to an economist, for example, that charities publicize the names of their donors. Some people do give anonymously, but how many buildings on your campus are named Anonymous Hall?

Big Idea Two: Good Institutions Align Self-Interest with the Social Interest

The story of the convict ships hints at a second lesson that runs throughout this book: When self-interest aligns with the broader public interest, we get good outcomes, but when self-interest and the social interest are at odds, we get bad outcomes, sometimes even cruel and inhumane outcomes. Paying the ship captains for every prisoner who walked off the ship was a good payment system because it created incentives for the ship captains to do the right thing, not just for themselves but also for the prisoners and for the government that was paying them.

It's a remarkable finding of economics that under the right conditions markets align self-interest with the social interest. You can see what we mean by thinking back to the supermarket example. The supermarket is stocked with products from around the world because markets channel and coordinate the self-interest of millions of people to achieve a social good. The farmer who woke at 5 AM to tend crops, the trucker who delivered the goods to the market, the entrepreneur who risked their capital to build the supermarket—all of these people acted in their own interest, but in so doing, they also acted in your interest.

In a striking metaphor, Adam Smith said that when markets work well, those who pursue their own interest end up promoting the social interest, as if led to do so by an "invisible hand." The idea that the pursuit of self-interest can be in the social interest—that at least sometimes, "greed is good"—was one of the most surprising discoveries of economic science, and after several hundred years this insight is still not always appreciated. Throughout this book, we emphasize ways in which individuals acting in their self-interest produce outcomes that were not part of their intention or design, but that nevertheless have desirable properties.

Not from benevolence but from self-interest

Markets, however, do not always align self-interest with the social interest. Sometimes the invisible hand is absent, not just invisible. Market incentives, for example, can be too strong. A firm that doesn't pay for the pollution that it emits into the air has too great an incentive to emit pollution. Fishermen sometimes have too strong an incentive to catch fish, thereby driving the stock of fish into collapse. In other cases, market incentives are too weak. Did you get your flu shot this year? The flu shot prevents you from getting the flu (usually), but it also reduces the chances that other people will get the flu. When deciding whether to get a flu shot, did you take into account the social interest or just your self-interest?

When markets don't properly align self-interest with the social interest, another important lesson of economics is that government can sometimes improve the situation by changing incentives with taxes, subsidies, or other regulations.

Big Idea Three: Trade-offs Are Everywhere

Vioxx users were outraged when Merck withdrew the arthritis drug from the market after a study showed that it could cause strokes and heart attacks. Vioxx had been on the market for five years and had been used by millions of people. Patients were angry at Merck and at the Food and Drug Administration (FDA). How could the FDA, which is charged with ensuring that new pharmaceuticals are safe and effective, have let Vioxx onto the market? Many people demanded more testing and safer pharmaceuticals. Economists worried that approved pharmaceuticals could become too safe.

Too safe! Is it possible to be too safe?! Yes, because trade-offs are everywhere. Researching, developing, and testing a new drug cost time and resources. On average, it takes about 12 years and $1 billion to bring a new drug to market. More testing means that approved drugs will have fewer side effects, but there are two important trade-offs: *drug lag* and *drug loss*.

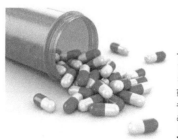

Are pharmaceuticals too safe?

Testing takes time so more testing means that good drugs are delayed, just like bad drugs. On average, new drugs work better than old drugs. So the longer it takes to bring new drugs to market, the more people are harmed who could have benefited if the new drugs had been approved earlier.[4] You can die because an unsafe drug is approved—you can also die because a safe drug has *not yet* been approved. This is *drug lag*.

Testing not only takes time; it is costly. The greater the costs of testing, the fewer new drugs there will be. The costs of testing are a hurdle that each potential drug must leap if it is to be developed. Higher costs mean a higher hurdle, fewer new drugs, and fewer lives saved. You can die because an unsafe drug is approved—you can also die because a safe drug is *never* developed. This is *drug loss*.

Thus, society faces a trade-off. More testing means the drugs that are (eventually) approved will be safer but it also means more drug lag and drug loss. When thinking about FDA policy, we need to look at both sides of the trade-off if we are to choose wisely.

The inevitability of trade-offs is the consequence of a big fact about the world, **scarcity**. We face trade-offs because we don't have enough resources to satisfy all of our wants—more of this means less of that. The **great economic problem** is how to arrange our scarce resources to satisfy as many of our wants as possible. So how do we solve this problem? One goal of this textbook is to explain the role of markets and prices in solving the great economic problem.

Trade-offs are closely related to another important idea in economics, opportunity cost.

Opportunity Cost

Every choice involves something gained and something lost. The **opportunity cost** of a choice is the value of the opportunities lost. Consider the choice to attend college. What is the cost of attending college? At first, you might calculate the cost by adding together the price of tuition, books, and room and board—that might be $22,000 or more a year. But that's not the opportunity cost of attending college. What opportunities are you losing when you attend college?

The main opportunity lost when you attend college is (probably) the opportunity to have a full-time job. Most of you reading this book could easily get a job earning $40,000 a year or maybe more. If you spend four years in college, that's $160,000 that you are giving up to get an education. The opportunity cost of college is probably higher than you thought. Perhaps you ought to ask more questions in class to get your money's worth! (But go back to the list of items we totaled earlier—tuition, books, and room and board. One of these items should *not* count as part of the opportunity cost of college. Which one? Answer: Room and board is not a cost of college if you would have to pay for it whether you go to college or not.)

The concept of opportunity cost is important for two reasons. First, if you don't understand the opportunities you are losing when you make a choice, you won't recognize the real trade-offs that you face. Recognizing trade-offs is the first step in making wise choices. Second, most of the time people do respond to changes in opportunity costs—*even when money costs have not changed*—so if you want to understand behavior, you need to understand opportunity cost.

What would you predict, for example, would happen to college enrollment during a recession? The price of tuition, books, and room and board doesn't fall during a recession but the opportunity cost of attending college does fall. Why? During a recession, the unemployment rate increases so it's harder to get a high-paying job. That means you lose less by attending college when the unemployment rate is high. It makes sense, therefore, that college enrollment tends to increase when the unemployment rate

A resource is **scarce** when there isn't enough to satisfy all of our wants.

The **great economic problem** is how to arrange our scarce resources to satisfy as many of our wants as possible.

The **opportunity cost** of a choice is the value of the opportunities lost.

increases; in opportunity costs terms, it is cheaper to go to college when jobs are hard to find.

Big Idea Four: Think on the Margin

Robert is cruising down Interstate 80 toward Des Moines, Iowa. Robert wants to get to his destination quickly and safely and he doesn't want to get a speeding ticket. The speed limit is 70 mph but he figures the risk of a ticket is low if he travels just a little bit faster, so Robert sets the cruise control to 72 mph. The road is straight and flat, and after 20 minutes he hasn't seen another car, so he thumbs it up a few clicks to 75. As he approaches Des Moines, Robert spots a police cruiser and thumbs it down to 70. After Des Moines it's nothing but quiet cornfields once again, so he thumbs it up to 72. Crossing the state line into Nebraska, Robert notices that the speed limit is 75, so he thumbs it up to 77 before thumbing it down again as he approaches Omaha.

Thinking on the margin A little bit faster? Or a little bit slower?

Robert and his thumb illustrate what economists mean by thinking on the margin. As Robert drives, he constantly weighs benefits and costs and makes a decision: a little bit faster or a little bit slower?

Thinking on the margin is just making choices by thinking in terms of marginal benefits and marginal costs, the benefits and costs of a little bit more (or a little bit less). Most of our decisions in life involve a little bit more of something or a little bit less, and it turns out that thinking on the margin is also useful for understanding how consumers and producers make decisions. Should the consumer buy a few more apples or a few less? Should the oil well produce a few more barrels of oil or a few less?

In this book, you will find lots of talk about marginal choices, including marginal cost (the additional cost from producing a little bit more), marginal revenue (the additional revenue from producing a little bit more), and marginal tax rates (the tax rate on an additional dollar of income). This point about margins is really just a way of restating the importance of trade-offs. If you wish to understand human behavior, look at the trade-offs that people face. Those trade-offs usually involve choices about a little bit more or a little bit less.

The importance of thinking on the margin did not become commonplace in economics until 1871, when marginal thinking was simultaneously described by three economists: William Stanley Jevons, Carl Menger, and Leon Walras. Economists refer to the "marginal revolution" to explain this transformation in economic thought. Marginal Revolution is also the name of a good blog you might want to check out!

Big Idea Five: Trade Makes People Better Off

When Alex and Shruti trade, both of them are made better off. (Alex does regret buying a certain polka-dot sweater, so take this as a general principle, not a mathematical certainty.) The principle is simple but important because exchange makes Alex and Shruti better off whether Alex and Shruti live in the same country and share the same language and religion or they live worlds apart geographically and culturally. The benefits of trade, however, go beyond those of exchange. The real power of trade is the power to increase production through specialization.

Few of us could survive if we had to produce our own food, clothing, and shelter (let alone our own cell phones and jet aircraft). Self-sufficiency is death. We survive and prosper only because specialization increases productivity. With specialization, the auto mechanic learns more about cars and the thoracic surgeon learns more about hearts than either could if each one of them needed to repair both cars and hearts. Through the division of knowledge, the sum total of knowledge increases and in this way so does productivity.

Trade also allows us to take advantage of economies of scale, the reduction in costs created when goods are mass-produced. No farmer could ever afford a combine harvester if he was growing wheat only for himself, but when a farmer grows wheat for thousands, a combine harvester reduces the cost of bread for all.

Martha Stewart may be the world's best ironer but she once sheepishly admitted that she doesn't always do her own ironing. Why not? The reason is that especially productive people can't do everything! Martha Stewart may be able to iron a blouse better than anyone else in the world, but she still hires people to do her ironing because for her an hour of ironing comes at the price of an hour spent running her business. Given the choice of spending an hour ironing or running her business, Martha Stewart is better off running her business. In other words, Martha Stewart's *opportunity cost* of ironing is very high.

The theory of comparative advantage says that when people or nations specialize in goods in which they have a low opportunity cost, they can trade to mutual advantage. Thus, Martha Stewart can benefit by buying ironing services even from people who are not as good at ironing as she is. Notice that the better Martha Stewart gets at running her business, the greater her cost of ironing. So when Martha becomes more productive, this increases her demand to trade. In a similar way, the greater the productivity of American business in producing jet aircraft or designing high-technology devices, the greater will be our demand to trade for textiles or steel.

Big Idea Six: Wealth and Economic Growth Are Important

Every year, several hundred million people contract malaria. In mild cases, malaria causes fever, chills, and nausea. In severe cases, malaria can cause kidney failure, coma, brain damage, and for about a million people a year—mostly children—death. Today, we think of malaria as a "tropical" disease, but malaria was once common in the United States. George Washington caught malaria, as did James Monroe, Andrew Jackson, Abraham Lincoln, Ulysses S. Grant, and James A. Garfield. Malaria was present in America until the late 1940s, when the last cases were wiped out by better drainage, removal of mosquito-breeding sites, and the spraying of insecticides. The lesson? Wealth—the ability to pay for the prevention of malaria—ended the disease in the United States. And wealth comes from economic growth. So the incidence of malaria is not just about geography; it's also about economics.

Malaria is far from the only problem that diminishes with wealth and economic growth. In the United States, one of the world's richest countries, 994 out of every 1,000 children born survive to the age of 5. In Somalia, one of the world's poorest countries, only about 886 children survive to age 5 (i.e., 114

FIGURE 1.1

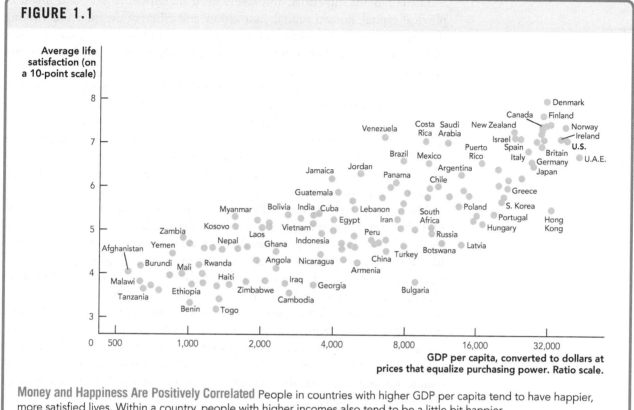

Money and Happiness Are Positively Correlated People in countries with higher GDP per capita tend to have happier, more satisfied lives. Within a country, people with higher incomes also tend to be a little bit happier.

Data from: Betsey Stevenson and Justin Wolfers, Wharton School at the University of Pennsylvania, as found in the *New York Times*, http://www.marketobservation.com/blogs/media/blogs/Statistics/ on 2/21/2014.

of every 1,000 children die before seeing their fifth birthday). Overall, it's the wealthiest countries that have the highest rates of infant survival.

Indeed, if you look at most of the things that people care about, they are much easier to come by in wealthier economies. Wealth brings us flush toilets, antibiotics, higher education, the ability to choose the career we want, fun vacations, and, of course, a greater ability to protect our families against catastrophes. Wealth also brings women's rights and political liberty, at least in most (but not all) countries. Wealthier economies lead to richer and more fulfilled, even happier lives, as seen in Figure 1.1. In short, *wealth matters, and understanding economic growth is one of the most important tasks of economics.*

Big Idea Seven: Institutions Matter

If wealth is so important, what makes a country rich? The most proximate cause is that wealthy countries have lots of physical and human capital per worker and they produce things in a relatively efficient manner, using the latest technological knowledge. But why do some countries have more physical and human capital and why is it organized well using the latest technological knowledge? In a word, incentives, which of course takes us back to Big Idea One.

Entrepreneurs, investors, and savers need incentives to save and invest in physical capital, human capital, innovation, and efficient organization. Among the most powerful institutions for supporting good incentives are property rights, political stability, honest government, a dependable legal system, and competitive and open markets.

Consider South and North Korea. South Korea has a per capita income more than 10 times greater than its immediate neighbor, North Korea. South Korea is a modern, developed economy, but North Koreans still starve or can go for months without eating meat. And yet both countries were equally poor in 1950 and, of course, the two countries share the same language and cultural and historical background. What differs is their economic systems and the incentives at work.

Macroeconomists are especially interested in the incentives to produce new ideas. If the world never had any new ideas, the standard of living would eventually stagnate. But entrepreneurs draw on new ideas to create new products like iPhones, new pharmaceuticals, self-driving cars, and many other innovations. Just about any device you use in daily life is based on a multitude of ideas and discoveries, the lifeblood of economic growth. New ideas, of course, require incentives and that means an active scientific community and the freedom and incentive to put new ideas into action. Ideas also have peculiar properties. One apple feeds one person but one idea can feed the world. Ideas, in other words, aren't used up when they are used and that has tremendous implications for understanding the benefits of trade, the future of economic growth, and many other topics.

Big Idea Eight: Economic Booms and Busts Cannot Be Avoided but Can Be Moderated

We have seen that growth matters and that the right institutions foster growth. But no economy grows at a constant pace. Economies advance and recede, rise and fall, boom and bust. In a recession, wages fall and many people are thrown into miserable unemployment. Unfortunately, we cannot avoid all recessions. Booms and busts are part of the normal response of an economy to changing economic conditions. When the weather is bad in India, for example, crops fail and the economy grows more slowly or perhaps not at all. The weather doesn't much affect the economy in the United States, but the U.S. economy is buffeted by other unavoidable shocks.

Although some booms and busts are part of the normal response of an economy to changing economic conditions, not all booms and busts are normal. The Great Depression (1929–1940) was not normal, but rather it was the most catastrophic economic event in the history of the United States. National output plummeted by 30%, unemployment rates exceeded 20%, and the stock market lost more than two-thirds of its value. Almost overnight the United States went from confidence to desperation. The Great Depression, however, didn't have to happen. Most economists today believe that if the government, especially the U.S. Federal Reserve, had acted more quickly and more appropriately, the Great Depression would have been shorter and less deep. At the time, however, the tools at the government's disposal—monetary and fiscal policy—were not well understood.

Today, the tools of monetary and fiscal policy are much better understood. When used appropriately, these tools can reduce swings in unemployment and GDP. Unemployment insurance can also reduce some of the misery that accompanies a recession. The tools of monetary and fiscal policy, however, are not all-powerful. At one time it was thought that these tools could end all recessions, but we know now that this is not the case. Furthermore, when used poorly, monetary and fiscal policy can make recessions worse and the economy more volatile.

A significant task of macroeconomic theory is to understand both the promise and the limits of monetary and fiscal policy in smoothing out the normal booms and busts of the macroeconomy.

Big Idea Nine: Inflation Is Caused by Increases in the Supply of Money

Yes, economic policy can be useful but sometimes policy goes awry, for instance, when **inflation** gets out of hand. Inflation, one of the most common problems in macroeconomics, refers to an increase in the general level of prices. Inflation makes people feel poorer but, perhaps more important, rising and especially volatile prices make it harder for people to figure out the real values of goods, services, and investments. For these and other reasons, most people (and economists) dislike inflation.

Inflation is an increase in the general level of prices.

But where does inflation come from? The answer is simple: Inflation is caused by a sustained increase in the supply of money. When people have more money, they spend it, and without an increase in the supply of goods, prices must rise. As Nobel laureate Milton Friedman once wrote, "Inflation is always and everywhere a monetary phenomenon."

The United States, like other advanced economies, has a central bank; in the United States that bank is called the Federal Reserve. The Federal Reserve has the power and the responsibility to regulate the supply of money in the American economy. This power can be used for good, such as when the Federal Reserve holds off or minimizes a recession. But the power also can be used for great harm if the Federal Reserve encourages too much growth in the supply of money. The result will be inflation and economic disruption.

A billionaire in Zimbabwe

In Zimbabwe, the government ran the printing presses at full speed for many years. By the end of 2007, prices were rising at an astonishing rate of 150,000% per year. The United States has never had a problem of this scope or anything close to it but inflation remains a common concern.

Amazingly, the inflation rate in Zimbabwe kept rising. In January of 2008, the government had to issue a 10-million-dollar bank note (worth about 4 U.S. dollars), and a year later they announced a 20-*trillion*-dollar note that bought about what 10 million dollars had a year earlier. In early 2009, the inflation rate leaped to billions of percent per month! Finally, in April of 2009, the government stopped issuing the Zimbabwean dollar altogether and permitted trade using foreign currencies such as the South African rand and U.S. dollar.

Big Idea Ten: Central Banking Is a Hard Job

The Federal Reserve ("the Fed") is often called on to combat recessions. But this is not always easy to do. Typically, there is a lag—often of many months—between when the Fed makes a decision and when the effects of that decision on the economy are known. In the meantime, economic conditions have changed so you should think of the Fed as shooting at a moving target. No one can foresee the future perfectly and so the Fed's decisions are not always the right ones.

As mentioned, too much money in the economy means that inflation will result. But not enough money in the economy is bad as well and can lead to a recession or a slowing of economic growth. These ideas are an important and extensive topic in macroeconomics, but the key problem is that a low or falling money supply forces people to cut their prices and wages and this adjustment doesn't always go smoothly.

The Fed is always trying to get it "just right," but some of the time it fails. Sometimes the failure is a mistake the Fed could have avoided, but other times it simply isn't possible to always make the right guess about where the world is headed. Thus, in some situations the Fed must accept a certain amount of either inflation or unemployment. Central banking relies on economic tools, but in the final analysis it is as much an art as a science.

Most economists think that the Fed does more good than harm. But if you are going to understand the Fed, you have to think of it as a highly fallible institution that faces a very difficult job.

The Biggest Idea of All: Economics Is Fun

When you put all these ideas and others together, you see that economics is both exciting and important. Economics teaches us how to make the world a better place. It's about the difference between wealth and poverty, work and unemployment, happiness and misery. Economics increases your understanding of the past, present, and future.

As you will see, the basic principles of economics hold everywhere, whether it is in a rice paddy in Vietnam or a stock market in São Paulo, Brazil. No matter what the topic, the principles of economics apply to all countries, not just to your own. Moreover, in today's globalized world, events in China and India influence the economy in the United States, and vice versa. For this reason, you will find that our book is truly international and full of examples and applications from Algeria to Zimbabwe.

But economics is also linked to everyday life. Economics can help you think about your quest for a job, how to manage your personal finances, and how to deal with debt, inflation, a recession, or a bursting stock market bubble. In short, economics is about understanding your world.

We are excited about economics and we hope that you will be too. Perhaps some of you will even become economics majors. If you are thinking about majoring, you might want to know that a bachelor's degree in economics is one of the best-paying degrees, with starting salaries just behind chemical and nuclear engineering. That reflects the value of an economics degree and the world's recognition of that value. But if your passion lies elsewhere, that's okay too; a course in the principles of economics will take you a long way toward understanding your world. With a good course, a good professor, and a good textbook, you'll never look at the world the same way again. So just remember: *See the Invisible Hand. Understand Your World.*

CHAPTER REVIEW

Go online to practice with more examples of these types of problems, including live links to videos, data sources, and feedback.

KEY CONCEPTS

incentives, p. 1

scarcity, p. 4

great economic problem, p. 4

opportunity cost, p. 4

inflation, p. 9

FACTS AND TOOLS

1. A headline[5] in the *New York Times*, read, "Study Finds Enrollment Is Up at Colleges Despite Recession." How would you rewrite this headline now that you understand the idea of opportunity cost?

2. When bad weather in India destroys the crop, does this sound like a fall in the total "supply" of crops or a fall in people's "demand" for crops? Keep your answer in mind as you learn about economic booms and busts later on.

3. How much did national output fall during the Great Depression? According to the chapter, which government agency might have helped to avoid much of the Great Depression had it acted more quickly and appropriately?

4. The chapter lists four things that entrepreneurs save and invest in. Which of the four are actual objects, and which are more intangible, like concepts or ideas or plans? Feel free to use Wikipedia or some other reference source to get definitions of unfamiliar terms.

5. Who has a better incentive to work long hours in a laboratory researching new cures for diseases: a scientist who earns a percentage of the profits from any new medicine they might invent, or a scientist who will get a handshake and a thank-you note from their boss if they invent a new medicine?

6. In the discussion of Big Idea Five, the chapter says that "self-sufficiency is death" because most of us would not be able to produce for ourselves the food and shelter that we need to survive. In addition to *death*, however, one could also say that self-sufficiency is *boredom* or *ignorance*. How does specialization and trade help you to avoid boredom and ignorance?

7. Aniyah is visiting her family over winter break. Her mom asks if she needs any household products before heading back to school. She tells her that she needs paper towels and suggests they go to the supermarket to get some. Aniyah's mom says that they should go to Costco instead. Her rationale is that while the total cost of the bulk package from Costco may be more expensive than a smaller package from the supermarket, the per unit price of each additional unit in the bulk package will be cheaper than at the supermarket. Which big idea of economics does this scenario illustrate? Briefly explain why.

8. Over the past six months, Ajay has become an avid disc golfer. Ajay's roommate, Thiago, initially introduced him to the sport, and he has loved it ever since. Knowing how excited Ajay is for his newfound hobby, Ajay's girlfriend and another of his friends decide to buy him the same disc-golfing bag for Christmas. Ajay does not need two of the same bag, so he decides to sell one of the bags to Thiago for lower than the market price—which both Ajay and Thiago think is a great deal. Which big idea of economics does this scenario illustrate? Briefly explain why.

THINKING AND PROBLEM SOLVING

9. In recent years, Venezuela has had hyperinflation, with the price of a cup of coffee increasing from 0.2 old bolivars in January 2018 to 8.7 million old bolivars in January 2022. (As a result, Venezuela was forced to devalue their currency in October 2021, removing six zeros. So the price of a cup of coffee was 8.7 new bolivars in January 2022. A previous devaluation in August 2018 had removed an additional five zeros from the currency, meaning the price of a cup of coffee in January 2022 in old, old bolivars would have been 0.87 trillion!) According to what you learned in this chapter, what do you think the government can do to end this hyperinflation?

10. Some people worry that machines will take jobs away from people, making people permanently unemployed. Only 150 years ago in the United States, most people were farmers. Now, machines do almost all of the farmwork, and fewer than 1.3% of Americans are farmers, yet that 1.3% produces enough food to feed the entire country while still exporting food overseas.

    a. What happened to all of those people who used to work on farms? Do you think most adult males in the United States are unemployed nowadays, now that farmwork is gone?

    b. Some people say that it's okay for machines to take jobs because we'll get jobs fixing the machines. Just from looking around, do you think that most working Americans are earning a living by fixing farm equipment? If not, what do you think most working people are doing instead? (We'll give a full answer later in this book.)

11. Let's connect Big Ideas Six and Nine: Do you think that people in poor countries are poor because they don't have enough money? In other words, could a country get richer by printing more pieces of paper called "money" and handing those out to its citizens?

12. Nobel Prize winner Milton Friedman said that a bad central banker is like a "fool in the shower." In a shower, of course, when you turn the faucet, water won't show up in the showerhead for a few seconds. So if a "fool in the shower" is always making big changes in the temperature based on how the water feels *right now*, the water is likely to swing back and forth between too hot and too cold. How does this apply to central banking?

13. According to the United Nations, there were roughly 300 million humans on the planet a thousand years ago. Essentially, all of them were living in extreme poverty by modern standards: They lacked antibiotics, almost all lacked indoor plumbing, and none traveled faster than a horse or a river could carry them. Today, roughly 700 million humans live in extreme poverty out of about 8 billion total humans. So over the last thousand years, what has happened to the *fraction* of humans who are living in extreme poverty: Did it rise, fall, or stay about the same? What

happened to the total *number* of people living in deep poverty: rise, fall, or no change?

14. A cell phone plan costs $50 per month for the first 1,000 minutes and $0.30 per minute for each additional minute after 1,000. What is the marginal cost of

    a. the 1st minute?

    b. the 500th minute?

    c. the 1,000th minute?

    d. the 1,001st minute?

    e. the 1,500th minute?

CHALLENGES

15. We claim that part of the reason the Great Depression was so destructive is because economists didn't understand how to use government policy very well in the 1930s. In your opinion, do you think that economists during the Great Depression would have agreed? In other words, if you had asked them why the Depression was so bad, would they have said, "Because the government ignored our wise advice," or would they have said, "Because we don't have any good ideas about how to fix this"? What does your answer tell you about the confidence of economists and other experts?

16. Some problems that economists try to solve are easy *as economic problems* but hard *as political problems*. Medical doctors face similar kinds of situations: Preventing most deaths from obesity or lung cancer is easy *as a medical problem* (eat less, exercise more, don't smoke) but hard *as a self-control problem*. With this in mind, how is ending hyperinflation like losing 100 pounds?

17. As Nobel Prize winner and *New York Times* columnist Paul Krugman has noted, the field of economics is a lot like the field of medicine: They are fields where knowledge is limited (both are new as real scientific disciplines) and where many cures are quite painful (opportunity cost) but where regular people care deeply about the issues. What are some other ways that economics and medicine are alike?

18. Economics is sometimes called "the dismal science." Of the big ideas in this chapter, which sound dismal—like bad news?

2

The Power of Trade and Comparative Advantage

Chaos, conflict, and war may dominate the news, but it's heartening to know that there is also an astounding amount of world *cooperation*. The next time you are in your local supermarket, stop and consider how many people cooperated to bring the fruits of the world to your table: kiwis from New Zealand, dried apricots from Turkey, dates from Egypt, mangoes from Mexico, bananas from Guatemala. How is it that farmers in New Zealand wake up at 5 AM to work hard tending their fields so that you, on the other side of the world, may enjoy a kiwi with your fruit salad?

This chapter is about a central feature of our world, trade. It's about how you eat reasonably well every day yet have little knowledge of farming, it's about how you cooperate with people whom you will never meet, and it's about how civilization is made possible.

We will focus on three of the benefits of trade:

1. Trade makes people better off when preferences differ.
2. Trade increases productivity through specialization and the division of knowledge.
3. Trade increases productivity through comparative advantage.

Trade and Preferences

In September 1995, Pierre Omidyar, a 28-year-old computer programmer, finished the code for what would soon become eBay. Searching around for a test item, Omidyar grabbed a broken laser pointer and posted it for sale with a starting price of $1. The laser pointer sold for $14.83. Astonished, Omidyar contacted the winning bidder to make sure he understood that the laser pointer was broken. "Oh yes," the bidder replied, "I am a collector of broken laser pointers." At that instant, Omidyar knew eBay was going to be a huge success. Within just a few years, he would become one of the richest men in the United States.

eBay profits by making buyers and sellers happy.

Today, eBay operates in more than 30 countries and earns billions of dollars in revenue. eBay's revenues, however, are a small share of the total value that is created for the hundreds of millions of buyers and sellers who trade everything on eBay from children's toys to the original Hollywood sign. Trade creates value by moving goods from people who value them less to people who value them more. Sam, for example, was going to trash the old Fisher Price garage that his kids no longer play with. Instead, Sam sells it on eBay to Jen who pays $65.50. What had been worth nothing is now worth at least $65.50. Value has been created. Trade makes Sam and Jen better off, and it makes eBay, the market maker who brought Sam and Jen together, better off. Trade makes people with different preferences better off.

Specialization, Productivity, and the Division of Knowledge

Simple trades of the kind found on eBay create value, but the true power of trade is discovered only when people take the next step, specialization. In a world without trade, no one can afford to specialize. People will specialize in the production of a single good only when they are confident that they will be able to trade that good for the many other goods that they want and need. Thus, as trade develops, so does specialization, and specialization turns out to vastly increase productivity.

How long could you survive if you had to grow your own food? Probably not very long. Yet most of us can earn enough money in a single day spent doing something other than farming to buy more food than we could grow in a year. Why can we get so much more food through trade than through personal production? The reason is that specialization greatly increases productivity. Farmers, for example, have two immense advantages in producing food compared with economics professors or students: Because they specialize, they know more about farming than other people, and because they sell large quantities, they can afford to buy large-scale farming machines. What is true for farming is true for just about every field of production—specialization increases productivity. Without specialization and trade, we would each have to produce our own food as well as other goods, and the result would be mass starvation and the collapse of civilization.

The human brain is limited and there is much to know. Thus, it makes sense to divide knowledge across many brains and then trade. In a primitive agricultural economy in which each person or household farms for themselves, each person has about the same knowledge as the person next door. In this case, the combined knowledge of a society of 1 million people barely exceeds that of a single person.[1] A society run with the knowledge of one brain is a poor and miserable society.

In a modern economy, many millions of times more knowledge is used than could exist in a single brain. In the United States, for example, we don't just have doctors—we have neurologists, cardiologists, gastroenterologists, gynecologists, and urologists, to name just a few of the many specializations in medicine.

The economist Thomas Sowell emphasizes that through specialization and trade, we each know less about many things but more about a few things, and in this way, "civilization is an enormous device for economizing on knowledge."

Knowledge increases productivity, so specialization increases total output. All of this knowledge is possible, however, only because each person can specialize in the production of one good and then trade for all other desired goods. Without trade, specialization is impossible.

MRU
mru.org/division-knowledge

How the Division of Knowledge Saved My Son's Life

The extent of specialization in a modern economy explains why no one knows the full details of how even the simplest product is produced. A Valentine's Day rose may have been grown in Kenya, flown through Amsterdam to the United States on a refrigerated airplane, and trucked to Topeka by drivers staying awake with Colombian coffee. Each person in this process knows only a small part of the whole, but with trade and market coordination, they each do their part and the rose is delivered without anyone needing to understand the whole process.

The extent of specialization in modern society is remarkable. We have already mentioned the many specializations in medicine. We also have dog walkers, closet organizers, and manicurists. It's common to dismiss the latter jobs as frivolous, but trade connects all markets. It's the dog walkers, closet organizers, and manicurists who give the otolaryngologists—specialists in the nose, ear, and throat—the time they need to perfect their skills.

The division of knowledge increases with specialization and trade. Economic growth in the modern era is primarily due to the creation of new knowledge. Thus, one of the most momentous turning points in the division of knowledge happens when trade is extensive enough to support large numbers of scientists, engineers, and entrepreneurs, all of whom specialize in producing new knowledge.

Every increase in world trade is an opportunity to increase the division of knowledge and extend the power of the human mind. During the Communist era, for example, China was like an island cut off from the world economy: 1 billion people who neither traded many goods nor many ideas with the rest of the world. After the fall of the Berlin Wall, Eastern Europe, Russia, and later China and India joined the world economy, adding to the world stock of scientists and engineers. Billions of minds were added to the division of knowledge and cooperation was extended further around the world than ever before.

Consider the many ideas and innovations that make life better, from antibiotics, to high-yield, disease-resistant wheat, to the semiconductor. Insofar as those goods have originated in one place and then been spread around the world, improving the lives of millions or billions, it is because of trade.

Reducing trade barriers, Berlin 1989

Comparative Advantage

A third reason to trade is to take advantage of differences. Brazil, for example, has a climate ideally suited to growing sugarcane, China has an abundance of low-skill workers, and the United States has one of the best-educated workforces in the world. Taking advantage of these differences suggests that world production can be maximized when Brazil produces sugar, China assembles iPads, and the United States devotes its efforts to designing the next generation of electronic devices.

Amanda Edwards/Getty Images

Comparative advantage: It's a good thing.
Martha Stewart may be the world's best ironer but she has admitted that she doesn't always do her own ironing. That's smart! Every hour Martha spends ironing is an hour less she has to run her billion-dollar business. The cost of ironing is too high for Martha Stewart, even if she is the world's best. Martha can be most productive if she does what she does most best.

Absolute advantage is the ability to produce the same good using fewer inputs than another producer.

A **production possibilities frontier** shows all the combinations of goods that a country can produce given its productivity and supply of inputs.

Taking advantage of differences is even more powerful than it looks. We say that a country has an **absolute advantage** in production if it can produce the same good using fewer inputs than another country. But to benefit from trade, a country need not have an absolute advantage. For example, even if the United States did have the world's best climate for growing sugar, it might still make sense for Brazil to grow sugar and for the United States to design iPads, if the United States had a bigger advantage in designing iPads than it did in growing sugar.

Here's another example of what economists call comparative advantage. Martha Stewart doesn't do her own ironing. Why not? Martha Stewart may, in fact, be the world's best ironer but she is also good at running her business. If Martha spent more time ironing and less time running her business, her blouses might be pressed more precisely but that would be a small gain compared with the loss from having someone else run her business. It's better for Martha if she specializes in running her business and then trades some of her income for other goods, such as ironing services, and of course many other goods and services as well.

The Production Possibility Frontier

The idea of comparative advantage is subtle but important. In order to give a precise definition, let's explore comparative advantage using a simple model. Suppose that there are just two goods, computers and shirts, and one input, labor. Assume that in Mexico, it takes 12 units of labor to make one computer and 2 units of labor to produce one shirt, and suppose that Mexico has 24 units of labor. Mexico, therefore, can produce 2 computers and 0 shirts or 0 computers and 12 shirts, or they can have any combination of computers and shirts along the line in the left panel of Figure 2.1 labeled Mexico's PPF. Mexico's PPF, short for Mexico's **production possibilities frontier**, shows all the combinations of computers and shirts that Mexico can produce given its productivity and supply of inputs. Mexico cannot produce outside of its PPF.

Similarly, assume that there are 24 units of labor in the United States but that in the United States it takes 1 unit of labor to produce either good. The United States therefore can produce 24 computers and 0 shirts, or 0 computers and 24 shirts, or any combination along the U.S. PPF shown in the right panel of Figure 2.1.

A PPF illustrates trade-offs. If Mexico wants to produce more shirts, it must produce fewer computers, and vice versa: It moves along its PPF. That's just another way of restating the fundamental principles of scarcity and opportunity cost.

Opportunity Costs and Comparative Advantage

In fact, there is a close connection between opportunity costs and the PPF. Remember, the opportunity cost of a choice is the value of the opportunities lost. Now look at the U.S. PPF in the right panel of Figure 2.1; notice that the slope, the rise over the run, is $-24/24 = -1$. In other words, for every additional shirt the United States produces, it must produce one fewer computer. One shirt has an opportunity cost of one computer and vice versa.

FIGURE 2.1

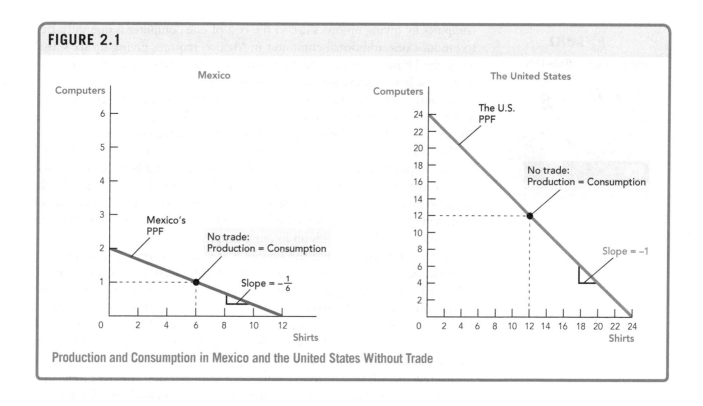

Production and Consumption in Mexico and the United States Without Trade

Now consider Mexico's PPF. The rise over the run is −2/12 = −1/6. In other words, for every additional shirt that Mexico produces, it must produce 1/6th less of a computer. Once again, the slope of the PPF tells us the opportunity cost. In Mexico, 1 shirt costs 1/6th of a computer, or 1 computer costs 6 shirts. We summarize the opportunity costs in Table 2.1.

Now here is the key. The (opportunity) cost of a shirt in the United States is one computer but the (opportunity) cost of a shirt in Mexico is just one-sixth of a computer. Thus, even though Mexico is less productive than the United States, Mexico has a lower cost of producing shirts! Since Mexico has the lower opportunity cost of producing shirts, we say that Mexico has a **comparative advantage** in producing shirts.

Now let's look at the opportunity cost of producing computers. Again, the trade-off for the United States is easy to see: It can produce one additional

A country has a **comparative advantage** in producing goods for which it has the lower opportunity cost.

TABLE 2.1 OPPORTUNITY COSTS

Country	Opportunity Cost of 1 Computer	Opportunity Cost of 1 Shirt
Mexico	6 shirts	1/6 of a computer
United States	1 shirt	1 computer

Mexico is the low-cost producer of shirts.

The United States is the low-cost producer of computers.

https://youtu.be/4rUfoU04QJM

Comparative Advantage

computer by giving up one shirt, so the cost of one computer is one shirt. But to produce one additional computer in Mexico requires giving up six shirts! Thus, the United States has the lower cost of producing computers or, economists say, it has a comparative advantage in producing computers.

We now know that the United States has a high cost of producing shirts and a low cost of producing computers. For Mexico, it's the reverse: Mexico has a low cost of producing shirts and a high cost of producing computers.

The theory of comparative advantage says that to increase its wealth, a country should produce the goods it can make at low cost and buy the goods that it can make only at high cost. Thus, the theory says the United States should make computers and buy shirts. Similarly, the theory says that Mexico should make shirts and buy computers. Let's use some numbers and some pictures to see whether the theory holds up in our example.

Suppose that Mexico and the United States each devote 12 units of labor to producing computers and 12 units to producing shirts. We can see from the PPFs that Mexico will produce one computer and six shirts and the United States will produce 12 computers and 12 shirts. At first, there is no trade, so production in each country is equal to consumption. We show the production–consumption point of each country with a black dot in Figure 2.1. Now, can Mexico and the United States make themselves better off through trade? Yes.

Imagine that Mexico moves 12 units of its labor out of computer production and into shirt production. Thus, Mexico specializes completely by allocating all 24 units of its labor to shirt production, thereby producing 12 shirts. Similarly, suppose that the United States moves 2 units of its labor out of shirt production and into computers—thus producing 14 computers and 10 shirts. Production in Mexico and the United States is now shown by the green points in Figure 2.2.

FIGURE 2.2

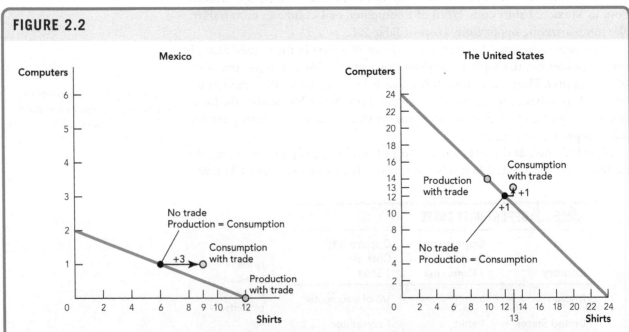

Production and Consumption in Mexico and the United States with Trade With no trade, Mexico produces and consumes 1 computer and 6 shirts and the United States produces and consumes 12 computers and 12 shirts. With specialization, Mexico produces 0 computers and 12 shirts and the United States produces 14 computers and 10 shirts. By trading 3 shirts for 1 computer, Mexico increases its consumption (compared with the no-trade situation) by 3 shirts and the United States increases its consumption by 1 computer and 1 shirt.

So, to finish the story, can you now see a way in which both Mexico and the United States can be made better off? Sure! Imagine that the United States trades one computer to Mexico in return for three shirts. Mexico is now able to consume one computer and nine shirts (three more shirts than before trade), while the United States is able to consume 13 computers (one more than before trade) and 13 shirts (one more than before trade).

Amazingly, both Mexico and the United States can now consume outside of their PPFs. In other words, before trade, Mexico could not have consumed one computer and nine shirts because this was outside their PPF. Similarly, before trade, the United States could not have consumed 13 computers and 13 shirts. But with trade, countries are able to increase their consumption beyond the range that was possible without trade.

Thus, when each country produces according to its comparative advantage and then trades, total production and consumption increase. Importantly, both Mexico and the United States gain from trade even though the United States is more productive than Mexico at producing *both* computers and shirts.

The theory of comparative advantage not only explains trade patterns but also tells us something remarkable: A country (or a person) will *always* be the low-cost seller of some good. The reason is clear: The greater the advantage a country has in producing A, the greater the cost to it of producing B. If you are a great pianist, the cost to you of doing anything else is very high. Thus, the greater your advantages in being a pianist, the greater the incentive you have to trade with other people for other goods. It's the same for countries. The more productive the United States is at producing computers, the greater its demand will be to trade for shirts. Thus, countries with high productivity can always benefit by trading with lower-productivity countries, and countries with lower productivity need never fear that higher-productivity countries will outcompete them in the production of all goods.

When people fear that a country can be outcompeted in everything, they are making a common mistake, namely confusing absolute advantage with comparative advantage. A producer has an absolute advantage over another producer if it can produce more output from the same input. But what makes trade profitable is differences in comparative advantage, and a country will always have some comparative advantage.

Thus, everyone can benefit from trade. From the world's greatest genius down to the person of below-average ability, no individuals or countries are so productive or so unproductive that they cannot benefit from inclusion in the worldwide division of labor. The theory of comparative advantage tells us something vital about world trade and about world peace. Trade unites humanity.

Comparative Advantage and Wages

Comparative advantage is a difficult story to grasp. Most of the world hasn't got it yet, so don't be too surprised if it takes you some time as well. You may at first be bothered by the fact that we did not explicitly discuss wages. Won't a country like the United States be uncompetitive in trade with low-wage countries like Mexico?

In fact, wages are in our model; we just need to bring them to the surface. Doing so will provide another perspective on comparative advantage.

TABLE 2.2 CONSUMPTION IN MEXICO AND THE UNITED STATES (NO SPECIALIZATION OR TRADE)

Country Labor Allocation (Computers, Shirts)	Computers	Shirts
Mexico (12, 12)	1	6
United States (12, 12)	12	12
Total consumption	13	18

TABLE 2.3 CONSUMPTION IN MEXICO AND THE UNITED STATES (SPECIALIZATION AND TRADE)

Country	Computers	Shirts
Mexico	1	9 = 6 + 3
United States	13 = 12 + 1	13 = 12 + 1
Total consumption	14	22

In our model, there is only one type of labor. In a free market, all workers of the same type will earn the same wage.* So, in this model there is just one wage in Mexico and one wage in the United States. We can calculate the wage in Mexico by summing up the total value of *consumption* in Mexico and dividing by the number of workers. (We calculate the value of consumption because at the end of the day workers care about what they consume, not what they produce.) We can perform a similar calculation for the United States. To do this, we need only a price for computers and a price for shirts. Let's suppose that computers sell for $300 and shirts for $100 (this is consistent with trading one computer for three shirts as we did earlier). Let's look first at the situation with no trade (see Table 2.2). The value of Mexican consumption is 1 × $300 plus 6 × $100 for a total of $900. Since there are 24 workers, the average wage is $37.50. The value of U.S. consumption is 12 × $300 + 12 × $100 = $4,800, so the U.S. wage is $200.

Now consider the situation with trade (see Table 2.3). The value of Mexican consumption is now 1 × $300 + 9 × $100 = $1,200 for a wage of $50, while the U.S. wage is now $216.67 (check it!). Wages in both countries have gone up, just as expected.

But notice that the wage in Mexico is lower than the wage in the United States, both before and after trade. The reason is that the productivity of labor is lower in Mexico. Ultimately, it's the productivity of labor that determines the wage rate. Specialization and trade let workers make the most of what they have—it raises wages as high as possible given productivity—but trade does not directly increase productivity.† Trade makes both Einstein and his less clever accountant better off, but it doesn't make the accountant a skilled scientist like Einstein.

In summary, workers in the United States often fear trade because they think that they cannot compete with low-wage workers in other countries. Meanwhile, workers in low-wage countries fear trade because they think that they cannot compete with high-productivity countries like the United States! But differences in wages reflect differences in productivity. High-productivity countries have high wages; low-productivity countries have low wages. Trade means that workers in both countries can raise their wages to the highest levels allowed by their respective productivities.

---

* In a free market, the same good will tend to sell for the same price everywhere. Imagine that the wages in computer manufacturing exceed the wages in shirt manufacturing. Everyone wants a higher wage, so workers in the shirt industry will try to move to the computer industry. As the supply of workers in computer manufacturing increases, however, wages in the computer sector will fall. And, as the supply of workers in shirt manufacturing decreases, wages in that sector will increase. Only when workers of the same type are paid the same wage is there no incentive for workers to move.

† Trade can increase productivity by improving the division of knowledge and by diffusing information about advanced production techniques. These advantages of trade are important but the logic of comparative advantage does not require an increase in productivity.

Adam Smith on Trade

Notice that we have so far talked about trade without distinguishing it much from "international trade." Adam Smith had an elegant summary connecting the argument for trade to that for international trade:

> It is the maxim of every prudent master of a family never to attempt to make at home what it will cost him more to make than to buy. The tailor does not attempt to make his own shoes, but buys them of the shoemaker. The shoemaker does not attempt to make his own clothes, but employs a tailor. What is prudence in the conduct of every private family can scarce be folly in that of a great kingdom. If a foreign country can supply us with a commodity cheaper than we ourselves can make it, better buy it of them with some part of the produce of our own industry employed in a way in which we have some advantage.[2]

Trade and Globalization

Does everyone always benefit from increased trade? No. In our simple model, workers within a country can easily switch between the shirt and computer sectors. In the real world, workers in the sector with increased demand (computers in the United States, shirts in Mexico) will see their wages rise while workers in the sector with decreased demand (shirts in the United States, computers in Mexico) will see their wages fall. Workers in sectors with falling wages will move to sectors with rising wages until wages in the sectors equalize, but the transition isn't always easy or quick. We will take another look at the gains and losses from trade in the chapter on international trade. Overall, however, greater trade increases total wealth. That typically brings benefits to a great many people in all parts of the trading world. We can see this theme throughout history.

Decreases in transportation costs, integration of world markets, and increased speed of communication have made the world a smaller place. But globalization is not new; rather, it has been a theme in human history since at least the Roman Empire, which knit together different parts of the world in a common economic and political area. When these trade networks later fell apart, the subsequent era was named "The Dark Ages."

Later, the European Renaissance arose from revitalized trade routes, the rebirth of commercially based cities, and the spread of science from China, India, and the Middle East. Periods of increased trade and the spread of ideas have been among the best for human progress. As economist Donald Boudreaux puts it: "Globalization is the advance of human cooperation across national boundaries."[3]

Takeaway

Simple trade makes people better off when preferences differ, but the true power of trade occurs when trade leads to specialization. Specialization creates enormous increases in productivity. Without trade, the knowledge used by an entire economy is approximately equal to the knowledge used by one brain. With specialization and trade, the total sum of knowledge used in an economy increases tremendously and far exceeds that of any one brain.

International trade is trade across political borders. The theory of comparative advantage explains how a country, just like a person, can increase its standard of living by specializing in what it can make at low (opportunity) cost and trading for

Bettmann/Getty Images

Adam Smith (1723–1790), author of *The Wealth of Nations* and one of the greatest economists of all time. When Smith could not finish teaching one semester, he told his students he would refund their tuition. When the students refused the refund saying they had learned so much already, Smith wept. We, however, will not refund the purchase price of this book even if you read only half of it. We are not as good economists as Adam Smith was.

CHECK YOURSELF

- What does specialization do to productivity? Why?
- How does trade let us benefit from the advantages of specialization?
- Usain Bolt is the world's fastest human. Usain could probably mow his lawn very quickly, much more quickly and at least as well as Harry, who mows lawns for a living. Why would Usain Bolt pay Harry to mow his lawn rather than do it himself?

what it can make only at high cost. When we apply the logic of opportunity cost to trade, we discover that everyone has a comparative advantage in something, so everyone can benefit from inclusion in the world market.

CHAPTER REVIEW

Go online to practice with more examples of these types of problems, including live links to videos, data sources, and feedback.

KEY CONCEPTS

absolute advantage, p. 16

production possibilities frontier, p. 16

comparative advantage, p. 17

FACTS AND TOOLS

1. Use the idea of the "division of knowledge" to answer the following questions:

   a. Which country has more knowledge: Utopia, where in the words of Karl Marx, each person knows just enough about hunting, fishing, and cattle raising to "hunt in the morning, fish in the afternoon, [and] rear cattle in the evening," or Experteisia, where one-third of the population learns only about hunting, one-third only about fishing, and one-third only about cattle raising?

   b. Which planet has more knowledge: Cloneia, each of whose 1 million inhabitants knows the same list of 1 million facts, or Differentia, whose 1 million inhabitants each know a different set of 1 million facts? How many facts are known in Cloneia? How many facts are known in Differentia?

2. In *The Wealth of Nations*, Adam Smith said that one reason specialization makes someone more productive is because "a man commonly saunters a little in turning his hand from one sort of employment to another." How can you use this observation to improve your pattern of studying for your four or five college courses this semester?

3. Opportunity cost is one of the tougher ideas in economics. Let's make it easier by starting with some simple examples. In the following examples, find the opportunity cost. Your answer should be a *rate*, as in "1.5 widgets per year" or "6 lectures per month." Ignoring Adam Smith's insight from the previous question, assume that these relationships are simple linear ones, so that if you put in twice the time, you get twice the output, and half the time yields half the output.

   a. Nikkita has a choice between two activities: She can repair one transmission per hour or she can repair two fuel injectors per hour. What is the opportunity cost of repairing one transmission?

   b. Ruby works at a customer service center and every hour she has a choice between two activities: answering 200 telephone calls per hour or responding to 400 emails per hour. What is the opportunity cost of responding to 400 emails?

   c. Deirdre has a choice between writing one more book this year or five more articles this year. What is the opportunity cost of writing half a book this year, in terms of articles?

4. a. American workers are commonly paid much more than Chinese workers. *True or false:* This is largely because American workers are typically more productive than Chinese workers.

   b. Julia Child, an American chef (and World War II spy) who reintroduced French cooking to Americans in the 1960s, was paid much more than most American chefs. *True or false:* This was largely because Julia Child was much more productive than most American chefs. (*Hint:* Do not think solely on kitchen production.)

5. It takes between 20 and 30 hours to assemble a vehicle in the United States, depending on

its size and quality. Let's use that fact plus a few invented numbers to sum up the global division of labor in auto manufacturing. In international economics, "North" is shorthand sometimes used to denote the high-tech developed countries of East Asia, North America, and Western Europe, while "South" is shorthand for the rest of the world. Let's use that shorthand here.

a. Consider the following productivity table: Which region has an absolute advantage at making high-quality cars? Low-quality cars?

	Number of Hours to Make One High-Quality Car	Number of Hours to Make One Low-Quality Car
North	30	20
South	60	30

b. Using the information in the productivity table, estimate the opportunity cost of making high- or low-quality cars in the North and in the South. Which region has a comparative advantage (i.e., lowest opportunity cost) for manufacturing high-quality cars? For low-quality cars?

	Opportunity Cost of Making One High-Quality Car	Opportunity Cost of Making One Low-Quality Car
North	__ low-quality cars	__ high-quality cars
South	__ low-quality cars	__ high-quality cars

c. Assume that 1 million hours of labor are available for making cars in the North, and another 1 million hours of labor are available for making cars in the South. In a no-trade world, let's assume that two-thirds of the auto industry labor in each region is used to make high-quality cars and one-third is used to make low-quality cars. Solve for how many of each kind of car will be produced in the North and South, and add up to determine the total global output of each type of car. (Why will both kinds of cars be made? Because the low-quality cars will be less expensive.)

	Output of High-Quality Cars	Output of Low-Quality Cars
North		
South		
Global output		

d. Now allow specialization. If each region completely specializes in the type of car in which it holds the comparative advantage, what will the global output of high-quality cars be? Of low-quality cars? In the following table, report your answers. Is global output in each kind of car higher than before? (We'll solve a problem with the final step of trade in the Work It Out problem.)

	Output of High-Quality Cars	Output of Low-Quality Cars
North		
South		
Global output		

6. It has been reported that John Lennon was once asked whether Ringo was the best drummer in the world, and he quipped, "He's not even the best drummer in the Beatles!" (Paul also drummed on some of the White Album.) Assuming that this story is true and that Lennon was correct, explain, using economics, why it could still make sense to have Ringo on drums.

THINKING AND PROBLEM SOLVING

7. Fit each of the following examples into one of these reasons for trade: division of knowledge or comparative advantage.

a. Two recently abandoned cats, Bingo and Tuppy, need to quickly learn how to catch mice in order to survive. If they also remain well groomed, they stand a better chance of surviving: Good grooming reduces the risk of disease and parasites. Each cat could go it alone, focusing almost exclusively on learning to catch mice. The alternative would be for Bingo to specialize in learning how to groom well and for Tuppy to specialize in learning how to catch mice well.

b. Supreme Court Chief Justice John Roberts hires attorneys who are less skilled than himself to do his taxes and routine legal work.

8. Nobel laureate Paul Samuelson said that comparative advantage is one of the few ideas in economics that is both "true and not obvious." Since it's not obvious, we should practice with it a bit. In each of the cases, determine the opportunity cost of each worker. Who has the absolute advantage at each task, and who has the comparative advantage?

a. In 30 minutes, Kana can either make miso soup or clean the kitchen. In 15 minutes, Nia can make miso soup; it takes Nia an hour to clean the kitchen.

b. In one hour, Ethan can bake 20 cookies or hang the drywall for two rooms. In one hour, Zara can bake 100 cookies or hang the drywall for three rooms.

c. Kara can build two glass sculptures per day or she can design two full-page newspaper advertisements per day. Sarah can build one glass sculpture per day or design four full-page newspaper ads per day.

d. Commander Data can write 12 excellent poems per day or solve 100 difficult physics problems per day. Riker can write one excellent poem per day or solve 0.5 difficult physics problems per day.

9. The federal education reform law known as the Every Student Succeeds Act (ESSA) requires every state to create standardized tests that measure whether students have mastered key subjects. Since the same test is given to all students in the same grade in the state, this encourages all schools within a state to cover the same material. According to the division of knowledge model, what are the costs of this approach?

10. In this chapter, we've often emphasized how specialization and exchange can create more *output*. But sometimes the output from voluntary exchange is difficult to measure and doesn't show up in GDP statistics. In each of the following cases, explain how the two parties involved might be able to make themselves *both* better off just by making a voluntary exchange.

a. Jing received two copies of *Gears of War 6* as birthday gifts. Jasmine received two copies of *Halo Infinite* as birthday gifts.

b. Nikhil has a free subscription to *Ring* magazine but isn't interested in boxing. Solange has a free

subscription to *The Source* but isn't all that interested in hip-hop, especially artists from Brooklyn.

c. Pat has a lot of love to give, but it is worthless unless received by another. Terry is in the same sad situation.

11. Many people talk about manufacturing jobs leaving the United States and going to other places, like China. Why isn't it possible for all jobs to leave the United States and go overseas (as some people fear)?

12. Refer to the figure. Assume that prior to trade, workers in both countries are allocated such that Japan is producing 2.25 tons of paper and 1.75 tons of sand, while New Zealand is producing 3.5 tons of paper and 4 tons of sand. Let's figure out what happens if both countries agree to trade.

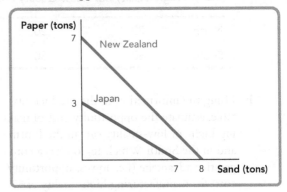

a. New Zealand's opportunity cost of producing 1 ton of sand is _____ ton(s) of paper. Japan's opportunity cost of producing 1 ton of sand is _____ ton(s) of paper.

b. Which country has the comparative advantage in paper production? Which country has the comparative advantage in sand production?

c. Suppose that each country fully specializes in the production of the good for which they have the comparative advantage. How many tons of paper are produced? How many tons of sand? Is this more or less than the pre-trade amounts?

13. Suppose that the following table shows the number of labor hours needed to produce airplanes and automobiles in the United States and South Korea but that one of the numbers is unknown.

	Number of Hours to Produce One Airplane	Number of Hours to Produce One Auto
South Korea	2,000	?
United States	800	5

a. Without knowing the number of labor hours required to produce an auto in South Korea, you can't figure out which country has the comparative advantage in which good. Can you give an example of a number for the empty cell of the table that would give the United States the comparative advantage in the production of airplanes? What about South Korea?

b. Who has the absolute advantage in the production of airplanes? What about autos?

c. What exact number would you have to place in the empty cell of the table for it to be impossible to determine which nation has a comparative advantage in airplanes or autos?

14. In the chapter, you saw how to create a production possibilities frontier for the United States and Mexico. Let's take a look at how to combine these PPFs to make one PPF for the U.S.–Mexico trade alliance. You'll use the same set of axes that was used in the chapter: computers on the vertical axis and shirts on the horizontal axis. Refer to Figure 2.1 and Table 2.1 as needed.

a. First, you need to plot the end points of the PPF by figuring out the maximum numbers of computers and shirts. If both the United States and Mexico produced only computers, how many would they produce? What if they produced only shirts? Plot these two points and label them as *A* (all computers) and *Z* (all shirts). The PPF for the U.S.–Mexico trade alliance is going to look a little different from the PPFs for the individual countries, so we don't want to simply connect the two points with a straight line. We need to figure out the rate at which the U.S.–Mexico trade alliance gives up computers to get shirts (or vice versa).

b. Starting at point *A*, if citizens of the United States or Mexico decided they wanted more shirts, where would those shirts be produced? Why? What do you think the PPF should look like as the U.S.–Mexico trade alliance initially moves away from point *A*?

c. Starting at point *Z*, if citizens of the United States or Mexico decided they wanted more computers, where would those computers be produced? Why? What do you think the PPF should look like as the U.S.–Mexico

trade alliance initially moves away from point *Z*?

d. Plot the point at which each country is completely specializing in the good for which it has the comparative advantage. Label this point *B*. Connect points *A*, *B*, and *Z*. This is the PPF for the U.S.–Mexico trade alliance. Can you describe how this PPF is a combination of the two nations' separate PPFs?

e. Suppose now that a third nation, Haiti, enters the trade alliance. In Haiti, the opportunity cost of a computer is 12 shirts, and Haiti has the labor necessary to produce 1 computer (or 12 shirts). Can you draw a new PPF for the U.S.–Mexico–Haiti trade alliance?

f. Okay, what will happen to the PPF as more and more countries join the trade alliance? What would it look like with an infinite number of countries?

CHALLENGES

15. In the computers and shirts example from the chapter, the United States traded one computer to Mexico in exchange for three shirts. This is not just an arbitrary ratio of shirts to computers, however. Let's explore the *terms of trade* a little bit more.

a. Why is trading away a computer for three shirts a good trade for the United States? Why is it also a good deal for Mexico?

b. What if, instead, the agreed-on terms of trade were one computer for eight shirts. Would this trade still benefit both the United States and Mexico?

c. What is the maximum (and minimum) number of shirts that a computer can trade for if both the United States and Mexico are to benefit from the trade?

16. Go to *www.Ted.com* and search for Thomas Thwaites's talk, "How I Built a Toaster—from Scratch." How much money and time do you think Thwaites spent building his toaster? How long do you think it would have taken Thwaites to earn enough money in, say, a minimum-wage job to buy a toaster? Comment on the division of labor and the importance of specialization in increasing productivity.

WORK IT OUT

For interactive, step-by-step help in solving the following problem, go online.

Here's another specialization and exchange problem. This problem is wholly made-up, so that you won't be able to use your intuition about the names of countries or the products to figure out the answer.

a. Consider the following productivity table: Which country has an absolute advantage at making rotids? At making taurons?

	Number of Hours to Make One Rotid	Number of Hours to Make One Tauron
Mandovia	50	100
Ducennia	150	200

b. Using the information in the productivity table, estimate the opportunity cost of making rotids and taurons in Mandovia and Ducennia. Which country has a comparative advantage at manufacturing rotids? At making taurons?

	Opportunity Cost of Making One Rotid	Opportunity Cost of Making One Tauron
Mandovia	— taurons	— rotids
Ducennia	— taurons	— rotids

c. One billion hours of labor are available for making products in Mandovia, and 2 billion hours of labor are available for making products in Ducennia. In a no-trade world, let's assume that half the labor in each country gets used to make each product. (In a semester-long international trade course, you'd build a bigger model that would determine just how the workers are divided up according to the forces of supply and demand.) Fill in the table.

	Output of Rotids	Output of Taurons
Mandovia		
Ducennia		
Total output		

d. Now allow specialization. If each country completely specializes in the product in which it holds the comparative advantage, what will the total output of rotids be? Of taurons? Is the total output of each product higher than before?

	Output of Rotids	Output of Taurons
Mandovia		
Ducennia		
Total output		

e. Finally, let's open up trade. Trade has to make both sides better off (or at least no worse off), and in this problem as in most negotiations, there's more than one price that can do so (just think about haggling over the price of a car or a house). Suppose the price that both sides agree to is three rotids for two taurons. Ship 5 million taurons in one direction and 7.5 million rotids in the other direction (you'll have to figure out on your own which way the trade flows). In the following table, calculate the amount that each country gets to consume. Who is better off under this set of prices?

	Consumption of Rotids	Consumption of Taurons
Mandovia		
Ducennia		
Total consumption		

f. This time, the trade negotiations turn out differently: It's two rotids for one tauron. Have the correct country ship 10 million rotids, have the other send 5 million taurons, and fill out the table. One way to make sure you haven't made a mistake is to make sure that "total consumption" is equal to "total output" from part d: We can't create rotids and taurons out of thin air! Are both countries better off than if there were no trade? Which country likes this trade deal better than the deal from part e?

	Consumption of Rotids	Consumption of Taurons
Mandovia		
Ducennia		
Total consumption		

3

Supply and Demand

The world runs on oil. Every day about 77 *million* barrels of "black gold" flow from the earth and the sea to fuel the world's demand. Changes in the demand for and supply of oil can plunge one economy into recession while igniting a boom in another. In capitals from Washington to Riyadh, politicians carefully monitor the price of oil and so do ordinary consumers. Gasoline is made from oil so when world events like war in Ukraine disrupt the oil supply, prices at the corner gas station rise. The oil market is arguably the single most important market in the world.

The most important tools in economics are supply, demand, and the idea of equilibrium. Even if you understand little else, you may rightly claim yourself economically literate if you understand these tools. Fail to understand these tools and you will understand little else. In this chapter, we use the supply and demand for oil to explain the concepts of supply and demand. In the next chapter, we use supply, demand, and the idea of equilibrium to explain how prices are determined. So pay attention: This chapter and the next one are important. Really important.

The Demand Curve for Oil

How much oil would be demanded if the price of oil were $5 per barrel? What quantity would be demanded if the price were $20? What quantity would be demanded if the price were $55? A demand curve answers these questions. A **demand curve** is a function that shows the quantity demanded at different prices.

In Figure 3.1 on the next page, we show a hypothetical demand curve for oil and a table illustrating how a demand curve can be constructed from information on prices and quantities demanded. The demand curve tells us, for example, that at a price of $55 per barrel buyers are willing and able to buy 5 million barrels of oil a day or, more simply, at a price of $55 the **quantity demanded** is 5 million barrels a day (MBD).

Demand curves can be read in two ways. Read "horizontally," we can see from Figure 3.2 that at a price of $20 per barrel demanders are willing and able to buy 25 million barrels of oil per day. Read "vertically," we can see that the maximum price that demanders are willing to pay for 25 million barrels of oil a day is $20 per barrel. Thus, demand curves tell us the quantity demanded at

A **demand curve** is a function that shows the quantity demanded at different prices.

The **quantity demanded** is the quantity that buyers are willing and able to buy at a particular price.

27

FIGURE 3.1

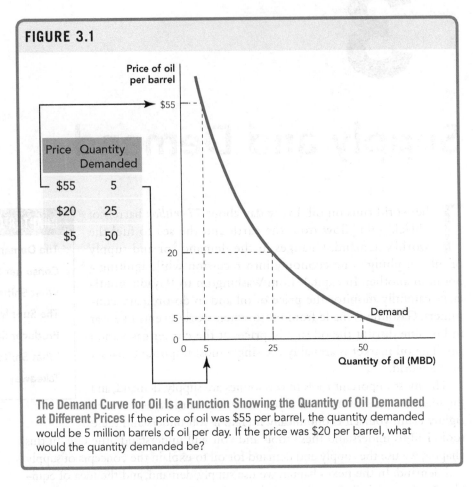

Price	Quantity Demanded
$55	5
$20	25
$5	50

The Demand Curve for Oil Is a Function Showing the Quantity of Oil Demanded at Different Prices If the price of oil was $55 per barrel, the quantity demanded would be 5 million barrels of oil per day. If the price was $20 per barrel, what would the quantity demanded be?

any price or the maximum willingness to pay (per unit) for any quantity. Some applications are easier to understand with one reading than with the other, so you should be familiar with both.

OK, a demand curve is a function that shows the quantity that demanders are willing to buy at different prices. But what does the demand curve *mean*?

FIGURE 3.2

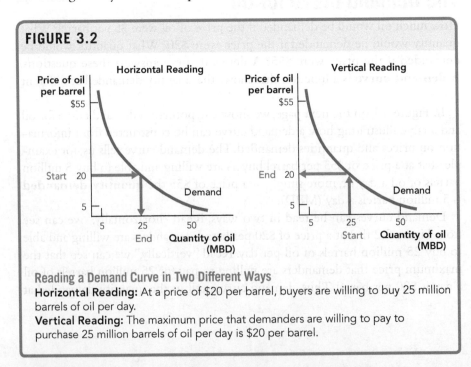

Reading a Demand Curve in Two Different Ways
Horizontal Reading: At a price of $20 per barrel, buyers are willing to buy 25 million barrels of oil per day.
Vertical Reading: The maximum price that demanders are willing to pay to purchase 25 million barrels of oil per day is $20 per barrel.

And why is the demand curve negatively sloped; that is, why is a greater quantity of oil demanded when the price is low?

Oil has many uses. A barrel of oil contains 42 gallons, and a little over half of that is used to produce gasoline (19.5 gallons) and jet fuel (4 gallons). The remaining 18.5 gallons are used for heating and energy generation and to make products such as lubricants, kerosene, asphalt, plastics, tires, and even rubber duckies (which are actually made not from rubber but from vinyl plastic).

Oil, however, is not equally valuable in all of its uses. Oil is more valuable for producing gasoline and jet fuel than it is for producing heating or rubber duckies. Oil is very valuable for transportation because in that use oil has few substitutes. There is no reasonable substitute for oil as jet fuel, for example, and although electric cars are becoming more popular, they are still a small share of the U.S. market. There are more substitutes for oil in heating and energy generation. In these fields, oil competes directly or indirectly against natural gas, coal, and electricity. Within each of these fields there are also more and less valuable uses. It's more valuable, for example, to raise the temperature in your house on a winter's day from 40 degrees to 65 degrees than it is to raise the temperature from 65 degrees to 70 degrees. Vinyl has high value as wire wrapping because it is fire-retardant, but we can probably substitute wooden toy boats for rubber duckies.

The fact that oil is not equally valuable in all of its uses explains why the demand curve for oil has a negative slope. When the price of oil is high, consumers will choose to use oil *only* in its most valuable uses (e.g., gasoline and jet fuel). As the price of oil falls, consumers will choose to also use oil in its less and less valued uses (heating and rubber duckies). Thus, a demand curve summarizes how millions of consumers choose to use oil given their preferences and the possibilities for substitution. Figure 3.3 illustrates these ideas with a demand curve for oil.

MRU

mru.org/demand

Why Does the Demand Curve Slope Down and Why Is This Important?

FIGURE 3.3

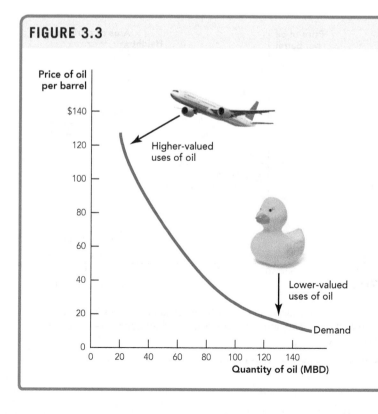

Price of oil per barrel

Higher-valued uses of oil

Lower-valued uses of oil

Demand

Quantity of oil (MBD)

The Demand for Oil Depends on the Value of Oil in Different Uses When the price of oil is high, oil will be used only in its higher-valued uses. As the price of oil falls, oil will also be used in lower-valued uses.

(Top: ssuaphotos/Shutterstock)
(Bottom: Lew Robertson/Corbis)

In summary, a demand curve is a function that shows the quantity that demanders are willing and able to buy at different prices. The lower the price, the greater the quantity demanded—this is often called the "law of demand."

Consumer Surplus

Consumer surplus is the consumer's gain from exchange, or the difference between the maximum price a consumer is willing to pay for a certain quantity and the market price.

Total consumer surplus is measured by the area beneath the demand curve and above the price.

If a consumer, say, the president of the United States, is willing to pay $80 per barrel to fuel his jet plane but the price of oil is only $20 per barrel, then the president earns a consumer surplus of $60 per barrel. If Joanne is willing to pay $25 and the price of oil is $20 per barrel, then Joanne earns a consumer surplus of $5 per barrel. For most of the products that you buy, you would probably be willing to pay more than the price, if you had to. The difference between what you are willing to pay and what you must pay (the price) is consumer surplus. **Consumer surplus** is the consumer's gain from exchange. Adding up consumer surplus for each consumer and for each unit, we can find **total consumer surplus**. On a graph, *total consumer surplus is the shaded area beneath the demand curve and above the price* (see Figure 3.4).

It's often convenient to approximate demand and supply curves with straight lines—this makes it easy to calculate areas like consumer surplus. The right panel of Figure 3.4 simplifies the left panel. Now we can calculate consumer surplus using a little high school geometry. Recall that the area of a triangle is $\frac{\text{Base} \times \text{Height}}{2}$. The base of the consumer surplus triangle is 90 million barrels and the height is $60 = $80 − $20, so consumer surplus equals $2,700 million ($\frac{1}{2} \times 90$ million $\times $60).

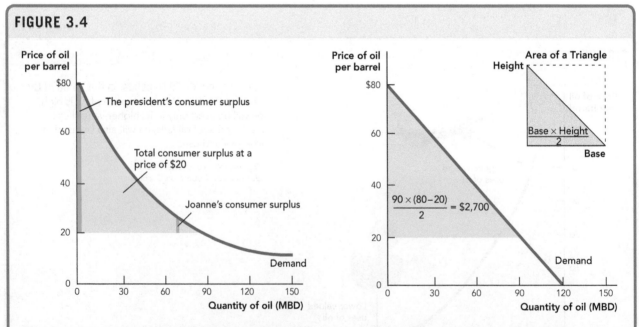

FIGURE 3.4

Total Consumer Surplus Is the Area Beneath the Demand Curve and Above the Price Total consumer surplus is the sum of consumer surplus of all buyers, the area beneath the demand curve and above the price. In the right panel, we show that consumer surplus is easy to calculate with a linear demand curve.

What Shifts the Demand Curve?

The demand curve for oil tells us the quantity of oil that people are willing to buy at a given price. Assume, for example, that at a price of $25 per barrel, the world demand for oil is 70 million barrels per day. An increase in demand means that at a price of $25, the quantity demanded increases to, say, 80 million barrels per day. Or, equivalently, it means that the maximum willingness to pay for 70 million barrels increases to say $50 per barrel. The left panel of Figure 3.5 shows an increase in demand. *An increase in demand shifts the demand curve outward, up and to the right.*

The right panel of Figure 3.5 shows a decrease in demand. *A decrease in demand shifts the demand curve inward, down and to the left.*

What kinds of things will increase or decrease demand? Unfortunately for economics students, a lot of things! Here is a list of some important demand shifters:

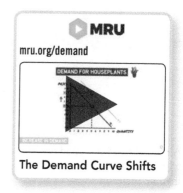

The Demand Curve Shifts

Important Demand Shifters

- Income
- Population
- Price of substitutes
- Price of complements
- Expectations
- Tastes

If you must, memorize the list. But keep in mind the question, "What would make people willing to buy a greater quantity at the same price?" Or equivalently, "What would make people willing to pay more for the same quantity?" With these questions in mind, you should always be able to come up with a fairly good list on your own.

FIGURE 3.5

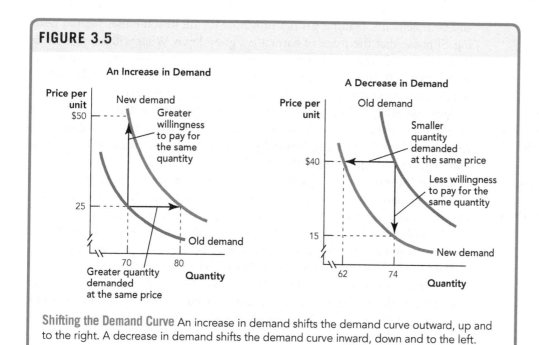

Shifting the Demand Curve An increase in demand shifts the demand curve outward, up and to the right. A decrease in demand shifts the demand curve inward, down and to the left.

Here are some examples of demand shifters in action.

Income When people get richer, they buy more stuff. In the United States, people buy bigger cars when their income increases and big cars increase the demand for oil. When income increases in China or India, many people buy their first car and that too increases the demand for oil. Thus, an increase in income will increase the demand for oil exactly as shown in the left panel of Figure 3.5.

When an *increase* in income *increases* the demand for a good, we say the good is a **normal good**. Most goods are normal; for example, cars, electronics, and restaurant meals are normal goods. Can you think of some goods for which an increase in income will *decrease* the demand? When we were young economics students, we didn't have a lot of money to go to expensive restaurants. For 50 cents and some boiling water, however, we could get a nice bowl of instant Ramen noodles. Ah, good times. When our income increased, however, our demand for Ramen noodles decreased—we don't buy Ramen noodles anymore! A good like Ramen noodles for which an *increase* in income *decreases* the demand is called an **inferior good**. What goods are you consuming now that you probably wouldn't consume if you were rich? Economic growth is rapidly increasing the incomes of millions of poor people in China and India. What goods do poor people consume in these countries today that they will consume less of 20 years from now?

Population More people, more demand. That's simple enough. Things get more interesting when some subpopulations increase more than others. The United States, for example, is aging. Today the 65-year-old-and-older crowd makes up about 17% of the population. By 2030, 19.4% of the population will be 65 years or older. In fact, demographers estimate that by 2030, 18.2 million people in the United States will be over 85 years of age![1] What sorts of goods and services will increase in demand with this increase in population? Which will decrease in demand? Entrepreneurs want to know the answers to these questions because big profits will flow to those who can anticipate new and expanded markets.

The Price of Substitutes and Complements Every good has substitutes and complements. Natural gas is a substitute for oil in some uses such as heating. Suppose that the price of natural gas goes down. What will happen to the demand for oil? When the price of natural gas goes down, some people will switch from oil furnaces to natural gas, so the demand for oil will decrease—the demand curve shifts down and to the left. Figure 3.6 illustrates.

More generally, a decrease in the price of a **substitute** will decrease demand for the other good. A decrease in the price of Pepsi, for example, will decrease the demand for Coca-Cola. Naturally, an increase in the price of a substitute will increase demand for the other good.

Complements are things that go well together such as ground beef and hamburger buns, sugar and tea, iPhones and iPhone apps. Demand for a good increases when the price of a complementary good decreases (and vice versa).

It sounds complicated, so just remember that ground beef and hamburger buns are complements. Suppose the price of beef goes down. What happens to the demand for hamburger buns? If the price of beef goes down, people buy more ground beef and they also increase their demand for hamburger buns; that is, the demand curve for hamburger buns shifts up and to the right. A supermarket having a sale on ground beef, for example, will also want to stock up on hamburger buns.

In explaining the basics of lobbying and regulation, the Nobel Prize–winning economist George Stigler said, "the butter producers wish to suppress margarine

---

A **normal good** is a good for which demand increases when income increases.

An **inferior good** is a good for which demand decreases when income increases.

Nastasic/Getty Images

Demographics and demand The number of old people in the United States is increasing. How will this increase in the elderly population shift the demand curve for different goods?

If two goods are **substitutes**, a decrease in the price of one good leads to a decrease in demand for the other good.

If two goods are **complements**, a decrease in the price of one good leads to an increase in the demand for the other good.

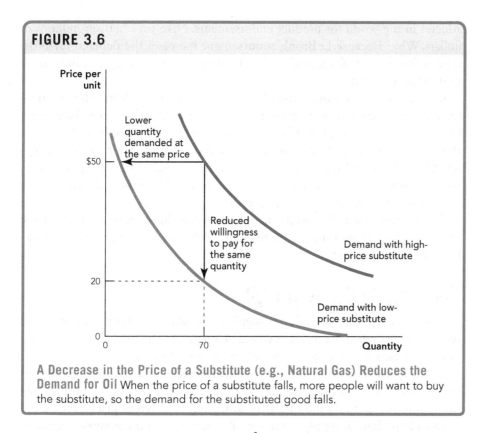

FIGURE 3.6

A Decrease in the Price of a Substitute (e.g., Natural Gas) Reduces the Demand for Oil When the price of a substitute falls, more people will want to buy the substitute, so the demand for the substituted good falls.

and encourage the production of bread."[2] More generally, firms want the substitutes for their products to be expensive and the complements to be cheap. So let's consider the last item in our list of complements, iPhones and iPhone apps. Does Apple want cheap apps or expensive apps? Apple wants cheap apps, so we can predict that Apple will make it easy to write iPhone apps and that it will promote a competitive marketplace in apps.

Expectations In July 2019, oil prices spiked upward after Iran seized two British oil tankers in the Strait of Hormuz. Is a single oil tanker or even two so critical to the world supply of oil? No. But Iran, Iraq, and Saudi Arabia shipped 21 million barrels of oil through the strait every *day* and demanders of oil feared that the Iranian seizures might have been the start of a large-scale disruption. Fear of future disruptions encouraged businesses and governments to buy more oil now and increase emergency stockpiles. In other words, *the expectation of a reduction in the future oil supply increased the demand for oil today.*

You have probably responded to expectations about future events in a similar way. When the weather forecaster predicts a big storm, many people rush to the stores to stock up on storm supplies. In the week before Hurricane Sandy hit New Jersey, for example, sales of flashlights and batteries skyrocketed.

Expectations are powerful—they can be as powerful in affecting demand (and supply) as events themselves.

Tastes Tastes are always changing. The keto diet increased the demand for beef and helped to make steakhouses such as Outback Steakhouse and the Brazilian-inspired Fogo De Chão popular. But in recent years, the "ethical eating" trend has increased the demand for less processed foods and more plant-based foods, including plant-based meat substitutes such as the Impossible™ Burger.

LeBron James's four NBA championships, four Most Valuable Player awards, and two Olympic gold medals have made him one of the most sought after

CHECK YOURSELF

- Google makes its Android operating system for smartphones available for free under an open source license. Why?

athletes in the world for product endorsements. Nike pays LeBron millions of dollars. Why? Because LeBron's endorsement increases the demand for Nike shoes. Changes in tastes caused by fads, fashions, and advertising can all increase or decrease demand.

Can tastes change something like the demand for oil? Sure. The environmental movement has made people more aware of global climate change and how the consumption of oil adds carbon dioxide to the atmosphere. As a result, the demand for hybrid cars has increased, more people are recycling things like plastic bags, and more people are considering installing solar power cells on their rooftops as an alternative source of energy. All of these changes can be understood as a change in tastes or preferences.

The bottom line is that while many factors can shape market demand, most of these factors should make intuitive sense. After all, you are, on a daily basis, part of market demand.

The Supply Curve for Oil

How much oil would oil producers supply to the world market if the price of oil were $5 per barrel? What quantity would be supplied if the price were $20? What quantity if the price were $55? A supply curve for oil answers these questions.

The **supply curve** for oil is a function showing the quantity of oil that suppliers would be willing and able to sell at different prices, or, more simply, the supply curve shows the **quantity supplied** at different prices. Figure 3.7 shows a hypothetical supply curve for oil. The price is on the vertical axis and

CHECK YOURSELF

• Economic growth in India is raising the income of Indian workers. What do you predict will happen to the demand for automobiles? What about the demand for charcoal bricks for home heating?

• As the price of oil rises, what do you predict will happen to the demand for mopeds?

The **supply curve** is a function that shows the quantity supplied at different prices.

The **quantity supplied** is the amount of a good that sellers are willing and able to sell at a particular price.

FIGURE 3.7

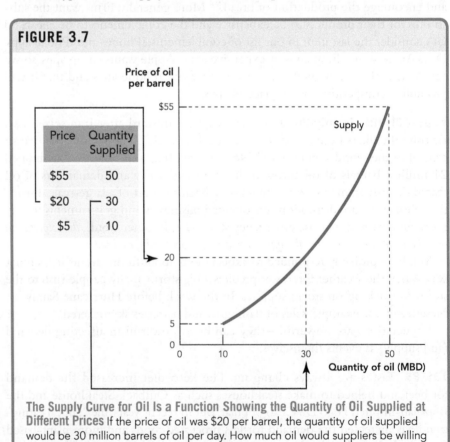

The Supply Curve for Oil Is a Function Showing the Quantity of Oil Supplied at Different Prices If the price of oil was $20 per barrel, the quantity of oil supplied would be 30 million barrels of oil per day. How much oil would suppliers be willing and able to sell at $55?

the quantity of oil is on the horizontal axis. The table beside the graph shows how a supply curve can be constructed from a table of prices and quantities supplied.

The supply curve tells us, for example, that at a price of $20 the quantity supplied is 30 million barrels of oil a day.

As with demand curves, supply curves can be read in two ways. Read "horizontally," Figure 3.8 shows that at a price of $20 per barrel suppliers are willing to sell 30 million barrels of oil per day. Read "vertically," the supply curve tells us that to produce 30 million barrels of oil a day, suppliers must be paid at least $20 per barrel. Thus, the supply curve tells us the maximum quantity that suppliers will supply at different prices or the minimum price at which suppliers will sell different quantities. The two ways of reading a supply curve are equivalent, but some applications are easier to understand with one reading and some with the other, so you should be familiar with both.

Our hypothetical supply curve is not realistic because we just made up the numbers. But now that we know the technical meaning of a supply curve—*a function that shows the quantity that suppliers would be willing and able to sell at different prices*—we can easily explain its economic meaning.

Saudi Arabia, the world's third-largest oil producer, produces about 9 million barrels of oil per day. The United States, currently the world's top oil producer, produces over 11 million barrels per day. But there is one big difference between Saudi oil and U.S. oil: U.S. oil costs much more to produce. The United States has been producing major quantities of oil since 1901 when, after drilling to a depth of 1,020 feet, mud started to bubble out of an oil well dug in Spindletop, Texas. Minutes later the drill bit exploded into the air and a fountain of oil leapt 150 feet into the sky. It took nine days to cap the well, and in the process a million barrels of oil were spilt. No one had ever seen so much oil. Within months the price of oil dropped from $2 per barrel to just 3 cents per barrel.[3]

It's safe to say that the United States will never see another gusher like Spindletop. Today the typical new well in the United States is drilled to a depth

FIGURE 3.8

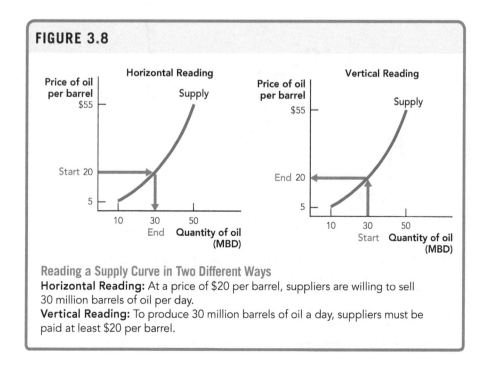

Reading a Supply Curve in Two Different Ways
Horizontal Reading: At a price of $20 per barrel, suppliers are willing to sell 30 million barrels of oil per day.
Vertical Reading: To produce 30 million barrels of oil a day, suppliers must be paid at least $20 per barrel.

mru.org/supply

Why Do (Most) Supply Curves Slope Up and Why Is This Important?

of roughly 1 mile. Instead of gushing, most of the wells must be pumped or flooded with water to push the oil to the surface.[4] All this makes oil production in the United States much more expensive than it used to be and much more expensive than in Saudi Arabia, where oil is more plentiful than anywhere else in the world.

In Saudi Arabia, lifting a barrel of oil to the surface costs about $2. Costs in Iran and Iraq are only slightly higher. Nigerian and Russian oil can be extracted at a cost of around $5 and $7 per barrel, respectively. Alaskan oil costs around $10 to extract. Oil from Britain's North Sea costs about $12 to extract. There is more oil in Canada's tar sands than in all of Iran, but it costs about $22.50 per barrel to get the oil out of the sand.[5] In the continental United States, one of the oldest and most developed oil regions in the world, lifting costs are about $27.50. At a price of $40 per barrel, it becomes profitable to "sweat" oil out of Oklahoma oil shale.

Putting all of this together, we can construct a simple supply curve for oil. At a price of $2 per barrel, the only oil that would be profitable to produce would be oil from the lowest-cost wells in places like Saudi Arabia. As the price of oil rises, oil from Iran and Iraq become profitable. When the price reaches $5, Nigerian and then Russian producers begin to just break even. As the price rises yet further toward $10, Alaskan oil starts to break even and then become profitable. North Sea, Canadian, and then Texan oil fields come online and increase production as the price rises further. At higher prices, it becomes profitable to extract oil using even more exotic technologies or deeper wells in more inhospitable parts of the world. Figure 3.9 illustrates.

FIGURE 3.9

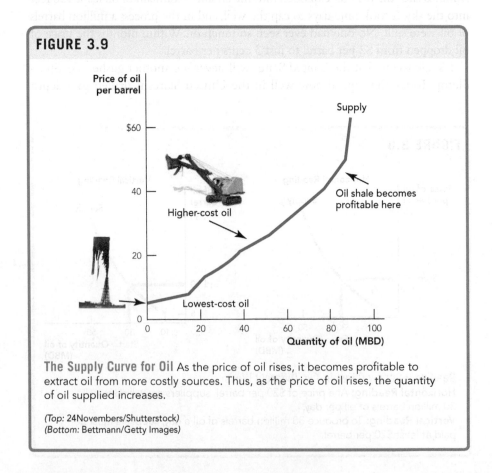

The Supply Curve for Oil As the price of oil rises, it becomes profitable to extract oil from more costly sources. Thus, as the price of oil rises, the quantity of oil supplied increases.

(Top: 24Novembers/Shutterstock)
(Bottom: Bettmann/Getty Images)

What's important to understand about Figure 3.9 is that as the price of oil rises, it becomes profitable to produce oil using methods and in regions of the world with higher costs of production. The higher the price of oil, the deeper the wells.

In summary, a supply curve is a function that shows the quantity that suppliers would be willing and able to sell at different prices. The higher the price, the greater the quantity supplied—this is often called the "law of supply."

Producer Surplus

Figure 3.9 suggests two other concepts of importance. If the price of oil is $40 per barrel and Saudi Arabia can produce oil at $2 per barrel, then we say that Saudi Arabia earns a **producer surplus** of $38 per barrel. Similarly, if the price of oil is $40 per barrel and Nigeria can produce at $5 a barrel, Nigeria earns a producer surplus of $35 per barrel. More generally, the difference between the lowest price that a producer is willing to sell a good for and the actual price is the producer's surplus, the producer's gain from exchange. Adding the producer surplus for each producer for each unit, we can find total producer surplus. Fortunately, this is easy to do on a diagram. *Total producer surplus is the area above the supply curve and below the price* (see Figure 3.10).

Consumer surplus measures the consumer's benefit from trade, and producer surplus measures the producer's benefit from trade. If we add the two surpluses together, we get a measure of the total gains from trade to market participants. All else equal, more benefits are better so throughout this text, we will be using consumer plus producer surplus as a measure of welfare to compare different institutions and policies such as markets, monopolies, price controls, quotas, taxes and subsidies. Which of these institutions maximizes total benefits and under what conditions? Of course, sometimes not all else is equal, and when we study externalities and ethics, we will look at situations where it's important to add to our measure of benefits (and costs) to take into account the effect of trade on bystanders and on broader social interests.

Producer surplus is the producer's gain from exchange, or the difference between the market price and the minimum price at which a producer would be willing to sell a particular quantity.

Total producer surplus is measured by the area above the supply curve and below the price.

FIGURE 3.10

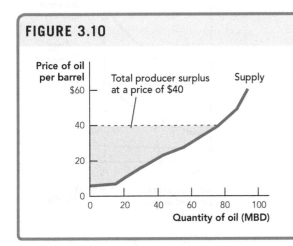

Total Producer Surplus Is the Area Above the Supply Curve and Below the Price
Total producer surplus is the sum of the producer surplus of each seller, the area above the supply curve and below the price.

What Shifts the Supply Curve?

The second important concept suggested by Figure 3.9 is the connection between the supply curve and costs. What happens to the supply curve when the cost of producing oil falls? Suppose, for example, that a technological innovation in oil drilling such as sidewise drilling allows more oil to be produced at the same cost. What happens to the supply curve? The supply curve tells us how much suppliers are willing to sell at a particular price. The new technology makes some oil fields profitable that were previously unprofitable, so *at any price* suppliers are now willing to supply a greater quantity. Equivalently, the new technology lowers costs, so suppliers will be willing to sell any given quantity at a lower price. Either way, economists say that a decrease in costs increases supply. In terms of the diagram, *a decrease in costs means that the supply curve shifts down and to the right*, which the left panel of Figure 3.11 illustrates. Of course, *higher costs mean that the supply curve shifts in the opposite direction, up and to the left*, as illustrated in the right panel of Figure 3.11.

Once you know that a decrease in costs shifts the supply curve down and to the right and an increase in costs shifts the supply curve up and to the left, then you really know everything there is to know about supply shifts. It can take a little practice, however, to identify the many factors that can change costs. Here are some important supply shifters:

Important Supply Shifters

- Technological innovations and changes in the price of inputs
- Taxes and subsidies
- Expectations
- Entry or exit of producers
- Changes in opportunity costs

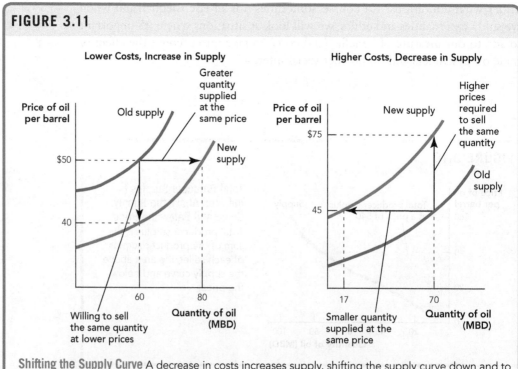

FIGURE 3.11

Lower Costs, Increase in Supply

Higher Costs, Decrease in Supply

Shifting the Supply Curve A decrease in costs increases supply, shifting the supply curve down and to the right. An increase in costs decreases supply, shifting the supply curve up and to the left.

It can also help in analyzing supply shifters to know that sometimes it's easier to think of cost changes as shifting the supply curve right or left, and other times it's a little easier to think of cost changes as shifting the supply curve up or down. These two methods of thinking about supply shifts are equivalent and correspond to the two methods of reading a supply curve, the horizontal and vertical readings, respectively. We will give examples of each method as we examine some cost shifters in action.

Technological Innovations and Changes in the Price of Inputs We have already given an example of how improvements in technology can reduce costs, thus increasing supply. A reduction in input prices also reduces costs and thus has a similar effect. A fall in the wages of oil rig workers, for example, will reduce the cost of producing oil, shifting the supply curve down and to the right as in the left panel of Figure 3.11. Alternatively, an increase in the wages of oil rig workers will increase the cost of producing oil, shifting the supply curve up and to the left as in the right panel of Figure 3.11.

Taxes and Subsidies We can get some practice using up or down shifts to analyze a cost change by examining the effect of a $10 oil tax on the supply curve for oil. As far as firms are concerned, a tax on output is the same as an increase in costs. If the government taxes oil producers $10 per barrel, this is exactly the same to producers as an increase in their costs of production of $10 per barrel.

In Figure 3.12, notice that before the tax, firms require $40 per barrel to sell 60 million barrels of oil per day (point *a*). How much will firms require to sell the same quantity of oil when there is a tax of $10 per barrel? Correct, $50. What firms care about is the take-home price. If firms require $40 per barrel to sell 60 million barrels of oil, that's what they require regardless of the tax. When the government takes $10 per barrel, firms must charge $50 to keep their take-home price at $40. Thus, in Figure 3.12, notice that the $10 tax shifts the supply curve up by exactly $10 at *every point* along the curve.

It's important to avoid one possible confusion. All we have said so far is that a $10 tax shifts the supply curve for oil up by $10. We haven't said anything about the effect of a tax on the *price* of oil—that's because we have not yet analyzed how market prices are formed. We are saving that topic for Chapter 4.

FIGURE 3.12

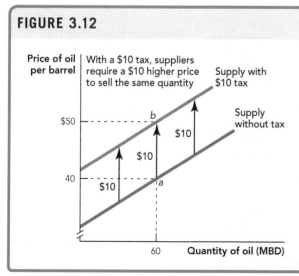

Price of oil per barrel | With a $10 tax, suppliers require a $10 higher price to sell the same quantity

Supply with $10 tax

Supply without tax

$50 ---- *b*

$10

$10

$10

40 ---- *a*

$10

60   **Quantity of oil (MBD)**

A Tax on Industry Output Shifts the Supply Curve Up by the Amount of the Tax When suppliers pay no tax, they are willing to supply 60 million barrels a day (MBD) of oil for a price of $40 per barrel. If they must pay a tax of $10 per barrel, they will be willing to supply 60 MBD for $10 more, or $50 a barrel. Thus, a tax shifts the supply curve up by the amount of the tax.

How does a subsidy, a tax benefit, or a write-off shift the supply curve? We will save that analysis for the end-of-chapter problems but here's a hint: A subsidy is the same as a negative or "reverse" tax.

Expectations Suppliers who expect that prices will increase in the future have an incentive to sell less today so that they can store goods for future sale. Thus, the expectation of a future price increase shifts today's supply curve to the left as illustrated in Figure 3.13. The shifting of supply in response to price expectations is the essence of *speculation*, the attempt to profit from future price changes.

Entry or Exit of Producers When the United States signed the North American Free Trade Agreement (NAFTA), reducing barriers to trade among the United States, Mexico, and Canada, Canadian producers of lumber entered the U.S. market and increased the supply of lumber. We can most easily think about this as a shift to the right of the supply curve.

In Figure 3.14, the domestic supply curve is the supply curve for lumber before NAFTA. The curve labeled domestic supply plus Canadian imports is the supply curve for lumber after NAFTA allowed Canadian firms to sell in the United States with fewer restrictions. The entry of more firms meant that

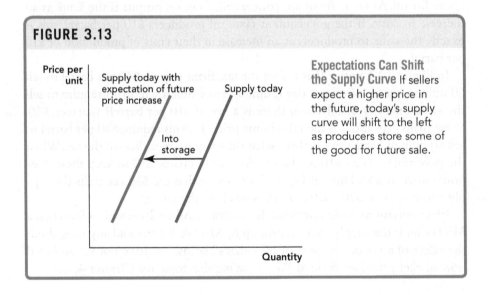

FIGURE 3.13

Expectations Can Shift the Supply Curve If sellers expect a higher price in the future, today's supply curve will shift to the left as producers store some of the good for future sale.

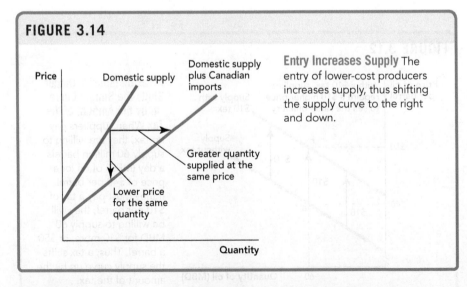

FIGURE 3.14

Entry Increases Supply The entry of lower-cost producers increases supply, thus shifting the supply curve to the right and down.

at any price a greater quantity of lumber was available; that is, the supply curve shifted to the right.[*]

In a later chapter, we discuss the effects of foreign trade at greater length.

Changes in Opportunity Costs The last important supply shifter, changes in opportunity costs, is the trickiest to understand. Recall from Chapter 1 that when the unemployment rates increase, more people tend to go to college. If you can't get a job, you aren't giving up many good opportunities by going to college. Thus, when the unemployment rate increases, the (opportunity) cost of college falls and so more people attend college. Notice that to understand how people behave, you must understand their opportunity costs.

Now suppose that a farmer is currently growing soybeans but that his land could also be used to grow wheat. If the price of *wheat* increases, then the farmer's opportunity cost of growing soybeans increases and the farmer will want to shift land from soybean production into the more profitable alternative of wheat production. As land is taken out of soybean production, the supply curve for soybeans shifts up and to the left.

In Figure 3.15, notice that before the increase in the price of wheat, farmers would be willing to supply 2,800 million bushels of soybeans at a price of $5 per bushel (point *a*). But when the price of wheat increases, farmers are willing to supply only 2,000 million bushels of soybeans at a price of $5 per bushel because an alternative use of the land (growing wheat) is now more valuable. Equivalently, before the increase in the price of wheat, farmers were

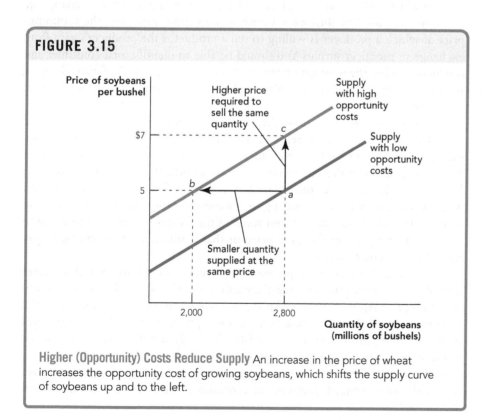

FIGURE 3.15

Higher (Opportunity) Costs Reduce Supply An increase in the price of wheat increases the opportunity cost of growing soybeans, which shifts the supply curve of soybeans up and to the left.

---

[*] It is equally correct to think of new entrants as shifting the supply curve down. Remember, it's ultimately costs that shift supply, and what increases supply is entry of *lower-cost* producers. Industry costs fell when Canadian producers entered the market because many Canadian producers had lower costs than some U.S. producers. As lower-cost Canadian producers entered the industry, higher-cost U.S. producers exited the industry, and industry costs decreased, thus shifting the supply curve down.

CHECK YOURSELF

- Technological innovations in chip making have driven down the costs of producing computers. What happens to the supply curve for computers? Why?
- The U.S. government subsidizes making ethanol as a fuel made from corn. What effect does the subsidy have on the supply curve for ethanol?

willing to sell 2,800 million bushels of soybeans for $5 per bushel, but after their opportunity costs increase, farmers require $7 per bushel to sell the same quantity (point *c*).

Similarly, a decrease in opportunity costs shifts the supply curve down and to the right. If the price of wheat falls, for example, the opportunity cost of growing soybeans falls and the supply curve for soybeans will shift down and to the right. It's just another example of a running theme throughout this chapter, namely that both supply and demand respond to incentives.

Takeaway

In this chapter, we have presented the fundamentals of the demand curve and the supply curve. The next chapter and much of the rest of this book build on these fundamentals. We thus give you fair warning. If you do not understand this chapter and the next, you will be lost!

A key point to know is that a demand curve is a function showing the quantity demanded at different prices. In other words, a demand curve shows how customers respond to higher prices by buying less and to lower prices by buying more. Another key point is that, similarly, a supply curve is a function showing the quantity supplied at different prices. In other words, a supply curve shows how producers respond to higher prices by producing more and to lower prices by producing less.

The difference between the maximum price a consumer is willing to pay for a product and the market price is the consumer's gain from exchange or consumer surplus. The difference between the market price and the minimum price at which a producer is willing to sell a product is the producer's gain from exchange or producer surplus. You should be able to identify total consumer and producer surplus, the total gain from exchange, on a diagram. In future chapters, we will be using total consumer plus total producer surplus to evaluate different institutions and policies.

When it comes to what shifts the supply and demand curves, we have listed some factors in this chapter. Yes, you should know these lists, but more fundamentally you should know that an increase in demand *means* that buyers want a greater quantity at the same price or, equivalently, they are willing to pay a higher price for the same quantity. Thus, anything that causes buyers to want more at the same price or be willing to pay more for the same quantity increases demand. In a pinch, just think about some of the factors that would cause you to want more of a good at the same price or that would make you willing to pay more for the same quantity.

Similarly, an increase in supply *means* that sellers are willing to sell a greater quantity at the same price or, equivalently, they are willing to sell a given quantity at a lower price. Again, what would make you willing to sell more of a good for the same price or sell the same quantity for a lower price? (Here's a hint—you might be willing to do this if your costs had fallen.) Supply and demand curves are not just abstract constructs, they also shape your life.

In the next chapter, we will use supply curves and demand curves to answer one of the most crucial questions in economics: How is the price of a good determined?

CHAPTER REVIEW

Go online to practice with more examples of these types of problems, including live links to videos, data sources, and feedback.

KEY CONCEPTS

demand curve, p. 27

quantity demanded, p. 27

consumer surplus, p. 30

total consumer surplus, p. 30

normal good, p. 32

inferior good, p. 32

substitutes, p. 32

complements, p. 32

supply curve, p. 34

quantity supplied, p. 34

producer surplus, p. 37

total producer surplus, p. 37

FACTS AND TOOLS

1. When the price of a good increases, the quantity demanded _____. When the price of a good decreases, the quantity demanded _____.

2. When will people search harder for substitutes for oil: when the price of oil is high or when the price of oil is low?

3. Your roommate just bought a Garmin GPS Smartwatch for $200. They would have been willing to pay $250 for a device that could improve their morning runs by measuring the speed, distance, and duration of the runs and calculating the calories burned. How much consumer surplus does your roommate enjoy from the watch?

4. What are three things that you'll buy less of once you graduate from college and get a good job? What kinds of goods are these called?

5. When the price of Apple MacBooks goes down, what probably happens to the demand for laptops that use Microsoft Windows as an operating system?

6. **a.** When the price of olive oil goes up, what probably happens to the demand for corn oil?

   b. When the price of petroleum goes up, what probably happens to the demand for natural gas? To the demand for coal? To the demand for solar power?

7. **a.** If everyone thinks that the price of tomatoes will go up next week, what is likely to happen to the demand for tomatoes today?

   b. If everyone thinks that the price of gasoline will go up next week, what is likely to happen to the demand for gasoline today? (*Note:* Is this change in demand caused by consumers or by gas station owners?)

8. Along a supply curve, if the price of oil falls, what will happen to the quantity of oil supplied? Why?

9. If the price of cars falls, are carmakers likely to make more or fewer cars, according to the supply curve? (Notice that the "person on the street" often thinks the opposite is true!)

10. When is a pharmaceutical business more likely to hire highly educated, cutting-edge workers and use new, experimental research methods: when the business expects the price of its new drug to be low or when it expects the price to be high?

11. Imagine that a technological innovation reduces the costs of producing high-quality steel. What happens to the supply curve for steel?

12. When oil companies expect the price of oil to be higher next year, what happens to the supply of oil today?

13. Do taxes usually increase the supply of a good or reduce the supply?

14. As the baby boom population ages, what is likely to happen to the demand for health care in the United States?

15. If the Netflix series *Cobra Kai* repopularizes karate among teenagers, what is the likely effect in the market for karate classes?

16. If an influx of American servicemen who were posted in Okinawa begin to open karate schools to teach the martial arts they learned overseas, what is the likely effect in the market for karate classes?

17. State whether each of the following will likely lead to an *increase* or a *decrease* in the demand for hair transplant surgery.

a. Jason Statham and Dwayne Johnson (both men with receding hairlines) star in blockbuster films as leading men.

b. There is a general increase in income, and men consider hair transplant surgery to be a normal good.

c. The population is aging.

d. Toupees increase in price.

e. Consumers expect new regulations in the industry that will increase the price of surgery the following year.

18. If changes in policy reduce the number of Canadian lumber producers who are able to sell their product in the United States, what impact does this have on the supply of lumber in the United States?

THINKING AND PROBLEM SOLVING

19. Consider the following demand curve for oil:

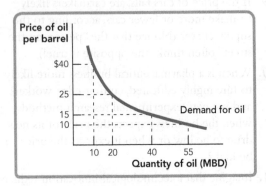

a. Using this demand curve, fill in the following table:

Price	Quantity Demanded
	55
$25	

b. If the price was $10, how much oil would be demanded?

c. What is the maximum price (per barrel) that demanders will pay for 20 million barrels of oil?

20. From the following chart, draw the demand curve for pencils (in hundreds):

Price	Quantity Demanded (100s)
$5	60
$15	45
$25	35
$35	20

21. If the price of glass dramatically increases, what are we likely to see a lot less of: glass windows or glass bottles? Why?

22. Let's think about the demand for LED TVs.

a. If the price for a 60-inch LED TV is $500 and Miguel would be willing to pay $3,000, what is Miguel's consumer surplus?

b. Consider the following figure for the total demand for LED TVs. At $500 per TV, 1,200 TVs are demanded. What is the total consumer surplus at that price? Calculate the total and identify it on the diagram.

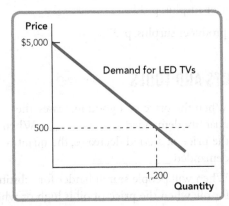

c. Where is Miguel in the figure?

23. If income increases and the demand for good X shifts as shown in the figure, then is good X a normal or an inferior good? Give an example of a good like good X.

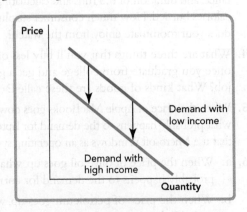

24. Assume that butter and margarine are substitutes. What will happen to the demand curve for butter if the price of margarine increases? Why?

25. SUVs and gasoline are complements. What will happen to the demand curve for gasoline if the price of SUVs decreases? Why? (*Hint:* What happens to the quantity demanded of SUVs?)

26. Suppose that the supply curve for solar panels is as shown in the diagram:

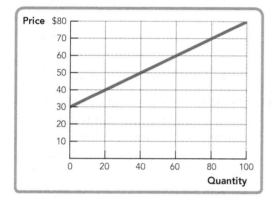

The government decides that it would like to increase the quantity of solar panels in use, so it offers a $20 subsidy per panel to producers. Draw the new supply curve. (*Hint:* Remember our analysis of how a tax affects supply, as shown in Figure 3.12, and bear in mind that a subsidy can be thought of as a "negative tax.")

27. A group of friends is trying to decide if they will each independently buy Hulu subscriptions. The table below gives each individual's maximum willingness to pay for a subscription.

Maximum Willingness to Pay	
Isabella	$20.00
Saitama	$15.00
Isaiah	$12.50
Aaliyah	$17.50

a. If the price of a Hulu subscription is $15, what will be the total amount of consumer surplus?

b. At this price, will every friend purchase a subscription? Why or why not?

28. Consider the following supply curve for oil. Note that MBD stands for "millions of barrels per day," the usual way informed people talk about the supply of oil:

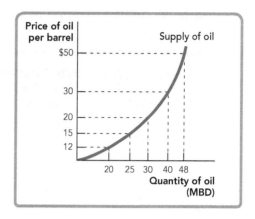

a. Based on this supply curve, fill in the table:

Price	Quantity Supplied
$12	
	40

b. If the price for a barrel of oil was $15, how much oil would oil suppliers be willing to supply?

c. What is the lowest price at which suppliers of oil would be willing to supply 20 MBD?

29. From the following table of prices per 100 pencils and quantities supplied (in hundreds of pencils), draw the supply curve for pencils:

Price	Quantity Supplied
$5	20
$15	40
$25	50
$35	55

30. Suppose Melvald's Illumination and National Lights are the only two suppliers of Christmas lights in Hawkins. Draw the supply curve for the Christmas lights industry in Hawkins from the following tables for the two companies. To create this "Christmas lights industry supply curve," note that you'll add up the *total* number of Christmas lights that the industry will supply at a price of $1 (15 Christmas lights)

and then do the same for the prices of $5, $7, and $10.

Price	Bulbs Supplied by Melvald's Illumination	Bulbs Supplied by National Lights
$1	10	5
$5	15	7
$7	25	15
$10	35	20

31. Using the following diagram, identify and calculate total producer surplus if the price of oil is $50 per barrel. Recall that for a triangle, Area = (1/2) × Base × Height. (You never thought you'd use that equation unless you became an engineer, did you?)

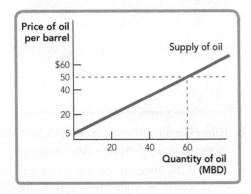

32. The supply curve for sugar is as follows:

Price (per 100-pound bag)	Quantity
$30	10,000
$50	15,000
$70	20,000

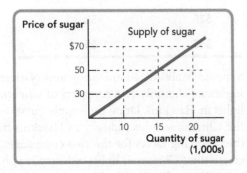

Under pressure from nutrition activists, the government decides to tax sugar producers with a $5 tax per 100-pound bag. Using the figure above, draw the new supply curve. After the tax is enacted, what price will result in quantities supplied of 10,000? 15,000? 20,000? Give your answers in the table:

Price (per 100-pound bag)	Quantity
	10,000
	15,000
	20,000

33. Consider the farmers talked about in the chapter who have land that is suitable for growing both wheat and soybeans. Suppose all farmers are currently farming wheat but the price of soybeans rises dramatically.

   a. Does the opportunity cost of producing wheat rise or fall?

   b. Does this shift the supply curve for wheat (as in one of the panels of Figure 3.11), or is it a movement along a fixed supply curve?

   What direction is this shift or movement? Illustrate your answer in the following figure:

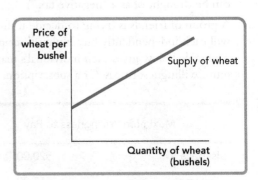

CHALLENGES

34. Jada is an economist. She loves being an economist so much that she would do it for a living even if she earned only $30,000 per year. Instead, she earns $103,000 per year. (*Note:* This is the average salary of new economists with a PhD degree.) How much producer surplus does Jada enjoy?

35. The economist Bryan Caplan recently found a pair of $10 arch supports that saved him from the pain of major foot surgery. As he stated on his blog (econlog.econlib.org), he would have been willing to pay $100,000 to fix his foot problem, but instead he paid only a few dollars.

   a. How much consumer surplus did Bryan enjoy from this purchase?

   b. If the sales tax was 5% on this product, how much revenue did the government raise when Bryan bought his arch supports?

   c. If the government could have taxed Bryan based on his *willingness to pay* rather than on how much he *actually* paid, how much sales tax would Bryan have had to pay?

36. For most young people, working full-time and going to school are substitutes: You tend to do one or the other. When it's tough to find a job, does that raise the opportunity cost of going to college, or does it lower it? When it's tough to find a job, does the demand for college rise or fall?

37. What should happen to the "demand for speed" (measured by the average speed on highways) once airbags are included on cars?

38. The industrial areas in northeast Washington, D.C., were relatively dangerous in the 1980s. Over the last three decades, the area has become a safer place to work (although there are still roughly six times more violent crimes per person in these areas compared with another D.C. neighborhood, Georgetown). When an area becomes a safer place to work, what probably happens to the "supply of labor" in that area?

Discovering DATA

39. The Federal Reserve Economic Data (FRED) database is available at https://fred.stlouisfed.org. Go to FRED and search for data on crude oil prices. You will find several series; click on one of them, such as Crude Oil Prices: West Texas Intermediate (WTI)—Cushing, Oklahoma. Adjust the dates to focus in on the time period from January 1, 2019, through April 15, 2020. The short recession induced by COVID-19 is shown by the shaded area.

   a. Print the graph.

   b. What happened to crude oil prices during the recession, especially as the recession continued?

   c. Do you think the change in price was driven more by a shift to demand or to supply? Using the lists of important demand and supply shifters from Chapter 3, what was the major factor shifting demand or supply?

   d. FRED has several series for the oil price. Why doesn't it matter which one we use?

   e. Optional: Using what you learn in the next chapter, draw a demand and supply diagram. Label the initial price the "pre-recession price." Show the new demand or supply curve. Label the new price the "recession price."

WORK IT OUT

For interactive, step-by-step help in solving the following problem, go online.

The supply curve for rice is as follows:

Price (per 100-pound bag)	Quantity
$40	10,000
$60	15,000
$80	20,000

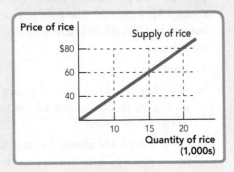

Under pressure from nutrition activists, the government decides to tax rice producers with a $5 tax per 100-pound bag. Using the preceding figure, draw the new supply curve. After the tax is enacted, what price will bring forth quantities of 10,000? 15,000? 20,000? Give your answers in the table:

Price (per 100-pound bag)	Quantity
	10,000
	15,000
	20,000

4

Equilibrium

How Supply and Demand Determine Prices

I n Chapter 3, we introduced the supply curve and the demand curve. In that chapter, we wrote things like "if the price is $20 per barrel, the quantity supplied will be 50 million barrels per day (MBD)" and "if the price is $50, the quantity demanded will be 120 MBD." But how is price determined?

We are now ready for the big event: equilibrium. Figure 4.1 puts the supply curve and demand curve for oil together in one diagram. Notice the one point where the curves meet. The price at the meeting point is called the equilibrium price and the quantity at the meeting point is called the equilibrium quantity.

The equilibrium price is $30 and the equilibrium quantity is 65 MBD. What do we mean by equilibrium? We say that $30 and 65 are the equilibrium price and quantity because at any other price and quantity, economic forces are put in play that push prices and quantities toward these values. The equilibrium price and quantity are the only price and quantity that in a free market are stable. The sketch at right gives an intuitive feel for what we mean by equilibrium—the force of gravity pulls the ball down the side of the bowl until it comes to a state of rest. We will now explain the economic forces that push and pull prices toward their equilibrium values.

Equilibrium and the Adjustment Process

Imagine that demand and supply were as in Figure 4.1, but the price was above the equilibrium price of $30, say at $50—we would then have the situation depicted in the left panel of Figure 4.2.

At a price of $50, suppliers want to supply 100, but at that price the quantity demanded by buyers is just 32, which creates an excess supply, or **surplus**, of 68. What will suppliers do if they cannot sell all of their output at a price of $50? Hold a sale! Each seller will reason that by pricing just a little bit below their competitors, they will be able to sell much more. *Competition will push prices down whenever there is a surplus.* As competition pushes prices down, the quantity demanded will increase and the quantity supplied will

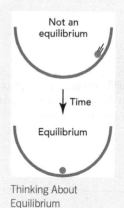

Thinking About Equilibrium

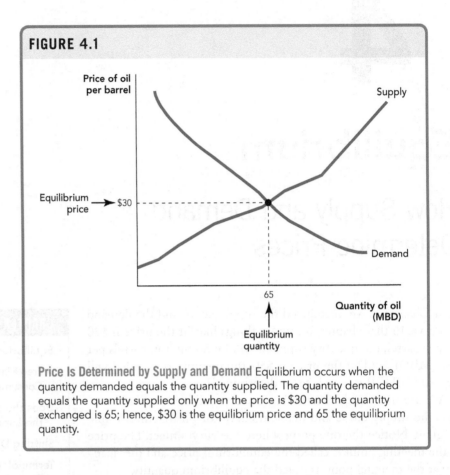

FIGURE 4.1

Price of oil per barrel

Equilibrium price → $30

Supply

Demand

65

Quantity of oil (MBD)

Equilibrium quantity

Price Is Determined by Supply and Demand Equilibrium occurs when the quantity demanded equals the quantity supplied. The quantity demanded equals the quantity supplied only when the price is $30 and the quantity exchanged is 65; hence, $30 is the equilibrium price and 65 the equilibrium quantity.

A **surplus** is a situation in which the quantity supplied is greater than the quantity demanded.

A **shortage** is a situation in which the quantity demanded is greater than the quantity supplied.

The **equilibrium price** is the price at which the quantity demanded is equal to the quantity supplied.

The **equilibrium quantity** is the quantity at which the quantity demanded is equal to the quantity supplied.

decrease. Only at a price of $30 will equilibrium be restored because only at that price does the quantity demanded (65) equal the quantity supplied (65).

What if price is below the equilibrium price? The right panel of Figure 4.2 shows that at a price of $15 demanders want 95 but suppliers are only willing to sell 24, which creates an excess demand, or **shortage**, of 71. What will sellers do if they discover that at a price of $15, they can easily sell all of their output and still have buyers asking for more? Raise prices! Buyers also have an incentive to offer higher prices when there is a shortage because when they can't buy as much as they want at the going price, they will try to outbid other buyers by offering sellers a higher price. *Competition will push prices up whenever there is a shortage.* As prices are pushed up, the quantity supplied increases and the quantity demanded decreases until at a price of $30 there is no longer an incentive for prices to rise and equilibrium is restored.

If competition pushes the price down whenever it is above the **equilibrium price** and it pushes the price up whenever it is below the equilibrium price, what happens at the equilibrium price? *The equilibrium price is stable because at the equilibrium price the quantity demanded is exactly equal to the quantity supplied.* Because every buyer can buy as much as they want at the equilibrium price, buyers don't have an incentive to push prices up. Since every seller can sell as much as they want at the equilibrium price, sellers don't have an incentive to push prices down. Of course, buyers would like lower prices, but any buyer who offers sellers a lower price will be scorned. Similarly, sellers would like higher prices, but any seller who tries to raise their asking price will quickly lose customers.

Finally, at the equilibrium price the quantity demanded is equal to the quantity supplied and that quantity is called the **equilibrium quantity**.

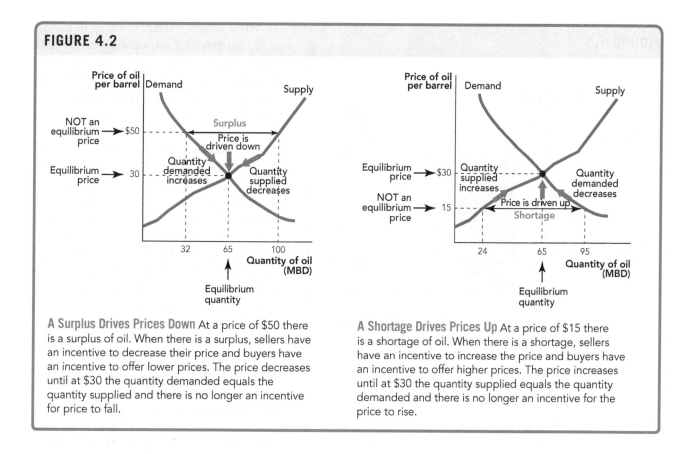

FIGURE 4.2

A Surplus Drives Prices Down At a price of $50 there is a surplus of oil. When there is a surplus, sellers have an incentive to decrease their price and buyers have an incentive to offer lower prices. The price decreases until at $30 the quantity demanded equals the quantity supplied and there is no longer an incentive for price to fall.

A Shortage Drives Prices Up At a price of $15 there is a shortage of oil. When there is a shortage, sellers have an incentive to increase the price and buyers have an incentive to offer higher prices. The price increases until at $30 the quantity supplied equals the quantity demanded and there is no longer an incentive for the price to rise.

Who Competes with Whom?

Sellers want higher prices and buyers want lower prices, so the person in the street often thinks that sellers compete *against* buyers.

But economists understand that regardless of what sellers want, what they do when they compete is lower prices. *Sellers compete with other sellers.* Similarly, buyers may want lower prices but what they do when they compete is raise prices. *Buyers compete with other buyers.*

If the price of a good that you want is high, should you blame the seller? Not if the market is competitive. Instead, you should "blame" other buyers for outbidding you.

A Free Market Maximizes Producer Plus Consumer Surplus (the Gains from Trade)

Figure 4.3 provides another perspective on the market equilibrium. Consider panel A. At a price of $15 suppliers will voluntarily produce 24 MBD. But notice that this is only enough oil to satisfy some of the buyers' wants. Which ones? The buyers will allocate what oil they have to their highest-valued wants. In panel A of Figure 4.3, the 24 MBD of oil will be used to satisfy the wants labeled "Satisfied wants." All other wants will remain unsatisfied. Now suppose that suppliers could be induced to sell just one more barrel of oil. How much would buyers be willing to pay for this barrel of oil? We can read the value of this additional barrel of oil by the height of the demand curve at

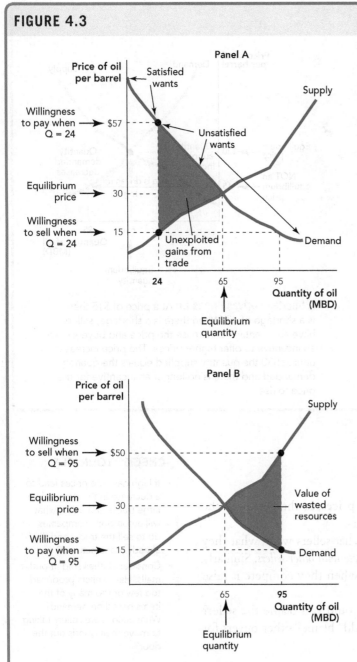

FIGURE 4.3

Panel A

Price of oil per barrel

Satisfied wants

Willingness to pay when Q = 24 → $57

Unsatisfied wants

Equilibrium price → 30

Willingness to sell when Q = 24 → 15

Unexploited gains from trade

Supply

Demand

24   65   95   Quantity of oil (MBD)

Equilibrium quantity

Panel B

Price of oil per barrel

Supply

Willingness to sell when Q = 95 → $50

Equilibrium price → 30

Value of wasted resources

Willingness to pay when Q = 95 → 15

Demand

65   95   Quantity of oil (MBD)

Equilibrium quantity

At the Equilibrium Quantity There Are No Unexploited Gains from Trade or Any Wasteful Trades

Panel A: Unexploited gains from trade exist when quantity is below the equilibrium quantity. Buyers are willing to pay as much as $57 for the 24th unit and sellers are willing to sell the 24th unit for as little as $15, so not trading the 24th unit leaves $42 in unexploited gain from trade. Only at the equilibrium quantity are there no unexploited gains from trade.

Panel B: Resources are wasted at quantities greater than the equilibrium quantity. Sellers want at least $50 for the 95th unit, but buyers are willing to pay only $15, so selling the 95th unit wastes $35 in resources. Only at the equilibrium quantity are there no wasted resources.

24 MBD. Buyers would be willing to pay up to $57 (or $56.99 if you want to be very precise), the value of the first unsatisfied want for an additional barrel of oil when 24 MBD are currently being bought. How much would sellers be willing to accept for one additional barrel of oil? We can read the lowest price at which sellers are willing to sell an additional barrel of oil by the height of the supply curve at 24 MBD. (Since sellers will be just willing to sell an additional barrel of oil when it covers their additional costs, we can also read this as the cost of producing an additional barrel of oil when 24 MBD are currently being produced.) Sellers would be willing to sell an additional barrel of oil for as little as $15.

Buyers are willing to pay $57 for an additional barrel of oil, and sellers are willing to sell an additional barrel for as little as $15. Trade at any price between $57 and $15 can make both buyers and sellers better off. There are potential gains from trade so long as buyers are willing to pay more than sellers are willing to accept. Now notice that *there are unexploited gains from trade at any quantity less than the* equilibrium quantity. Economists believe that in a free market unexploited gains from trade won't last for long. We expect, therefore, that in a free market the quantity bought and sold will increase until the equilibrium quantity of 65 is reached.

We have shown that gains from trade push the quantity toward the equilibrium quantity. What about a push for trade coming from the other direction? In a free market, why won't the quantity bought and sold *exceed* the equilibrium quantity?

Now consider panel B of Figure 4.3. Suppose that for some reason suppliers produce a quantity of 95. At that quantity it costs suppliers $50 to produce the last barrel of oil (say, by squeezing it out of the Athabasca tar sands). How much is that barrel of oil worth to buyers? Again, we can read this from the height of the demand curve at 95 MBD. It's only $15 (they get a few extra rubber duckies). So if quantity supplied exceeds the equilibrium quantity, it costs the sellers more to produce a barrel of oil than that barrel of oil is worth to buyers.

In a free market, suppliers won't spend $50 to produce something they can sell for at most $15—that's a recipe for bankruptcy.[*] We expect, therefore, that in a free market, the quantity bought and sold will decrease until the equilibrium quantity of 65 MBD is reached.

Suppliers won't try to drive themselves into bankruptcy, but if they did, would this be a good thing? Even at the equilibrium quantity, buyers have unsatisfied wants. Wouldn't it be a good idea to satisfy even more wants? No. The reason is that resources are wasted if the quantity exceeds the equilibrium quantity.

Imagine once again that suppliers were producing 95 units and thus were producing many barrels of oil whose cost exceeded their worth. This would be a loss not just to the suppliers but also to society. Producing oil takes resources—labor, trucks, pipes, and so forth. Those resources, or the value of those resources, could be used to produce something people really are willing to pay for—economics textbooks, for example, or iPads. If we waste resources producing barrels of oil for $50 that are worth only $15, we have fewer resources to produce goods that cost only $32 but that people value at $75. We have only a limited number of resources and getting the most out of those resources means producing neither too little of a good (as in panel A of Figure 4.3) nor too much of a good (as in panel B). Markets can help us to achieve this goal.

Figure 4.3 shows why in a free market there tends not to be unexploited gains from trade—at least not for long—or wasteful trades. Put these two things together and we have a remarkable result. *A free market maximizes the gains from trade.* The gains from trade can be broken down into producer surplus and consumer surplus, so we can also say that *a free market maximizes producer plus consumer surplus.*

Figure 4.4 illustrates how the gains from trade—producer plus consumer surplus—are maximized at the equilibrium price and quantity. Maximizing the gains from trade, however, requires more than just producing at the equilibrium price and quantity. In addition, goods must be produced at the lowest possible cost and they must be used to satisfy the highest value demands. In Figure 4.4, for example, notice that every seller has lower costs than every nonseller. Also, every buyer has a higher willingness to pay for the good than every nonbuyer.

Imagine if this claim were not true; suppose, for example, that Joe is willing to pay $50 for the good and there are two sellers: Abella with costs of $40 and Barbara with costs of $20. It's possible that Joe and Abella could make a deal, splitting the gains from trade of $10. But this trade would not maximize the gains from trade because if Joe and Barbara trade, the gains from trade are much higher, $30. Over time, both Joe and Barbara will figure this out, so in equilibrium, we expect Joe to trade with Barbara, not Abella. Thus, when we say that a free market maximizes the gains from trade, we mean three closely related things:

1. The goods are bought by the buyers with the highest willingness to pay.

2. The goods are sold by the sellers with the lowest costs.

3. There are no unexploited gains from trade and no wasteful trades.

MRU

mru.org/equilibrium

Equilibrium and the Gains from Trade

---

[*] Can you think of when suppliers might do this? What about if they were being subsidized by the government? In that case, the buyers might value the good less than the cost to sellers, but so long as the government makes up the difference, the sellers will be happy to sell a large quantity.

FIGURE 4.4

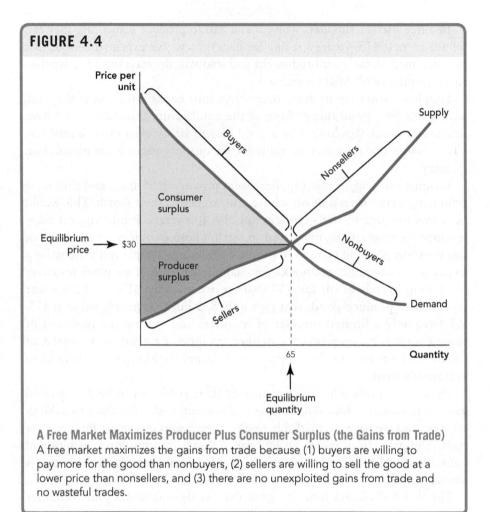

A Free Market Maximizes Producer Plus Consumer Surplus (the Gains from Trade)
A free market maximizes the gains from trade because (1) buyers are willing to pay more for the good than nonbuyers, (2) sellers are willing to sell the good at a lower price than nonsellers, and (3) there are no unexploited gains from trade and no wasteful trades.

CHECK YOURSELF

• As the price of cars goes up, which marketplace wants will be the first to go unsatisfied? Give an example.

• In the late 1990s, telecommunication firms laid a greater quantity of fiber-optic cable than the market equilibrium quantity (as proved by later events). Describe the nature of the losses from too much investment in fiber-optic cable. What market incentives exist to avoid these losses?

• Suppose that Kiran values a good at $50. Store A is willing to sell the good for $45, and store B is willing to sell the same good for $35. In a free market, what will be the total consumer surplus? Now suppose that store B is prevented from selling. What happens to the total consumer surplus?

Together, these three conditions imply that the gains from trade are maximized.

One of the remarkable lessons of economics is that under the right conditions, the pursuit of self-interest leads not to chaos but to a beneficial order. The maximization of consumer plus producer surplus in markets populated solely by self-interested individuals is one application of this central idea.

Does the Model Work? Evidence from the Laboratory

It's easy to see the equilibrium price and quantity when we draw textbook supply and demand curves, but in a real market the demanders and sellers do not know the true curves. Moreover, the conditions required to maximize the gains from trade are quite sophisticated. So how do we know whether the model really works?

In 1956, Vernon Smith launched a revolution in economics by testing the supply and demand model in the lab. Smith's early experiments were simple. He took a group of undergraduate students and broke them into two groups, buyers and sellers. Buyers were given a card that indicated their maximum willingness to pay. Sellers were given a card that indicated their cost, the minimum price at which they would be willing to sell. The buyers and sellers were then instructed to call out bids and offers ("I will sell for $3.00" or "I will pay $1.50"). Each student could earn a profit by the difference between their willingness to pay or sell and the contract price. For example, if you were a buyer and your card said $3.00 and you were able to make a deal with a seller to buy for $2.00, then you would have made a $1.00 profit.

The students knew only their own willingness to pay or to sell, but Vernon Smith knew the actual shape of the supply and demand curves. Smith knew the curves because he knew exactly what cards he had handed out. Data from one of Smith's first experiments are shown in Figure 4.5. Smith handed out 11 cards to sellers and 11 to buyers. The lowest-cost seller had costs of 75 cents, the next lowest-cost seller had costs of $1.00. Thus, at any price below 75 cents the quantity supplied on the market supply curve was zero; between 75 cents and $1, the quantity supplied was 1 unit; between $1.00 and $1.25, the next highest cost, 2 units; and so forth. Looking at the figure can you see how many units demanders were willing to buy at a price of $2.65? At a price of $2.65, the quantity demanded is 3 units. (To test yourself, identify, by their willingness to pay, exactly which three buyers are willing to buy at a price of $2.65.)

Smith knew from the graph that the equilibrium price and quantity as predicted by the supply and demand model were $2.00 and 6 units, respectively. But what would happen in the real world? Smith ran his experiment for 5 periods, each period about 5 minutes long. The right side of the figure shows the price for each completed trade in each period. The prices quickly converged toward the expected equilibrium price and quantity so that in the last period the average price was $2.03 and the quantity exchanged was 6 units.

Smith's market converged rapidly to the equilibrium price and quantity exactly as predicted by the supply and demand model. But recall that the

FIGURE 4.5

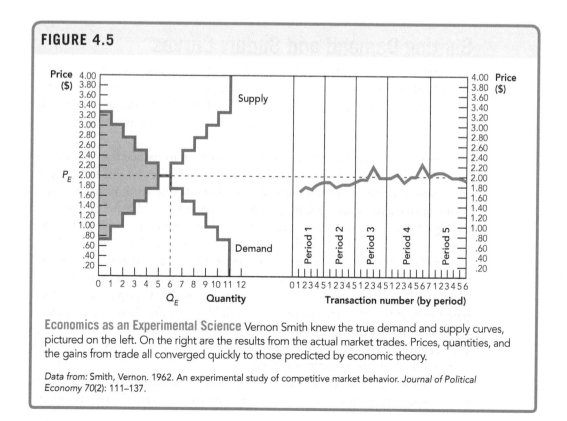

Economics as an Experimental Science Vernon Smith knew the true demand and supply curves, pictured on the left. On the right are the results from the actual market trades. Prices, quantities, and the gains from trade all converged quickly to those predicted by economic theory.

Data from: Smith, Vernon. 1962. An experimental study of competitive market behavior. *Journal of Political Economy* 70(2): 111–137.

The idea of economics as an experimental science came to Vernon Smith in a fit of insomnia in 1956. Nearly 50 years later, Smith was awarded the 2002 Nobel Prize in Economics.

model also predicts that a free market will maximize the gains from trade. Remember our conditions for efficiency, which in this context are that the supply of goods must be bought by the demanders with the highest willingness to pay, the supply of goods must be sold by the suppliers with the lowest costs, and the quantity traded should be equal to 6 units, neither more nor less.

So what happened in Smith's test of the market model? In the final period, 6 units were bought and sold and the buyers had the six highest valuations and the sellers the six lowest costs—exactly as predicted by the supply and demand model. Producer plus consumer surplus or total surplus was maximized. In fact, in the entire experiment only once was a seller with a cost greater than equilibrium price able to sell and only once was a buyer with a willingness to pay less than the equilibrium price able to buy—so total surplus was very close to being maximized throughout the experiment.

Vernon Smith began his experiments thinking that they would prove the supply and demand model was wrong. Decades later he wrote:

> I am still recovering from the shock of the experimental results. The outcome was unbelievably consistent with competitive price theory. . . . But the results *can't* be believed, I thought. It must be an accident, so I must take another class and do a new experiment with different supply and demand schedules.[1]

Many thousands of experiments later, the supply and demand model remains of enduring value. In 2002, Vernon Smith was awarded the Nobel Prize in Economics for establishing laboratory experiments as an important tool in economic science.

Shifting Demand and Supply Curves

Another way of testing the supply and demand model is to examine the model's predictions about what happens to equilibrium price and quantity when the supply or demand curves shift. Even if the model doesn't give us precise predictions (outside the lab), we can still ask whether the model helps us to understand the world.

Imagine, for example, that technological innovations reduce the costs of producing a good. As we know from Chapter 3, a fall in costs shifts the supply curve down and to the right as shown in Figure 4.6. The result of lower costs is a lower price and an increase in quantity. Begin at the Old Equilibrium Price and Quantity at point *a*. Now a decrease in costs shifts the Old Supply curve down and to the right out to the New Supply curve. Notice at the Old Equilibrium Price there is now a surplus—in other words, now that their costs have fallen, suppliers are willing to sell more at the old price than demanders are willing to buy. The excess supply, however, is temporary. Competition between sellers pushes prices down, and as prices fall, the quantity demanded increases. Prices fall and quantity demanded increases until the New Equilibrium Price and Quantity are established at point *b*. At the new equilibrium, the quantity demanded equals the quantity supplied.

We can see this process at work throughout the economy. As technological innovations reduce the price of computer chips, for example, prices fall and

FIGURE 4.6

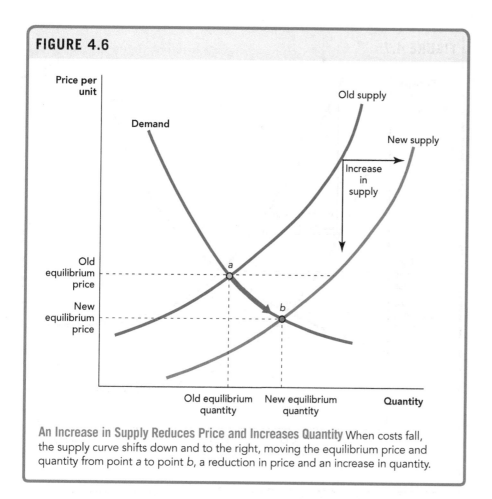

An Increase in Supply Reduces Price and Increases Quantity When costs fall, the supply curve shifts down and to the right, moving the equilibrium price and quantity from point *a* to point *b*, a reduction in price and an increase in quantity.

the quantity of chips—used in everything from computers to cell phones to toys—increases.

What about a decrease in supply? A decrease in supply will raise the market price and reduce the market quantity, exactly the opposite effects to an increase in supply. But don't take our word for it. Draw the diagram. The key to learning demand and supply is not to try to memorize everything that can happen. Instead, focus on learning how to use the tools. If you know how to use the tools, then simply by drawing a few pictures, you can deduce what happens to price and quantity for any configuration of demand and supply and for any set of shifts.

Figure 4.7 shows the same process for an increase in demand. Begin with the Old Equilibrium Price and Quantity at point *a*. Now suppose that demand increases to New Demand. As a result, the price and quantity are driven up to the New Equilibrium Price and Quantity at point *b*. Notice this time we omitted discussion of the temporary transition. So here's a good test of your knowledge. Can you explain *why* the price and quantity demanded increased with an increase in demand? (*Hint:* What happens at the Old Equilibrium Price after Demand has increased to New Demand?)

Of course, if we can analyze an increase in demand, then a decrease in demand is just the opposite: A decrease in demand will tend to decrease price and quantity. Once again, draw the diagram!

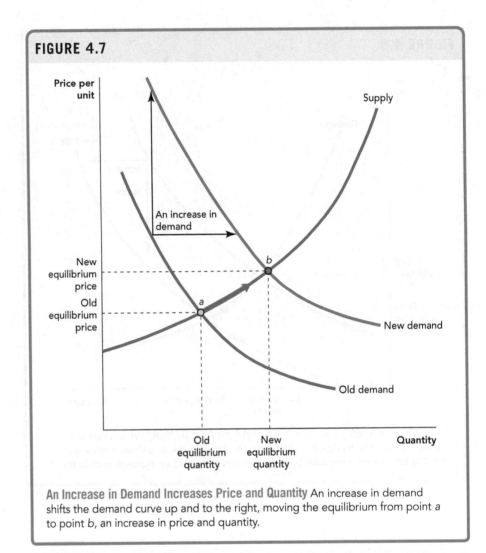

FIGURE 4.7

An Increase in Demand Increases Price and Quantity An increase in demand shifts the demand curve up and to the right, moving the equilibrium from point *a* to point *b*, an increase in price and quantity.

Do you recall the list of demand and supply shifters that we presented in Chapter 3? We can now put all that knowledge to good use. With demand, supply, and the idea of equilibrium, we have powerful tools for analyzing how changes in income, population, expectations, technologies, input prices, taxes and subsidies, alternative uses of industry inputs, and other factors will change market prices and quantities. In fact, with our tools of demand, supply, and equilibrium, we can analyze and understand *any* change in *any* competitive market.

Terminology: Demand Compared with Quantity Demanded and Supply Compared with Quantity Supplied

Sometimes economists use very similar words for quite different things. (We're sorry but unfortunately it's too late to change terms.) In particular, there is a big difference between *demand* and *quantity demanded*. For example, an increase in the quantity demanded is a movement *along* a fixed demand curve.

An increase in demand is a *shift* of the entire demand curve (up and to the right).

Don't worry: You are *already* familiar with these differences; we just need to point them out to you and explain the associated differences in terminology. Panel A of Figure 4.8 is a repeat of Figure 4.6, showing that an increase in supply reduces the equilibrium price and increases the equilibrium quantity. But now we emphasize something a little different—the increase in supply pushes the price down, thereby causing an increase in the *quantity demanded* from 70 units to 90 units. Notice that the increase in the quantity demanded is a

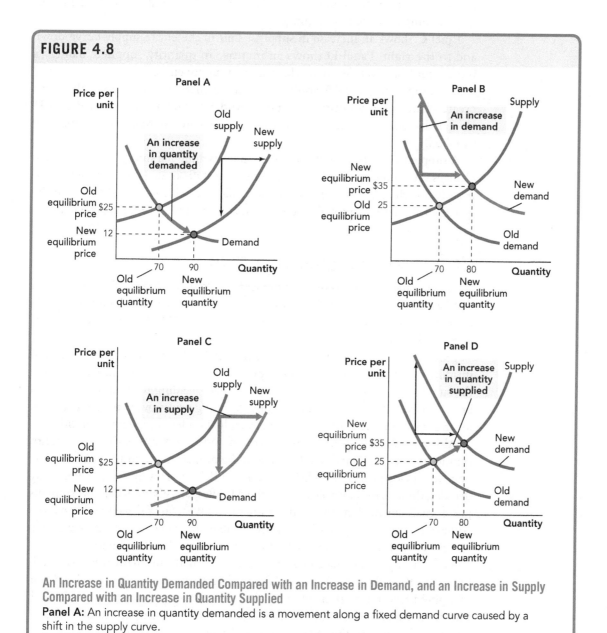

FIGURE 4.8

An Increase in Quantity Demanded Compared with an Increase in Demand, and an Increase in Supply Compared with an Increase in Quantity Supplied

Panel A: An increase in quantity demanded is a movement along a fixed demand curve caused by a shift in the supply curve.
Panel B: An increase in demand is a shift in the demand curve up and to the right.
Panel C: An increase in supply is a shift in the supply curve down and to the right.
Panel D: An increase in quantity supplied is a movement along a fixed supply curve caused by a shift in the demand curve.

movement along the demand curve. In panel A, the demand has not changed, only the quantity demanded.

Panel B is a repeat of Figure 4.7 and it shows an *increase in demand*. Notice that an increase in demand is a shift in the entire demand curve up and to the right. Indeed, we can also think about an increase in demand as the creation of a new demand curve, appropriately labeled New Demand.

Similarly, an increase in supply is a *shift* of the entire supply curve, whereas an increase in quantity supplied is a movement *along* a fixed supply curve. If you look closely at panels A and B, you will see that we have already shown you a shift in supply and a change in quantity supplied! But to make things clear, we repeat the analysis for supply in panels C and D: The graphs are the same but now we emphasize different things.

Panel C shows an increase in supply, a shift in the entire supply curve down and to the right. Panel D shows an increase in quantity supplied, namely a movement from 70 to 80 units along a fixed supply curve.

By comparing panels A and C, we can see that shifts in the supply curve create changes in quantity demanded. And by comparing panels B and D, we can see that shifts in the demand curve create changes in the quantity supplied.

A simple rule of thumb which will help everything fall into place is that what changes the equilibrium price and quantity are shifts in demand and supply, and *that's it*. So whenever you are asked, "Why did the price rise?" or "Why did the quantity fall?" always start with a shift in demand or supply. Everything else follows.

Understanding the Price of Oil

We can use the supply and demand model to understand some of the major events that have determined the price of oil over the past half century. Figure 4.9 shows the *real price* of oil in 2016 dollars between 1960 and 2022. (The real price corrects prices for inflation.)

From the early twentieth century to the 1970s, the demand for oil increased steadily, but major discoveries and improved production techniques meant that the supply of oil increased at an even faster pace, leading to modest declines in price. Contrary to popular belief, slightly declining prices over time are common for minerals and other natural resources supplied under competitive conditions.

Although the streets of Baghdad were paved with tar as early as the eighth century, the discovery and development of the modern oil industry in the Middle East were made primarily by U.S., Dutch, and British firms much later. For many decades, these firms controlled oil in the Middle East, giving local governments just a small cut of their proceeds. It's hard to take your oil well and leave the country, however, so the major firms were vulnerable to taxes and nationalization.

The Iranian government nationalized the British oil industry in Iran in 1951.[*] The Egyptians nationalized the Suez Canal, the main route through which oil flowed to the West, in 1956, leading to the Suez Crisis—a brief war that pitted Egypt against an alliance of the United Kingdom, France, and Israel. Further nationalizations and increased government control of the oil industry occurred throughout the 1960s and early 1970s.

---

[*] The nationalization was reversed in 1953 when the government of Mohammad Mosaddeq was toppled by a CIA-backed coup that brought the king, Mohammad Reza Pahlavi, back to power. The coup would have repercussions a quarter century later with the coming of the Iranian Revolution, when the American-backed government was overthrown by Islamic radicals.

FIGURE 4.9

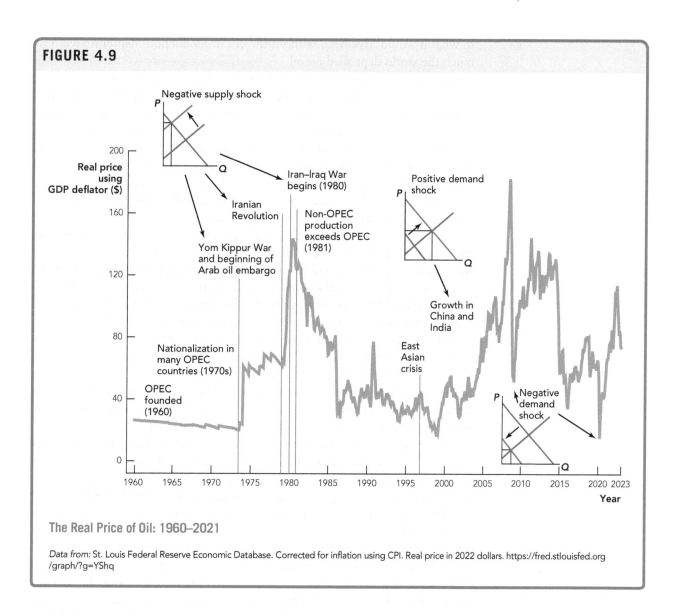

The Real Price of Oil: 1960–2021

Data from: St. Louis Federal Reserve Economic Database. Corrected for inflation using CPI. Real price in 2022 dollars. https://fred.stlouisfed.org/graph/?g=YShq

OPEC, the Organization of the Petroleum Exporting Countries, was formed in 1960.* Initially, OPEC restricted itself to bargaining with the foreign nationals for a larger share of their oil revenues. By the early 1970s, however, further nationalizations in the OPEC countries made it possible for OPEC countries to act together to reduce supply and raise prices.

A triggering event for OPEC was the Yom Kippur War. Egypt and Syria attacked Israel in 1973 in an effort to regain the Sinai Peninsula and the Golan Heights, which Israel had captured in 1967. In an effort to punish Western countries that had supported Israel, a number of Arab exporting nations cut oil production. Supply had been increasing by about 7.5% per year in the previous decade, but between 1973 and 1974 production was dead flat. Prices tripled in just one year. The large increase in price from a small decline in supply (relative

---

* OPEC was founded by Iran, Iraq, Kuwait, Saudi Arabia, and Venezuela, later joined by Qatar (1961), Indonesia (1962–2009, 2016), Libya (1962), the United Arab Emirates (1967), Algeria (1969), Nigeria (1971), Ecuador (1973–1992), Gabon (1975–1994), and Angola (2007). Ecuador rejoined OPEC in 2007 and Gabon rejoined in 2016, while Qatar quit OPEC in 2019.

to what it would have been without the cut in production) demonstrated how much the world depended on oil.

Prices stabilized, albeit at a much higher level, after 1974, but political unrest in Iran in 1978, followed by revolution in 1979, cut Iranian oil production. This time the reduction in supply was accidental rather than deliberate, but the result was the same—sharply higher prices. When Iraq attacked Iran in 1980, production in both countries diminished yet again, pushing prices to their highest level in the twentieth century—$180 in 2022 dollars. Prices might have been driven even higher if demand had not been reduced by a recession in the United States.

Higher prices attract entry. In 1972, the United Kingdom produced 2,000 barrels of oil per day. By 1978, with the opening of the North Sea wells, the United Kingdom was producing 1 million barrels per day. In the same period, Norway increased production from 32,000 to 356,000 barrels per day and Mexico more than doubled its production from 465,000 barrels per day to a little more than 1.2 million barrels per day. By 1982, non-OPEC production exceeded OPEC production for the first time since OPEC was founded. Iranian production also began to recover, increasing by 1 million barrels per day in 1982. Prices began to fall during the 1980s and 1990s.

Prices can also fluctuate with shifts in demand. A sharp fall in the price of oil came in 2009 when the United States and many of the major economies in the world were in the trough of a deep recession. Incomes fell, reducing the demand for oil and reducing the price. As the United States slowly recovered, however, the demand for oil increased, driving up the price.

The economies of China and India have surged in the early twenty-first century to the point where millions of people are for the first time in the history of their country able to afford an automobile. In 1949, the Communists confiscated all the private cars in China. As late as 2000, there were just 6 million cars in all of China, but by 2010 more vehicles were bought in China than in the United States, almost 18 million in that one year alone. Total highway miles quadrupled between 2000 and 2010.[2] This increased demand for oil pushed prices up to levels not seen since the 1970s.[*] Moreover, unlike temporary events such as the Iranian Revolution and the Iran–Iraq War, the increase in demand in China and in other newly developing nations will not reverse soon. In the United States, there's nearly one car for every two people. China has a population of 1.3 billion people, so there is plenty of room for growth in the number of cars and thus the demand for oil. On the other hand, new discoveries and techniques such as fracking are increasing the supply of oil. Electric cars may also reduce the demand for oil. As you can see from the graph, oil prices are difficult to predict; the reason is that the social, technological, and geopolitical factors that shift the demand and supply curves are difficult to predict. Nevertheless, demand and supply analysis is extremely useful in understanding how shifts in these factors influence the price of oil.

Takeaway

Now that you have finished reading this chapter, you should read it again. Really. Understanding supply and demand is critical to understanding economics, and in this chapter we have covered the most important aspects

CHECK YOURSELF

- In Figure 4.9, you will notice a jump in oil prices around 1991. What happened in this year to increase price? Was it a supply shock or a demand shock?
- In Figure 4.9, during what period would you include a small figure for positive supply shocks (increases in supply)? Explain the causes behind the positive supply shocks and the effect of these shocks on the price of oil.

---

[*] Improved technology is continually lowering the cost of discovering and producing oil (shifting the supply curve down and to the right), so what has happened in recent years is not simply an increase in demand but an increase in demand that has outstripped the increase in supply.

of the supply and demand model, namely how supply and demand together determine equilibrium price and quantity. You should understand, among other ideas, the following:

1. Market competition brings about an equilibrium in which the quantity supplied is equal to the quantity demanded.

2. Only one price/quantity combination is a market equilibrium and you should be able to identify this equilibrium in a diagram.

3. You should understand and be able to explain the incentives that enforce the market equilibrium. What happens when the price is above the equilibrium price? Why? What happens when the price is below the equilibrium price? Why?

4. The sum of consumer and producer surplus (the gains from trade) is maximized at the equilibrium price and quantity, and no other price/quantity combination maximizes consumer plus producer surplus.

5. You should know from Chapter 3 the major factors that shift demand and supply curves and from this chapter be able to explain and predict the effect of any such shift on the equilibrium price and quantity.

6. A "change in demand [the demand curve]" is not the same thing as "a change in quantity demanded"; a "change in supply [the supply curve]" is not the same thing as "a change in quantity supplied."

Most important, you should be able to work with supply and demand to answer questions about the world.

CHAPTER REVIEW

Go online to practice with more examples of these types of problems, including live links to videos, data sources, and feedback.

KEY CONCEPTS

surplus, p. 49

shortage, p. 50

equilibrium price, p. 50

equilibrium quantity, p. 50

FACTS AND TOOLS

1. If the price in a market is above the equilibrium price, does this create a surplus or a shortage?

2. When the price is above the equilibrium price, does self-interest (or greed) tend to push the price down or up?

3. Robin is on eBay, bidding for a first edition of the influential Frank Miller graphic novel *Batman: The Dark Knight Returns*. In this market, who is Robin competing with: the seller of the graphic novel or the other bidders?

4. Now, Robin is in Japan, trying to get a job as a full-time translator; he wants to translate English TV shows into Japanese and vice versa. Robin notices that the wage for translators is very low. Who is the "competition" pushing the wage down: Does the competition come from businesses who hire the translators or from the other translators?

5. Jules wants to purchase a Royale with cheese from Vincent. Vincent is willing to offer this tasty burger for $3. However, Jules is willing to pay up to $8 for it (after all, his girlfriend is a vegetarian, so he doesn't get many opportunities for tasty burgers).

   a. How large are the potential gains from trade if Jules and Vincent agree to make this trade? In other words, what is the sum of producer and consumer surplus if the trade happens?

b. If the trade takes place at $4, how much producer surplus goes to Vincent? How much consumer surplus goes to Jules?

c. If the trade takes place at $7, how much producer surplus goes to Vincent? How much consumer surplus goes to Jules?

6. What happened in Vernon Smith's lab? Choose the right answer:

a. The price and quantity were close to equilibrium but gains from trade were far from the maximum.

b. The price and quantity were far from equilibrium and gains from trade were far from the maximum.

c. The price and quantity were far from equilibrium but gains from trade were close to the maximum.

d. The price and quantity were close to equilibrium and gains from trade were close to the maximum.

7. When supply falls, what happens to quantity demanded in equilibrium? (This should get you to notice that both suppliers and demanders change their behavior when one curve shifts.)

8. **a.** When demand increases, what happens to price and quantity in equilibrium?

b. When supply increases, what happens to price and quantity in equilibrium?

c. When supply decreases, what happens to price and quantity in equilibrium?

d. When demand decreases, what happens to price and quantity in equilibrium?

9. **a.** When demand increases, what happens to price and quantity in equilibrium?

b. When supply increases, what happens to price and quantity in equilibrium?

c. When supply decreases, what happens to price and quantity in equilibrium?

d. When demand decreases, what happens to price and quantity in equilibrium?

No, this is not a mistake. Yes, it is that important.

10. What's the best way to think about the rise in oil prices in the 1970s, when wars and oil embargoes wracked the Middle East? Was it a rise in demand, a fall in demand, a rise in supply, or a fall in supply?

11. What's the best way to think about the rise in oil prices prior to the Great Recession, a time when China and India were rapidly becoming richer?

Was it a rise in demand, a fall in demand, a rise in supply, or a fall in supply?

12. What's the best way to think about high oil prices in 2022 that have coincided with the Russian invasion of Ukraine, global transportation issues, and resumed consumption as the world has started to move out of a pandemic? Is it a rise in demand, a fall in demand, a rise in supply, a fall in supply, or some combination of the above?

THINKING AND PROBLEM SOLVING

13. Suppose the market for batteries looks as follows:

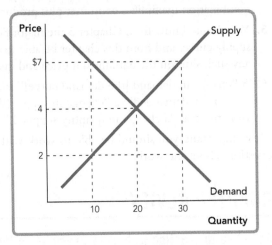

What are the equilibrium price and quantity?

14. Consider the following supply and demand tables for bread. Draw the supply and demand curves for this market. What are the equilibrium price and quantity?

Price of One Loaf	Quantity Supplied	Quantity Demanded
$0.50	10	75
$1	20	55
$2	35	35
$3	50	25
$5	60	10

15. If the price of a one-bedroom apartment in Washington, D.C., is currently $2,000 per month, but the supply and demand curves look as follows, then is there a shortage or surplus of apartments? What would we expect to happen to prices? Why?

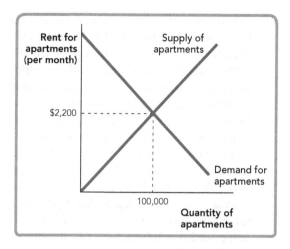

16. Determine the equilibrium quantity and price of Good X without drawing a graph.

Price of Good X	Quantity Supplied	Quantity Demanded
$22	100	225
$25	115	200
$30	130	175
$32	150	150
$40	170	110

17. In the following figure, how many pounds of sugar are sellers willing to sell at a price of $20? How much is demanded at this price? Does this result in a surplus or a shortage of sugar and of how much? What is the buyer's willingness to pay when the quantity is 20 pounds? Is this combination of $20 per pound and a quantity of 20 pounds an equilibrium? If not, identify the unexploited gains from trade.

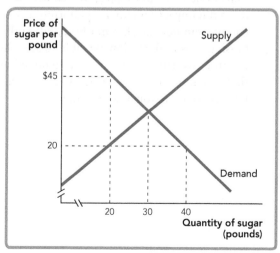

18. The market for action figures is represented in the following graph. What is the total producer surplus? The total consumer surplus? What are the total gains from trade?

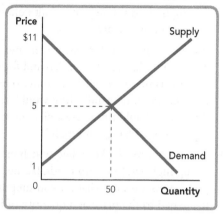

19. Suppose you decide to follow in Vernon Smith's footsteps and conduct your own experiment with your friends. You give out 10 cards: 5 cards to buyers with the figures for willingness to pay of $1, $2, $3, $4, and $5, and 5 cards to sellers with the amounts for costs of $1, $2, $3, $4, and $5. The rules are the same as Vernon Smith implemented.

 a. Draw the supply and demand curves for this market. At a price of $3.50, how many units are demanded? And supplied?

 b. Assuming the market works as predicted, and the market moves to equilibrium, will the buyer who values the good at $1 be able to purchase? Why or why not?

20. If the price of margarine decreases, what happens to the demand for butter? What happens to the equilibrium quantity and price for butter? What would happen if butter and margarine were not substitutes? Use a supply and demand diagram to support your answer.

21. The market for sugar is diagrammed:

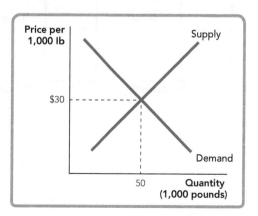

a. What would happen to the equilibrium quantity and price if the wages of sugar cane harvesters increased?

b. What if a new study was published that emphasized the negative health effects of consuming sugar?

22. If a snowstorm was forecast for the next day, what would happen to the demand for snow shovels? Is this a change in quantity demanded or a change in demand? How would this affect the price? Would this cause a change in quantity supplied or a change in supply?

23. In recent years, the keto diet, which emphasizes eating high-fat, low-carb foods, has become very popular. As a result, what do you suppose has happened to the price and quantity of bread? Use supply and demand analysis to support your answer.

24. In 2021, several handheld clothes steamers were recalled due to defects, leading to users receiving serious burns. Once this was reported in the media, what probably happened to the demand for handheld clothes steamers? As a result, what likely happened to the equilibrium price and quantity traded of handheld clothes steamers? Are the manufacturers of handheld clothes steamers probably better or worse off when such news comes out?

25. Here's a quick problem to test whether you really understand what producer surplus and consumer surplus mean, rather than just relying on the geometry of demand and supply. For each of the two diagrams that follow, calculate producer surplus, consumer surplus, and total surplus. Assume the curves are perfectly vertical and perfectly horizontal.

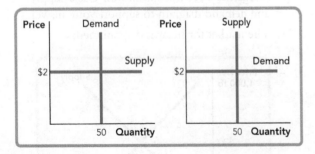

26. The diagram that follows shows the market for agricultural products. The shift from the old supply curve to the new supply curve is the result of technological and scientific advances in farming, including the production of more resilient and productive seeds. Calculate the change in consumer surplus and the change in producer surplus caused by these technological advances. Are buyers better or worse off as a result of these advancements? What about sellers? (Note that you cannot calculate consumer surplus directly with the information given in the diagram, but you don't need that information to calculate the *change* in consumer surplus.)

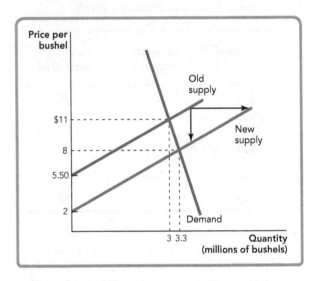

27. Now that you've mastered interpreting shifts in demand and supply, it's time to add another wrinkle: simultaneous shifts in both demand and supply. When we explore simultaneous shifts of demand and supply, we can determine the impact on either equilibrium price *or* equilibrium quantity, but not both. Fill in the missing cells in the following table to see why. Because two curves can shift in two directions, there are four cases to consider. The first column is done for you as an example.

	Case 1	Case 2	Case 3	Case 4
Change in demand	Increase	Increase	Decrease	Decrease
How demand change affects price	↑			
How demand change affects quantity	↑			
Change in supply	Increase	Decrease	Increase	Decrease
How supply change affects price	↓			
How supply change affects quantity	↑			
Combined effect of demand and supply on price	?			
Combined effect of demand and supply on quantity	↑			

28. In the last problem, you saw how simultaneous shifts in demand and supply can leave us with uncertainty about the impact on price or on quantity. An increase in both demand and supply will increase equilibrium quantity but have an ambiguous effect on equilibrium price. However, if we knew that there was a *significant* increase in demand and only a *small* increase in supply, we could conclude that the price would probably rise overall, albeit not by as much as would have been the case if supply had not increased slightly.

In each of the following examples, there are a *major* event and a *minor* event. Determine whether each change relates to demand or to supply, and then figure out the impact on price and quantity; be sure to say something about the relative magnitudes of the price and quantity changes.

a. *Market:* Rock salt

Major event: A bitterly cold and unusually snowy winter season has significantly depleted the amount of available rock salt.

Minor event: There is another snowstorm, and roads and sidewalks need to be salted.

b. *Market:* Smartphones

Major event: The proliferation of fast, reliable, affordable (or free) Wi-Fi and cellular signals increases the usability of smartphones.

Minor event: The production of smartphones is marked by modest technological advances.

c. *Market:* Canned tomatoes

Major event: A large canned tomato manufacturer begins to use cheap imported tomatoes from Mexico rather than domestic tomatoes.

Minor event: This causes a public relations fiasco, resulting in an organized effort to boycott canned tomatoes.

CHALLENGES

29. For many years, it was illegal to color margarine yellow (margarine is naturally white). In some states, margarine manufacturers were even required to color margarine pink! Who do you think supported these laws? Why? (*Hint:* Your analysis in question 20 from the previous section is relevant!)

30. Think about two products: "safe cars" (a heavy car such as an Audi A6 with speed-sensitive steering, four-wheel independent suspension, electronic stability control, high-intensity discharge headlights, a lane departure system, and front and rear parking cameras) and "dangerous cars" (a lightweight car such as _____ [name removed for legal reasons, but you can fill in as you wish]).

a. Are these two products substitutes or complements?

b. If new research makes it easier to produce safe cars, what happens to the supply of safe cars? What will happen to the equilibrium price of safe cars?

c. Now that the price of safe cars has changed, how does this impact the demand for dangerous cars?

d. Now let's tie all these links into one simple sentence:

In a free market, as engineers and scientists discover new ways to make cars safer, the number of dangerous cars sold will tend to

_____.

31. Many clothing stores often have clearance sales at the end of each season. Using the tools you learned in this chapter, can you think of an explanation why?

32. **a.** If oil executives read in the newspaper that massive new oil supplies have been discovered under the Pacific Ocean but will likely only be useful in 10 years, what is likely to happen to the supply of oil *today*? What is the likely equilibrium impact on the price and quantity of oil *today*?

    b. If oil executives read in the newspaper that new solar-power technologies have been discovered but will likely only become useful in 10 years, what is likely to happen to the supply of oil *today*? What is the likely equilibrium impact on the price and quantity of oil *today*?

    c. What's the short version of these scenarios? Fill in the blank: If we learn *today* about promising *future* energy sources, today's price of energy will _____ and today's quantity of energy will _____.

33. **a.** Due to supply chain issues resulting from the global pandemic, the prices of computer chips increased greatly, and delivery of computer chips was often delayed. How did this likely affect the supply of new cars?

    b. Given your answer to part a, what was the likely knock-on effect in the demand for used cars?

    c. Rental car companies are a major supplier of used cars, as they sell some of their fleet each year and replace them with new vehicles. In anticipation of high new car prices (and their potential unavailability), many rental car companies chose not to sell any of their fleet during the pandemic. What impact did this likely have on the supply of used cars?

    d. Given your answers to parts b and c, what do you expect happened to the price of used cars?

34. Economists often say that prices are a "rationing mechanism"; that is, they serve the function of determining who will receive a scarce resource. If the supply of a good falls, how do prices "ration" these now scarce goods in a competitive market?

35. When the crime rate falls in the area around a factory, what probably happens to wages at that factory?

36. Let's take the idea from the previous question and use it to explain why businesses sometimes try to make their employees happy. If a business can make a job seem fun (by offering inexpensive pizza for lunch or having an employee game room for use during breaks) or at least safe (by nagging the city government to put police patrols around the factory), what probably happens to the supply of labor? What happens to the equilibrium wage if a factory or office or laboratory becomes a great place where people "really want to work"? How does this explain why the hourly wage for the median radio or television announcer is only around $18 per hour, lower than almost any other job in the entertainment or broadcasting industry?

WORK IT OUT

For interactive, step-by-step help in solving the following problem, go online.

Consider the following supply and demand tables for milk. Draw the supply and demand curves for this market. What are the equilibrium price and quantity?

Price of One Gallon	Quantity Supplied	Quantity Demanded
$1	20	150
$2	40	110
$4	70	70
$6	100	50
$10	120	20

5

Elasticity and Its Applications

"Guns for groceries" is how the Los Angeles Police Department advertises their annual gun buyback program. A handgun will get you a $100 gift card good for groceries at a local store, and an assault weapon is worth a $200 gift card. The guns can be turned in "no questions asked." You don't even have to go to the police station; the LAPD set up a drive-through at a local shopping mall. One Christmas, the program was so popular that it created traffic congestion and long lines. Gun buybacks have been held in recent years in Baltimore, Santa Fe, Camden, New Jersey, and many other cities across the nation. But do the programs work?

In this chapter, we develop the tools of demand and supply elasticity. To be honest, at first these tools will seem dry and technical. Stick with us, however, and you will see how the concept of elasticity is useful for dealing with important questions such as why local gun buybacks are unlikely to work, why the war on drugs can generate violence, why housing prices have increased so much in some U.S. cities, and how to evaluate proposals to increase drilling in the Arctic National Wildlife Refuge (ANWR).

In Chapter 4, we discussed how to shift the supply and demand curves to produce qualitative predictions about changes in prices and quantities. Estimating elasticities of demand and supply is the first step in quantifying how changes in demand and supply will affect prices and quantities.

The Elasticity of Demand

When the price of a good increases, individuals and businesses will buy less. But how much less? A lot or a little? The **elasticity of demand** measures how responsive the quantity demanded is to a change in price—the more responsive quantity demanded is to a change in the price, the more elastic is the demand curve. Let's start by comparing two different demand curves.

In Figure 5.1, when the price increases from $40 to $50, the quantity demanded decreases from 100 to 20 along demand curve E but only from 100 to 95 along demand curve I—thus, demand curve E is more elastic than demand curve I.

Elasticity is not the same thing as slope, but they are related and for our purposes you won't make any mistakes if you follow the elasticity rule:

> *Elasticity rule:* If two linear demand (or supply) curves run through a common point, then at any given quantity the curve that is flatter is more elastic.

The **elasticity of demand** measures how responsive the quantity demanded is to a change in price; more responsive equals more elastic.

Determinants of the Elasticity of Demand

Of the two curves in Figure 5.1, which do you think would best represent the demand curve for oil?

There are few substitutes for oil in its major use, transportation, so when the price increases by a lot, the quantity demanded falls by only a little. Thus, the demand curve for oil is not very elastic and would be best represented by demand curve I.

The fundamental determinant of the elasticity of demand is how easy it is to substitute one good for another. The fewer substitutes for a good, the less elastic the demand. The more substitutes for a good, the more elastic the demand.

When the price of oil goes up, people grumble but few stop using cars, at least not right away. But what happens to the elasticity of the demand for oil over time? The demand for oil tends to become more elastic over time because the more time people have to adjust to a price change, the better they can substitute one good for another. In other words, there are more *substitutes* for oil in the long run than in the short run. Since the OPEC oil price increases in the 1970s (see Figure 4.9 in Chapter 4), the world economy has slowly substituted away from oil by moving toward other sources of energy such as coal, nuclear, and hydroelectric. It took many years, but today the world uses about one-fourth the amount of oil per dollar of GDP than it did in the 1970s.[1]

In the long run, there are even substitutes for oil in transportation. One reason that mopeds are more popular and SUVs less popular in Europe than in the United States is that taxes make the price of gasoline much higher in Europe than in the United States. Europeans have adjusted by buying more mopeds

FIGURE 5.1

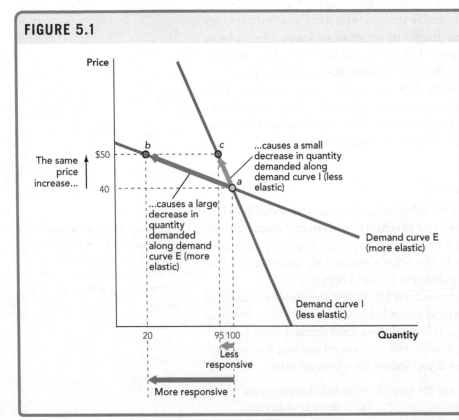

The More Responsive Quantity Demanded Is to a Change in Price, the More Elastic Is the Demand Curve Beginning at point *a*, an increase in price from $40 to $50 causes a big decrease in quantity demanded along demand curve E, from 100 units to 20 units at point *b*. But the same increase in price causes only a small decrease in quantity demanded along demand curve I from 100 to 95 units at point *c*. Since the quantity demanded is more responsive to a change in price along demand curve E, demand curve E is more elastic than demand curve I.

and smaller cars and driving fewer miles—Americans would do the same if the price of gasoline were expected to increase permanently.

If the price of oil increases by a significant amount for a long period, then even the organization of cities will change as people move from suburbia toward apartments and townhouses located closer to work. It may seem odd to think of moving closer to work as a "substitute for oil," but people adjust to price increases in many ways and economists think of all these adjustments as involving substitutes. If the price of cigarettes goes up and people decide to satisfy their oral cravings by chewing carrots, then carrots are a substitute for cigarettes.

In short, the more time people have to adjust to a change in price, the more elastic the demand curve will be.

Let's compare the demand for Orange Crush, a particular brand of orange soda, with the demand for orange soda. There are many good substitutes for Orange Crush, including Orangina, Fanta, and Slice (Wikipedia lists 53 types of orange soda). As a result, the demand for Orange Crush is very elastic because even a small increase in the price of Orange Crush will result in a large decrease in the quantity demanded as people switch to the substitutes. The demand curve for orange soda, however, is less elastic because there are fewer substitutes for orange soda than there are for Orange Crush and the substitutes such as root beer or cola are not as good. We illustrate this in Figure 5.2. The general point is that the demand for a specific brand of a product is more elastic than the demand for a product category. We will come back to this point when we look in more depth at competition and monopoly in Chapters 12 and 13.

What counts as a good substitute depends on a buyer's preferences, as well as on objective properties of the good. If the price of Coca-Cola increases at the supermarket, many people will buy Pepsi but others will keep on buying Coca-Cola because for them Pepsi is *not* a good substitute. So, some people have a more elastic demand for Coca-Cola, while other people have a less elastic demand. A closely related idea is that demand is less elastic for goods that people consider to be "necessities" and is more elastic for goods that are considered "luxuries." Of course, for some people their morning coffee at Starbucks *is* a necessity and for others it's a luxury. Let's summarize by saying that the demand for necessities—however a person defines that term—tends to be less elastic and the demand for luxuries tends to be more elastic.

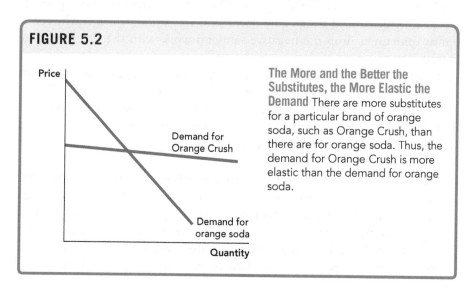

FIGURE 5.2

The More and the Better the Substitutes, the More Elastic the Demand There are more substitutes for a particular brand of orange soda, such as Orange Crush, than there are for orange soda. Thus, the demand for Orange Crush is more elastic than the demand for orange soda.

TABLE 5.1 SOME FACTORS DETERMINING THE ELASTICITY OF DEMAND

Less Elastic	More Elastic
Fewer substitutes	More substitutes
Short run (less time)	Long run (more time)
Categories of product	Specific brands
Necessities	Luxuries
Small part of budget	Large part of budget

The higher a person's income, the less concerned they are likely to be with the price of an item; thus, higher income makes demand less elastic. In 2008, the price of wheat tripled, and many people all around the world bought less bread. But neither of the authors of this book cut back much on our consumption of bread. The price of bread is too small a portion of our budgets to worry very much about its price, so our consumption of bread is not very elastic. On the other hand, when the price of housing increases, we buy smaller houses just like everyone else. Thus, the larger the share of a person's budget devoted to a good, the more elastic their demand for that good is likely to be.

We summarize the determinants of the elasticity of demand in Table 5.1.

Calculating the Elasticity of Demand

The elasticity of demand has a precise definition with important properties. The elasticity of demand is the percentage change in the quantity demanded divided by the percentage change in price.

$$\text{Elasticity of demand} = E_d = \frac{\textbf{Percentage change in quantity demanded}}{\textbf{Percentage change in price}}$$

$$= \frac{\%\Delta Q_{\text{Demanded}}}{\%\Delta \textbf{Price}}$$

where Δ (delta) is the mathematical symbol for "change in."

- If the price of oil increases by 10% and over a period of several years the quantity demanded falls by 5%, then the long-run elasticity of demand for oil is −5%/10% = −0.5, or 0.5 in absolute terms.

- If the price of Minute Maid orange juice falls by 10% and the quantity of Minute Maid orange juice demanded increases by 17.5%, then the elasticity of demand for Minute Maid orange juice is 17.5%/−10% = −1.75, or 1.75 in absolute terms.[2]

Elasticities of demand are always negative because when the price goes up, the quantity demanded always goes down (and vice versa), which is why economists sometimes drop the negative sign and work with the absolute value instead.

When the absolute value of the elasticity is less than 1, the demand is not very elastic or economists say the demand is **inelastic**; if it is greater than 1, economists say that demand is **elastic**; and if it is exactly equal to 1, economists say that demand is **unit elastic**. So in our calculations, oil has inelastic demand and Minute Maid orange juice has elastic demand.

Using the Midpoint Method to Calculate the Elasticity of Demand

To calculate an elasticity, you need to know how to calculate the percentage change in quantity and the percentage change in price. That is a bit trickier than it sounds. To see why, let's suppose that you observe the price and quantity pairs shown in the table on the next page (careful readers will note that these points correspond to points *a* and *b* along demand curve E in Figure 5.1).

The **elasticity of demand** is a measure of how responsive the quantity demanded is to a change in price. It is computed by

$$E_d = \frac{\%\Delta Q_{\text{Demanded}}}{\%\Delta \textbf{Price}}$$

$$|E_d| > 1 = \textit{Elastic}$$
$$|E_d| < 1 = \textit{Inelastic}$$
$$|E_d| = 1 = \textit{Unit elastic}$$

If you think of moving from point *a* to point *b* (let's call this moving from "before" to "after"), then the quantity demanded falls from 100 to 20 so the change in quantity demanded is −80. What is the percentage change in quantity demanded?

	Price	Quantity Demanded
Point *a*	$40	100
Point *b*	$50	20

If the beginning quantity, Q_{Before}, is 100 and the ending quantity, Q_{After}, is 20, it seems natural to calculate the percentage change in quantity like this:

$$\frac{\Delta Q}{Q} = \frac{Q_{After} - Q_{Before}}{Q_{Before}} = \frac{20 - 100}{100} = \frac{-80}{100} = -0.8 = -80\%$$

But now think of moving from point *b* to point *a*. In this case, quantity demanded increases from 20 to 100 and it now seems natural to calculate the percentage change in quantity like this:

$$\frac{\Delta Q}{Q} = \frac{Q_{After} - Q_{Before}}{Q_{Before}} = \frac{100 - 20}{20} = \frac{80}{20} = 4 = 400\%$$

In the first case, we are thinking of a percentage decrease in quantity and in the second of a percentage increase in quantity so it's easy to see why one number is negative and the other positive. But why are the numbers so different when we are calculating exactly the same change?

The different values occur because the base of the calculation changes. If you are driving 100 mph and decrease speed to 20 mph, it's natural to say that your speed went down by 80% because you calculate using a base of 100. But if you are driving 20 mph and you increase speed to 100 mph, it's natural to say that you increased your speed by 400% since you now use 20 as the base. Economists would like to calculate the same number for elasticity whether the quantity (or speed) decreases from 100 to 20 or increases from 20 to 100.

To avoid problems with the choice of base, economists calculate the percentage change in quantity by dividing the change in quantity by the *average* or *midpoint quantity*—the base is thus the same whether you think about quantity as increasing or decreasing.

Here is the formula:

$$\textbf{Elasticity of demand} = E_d = \frac{\%\Delta Q_{Demanded}}{\%\Delta \textbf{Price}}$$

$$= \frac{\dfrac{\textbf{Change in quantity demanded}}{\textbf{Average quantity}}}{\dfrac{\textbf{Change in price}}{\textbf{Average price}}} = \frac{\dfrac{Q_{After} - Q_{Before}}{(Q_{After} + Q_{Before})/2}}{\dfrac{P_{After} - P_{Before}}{(P_{After} + P_{Before})/2}}$$

In this case, we calculate the percentage change in quantity demanded as $\frac{-80}{(100+20)/2} \times 100 = -133.3\%$ and we also use the midpoint formula for the percentage change in price, which is $\frac{50-40}{(50+40)/2} \times 100 = 22.2\%$. With these two numbers, we can now calculate the elasticity of demand over this portion of the demand curve:

$$E_d = \frac{-133.3\%}{22.2\%} = -6$$

Notice absolute value of the elasticity, 6, is greater than 1, so the demand is elastic over this range.

It's most important that you understand the concept of elasticity. To calculate an elasticity, don't worry too much; just locate the formula and plug in the numbers.

Total Revenues and the Elasticity of Demand

A firm's revenues are equal to price per unit times quantity sold.

Revenue = Price × Quantity, or $R = P \times Q$

Elasticity measures how much Q goes down when P goes up, so you might suspect that there is a relationship between elasticity and revenue. Indeed, the relationship is remarkably useful: If the demand curve is inelastic, then revenues go up when the price goes up. If the demand curve is elastic, then revenues go down when the price goes up.

Let's give some intuition for this result. Imagine that the demand curve is inelastic, thus not responsive to price. This means that when P goes up by a lot, Q goes down by a little, like this:

$$\overset{\uparrow}{P} \times \underset{\downarrow}{Q}$$

So when the demand curve is inelastic, what will happen to revenues? If P goes up by a lot and Q goes down by a little, then revenues will go up.

$$\overset{\uparrow}{R} = \overset{\uparrow}{P} \times \underset{\downarrow}{Q}$$

Thus, when the demand curve is inelastic, revenues go up when the price goes up and, of course, revenues will go down when the price goes down.

We can also show the relationship in a diagram. Figure 5.3 shows an inelastic demand curve on the left and an elastic demand curve on the right.[*] Revenue is $P \times Q$, so revenue is equal to the area of a rectangle with height equal to price and width equal to the quantity; for example, when the price is $40 and the quantity is 100, revenues are $4,000, or the area of the blue rectangle (note that the blue and green rectangles overlap).

In both diagrams, the blue rectangles show revenue at a price of $40 and the green rectangles show revenues at the higher price of $50. Compare the size of the blue and green rectangles when the demand curve is inelastic (on the left) and when the demand curve is elastic (on the right). What do you see? When the demand curve is inelastic, an increase in price increases revenues (the green rectangle is bigger than the blue rectangle), but when the demand curve is elastic, an increase in price decreases revenues (the green rectangle is smaller than the blue rectangle).

Of course, the relationships hold in reverse as well. If the demand curve is inelastic, a price decrease causes a decrease in revenues, and if the demand curve is elastic, a price decrease causes an increase in revenues.

Can you guess what happens to revenues when price increases or decreases and the demand curve is unit elastic? Right, nothing! When the demand curve

---

[*] These curves are the same curves as in Figure 5.1, so they run through a common point, and thus we can apply our elasticity rule, which tells us that at any given quantity the flatter curve is more elastic than the steeper curve.

FIGURE 5.3

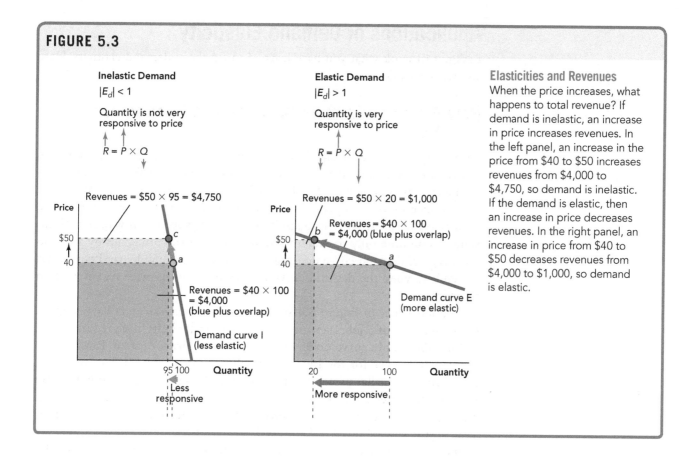

Inelastic Demand

$|E_d| < 1$

Quantity is not very responsive to price

$R = P \times Q$

Revenues = $50 × 95 = $4,750

Revenues = $40 × 100 = $4,000 (blue plus overlap)

Demand curve I (less elastic)

Less responsive

Elastic Demand

$|E_d| > 1$

Quantity is very responsive to price

$R = P \times Q$

Revenues = $50 × 20 = $1,000

Revenues = $40 × 100 = $4,000 (blue plus overlap)

Demand curve E (more elastic)

More responsive

Elasticities and Revenues

When the price increases, what happens to total revenue? If demand is inelastic, an increase in price increases revenues. In the left panel, an increase in the price from $40 to $50 increases revenues from $4,000 to $4,750, so demand is inelastic. If the demand is elastic, then an increase in price decreases revenues. In the right panel, an increase in price from $40 to $50 decreases revenues from $4,000 to $1,000, so demand is elastic.

is unit elastic, a change in price is exactly matched by an equal and opposite percentage change in quantity so revenues stay the same. Unit elasticity is the dividing point between elastic and inelastic curves.

You should be able to use all of these relationships on an exam. Table 5.2 summarizes what we have covered so far.

If you must, memorize the table. At least one of your textbook authors, however, can never remember the relationship between elasticity and total revenue. So, instead of memorizing the relationship, he always derives it by drawing little diagrams like those in Figure 5.3. If you can easily duplicate these diagrams, you too will always be able to answer questions involving elasticity and total revenue.

TABLE 5.2 ELASTICITY AND REVENUE

Absolute Value of Elasticity	Name	How Revenue Changes with Price
$|E_d| < 1$	Inelastic	Price and revenue move together.
$|E_d| > 1$	Elastic	Price and revenue move in opposite directions.
$|E_d| = 1$	Unit elastic	When price changes, revenue stays the same.

Applications of Demand Elasticity

Let's put to work what you have learned so far about demand elasticity. Here are two applications.

How American Farmers Have Worked Themselves Out of a Job

Using the same inputs of land, labor, and capital, American farmers can produce nearly three times as much food today as they could in 1950—that's an amazing increase in productivity. The increase in productivity means that Americans can produce more food per person today than in 1950. But how much more food can Americans eat? Although it doesn't always seem this way, Americans want to consume only so much more food even if the price falls by a lot. So what type of demand curve does this suggest? An inelastic demand curve; and remember, when the demand curve is inelastic, a fall in price means a fall in revenues.

The left panel of Figure 5.4 shows how American farmers have worked themselves out of a job. Increases in farming productivity have reduced cost, shifting the supply curve down and reducing the price of food. But because the demand curve for food is inelastic, the quantity of food demanded has increased by a smaller percentage than the price has fallen. As a result, farming revenues have declined. Notice that in the left panel of Figure 5.4, the blue rectangle (farm revenues today) is smaller than the green rectangle (revenues in 1950)—just as we showed in Figure 5.3.

Increases in productivity, however, do not always mean that revenue falls. In the past several decades, productivity has increased in computer chips even faster than in farming. But as the price of computer chips has fallen, the quantity of computer chips demanded has increased even more. Computer chips are now not just in computers but in phones, televisions, automobiles, and toys.

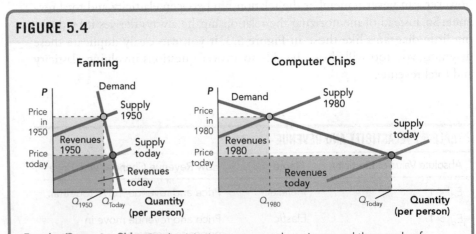

FIGURE 5.4

Farming/Computer Chips Productivity improvements have increased the supply of food and the supply of computer chips, thus reducing the prices of these goods. The demand for food, however, is inelastic, while the demand for computer chips is elastic. As a result, the decrease in the price of food has driven down farm revenues, while the decrease in the price of computer chips has driven up computer chip revenues.

As a result, revenues for the computer chip industry have increased and made computing a larger share of the American economy. What type of demand curve does this suggest? An elastic demand curve. The right panel in Figure 5.4 illustrates how an increase in productivity in computing has shifted the supply curve down and reduced prices, but the quantity of computer chips demanded has increased by an even greater percentage than the price has fallen. As a result, computer chip revenues have increased.

The lesson is that whether a demand curve is elastic or inelastic has a tremendous influence on how an industry evolves over time. If you want to be in on a growing industry, it helps to know the elasticity of demand.

Why the War on Drugs Is Hard to Win

It's hard to defeat an enemy that grows stronger the more you strike against them. (See the movies *Rocky I, II, III, IV, V, Rocky Balboa,* and *Creed I, II, III.*) The war on drugs is like that. We illustrate with a simple model.

The U.S. government spends more than $50 billion a year arresting more than 1.5 million people and deterring the supply of drugs with police, prisons, and border patrols. This, in turn, increases the cost of smuggling and dealing drugs. (The war on drugs also increases the costs of buying drugs. We could include this factor in our model, but to keep the model simple, we will focus on increases in the costs of supplying drugs.) When costs go up, suppliers require a higher price to supply any given quantity so the supply curve shifts up—in Figure 5.5 from "Supply with no prohibition" to "Supply with prohibition."[*]

The most important assumption in Figure 5.5 is that the demand curve is inelastic. It's hard to get good data on how the quantity of drugs demanded varies with the price, but most studies suggest that the demand for illegal drugs is quite inelastic, approximately 0.5. Inelastic demand is also plausible from what we know intuitively about how much people are willing to pay for drugs

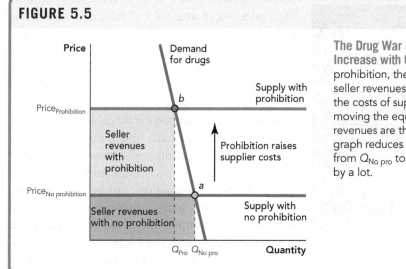

FIGURE 5.5

The Drug War Is Hard to Win Because Seller Revenues Increase with Greater Enforcement Without drug prohibition, the market equilibrium is at point *a* with seller revenues given by the blue area. Prohibition raises the costs of supply, pushing up the supply curve and moving the equilibrium to point *b*. At point *b*, seller revenues are the larger green area. Prohibition in this graph reduces the quantity of drugs consumed a little, from $Q_{No\,pro}$ to Q_{Pro}, but it raises seller revenues by a lot.

[*]Note that we have assumed that the supply of drugs is perfectly horizontal, which is plausible for an agricultural product whose production can be expanded or contracted very easily without an increase in costs. We discuss the elasticity of supply at greater length in the next section.

even when the price rises. Economists have much better data on the elasticity of demand for cigarettes, which one can think of as the elasticity of demand for the drug nicotine and it too is about 0.5.[3]

What happens to seller revenues when the demand curve is inelastic and the price rises? (Review Figure 5.3 if you don't know immediately.) When the demand curve is inelastic, an increase in price increases seller revenues. In Figure 5.5, the blue rectangle is seller revenues at the no-prohibition price; the much larger green rectangle is seller revenues with prohibition. Prohibition increases the cost of selling drugs, which raises the price, but at a higher price, revenues from drug selling are greater even if the quantity sold is somewhat smaller.

The more effective prohibition is at raising costs, the greater are drug industry revenues. So, more effective prohibition means that drug sellers have more money to buy guns, pay bribes, fund the dealers, and even research and develop new technologies in drug delivery (like crack cocaine). It's hard to beat an enemy that gets stronger the more you strike against them.

The war on drugs is difficult to win, but that doesn't necessarily mean that it's not worth fighting. Nobel Prize–winning economist Gary S. Becker, however, suggests a change in tactics. Suppose drugs were legal but taxed, much as alcohol is today. Becker suggests that the tax could be set so that it raised seller costs exactly as much as did prohibition (in Figure 5.5 simply relabel "Supply with prohibition" as "Supply with tax"). Since the tax raises costs by the same amount, the quantity of drugs sold would be the same under the tax as under prohibition. The only difference would be that instead of increasing seller revenues, a tax would increase government revenues (by the green rectangle *not* including the overlap with the blue rectangle). Many of the unfortunate spillovers of the war on drugs—things like gangs, guns, and corruption—could be greatly reduced under a "legal but taxed" system.[*]

We are moving toward this kind of system in the United States, at least for marijuana. As of 2022, recreational marijuana was legal in 19 states including California, Colorado, Massachusetts, and Washington. (Marijuana use, however, remains illegal under federal law.) In Colorado, legal sales began in 2014 and sales and other taxes on marijuana raise over $300 million annually. Not surprisingly, arrests for marijuana use have fallen by roughly 70%, so Colorado is also saving money on police, courts, and prisons. The price of marijuana in Colorado is about the same or a bit higher than in states where marijuana is illegal but the quality and variety of marijuana and methods of delivery (e.g., edibles) has increased tremendously. One worry is that as with alcohol, a minority of consumers account for a majority of use. In Colorado, for example, daily users account for 69% of total marijuana consumption so serious problems can develop in a minority even when the majority of people enjoy casual use.[4] Outright prohibition of

Theo Stroomer/Getty Images

In many states recreational marijuana use is now legal and the government, rather than criminals, is profiting from marijuana sales.

---

[*] On the benefits of a tax system for currently illegal drugs, see Becker, Gary S., Kevin M. Murphy, and Michael Grossman. 2006. The market for illegal goods: The case of drugs. *Journal of Political Economy* 114(1): 38–60.

marijuana appears to be ending but much work remains to be done on pre-cisely how marijuana and other drugs will be taxed and regulated.

Let's turn now to the elasticity of supply.

The Elasticity of Supply

When the price of a good like oil increases, suppliers will increase the quantity supplied, but by how much? Will the quantity supplied increase by a lot or by a little? The **elasticity of supply** measures how responsive the quantity supplied is to a change in price. To see the intuition, let's take a look at Figure 5.6, which shows two different supply curves.

In Figure 5.6, when the price increases from $40 to $50, the quantity supplied increases from 80 to 85 along supply curve I but by the much larger amount from 80 to 170 along supply curve E. Since the quantity supplied is more respon-sive to a change in price, supply curve E is more elastic than supply curve I.

Determinants of the Elasticity of Supply

Which supply curve, supply curve I or supply curve E, do you think would better represent the supply curve for oil? Even large increases in the price of oil will not increase the quantity of oil supplied by very much because it's not easy

The **elasticity of supply** measures how responsive the quantity supplied is to a change in price.

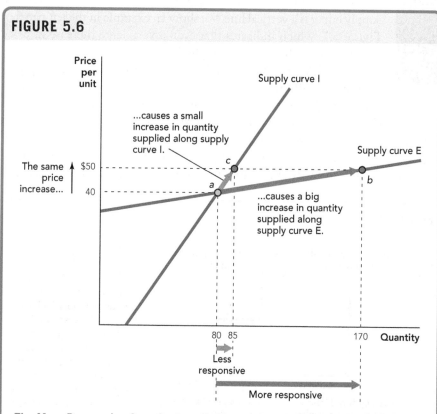

FIGURE 5.6

The More Responsive Quantity Supplied Is to a Change in Price, the More Elastic the Supply Curve Beginning at point *a*, an increase in price from $40 to $50 causes a small increase in quantity supplied along supply curve I, from 80 to 85 units (at point *c*). But the same increase in price causes a big increase in quantity supplied along supply curve E, from 80 to 170 units (at point *b*). Since the quantity supplied is more responsive to a change in price, supply curve E is more elastic than supply curve I.

to quickly increase the production of oil. Producing more oil requires time and a significant increase in the costs of exploration and drilling. Thus, the supply curve for oil is not very elastic (we could also say inelastic) and would be better represented by supply curve I.

The fundamental determinant of the elasticity of supply is how quickly per-unit costs increase with an increase in production. If increased production requires much higher per-unit costs, then supply will be less elastic—or inelastic. If production can increase without much increasing per-unit costs, then supply will be elastic.

Pablo Picasso 1881–1973

It's usually difficult to increase the supply of raw materials such as oil, coal, and gold without increasing costs—remember from Chapter 3 that the higher the price, the deeper the mine—so the supply of raw materials is often inelastic. The supply of manufactured goods is usually more elastic since production can often be increased at similar costs per unit by building more factories. To fully understand the elasticity of supply, let's consider two goods that represent polar cases of the elasticity of supply: Picasso paintings and toothpicks.

Picasso won't be painting any more canvases no matter how high the price of his paintings rises so the supply of Picasso paintings is not at all elastic—perfectly inelastic would be a good working assumption.* A perfectly inelastic supply curve is a vertical line. We show an example in the left panel of Figure 5.7, which indicates that even a very large increase in price won't increase the quantity supplied.

Toothpick manufacturers, however, can increase the supply of toothpicks without an increase in their costs per toothpick by cutting down just a few more trees and running them through the mill. Thus, a small increase in the price of toothpicks will generate a large increase in quantity supplied; that is, the supply of toothpicks will be very elastic—perfectly elastic would be a good working assumption. A perfectly elastic supply curve is flat, which indicates that even a tiny increase in price increases the quantity

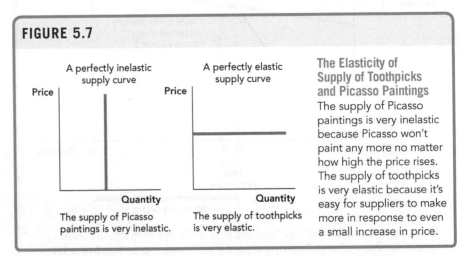

FIGURE 5.7

A perfectly inelastic supply curve

Price

Quantity

The supply of Picasso paintings is very inelastic.

A perfectly elastic supply curve

Price

Quantity

The supply of toothpicks is very elastic.

The Elasticity of Supply of Toothpicks and Picasso Paintings The supply of Picasso paintings is very inelastic because Picasso won't paint any more no matter how high the price rises. The supply of toothpicks is very elastic because it's easy for suppliers to make more in response to even a small increase in price.

* Why isn't the supply of Picasso paintings perfectly inelastic for certain? The supply of newly created Picasso paintings is perfectly inelastic, but with a higher price more people will be induced to sell their Picasso paintings, so the market supply of Picasso paintings will be very inelastic but not necessarily perfectly inelastic.

supplied by a very large amount. We show a perfectly elastic supply curve in the right panel of Figure 5.7.

It's easy to expand the supply of toothpicks because even if the toothpick industry doubles in size, the increases in the demand for wood will be negligible, so the toothpick industry can expand without pushing up the price of its primary input, wood. But if the housing industry were to double in size, the demand for wood would increase dramatically, and since it takes time to plant and harvest new trees, the price of wood and thus the price of houses would increase in the short run. More generally, supply is more elastic when the industry can be expanded without causing a big increase in the demand for that industry's inputs.

A closely related point is that the local supply of a good is much more elastic than the global supply. The supply of oil to the world is inelastic because world production won't increase without a significant increase in the cost of production per barrel. But imagine that more people move to Austin, Texas, increasing the demand for oil in that city. It's very easy to ship more oil to Austin from other parts of the United States so the supply of oil to Austin is well approximated by a perfectly elastic supply curve.

As with demand, supply tends to be more elastic in the long run than in the short run because in the long run, suppliers have more time to adjust. Suppliers can respond to an increase in the price of bicycles fairly quickly by running currently existing factories at higher capacity. Given more time, however, suppliers can increase output at lower cost by building new factories.

For some goods, it's almost impossible to increase output much in the short run. The best Scotch whisky, for example, is aged in oak barrels for 10, 20, or even 30 years. If the price of such high-quality Scotch whisky increases today, it will be at least 10 years before supply can increase.

We summarize the primary factors that determine the elasticity of supply in Table 5.3.

TABLE 5.3 PRIMARY FACTORS DETERMINING THE ELASTICITY OF SUPPLY

Less Elastic	More Elastic
Difficult to increase production at constant unit cost (e.g., some raw materials)	Easy to increase production at constant unit cost (e.g., some manufactured goods)
Large share of market for inputs	Small share of market for inputs
Global supply	Local supply
Short run	Long run

Calculating the Elasticity of Supply

The elasticity of supply also has a precise definition. The **elasticity of supply** is the percentage change in the quantity supplied divided by the percentage change in price.

The **elasticity of supply** is a measure of how responsive the quantity supplied is to a change in price. It is computed by

$$E_s = \frac{\%\Delta Q_{Supplied}}{\%\Delta Price}$$

Examples:

- If the price of soybeans rises by 10% and the quantity supplied increases by 20%, then the elasticity of supply for soybeans is $\frac{20\%}{10\%} = \mathbf{2}$.

- If the price of coffee falls by 10% and the quantity supplied of coffee falls by 1.5%, then the elasticity of supply for coffee is $\frac{-1.5\%}{-10\%} = \mathbf{0.15}$.[5]

Using the Midpoint Method to Calculate the Elasticity of Supply As with demand elasticities, it's important to calculate percent changes for supply elasticities using the midpoint method. Here is the midpoint formula for the elasticity of supply.

$$\text{Elasticity of supply} = E_s = \frac{\%\Delta Q_{\text{Supplied}}}{\%\Delta \text{Price}}$$

$$= \frac{\dfrac{\text{Change in quantity supplied}}{\text{Average quantity}}}{\dfrac{\text{Change in price}}{\text{Average price}}} = \frac{\dfrac{Q_{\text{After}} - Q_{\text{Before}}}{(Q_{\text{After}} + Q_{\text{Before}})/2}}{\dfrac{P_{\text{After}} - P_{\text{Before}}}{(P_{\text{After}} + P_{\text{Before}})/2}}$$

Applications of Supply Elasticity

Let's examine two important issues in public policy, gun buybacks and the economics of housing. In both cases, understanding the elasticity of supply is critical if we are to evaluate these policies wisely.

Gun Buyback Programs

Let's return to the question we introduced in the opening. Will local gun buybacks reduce the number of guns on the street and increase safety? The theory of gun buybacks is that (1) gun buybacks reduce the number of guns in circulation and (2) reductions in the number of guns in circulation reduce crime. It's not obvious that point (2) is true—guns are used for self-defense as well as for crime so fewer guns could mean more crime. But we don't have to decide that controversial question here because simple economic theory suggests that point (1) is false—gun buybacks in a city like Los Angeles are unlikely to reduce the number of guns in circulation. Let's see why.

We can analyze the effect of this program with a few questions. What kinds of guns are most likely to be sold at the gun buyback, high-quality or low-quality guns? And, what is the elasticity of supply of such guns to a city like Los Angeles?

The best gun to sell at a buyback is one that you can't sell anywhere else, so buybacks attract low-quality guns. In one Seattle buyback, 17% of the guns turned in didn't even fire.[6]

Now here is the key question: What is the elasticity of supply of low-quality guns to a city like Los Angeles? Recall from Table 5.3 that local supply curves are typically more elastic than global or national supply curves. It's estimated that there are hundreds of millions of guns in the United States, so there are plenty of low-quality guns—so many that the supply of such guns to Los Angeles will

Only in America: A drive-through gun buyback program.

be very elastic—elastic enough to make perfectly elastic a good working assumption.

Now that we know that the supply of low-quality guns to Los Angeles is very elastic, let's draw the diagram and analyze the policy. In Figure 5.8, we draw a perfectly elastic supply curve. With no buyback, the price of a low-quality, used gun is $84 and 1,000 guns are traded in Los Angeles. The gun buyback program increases the demand for used guns, shifting the demand curve outward, and the increase in demand pushes up the quantity of guns supplied in Los Angeles to 6,000 units. But the supply is so elastic that the price of guns doesn't increase, so even though the police buy 5,000 guns, the quantity of guns traded on the streets stays at 1,000. In other words, there is no net change in the number of guns on the streets of Los Angeles.

If this seems difficult to believe, imagine that instead of guns, the Los Angeles police decided to buy back shoes. Remember, the idea of a gun buyback is to reduce the number of guns in Los Angeles. Now, do you think that a shoe buyback would reduce the number of shoes in Los Angeles? Of course not. What will happen? People will sell their old shoes, the ones they don't wear anymore. Some enterprising individuals might even buy old shoes from thrift shops and sell those to the police. (In one Oakland gun buyback, some enterprising gun dealers from Reno, Nevada, drove to Oakland and sold the police more than 50 low-quality guns.[7]) The shoe buyback is unlikely to cause people to go shoeless, and for the same reasons a gun buyback is unlikely to cause people to go gunless.

The key point is that if the police can't drive up the price of guns, then they can't reduce the quantity of guns demanded on the streets. And the price of guns is determined not in Los Angeles, but in the national market for guns where millions of guns are bought and sold; thus a police buyback of a few thousand guns is too small to influence the price.

It's even possible that gun buybacks will *increase* the number of guns in circulation. Suppose that gun buybacks become a common and permanent feature of the market for guns. Before the gun buyback, a purchaser of a new gun expects that it will eventually wear out or otherwise fall in value until it

FIGURE 5.8

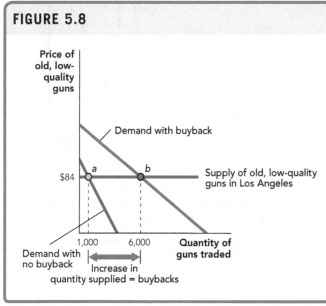

Elasticity and Gun Buybacks In the initial equilibrium at point *a*, 1,000 low-quality guns are traded. When police buy guns, the demand for guns increases, but since the supply of guns to a local region is very elastic, the street price of guns does not increase. As a result, the police can buy as many guns as they want, but there is no decrease in the number of guns on the street.

becomes worthless. But when gun buybacks are common, someone buying a gun knows that if it stops working, he can always sell it to the government. A buyback makes new guns more valuable; now they come with an insurance policy protecting against declines in value, which increases the demand for new guns.[8] You have probably experienced the same effect—students are more willing to buy an expensive textbook if they know they can easily sell it at the end of the semester (but do keep *this* book forever!).

Given the economic analysis, it's not surprising that studies of local gun buybacks have shown them to be ineffective at reducing crime.[9]

The Economics of Housing Supply

The price of housing has increased dramatically in the United States. Why? One possible answer might be that population and income have increased demand, pushing up housing prices. Figure 5.9, however, shows that although housing prices fluctuated between 1950 and 1999, they didn't increase very much on average, despite large increases in population and income. Why didn't housing prices increase? The simple answer is that the United States built a lot more housing during this period.

Economists Edward Glaeser and Joseph Gyourko argue that housing prices have been increasing in recent years because regulation has made it much more difficult to build new housing, especially in a handful of large, important cities such as San Francisco, Los Angeles, Boston, and New York.[10] Glaeser and Gyourko point out that house prices haven't increased in every city. In Atlanta, for example, house prices haven't increased anywhere near as much as in other cities in the United States, despite a big increase in population, because Atlanta has built more housing.

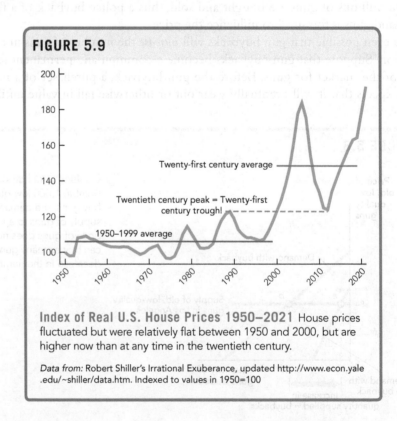

FIGURE 5.9

Index of Real U.S. House Prices 1950–2021 House prices fluctuated but were relatively flat between 1950 and 2000, but are higher now than at any time in the twentieth century.

Data from: Robert Shiller's *Irrational Exuberance,* updated http://www.econ.yale.edu/~shiller/data.htm. Indexed to values in 1950=100

FIGURE 5.10

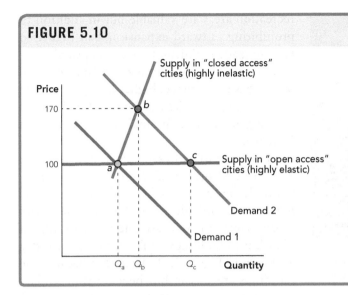

When Increased Demand Meets Inelastic Supply, Prices Rise Closed access and open access cities respond very differently to an increase in the demand for housing. In a closed access city, an increase in demand mostly increases prices—moving the equilibrium from point *a* to point *b*. In an open access city, an increase in demand mostly increases quantities—moving the equilibrium from point *a* to point *c*.

Let's call cities where it's difficult to build new housing, "closed access" cities. In these cities, the supply of housing is inelastic. We will call cities like Atlanta where building new housing is less restricted, "open access" cities. In these cities, the supply of housing is elastic. Figure 5.10 shows what happens when demand increases in a closed access city compared with an open access city. When demand increases in a closed access city, the equilibrium moves from point *a* to point *b*. Notice that prices increase a lot and the quantity of housing increases only slightly. In comparison when demand increases in an open access city, the equilibrium moves from point *a* to point *c* where the quantity of housing increases a lot and prices increase only slightly.

One study estimated that in Atlanta the elasticity of housing supply was 21.6 while in San Francisco it was only 0.14![11] Suppose that we would like to increase the supply of housing by 10%. How much will prices have to rise in Atlanta? What about in San Francisco?

To answer this question remember that the elasticity of supply is defined as the percentage change in quantity supplied divided by the percentage change in price, $E_S = \dfrac{\%\Delta Q_S}{\%\Delta P}$. In Atlanta we know that $E_S = 21.6$ and we are interested in calculating what must happen to prices if the quantity of housing increases by 10% so we can write: $E_S = 21.6 = \dfrac{10\%}{\%\Delta P}$ *or* $\%\Delta P = \dfrac{10\%}{21.6} = 0.46\%$. In other words, in Atlanta a less than 1% increase in prices will be enough to increase the quantity of housing supplied by 10%. What about in San Francisco? We will leave it to you to check the calculation but in San Francisco prices will have to rise by 71.4% to increase the quantity of housing supplied by 10%!

What's going on? Part of the issue is that Atlanta is surrounded by land, so the Atlanta metropolitan region can expand in any direction, but San Francisco is on a peninsula so there is less room to expand. San Francisco and California, however, have also prevented expansion by prohibiting housing along much of the coast north and south of San Francisco. Of course, parks and

Steve Proehl/The Image Bank/Getty Images

Zoning restrictions in San Francisco make it illegal or difficult to get approval to build multistory apartments, that is, to build up. Apartments are allowed only in the downtown area seen in the distance.

CHECK YOURSELF

- A computer manufacturer makes an experimental computer chip that critics praise, leading to a huge increase in the demand for the chip. How elastic is supply in the short run? What about the long run?
- Will the same increase in the demand for housing increase prices more in Manhattan or in Des Moines, Iowa?

recreation areas are valuable but in addition to prohibiting outward expansion, San Francisco has also made it difficult to expand upward!

Taller buildings economize on land so when building is unrestricted, higher land prices result in taller buildings. Tall buildings and multifamily housing, however, are prohibited in much of San Francisco.

In contrast to San Francisco and many other cities around the world, New York does allow tall buildings but a similar analysis shows how much more difficult it is to build in New York today than in the past. By one estimate, 40% of New York's buildings could not be built today, as shown in Figure 5.11. That's not because the buildings are unsafe but because they violate zoning restrictions on height or distance to the street. The zoning restrictions may result in a more aesthetically pleasing city (it's debatable) but they do make it more expensive to build, which in turn raises the price of housing.

Restrictions on building in cities such as San Francisco, Los Angeles, Boston, and New York have become an increasingly important issue in the United States. Contrary to what many people expected, cities have become more important in the Internet age, not less important. As a result, many highly educated workers want to move to cities for high-wage jobs but higher prices for housing eat up much of the gain. At the same time, less educated and less skilled workers can't afford to live in cities at all, which increases income inequality. How the United States chooses to address these issues has significant economic and political consequences.

FIGURE 5.11

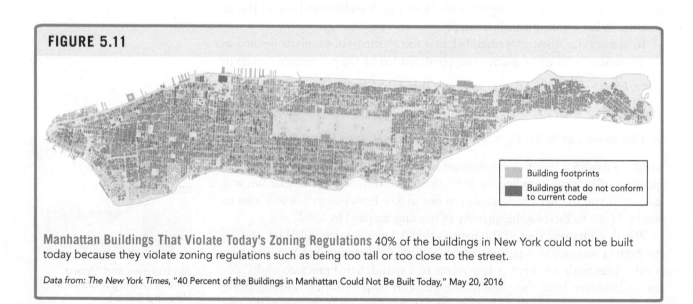

Building footprints

Buildings that do not conform to current code

Manhattan Buildings That Violate Today's Zoning Regulations 40% of the buildings in New York could not be built today because they violate zoning regulations such as being too tall or too close to the street.

Data from: The New York Times, "40 Percent of the Buildings in Manhattan Could Not Be Built Today," May 20, 2016

Using Elasticities for Quick Predictions (Optional)

Economists are often asked to predict how shifts in demand and supply will change market prices. Two simple price-change formulas make it possible to make quick predictions for price changes using elasticities.[13]

■ Percent change in price from a shift in demand $= \dfrac{\text{Percent change in demand}}{|E_d| + E_s}$

■ Percent change in price from a shift in supply $= -\dfrac{\text{Percent change in supply}}{|E_d| + E_s}$

These formulas are approximations that work well when the percent change in demand or supply is small, say, 10% or less.[14] Let's apply the formula to an interesting problem.

How Much Would the Price of Oil Fall If the Arctic National Wildlife Refuge Were Opened Up for Drilling?

The Arctic National Wildlife Refuge (ANWR) is the largest of Alaska's 16 national wildlife refuges. It is believed to contain significant deposits of petroleum. Former President George W. Bush argued in favor of drilling in ANWR.

> Increasing our domestic energy supply will help lower gasoline prices and utility bills. We can and should produce more crude oil here at home in environmentally responsible ways. The most promising site for oil in America is a 2,000 acre site in the Arctic National Wildlife Refuge, and thanks to technology, we can reach this energy with little impact on the land or wildlife.[15]

Some environmentalists disagree about whether the oil can be produced in environmentally responsible ways. We will leave that debate to others. What do economists say about the former president's assertion that "Increasing our domestic energy supply will help lower gasoline prices and utility bills"? An increase in supply will lower prices, but by how much?

The Department of Energy's Energy Information Service (EIS) predicts that production from ANWR will average about 900,000 barrels per day at its peak, or roughly 1% of worldwide oil production. Let's suppose that ANWR increases world supply by 1%. Since the elasticity of demand for oil is about −0.5 and in the long run the best estimate of the elasticity of supply is about 0.3, using our price formula, we have

At what price should we drill for oil in ANWR?

Steven J. Kazlowski/Alamy Stock Photo

$$\text{Percent change in price of oil from a 1\% increase in supply} = -\frac{1\%}{0.5 + 0.3}$$

$$= -1.25\%$$

A 1.25% fall in price won't seem like very much when you are gassing up at the pump, but don't forget that *every user of oil in the world* will benefit from the fall in price—so a fall of 1.25% is nothing to sneeze at.

So should we drill for oil in ANWR or not? The answer will depend on the value of conservation, the costs of drilling for oil (including the costs of a potential oil spill such as occurred in the Gulf of Mexico), and the price and quantity of oil that can be recovered. Not an easy calculation! You may be interested to know that President Trump opened up ANWR to drilling but before drilling began, President Biden reversed that decision.

Takeaway

The elasticity of demand measures how responsive the quantity demanded is to a change in price—the more responsive, the more elastic the demand. Similarly, the elasticity of supply measures how responsive the quantity supplied is to a change in price—the more responsive, the more elastic the supply.

In Chapter 4, we learned how to shift the supply and demand curves to produce *qualitative* predictions about changes in prices and quantities. Estimating elasticities of demand and supply is the first step in *quantifying* how changes in demand and supply will affect prices and quantities. You should know how to calculate elasticities of demand and supply using data on prices and quantities.

The elasticity of demand tells you how revenues respond to changes in price along a demand curve. If the $|E_d| < 1$, then price and revenue move together, and if $|E_d| > 1$, then price and revenue move in opposite directions. We used these relationships to explain why decreases in the price of food have made farming a smaller share of the economy, but decreases in the price of computer chips have made computing a larger share of the economy. We also used the same relationship to explain why the war on drugs can strengthen the very people it is trying to weaken.

You don't need to do statistical studies of demand and supply to get useful information about elasticities. Once you understand the concept, a little common sense will tell you that the supply curve for low-quality guns in Los Angeles is very elastic. And, if you can reason that the supply of low-quality guns to Los Angeles is very elastic, a little economics will tell you that gun buyback programs are a waste of taxpayer dollars. Similar reasoning suggests that when regulations make it expensive to build more housing, an increase in demand will result in an increase in price. Prices rise where apartments can't.

Elasticity is a bit dry but it's a very useful concept, and it will appear again when we come to discuss taxes in Chapter 6 and monopoly in Chapter 13.

CHAPTER REVIEW

Go online to practice with more examples of these types of problems, including live links to videos, data sources, and feedback.

KEY CONCEPTS

elasticity of demand, p. 69

inelastic, p. 72

elastic, p. 72

unit elastic, p. 72

elasticity of supply, p. 81

FACTS AND TOOLS

1. For each of the following pairs, which of the two goods is more likely to be inelastically demanded and why? Table 5.1 should help.

   a. Demand for tangerines vs. demand for fruit

   b. Demand for beef next month vs. demand for beef over the next decade

   c. Demand for Exxon gasoline at the corner of 7th and Grand vs. demand for gasoline in the entire city

   d. Demand for insulin vs. demand for vitamins

2. For each of the following pairs, which of the two goods is more likely to be elastically supplied? Table 5.3 should help.

   a. Supply of apples over the next growing season vs. supply of apples over the next decade

   b. Supply of construction workers in Binghamton, New York, vs. supply of construction workers in New York State

   c. Supply of breakfast cereal vs. supply of food

   d. Supply of gold vs. supply of computers

3. Indicate whether the demand for the good would become more elastic or less elastic after each of the following changes. (Note that in each of these cases, the demand curve may also shift inward or outward, but in this question we are interested in whether demand becomes more or less elastic.) Briefly justify your answer.

   a. The demand curve for soap after wide understanding that bacteria and other organisms cause and spread disease

   b. The demand curve for coal after the invention of nuclear power plants

   c. The demand curve for cars as more employers allow employees to work remotely

   d. The demand curve for a new television during an economic boom

4. For each of the following, indicate if the supply for the good would become more elastic or less elastic as a result of each change, and briefly justify your answer. (Once again, in each case the supply curve will also shift, but we are interested in changes in the elasticity.)

   a. The supply curve for diamonds if a new process for *manufacturing* diamonds is created

   b. The supply curve for food if pesticides and fertilizers were banned

   c. The supply curve for plastic if the share of total oil output that is used to make plastic increases

   d. The supply curve for nurses after several years of increasing wages in nursing

5. Let's work out a few examples to get a sense of what elasticity of demand means in practice. Remember that in all of these cases, we're moving along a fixed demand curve—so think of supply increasing or decreasing, while the demand curve is staying in the same place.

   a. If the elasticity of demand for college textbooks is −0.1 and the price of textbooks increases by 20%, how much will the quantity demanded change, and in what direction?

   b. In your answer to part a, was your answer in percentages or in total number of textbooks?

   c. If the elasticity of demand for spring break packages to Cancun is −5, and if you notice that this year the quantity of packages demanded increased by 10%, then what happened to the price of Cancun vacation packages?

   d. In your college town, real estate developers are building thousands of new student-friendly apartments close to campus. If you want to pay the lowest rent possible, should you hope that demand for apartments is relatively elastic or relatively inelastic?

   e. In your college town, the local government decrees that thousands of apartments close to campus are uninhabitable and must be torn down next semester. If you want to pay the lowest rent possible, should you hope that demand for apartments is relatively elastic or relatively inelastic?

   f. If the elasticity of demand for ballpoint pens with blue ink is −20, and the price of ballpoint pens with blue ink rises by 1%, what happens to the quantity demanded?

   g. What's an obvious substitute for ballpoint pens with blue ink? (This obvious substitute explains why the demand is so elastic.)

6. It's an important tradition in the Santos family that they eat the same meal at their favorite restaurant every Sunday. By contrast, the Chen

family spends exactly $50 for their Sunday meal at whatever restaurant sounds best.

a. Which family has a more elastic demand for restaurant food?

b. Which family has a unit elastic demand for restaurant food? (*Hint:* How would each family respond to an increase in food prices?)

7. The U.S. Department of Agriculture (USDA) has been concerned that Americans aren't eating enough fruits and vegetables, and they've considered coupons and other subsidies to encourage people—especially lower-income people—to eat these healthier foods. Of course, if people's demand for fruits and vegetables is perfectly inelastic, then there's no point in giving out coupons (thought question: why?). If instead the demand is only somewhat elastic, there may be better ways to spend taxpayer dollars.

This is clearly a situation where you'd want to know the elasticity of fruit and vegetable demand: If people respond a lot to small changes in price, then government-funded fruit and vegetable coupons *could* make poorer Americans a lot healthier, which *might* save taxpayers money *if* they don't have to pay for expensive medical treatments for unhealthy eaters. There are a lot of links in this chain of reasoning—all of which are covered in more advanced economics courses—but the first link is whether people actually have elastic demand for fruits and vegetables. The USDA's Economic Research Service employs economists to answer these sorts of questions, and a report from 2009 contained the following estimated elasticities (*Source:* Diansheng Dong and Biing-Hwan Lin. 2009. Fruit and vegetable consumption by low-income Americans: Would a price reduction make a difference? *Economic Research Report* 70, USDA).

Fruit	Elasticity of Demand
Apple	–0.16
Banana	–0.42
Grapefruit	–1.02
Grapes	–0.91
Orange	–1.14

a. Based on these demand elasticity estimates, which fruit is most inelastically demanded? Which is most elastically demanded?

b. For which of these fruits would a 10% drop in price cause an increase in total revenue from the sale of that fruit?

c. If the government could offer "10% off" coupons for only three of these fruits, and it wanted to have the biggest possible effect on quantity demanded, which three fruits should get the coupons?

d. Overall, the authors found that for the average fruit, the elasticity of demand was about –0.52. Is the demand for fruit elastic or inelastic?

8. On average, old cars pollute more than newer cars. Therefore, every few years, a politician proposes a cash for clunkers program: The government offers to buy up and destroy old, high-polluting cars. If a cash for clunkers program buys 1,000 old, high-polluting cars, is this the same as saying that there are 1,000 fewer old, high-polluting cars on the road? Why or why not?

9. As we noted in the chapter, many economists have estimated the short-run and long-run elasticities of oil demand. Let's see if a rise in the price of oil hurts oil revenues in the long run. One economist found that in the United States, the long-run elasticity of oil demand is –0.5.

a. If the price of oil rises by 10%, how much will the quantity of oil demanded fall: by 5%, by 0.5%, by 2%, or by 20%?

b. Does a 10% rise in oil prices increase or decrease total revenues to the oil producers?

c. Some policymakers and environmental scientists would like to see the United States cut back on its use of oil in the long run. We can use this elasticity estimate to get a rough measure of how high the price of oil would have to permanently rise in order to get people to make big cuts in oil consumption. How much would the price of oil have to permanently rise in order to cut oil consumption by 50%?

d. France has the largest long-run elasticity of oil demand (–0.6) of any of the large, rich countries, according to Cooper's estimates. Does this mean that France is better at responding to long-run price changes than other rich countries, or does it mean France is worse at responding?

10. Guess whether the demand for cigarettes is elastic or inelastic. Explain your reasoning. How do you think vaping changed the elasticity of demand for cigarettes?

THINKING AND PROBLEM SOLVING

11. Suppose that 200,000 Uber trips are taken every day in New York City and suppose that the elasticity of demand for an Uber trip is −0.5. If the price increased by 10% how many Uber trips would be taken in a day?

12. A movie theatre owner runs an experiment. She decreases prices 2% and discovers that ticket sales increase by 5%. Also, she increases prices by 1% and discovers that sales decrease by 2%. What should the owner do to maximize revenue?

13. In Figure 5.1 we showed two demand curves. On the demand curve labeled E for more elastic, the quantity demanded was 100 at a price of $40 and 20 at a price of $50. For the demand curve labeled I for less elastic or inelastic, the quantity demanded was 100 at a price of $40 and 95 at a price of $50. Using the midpoint formula, calculate the elasticity of demand for these two curves and check that they were labeled correctly.

14. During the Middle Ages, the African city of Taghaza quarried salt in 200-pound blocks to be sent to the salt market in Timbuktu, in present-day Mali. Travelers report that Taghazans used salt instead of wood to construct buildings.

    Compared with other towns without big salt mines, was the demand for *wood* more elastic or less elastic in Taghaza? How do you know?

15. Suppose that drug addicts pay for their addiction by stealing, so the higher the total revenue of the illegal drug industry, the higher the amount of theft. If a government crackdown on drug suppliers leads to a higher price of drugs, what will happen to the amount of theft if the demand for drugs is elastic? What if the demand for drugs is inelastic?

16. Henry Ford famously mass-produced cars at the beginning of the twentieth century, starting Ford Motor Company. He made millions because mass production made cars cheap to make, and he passed some of the savings to the consumer in the form of a low price. Cars became a common sight in the United States thereafter. Keeping total revenue and its relationship with price in mind, do you expect the demand for cars to be elastic or inelastic given the story of Henry Ford?

17. In Chapter 10, you'll see that we purchased permits to pollute the air with sulfur dioxide (SO_2). We didn't use the permits. Instead, we threw them out. In other words, we bought permits for the same reason the government buys guns in gun buyback programs—to prevent what we bought from being used. As we discussed in the chapter, gun buyback programs have failed. So why is our plan to buy permits more likely to get SO_2 out of the air than the government's plan to get guns off the street? (*Hint:* Think in terms of elasticities and keep in mind that only a fixed number of pollution permits are available.)

18. How might elasticities help to explain why people on vacation tend to spend more for food and necessities than the local population?

19. In the short run, the price elasticity of the demand and supply of electricity can be very low.

    a. How might revenue for the electricity industry change if one power plant were shut down for maintenance, reducing supply?

    b. If one power company owned many power plants, would it have a short-term incentive to keep all of its plants running, or could it have a short-term incentive to shut down a power plant now and then?

20. Immigration is a fact of life in the United States. Over time, this will lead to an increase in the labor supply. What field would you rather be in: a field where the demand for your kind of labor is elastic or a field where the demand for your kind of labor is inelastic?

21. In the world of fashion, the power to imitate a trendy look is the power to make money. Stores such as H&M and Forever 21 focus on imitating fashions wherever possible: As soon as they see that a new look is coming along, something people are willing to pay a high price for, they start cranking out that look.

Do these imitation-centered stores make the supply of clothing more elastic or less elastic? How can you tell?

22. The relationship between elasticity of demand and total revenue can be a helpful shortcut, particularly if your professor likes to give multiple-choice exams. For each of the following examples, calculate how much money each consumer spends at the low price and at the high price, and decide whether the right answer for a question asking for the price elasticity of demand on a multiple-choice exam would be (a) −2.33, (b) −1.17, (c) −1.00, or (d) −0.56. Remember, if the consumer spends more money at the lower price, demand must be

elastic. (*Warning:* Two of these will require a bit of guesstimation.)

a. When the price of a movie ticket rises from $6 to $8 for senior citizens, Gary (a senior citizen) decides to go to the movies every other day (15 times per month) instead of every day (30 times per month).

b. When the price of a large specialty coffee drink rises from $3 to $4, Gabriela reduces her weekly consumption from 7 to 5.

c. When $P_X = \$10.00$, $Q_X^D = 30$. When $P_X = \$7.50$, $Q_X^D = 40$.

23. Let's practice the midpoint formula. Calculate the elasticity of demand for each of the goods or services in the table that follows.

Good or Service	Beginning Price	Beginning Quantity	Ending Price	Ending Quantity	Elasticity
Daily movie ticket sales in Denver, Colorado	$6	50,000	$10	40,000	
Weekly milk sales at Loma Vista Elementary School	$1	1,000	$1.50	800	
Weekly round-trip ticket sales, New York to San Francisco	$500	10,000	$1,000	9,000	
Annual student enrollments, Upper Tennessee State University	$6,000	40,000	$9,000	39,000	

24. Consider the graph below:

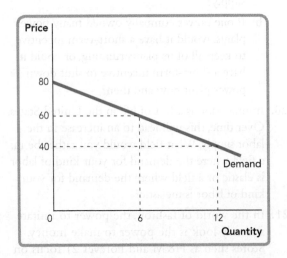

a. If price falls from $60 to $40, what happens to total revenue? Given this answer, is the demand curve elastic or inelastic over this range?

b. Calculate the price elasticity of demand using the midpoint formula. Does your answer coincide with that of part a?

CHALLENGES

25. In this chapter, we've emphasized that the elasticity of supply is higher in the long run than in the short run. In a lot of cases, this is surely true: If you see that jobs pay more in the next state over, you won't move there the next week but you might move there next year. But sometimes the short-run elasticity will be *higher* than the long-run elasticity.

Austan Goolsbee found an interesting example of this when he looked at the elasticity of income of highly paid executives with respect to taxes. In 1993, then President Bill Clinton passed a law raising income taxes. This tax hike was fully expected: He campaigned on it in 1992.

a. What do you expect happened to executive income in the first year of the tax increases? What about in subsequent years? (*Source:* Goolsbee, Austan. 2000. What happens when you tax the rich? Evidence from executive compensation. *Journal of Political Economy* 108(2): 352–378. For a book on the topic written by a leading economist, see Joel Slemrod (Ed.), 2000. *Does Atlas Shrug?* [Cambridge, MA: Harvard University Press].)

(*Hint:* Top executives have a lot of power over when they get paid for their work: They can ask for bonuses a bit earlier, or they can cash out their stock options a bit earlier. Literally, this isn't their "labor supply"; it's more like their "income supply.")

b. Goolsbee estimated that the short-run elasticity of "income supply" for these executives was 1.4, while the long-run elasticity of "income supply" was 0.1. (*Note:* Goolsbee used a variety of statistical methods to look for these elasticities, and all came to roughly the same result.) If taxes pushed down their take-home income by 10%, how much would this cut the amount of income supplied in the short run? In the long run?

c. You are a newspaper reporter. Your editor tells you to write a short feature story with this title: "Goolsbee's research proves that tax hikes make the rich work less." Make your case in one sentence.

d. You are a newspaper reporter. Your editor tells you to write a short feature story with this title: "Goolsbee's research proves that tax hikes have little effect on work by the wealthy." Make your case in one sentence.

e. Which story is more truthful?

26. We saw that a gun buyback program was unlikely to work in Los Angeles. If the entire United States ran a gun buyback program, would that be better at eliminating guns or worse? Why? What about if the gun buyback was also accompanied by a law making (at least some) guns illegal?

27. Using the data from the ANWR example, what will be the percentage increase in quantity supplied if ANWR raises supply by 1%? No, this isn't a trick question, and the formula is already there in the chapter. Why isn't this number just 1%?

Discovering DATA

28. Using the FRED economic database (https://fred.stlouisfed.org), let's compare expenditures on cell phones with the price of phones. Unfortunately, as is often the case, it's difficult to find data on exactly what we want, but if you search for "real expenditures telephone," you will find a series for expenditure on telephone and related communication equipment. Then click Edit Graph and Add Line. Search for "expenditures telephone price," and you should find a price series (make sure it says "chain type price index") for telephones and communication equipment. To make comparisons easier, change the units to Index and set the index equal to "Index 2012=100" for both series and then set the dates from 2010-01-01 to 2021-01-01.

a. Between 2010 and 2021, what happened to expenditures? Prices?

b. Is the demand for telephones elastic or inelastic?

29. Suppose the elasticity of housing demand is 1 and the elasticity of housing supply is 20 in Atlanta and 0.15 in San Francisco. If the demand for housing increases by 10% in both cities, by approximately how much will prices rise in each city? (*Hint:* Use the formulas in the section, Elasticities for Quick Predictions.)

30. The world was horrified when it learned that slavery was being practiced in Sudan as part of the Second Sudanese Civil War (1983–2005). In 1995, the humanitarian group Christian Solidarity International began a controversial program to buy the freedom of thousands of people who had been enslaved. Other humanitarian groups opposed these programs because they believed that "redemption" programs could increase the incentive of suppliers to enslave more people. Under what conditions on the elasticity of supply will the slave redemption program be most effective? Draw a figure. Under what conditions on the elasticity of supply will the redemption program be less effective? Draw a figure and discuss the dilemma created by redemption programs.

WORK IT OUT

For interactive, step-by-step help in solving the following problem, go online.

Figure 5.3 and Table 5.2 both set out some important but tedious rules. Let's practice them, since they are quite likely to be on an exam. For each of the following cases, state whether the demand curve is relatively steep or flat and whether a *fall* in price will raise total revenue or lower it. In this case,

note that we present the elasticity in terms of its absolute value.

a. Elasticity of demand = 0.7

b. Elasticity of demand = 3.0

c. Elasticity of demand = 20.0

d. Elasticity of demand = 1.05

e. Elasticity of demand = 0.95

CHAPTER 5 APPENDIX

Other Types of Elasticities

Economists often compute elasticities any time one variable is related to another variable. Klick and Tabarrok, for example, find that a 50% increase in the number of police on the streets reduces automobile theft and theft from automobiles by 43%, so the elasticity of auto crime with respect to police is −43%/50% = −0.86. Gruber, who studies church attendance, finds an interesting relationship: The more people give to their church, the less likely they are to attend! In other words, people regard money and time as substitutes and those who give more of one are likely to give less of the other. Gruber calculates that a 10% increase in giving leads to an 11% decline in attendance or an elasticity of attendance with respect to giving of −11%/10% = −1.1.[16]

Thus, any time there is a relationship between two variables A and B, you can always express the relationship in terms of an elasticity. Two other frequently used elasticities in economics are the cross-price elasticity of demand and the income elasticity of demand.

The Cross-Price Elasticity of Demand

The cross-price elasticity of demand measures how responsive the quantity demanded of good A is to the price of good B.

$$\frac{\text{Percentage change in quantity demanded of good } A}{\text{Percentage change in price of good } B} = \frac{\%\Delta Q_{\text{Demanded},A}}{\%\Delta P_B}$$

Given data on the quantity demanded of good A at two different prices of good B, the cross-price elasticity can be calculated using the following formula:

$$= \frac{\dfrac{\text{Change in quantity demanded } A}{\text{Average quantity } A}}{\dfrac{\text{Change in price } B}{\text{Average price } B}} = \frac{\dfrac{Q_{\text{After},A} - Q_{\text{Before},A}}{(Q_{\text{After},A} + Q_{\text{Before},A})/2}}{\dfrac{P_{\text{After},B} - P_{\text{Before},B}}{(P_{\text{After},B} + P_{\text{Before},B})/2}}$$

The cross-price elasticity of demand is closely related to the idea of substitutes and complements. If the cross-price elasticity is positive, an increase in the price of good B increases the quantity of good A demanded so the two goods are substitutes. If the cross-price elasticity is negative, an increase in the price of good B decreases the quantity of good A demanded so the two goods are complements.

- If the cross-price elasticity > 0, then goods A and B are substitutes.
- If the cross-price elasticity < 0, then goods A and B are complements.

The Income Elasticity of Demand

The income elasticity of demand measures how responsive the quantity demanded of a good is with respect to changes in income.

$$\text{Income elasticity of demand} = \frac{\text{Percentage change in quantity demanded}}{\text{Percentage change in income}}$$

$$= \frac{\%\Delta Q_{\text{Demanded}}}{\%\Delta \text{Income}}$$

As usual, given data on the quantity demanded at two different income levels, the income elasticity of demand can be calculated as

$$\frac{\dfrac{\text{Change in quantity demanded}}{\text{Average quantity}}}{\dfrac{\text{Change in income}}{\text{Average income}}} = \frac{\dfrac{Q_{\text{After}} - Q_{\text{Before}}}{(Q_{\text{After}} + Q_{\text{Before}})/2}}{\dfrac{I_{\text{After}} - I_{\text{Before}}}{(I_{\text{After}} + I_{\text{Before}})/2}}$$

The income elasticity of demand can be used to distinguish normal from inferior goods. Recall from Chapter 3 that when an *increase* in income *increases* the demand for a good, we say the good is a *normal good*. And a good like Ramen noodles, for which an *increase* in income *decreases* the demand, is called an *inferior good*.

■ If the income elasticity of demand > 0, then the good is a normal good.

■ If the income elasticity of demand < 0, then the good is an inferior good.

Sometimes economists also distinguish normal from "luxury" goods, defined as one where, say, a 10% increase in income causes more than a 10% increase in the quantity of the good demanded. Thus,

■ If the income elasticity of demand > 1, then the good is a luxury good.

Discovering DATA

Using the FRED economic database (https://fred.stlouisfed.org/), let's compare people's purchases of groceries with their purchases of electronics and appliances. At FRED, search for "retail trade grocery," then click on Edit Graph and Add Line; search for "retail trade electronics." Both series should be in millions of dollars, but since grocery stores sell much more than electronics stores, the scales make it difficult to see the changes. Switch units to Index and then set the index equal to 100 in December of 2007, the beginning of the 2007–2009 recession. Do this for both series. Print the graph.

a. What happened to food sales over the 2007–2009 recession? What about sales of electronics?

b. What does your answer to part (a) suggest about the income elasticity of food and electronics?

c. The data include electronics and appliance stores. Why might appliance purchases be especially income elastic compared with food purchases, at least over the short run?

6

Taxes and Subsidies

Billionaire hedge fund manager David Tepper paid so much in state income taxes that when he moved from New Jersey to Florida, the state of New Jersey had to scramble to adjust its budget calculations. Tepper may have moved for the better weather, but by moving he also saved hundreds of millions of dollars since Florida does not have a personal income tax. Tepper, who is in his early 60s, may also have been thinking about the future. If Tepper dies as a resident of Florida instead of New Jersey, his heirs stand to inherit billions more because, unlike New Jersey, Florida has no estate tax. (Unless he moves abroad, however, Tepper will still have to pay the federal estate tax.) It's not just billionaires who pay attention to estate taxes, however. There is a small but noticeable trend for elderly wealthy people to move from high estate-tax states to low estate-tax states.[1] Elderly wealthy people can reduce their estate tax by changing *where* they die. Could they also change the estate tax by changing *when* they die?

In fact, two economists, Joshua Gans and Andrew Leigh, found that in Australia a potential $10,000 reduction in the estate tax prompted people to postpone death by about a week! If that sounds incredible, it may help to know that there is also a small but noticeable trend for people to live until after their birthdays or other major events. New York hospitals, for example, reported fewer deaths than usual in the last week of 1999—the last week of the twentieth century—and more deaths than usual in the first week of the twenty-first century. If death can be postponed for major events, then why not postpone death to save on taxes? Or if that fails, don't call the coroner until the lower tax rate is in effect.

If all this seems a bit macabre, don't worry—not only can deaths be postponed for tax reasons, births can also be advanced. Parents get a tax deduction for dependents like children, and so long as the child is born before the clock strikes midnight on December 31, the family gets the deduction for the entire year. Thus, compared with a child born in early January, a child born in late December can save parents thousands of dollars. Journalist David Leonhardt wrote about this incentive in the *New York Times*:

> Unless you're a cynic, or an economist, I realize you might have trouble believing that the intricacies of the nation's tax code would impinge on something as sacred as the birth of a child. But it appears that you would be wrong.

Not only are more children born in late December than in early January, but also the extra births appear to be clustered among those who have the most to gain from a tax deduction, exactly as a cynic or an economist would predict. Leonhardt coined the term "national birth day" to indicate the day of the year on which the largest number of births occurs. For a long time, "national birth day" was around mid-September (probably because it was cold and dark the previous December!). But amazingly, as induced labor, Caesarian sections, and taxes have all increased, the day of the year on which the largest number of births occur has now moved to late December![2]

In this chapter, we examine taxes and also subsidies, which are payments from the government for production. The analysis will draw on our understanding of demand and supply and also on our understanding of elasticity from the last chapter.

Commodity Taxes

Commodity taxes are taxes on goods. Well-known commodity taxes include those on fuel, liquor, and cigarettes, although in the United States most commodities are taxed in one way or another. We will emphasize the following truths about commodity taxation:

1. Who ultimately pays the tax does *not* depend on who writes the check to the government.

2. Who ultimately pays the tax *does* depend on the relative elasticities of demand and supply.

3. Commodity taxation raises revenue and creates deadweight loss (i.e., reduces the gains from trade).

Who Ultimately Pays the Tax Does Not Depend on Who Writes the Check

Imagine that the government is considering a tax on apples. The government can collect the tax in either of two ways (assume that each method is equally costly to implement). The government can tax apple sellers $1 for every basket supplied, or they can tax apple buyers $1 for every basket of apples bought. Which tax scheme is better for apple buyers?

Surprisingly, the answer is that the tax has exactly the same effects whether it is "paid" for by sellers or "paid" for by buyers. Who ultimately pays a tax is determined not by the laws of Congress but by the laws of supply and demand.

Let's consider the effect of a $1 tax on apple sellers, which we analyze beginning with panel A of Figure 6.1. As discussed in Chapter 3, as far as sellers are concerned, a tax is the same as an increase in costs. Thus, if with no tax sellers require a minimum of $1 per basket to sell 250 baskets of apples, then with a $1 tax they will require $2 per basket to sell the same quantity—$1 for their regular costs and $1 for their tax cost. Similarly, if with no tax sellers require a minimum of $3 per basket to sell 1,250 baskets, then with a $1 tax they will require $4 per basket. Following through on this logic, we see that a $1 tax shifts the supply curve up at every quantity by exactly $1.

Panel B of Figure 6.1 adds a demand curve to show the effect of the tax on the market for apples. With no tax, the equilibrium is at point *a* with a price of $2 per basket and a quantity of 700. If apple sellers must pay a $1 tax for every

FIGURE 6.1

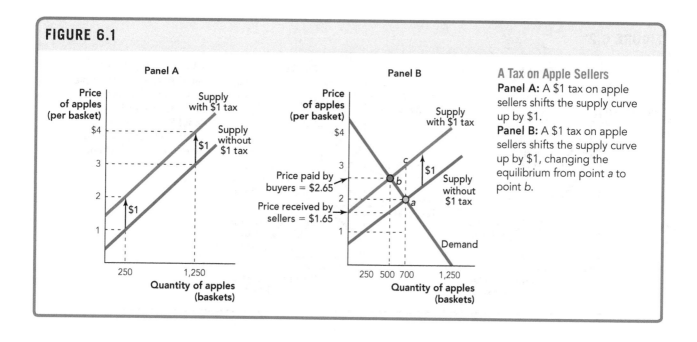

Panel A

Panel B

A Tax on Apple Sellers
Panel A: A $1 tax on apple sellers shifts the supply curve up by $1.
Panel B: A $1 tax on apple sellers shifts the supply curve up by $1, changing the equilibrium from point *a* to point *b*.

basket supplied, the supply curve shifts up by $1 and the new equilibrium is at point *b* with a higher price of $2.65 and a smaller quantity consumed of 500.

Students are sometimes surprised that a $1 tax does not necessarily raise the price by $1. To see why, imagine that the price did rise by $1. In that case, the price would rise to $3 at point *c*. But is point *c* an equilibrium?

No. Point *c* is not an equilibrium because at point *c*, the quantity supplied is greater than the quantity demanded. In other words, apple sellers in this market find that if they try to pass all of the tax onto apple buyers by raising the price to $3 per basket, there are not enough buyers to purchase 700 baskets, so sellers have excess supply. What incentives does this create? As they compete to obtain buyers, sellers must bid the price down. As the price falls, sellers supply fewer apples until the new equilibrium is reached at point *b*.

With the tax, buyers pay $2.65 per basket and sellers receive $1.65 per basket ($2.65 minus the $1 tax they must send to the government). Notice that the difference between the price that buyers pay and the price that sellers receive is equal to the tax. In fact, so long as the tax doesn't drive the industry out of existence, it will always be the case that

The tax = Price paid by buyers − Price received by sellers

What happens if instead of taxing sellers, the government taxes buyers? We illustrate beginning with panel A of Figure 6.2. Imagine that before the tax buyers were willing to pay up to $4 per basket to purchase 100 baskets. If buyers must pay a $1 tax *on top of the price*, what is the most that they will now be willing to pay? Correct, $3. That is, if the buyers value the apples at $4 per basket but they must pay a tax of $1 to the government, then the most the buyers will be willing to pay the apple suppliers is $3 per basket (since the total price including the tax will now be $4). Similarly, if before the tax buyers were willing to pay up to $2 per basket to purchase 700 baskets, then after the $1 tax they will be willing to pay to the sellers at most $1 per basket for the same quantity. Following through on this logic, we see that a tax of $1 on buyers shifts the demand curve down at every quantity by $1.

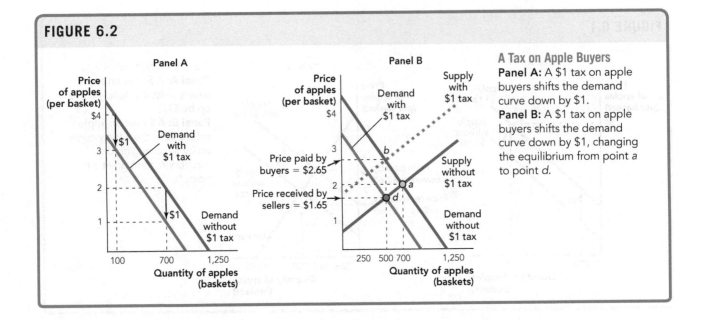

FIGURE 6.2

The burden of a tax can be transmitted far from where the tax initially hits.

Panel B shows the market for apples. With no tax, the equilibrium is at point *a* with a price of $2 and a quantity of 700. With the $1 tax on apple buyers, the demand curve shifts down by $1 and the new equilibrium is at point *d* with a price of $1.65 and a quantity of 500.

Notice that with the tax, apple buyers pay a total price of $2.65 ($1.65 in market price plus $1 tax) and apple sellers receive $1.65. In other words, the price buyers pay, the price sellers receive, and the quantity traded (500 baskets) are identical to what they were when the tax was placed on apple sellers.

We can see what is going on by showing in panel B of Figure 6.2 a dotted supply curve, the supply curve *if* there were a $1 tax on sellers (exactly as in Figure 6.1). If the $1 tax is placed on sellers, the equilibrium is at point *b*. If the tax is placed on buyers, the equilibrium is at point *d*. The only difference between points *b* and *d* is that when the tax is placed on suppliers, the market price ($2.65) *includes* the tax, but when the tax is placed on buyers, the market price ($1.65) does not include the tax. The tax must be paid, however, so in either case the final price paid by buyers is $2.65 and the final price received by sellers is $1.65.

We have just shown something quite surprising. Who pays a tax does not depend on who must send the check to the government. Don't be fooled; a tax on apple sellers has exactly the same effects as a tax on apple buyers.

Who Ultimately Pays the Tax Depends on the Relative Elasticities of Supply and Demand

We have just seen that whether the $1 apple tax is placed on buyers or sellers, the price to buyers ends up being $2.65 and the price received by sellers ends up being $1.65. But why is it that with the tax, buyers pay 65 cents more ($2.65 − $2), while sellers receive 35 cents less ($2 − $1.65)? What determines how the burden of the tax is shared between buyers and sellers? To answer this question, we introduce the *wedge shortcut*.

The Wedge Shortcut

The most important effect of a tax is to drive a tax wedge between the price paid by buyers and the price received by sellers. Recall that

The tax = Price paid by buyers − Price received by sellers

If we focus on the wedge aspect of a tax, we can simplify our tax analysis. In Figure 6.3, instead of shifting curves, we start with a tax of $1 and we "push" this vertical "tax wedge" into the diagram until the top of the wedge just touches the demand curve and the bottom of the wedge just touches the supply curve. The top of the wedge at point *b* gives us the price paid by the buyers ($2.65), the bottom of the wedge at point *d* gives us the price received by sellers ($1.65), and the quantity at which the wedge "sticks" is 500 baskets, exactly as before.

Using the wedge shortcut, we show that whether buyers or sellers pay a tax is determined by the relative elasticities of demand and supply. Recall from Chapter 5 that the elasticity of demand measures how responsive the quantity demanded is to a change in price and the elasticity of supply measures how responsive the quantity supplied is to a change in price. We show that *when demand is more elastic than supply, demanders pay less of the tax than sellers. When supply is more elastic than demand, suppliers pay less of the tax than buyers.*

In panel A of Figure 6.4, we draw a demand curve that is more elastic than the supply curve. So who will pay most of the tax? Sellers. To see why sellers will pay most of the tax, push the tax wedge into the diagram. Notice that at the quantity that the tax wedge sticks, the price paid by buyers is only a small amount above the price with no tax. The price received by sellers, however, falls well below the price with no tax. Thus, when demand is more elastic than supply, buyers pay less of the tax than sellers.

FIGURE 6.3

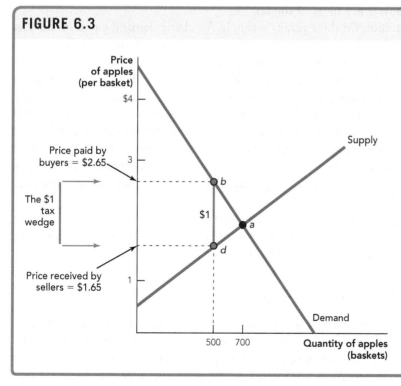

The Tax Wedge If the tax is $1, the price paid by the buyers must be $1 higher than the price received by the sellers. Driving a $1 tax wedge into the diagram shows us the new equilibrium must be where the price paid by the buyers is $2.65, the price received by the sellers is $1.65, and the quantity traded is 500.

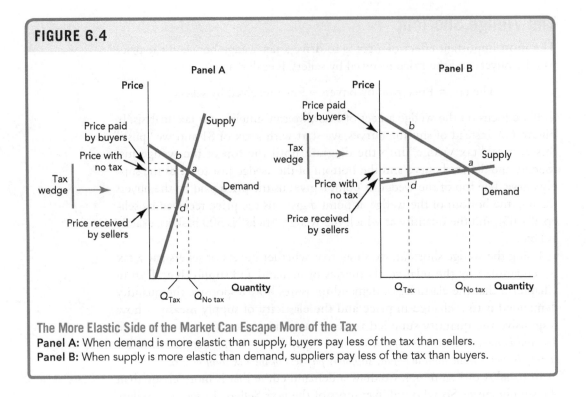

FIGURE 6.4

Panel A

Panel B

The More Elastic Side of the Market Can Escape More of the Tax
Panel A: When demand is more elastic than supply, buyers pay less of the tax than sellers.
Panel B: When supply is more elastic than demand, suppliers pay less of the tax than buyers.

In panel B of Figure 6.4, we draw a supply curve that is more elastic than the demand curve. So who will pay most of the tax? Buyers. To see why buyers will pay most of the tax, take the tax wedge and push it into the diagram. At the point that the wedge "sticks," notice that the price paid by buyers has risen far above the price with no tax. The price received by sellers, however, has fallen only just below the price with no tax. Thus, when supply is more elastic than demand, buyers pay more of the tax.

The intuition for these results is simple. An elastic demand curve means that demanders have lots of substitutes and you can't tax someone who has a good substitute because they will just buy the substitute! Thus, when demand is elastic, sellers will end up paying most of the tax. An elastic supply curve has a similar interpretation. It means that the workers and capital in the industry can easily find work in another industry—so if you try to tax an industry with an elastic supply curve, the industry inputs will escape to other industries. Just remember, therefore, that *elasticity = escape*. So long as the industry is not taxed out of existence, someone must pay the tax, so whether buyers or sellers pay more depends on who can escape the best—that is, which curve is *relatively* more elastic.

Elasticity = Escape

Bearing in mind our rule that the more elastic side of the market can better escape the tax, let's take a look at some taxes to see whether it is buyers or sellers who will bear the greater burden.

Health Insurance Mandates and Tax Analysis

One of the provisions of the 2010 Patient Protection and Affordable Care Act, popularly known as the Affordable Care Act (ACA) or "Obamacare," was a mandate that required large employers to pay for employee health insurance or face a penalty. The ACA was modeled on a similar act passed in Massachusetts in 2006. It's good to have health insurance, and it's even better if someone else is paying for it. But who really pays? The ACA and Massachusetts laws required that firms buy health insurance for every full-time worker hired so we can think of these mandates as a tax on labor. Who pays the tax? As we now know, who pays more of the tax depends on whether supply or demand is more elastic. So consider, is it easier for firms to escape the tax by not employing or for workers to escape the tax by not working?

Can firms escape the tax? Yes, in a lot of ways. If the tax on labor gets too high, firms can substitute capital (machines) for labor, they can move overseas, or they can close up shop altogether. Can workers escape the tax? It's not so easy. Most workers would continue to work even if their wages were lower because the costs of leaving the labor force are high. Thus, for most workers, the elasticity of labor supply is low (this is especially true for working-age men; men nearing retirement and married women tend to have higher elasticities of labor supply). The demand for labor, therefore, is likely to be more elastic than the supply of labor. Remember that when demand is more elastic than supply, sellers (i.e., workers = sellers of labor) will pay most of the tax in the form of lower wages. This is the situation depicted in panel A of Figure 6.4. Nevertheless, are there any succinct conclusions regarding the tax burden of the act? Yes.

Studies of the Massachusetts mandate estimate that the wages of workers who gained health insurance because of the law fell by about the same amount as the cost of the coverage to firms.[3] In other words, most of the burden of the law fell on workers through lower wages, exactly as our model predicts. Broadly speaking the same thing is true of the ACA. In addition to an employer mandate, the national ACA also involves an individual mandate, taxpayer-funded subsidies for purchase of health insurance by low-income individuals, and an expansion in taxpayer-funded Medicaid. Thus the burden of the entire Act is complicated. The Congressional Budget Office, however, estimates that when employers add insurance coverage because of the law, "workers' wages will adjust by roughly the employers' cost of providing that coverage."[4]

Just because workers bear the costs of a law requiring firms to purchase health insurance, doesn't mean that the law is a bad idea. It's quite reasonable to want everyone in society to have health insurance and requiring employers to purchase health insurance is one way, albeit not necessarily the best way, to move toward this goal. What is important is that citizens not be fooled into thinking that the law is a free lunch at the expense of their employer. Tax analysis is useful because it helps us to see the true benefits and costs of economic policy and thus to choose wisely.

Who Pays the Cigarette Tax?

States tax cigarettes at very different rates. New Jersey, for example, taxes cigarettes at $2.70 per pack while South Carolina taxes cigarettes at just 57 cents per pack (2023 rates). Who ultimately pays the cigarette tax? Buyers or sellers? As usual, who pays depends on the relative elasticities of demand and supply.

As you might expect, given the addictive nature of nicotine, smokers have an inelastic demand for cigarettes, around −0.5. What about suppliers? Before you answer, remember that we are analyzing *state* cigarette taxes so the relevant question is how easily can a cigarette manufacturer escape a state tax?

A manufacturer can easily escape a state tax by selling elsewhere. In fact, because it's so easy for a cigarette manufacturer to ship its product around the country, the

Envision/Getty Images

What a drag it is being taxed Heavy taxes encourage smokers to smoke fewer cigarettes, but they also encourage smokers to choose cigarettes with higher nicotine levels. High cigarette taxes have also been shown to increase smoking intensity—when taxes are high, smokers inhale more deeply and they smoke down to the butt.

elasticity of supply to any one state is very large, which means that buyers will bear almost all of the tax—as illustrated in panel B of Figure 6.4.

If the price paid by buyers increases by almost the amount of the tax, then the price received by sellers must be almost the same in all states regardless of the tax. To see why this makes sense, imagine what would happen if manufacturers earned less money per pack selling cigarettes in a high-tax state like New Jersey than in a low-tax state like South Carolina. If this happened, manufacturers would ship fewer cigarettes to New Jersey and more to South Carolina, and this would continue until the after-tax price was the same in both states.

We can easily test this theory. A pack of cigarettes sold for about $5.57 in South Carolina and $8.06 in New Jersey (2023), so the price to buyers was 45% higher in New Jersey. But the after-tax price received by sellers was about the same, $5.00 in South Carolina ($5.57 − $0.57) versus $5.36 in New Jersey ($8.06 − $2.70). (The small differences can probably be accounted for by other costs of doing business that differ between New Jersey and South Carolina.)

By the way, one argument for high cigarette taxes is that the government should discourage smoking. State taxes, however, are a bad method of discouraging smoking in the United States. A New Jersey tax will discourage smoking by residents of New Jersey but, as we have seen, to escape the New Jersey tax, cigarette manufacturers will ship more cigarettes to other states, which pushes cigarette prices down in those states, thereby increasing the quantity demanded. A New Jersey tax, therefore, will decrease smoking in New Jersey but this will be partially offset by increased smoking in other states. It's more difficult for cigarette manufacturers to escape federal taxes than state taxes so if the goal is to reduce national consumption, a federal tax is superior to a state tax.

A Commodity Tax Raises Revenue and Reduces the Gains from Trade (Creates a Deadweight Loss)

A tax generates revenues for the government but also reduces the gains from trade. In the left panel of Figure 6.5, we show the apple market with no tax; the equilibrium price is $2 and the equilibrium quantity is 700. Consumer surplus is shown in green and producer surplus is shown in blue. As emphasized in Chapter 4, in a free market trade occurs whenever the buyer's willingness to pay exceeds the supplier's willingness to sell (i.e., whenever the demand curve lies above the supply curve). A free market maximizes the gains from trade, the sum of consumer and producer surplus.

In the right panel, we show the same market with a $1 tax (this is identical to Figure 6.3 only this time we have labeled some of the areas). The tax is $1 per basket and 500 baskets are traded, so tax revenues are shown by the purple rectangle and are equal to $500 = $1 × 500.

The tax decreases consumer and producer surplus, as you can see by comparing the green and blue areas in the left and right panels. *Some* of the consumer and producer surplus is transferred to the government in the form of tax

mru.org/tax-revenue

Understanding Tax Revenue and Deadweight Loss

FIGURE 6.5

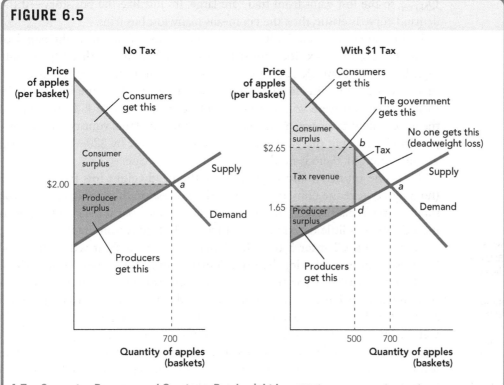

A Tax Generates Revenue and Creates a Deadweight Loss With no tax, producer plus consumer surplus is maximized in the left panel. With the tax, consumer surplus and producer surplus are smaller and tax revenues are larger. But tax revenues increase by less than producer and consumer surplus fall. As a result, the tax creates the deadweight loss shown by the gray area (triangle *abd*) in the right panel.

revenues, but notice that consumer and producer surplus together decrease by more than government revenue increases—the difference is the gray triangle (*abd*) labeled "deadweight loss." A **deadweight loss** is the reduction in total surplus caused by a market distortion or inefficiency. In this case the deadweight loss is caused by the tax.

To understand why a tax creates a deadweight loss, let's take a simple case. Imagine that you are willing to pay $50 for a bus ride to New York City when the price of a ticket is $40. Thus, you take the trip and earn $10 in consumer surplus ($50 − $40). Now suppose the government imposes a $20 tax, which increases the price of the ticket to $60. Do you take the trip? No, since the price of the ticket now exceeds your willingness to pay, you do not go to New York City. Thus, you lose $10 in consumer surplus. Does the government gain any tax revenue? No. Your loss of $10 is not compensated for by any increase in government revenue and thus is a deadweight loss. In short, the deadweight loss of a tax is the lost gains from the trips (trades) that do not occur because of the tax.

*A **deadweight loss** is the reduction in total surplus caused by a market distortion or inefficiency.*

Elasticity and Deadweight Loss

A key factor determining deadweight loss is the elasticities of supply and demand. Figure 6.6, for example, shows that the deadweight loss from taxation is larger the more elastic the demand curve. To understand why, remember that deadweight loss is the lost gains from trade. If the demand curve is relatively elastic, as in the left panel of Figure 6.6, then the tax deters a lot of trades, Q_{Tax} is much less than

$Q_{\text{No tax}}$, so the lost gains from trade are large. It's just like the bus story—if the demand curve is elastic, then the tax means many lost bus trips.

If the demand is relatively inelastic, however, as in the right panel of Figure 6.6 then the tax does not deter many trades. Notice that Q_{Tax} is only slightly smaller than $Q_{\text{No tax}}$. Since nearly the same number of trades occur, there are few lost gains from trade. Again, let's go back to the bus example. Imagine that you were willing to pay $100 to go to New York. In that case, if the government taxes you $20, you still take the trip. True, your consumer surplus falls by $20, but the government's revenues increase by $20—since the trip was not deterred, there is no deadweight loss in this case.

The same intuition also explains why the deadweight loss from taxation (holding tax revenue constant) is lower the less elastic the supply curve. If the supply curve is elastic, then the tax deters many trades, but if the supply curve is inelastic, there is little deterrence and thus few lost gains from trade.

Recall from Chapter 5 that the demand curve for fruit will tend to be less elastic (more inelastic) than the demand curve for apples because there are fewer substitutes for fruit than there are for apples. Thus, an equal-revenue tax on fruit would generate less deadweight loss than a tax on apples. By the same reasoning, a tax on food would generate less deadweight loss than one on fruit, and a tax on all consumption goods would generate even less deadweight loss than an equal-revenue tax on food. The lesson is that broad-based taxes will tend to create less deadweight loss than more narrowly based taxes. Of course, there can be exceptions. We might want to tax "bads," such as pollution, more than "goods." We take up the taxation of bads in Chapter 10.

Even though taxes create a deadweight loss, they also pay for beneficial goods and services. In Chapter 19, we discuss in more detail when the goods that taxation provides are likely to have benefits that exceed the deadweight loss caused by taxation.

CHECK YOURSELF

- Suppose that the government taxes insulin producers $50 per dose produced. Who is likely to ultimately pay this tax?
- Although the government taxes almost everything, would the government rather tax items that have relatively inelastic or relatively elastic demands and supplies? Why?
- A tax transfers some consumer and some producer surplus into government revenue. Show that when demand is more elastic than supply, producers lose more surplus than consumers lose. And who loses more when supply is more elastic than demand?

FIGURE 6.6

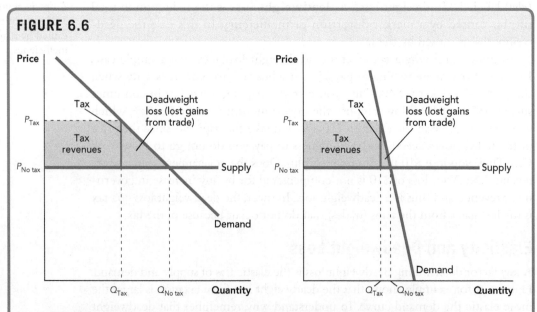

The Deadweight Loss from Taxation Is Larger the More Elastic the Demand Curve The tax rate and tax revenues are the same but the deadweight loss is larger in the left panel where the demand curve is more elastic.

Subsidies

A subsidy is a reverse tax: Instead of taking money away from consumers (or producers), the government gives money to consumers (or producers). The close connection between subsidies and taxes means that their effects are analogous. We emphasize the following facts about commodity subsidies:

1. Who gets the subsidy does *not* depend on who gets the check from the government.
2. Who benefits from a subsidy *does* depend on the relative elasticities of demand and supply.
3. Subsidies must be paid for by taxpayers and they create inefficient *increases* in trade (deadweight loss).

With a tax, the price paid by the buyers exceeds the price received by sellers. A subsidy reverses this relationship so the price received by sellers exceeds the price paid by buyers, the difference being the amount of the subsidy. In other words:

The subsidy = Price received by sellers − Price paid by buyers

We can analyze subsidies using the same wedge shortcut as before, except now we push the wedge from the right side of the diagram toward the left side. In Figure 6.7, we show that with a $1 subsidy, sellers of apples will receive

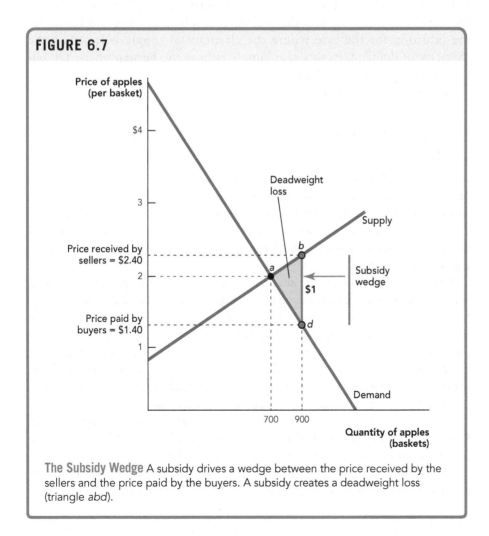

FIGURE 6.7

The Subsidy Wedge A subsidy drives a wedge between the price received by the sellers and the price paid by the buyers. A subsidy creates a deadweight loss (triangle *abd*).

$2.40 per basket, but buyers will pay only $1.40, the difference of $1 being the subsidy amount.

A subsidy means that the sellers are receiving more than buyers are paying, so who is making up the difference? Taxpayers. The cost to taxpayers is the amount of the subsidy times the number of units subsidized. In Figure 6.7: $1 × 900 or $900.

Just like a tax, a subsidy also creates a deadweight loss. A tax creates a deadweight loss because with the tax, some beneficial trades fail to occur. A subsidy creates a deadweight loss for the reverse reason: With the subsidy, some nonbeneficial trades do occur. In Figure 6.7, notice that for the baskets between 700 and 900, the supply curve lies above the demand curve (i.e., line segment *ab* lies above line segment *ad*). The height of the supply curve tells us the cost of producing these baskets. The height of the demand curve tells us the value of these baskets to buyers. Producing baskets for which the cost exceeds the value creates waste, a deadweight loss measured by the triangle *abd*. In other words, the resources used to produce those extra baskets have an opportunity cost, and they could produce more value in some other part of the economy.

As with taxes, the wedge analysis shows that it doesn't make a difference whether buyers are subsidized $1 for every unit bought or sellers are subsidized $1 for every unit sold.

Similarly, we showed that who bears the burden of a tax depends on the relative elasticities of supply and demand. Exactly the same forces determine who gets the benefit of a subsidy. The rule is simple: Whoever bears the burden of a tax receives the benefit of a subsidy. Figure 6.8 illustrates the intuition for the case where the elasticity of supply is less than the elasticity of demand. In this case, suppliers bear the burden of the tax but receive the benefit of a subsidy.

Let's analyze two examples of subsidies in action.

King Cotton and the Deadweight Loss of Water Subsidies

In California, Arizona, and other western states, there are very large subsidies to water used in agriculture. In California, for example, cotton, alfalfa, and rice farmers in the Central Valley area typically pay $20–$50 an acre-foot for water that costs $200–$500 an acre-foot (an acre-foot is the amount of water needed to cover 1 acre 1 foot deep). The difference is made up by a government subsidy.

Farmers use the subsidized water to transform desert into prime agricultural land. But turning a California desert into cropland makes about as much sense as building greenhouses in Alaska! America already has plenty of land on which cotton can be grown cheaply. Spending billions of dollars to dam rivers and transport water hundreds of miles to grow a crop that can be grown more cheaply in Georgia is a waste of resources, a deadweight loss. The water used to grow California cotton, for example, has much higher value producing silicon chips in San Jose or as drinking water in Los Angeles than it does as irrigation water.

Recall from Chapter 4 that one of the conditions for maximizing the gains from trade in a free market is that there are no wasteful trades. We can now see how in some situations a subsidy can create wasteful trades.

The waste created by water subsidies is compounded with a variety of agricultural subsidies. Some farmers in the Central Valley are "double-

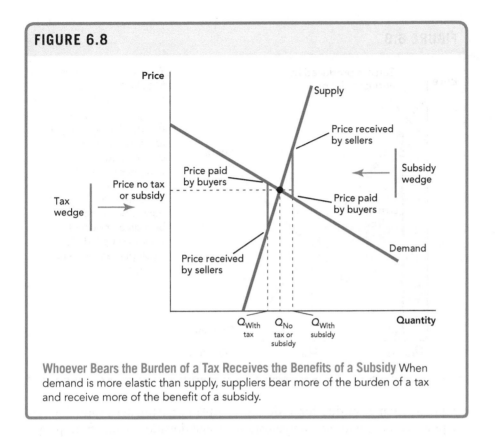

FIGURE 6.8

Whoever Bears the Burden of a Tax Receives the Benefits of a Subsidy When demand is more elastic than supply, suppliers bear more of the burden of a tax and receive more of the benefit of a subsidy.

dippers"—they use subsidized water to grow subsidized cotton. Some are even "triple-dippers"—they use subsidized water to grow subsidized corn to feed cows to produce subsidized milk!

Who benefits from the water subsidy? Is it California cotton suppliers or cotton buyers? Remember that suppliers receive more of the benefit of a subsidy than buyers when the elasticity of demand is greater than the elasticity of supply (as in Figure 6.8). Can you explain why the elasticity of demand for California cotton is much greater than the elasticity of supply? The elasticity of demand for *California* cotton is very high since cotton grown elsewhere is almost a perfect substitute. In other words, the price of cotton is determined on the world market for cotton, and California production is too small to have much of an influence on the world price. It's not surprising, therefore, that it's not cotton consumers who lobby for water subsidies but the farmers in California's Central Valley. Central Valley California farmers are politically powerful and they have been subsidized since 1902!

The Economics of Free Goods

Are free goods good? Not necessarily. There are two potential problems with free goods: too few goods or too many! Let's look at two ways of making a good "free": (1) making it illegal to sell the good for money, that is, legislating that the price cannot be above zero, or (2) subsidizing production so much that the price is driven to zero.

The National Organ Transplant Act (NOTA) makes it illegal to compensate someone for donating a human organ for transplant. You can probably guess one consequence, namely, too few organs for donation. Every year, some 5,000

CHECK YOURSELF

• Who is more likely to lobby for subsidies: coal miners or restaurant workers?

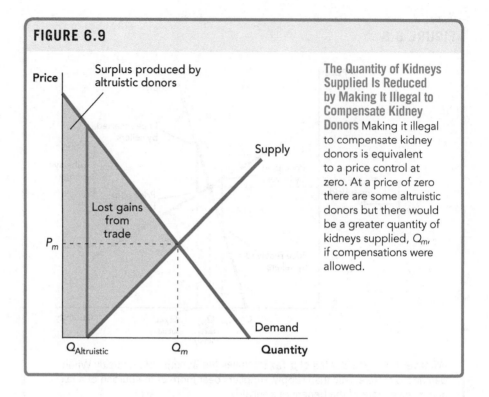

FIGURE 6.9

Price

Surplus produced by
altruistic donors

Supply

Lost gains
from
trade

P_m

Demand

$Q_{\text{Altruistic}}$ Q_m **Quantity**

The Quantity of Kidneys Supplied Is Reduced by Making It Illegal to Compensate Kidney Donors Making it illegal to compensate kidney donors is equivalent to a price control at zero. At a price of zero there are some altruistic donors but there would be a greater quantity of kidneys supplied, Q_m, if compensations were allowed.

people die while waiting for a kidney transplant. Fortunately, some kidneys are provided even with no compensation—some donations come from people who died young and who had signed their organ donor cards, while others come from living donors, a small group of wonderful people who donate one of their kidneys to someone in need (it's quite possible to live a long life with just one kidney). But the quantity of kidneys supplied would likely be much larger if it were legal to compensate donors.

Figure 6.9 shows the story in a diagram. When compensation for donors is illegal, a small number of altruistic donors continue to donate ($Q_{\text{Altruistic}}$) and create substantial value (the gray area), but the total quantity supplied is far below the quantity that would be supplied with compensation (Q_m), and there are substantial lost gains from trade (the purple area, which in this case can be thought of as lost lives).

In Iran, organ donors are compensated, and Iran is one of the few places in the world where there isn't a shortage of kidneys. Blood plasma is another interesting example; it is illegal to compensate donors in most of the world, but it is legal to compensate donors in the United States. As a result, the United States is sometimes called the OPEC of blood plasma because it exports plasma to many countries where compensating plasma donors is illegal.

Making it illegal to compensate organ donors is an example of a price control, where in this case the price is controlled at zero. We return to price controls in Chapter 8 and also discuss the ethics of compensating kidney donors at greater length in Chapter 21.

Another way of making a good free is to subsidize production enough so that the price is driven down to zero. Figure 6.10 illustrates this.

The story is the same as we discussed for water subsidies. When the government subsidizes water, farmers will use water that costs $500 to irrigate crops that are worth only $10. Indeed, if the price is driven to zero, farmers will continue to use water until the last drop has zero value.

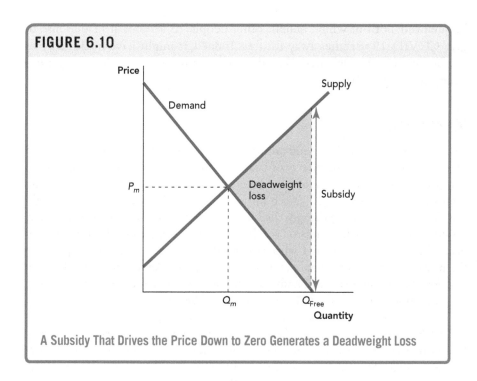

FIGURE 6.10

A Subsidy That Drives the Price Down to Zero Generates a Deadweight Loss

Comparing the lost gains from trade in Figure 6.9 and the deadweight loss in Figure 6.10, notice that producing too many goods can be worse than producing too few!

Many people argue that health care should be available for free. But how much health care? If people could consume as much health care as they wanted at a zero price (Q_{free} in Figure 6.10), the deadweight losses would be very high. As a result, "free" health care usually comes with quantity or quality restrictions. In Great Britain, for example, health care is essentially free, but how much and what health care is available is decided by the National Institute for Care Excellence (NICE). NICE compares the costs of treatments with an estimate of what are called quality-adjusted life years (QALYs). One year of excellent health is 1 QALY. One year of health for a patient on dialysis is estimated at 0.56 QALYs because dialysis takes many hours in a day and results in a lower quality of life. NICE is willing to pay about up to about $40,000 to buy a QALY. So if a treatment costs less than $40,000 and will give a patient one extra year of life in excellent health or two extra years at 0.5 health, that treatment will be approved. But if the treatment costs more than $40,000, it will not be approved. The details of the NICE system are less important than the principle that all economic systems must deal with scarcity.

We showed in Chapter 4 (see Figure 4.3) that the market price maximizes the gains from trade, that is producer plus consumer surplus. Our discussion of the deadweight loss of taxes and subsidies is really an application of this principle. But there is an important qualifier. What if people other than the producers and suppliers bear some of the costs or benefits of production? We will give just one example here.

COVID-19 vaccines were given away for free during the pandemic. Did that create a large deadweight loss? No. Vaccinated people are somewhat less likely to spread COVID-19 and significantly more likely not to become

CHECK YOURSELF

- To promote energy independence, the U.S. government provides a subsidy to corn growers if they convert the corn to ethanol, a fuel used in some cars. Because of this subsidy, what happens to the quantity supplied of ethanol, and what happens to the price received by corn growers and the price paid by ethanol buyers?

- The U.S. government subsidizes college education in the form of Pell grants and lower-cost government Stafford loans. How do these subsidies affect the price of college education? Which is relatively more elastic: supply or demand? Who benefits the most from these subsidies: suppliers (colleges) or demanders of education (students)?

hospitalized, both of which benefit other people. As a result, it made sense to give COVID-19 vaccines away for free. Indeed, it might have made sense to pay people to get vaccinated! We take up the issue of externalities at greater length in Chapter 10.

Takeaway

The tools of supply and demand are very powerful. In this chapter we have used these tools to explain the effects of taxes and subsidies. Using the wedge shortcut, you should be able to show that taxes decrease the quantity traded, subsidies increase the quantity traded, and both taxes and subsidies create a deadweight loss. We showed that, surprisingly, the burden of a tax and the benefit of a subsidy do not depend on who sends or receives the government check. Instead, who bears the burden of a tax and who receives the benefit of a subsidy depend on the relative elasticities of supply and demand. In particular, if you remember that *elasticity = escape*, then you will know that the side of the market (buyers or sellers) with the more elastic curve will escape more of the tax.

We also showed that elasticities of demand and supply determine the deadweight loss of a tax. The more elastic either the demand or the supply curve is, the more a tax deters trade, and the more trades that are deterred, the greater the deadweight loss (for a given amount of tax revenue). As a result, it is better to tax goods with inelastic demands. Equal-revenue taxes on broad-based goods (for example, food) tend to have lower deadweight loss than taxes on narrowly based goods (for example, apples) because broad-based goods have more inelastic demands.

CHAPTER REVIEW

Go online to practice with more examples of these types of problems, including live links to videos, data sources, and feedback.

KEY CONCEPTS

deadweight loss, p. 105

FACTS AND TOOLS

1. As we saw in Chapter 4, economists' idea of equilibrium borrows a lot from physics. Let's push the physics metaphors a bit further. Here, we focus just on the supply side. For each set of words in brackets, circle the correct choice:

    a. When the government subsidizes an activity, resources such as labor, machines, and bank lending will tend to gravitate [toward/away from] the activity that is subsidized and will tend to gravitate [toward/away from] activity that is not subsidized.

    b. When the government taxes an activity, resources such as labor, machines, and bank lending will tend to gravitate [toward/away from] the activity that is taxed and will tend to gravitate [toward/away from] activity that is not taxed.

2. Junk food has often been criticized for being unhealthy and too cheap, enticing the poor to adopt unhealthy lifestyles. In response, some cities, such as Philadelphia, Seattle, and San Francisco, have implemented taxes on sugar-sweetened beverages to try to discourage

consumers from purchasing them, while the countries of Mexico and Hungary have imposed broader taxes on a wider variety of junk foods.

a. What needs to be true for the tax to actually deter people from eating junk food: Should junk food demand be elastic or should it be inelastic?

b. If the governments of Hungary and Mexico want to strongly discourage people from eating junk food, when will they need to set a higher tax rate: when junk food demand is elastic or when it is inelastic? (The junk food tax rates in Hungary and Mexico are 4% and 8%, respectively.)

c. But hold on a moment: The supply side matters as well. If junk food supply is highly elastic—perhaps because it's not that hard to start selling salads with low-fat dressing instead of cheese-laden burgers—does that mean that a junk food tax will have a bigger effect than if supply were inelastic? Or is it the other way around?

d. Let's combine these stories now. If a government is hoping that a small tax can actually discourage a lot of junk food purchases, it should hope for:

    I. Elastic supply and inelastic demand

    II. Elastic supply and elastic demand

    III. Inelastic supply and elastic demand

    IV. Inelastic supply and inelastic demand

3. As we saw in the chapter, understanding elasticity is crucial for understanding the impacts of business and government decisions. Decades ago, Washington, D.C., a fairly small city, wanted to raise more revenue by increasing the gas tax. Washington, D.C., shares borders with Maryland and Virginia, and it's very easy to cross the borders between D.C. and one or both states without even really noticing: The suburbs just blend together.

a. How elastic is the demand for gasoline *sold at stations within D.C.*? In other words, if the price of gas in D.C. rises, but the price in Maryland and Virginia stays the same, will gasoline sales at D.C. stations fall a little, or will they fall a lot?

b. Take your answer to part a into account when answering this question. So, when Washington, D.C., increased its gasoline tax, how much revenue did it raise: Did it raise

a little bit of revenue, or did it raise a lot of revenue?

c. How would your answer to part b change if D.C., Maryland, and Virginia all agreed to raise their gas tax simultaneously? These states have heavily populated borders with each other, but they don't have any heavily populated borders with other states.

4. In Figure 6.5, what is the total revenue raised by the tax, in dollars? What is the deadweight loss from the tax, in dollars? (*Note:* You've seen the formula for the latter before. We'll let you look around a little for this one.)

5. **a.** Once again: Why does the text say that *elasticity = escape*? (This is worth remembering: Elasticity is one of the toughest ideas for most economics students.)

b. Which two groups of workers did we say have a relatively high elasticity of labor supply? Keep this in mind as politicians debate raising or lowering taxes on different types of workers: These two groups are the ones most likely to make big changes in their behavior.

6. Suppose that Maria is willing to pay $40 for a haircut, and her stylist Juan is willing to accept as little as $25 for a haircut.

a. What possible prices for the haircut would be beneficial to both Maria and Juan? How much total surplus (i.e., the sum of consumer and producer surplus) would be generated by this haircut?

b. If the state where Maria and Juan live instituted a tax on services that included a $5 per haircut tax on stylists and barbers, what happens to the range of haircut prices that benefit both Maria and Juan? Will the haircut still happen? Will this tax alter the total economic benefit of this haircut?

c. What if instead the tax was $20?

THINKING AND PROBLEM SOLVING

7. Some people with diabetes absolutely need to take insulin on a regular basis to survive, while pharmaceutical companies that make insulin have a lot of other options for generating revenue.

a. If the U.S. government imposes a tax on insulin producers of $10 per cubic centimeter of insulin, payable every month to the U.S. Treasury, who will bear most of the burden of the tax: insulin producers or people with diabetes? Or do you need more information to answer this question?

b. Suppose instead that because of government corruption, the insulin manufacturers convince the U.S. government to pay the insulin makers $10 per cubic centimeter of insulin, payable every month *from* the U.S. Treasury. Who will get more of the benefit of this subsidy: insulin producers or people with diabetes? Or do you need more information to answer this question?

8. Let's see if we can formulate any real laws about the economics of taxation. Which of the following *must* be true, as long as supply and demand curves have their normal shape (i.e., they aren't perfectly vertical or horizontal, and demand curves have a negative slope while supply curves have a positive slope). More than one may be true.

If there is a tax:

a. The equilibrium quantity must fall, and the price that buyers pay must rise.

b. The equilibrium quantity must rise, and the price that sellers pay must rise.

c. The equilibrium quantity must fall, and the price that sellers receive must fall.

d. The equilibrium quantity must rise, and the price that buyers receive must fall.

(*Note:* The correct answer[s] to this question was [were] actually controversial until Nobel laureate Paul Samuelson created a simple mathematical proof in his legendary graduate textbook, *Foundations of Economic Analysis*.)

9. Using the following diagram, use the wedge shortcut to answer these questions:

a. If a tax of $2 were imposed, what price would buyers pay and what price would suppliers receive? How much revenue would be raised by the tax? How much deadweight loss would be created by the tax?

b. If a subsidy of $5 were imposed, what price would buyers pay and what price would suppliers receive? How much would the subsidy cost the government? How much deadweight loss would be created by the subsidy?

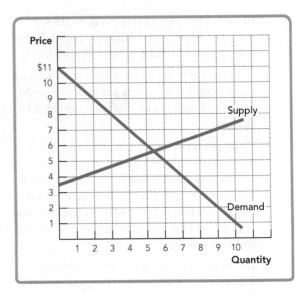

10. When a government is trying to raise tax revenue, it sometimes attempts to target higher-income people because they are in a better position to bear the burden of a tax. However, it can be very difficult to earn tax revenue from wealthy people, as we will discuss in this problem.

a. Consider the progressive nature of the U.S. federal income tax system: It's designed so that higher incomes are taxed at higher tax rates. Thinking about the elasticity of labor supply, why might it be more difficult to collect tax revenue from a wealthy individual than from a poor person, all else equal?

b. Another way governments have tried to collect taxes from the wealthy is through the use of luxury taxes, which are exactly what they sound like: taxes on goods that are considered luxuries, like jewelry or expensive cars and real estate. What is true about the demand for luxuries? Consider jewelry. Is a luxury tax more likely to hurt the buyers of jewelry or the sellers of jewelry?

c. The chapter began by discussing another tax that targets wealthy individuals: the estate tax. Comment on the effectiveness of this tax (in terms of government revenue), considering the demand of wealthy individuals for leaving an inheritance.

11. As we learned in Chapter 4, the competitive market equilibrium maximizes gains from trade. Taxes and subsidies, by altering the market outcome, reduce the gains from trade. Does this happen because of the impact of taxes and subsidies on *prices* or the impact of taxes and subsidies on *quantities*?

12. Consider the following diagram of a tax. The triangular area representing deadweight loss is highlighted, and its dimensions are labeled "Base" and "Height" (recall that the formula for the area of a triangle is $\frac{1}{2} \times$ Base $\times$ Height).

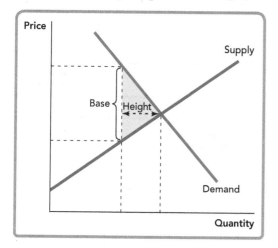

   a. In order to calculate the deadweight loss of a tax, you don't need the entire demand and supply diagram; you just need to know two numbers, the *base* and *height* of the deadweight loss triangle. What is the real-life meaning of the base? What about the height?

   b. Can you turn your answers to part a into general rules about the deadweight loss associated with taxes? Try phrasing it like this but replacing the part in brackets: "The larger the [base or height], the more deadweight loss is generated by a given tax."

   c. Holding the base constant, the height and thus the deadweight loss would get larger if the demand curve or the supply curve were more _____.

   d. Without having a diagram as a reference, can you answer the preceding questions for a subsidy?

13. Suppose your state government has decided to tax doughnuts. Currently, in your state, 300,000 doughnuts are sold every day. Three possible taxes are being considered by lawmakers: a 20-cent-per-doughnut tax, which would decrease doughnut sales by 50,000 per day; a 25-cent-per-doughnut tax, which would decrease doughnut sales by 100,000 per day; and a 50-cent-per-doughnut tax, which would decrease doughnut sales by 150,000 doughnuts per day.

   a. Calculate the amount of tax revenue generated by each tax and the deadweight loss caused by each tax.

   b. If the goal of your state government is to raise tax revenue in the most efficient manner (with the least deadweight loss per dollar of revenue), which tax is preferable?

   c. If the goal of your state government is simply to raise the most tax revenue, which tax is preferable?

   d. What other goal might your state government have when creating this kind of tax besides raising tax revenue? (*Hint:* See question 2.)

14. How is it that a tax creates a deadweight loss by *decreasing* quantity, but a subsidy creates a deadweight loss by *increasing* quantity?

15. Refer to the figure.

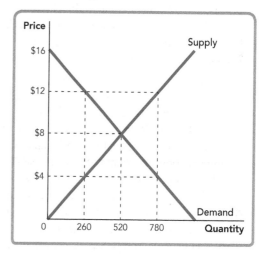

   a. Following the imposition of an $8 subsidy, calculate the change in consumer surplus and the change in producer surplus resulting from the subsidy. How much does the subsidy cost the government? Finally, add up the benefit to consumers and producers and subtract out the cost to the government.

   b. Calculate the deadweight loss directly, as in question 12. How does this answer compare to your answers from part a?

Discovering DATA

16. Go to the FRED Economic Database (https://fred.stlouisfed.org/) and find tobacco taxes in Texas. In what year (1991–2021) would you guess Texas raised the sales tax on tobacco?

CHALLENGES

17. Let's apply the economics of taxation to romantic relationships.

    a. What does it mean to have an inelastic demand for your boyfriend or girlfriend? How about an elastic demand?

    b. Sometimes relationships have taxes. Suppose that you and your boyfriend or girlfriend live one hour apart. Using the tools developed in the chapter, how can you predict which one of you will do most of the driving? That is, which one of you will bear the majority of the relationship tax?

18. a. The sale of "loosies," black market single cigarettes, is common in some cities, and this market is at least partially fed by interstate smuggling operations. Which way do you suspect the smugglers move the cigarettes based on economic theory? From the high-tax North to the low-cost South, or vice versa?

    b. In our discussion of taxation, we've acted as if it were effortless to pass and enforce tax laws. But of course, law enforcement officials, including the Internal Revenue Service, put a lot of effort into enforcing tax laws. Let's think for a moment about what kind of taxes are easiest to collect, just based on the basic ideas we've covered. Who will make the most effort to escape a tax: the party who is elastic or the party who is inelastic? (*Hint:* It doesn't matter whether we're talking about suppliers or demanders.)

    (*Note:* Public administration researchers know the most about this topic. Carolyn Webber and Aaron Wildavsky's surprisingly enjoyable classic, *A History of Taxation and Expenditure in the Western World*, sets out just how difficult it's been for most Western governments to collect taxes.)

19. Let's get some practice with the "wedge trick" and use it to learn about the relationship between subsidies and lobbying. The U.S. government has many subsidies for alternative energy development: Some are just called subsidies; some are called tax breaks instead. Either way, they work just like the subsidies we studied in this chapter. We'll look at the market for wind turbines.

    a. In the two figures, one is a case where the sellers of wind turbines have an elastic supply and the buyers of wind turbines (local

power companies) have inelastic demand. In the other case, the reverse is true. Which is which?

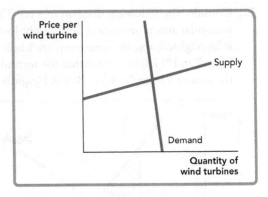

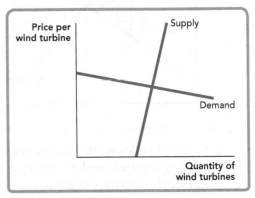

    b. In which case will a subsidy cut the price paid by the buyers the most: when demand is elastic or when it is inelastic? (It'll be easiest if you use the wedge trick.) Is this the first or second graph?

    c. In which case will a subsidy increase the price received by the sellers more: when supply is elastic or when it is inelastic? Again, which graph is this?

    d. Now look at how producer surplus and consumer surplus change in these two cases. To see this, remember that producer surplus is the area *above* the supply curve and below the price, and consumer surplus is the area *below* the demand curve and above the price. So in the first graph, who gets the lion's share of any subsidy-driven extra surplus: suppliers or demanders? Is that the inelastic group or the elastic group? In other words, whose surplus triangle gets bigger faster as the quantity increases? (You might try shading in these triangles just to be sure.)

    e. Now it's time for the second graph. Again, who gets the lion's share of any subsidy-driven extra surplus: suppliers or demanders? Is that the inelastic group or the elastic group?

f. There's going to be a pattern here in parts d and e: The more (elastic or inelastic?) side of the market gets more of the extra surplus from the subsidy.

g. When Congress gives subsidies for the alternative energy market, it is hoping that a small subsidy can get a big increase in output: In other words, they are hoping that the equilibrium quantity will be *elastic*. At the same time, the groups most likely to lobby Congress for a big alternative energy subsidy are going to be the groups that get the most extra surplus from any subsidy. After all, if the subsidy doesn't give them much surplus, they're not likely to ask Congress for it.

So here's the big question: Will the groups that are most likely to *lobby* for a subsidy be the same groups that are most likely to *respond to* the subsidy? (*Note:* This is a general lesson about the incentives for lobbying: It's not just a story about the alternative energy industry.)

20. As you learned in the chapter, the elasticities of demand and supply are crucial in determining how the burden of a tax (or the benefit of a subsidy) is divided between buyers and sellers. Under what conditions for supply or demand would a seller actually be able to avoid bearing any of the burden of a tax? Under what conditions would a subsidy benefit only the sellers of a good?

21. In the chapter, most of the taxes we discussed were equal to a certain dollar amount per unit. In this case, a tax on sellers results in a parallel upward shift of the supply curve; a tax on buyers results in a parallel downward shift of the demand curve. In reality, however, many taxes are expressed as a percentage. Graphically, how would you show a 100% tax on the sellers of a good? How would you show a 100% tax on the buyers of a good? One of the results of this chapter is that it doesn't matter on whom the tax is levied; the outcome is the same. Show graphically that this also applies to *percentage* taxes.

WORK IT OUT

For interactive, step-by-step help in solving this problem, go online.

Consider the following supply and demand diagram. In this market, the government subsidizes the production of this good, and the subsidy wedge is indicated.

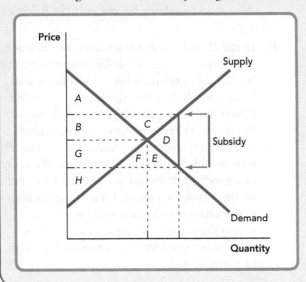

a. Without the subsidy, which area(s) represent(s) the total gains from trade?

b. After the subsidy, which area(s) represent(s) consumer surplus? Which area(s) represent(s) producer surplus? Which area(s) represent(s) total government spending on this subsidy?

c. Which area(s) in part b showed up in the answer to more than one of the questions? Can you explain this?

7

The Price System: Signals, Speculation, and Prediction

A price is a signal wrapped up in an incentive. That may sound a little abstract, but it's one of the most fundamental insights in economics. Prices convey important information and they create an incentive to respond to that information in socially useful ways. In this chapter, you'll see how one market influences another and then how an entire series of markets in a global economy fit together. Prices are the key force integrating markets and motivating entrepreneurs. We will have plenty of examples in this chapter, but keep your eye on the primary theme: The price system creates rich connections between markets and enables societies to mobilize vast amounts of knowledge toward common ends, yet without a central planner.

Markets Link the World

Let's take a closer look at the story of just one product. It's Valentine's Day. You have just given your partner a beautiful, single-stemmed rose, one of 250 million that will be sold today.[1] Where did the rose come from and how did it get into your hands?

Chances are good that your rose was grown in Kenya in the Lake Naivasha area to the northwest of Nairobi.[2] Over 150,000 tons of roses are grown in Kenya every year, almost all for export. The Kenyan women who do most of the fieldwork know very little about the strange Western celebration of love called Saint Valentine's Day, but they don't have to. What they do know is that they get paid more when the roses are debudded so that they bloom just in time for delivery on February 14.

No one wants to give (or receive) a wilted rose, so everyone involved in the rose business has an incentive to move quickly. In a matter of hours after picking, the roses travel in cooled trucks from the field to the airport in Nairobi, where they are loaded onto refrigerated aircraft. Within a day, the flowers are in Aalsmeer, Holland.

Aalsmeer is the home of the world's largest flower market. On a typical working day, 20 million flowers are flown into this tiny Dutch town.

MRU

mru.org/rose

How Does the Invisible Hand Deliver Roses?

The flowers are paraded in lots before large clocks, clocks that measure not time but prices. Beginning with a high price, the clocks quickly tick downward until a bidder stamps a button indicating that they are willing to buy at that price. By the end of the day, 20 million flowers have been sold, and they are once again packed onto cooled airplanes to be flown to the world's buyers in London, Paris, New York, and Topeka. From Kenya to your partner's hand in 72 hours.[3]

The worldwide market links romantic American teenagers with Kenyan flower growers, Dutch clocks, British airplanes, Colombian coffee (to keep the pilots awake), Korean cell phones, and much, much more. To bring just one product to your table requires the cooperative effort of millions.

Moreover, this immense cooperation is voluntary and undirected. Each of millions of people acting in their self-interest play a role, but no one knows the full story of how a Kenyan rose becomes a gift of love in Topeka because the full story is too complex. Nevertheless, every Valentine's Day you can count on the fact that your local florist will have roses for sale.

The market is the original Web, and it's more dense, interconnected, and alive with intelligence than its computer analog.

Markets Link to One Another

In Chapters 3 and 4, we showed how the supply and demand for oil determine the price of oil. Now we return to oil but this time as an example of how shifts in supply and demand in one market ripple across the worldwide market, changing distant people and products in ways that no one can foresee.

The Kenyan flower industry was one unforeseen consequence of changes in the market for oil. Prior to the 1970s, roses were grown in American greenhouses. Higher prices for oil raised heating costs so much that it became cheaper to grow roses in warm countries and ship them to cold countries.[*] If roses had been heavier, the higher costs of transportation might have outweighed the lower costs of heating, but even with higher fuel costs, transportation costs in the modern world have been falling.

It's not obvious that the right way to respond to an increased scarcity of oil is to move flower production from California to Kenya. No one planned such a response in advance. Instead, creative entrepreneurs responded to the increase in the price of oil in ways that no one predicted or planned. Entrepreneurs are constantly on the lookout for ways to lower costs, and their cost-cutting measures link markets that at first seem like they are a world away.

The world is linked in fascinating ways. In Peru, workers roam the hillsides collecting millions of female cochineal bugs from their cactus pad nests. After dunking in hot water, drying, and grinding, the bugs make an excellent red dye. The dye is used to color many products including yogurt (look for carmine in the ingredients), red Smarties, and even lipstick!

Holger Scheibe/Getty Images

From Oil to Candy Bars and Brick Driveways

How does the price of oil affect the price of candy bars? One way is obvious: Higher energy costs increase the cost of producing most products, including

---

[*] The shift of flower production from America to Kenya and other equatorial countries like Colombia and Ecuador in the 1980s is part of a trend. Two decades earlier, declines in transportation costs and increases in the relative costs of heating, land, and labor moved flower production from New York and Pennsylvania to Florida and California. On the evolution of the cut flower industry, see Mendez, Jose A. 1991. *The Development of the Colombian Cut Flower Industry.* The World Bank. WPS 660.

candy bars. But the market also links oil and candy bars in more subtle ways. For instance, ethanol is the active ingredient in alcoholic beverages, but it's also a good fuel that can be made from a variety of crops like corn or sugarcane. Brazil is the second-largest producer and consumer of fuel ethanol in the world, and it has greatly reduced its gasoline consumption through the adoption of flexible fuel vehicles that can run on ethanol, gasoline, or any combination of the two; the country now uses as much ethanol as gasoline in its light vehicle fleet.[4] Brazil is also the largest producer of sugar in the world.

Surprised? Corn and oil are substitutes.

Can you see the connection between the price of oil and the price of candy bars now? As the price of oil has increased, the Brazilians have shifted sugar cane from sugar production to ethanol production, thereby holding down fuel costs but increasing the price of sugar.[5]

What about brick driveways? A 42-gallon barrel of crude oil is refined into approximately 19.5 gallons of gasoline, 9.2 gallons of fuel oil, 4 gallons of jet fuel, 1.3 gallons of asphalt, and a number of other products.[6] To some extent, these divisions are fixed. (Asphalt is what you get after you separate out the other products.) But oil refiners do have some flexibility, and when the price of gasoline is relatively high, it pays for them to pull every last drop of gasoline out of a barrel of crude, leaving less crude to make the remaining products. A higher price of gasoline, therefore, means a reduced supply of asphalt. A reduced supply of asphalt pushes up the price of asphalt. So, when the price of oil rises, the price of using asphalt to pave an average-sized driveway rises.[7] Seeing the higher price, homeowners turn to substitutes such as concrete, cobblestones, and brick.

Solving the Great Economic Problem

Markets around the world are linked to one another. A change in supply or demand in one market can influence markets for entirely different products thousands of miles away. But what does all this linking accomplish? The **great economic problem** is to arrange our scarce resources to satisfy as many of our wants as possible. Let's imagine that war in the Middle East reduces the supply of oil. We must economize on oil. But how? It would be foolish to reduce oil equally in all uses—oil is more valuable in some uses than in others. We want to shift oil out of low-valued uses, where we can do without or where good substitutes for oil exist, so that we can keep supplying oil for high-valued uses, where oil has few good substitutes.

One way to make this shift would be for a central planner to issue orders. The central planner would order so much oil to be used in the steel industry, so much for heating, and so much for Sunday driving. But how would the central planner know the value of oil in each of its millions of uses? No one knows for certain all the uses of oil, let alone which uses of oil are high-valued uses and which are low-valued uses. Is the oil used to produce steel more valuable than the oil used to produce vegetables? Even if steel is worth more than vegetables, the answer isn't obvious because electricity might be a good substitute for oil in producing steel but not for producing vegetables. To estimate the value of oil in different uses, therefore, the central planner would have to gather information about all the uses of oil and all of the substitutes for oil in each use (and all of the substitutes for the substitutes!). Using this

CHECK YOURSELF

- The U.S. government offers a subsidy for converting corn to ethanol. If farmers receive a higher price for turning corn into ethanol, what will happen to the price of corn used in cornbread? How will cafeterias and restaurants respond?
- Sawdust is used for bedding milk cows. What did the end of the housing boom in 2007 do to the price of milk? Search for "sawdust" at https://www.MarginalRevolution.com if you need a hint.

The **great economic problem** is to arrange our scarce resources to satisfy as many of our wants as possible.

mru.org/price-signals

A Price Is a Signal Wrapped Up in an Incentive

information, the central planner would then have to somehow compute the optimal allocation of oil and then send out thousands of orders directing oil to its many uses in the economy.

The task of central planning is impossibly complex and we haven't yet discussed incentives. Why would anyone have an incentive to send truthful information to the central planner? Each user of oil would surely announce that their use is the high-valued use for which no substitute is possible. And what incentive would the central planner have to actually direct oil to its high-value uses?

The U.S. government briefly tried to centrally plan the allocation of oil during the 1973–1974 oil crisis. President Nixon even went so far as to forbid gas stations from opening on Sundays in an attempt to reduce Sunday driving! We describe the consequences of this approach to the oil crisis at greater length in the next chapter. The Soviet Union and China went much further than the United States and tried to centrally plan entire economies. Central planning on a large scale, however, failed and has now been abandoned throughout virtually all the world (Cuba and North Korea, both very poor countries, are the exceptions).

The central planning approach failed because of problems of *information* and *incentives*. We need a better approach.

Users of oil have a lot of information about the value of oil in their own uses, much more information than could ever be communicated to a central planner. We need to take advantage of this information without attempting to communicate it to a central bureaucracy. Ideally, each user of oil would compare the value of oil in their use with the value of oil in alternative uses, and each user of oil would have an incentive to give up the oil if it has a lower value in their use than in alternative uses. This is exactly what the price system accomplishes.

Let's go back to the person thinking about whether to pave the driveway with asphalt or brick. This person knows the value of a paved driveway but doesn't know what uses the asphalt has elsewhere in the economy. They do know the price of asphalt, and *in a free market, the price of asphalt is equal to the value of the asphalt in its next highest-value use.* Take a look at Figure 7.1, which is just the now-familiar supply and demand diagram. Remember that the value of a good in its various uses is given by the height of the demand curve. Notice that the equilibrium price splits the uses of the good into two—above the equilibrium price are the high-value, satisfied demands; below the price are the low-value, unsatisfied demands. Now what is the value of the highest-value demand that is not satisfied? It's just equal to the market price (or if you like, "just below" the market price). In other words, if one more barrel of oil became available, the highest-value use of that barrel would be to satisfy the first presently unsatisfied demand. The market price tells us the value of the good in its next highest-valued use.

When a consumer compares the price of asphalt to the value of asphalt for paving their driveway, they are comparing *the value of asphalt on their driveway to its opportunity cost.* And remember, because markets are linked, the price of asphalt is linked to the price of oil, and the price of oil is linked to the demand for automobiles in China and the supply of ethanol and the price of sugar. So when the consumer compares the value of asphalt in

The true cost of a motorcycle is not its money price but rather a lawnmower. The true cost is the *opportunity cost*—what the resources that went into the motorcycle could have produced had the motorcycle not been built.

It is part of the marvel of a free market that, under the right conditions, the money price of the motorcycle exactly represents the value of the resources that went into producing the motorcycle, namely the value those resources would have had in their next highest-valued use.

FIGURE 7.1

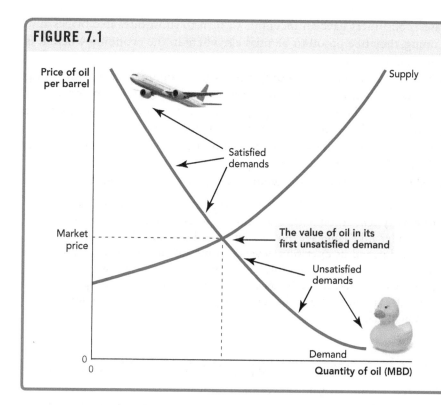

The Market Price and Opportunity Cost The market price splits the uses of oil into two. Above the price are the uses of oil whose value is greater than the price; in a free market, these demands will be satisfied. Below the price are the uses of oil whose value is less than the price; in a free market, these are the unsatisfied demands. Notice that the value of oil in the first unsatisfied demand is just slightly below the market price.

(Top: ssuaphotos/Shutterstock)
(Bottom: Lew Robertson/Corbis)

paving their driveway to the price of asphalt, they may be comparing the value of asphalt in paving their driveway to the value of 500 gallons of gasoline used by a motorist in Brazil. Or, in other words, when you decide whether to drive to school or take the bus, you are deciding whether your use of oil is more valuable than the billions of other uses of oil in the world that are presently unsatisfied!

The market solves the information problem by collapsing all the relevant information in the world about the uses of oil into a single number, the price. As Nobel laureate Friedrich Hayek wrote:*

> The most significant fact about this system is the economy of knowledge with which it operates . . . by a kind of symbol [the price], only the most essential information is passed on and passed on only to those concerned. . . . The marvel is that in a case like that of a scarcity of one raw material, without an order being issued, without more than perhaps a handful of people knowing the cause, tens of thousands of people whose identity could not be ascertained by months of investigation, are made to use the material or its products more sparingly; i.e., they move in the right direction.

In addition to solving the information problem, the price system also solves the incentive problem. It's in a consumer's interest to pay attention to prices! When the price of an oil product like asphalt

Friedrich A. Hayek (1899–1992) explained the marvel of the price system.

Hulton Archive/Getty Images

---

* Hayek's classic paper, "The Use of Knowledge in Society," is deep but easy to read. You can find it online by searching for "Hayek use of knowledge in society." The original citation is Hayek, Friedrich A., 1945. The use of knowledge in society. *American Economic Review* 35(4): 519–530. Copyright American Economic Association; reproduced with permission of the *American Economic Review.*

CHECK YOURSELF

- Peanuts are used primarily for food dishes, but they are also used in bird feed, paint, varnish, furniture polish, insecticides, and soap. Rank these uses from higher to lower value taking into account in which use the peanuts are critical and in which uses there are good substitutes. Don't obsess over this: We know you are not a peanut expert, but see if you can come up with a sense of higher and lower values.

- Imagine that there is a large peanut crop failure in China, which produces more than one-third of the world's supply. Which of the uses that you ranked in the previous question will be cut back?

increases, consumers have an incentive to turn to substitutes like bricks and, in so doing, they free up oil to be used elsewhere in the economy where it is of higher value.

The worldwide market accomplishes this immense task of allocating resources without any central planning or control. No one knows or understands all the links between oil, sugar, and brick driveways, but the links are there and the market works even without anyone's understanding or knowledge. Amazed by what he saw, Adam Smith said the market works as if "an invisible hand" guided the process.

Nobel laureate Vernon Smith, whom we met in Chapter 4, put it this way:

> At the heart of economics is a scientific mystery: How is it that the pricing system accomplishes the world's work without anyone being in charge? Like language, no one invented it. None of us could have invented it, and its operation depends in no way on anyone's comprehension or understanding of it. . . . The pricing system—How is order produced from freedom of choice?—is a scientific mystery as deep, fundamental and inspiring as that of the expanding universe or the forces that bind matter.[8]*

A Price Is a Signal Wrapped Up in an Incentive

How is order produced from freedom of choice? That is a scientific mystery, and prices are the biggest clue to the solution. Prices do much more than tell people how much they must shell out for a burger and fries. Prices are incentives, prices are signals, prices are predictions. To understand the market, you need to better understand prices.

When the price of oil rises, all users of oil are encouraged to economize—perhaps by simply using less but also by thinking about substitutes: everything from electric cars to moving flower cultivation overseas. An increase in the price of oil is also a signal to suppliers to invest more in exploration, to look for alternatives like ethanol, and to increase recycling. Do you know the most recycled product in America? It's asphalt.[9]

Politicians and consumers sometime fail to understand the signaling role of prices. After a hurricane, the prices of ice, generators, and chainsaws often skyrocket. Consumers complain of price gouging, and politicians call for price controls. That's understandable, because it can seem doubly harsh to be hit by a hurricane *and* high prices. But the price system is just doing its job. A skyrocketing price is like a flare being shot into the night sky that shouts—bring ice here! A price control eliminates the signal to bring ice into the devastated area as quickly as possible.

The high price of ice in a hurricane-devastated area signals a profit opportunity for ice suppliers. Buy ice where the price is low and deliver it to where the price is high. As the supply of ice in the hurricane-devastated area increases, the price will fall. More generally, price

A skyrocketing price is a signal to bring resources here!

South_agency/E+/Getty Images

* Credit for quotation: Smith, Vernon. 1982. Microeconomic systems as an experimental science. *American Economic Review* 72: 923–955. Copyright American Economic Association; reproduced with permission of the *American Economic Review*.

signals and the accompanying profits and losses tell entrepreneurs what areas of the economy consumers want expanded and what areas they want contracted. If consumers want more computers, prices and profits in the computer industry will increase and the industry will expand.

Losses may be an even more important signal than profits. Entrepreneurs who fail to compete with lower costs and better products take losses and their businesses contract or even go bankrupt. Bankruptcy is bad for a business but can be good for capitalism. Ever heard of Smith Corona, Polaroid, Pan Am, or Hechingers? At one point, each of these companies led its industry, but today all are either bankrupt or much smaller than at their peak. In a free market, no firm is so powerful that it does not daily face the market test. As a result, *in a successful economy there will be many unsuccessful firms.*

Arbitrage and Speculation

Every morning, fishermen in the Indian state of Kerala bring their catch to one of many beach markets strung along the coast. In the past, the fishermen were sometimes frustrated when they would arrive at a market to find that all the buyers had already left, having bought enough from other fishermen. By the time they arrived at one market it was usually too late to set sail for another market further up or down the coast, so they simply dumped their catch into the sea. At the same time, at other markets, which didn't receive any or enough fish to sell, there were frustrated buyers who went home without any fish.

The problem the fishermen faced was one of limited information. While they were out at sea, the fishermen had no way of learning about price differences between the many coastal markets. In the late 1990s, however, a new technology arrived in Kerala, cell phones. Cell phone stations along the coasts let fishermen check prices and the state of demand while they were still far from shore. If prices were low in one market, the fishermen would head to a different market where prices were higher. But notice that as fishermen sell more in markets with high prices the price falls, and as fishermen sell less in markets with low prices the price rises. Thus, in seeking the highest price, the fishermen move prices until the prices in all markets are roughly the same.

We can see the dramatic effect of cell phones on price dispersion in the two graphs in Figure 7.2. The top graph shows that most fishermen bought cell phones within weeks of their becoming available. The bottom graph shows that as cell phones became available prices in different markets became much less dispersed. Robert Jensen, the economist who studied these issues, also found that waste declined from 5% to 8% of the daily catch before cell phones to virtually nothing after the introduction of cell phones. In addition, fishermen profits and consumer surplus both increased.

The introduction of cell phones allowed the fishermen to perform a kind of arbitrage, taking advantage of price differences for the same good in different markets by buying (or in the case of the fishermen not selling) where the price is low and selling where the price is high. Let's show the general process in Figure 7.3.

What's the market price of fish today?

Boris Breuer/The Image Bank/Getty Images

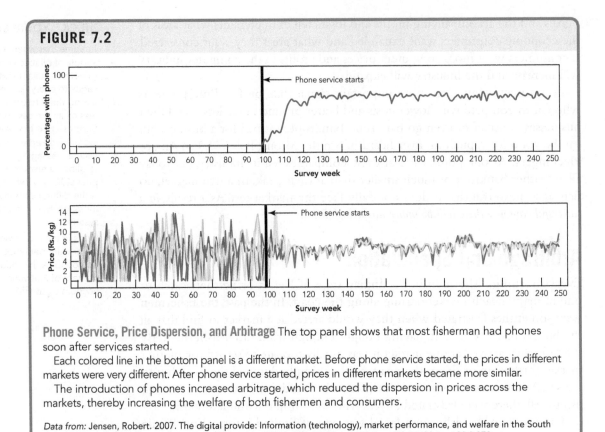

FIGURE 7.2

Phone Service, Price Dispersion, and Arbitrage The top panel shows that most fisherman had phones soon after services started.

Each colored line in the bottom panel is a different market. Before phone service started, the prices in different markets were very different. After phone service started, prices in different markets became more similar.

The introduction of phones increased arbitrage, which reduced the dispersion in prices across the markets, thereby increasing the welfare of both fishermen and consumers.

Data from: Jensen, Robert. 2007. The digital provide: Information (technology), market performance, and welfare in the South Indian fisheries sector. *Quarterly Journal of Economics* 122(3): 879–924. https://doi.org/10.1162/qjec.122.3.879

The top panel of Figure 7.3 shows two markets, the North Market and the South Market. The price in the North Market is low because the quantity supplied is high (e.g., all the fishermen in an area have a good catch and arrive at the market to find lots of supply and low prices). In the South Market, however, the quantity supplied is low and the price is high.

Arbitrage means buying low and selling high, in this case buying in the North Market and selling in the South Market. In the bottom panel of Figure 7.3, we show that when the arbitragers buy in the North Market the price rises and the equilibrium moves from point *a* to point *c*. Similarly, as the arbitragers ship goods for sale to the South Market the price in the South Market falls, moving the equilibrium from point *b* to point *d*. Arbitragers will continue to buy in the North Market and sell in the South Market until the two prices are equal (we ignore transportation costs for simplicity).

Notice that arbitragers ship goods from where the value is low to where the value is high, so arbitrage increases total welfare. In the bottom panel of Figure 7.3, notice that the loss in value from reduced consumption in the North Market is smaller than the gain in value from increased consumption in the South Market, as shown by the relative size of the blue-shaded areas.

In Figure 7.3 we show the North Market with high supply and low prices and the South Market with low supply and high prices but, as in Kerala, which market has high and which has low prices can change every day so the idea is that arbitrage tends to smooth prices and quantities in both markets over time.

FIGURE 7.3

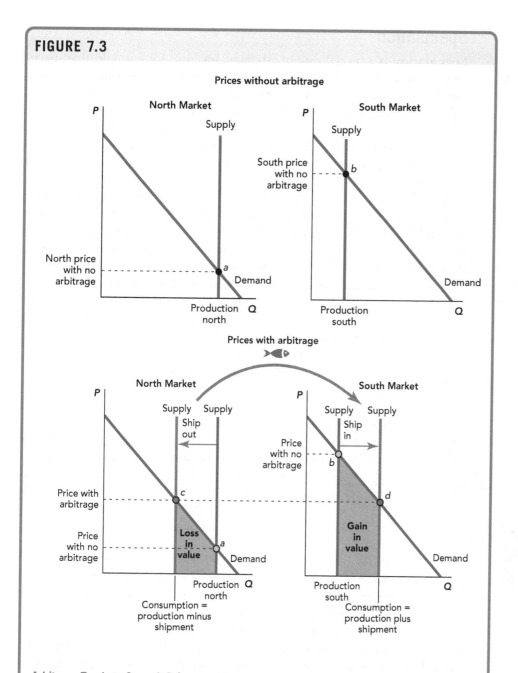

Arbitrage Tends to Smooth Prices and Increase Welfare The top panel shows the price of fish in the North and South Market when there is no arbitrage.

The bottom panel shows what happens with arbitrage. In the left panel, fishermen from North Market learn that the price is higher in South Market and so they ship fish from where the price is low, North Market, to where the price is high, South Market—as a result, the price of fish increases in North Market and decreases in South Market until the prices equalize. Higher prices in North Market cause consumers to reduce consumption, causing gains from trade to fall by the blue area in the left panel, but lower prices in South Market cause consumers to increase consumption, causing gains from trade to increase by the blue area in the right panel. Total welfare (gain in value plus loss in value) increases, because prices incentivized the fishermen to ship fish from where the value was low to where the value was high.

The analysis of speculation through time is similar, with North Market representing "today," and South Market representing "the future." To complete the analogy you can think of storing a good as "shipping it to the future."

Speculation

Speculation is the attempt to profit from future price changes.

Speculation is a special case of arbitrage. Imagine, for example, that speculators believe that a war in the Middle East is likely in the near future. How can the speculators make money? The way to make money is to buy low and sell high, so speculators should buy oil today when the price is low, store the oil, and then sell it when war breaks out and the price is high. The analysis is very similar to that shown in Figure 7.3—just interpret the North Market as "today," South Market as "the future," and storing the good as "shipping it to the future."

Speculation is arbitrage through time. Speculation is an especially risky type of arbitrage because the speculators could be wrong; perhaps the war in the Middle East never happens. If the speculators guess wrong, they will lose money and society will be worse off. But speculators have strong incentives to be as accurate as possible because they put their money where their mouth is. When speculators are wrong, they lose money—a lot of money. Bad speculators soon find themselves out of a job. Anyone who is able to be a speculator for a long time is either very, very lucky or just very good. So, like other forms of arbitrage, speculation tends to smooth prices over time and increase welfare, even though in particular instances speculators can be wrong.

Futures are standardized contracts to buy or sell specified quantities of a commodity or financial instrument at a specified price with delivery set at a specified time in the future.

You can also see in Figure 7.3 why speculators have an image problem. Speculators raise prices today but lower prices in the future. The media often report when speculators raise prices but rarely do they report when speculators lower prices.

Speculators typically buy and sell in special markets called futures markets. Oil **futures**, for example, are contracts to buy or sell a given quantity of oil at a specified price with delivery set at a specified time and place in the future. On the New York Mercantile Exchange (NYMEX), you can buy futures for light, sweet crude oil to be delivered at 30, 36, 48, 72, or 84 months in the future at a price agreed on today.

Futures markets are used not only for speculation but also for reducing risk. An airline that wants to know in advance what its fuel costs are going to be next year can lock in the price by buying oil on the futures market. Instead of buying futures, farmers can sell futures. A soybean farmer plants the crop today but does not harvest it until next year when the soybean price could be quite different from today's spot price. To avoid the price risk, the farmer can sell futures, that is, agree to sell so many soybeans at harvest time at a price agreed on today. Futures markets are also common in currencies. Suppose that Ford expects to sell 1,000 cars in Germany for 25,000 euros each. At the end of the year, how many dollars will Ford make? Ford doesn't know because the euro/dollar exchange rate can fluctuate. By selling euro futures, Ford can lock in the exchange rate.

Douglas Pulsipher/Acclaim Images

Markets see the future with futures markets.

CHECK YOURSELF

- Speculation occurs in stocks as well as commodities. In 2008, Lehman Brothers, a Wall Street investment banking firm, complained that speculators were driving the price of its stock lower and lower. During this time, Lehman continued to give rosy forecasts. Later in 2008, Lehman Brothers went bankrupt. Why was the forecast of the speculators more informative on net than the statements being issued from Lehman?

Signal Watching

Speculators who think that a war in the Middle East is likely will buy oil futures, pushing up the futures price (the price agreed on today for delivery in the future). If the futures price is much higher than the spot or current price, that is a sign that smart people with money on the line think that supply disruptions may soon occur. Futures prices for oil, currencies, and many commodities can be found in a newspaper or online, so anyone who wants to forecast events in the Middle East can benefit from reading price signals.

Futures prices can be extraordinarily informative about future events. The major factor determining the price of orange juice futures, for example, is the weather. If bad weather is expected to cause a frost destroying many oranges, the price of orange juice futures will be high. If good weather and a bumper crop are expected, the price will be low. The economist Richard Roll found that the futures price for orange juice was so sensitive to the weather that it could be used to improve the predictions of the National Weather Service![10]

It's not hard to see the future if you know where to look. In December 1991, the United Nations and the Worldwatch Institute warned that wheat would be very scarce in the coming year. Economist Paul Heyne looked in the newspaper and found that on that day the price of wheat was $4.05 a bushel. But the futures price for the following December was $3.51. Speculators, unlike the Worldwatch Institute, were not forecasting increased scarcity. In whose forecast would you put more confidence: that of the Worldwatch Institute or that of wheat speculators? Why?*

The futures price of oil can be used to predict war in the Middle East, but that is a side benefit of the futures market and not its purpose. Factors other than war (e.g., the decisions of OPEC, oil discoveries, and the demand for oil) also affect oil futures, so the futures price of oil is a *noisy signal* of war in the Middle East. A phone line with static—that's a noisy signal. Electrical engineers work to increase the signal-to-noise ratio on cell phones. More recently, economic engineers have begun to design markets to increase the signal-to-noise ratio of prices.

Prediction Markets

If markets are good at predicting the future even though they evolved to do something else, imagine how useful they might be if they were designed to predict. Beginning in the late 1980s, economic engineers began to design **prediction markets**, speculative markets designed so that prices can be interpreted as probabilities and used to make predictions.[11]

A **prediction market** is a speculative market designed so that prices can be interpreted as probabilities and used to make predictions.

The best-known prediction market is the Iowa Electronic Markets. The Iowa market lets traders use real money to buy and sell "shares" of political candidates. During the 2016 election, for example, traders on the Iowa Electronic Markets could buy shares in Donald Trump and Hillary Clinton. A share in Clinton, for example, would pay $1 if Clinton won the election and nothing otherwise. Suppose that the market price of a Clinton share is 75 cents. What does this market price suggest about the probability of Clinton winning the election?

To answer this question, think about each share as a bit like a lottery ticket. The ticket pays $1 if Clinton wins and nothing if she loses. How much would you be willing to pay for this lottery ticket if Clinton has a 20% chance of winning? How much would you be willing to pay for this lottery ticket if Clinton has a 75% chance of winning? If Clinton has a 20% chance of winning, then a

---

* By the way, Heyne's forecast was correct—wheat was not especially scarce in 1992. Did you put your confidence in the right place?

On November 1, 2016, a share that paid $1 if Donald Trump won the U.S. presidential election was selling for 40 cents and a share that paid $1 if Hillary Clinton won the U.S. presidential election was selling for 60 cents. What was the market predicting?

lottery ticket that pays $1 if she wins, and nothing otherwise, is worth about 20 cents on average ($0.2 \times \$1$). If Clinton has a 75% chance of winning, then the lottery ticket is worth about 75 cents ($0.75 \times \$1$). Thus, working backward, if we see that people are willing to pay 75 cents for a Clinton lottery ticket, we can infer that they think that Clinton has about a 75% probability of winning the election. In this way, we can use market prices to predict elections!

On November 1, a week before the election on November 8, the polls were predicting a Clinton victory, as were the Iowa markets. Statistician Nate Silver's model, which was based on national and state polls, gave Trump a 29% chance of winning. The prediction markets suggested a Trump victory was more likely, 40%, but still less likely than a Clinton victory. In fact, Trump won the election in what to most people was a surprise. The markets appeared to be a bit better than the polls but were the markets still wrong? Not necessarily. Events with a 40% chance are predicted to happen 40% of the time! To evaluate the markets, we have to examine many predictions. In fact, in more than 20 years of predicting U.S. and foreign elections, primaries, and other political events, the Iowa Electronic Markets have proven to be more accurate on average than polls. Uncertainty will always be with us and social scientists have to remain humble about our ability to predict the future. But markets are a good way of aggregating information and prediction markets have performed well relative to other methods of predicting the future.

The Hollywood Stock Exchange (https://www.HSX.com) is also proving that the innovative use of markets can be profitable. The Hollywood Exchange lets traders buy and sell shares and options in movies, music, and Oscar contenders. Trading on the Hollywood Exchange is conducted in make-believe "Hollywood Dollars," but the goal of the HSX—which is owned by a subsidiary of the Wall Street firm Cantor Fitzgerald—is profit. Some 800,000 people trading on HSX for fun have proven that HSX prices are reliable predictors of future film profits. Figure 7.4 graphs market predictions of opening revenues on the horizontal axis against actual opening revenues on the vertical axis. If all predictions were perfect, then predicted revenues would be exactly equal to actual revenues and all the observations would lie on the 45-degree red line. No one can predict the future perfectly, of course. Movies above the red line did better than predicted and movies below the red line did worse than predicted. The market predicted that *The Adventures of Pluto Nash*, a 2002 movie starring Eddie Murphy, would take in opening weekend revenues of over $10 million. In fact, *The Adventures of Pluto Nash* was one of the biggest financial bombs of all time with costs of $100 million and revenues of $7.1 million, much of that generated on the opening weekend before word of mouth sent it straight to the reject pile. *The Fast and the Furious*, however, was an unexpected hit, earning opening revenues of $41.6 million when less than half that amount, just $19.6 million, had been predicted. You know which movie resulted in lots and lots of sequels.

Although market predictions are sometimes a little high and sometimes a little low, they are centered on the 45-degree line, which means that they are

https://youtu.be/j9woif4gpew

Prediction Markets

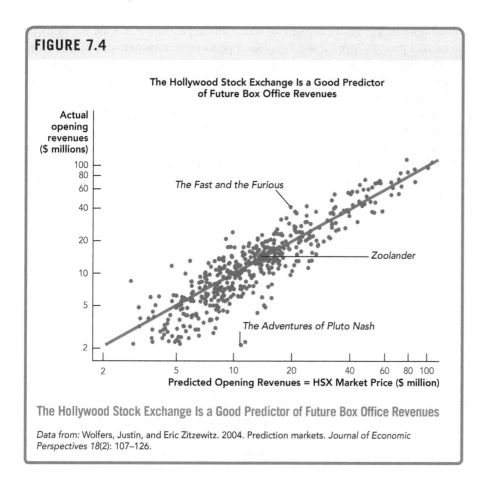

FIGURE 7.4

The Hollywood Stock Exchange Is a Good Predictor of Future Box Office Revenues

The Hollywood Stock Exchange Is a Good Predictor of Future Box Office Revenues

Data from: Wolfers, Justin, and Eric Zitzewitz. 2004. Prediction markets. *Journal of Economic Perspectives* 18(2): 107–126.

correct on average. The market, for example, predicted that *Zoolander* would have opening revenues of $15.03 million and actual revenues were $15.7 million. Perhaps the biggest sign of the accuracy of the HSX market is that HSX sells its data to Hollywood studios eager to improve their predictions about future blockbusters.

The use of prediction markets is expanding rapidly, but what's important for our purposes is that prediction markets help to illustrate how *all* markets work. Market prices are signals that convey valuable information. Buyers and sellers have an incentive to pay attention to and respond to prices and in so doing they direct resources to their highest-value uses. That means everyone can make the most out of limited resources.

Takeaway

No market is an island. Markets are linked geographically, through time and across different goods. The price of gasoline at your local gasoline station is linked to the market for oil in China. The price of oil today is linked to the expectations about the market for oil in the future and, through investment, to the market for oil in the past. Markets in one good are linked to markets in other goods. The supply and demand of flowers, asphalt, and candy bars are all linked through the worldwide market.

The worldwide market is neither designed nor, because it is so complex, ever completely understood. The market acts like a giant computer to arrange our limited resources to satisfy as many of our wants as possible. Prices are the heart of the market process. A price is a signal wrapped up in an incentive because prices signal the value of resources to consumers, suppliers, and entrepreneurs, and they incentivize everyone to take appropriate actions to respond to scarcity and changing circumstances.

Free market prices work as signals because through buying and selling, prices come to reflect important pieces of information. The futures price of oil, for example, can signal war in the Middle East and the futures price of orange juice can tell us about the weather in Florida. Market prices can be so informative that new markets (prediction markets) are being created to help businesses, governments, and scientists predict future events.

CHAPTER REVIEW

Go online to practice with more examples of these types of problems, including live links to videos, data sources, and feedback.

KEY CONCEPTS

great economic problem, p. 121

speculation, p. 128

futures, p. 128

prediction market, p. 129

FACTS AND TOOLS

1. For each of the following statements, state whether they are true or false. For those that are not true, state why they are false.

    a. The price of a good contains information about the cost of producing the good but not about its value to consumers.

    b. If the price of a resource significantly decreased in one country, we would expect domestic suppliers in that country to export more of the resource to other countries.

    c. Prices change in markets as people adjust their behavior.

    d. Worldwide markets cannot solve very large resource-allocation problems simply by using prices.

    e. Central planning usually fails because of information and incentive problems.

2. **a.** Suppose you'd like to do five different things, each of which requires exactly one orange. Complete the following table, ranking your highest-valued orange-related activity (1) to your lowest-valued activity (5).

Activity	Rank of Preference
Give a friend the orange.	
Throw the orange at a person you don't like.	
Eat the orange.	
Squeeze the orange to drink the juice.	
Use the orange as decorative fruit.	

    b. Suppose the price per orange is high enough that you buy only four. What activity do you not do?

    c. How low would the price of oranges have to fall for you to purchase five oranges? What does the price at which you would just purchase the fifth orange tell us about the value you receive from the fifth-ranked activity?

3. The supply and demand for copper change constantly. New sources are discovered, mines

collapse, workers go on strike, products that use it wane in and out of popularity, weather affects shipping conditions, and so on.

   a. Suppose you learned that growing political instability in Chile (the largest producer of copper) will greatly reduce the productivity of its mines in two years. Ignoring all other factors, which curve (demand or supply) will shift in the market for copper two years from now and in which direction?

   b. Will the price rise or fall as a result of this curve shift?

   c. Given your answer in part b, would a reasonable person buy copper to store for later? Why or why not? Ignore storage costs.

   d. As a result of many people imitating your choice in part c, what happens to the current price of copper?

   e. Does the action in parts c and d encourage people to use more copper today or less copper today?

4. In this chapter, we noted that successful economies are more likely to have many failing firms. If a nation's government instead made it impossible for inefficient firms to fail by giving them loans, cash grants, and other bailouts to stay in business, why is that nation likely to be poor? (*Hint:* Steven Davis and John Haltiwanger. 1999. "Gross Job Flows." In *Handbook of Labor Economics* [Amsterdam: North-Holland] found that in the United States, 60% of the increase in U.S. manufacturing efficiency was caused by people moving from weak firms to strong firms.)

5. For you, personally, what is your opportunity cost of doing this homework?

6. Suppose you are bidding on a used car and someone else bids above the highest amount that you are willing to pay. What can you say for sure about that person's monetary value of the good compared to yours?

7. Sometimes speculators get it wrong. In the months before the Persian Gulf War, speculators drove up the price of oil: The average price in October 1990 was $36 per barrel, more than double its price in 1988. Oil speculators, like many people around the world, expected the Gulf War to last for months, disrupting the oil supply throughout the Gulf region. Thus, speculators either bought oil on the open market (almost always at the high speculative price) or already owned oil and just kept it in storage. Either way, their plan was the same: to sell it in the future, when prices might be even higher.

   As it turned out, the war was swift: After one month of massive aerial bombardment of Iraqi troops and a 100-hour ground war, then President George H. W. Bush declared a cessation of hostilities. Despite the fact that Saddam Hussein set fire to many of Kuwait's oil fields, the price of oil plummeted to about $20 per barrel, a price at which it remained for years.

   a. Is buying oil for $36 a barrel and selling it for $20 per barrel a good business plan? How much profit did speculators earn, or how much money did they lose, on each barrel?

   b. Why did the speculators follow this plan?

   c. When the speculators sold their stored oil in the months after the war, did this massive resale tend to increase the price of oil or decrease it?

   d. Do you think that many consumers complained about speculators or even realized that speculators were influencing the price of oil in spring 1991?

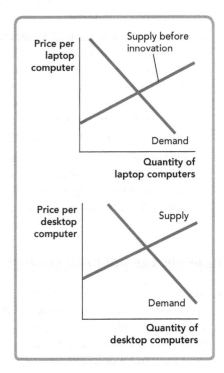

8. You manage a department store in Florida, and one winter day you read in the newspaper that orange juice futures have fallen dramatically in

price. Should your store stock up on more sweaters than usual, or should your store stock up on more Bermuda shorts?

9. Take a look at Figure 7.4. If investors in the Hollywood Stock Exchange were too optimistic on average, would the dots tend to cluster above the red diagonal line or below it? How can you tell?

10. Let's see if the forces of the market can be as efficient as a benevolent dictator. Since laptop computers are increasingly easy to build and since they allow people to use their computers wherever they like, an all-wise benevolent dictator would probably decree that most people buy laptops rather than desktop computers. This is especially true now that laptops are about as powerful as most desktops. In answering questions a–c, answer in words as well as by shifting the appropriate curves in the following figures.

   a. Since it's become much easier to build better laptops in recent years, laptop supply has increased. What does this do to the price of laptops?

   b. Laptops and desktops are substitutes. Now that the price of laptops has changed, what does this do to the demand for desktop computers?

   c. And how does that affect the quantity supplied of desktop computers?

   d. Now let's look at the final result: Once it became easier to build good laptops, did "invisible hand" forces push more of society's resources into making laptops and push resources away from making desktops? (*Note:* Laptop sales first outnumbered desktop sales in 2008, and by 2020, laptop sales were roughly double desktop sales.)

   e. Do you foresee a similar shift in resources away from laptop sales in the future? If so, where do you believe the resources will likely shift? Will the market dynamics follow a similar pattern as above?

THINKING AND PROBLEM SOLVING

11. Yusef enters into a futures contract, allowing him to sell 5,000 troy ounces of gold at $1,000 per ounce in 36 months. After that time passes, the market price of gold is $950 per troy ounce. How much does Yusef make or lose?

12. Circa 1200 BCE, a decreasing supply of tin resulting from wars and the breakdown of trade led to a drastic increase in the price of bronze in the Middle East and Greece (tin being necessary for its production). It is around this time that blacksmiths developed iron- and steel-making techniques (as substitutes for bronze).

   a. How is the increasing price of bronze a signal?

   b. How is the increasing price an incentive?

   c. How do your answers in parts a and b help explain why iron and steel became more common around the same time as the increase in price?

   d. After the development of iron, did the supply or demand for bronze shift? Which way did it shift? Why?

13. In 1980, University of Maryland economist Julian Simon bet Stanford entomologist Paul Ehrlich that the price of any five metals of Ehrlich's choosing would fall over 10 years. Ehrlich believed that resources would become scarcer over time as the population grew, while Simon believed that people would find good substitutes, just as earlier people developed iron as a substitute for scarce bronze. The price of all five metals that Ehrlich chose (nickel, tin, tungsten, chromium, and copper) fell over the next 10 years and Simon won the bet. Ehrlich, an honorable man, sent a check in the appropriate amount to Simon.

   a. What does the falling price tell us about the relative scarcity of these metals?

   b. What *could have* shifted to push these prices down: demand or supply? And would demand have increased or decreased to produce this effect? What about supply?

14. In this chapter, we explored how prices tie all goods together. To illustrate this idea, suppose new technologies drastically increase the productivity of producing electric cars.

   a. Given this change, how would the price of electric cars change?

   b. Given your answer in part a, how would the price of batteries change?

   c. Given your answer in part b, how would the price of lithium (which is used in rechargeable batteries) change?

   d. Given your answer in part c, how would the price of heat-resistant glass and ceramics change? (*Hint:* Lithium is a key component used in the production of both products.)

   e. Given your answer in part d, how would the quantity of sand (used in glass production) consumed change?

15. The law of one price states that if it's easy to move a good from one place to another, the price of identical goods will be the same because traders will buy low in one region and sell high in another. How is our story about the effect of speculators similar to the lesson about the law of one price?

16. Let's build on this chapter's example of asphalt. Suppose a new invention comes along that makes it easier and much less expensive to recycle clothing: Perhaps a new device about the size of a washing machine can bleach, reweave, and redye cotton fabric to closely imitate any cotton item you see in a fashion magazine. Head into the laundry room, drop in a batch of old clothes, scan in a couple of pages from *Vogue*, and come back in an hour.

    a. If you think of the "market for clothing" as "the market for new clothing," does this shift the demand or the supply curve, and in which direction?

    b. If you think of the "market for clothing" as "the market for clothing, whether it's new or used," does this shift the demand or the supply curve, and in which direction?

    c. What will this do to the price of new, unrecycled clothing?

    d. After this invention, will society's scarce productive resources (machines, workers, retail space) flow *toward* the "new clothing" sector or away from it?

    (*Note:* This question might sound fanciful but three-dimensional printers, which can create plastic or plaster prototypes of small items such as toys, cups, etc., have fallen dramatically in price. Every day, you're getting just a little bit closer to having your own personal *Star Trek* replicator.)

17. Robin is planning to ask Peggy to the Homecoming dance. Before he asks her, he wants to know what the chances are that she'll say yes. Robin is a scientist so he considers two paths to estimate the probability that Peggy will say yes.

    I. Ask 10 of his friends, "Do you think she'll really say yes?"

    II. Tell another 10 of his friends, "I'm starting a betting market. I'll pay $10 if she says yes, $0 if she says no. I'm offering this bet only once, to the highest bidder. Start bidding against each other for a chance at $10!"

    a. According to the evidence in this chapter, one of these methods will work better. Which one, and why?

    b. If the highest bid from Group II is $1 (along with a few lower bids of $0.75, $0.50, and zero), then roughly what's the chance that Peggy will say yes to Robin?

    c. If the highest bid from Group II quickly shoots up to about $9, then what's the chance that Peggy will say yes to Robin?

18. A classic essay about how markets link to each other is entitled "I, Pencil," written by Leonard E. Read (his real name). It is available for free online at the *Library of Economics and Liberty*. As you might suspect, it is written from the point of view of a pencil. One line is particularly famous: "No single person on the face of this earth knows how to make me." Based on what you've learned in this chapter about how markets link the world, how is this true?

CHALLENGES

19. In *The Fatal Conceit*, economist Friedrich A. Hayek, arguing against central planning, wrote, "The curious task of economics is to demonstrate to men how little they really know about what they imagine they can design." In other words, people generally assume that they can plan out the best procedure for producing a good (such as the Valentine's Day rose mentioned at the beginning of the chapter), but as we learned, that's not true. What are some of the different roles that the price system plays in creating this order? (*Hint:* Key words are "links," "signals," and "incentives.")

20. One question that economics students often ask is, "In a market with a lot of buyers and

sellers, who sets the price of the good?" There are two possible correct answers to this question: "Everyone" and "No one." Choose one of the two as your answer, and explain in one or two sentences why you are correct.

21. This chapter emphasized the ability of an orderly system to emerge without someone explicitly designing the entire system. How does the evolution of language illustrate a type of spontaneous order?

22. Are you in favor of "price gouging" during natural disasters? Why or why not?

23. What is the opportunity cost of the economics profession?

WORK IT OUT

For interactive, step-by-step help in solving this problem, go online.

Two major-party presidential candidates are running against each other in the 2020 election. The Democratic Party candidate promises more money for corn-based ethanol research, and the Republican Party candidate promises more money for defense contractors. In the weeks before the election, defense stocks take a nosedive.

a. Who is probably going to win the election: the pro-ethanol candidate or the pro–defense spending candidate?

b. We talked about how price signals are sometimes noisy. Think of two or three other markets you might want to look at to see if your answer to part a is correct.

8

Price Ceilings and Floors

On a quiet Sunday in August of 1971, President Richard Nixon shocked the nation by freezing all prices and wages in the United States. It was now illegal to raise prices—even if both buyers and sellers voluntarily agreed to the change. Nixon's order, one of the most significant peacetime interventions into the U.S. economy ever to occur, applied to almost all goods, and even though it was supposed to be in effect for only 90 days, it would have lasting effects for more than a decade.

In Chapter 7, we explained how a price is "a signal wrapped up in an incentive"; that is, we explained how prices signal information and create incentives to economize and seek out substitutes. We also explained how markets are linked geographically, across different products, and through time. In this chapter, we show how price controls—laws making it illegal for prices to move above a maximum price (price ceilings) or below a minimum price (price floors)—interfere with all of these processes. We begin by explaining how a price control affects a single market, and then we turn to how price controls delink some markets and link others in ways that are counterproductive.

Price Ceilings

Nixon's price controls didn't have much effect immediately because prices were frozen near market levels. But the economy is in constant flux and market prices soon shifted. At the time of the freeze, prices were rising because of inflation, so the typical situation came to resemble that in Figure 8.1, with the controlled price below the uncontrolled or market equilibrium price.

When the maximum price that can be legally charged is below the market price, we say that there is a **price ceiling**. Economists call it a price ceiling because prices cannot legally go higher than the ceiling. Price ceilings create five important effects:

1. Shortages
2. Reductions in product quality
3. Wasteful lines and other search costs
4. A loss of gains from trade
5. A misallocation of resources

A **price ceiling** is a maximum price allowed by law.

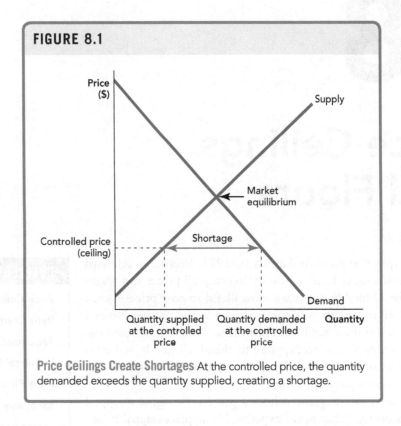

FIGURE 8.1

Price Ceilings Create Shortages At the controlled price, the quantity demanded exceeds the quantity supplied, creating a shortage.

A shortage of vinyl in 1973 forced Capitol Records to melt down slow sellers so they could keep pressing Beatles' albums.

Shortages

When prices are held below the market price, the quantity demanded exceeds the quantity supplied. Economists call this a shortage. Figure 8.1 shows that the shortage is measured by the difference between the quantity demanded at the controlled price and the quantity supplied at the controlled price. Notice also that the lower the controlled price is relative to the market equilibrium price, the larger the shortage.

In some sectors of the economy, shortages appeared soon after prices were controlled in 1971. Increased demand in the construction industry, for example, meant that price controls hit that sector especially hard. Ordinarily, increased demand for steel bars, for example, would increase the price of steel bars, encouraging more production. But with a price ceiling in place, demanders could not signal their need to suppliers nor could they provide suppliers with an incentive to produce more. As a result, shortages of steel bars, lumber, toilets (for new homes), and other construction inputs were common. By 1973, there were shortages of wool, copper, aluminum, vinyl, denim, paper, plastic bottles, and more.

Reductions in Quality

At the controlled price, demanders find that there is a shortage of goods—they cannot buy as much of the good as they would like. Equivalently, at the controlled price, sellers find that there is an excess of demand or, in other words, *sellers have more customers than they have goods.* Ordinarily, this would be an opportunity to profit by raising prices, but when prices are controlled, sellers can't raise prices without violating the law. Is there another way that sellers can increase profits? Yes. It's much easier to evade the law by cutting quality than by raising price, so when prices are held below market levels, quality declines.

Thus, even when shortages were not apparent, quality was reduced. Books were printed on lower-quality paper, $2'' \times 4''$ lumber shrank to $1\frac{5}{8}'' \times 3\frac{5}{8}''$, and new automobiles were painted with fewer coats of paint. To help deal with the shortage of paper, some newspapers even switched to a smaller font size.[1]

Another way quality can fall is with reductions in service. Ordinarily, sellers have an incentive to please their customers, but when prices are held below market levels, sellers have more customers than they need or *want*. Customers without potential for profit are just a pain so when prices cannot rise, we can expect service quality to fall. The full-service gasoline station, for example, disappeared with price controls in 1973, and instead of staying open for 24 hours, gasoline stations would close whenever the owner wanted a lunch break.

The Great Matzo Ball Debate In 1972, AFL-CIO boss George Meany complained that the number of matzo balls in his favorite soup had sunk from four to three, in effect raising the price.

C. Jackson Grayson, chairman of the U.S. Price Commission, was worried about the bad publicity, so on *Face the Nation* he triumphantly held aloft a can of Mrs. Adler's Soup, claiming that his staff had opened many cans and concluded there were still four balls per can.

Whoever was right about the soup, Meany was certainly the better economist: Price ceilings reduce quality.

Wasteful Lines and Other Search Costs

The most serious shortage during the 1970s was for oil. The OPEC embargo in 1973 and the reduction in supply caused by the Iranian Revolution in 1979 increased the world price of oil, as we saw in Chapter 4. In the United States, however, price controls on domestically produced oil had not been lifted and the United States thus faced intense shortages of oil and long lines to purchase gasoline.

The long lines were not an accident. Figure 8.2 on the next page shows that wasteful lines are caused by price ceilings.

At the controlled price of $1, sellers supply Q_s units of the good. How much are demanders willing to pay (per unit) for these Q_s units? Recall that the demand curve shows the willingness to pay, so follow a line from Q_s up to the demand curve to find that demanders are willing to pay $3 per unit for Q_s units. The price controls, however, make it illegal for demanders to offer sellers a price of $3, but there are other ways of paying for gas.

Knowing that there is a shortage, some buyers might bribe station owners (or attendants) to fill up their tanks. Suppose that the average tank holds 20 gallons. Buyers would then be willing to pay $60 for a fill-up, the legal price of $20 plus a $40 under-the-table bribe. Thus, if bribes are common, the total price of gasoline—the legal price plus the bribe price—will rise to $3 per gallon ($60/20 gallons).

Corruption and bribes can be common, especially when price controls are long-lasting, but they were not a major problem during the gasoline shortages of the 1970s. Nevertheless, the total price of gasoline did rise well above the controlled price. Instead of competing by paying bribes, buyers competed by their willingness to wait in line. Remember that at the controlled price the quantity of gasoline demanded is greater than the quantity supplied, so some buyers are going to be disappointed—they are going to get less gasoline than they want and some buyers may get no gasoline at all. Buyers will compete to avoid being left with nothing. Let's assume that all gasoline station owners refuse bribes. Unfortunately, honesty does not eliminate the shortage.

MRU

mru.org/price-ceilings

Price Ceilings

FIGURE 8.2

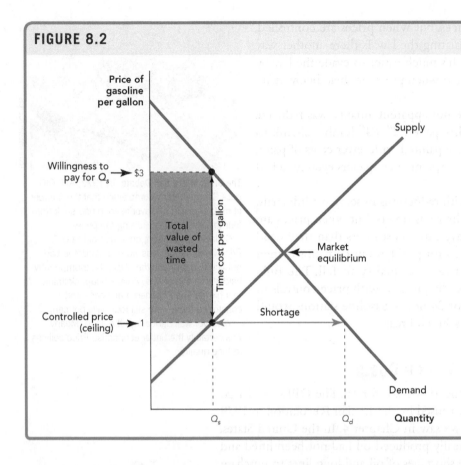

Price Ceilings Create Wasteful Lines At the controlled price, the quantity of gasoline supplied is Q_s and buyers are willing to pay as much as $3 for a gallon of gasoline. But the maximum price that sellers can charge is $1. The difference between what buyers are willing to pay and what sellers can charge encourages buyers to line up to buy gasoline. Buyers will line up until the total price of gasoline, the out-of-pocket price plus the time cost, increases to $3 per gallon. Time spent waiting in line is wasted time. The total value of wasted time is given by the time cost per gallon multiplied by the quantity of gallons bought.

A first-come/first-served system is honest, but buyers who get to the gasoline station early will get the gas, leaving the latecomers with nothing. In this situation, how long will the lineups get?

Suppose that buyers value their time at $10 an hour and, as before, the average fuel tank holds 20 gallons. Eager to obtain gas during the shortage, a buyer arrives at the station early, perhaps even before it opens, and must wait in line for an hour before they are served. Their total price of gas is $30: $1 per gallon for 20 gallons in out-of-pocket cost plus $10 in time cost. Since the total value of the gas is $60, that's still a good deal. But if it's a good deal for them, it's probably a good deal for other buyers, too, so the next time they want to fill up, they are likely to discover that others have come before and now they have to wait longer. How much longer? Following the logic to its conclusion, we can see that the line will lengthen until the total cost for 20 gallons of gasoline is $60: $20 in cash paid to the station owner plus $40 in time costs (4 hours' worth of waiting). The price per gallon, therefore, rises to $3 ($60/20 gallons)—exactly as occurred with bribes!

Price controls do not eliminate competition. They merely change the form of competition. Is there a difference between paying in bribes and paying in time? Yes. Paying in time is much more wasteful. When a buyer bribes a gasoline station owner $40, at least the gasoline station owner gets the bribe. But when a buyer spends $40 worth of time or four hours waiting in line, the gasoline station owner doesn't get to add four hours

When the quantity demanded exceeds the quantity supplied, someone is going to be disappointed.

to their life. The bribe is transferred from the buyer to the seller, but the time spent waiting in line is simply lost. Figure 8.2 shows that when the quantity supplied is Q_s, the total price of gasoline will tend to rise to $3: a $1 money price plus a time price of $2 per gallon. The total amount of waste from waiting in line is given by the shaded area, the per gallon time price ($2) multiplied by the number of gallons bought (Q_s).*

Lost Gains from Trade (Deadweight Loss)

Price controls also reduce the gains from trade. In Figure 8.3, at the quantity supplied Q_s, how much would demanders pay for one *additional* gallon of gasoline? The willingness to pay for a gallon of gas at Q_s is $3, so demanders would be willing to pay just a little bit less, say, $2.95, for an additional gallon. How much would suppliers require to sell an additional gallon? Supplier cost is read off the supply curve, so reading up from the quantity Q_s to the supply curve, we find that the willingness to sell at Q_s is $1; suppliers would be willing to supply an additional unit for just a little bit more, say, $1.05.

Demanders are willing to pay $2.95 for an additional gallon of gas, suppliers are willing to sell an additional gallon for $1.05, and so there is $1.90 of

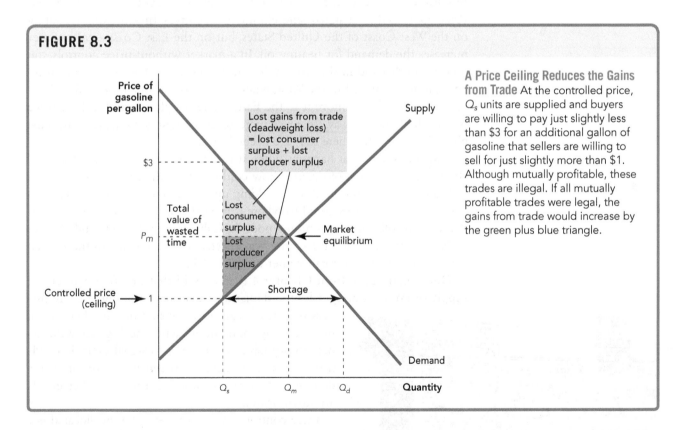

FIGURE 8.3

A Price Ceiling Reduces the Gains from Trade At the controlled price, Q_s units are supplied and buyers are willing to pay just slightly less than $3 for an additional gallon of gasoline that sellers are willing to sell for just slightly more than $1. Although mutually profitable, these trades are illegal. If all mutually profitable trades were legal, the gains from trade would increase by the green plus blue triangle.

* We need to qualify this slightly. If *every* buyer has a time value of $10 per hour, then the total time wasted will be the area as shaded in the diagram. If some buyers have a time value lower than $10, say, $5 per hour, they will wait in line for four hours, paying $20 in out-of-pocket costs but only $20 in time costs. If these buyers value the gasoline as highly as does the marginal buyer, at $60 for 20 gallons, they will earn what economists call a "rent" of $20; thus, not all of the rectangle would be wasted. Regardless of whether all of the rectangle or just some of the rectangle is wasted, it's important to see that (1) price ceilings generate shortages and lineups, (2) the lineups mean that the total price of the controlled good is higher than the controlled price (and perhaps even higher than the uncontrolled price), and (3) the time spent waiting in line is wasted.

potential gains from trade to split between them. But it's illegal for suppliers to sell gasoline at any price higher than $1. Buyers and sellers want to trade, but they are prevented from doing so by the threat of jail. If the price ceiling were lifted and trade were allowed, the quantity traded would expand from Q_s to Q_m and buyers would be better off by the green triangle labeled "Lost consumer surplus," while sellers would be better off by the blue triangle labeled "Lost producer surplus." But with a price ceiling in place, the quantity supplied is Q_s and together the lost consumer and producer surplus are lost gains from trade (economists also call this a **deadweight loss**).

A **deadweight loss** is the reduction in total surplus caused by a market distortion or inefficiency.

Recall from Chapter 4 that we said that in a free market the quantity of goods sold maximizes the sum of consumer and producer surplus. We can now see that in a market with a price ceiling, the sum of consumer and producer surplus is not maximized because the price control prevents mutually profitable gains from trade from being exploited.

In addition to these losses, price controls cause a misallocation of scarce resources; let's see how that works in more detail.

Misallocation of Resources

In Chapter 7, we explained how a price is a signal wrapped up in an incentive. Price controls distort signals and eliminate incentives. Imagine that it's sunny on the West Coast of the United States, but on the East Coast a cold winter increases the demand for heating oil. In a market without price controls, the increase in demand in the East pushes up prices in the East. Eager for profit, entrepreneurs buy oil in the West, where the oil is not much needed and the price is low, and they move it to the East, where people are cold and the price of oil is high. In this way, the price increase in the East is moderated and supplies of oil move to where they are needed most.

Now consider what happens when it is illegal to buy or sell oil at a price above a price ceiling. No matter how cold it gets in the East, the demanders of heating oil are prevented from bidding up the price of oil, so there's *no signal* and *no incentive* to ship oil to where it is needed most. Price controls mean that oil is misallocated. Swimming pools in California are heated, while homes in New Jersey are cold. In fact, this was exactly what happened in the United States, especially in the harsh winter of 1972–1973.

Once again recall from Chapter 4 that we said that in a free market the supply of goods is bought by the demanders who have the highest willingness to pay. We can now see that in a market with a price ceiling, demanders with the highest willingness to pay have no easy way to signal their demands nor do suppliers have an incentive to supply their demands. As a result, in a controlled market goods are misallocated.

Price controls cause resources to be misallocated not just geographically, but also across different uses of oil. Recall from Chapter 3 that the demand curve for oil shows the uses of oil from the highest-valued to the lowest-valued uses. In case you forgot, Figure 8.4 shows the key idea: High-valued uses are at the top of the curve and low-valued uses at the bottom. Without market prices, however, we have no guarantee that oil will flow to its

Distorted signals cause resources to be misallocated.

highest-valued uses. As we have just seen, in a situation with price controls, it's possible to have plenty of oil to heat swimming pools in California (hello, rubber ducky!) and not enough oil for heating cold homes in New Jersey. Similarly, in 1974 *Business Week* reported, "While drivers wait in three-hour lines in one state, consumers in other states are breezing in and out of gas stations."[2]

Figure 8.5 illustrates the problem more generally. As we know, at the controlled price, the quantity demanded Q_d exceeds the quantity supplied Q_s and there is a shortage. Ideally, we would like to allocate the quantity of oil supplied, Q_s, to its highest-valued uses; these are illustrated at the top of the demand curve by the thick line. But the potential consumers of the oil with the highest-valued uses are legally prevented from signaling their high value by offering to pay oil suppliers more than the controlled price. Oil suppliers, therefore, have no incentive to supply oil to just the highest-valued uses. Instead, oil suppliers will give the oil to any user who is willing to pay the controlled price—but most of these users of oil have lower-valued uses. Like the lines at the

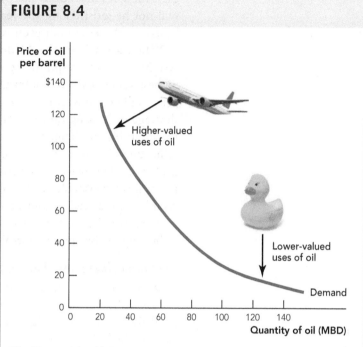

FIGURE 8.4

The Demand for Oil Depends on the Value of Oil in Different Uses
When the price of oil is high, oil will only be used in the higher-valued uses. As the price falls, oil will also be used in lower-valued uses.

(Top: ssuaphotos/Shutterstock)
(Bottom: Lew Robertson/Corbis)

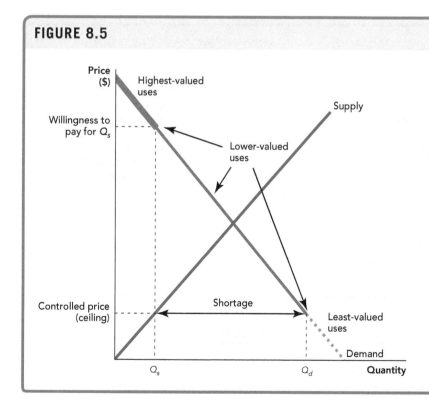

FIGURE 8.5

When Prices Are Controlled, Resources Do Not Flow to Their Highest-Valued Uses
Gains from trades are maximized when goods flow to their highest-valued uses. A price control prevents the highest-valued uses from outbidding lower-valued uses, so some oil flows to lowered-value uses, even though it would be more valuable if used elsewhere.

gas station, it's first come/first served. In fact, the only uses of oil that definitely will not be satisfied are the least-valued uses. (Why not? The users with the least-valued uses are not even willing to pay the controlled price.)

When a crisis in the Middle East reduces the supply of oil, the price system rationally responds by reallocating oil from lower-valued uses to the highest-valued uses. In contrast, when the supply of oil is reduced and there are price ceilings, oil is allocated according to random and often trivial factors. The shortage of heating oil in 1971, for example, was exacerbated by the fact that President Nixon happened to impose price controls in *August* when the price of heating oil was near its seasonal low.[3] Since the price of heating oil was controlled at a low price, while gasoline was controlled at a slightly higher price, it was more profitable to turn crude oil into gasoline than into heating oil. As winter approached, the price of heating oil would normally have risen and refiners would have turned away from gasoline production to the production of heating oil, but price controls removed the incentive to respond rationally.

Advanced Material: The Loss from Random Allocation If there were no misallocation, then under a price control, consumer surplus would be the area between the demand curve and the controlled price up to the quantity supplied, the green area in Figure 8.6. (Of course, some of this surplus will likely be eaten up by bribes, time spent waiting in line, and so forth as explained earlier.)

Under a price control, however, the good is not necessarily allocated to the highest-valued uses. As a result, consumer surplus will be less than the green area—but how much less? The worst-case scenario would occur if all the goods were allocated to the lower-valued uses, but that seems unlikely. A more realistic assumption is that under price controls, goods are allocated randomly so that a high-valued use is as likely as a low-valued use to be satisfied.

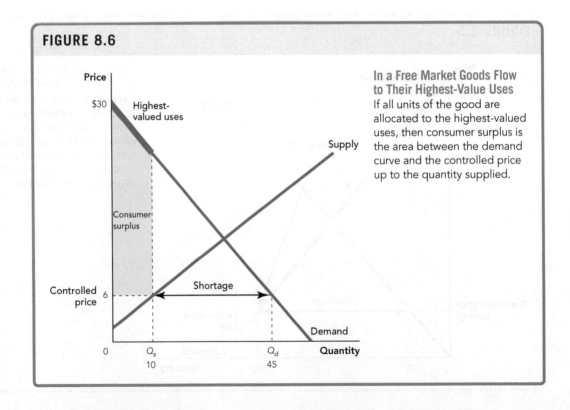

FIGURE 8.6

In a Free Market Goods Flow to Their Highest-Value Uses If all units of the good are allocated to the highest-valued uses, then consumer surplus is the area between the demand curve and the controlled price up to the quantity supplied.

FIGURE 8.7

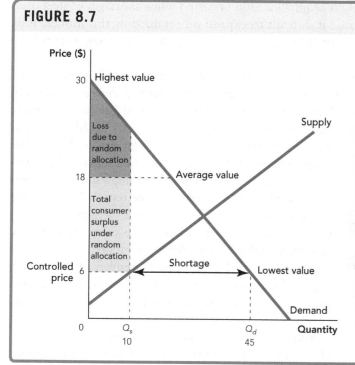

Consumer Surplus Falls Under Random Allocation When there is a price control, the buyers with the highest-valued uses cannot outbid other buyers, so goods will flow to any buyer willing to pay more than the controlled price of $6. If goods are allocated randomly to buyers with values between $30 and $6, the average value will be $18. Consumer surplus under random allocation is the green area. If goods were allocated to the highest-valued uses, consumer surplus would be larger, the red plus green areas. Thus, a price control misallocates resources, reducing consumer surplus.

In Figure 8.7 we show two uses. The highest-valued use has a value of $30 and the lowest-valued use has a value of $6. Now imagine that one unit of the good is allocated randomly between these two uses. Thus, with a probability of $\frac{1}{2}$, it will be allocated to the use with a value of 30, and with a probability of $\frac{1}{2}$, it will be allocated to the use with a value of 6. On average, how much value will this unit create? The average value will be

$$\text{Average value} = \frac{1}{2} \times \$30 + \frac{1}{2} \times \$6 = \$18$$

Extending this logic, it can be shown that if every use between the highest-valued use and the lowest-valued use is *equally* likely to be satisfied, then the average value is $18. Thus on average, a randomly allocated unit of the good will create a value of $18. If there are, say, 10 units allocated, then the total value of those units will be 10 × $18 = $180. Since the average value is $18 and the controlled price is $6, consumer surplus is the green area in Figure 8.7 labeled total consumer surplus under random allocation. But notice that the green area in Figure 8.7, consumer surplus under random allocation, is much less than the green area in Figure 8.6, consumer surplus under allocation to the highest-valued uses. The difference is the red area in Figure 8.7, the loss due to random allocation.

Misallocation and Production Chaos Shortages in one market create breakdowns and shortages in other markets, so the chaos of price controls expands even into markets without price controls. In ordinary times, we take it for granted that products will be available when we want them, but in an economy with many price controls, shortages of key inputs can appear at any time. In 1973, for example, million-dollar construction projects were delayed because a few thousand dollars' worth of steel bar was unavailable.[4]

Perhaps the height of misallocation occurred when shortages of steel drilling equipment made it difficult to expand oil production; this mistake took place even as the United States was undergoing the worst energy crisis in its history.[5]

As the shortages and misallocations grew worse, schools, factories, and offices were forced to close, and the government stepped in to allocate oil by command. President Nixon ordered gasoline stations to close between 9 PM Saturday and 12:01 AM Monday.[6] The idea was to prevent "wasteful" Sunday driving, but the ban simply encouraged people to fill their tanks earlier. Daylight savings time and a national 55-mph speed limit were put into place (the latter not to be repealed until 1995). Some industries, such as agriculture, were given priority treatment for fuel allocation, while others were forced to endure cutbacks. Fuel for noncommercial aircraft, for example, was cut by 42.5% in November of 1973, sending the local economy of Wichita, Kansas, where aircraft producers Cessna, Beech, and Lear were located, into a tailspin.[7]

The Everett Collection

President Nixon said no to commercial holiday lights during the Christmas of 1973.

Some of these ideas for conserving fuel were probably sensible while others were not, but without market prices, it's hard to tell which is which. The subtlety of the market process in allocating oil and taking advantage of links between markets is difficult, even impossible, to duplicate. C. Jackson Grayson was chairman of President Nixon's Price Commission, but after seeing how controls worked in practice, he said:

> Our economic understanding and models are simply not powerful enough to handle such a large and complex economic system better than the marketplace.[8]

The End of Price Ceilings

Price controls for most goods were lifted by April 1974, but controls on oil remained in place. Over the next seven years, controls on oil would be eased but at the price of substantial increases in complexity and bureaucracy. In September 1973, for example, price controls were lifted on new oil. "New oil" was defined as oil produced on a particular property in excess of the amount that had been produced in 1972. Decontrol of new oil was a good idea because it increased the incentive to develop new deposits. The two-tier system, however, also created wasteful gaming as firms shut down some oil wells only to drill "new" wells right next door.[9] The battle between entrepreneurs and regulators was met with increasingly complex rules. Thus, the two-tier program was extended to three tiers, then five, then eight, then eleven.

Price controls on oil ended as abruptly as they had begun when on the morning of January 20, 1981, Ronald Reagan was inaugurated as president, and before lunch with Congress, he performed his first act as president—eliminating all controls on oil and gasoline. As expected, the price of oil in the United States rose a little but the shortage ended overnight. Within a year, prices began to fall as supply increased and within a few years they were well below the levels of 1979. Fluctuations in the price of oil have continued to occur, of course, but since the ending of controls, there has been no shortage of oil in the United States.

Does Uber Price Gouge?

Price controls continue to be debated. Consider the ride-sharing service Uber. Uber brings together demanders and suppliers of car rides.

In setting the price for each ride, Uber considers local information about supply and demand. If a big concert has just ended or if it's raining, then demand may be especially high and Uber will often charge a higher price—called the surge price. Because Uber drivers get a share of the price, higher prices incentivize drivers to drive where and when demand has increased—where the big concert is getting out or when it's raining, for example. After a spike in demand following an Ariana Grande concert at Madison Square Garden, for example, Uber prices surged and the number of Uber drivers in that area increased by more than 75%.[10] Similarly, when it's raining in New York City, it's been estimated that the number of Uber rides goes up by about 22%. In contrast, taxis, which are fixed in number and do not have surge pricing, increase their number of rides by only 5% when it's raining.[11]

Surge pricing means the number of Uber rides increases when it's raining.

The higher price also reduces the number of people who want a ride. The higher the price, the more likely you will just walk, take your bike, or go an hour later when overall demand is lower. You could even try another ride-sharing service or call a cab. One study estimated that if the Uber price goes up by 10%, the quantity demanded falls by about 5.1%, for an implied price elasticity of −0.51 (i.e., −5.1%/10%).[12] The net result of Uber adjusting prices is that the quantity supplied and the quantity demanded are equalized. Even in busy times, anyone can get a ride fairly quickly so long as they are willing to pay the price.

Not everyone, however, likes surge pricing. Laws to restrict surge pricing have been proposed and have even passed in some places such as New Delhi, India. The problem with restricting surge pricing is that when users need rides the most, the price would be kept low by the law, and the quantity demanded would exceed the quantity supplied, as in Figure 8.1. The shortage would mean a long wait before you can get a ride. Indeed, the reason Uber introduced surge pricing was precisely to reduce the shortages and long waits that had often occurred when the demand for service increased with bad weather or when popular events concluded.

By the way, the same study showed that if consumers spend a dollar on Uber, they receive about an extra $1.60 in consumer surplus, and that is with surge pricing. Indeed, that is in part *because* surge pricing allocates rides to the high demanders. A price control would mean that the people with the highest demand for a ride would no longer have a way to signal that demand and rides would be allocated randomly instead of to those who value them the most. The net result would be a loss due to misallocation, as was shown in Figure 8.7.

CHECK YOURSELF

- Nixon's price controls set price ceilings below the market price. What would have happened if the price ceilings had been set above market prices?

- Under price controls, why were the shortages of oil in some local markets much more severe than in others?

A **rent control** is a price ceiling on rental housing.

Rent Controls

A **rent control** is a price ceiling on rental housing, such as apartments, so everything we have learned about price ceilings also applies to rent controls. Rent controls create shortages, reduce quality, create wasteful lines and increase the costs of search, cause a loss of gains from trade, and misallocate resources.

Shortages

Rent controls usually begin with a "rent freeze," which prohibits landlords from raising rents. Since rent controls are often put into place when rents are rising, the situation quickly comes to look like Figure 8.8, with the controlled rent below the market equilibrium rent.

Apartments are long-lasting goods that cannot be moved, so when rent controls are first imposed, owners of apartment buildings have few alternatives but to absorb the lower price. In other words, the short-run supply curve for apartments is inelastic. Thus, Figure 8.8 shows that even though the rent freeze may result in rents well below the market equilibrium level, there is only a small reduction in the quantity supplied in the short run.

In the long run, however, fewer new apartment units are built and older units are turned into condominiums or torn down to make way for parking garages or other higher-paying ventures. Rent controls introduced into San Francisco in 1994 encouraged landlords to reduce the stock of rental housing by 15%. Renters who had an apartment in 1994 benefited but at the expense not just of landlords but of future renters who had to pay higher prices in the market sector.[13] Thus, the long-run supply curve is much more elastic than the short-run supply curve, and the shortage grows over time from the short-run shortage to the long-run shortage.

FIGURE 8.8

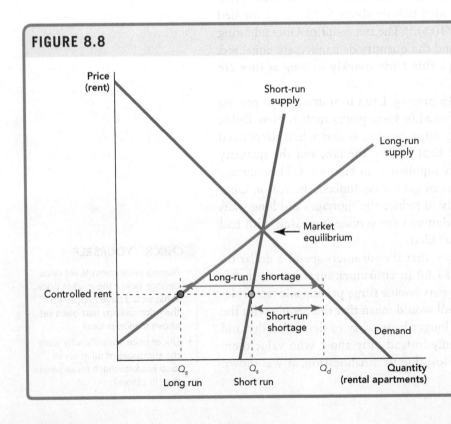

Rent Control Creates Larger Shortages in the Long Run Than in the Short Run A rent control below the equilibrium price generates a shortage. The short-run shortage is small since the apartment units are already built. In the long run, fewer new units are built and old apartments are torn down or turned into condominiums so the long-run shortage is much greater.

Although old apartment buildings can't disappear overnight, future apartment buildings can. Developers look for profits over a 30-year or longer time frame, so even a modest rent control can sharply reduce the value of new apartment construction.

Reductions in Product Quality

Rent controls also reduce housing quality, especially the quality of low-end apartments. When the price of apartments is forced down, owners attempt to stave off losses by cutting their costs. With rent controls, for example, owners mow the lawns less often, replace lightbulbs more slowly, and don't fix the elevators so quickly. When the controls are strong, cheap but serviceable apartment buildings turn into slums and then slums turn into abandoned and hollowed-out apartment blocks. Rent controls in European countries have tended to be more restrictive than in the United States, leading the economist Assar Lindbeck to remark, "Rent control is the most effective method we know for destroying a city, except for bombing it."[14] Lindbeck, however, was wrong, at least according to Vietnam's foreign minister, who in 1989 said, "The Americans couldn't destroy Hanoi, but we have destroyed our city by very low rents."[15] The same thing has happened in Mumbai, India, where rents were fixed for decades at rates so low that maintenance was unprofitable. The result has been severe deterioration of the housing stock and even the collapse of some apartment buildings.

MRU
https://youtu.be/2fh4tPWYeks

Rent Control in Mumbai

Wasteful Lines, Search Costs, and Lost Gains from Trade

Lines for apartments are not as obvious as for gasoline, but finding an apartment in a city with extensive rent controls usually involves a costly search. New Yorkers have developed a number of tricks to help them, as the character played by Billy Crystal explained in the movie *When Harry Met Sally:*

> What you do is, you read the obituary column. Yeah, you find out who died, and go to the building and then you tip the doorman. What they can do to make it easier is to combine the obituaries with the real estate section. Say, then you'd have "Mr. Klein died today leaving a wife, two children, and a spacious three-bedroom apartment with a wood-burning fireplace."

The search can be especially costly for people who landlords think are not "ideal renters." At the controlled price, landlords have more customers than they have apartments, so they can pick and choose among prospective renters. Landlords prefer to rent to people who are seen as being more likely to pay the rent on time and not cause trouble for other tenants, for example, older, richer couples without children or dogs. Landlords might also discriminate on racial or other grounds. Indeed, a landlord who doesn't like your looks can turn you down and immediately rent to the next person in line. Landlords can discriminate even if there are no rent controls, but without rent

A rent-controlled apartment—furnished

JG Photography/Alamy Stock Photo

controls, the vacancy rate will be higher because the quantity of apartments will be larger and turnover will be more common, so landlords who turn down prospective renters will lose money as they wait for their ideal renter. Rent controls reduce the price of discrimination, so remember the law of demand: When the price of discrimination falls, the quantity of discrimination demanded will increase.

Bribing the landlord or apartment manager to get a rent-controlled apartment is also common. Bribes are illegal but they can be disguised. An apartment might rent for $500 a month but come with $5,000 worth of "furniture." Renters refer to these kinds of tie-in sales as paying "key money," as in the rent is $500 a month but the key costs are extra.

Are Oust studied rent controls in Oslo, Norway and found that during the rent control era it was common for landlords to require their tenants to be of a certain gender, age, occupation, and even religion (which would be illegal in the United States). Landlords would also find ways to charge extra by asking renters for extra services such as child care, garden work, or snow clearing. When rent control was eliminated, however, the number of apartments increased and landlords no longer advertised these kinds of requirements. Perhaps most telling, in the rent-control era it was common for renters to advertise "Apartment Wanted" but when rent controls were lifted it became much more common for landlords to advertise "Apartments for Rent."[16]

The analysis of lost gains from trade from rent controls is exactly the same as we showed in Figure 8.3 for price controls on gasoline. At the quantity supplied under rent control, demanders are willing to pay more for an apartment than sellers would require to rent the apartment. If buyers and sellers were free to trade, they could both be better off, but under rent control, these mutually profitable trades are illegal and the benefits do not occur.

Misallocation of Resources

As with gasoline, apartments under rent control are allocated haphazardly—some people with a high willingness to pay can't buy as much housing as they want, even as others with a low willingness to pay consume more housing than they would purchase at the market rate. The classic example is the older couple who stay in their large rent-controlled apartment even after their children have moved out. It's a great deal for the older couple, but not so good for the young couple with children who as a result are stuck in a cramped apartment with nowhere to go.

Economists can estimate the amount of misallocation by comparing the types of apartments that renters choose in cities like New York, which has had rent controls since they were imposed as a "temporary" measure in World War II, with the types of apartments that people choose in cities like Chicago, which has a free market in rental housing. In one study of this kind, Edward Glaeser and Erzo Luttmer found that as many as 21% of the renters in New York City live in an apartment that has more or fewer rooms than they would choose if they lived in a city without rent controls.[17] This misallocation of resources creates significant waste and hardship.

Rent Regulation

In the 1990s, many American cities with rent control changed policy and began to eliminate or ease rent controls. Some economists refer to these new policies not as rent control but as "rent regulation." A typical rent regulation limits price increases without limiting prices. Price increases, for example, might be limited to, say, 10% per year. Thus, rent regulations can protect tenants from sharp increases in rent, while still allowing prices to rise or fall over several years in response to market forces. Rent regulation laws usually also allow landlords to pass along cost increases so the incentive to cut back on maintenance is reduced. Economists are almost universally opposed to rent controls but some economists think that moderate rent regulation could have some benefits.[18]

Arguments for Price Ceilings

Without price controls on oil in 1973, some people might not have been able to afford to heat their homes. Without rent controls, some people may not be able to afford appropriate housing. It's not obvious that the poor are better off with shortages than with high prices. Nevertheless, *if* price controls were the *only* way to help the poor, then this would be an argument in favor of price controls.

Price controls, however, are never the only way to help the poor and they are rarely the best way. If affordable housing is a concern, for example, then a better policy than rent controls is for the government to provide housing vouchers. Housing vouchers, which are used extensively in the United States, give qualifying consumers a voucher worth, say, $500 a month that can be applied to any unit of housing.[19] Unlike rent controls, which create shortages, vouchers *increase* the supply of housing. Vouchers can also be targeted to consumers who need them, whereas rent controls in New York City have subsidized millionaires.

There are a few other sound arguments for price controls. The best case for price controls is to discipline monopolies. Alas, this explanation does not fit price controls on gasoline, apartments, bread, or almost all of the goods that price controls are routinely placed on. We will look at this special case more extensively in Chapter 13.

One of the primary reasons for price controls may be that the public, unlike economists, does not see the consequences of price controls. People who have not been trained in economics rarely connect lineups with price controls. During the gasoline shortages of the 1970s, probably not one American in ten understood the connection between the controls and the shortage—most consumers blamed big oil companies and rich Arab sheiks.

Universal Price Controls

We have seen that price controls in the United States caused shortages, lineups, delays, quality reductions, misallocations, bureaucracy, and corruption. And the U.S. experience with extensive price controls was short, just a few months for most goods, and a few years for oil and a handful of other goods. What would happen if price controls on all goods remained in place for a lengthy period of time? An economy with permanent, universal price controls is in essence a "command economy," much as existed in the Communist countries

Peter Turnley/Getty Images

In the former Soviet Union, never-ending shortages meant that lining up for hours to get bread, shoes, or other goods was normal.

prior to the fall of the Berlin Wall. In *The Russians*, Hedrick Smith described what it was like for consumers living in the Soviet Union in 1976:[20]

> The list of scarce items is practically endless. They are not permanently out of stock, but their appearance is unpredictable.... Leningrad can be overstocked with cross-country skis and yet go several months without soap for washing dishes. In the Armenian capital of Yerevan, I found an ample supply of accordions but local people complained that they had gone for weeks without ordinary kitchen spoons or tea samovars. I knew a Moscow family that spent a frantic month hunting for a child's potty while radios were a glut on the market....

> The accepted norm is that the Soviet woman daily spends two hours in line, seven days a week.... I have known of people who stood in line 90 minutes to buy four pineapples ... three and a half hours to buy three large heads of cabbage only to find the cabbages were gone as they approached the front of the line, 18 hours to sign up to purchase a rug at some later date, all through a freezing December night to register on a list for buying a car, and then waiting 18 months for actual delivery, and terribly lucky at that.

The never-ending shortage of goods in the former Soviet Union suggests another reason why price controls are not eliminated even when doing so would make most people better off. Shortages were beneficial to the very same party elite who controlled prices. With all goods in permanent shortage, how did anyone in the Soviet Union obtain goods? By using *blat*. *Blat* is a Russian word meaning one has connections that can be used to get favors. As Hedrick Smith put it:

> In an economy of chronic shortages and carefully parceled-out privileges, blat is an essential lubricant of life. The more rank and power one has, the more blat one normally has ... each has access to things or services that are hard to get and that other people want or need.

Consider the manager of a small factory that produces radios. Music may be the food that feeds people's souls but the manager would also like some beef. Shortages mean that the manager's salary is almost useless in helping them to obtain beef but what do they have of value? They have access to radios. If the manager can find a worker in a beef factory who loves music, they will have *blat*, a connection and something to trade. Even if they can't find someone with the exact opposite wants as they have, access to radios gives the manager power because people will want to do favors for them. But notice that the manager of the radio factory has *blat* only because of a shortage of radios. If radios were easily available at the market price, then the manager's access would no longer be of special value. The manager of the radio factory wants low prices because then they can legally buy radios at the official price and use them to obtain goods that they want. Ironically, the managers and producers of beef, purses, and televisions all want shortages of their own good even though all would benefit if the shortages of all goods were eliminated.

Blat is a Russian word but it's a worldwide phenomena. Even in the United States, where by world standards corruption is low, *blat* happens. During the 1973–1974 oil crisis, for example, when the Federal Energy Office controlled the allocation of oil, it quickly became obvious that the way to get more oil was to use *blat*. Firms began to hire former politicians and bureaucrats who used their connections to help the firms get more oil. Today, the *blat* economy is much larger—over half of all federal politicians who leave office for the private sector become lobbyists.

Price Floors

When governments control prices, it is usually with a price ceiling designed to keep prices below market levels, but occasionally the government intervenes to keep prices above market levels. Can you think of an example? Here's a hint. Buyers usually outnumber sellers, so it's probably no accident that governments intervene to keep prices below market levels more often than they intervene to keep prices above market levels. The most common example of a price being controlled above market levels is the exception that proves the rule because it involves a good for which sellers outnumber buyers. Here's another hint. You own this good.

The good is labor, and the most common example of a price that is controlled above the market level is the minimum wage.

When the minimum price that can be legally charged is above the market price, we say that there is a **price floor**. Economists call it a price floor because prices cannot legally go below the floor. Price floors create four important effects:

A **price floor** is a minimum price allowed by law.

1. Surpluses
2. Lost gains from trade (deadweight loss)
3. Wasteful increases in quality
4. A misallocation of resources

Surpluses

Figure 8.9 graphs the demand and supply of labor and shows how a price held above the market price creates a surplus, a situation in which the quantity of

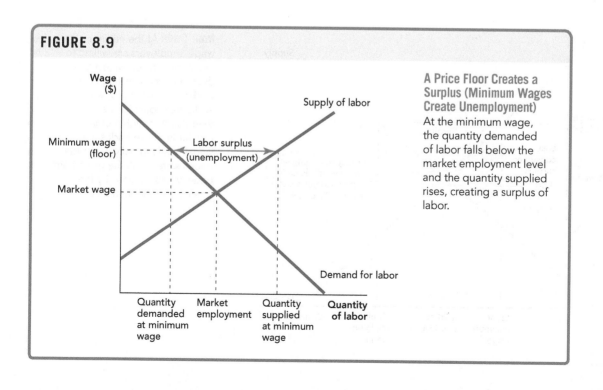

FIGURE 8.9

A Price Floor Creates a Surplus (Minimum Wages Create Unemployment) At the minimum wage, the quantity demanded of labor falls below the market employment level and the quantity supplied rises, creating a surplus of labor.

labor supplied exceeds the quantity demanded. We have a special word for a surplus of labor: unemployment.

The idea that a minimum wage creates unemployment should not be surprising. If the minimum wage did not create unemployment, the solution to poverty would be easy—raise minimum wages to $10, $20, or even $100 an hour! But at a high enough wage, none of us would be worth employing.

Can a more moderate minimum wage also create unemployment? Yes. A minimum wage of $7.25 an hour, the federal minimum in 2022, won't affect most workers who, because of their productivity, already earn more than $7.25 an hour. In the United States, for example, more than 95% of all workers paid by the hour already earn more than the minimum wage. A minimum wage, however, will decrease employment among low-skilled workers. The more employers have to pay for low-skilled workers, the fewer low-skilled workers they will hire.

Young people, for example, often lack substantial skills and are more likely to be made unemployed by the minimum wage. About 20 percent of all workers earning the minimum wage are teenagers (ages 16–19) and about half are less than 25 years of age.[21] Studies of the minimum wage verify that the unemployment effect is concentrated among teenagers.[22]

In addition to creating surpluses, a price floor, just like a price ceiling, reduces the gains from trade.

Lost Gains from Trade (Deadweight Loss)

Notice in Figure 8.10 that at the minimum wage employers are willing to hire Q_d workers. Employers would hire more workers if they could offer lower wages and, importantly, workers would be willing to work at lower wages if they were allowed to do so. If employers and workers could bargain freely, the

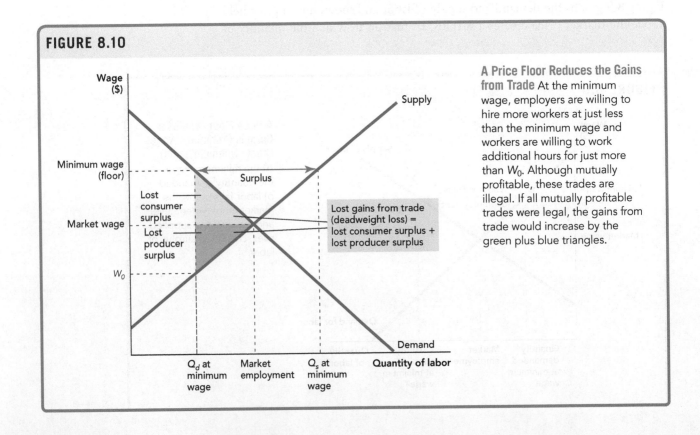

FIGURE 8.10

A Price Floor Reduces the Gains from Trade At the minimum wage, employers are willing to hire more workers at just less than the minimum wage and workers are willing to work additional hours for just more than W_0. Although mutually profitable, these trades are illegal. If all mutually profitable trades were legal, the gains from trade would increase by the green plus blue triangles.

wage would fall and the quantity of labor traded would increase to the level of market employment. Notice that at the market employment level, the gains from trade increase by the green and blue triangles. The green triangle is the increase in consumer surplus (remember that in this example it is the employers who are the consumers of labor) and the blue triangle is the increase in producer (worker) surplus. Since the minimum wage prevents employment from reaching the market employment level, there is a loss of consumer and producer surplus.

Should the minimum wage be called the "Robot Employment Act"?

Although the minimum wage creates some unemployment and reduces the gains from trade, the influence of the minimum wage in the American economy is very small. Even for the young, the minimum wage is not very important because although most workers earning the minimum wage are young, most young workers earn more than the minimum wage. As noted, about half of the workers earning the minimum wage are younger than 25 years old but more than 90% of workers younger than 25 earn more than the minimum wage.[23]

These facts may surprise you. The minimum wage is hotly debated in the United States. Democrats often argue that the minimum wage must be raised to help working families. Republicans respond that a higher minimum wage will create unemployment and raise prices as firms pass on higher costs to customers. Neither position is realistic. At best, the minimum wage will raise the wages of some teenagers and young workers whose wages would increase anyway as they improve their education and become more skilled. At worst, the minimum wage will raise the price of a hamburger and create unemployment among teenagers, many of whom will simply choose to stay in school longer (not necessarily a bad thing). The minimum wage debate is more about rhetoric than reality.

Even though small increases in the U.S. minimum wage won't change much, large increases would cause serious unemployment.

Keep in mind that there are substitutes for minimum wage workers. Higher minimum wages, for example, increase the incentive to move production to other cities, states, or countries where wages are lower. The United States imports lots of fruits and vegetables because it is cheaper to produce these abroad and ship them to the United States than it is to produce them here. Many minimum wage jobs are service jobs that cannot be moved abroad but firms can substitute capital—in the form of machines—for labor. If the minimum wage were to increase substantially, we might even see robots flipping burgers.[24]

To explain the other important effects of price floors—wasteful increases in quality and a misallocation of resources—we turn from minimum wages to airline regulation.

Wasteful Increases in Quality

Many years ago, flying on an airplane was pleasurable; seats were wide, service was attentive, flights weren't packed, and the food was good. So airplane travel in the United States must have gotten worse, right? No, it has gotten better. Let's explain.

The Civil Aeronautics Board (CAB) extensively regulated airlines in the United States from 1938 to 1978. No firm could enter or exit the market, change prices, or alter routes without permission from the CAB. The CAB kept prices well above market levels, sometimes even denying requests by firms to lower prices!

We know that prices were kept above market levels because the CAB only had the right to control airlines operating *between* states. In-state airlines were largely unregulated. Using data from large states like Texas and California, it was possible to compare prices on unregulated flights to prices on regulated flights of the same distance. Prices on flights between San Francisco and Los Angeles, for example, were half the price of similar-length flights between Boston and Washington, D.C.

In Figure 8.11, firms are earning the CAB-regulated fare on flights that they would be willing to sell at the much lower price labeled "Willingness to sell." Initially, therefore, regulation was a great deal for the airlines, who took home the red area as producer surplus.

A price floor means that prices are held *above* market levels, so firms want more customers. The price floor, however, makes it illegal to compete for more customers by lowering prices. So how do firms compete when they cannot lower prices? Price floors cause firms to compete by offering customers higher quality.

When airlines were regulated, for example, they competed by offering their customers bone china, fancy meals, wide seats, and frequent flights. Sounds good, right? Yes, but don't forget that the increase in quality came at a price. Would you rather have a fine meal on your flight to Paris or a modest meal and more money to spend at a real Parisian restaurant?

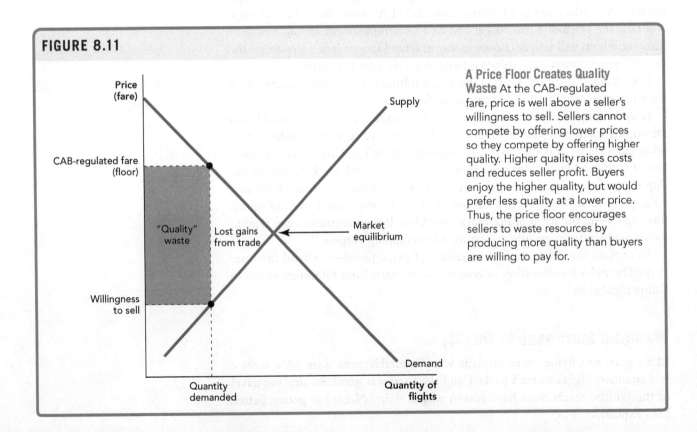

FIGURE 8.11

A Price Floor Creates Quality Waste At the CAB-regulated fare, price is well above a seller's willingness to sell. Sellers cannot compete by offering lower prices so they compete by offering higher quality. Higher quality raises costs and reduces seller profit. Buyers enjoy the higher quality, but would prefer less quality at a lower price. Thus, the price floor encourages sellers to waste resources by producing more quality than buyers are willing to pay for.

If consumers were willing to pay for fine meals on an airplane, airlines would offer that service. But if you have flown recently, you know that consumers would rather have a lower price. An increase in quality that consumers are not willing to pay for is a wasteful increase in quality. Thus, as firms competed by offering higher quality, the initial producer surplus was wasted away in frills that consumers liked but would not be willing to pay for—hence, the red area in Figure 8.11 is labeled "'Quality' waste."

Airline costs increased over time for another reason. The producer surplus initially earned by the airlines was a tempting target for unions who threatened to strike unless they got their share of the proceeds. The airlines didn't put up too much of a fight because, when their costs rose, they could apply to the CAB for

Despite being more efficient than its rivals, airline regulation prevented Southwest from entering the national market until deregulation in 1978. Today, Southwest Airlines is one of the largest airlines in the world.

an increase in fares, thus passing along the higher costs to consumers. Many of the problems that older airlines have faced in recent times are due to generous pension and health benefits they are paying out, benefits that were granted when prices of flights were regulated above market levels.

By 1978, costs had increased so much that the airlines were no longer benefiting from regulation and were willing to accede to deregulation.[25] Deregulation lowered prices, increased quantity, and reduced wasteful quality competition.[26] Deregulation also reduced waste and increased efficiency in another way—by improving the allocation of resources.

The Misallocation of Resources

Regulation of airline fares could not have been maintained for 40 years if the CAB had not also regulated entry. Firms wanted to enter the airline industry because the CAB kept prices high, but the CAB knew that if entry occurred, prices would be pushed down. So under the influence of the older airlines, the CAB routinely prevented new competitors from entering. In 1938, for example, there were 16 major airlines; by 1974, there were just 10 despite 79 requests to enter the industry.

Restrictions on entry misallocated resources because low-cost airlines were kept out of the industry. Southwest Airlines, for example, began as a Texas-only airline because it could not get a license from the CAB to operate between states. (Lawsuits from competitors also nearly prevented Southwest from operating in Texas.) Southwest was able to enter the national market only after deregulation in 1978.

The entry of Southwest was not just a case of increasing supply. One of the virtues of the market process is that it is open to new ideas, innovations, and experiments. Southwest, for example, pioneered consistent use of the same aircraft to lower maintenance costs, greater use of smaller airports like Chicago's Midway, and long-term hedging of fuel costs. Southwest's innovations have made it one of the most profitable and largest airlines in the United States. Southwest's innovations have spread, in turn, to other firms such as JetBlue Airways, easyJet (Europe), and WestJet (Canada). Regulation of entry didn't just increase prices; it increased costs and reduced innovation. Deregulation improved the allocation of resources by allowing low-cost,

CHECK YOURSELF

- The European Union guarantees its farmers that the price of butter will stay above a floor. The floor price is often above the market equilibrium price. What do you think has been the result of this?
- The United States has set a price floor for milk above the equilibrium price. Has this led to shortages or surpluses? How do you think the U.S. government has dealt with this? (*Hint:* Remember the cartons of milk you had in elementary school and high school? What was their price?)

innovative firms to expand nationally. Deregulation is the major reason why, today, flying is an ordinary event for most American families, rather than the province of the wealthy.

Takeaway

Price ceilings have several important effects: They create shortages, reductions in quality, wasteful lines and other search costs, a loss of gains from trade, and a misallocation of resources.

After reading this chapter, you should be able to explain all of these effects to your uncle. Also, to do well on the exam, you should be able to draw a diagram showing the price ceiling and correctly labeling the shortage. On the same diagram, can you locate the wasteful losses from waiting in line and the lost gains from trade? Review Figures 8.2 and 8.3 if you are having trouble with these questions. You should also understand why a price ceiling reduces product quality and how price ceilings misallocate resources, not just in the market with the price ceiling but potentially throughout the economy.

Price floors create surpluses, a loss of gains from trade, wasteful increases in quality, and a misallocation of resources.

After reading this chapter, you should be able to explain all of these effects to your aunt. Can you show, using the tools of supply and demand, why a price floor creates a surplus, a deadweight loss, and a wasteful increase in quality? You should be able to label these areas on a diagram. You should also be able to explain how price floors cause resources to be misallocated.

CHAPTER REVIEW

Go online to practice with more examples of these types of problems, including live links to videos, data sources, and feedback.

KEY CONCEPTS

price ceiling, p. 137

deadweight loss, p. 142

rent control, p. 148

price floor, p. 153

FACTS AND TOOLS

1. How does a free market eliminate a shortage?

2. When a price ceiling is in place keeping the price below the market price, what's larger: quantity demanded or quantity supplied? How does this explain the long lines and wasteful searches we see in price-controlled markets?

3. Suppose that the quantity demanded and quantity supplied in the market for milk is as follows:

Price per Gallon	Quantity Demanded	Quantity Supplied
$5	1,000	5,000
$4	2,000	4,500
$3	3,500	3,500
$2	4,100	2,000
$1	6,000	1,000

a. What is the equilibrium price and quantity of milk?

b. If the government places a price ceiling of $2 on milk, will there be a shortage or a surplus of milk? How large will it be? How many gallons of milk will be sold?

4. If a government decides to make health insurance affordable by requiring all health insurance companies to cut their prices by 30%, what will probably happen to the number of people covered by health insurance?

5. The Canadian government has wage controls for medical doctors. To keep things simple, let's assume that they set one wage for all doctors: $100,000 per year. It takes about 6 years to become a general practitioner or a pediatrician, but it takes about 8 or 9 years to become a specialist like a gynecologist, surgeon, or ophthalmologist. What kind of doctor would you want to become under this system? (*Note:* The actual Canadian system does allow specialists to earn a bit more than general practitioners, but the difference isn't big enough to matter.)

6. Between April 2020 and May 2022, the price of oil increased from $22 per barrel to $116 per barrel, and the price of gasoline in the United States rose from about $1.90 per gallon to nearly $5.00 per gallon. However, unlike in the 1970s, when oil prices spiked, there were no long lines outside gas stations in 2022. Why?

7. Price controls distribute resources in many unintended ways. In the following cases, who will probably spend more time waiting in line to get scarce, price-controlled goods? Choose one from each pair:

   a. Working people or retired people?

   b. Lawyers who charge $800 per hour or fast-food employees who earn $8 per hour?

   c. People with desk jobs or people who can disappear for a couple of hours during the day?

8. In the chapter, we discussed how price ceilings can put goods in the wrong *place*, as when too little heating oil wound up in New Jersey during a harsh winter in the 1970s. Price controls can also put goods in the wrong *time* as well. If there are price controls on gasoline, can you think of some periods during which the shortage will get worse? (*Hint:* Gas prices typically rise during the busy Memorial Day and Labor Day weekends.)

9. a. Consider Figure 8.8. In a price-controlled market like this one, when will consumer surplus be larger: in the short run or in the long run?

   b. In this market, supply is more elastic, more flexible, in the long run. In other words, in the longer term, landlords and home builders can find something else to do for a living. In light of this and in light of the geometry of producer surplus in this figure, do rent controls hurt landlords and home builders more in the short run or in the long run?

10. Business leaders often say that there is a "shortage" of skilled workers, and so they argue that immigrants need to be brought in to do these jobs. For example, a recent article was titled "Michigan leans on migrant workers amid labor shortage" and went on to point out that special U.S. visa programs, the H-2A and H-2B programs, "partially fill the gap with workers from other countries." (*Source:* Moore, Lindsay, and Barrett, Malachi. September 27, 2021. Michigan leans on migrant workers amid labor shortage. *Michigan Live.*)

    a. How do unregulated markets cure a "labor shortage" when there are no immigrants to boost the labor supply?

    b. Why don't businesses want to let unregulated markets cure the shortage?

11. a. If the government forced all bread manufacturers to sell their products at a "fair price" that was half the current, free-market price, what would happen to the quantity supplied of bread?

    b. To keep it simple, assume that people must wait in line to get bread at the controlled price. Would consumer surplus rise, fall, or can't you tell with the information given?

    c. With these price controls on bread, would you expect bread *quality* to rise or fall?

12. A review of the jargon: Is the minimum wage a "price ceiling" or a "price floor"? What about rent control?

13. How do U.S. business owners change their behavior when the minimum wage rises? How does this impact teenagers?

14. The basic idea of deadweight loss is that a willing buyer and a willing seller can't find a way to make an exchange. In the case of the minimum wage law, the reason they can't make an exchange is because it's illegal for the buyer (the firm) to hire the seller (the worker) at any wage below the legal minimum. But how can this really be a "loss" from the worker's point of view? It's obvious why business owners would love to hire workers for less than the minimum wage, but if all companies obey the minimum wage law, why are some workers still willing to work for less than that?

Discovering DATA

15. Go to the FRED economic database (https://fred.stlouisfed.org/) and search for "percent hourly paid minimum wage."

    a. In 2021, what percent of hourly workers were paid the minimum wage or less?

    b. Hourly wage workers are about three-fifths of total workers (the remainder work on salary). Almost all salaried workers earn above the minimum wage. So what percent of all workers earn the minimum wage or less?

THINKING AND PROBLEM SOLVING

16. In rich countries, governments almost always set the fares for taxi rides. The prices for taxi rides are the same in safe neighborhoods and in dangerous neighborhoods. Where is it easier to find a cab? Why? If these taxi price controls were ended, what would probably happen to the price and quantity of cab rides in dangerous neighborhoods? (*Aside:* How do you think ride-sharing apps like Uber and Lyft have affected this problem?)

17. When the United States had price controls on oil and gasoline, some parts of the United States had a lot of heating oil, while other states had long lines. As in the chapter, let's assume that winter oil demand is higher in New Jersey than in California. If there had been no price controls, what would have happened to the prices of heating oil in New Jersey and in California and how would "greedy businesspeople" have responded to these price differences?

18. On January 31, 1990, the first McDonald's opened in Moscow, capital of the then Soviet Union. Economists often described the Soviet Union as a "permanent shortage economy," where the government kept prices permanently low in order to appear "fair."

    An American journalist on the scene reported the customers seemed most amazed at the "simple sight of polite shop workers . . . in this nation of commercial boorishness."

    a. Why were most Soviet shop workers "boorish" when the McDonald's workers in Moscow were "polite"?

    b. What does your answer to the previous question tell you about the power of economic incentives to change human behavior? In other words, how entrenched is "culture"?

19. Let's calculate the value of lost gains from trade in a regulated market. The government decides it wants to make basic bicycles more affordable, so it passes a law requiring that all one-speed bicycles sell for $30, well below the market price. Use the following data to calculate the lost gains from trade, just as in Figure 8.3. Supply and demand are straight lines.

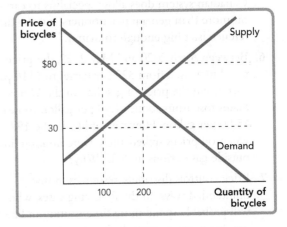

    a. What is the total value of wasted time in the price-controlled market?

    b. What is the value of the *lost gains from trade* resulting from the price ceiling?

    c. Note that we haven't given you the original market price of simple bicycles—why don't you need to know it? (*Hint:* The answer is a mix of geometry and economics.)

20. During a crisis such as Hurricane Dorian governments often make it illegal to raise the price of emergency items like flashlights and bottled water. In practice, this means that these items get sold on a first-come/first-served basis.

    a. If a person has a flashlight that she values at $5 and another person would be willing to pay $40 for the flashlight on the black market, what gains from trade are lost if the government shuts down the black market?

    b. Why might a person want to sell a flashlight for $40 during an emergency?

    c. Why might a person be willing to pay $40 for a flashlight during an emergency?

d. When will entrepreneurs be more likely to fill up their pickup trucks with flashlights and drive into a disaster area: when they can sell their flashlights for $5 each or when they can sell them for $40 each?

21. A "black market" is a place where people make illegal trades in goods and services. For instance, in Cuba, it is common for travelers to return home with clothing, electronics, and other items that they then sell at high prices on the illegal black market, while government workers may steal items from work that they can use to produce goods valued in the illegal markets.

Consider the following claim: "Price-controlled markets tend to create black markets." Let's illustrate with the following figure. If there is a price ceiling in the market for cancer medication of $50 per pill, what is the *widest* black market price range within which you can *definitely* find both a buyer and a seller who would be willing to illegally exchange a pill for money? (There is only one correct answer.)

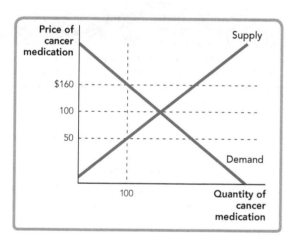

22. So, knowing what you know now about price controls, are you in favor of setting a $2 per gallon price ceiling on gasoline? Create a pro–price control and an anti–price control answer.

23. a. As we noted, Assar Lindbeck once said that short of aerial bombardment, rent control is the best way to destroy a city. What do you think Lindbeck might mean by this?

b. How does paying "key money" to a landlord reduce the severity of Lindbeck's "bombardment"?

24. In the town of Freedonia, the government declares that all street parking must be free: There can be no parking meters. In an almost identical town of Meterville, parking costs $5 per hour (or $1.25 per 15 minutes).

a. Where will it be easier to find parking: in Freedonia or Meterville?

b. One town will tend to attract shoppers who hate driving around looking for parking. Which one?

c. Why will the town from part b also attract shoppers with higher incomes?

25. In the late 1990s, the town of Santa Monica, California, made it illegal for banks to charge people ATM fees. As you probably know, it's almost always free to use your own bank's ATMs, but there's usually a fee charged when you use another bank's ATM. (*Source:* The war on ATM fees, *Time*, November 29, 1999.) As soon as Santa Monica passed this law, Bank of America stopped allowing customers from other banks to use their ATMs: In bank jargon, Bank of America banned "out-of-network" ATM usage.

In fact, this ban lasted for only a few days, after which a judge allowed banks to continue to charge fees while awaiting a full court hearing on the issue. Eventually, the court declared the fee ban illegal under federal law. But let's imagine the effect of a full ban on out-of-network fees.

a. In the figure, indicate the new price per out-of-network ATM transaction after the fee ban. Also clearly label the shortage.

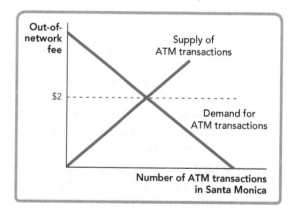

b. Calculate the exact amount of producer and consumer surplus in the out-of-network ATM market in Santa Monica after the ban. How large is producer surplus? How large is consumer surplus?

26. Rent control creates a shortage of housing, which makes it hard to find a place to live. In a price-controlled market, people have to waste a lot of time trying to find these scarce, artificially cheap products. Yet Congressman Charles B. Rangel, the chairman of the powerful House Ways and Means Committee, lived in *four* rent-stabilized apartments in Harlem (one of which he illegally used as his campaign headquarters). Why are powerful individuals often able to "find" price-controlled goods much more often than the nonpowerful? What does this tell us about the political side effects of price controls? (*Information from:* Republicans question Rangel's tax break support, *New York Times,* November 25, 2008.)

27. In the 1970s, AirCal and Pacific Southwest Airlines flew only within California. As we mentioned, the federal price floors didn't apply to flights within just one state. A major route for these airlines was flying from San Francisco to Los Angeles, a distance of 350 miles. This is about the same distance as from Chicago, Illinois, to Cleveland, Ohio. Do you think AirCal flights had nicer meals than flights from Chicago to Cleveland? Why or why not?

28. President Jimmy Carter didn't just deregulate airline prices. He also deregulated much of the trucking industry as well. Trucks carry almost all of the consumer goods that you purchase, so almost every time you purchase something, you're paying money to a trucking company.

   a. Based on what happened in the airline industry after prices were deregulated, what do you think happened in the trucking industry after deregulation? You can find some answers here: https://www.econlib .org/library/Enc/TruckingDeregulation.html. For another look that is critical of trucking deregulation but comes to basically the same answers, see Michael Belzer, 2000. *Sweatshops on Wheels: Winners and Losers in Trucking Deregulation.* Thousand Oaks, CA: Sage.

   b. Who do you think asked Congress and the president to keep price floors for trucking: consumer groups, retail shops like Walmart, or the trucking companies?

29. Suppose you're doing some history research on shoe production in ancient Rome, during the reign of the famous Emperor Diocletian. Your documents tell you how many shoes were produced each year in the Roman Empire, but they don't tell you the price of shoes. You find a document stating that in the year 301, Emperor Diocletian issued an "edict on prices," but you don't know whether he imposed price *ceilings* or

price *floors*—your Latin is a little rusty. However, you can clearly tell from the documents that the number of shoes actually exchanged in markets fell dramatically, and that both potential shoe sellers and potential shoe buyers were unhappy with the edict. With the information given, can you tell whether Diocletian imposed a ceiling or a floor? If so, which is it? (Yes, there really was an edict of Diocletian, and Wikipedia has excellent coverage of ancient Roman history.)

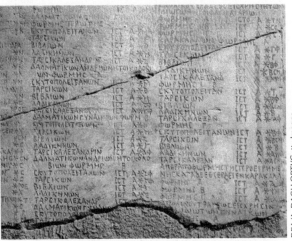

Emperor Diocletian issued an Edict on Maximum Prices in the year 301 in an effort to control inflation. As usual, the edict created shortages, disruptions in trade, and a black market. Copia et demanda legi parendum.

30. In the market depicted in the figure, there is either a price ceiling or a price floor—surprisingly, it doesn't matter which one it is: Whether it's an $80 price floor or a $30 price ceiling, the chart looks the same.

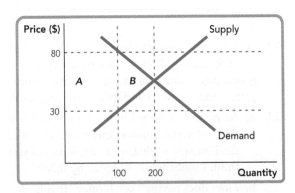

In the chart, there's a rectangle and a triangle. One represents the value lost from "deals that don't get made" and one represents the value wasted in "deals that do get made." Which is which?

31. We noted that in the 1970s price floors on airline tickets caused wasteful increases in the quality of airline trips. Does the minimum wage cause wasteful increases in the quality of workers? If so, how? In other words, how are minimum-wage workers like airplane trips?

32. The city of Mumbai in India imposed rent controls on apartments in 1947. Despite inflation and changes in land value, allowable rents have hardly increased since that time (although there have been some recent attempts at market reform with the 2021 Model Tenant Act)! Use what you know about rent controls to speculate about the quality of rent-controlled buildings in Mumbai.

CHALLENGES

33. a. If a government decided to impose price controls on gasoline, what could it do to avoid the time wasted waiting in lines? There is surely more than one solution to this problem.

  b. Does part a have any parallels to the markets for toilet paper, disinfectant wipes, and hand sanitizer that occurred at the beginning of the COVID-19 pandemic?

34. In New York City, some apartments are under strict rent control, while others are not. This is a theme in many novels, television shows, and movies about New York, including *Bonfire of the Vanities, Sex and the City*, and *When Harry Met Sally*. One predictable side effect of rent control is the creation of a black market. Let's think about whether it's a good idea to allow this black market to exist.

  a. Harry is lucky enough to get a rent-controlled apartment for $300 per month. The market rent on such an apartment is $3,000 per month. Harry himself values the apartment at $2,000 per month, and he'd be equally happy with a regular $2,000-per-month New York apartment. If he stays in the apartment, how much consumer surplus does he enjoy?

  b. If he illegally subleases his apartment to Sally on the black market for $2,500 per month and instead rents a $2,000 apartment, is he better off or worse off than if he obeyed the law?

35. Let's measure consumer surplus if the government imposes price controls and goods ended up being randomly allocated among those consumers willing to pay the controlled price. If the demand and supply curves are as in the figure, then:

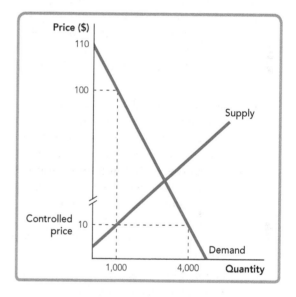

  a. What is consumer surplus under the price control?

  b. Now suppose that consumers who are not allocated the good are allowed to purchase the good from those who do receive the good. Which consumers will ultimately end up with the good in this situation? What will the price for the good be in the secondary market? How much profit will the secondary sellers earn? (For simplicity, assume that all of the goods are originally allocated to consumers who value the good for less than $100.)

36. Antibiotics are often given to people with colds (even though they are not useful for that purpose), but they are also used to treat life-threatening infections. If there was a price control on antibiotics, what do you think would happen to the allocation of antibiotics across these two uses?

37. In a command economy, such as North Korea, there are no prices for almost all goods. Instead, goods are allocated by a central planner. Suppose that a good like oil becomes more scarce. What problems would a central planner face in reallocating oil to maximize consumer plus producer surplus?

38. Labor unions are some of the strongest proponents of the minimum wage. Yet in 2021, the median full-time union member earned $1,169 per week, an average of over $29 per hour (https://www.afscme.org/blog/afscme-president-union-membership-report-proves-the-union-difference-in-pay). Therefore, a rise in the minimum wage doesn't directly raise the wage of many union workers. So why do unions support minimum-wage laws? Surely, there's more than one reason why this is so, but let's see if economic theory can shed some light on the subject.

   a. Skilled and unskilled labor are substitutes: For example, imagine that you can hire four low-skilled workers to move dirt with shovels at $7 an hour, or you can hire one skilled worker at $30 an hour to move the same amount of dirt with a skid loader. Using the tools developed in Chapter 3, what will happen to the demand for skilled labor if the price of unskilled labor increases to $10 per hour?

   b. If the minimum wage rises, will that increase or decrease the demand for the average union worker's labor? Why?

   c. Now, let's put the pieces together: Why might high-wage labor unions support an increase in the minimum wage?

39. In our Uber example, we said that after a spike in demand around Madison Square Garden, the number of Uber rides increased by more than 75% in the surrounding area, but when it starts to rain, Uber rides increase by the still substantial but lesser amount of 22%. Can you suggest one reason why the supply response is different in the two situations? (*Hint:* Think about the determinants of supply elasticity.)

40. In the market for kidneys, people are only allowed to donate kidneys to those in need of a transplant. They are not allowed to receive payments. How can this example be put into the language from this chapter? Given this, what do you expect to observe in the kidney market?

41. NFTs, or non-fungible tokens, are digital artworks sold on a blockchain that indicate membership in a club. In order to generate excitement, the sellers of NFTs sometimes offer them on a first-come/first-served basis at a price *below* the expected market price. For example, an NFT might be priced at 0.1 ETH (ETH is the Ethereum currency) when its market price was likely to be 0.4 ETH. What would you predict are some of the consequences of this policy? How much do you expect buyers will end up paying for their NFTs?

WORK IT OUT

For interactive, step-by-step help in solving this problem, go online.

Suppose that the market for coats can be described as follows:

Price	Quantity Demanded (millions)	Quantity Supplied (millions)
$120	16	20
$100	18	18
$80	20	16
$60	22	14

   a. What are the equilibrium price and quantity of coats?

   b. Suppose the government sets a price ceiling of $80. Will there be a shortage, and if so, how large will it be?

   c. Given that the government sets a price ceiling of $80, how much will demanders be willing to pay per unit of the good (i.e., what is the true price)? Suppose that people line up to get this good and that they value their time at $10 an hour. For how long will people wait in line to obtain a coat?

9

International Trade

International trade increased rapidly in the century before World War I. Tariffs and trade barriers fell throughout much of the nineteenth century and it was even possible to move about large parts of the world without a passport. The first era of globalization, however, ended with World War I, which brought passport requirements and numerous tariffs, quotas, and other barriers to international trade. After World War I, not much was done to bring the world back together, and with the coming of the Great Depression and then World War II, protectionism grew stronger yet.

After World War II, however, a commitment was made among most of the leading nations of the world to reduce barriers to international trade. In 1947 the second era of globalization began when 23 nations signed the General Agreement on Tariffs and Trade (GATT). The goal of the GATT was not only to increase trade but also to bring former enemies together in peaceful cooperation. As one prominent supporter of GATT put it,

> *When goods don't cross borders, armies will.*

In recognition of this goal, Germany and Japan joined the GATT shortly after the initial signatories. Under GATT tariffs fell and trade increased. By the beginning of the twenty-first century, the average level of tariffs among the United States, the European Union, and Japan was under 5%. Despite occasional skirmishes, trade policy was mostly handled through international agreements and the World Trade Organization, and those institutions helped keep tariff and other trade barriers low.

The expansion of world trade was especially beneficial to China and other developing nations, which were able to lift billions of people out of poverty, in part by increasing manufacturing exports to the developed world. Globalization, however, was not without its critics. Low- to medium-skilled jobs in the U.S. manufacturing sector came under pressure, not only from exporting countries such as China, but also from technology, as many American factory jobs were automated. Those pressures became politically influential in the United States with the inauguration of President Donald Trump.

In early 2018, President Trump imposed big new tariffs on washing machines from abroad. By the end of the year, tariffs had increased on over 12,000 products covering $303 billion of U.S. imports, mostly from China but also including Scotch whisky, Irish butter, French wine, and Canadian steel.[1] The Trump tariffs were the largest increase in U.S. tariffs since the 1930 Smoot-Hawley Act

CHAPTER OUTLINE

Analyzing Trade with Supply and Demand

The Costs of Protectionism

International Trade and Jobs

The Washing Machine Tariffs

The Economics and Politics of a Trade War

The U.S. Politics of Protectionism

Arguments Against International Trade

Takeaway

and they started a trade war with China, which soon retaliated with tariffs of its own.

In this chapter, we will explain how to analyze tariffs and other forms of protectionism using the tools of supply and demand. We will discuss who wins and who loses from international trade, and we will discuss how the economic consequences of trade can drive the politics of trade. We will then return to the Trump tariffs and look in more detail at what happened in the market for washing machines and then more generally we will look at the consequences of the trade war on the United States and world economy.

Analyzing Trade with Supply and Demand

Let's look at trade—and trade restrictions—using tools that you are already familiar with: demand and supply.

Figure 9.1 shows a domestic demand curve and a domestic supply curve for semiconductors. If there were no international trade, the equilibrium would be, as usual, at $P^{\text{No trade}}$, $Q^{\text{No trade}}$. Suppose, however, that this good can also be bought in the world market at the world price. To simplify our diagram, we will assume that the U.S. market is small relative to the world market, so U.S. demanders can buy as many semiconductors as they want without pushing up the world price. In terms of our diagram, the world supply curve is flat (perfectly elastic) at the world price. Later in the chapter we will discuss the results, which are similar, when this assumption does not hold.

Given that U.S. consumers can buy as many semiconductors as they want at the world price, how many will they buy? As usual, we read the quantity demanded off the domestic demand curve so at the world price, U.S. consumers will demand $Q_d^{\text{Free trade}}$ semiconductors. How many semiconductors will

---

FIGURE 9.1

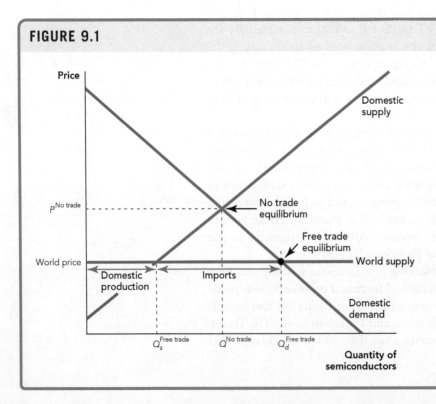

International Trade Using Demand and Supply If there were no international trade, the equilibrium would be found, as usual, at the intersection of the domestic demand and domestic supply curves at $P^{\text{No trade}}$ and $Q^{\text{No trade}}$. With trade, U.S. consumers can buy as many semiconductors as they want at the world price, and at this price U.S. consumers demand $Q_d^{\text{Free trade}}$ units. At the world price, the difference between domestic demand, $Q_d^{\text{Free trade}}$, and domestic supply, $Q_s^{\text{Free trade}}$, is made up by imports.

be supplied by *domestic* suppliers? As usual, we read the quantity supplied off the domestic supply curve so domestic suppliers will supply $Q_s^{\text{Free trade}}$ units. Notice that $Q_d^{\text{Free trade}} > Q_s^{\text{Free trade}}$, so where does the difference come from? From imports. In other words, with international trade, domestic consumption is $Q_d^{\text{Free trade}}$ units; $Q_s^{\text{Free trade}}$ of these units are produced domestically and the remainder, $Q_d^{\text{Free trade}} - Q_s^{\text{Free trade}}$, are imported.

Analyzing Tariffs with Demand and Supply

Many countries, including the United States, restrict international trade with tariffs, quotas, or other regulations that burden foreign producers but not domestic producers—this is called **protectionism.** A **tariff** is simply a tax on imports. A **trade quota** is a restriction on the quantity of foreign goods that can be imported: Imports greater than the quota amount are forbidden or heavily taxed.

Figure 9.2 shows how to analyze a tariff. The figure looks imposing but it's really the same as Figure 9.1 except that now we analyze domestic consumption, production, and imports before and after the tariff. Before the tariff, the situation is exactly as in Figure 9.1: $Q_d^{\text{Free trade}}$ units are demanded, $Q_s^{\text{Free trade}}$ units are supplied by domestic producers, and imports are $Q_d^{\text{Free trade}} - Q_s^{\text{Free trade}}$.

The tariff is a tax on imports so—just as you learned in Chapter 3—the tariff (tax) shifts the world supply curve up by the amount of the tariff. For example, if the world price of semiconductors is $2 per unit and a new tariff of $1 per semiconductor is imposed, then the world supply curve shifts up to $3 per unit.

At the new, higher price of semiconductors, two things happen. First, there is an increase in the domestic production of semiconductors as domestic suppliers respond to the higher price by increasing production. In the diagram, domestic production increases from $Q_s^{\text{Free trade}}$ to Q_s^{Tariff}. Second, there is a decrease in domestic consumption from $Q_d^{\text{Free trade}}$ to Q_d^{Tariff} as domestic consumers respond to the higher price by buying fewer semiconductors. Since the quantity produced by domestic suppliers rises and the quantity demanded by

Protectionism is the economic policy of restraining trade through quotas, tariffs, or other regulations that burden foreign producers but not domestic producers.

A **tariff** is a tax on imports.

A **trade quota** is a restriction on the quantity of goods that can be imported: Imports greater than the quota amount are forbidden or heavily taxed.

MRU

mru.org/tariffs

Tariffs and Protectionism

FIGURE 9.2

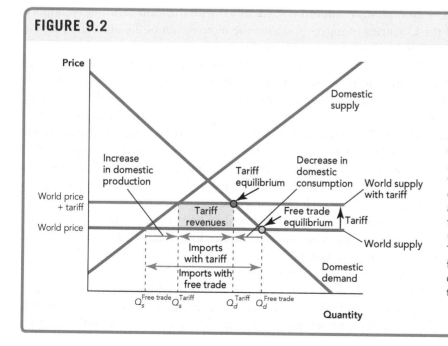

International Trade Using Demand and Supply: Tariffs A tariff shifts the world supply curve up by the amount of the tariff, thus raising the world price. In response to the higher price, consumers reduce their purchases from $Q_d^{\text{Free trade}}$ to Q_d^{Tariff} and domestic suppliers increase their production from $Q_s^{\text{Free trade}}$ to Q_s^{Tariff}. Since domestic consumption decreases and domestic production increases, the quantity of imports falls from $Q_d^{\text{Free trade}} - Q_s^{\text{Free trade}}$ to $Q_d^{\text{Tariff}} - Q_s^{\text{Tariff}}$. The government collects revenues from the tariff equal to the tariff × the quantity of imports, which is shown as the blue area.

domestic consumers falls, the quantity of imports falls. Specifically, imports fall from $Q_d^{\text{Free trade}} - Q_s^{\text{Free trade}}$ to the smaller amount $Q_d^{\text{Tariff}} - Q_s^{\text{Tariff}}$.

Figure 9.2 illustrates one more important idea. A tariff is a tax on imports so tariffs raise tax revenue for the government. The revenue raised by a tariff is the tariff amount times the quantity of imports (the quantity taxed). Thus, in Figure 9.2 the tariff revenue is given by the blue area.

The Costs of Protectionism

Now that we know that a tariff on an imported good will increase domestic production and decrease domestic consumption, we can analyze in more detail the costs of protectionism. The U.S. government, for example, greatly restricts the amount of sugar that can be imported into the United States. As a result, U.S. consumers typically pay 50% to 100% more for sugar than the world price, depending on the year. So, let's look in more detail at the costs of sugar protectionism.

To simplify our analysis, we make two assumptions. First, we assume that the tariff is so high that it completely eliminates all sugar imports. Although a small amount of sugar is allowed into the United States at a low tariff rate, anything above this small amount is taxed so heavily that no further imports occur. Our assumption that the tariff eliminates all sugar imports is not a bad approximation to what actually happens. Second, we assume that if we had complete free trade, all sugar would be imported. This is also a reasonable assumption because, as we will explain shortly, sugar can be produced elsewhere at much lower cost than in the United States. Making these two assumptions will focus attention on the key ideas. See Challenge question 17 at the end of the chapter for a more detailed analysis.

In Figure 9.3, we show the market for sugar. If there were complete free trade in sugar, U.S. consumers would be able to buy at the world price of 9 cents per pound and they would purchase 24 billion pounds. U.S. producers cannot compete with foreign producers at a price of 9 cents per pound so with free trade all sugar would be imported.

The tariff on sugar imports is so high that with the tariff there are no imports and the U.S. price of sugar—found at the intersection of the domestic demand and domestic supply curve—rises to 20 cents per pound.

Recall that a tariff has two effects: It increases domestic production and reduces domestic consumption. Each of these effects has a cost. First, the increase in domestic production may sound good—and it is good for domestic producers—but domestic producers have higher costs of production than foreign producers. Thus, the tariff means that sugar is no longer supplied by the lowest-cost sellers, and resources that could have been used to produce other goods and services are instead wasted producing sugar. Second, due to higher costs, the price of sugar rises and fewer people buy sugar, reducing the gains from trade. Let's look at each of these costs.

Sugar costs more to grow in the United States than in, say, Brazil, the world's largest producer of sugar, because the climate in the U.S. mainland is not ideal for sugar growing and because land and labor in Florida, where a lot of U.S. sugar is grown, have many alternative uses that are high in value. Sugar farmers in Florida, for example, have to douse their land with expensive fertilizers to increase production—in the process creating environmental damage in the Florida Everglades.[2] The excess resources—the fertilizer, land, and labor—that go into

FIGURE 9.3

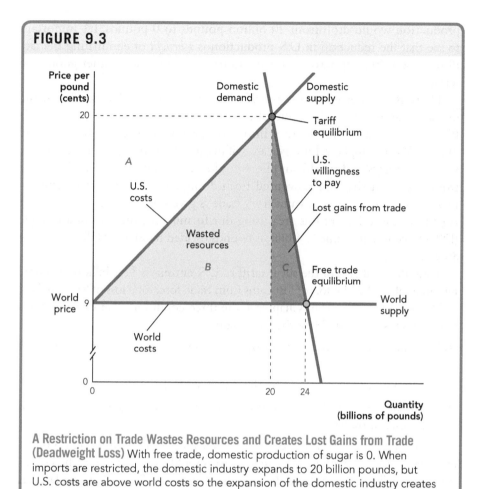

A Restriction on Trade Wastes Resources and Creates Lost Gains from Trade (Deadweight Loss) With free trade, domestic production of sugar is 0. When imports are restricted, the domestic industry expands to 20 billion pounds, but U.S. costs are above world costs so the expansion of the domestic industry creates wasted resources (area *B*). Together, wasted resources and lost gains from trade (area *C*) represent the deadweight loss from trade restrictions.

producing U.S. sugar could have been used to produce other goods like oranges and theme parks for which the United States and Florida are better suited.

Recall from Chapter 3 that the supply curve tells us the cost of production so at the equilibrium price the cost of producing an additional pound of sugar in the United States is exactly 20 cents. In other words, in the United States it takes 20 cents worth of resources like land and labor to produce one additional pound of sugar. That same pound of sugar could be bought in the world market for just 9 cents so the tariff causes 11 cents worth of resources to be wasted in producing that last pound of sugar.

The total value of wasted resources is shown in Figure 9.3 by the yellow area labeled "Wasted resources"; that area represents the difference between what it costs to produce 20 billion pounds of sugar in the United States and what it would cost to buy the same amount from abroad. We can calculate the total value of wasted resources using our formula for the area of a triangle.

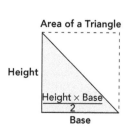

The height of the yellow triangle is 20 − 9 or 11 cents per pound, the base is 20 billion pounds, so the area is 110 billion cents, or $1.1 billion. The sugar tariff wastes $1.1 billion worth of resources.

Notice that if the sugar tariff were eliminated, the price of sugar in the United States would fall to the world price of 9 cents per pound and U.S.

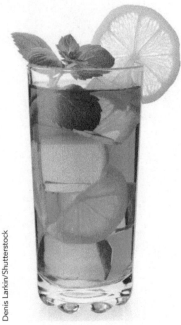

How to smuggle sugar The high price of U.S. sugar has encouraged smuggling and attempts to circumvent the tariff. In the 1980s when the U.S. price was four times the world price, Canadian entrepreneurs created super-high-sugar iced tea. The "tea" was shipped into the United States and then sifted for the sugar, which was resold. To combat this entrepreneurship, the U.S. government created even more tariffs for sugar-containing products like iced tea, cake mixes, and cocoa.

Denis Larkin/Shutterstock

production would drop from 20 billion pounds to 0 pounds. It's important to see that the reduction in U.S. production is a *benefit* of eliminating the tariff because it frees up resources that can be used to produce other goods and services.

There is another cost to the tariff. Remember from Chapter 3 that the demand curve tells us the value of goods to the demanders, so at the equilibrium price demanders are willing to pay up to 20 cents for a pound of sugar. World suppliers, however, are willing to sell sugar at 9 cents per pound. U.S. consumers and world suppliers could make mutually profitable gains from trade, but they are prevented from doing so by the threat of punishment. The value of the lost gains from trade is given by the pink area (area C). Again, we can calculate this area using our formula for the area of a triangle ([20 − 9] cents per pound × 4 billion pounds divided by 2) = 22 billion cents or $0.22 billion.

Thus, the total cost of the sugar tariff to U.S. citizens is $1.1 billion of wasted resources plus $0.22 billion of lost gains from trade for a total loss of $1.32 billion.

Do you remember from Chapter 4, the three conditions that explain why a free market is efficient? Here they are again:

1. The supply of goods is bought by the buyers with the highest willingness to pay.

2. The supply of goods is sold by the sellers with the lowest costs.

3. Between buyers and sellers, there are no unexploited gains from trade or any wasteful trades.

A tariff or quota that restricts consumers from trading with foreign producers means that the market is not free, so we should expect some of the conditions in our list to be violated. In this case, conditions 2 and 3 are violated. A tariff reduces efficiency because the supply of goods is no longer sold by the sellers with the lowest costs, and with a tariff, there are unexploited gains from trade between buyers and sellers.

Winners and Losers from Trade

We can arrive at this same total loss in another revealing way. The sugar tariff raises the price of sugar to U.S. consumers, which reduces consumer surplus. Recall from Chapter 3 that consumer surplus is the area underneath the demand curve and above the price. Thus, consumer surplus with the tariff is the area above the price of 20 cents and below the demand curve (not all of which is shown in Figure 9.3). As the price falls from 20 cents to 9 cents, consumer surplus increases by area $A + B + C$, which has a value (check it!) of $2.42 billion. Or, put differently, the tariff costs consumers $2.42 billion in lost consumer surplus.

The tariff increases price, which increases producer surplus, the area above the supply curve and below the price. Thus, the tariff increases U.S. producer surplus by area A, which has a value of $1.10 billion.

Notice that U.S. consumers lose more than twice as much from the tariff as U.S. producers gain. The total loss to U.S. citizens is the $2.42 billion loss to consumers minus the $1.10 billion gain to producers, for a total loss of $1.32 billion a year, *exactly as we found before*.

Our two methods of analyzing the cost of the sugar tariff are equivalent, but they emphasize different things. The first method emphasizes where the loss comes from: wasted resources and lost gains from trade. The second method focuses on *who* gains and *who* loses. Domestic producers gain but U.S. consumers lose even more.

International Trade and Jobs

Many people believe that protectionism increases the number of U.S. jobs. Economists, however, argue that trade has no major effects on the overall number of jobs in an economy. A tariff on washing machines will create jobs in the domestic washing machine industry, but what the person in the street has difficulty seeing is that tariffs on washing machines will reduce the number of jobs elsewhere in the economy. Let's take a closer look.

A tariff reduces the sales of foreign producers of washing machines. But why were workers and firms in China, for example, making washing machines to sell to the United States? Workers in China want to be paid for their work. Initially, workers in China are paid with U.S. dollars. But dollars are just pieces of paper! We use money to make trade easier, but, ultimately trade is about trading goods and services for other goods and services. People work to consume. Thus, our thought experiment reveals an important principle:

We pay for our imports with exports.

You are undoubtedly familiar with this principle in your own life. If you want to consume more (import), you must produce more (export). That's not quite right because of gifts and other transfers. By borrowing you can also consume more today without producing more today, so long as you produce more tomorrow. These complications also apply to international trade. Nevertheless, the principle is an important one and it tells us that if we import more we must eventually export more.

If we import more, we will export more. The reverse is also true. If we import less, we will export less. If we buy less from them, they will buy less from us. As a result, a tariff on our imports means fewer exports and fewer jobs in export industries. The jobs created by a tariff are easy to see. The jobs in our export industries that are destroyed by a tariff are harder to see but no less real.

We pay for our imports with exports but we may import and export very different goods and that has implications for how the benefits and costs of international trade are distributed. Let's go back to the idea of comparative advantage from Chapter 2. Compared to the rest of the world, the United States has a lot of highly educated, skilled workers, so the United States is likely to have a comparative advantage in producing complex goods like aircraft, entertainment, specialized computer chips, research and design, and other services. Other countries, such as China, have an abundance of less skilled workers. So China, at least compared to the United States, has a comparative advantage in producing less complex goods such as clothing, footwear, and simpler manufactured goods, and that includes doing the final stages of assembly on more complex manufactured goods, such as iPhones.

Increased trade with a country such as China, therefore, will shift U.S. production towards aircraft production and research and design services and away from producing shoes and washing machines. More generally, increased trade with China will increase the demand for skilled workers, driving up their wages, and it will decrease the demand for unskilled workers, driving down their wages.

Between 1996 and 2006, imports from China increased by a factor of six, from about $50 billion per year to $300 billion per year, a large change in a short period of time. The economists Nicholas Bloom, Kyle Handley, André Kurmann, and Philip Luck study this "China shock" and they find that, as theory predicts, there was an increase in demand for high-skilled American workers in complex export industries. Similarly, there was a decrease in demand for low-skilled workers in simple manufacturing industries where Chinese production was very competitive. The increased demand for skilled labor driven by the "China shock" increased the wages for *all* skilled workers, not just skilled workers in export industries. The demand for skilled workers increased first in export industries, but to attract those workers the export industries had to raise wages and pull workers away from other sectors and that pushed up the wages of all skilled workers. Similarly, competition from Chinese imports forced some domestic firms out of business, which initially increased unemployment among low-skilled workers. But, as the newly unemployed workers competed to obtain new jobs in other sectors, the wages of *all* unskilled workers fell. Adjusting took time, but overall just as many jobs were created as were lost and the newly created jobs were in higher-paying industries.

Low- and high-skilled workers, however, tend to live in different parts of the country so the shift in demand had geographic and later political consequences. The decreased demand for low-skill workers hurt the South and the Appalachian region of the United States where college educated workers are in the minority while the increased demand for skilled workers benefitted places such as on the coasts where college educated workers are in the majority.

We will return to the politics of trade a bit later, but you probably already guessed one connection—the areas which were hardest hit by the "China shock" tended to vote for Donald Trump in the 2016 election.[3]

The Washing Machine Tariffs

Now that you know how to analyze international trade using demand and supply, let's see how well the theory holds up by looking at what happened in the market for washing machines after the Trump tariffs were put into place in January of 2018. The tariff came in two parts. The first 1.2 million washing machines were taxed at a rate of 20% and all remaining imports were taxed at a rate of 50%. The tariffs were put in place for three years with slight declines (to 18% and 45% and 16% and 40%) in the 2nd and 3rd year respectively. A 50% tariff on washing machine parts was also included to prevent manufacturers from avoiding the duty by shipping parts to the United States for quick assembly.

Before the tariffs, about 3.8 million washing machines were imported per year. Once the tariffs began, imports declined by 1.2 million units to approximately 2.6 million washing machines per year. Figure 9.4 shows the price index for laundry equipment in the United States. Prices for washer and dryers had been declining since at least 2013, but the moment tariffs were imposed prices jumped dramatically. (Slight declines in prices were also seen in 2019 when the tariff rate decreased modestly.)

Economists estimate that the tariff increased the price of washing machines by about 12%. That's actually a smaller increase in price than one might guess

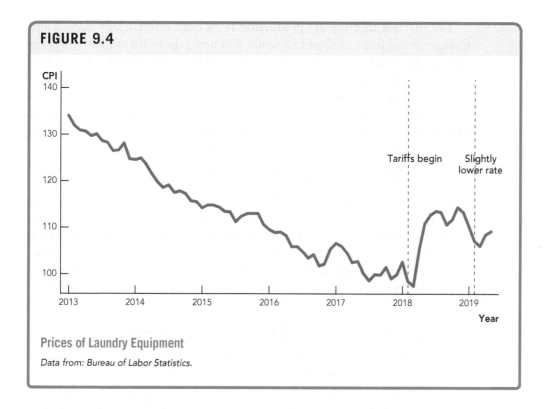

FIGURE 9.4

Tariffs begin

Slightly lower rate

Prices of Laundry Equipment

Data from: Bureau of Labor Statistics.

from the size of the tariff but it turns out that dryer prices also increased by about 12%. Dryers were not subject to the tariff. So why did dryer prices increase? Washers and dryers are typically bought together in a package. Manufacturers, therefore, tend to focus on the package price and they "smoothed" out the washer tariff over both washers and dryers. Looking at thousands of goods, economists estimated that the Trump tariffs were on average entirely passed on to consumers, just as our supply and demand model with a horizontal supply curve predicts (see Figure 9.2).

Another important prediction of the supply and demand model is that the tariff will increase the prices of *all* washing machines, whether produced domestically or imported. When the tariff is first put into place, domestic producers have lower costs than foreign producers and, as a result, they sell more and increase output. As domestic producers increase their output, however, their costs rise until in equilibrium domestic and foreign producers are, once again, selling for the same price. In fact, this is exactly what happened. Domestic producers like Whirlpool raised their prices at least as much as did foreign producers.

The Trump tariffs did have one unexpected consequence. In the model, it's natural to think of domestic producers as being domestically owned firms, but that is not necessarily the case. Whirlpool, a domestic producer of washing machines, did produce more because of the tariffs but something else happened. The foreign producers, Samsung and LG, expanded their U.S. factories! That's good for U.S. workers in the washer and dryer industry. Nevertheless, the expansion of Samsung and LG was probably an unwelcome surprise to Whirlpool, which may have expected that the tariffs would give them more of a competitive advantage in the domestic market than they ended up getting.

The increase in domestic production from both domestically owned and foreign owned firms resulted in about 1,800 new jobs in the washer and dryer industry. Remember trade policy does not influence the total number of jobs in an economy. The jobs created in the washer and dryer industry came at the expense of jobs lost in U.S. export industries. The new jobs in the protected industry, however, are visible and they are important politically, because a President can point to them as a benefit of their policies. Thus, it's an interesting question to ask, how much did consumers pay to create these jobs?

The tariffs increased washer and dryer prices by about 12% or $88 each on combined sales of 17.4 million units. The total cost to consumers, therefore, was approximately $1.56 billion per year. The government took in an extra $82.2 million in tariff revenues, which we count as a plus, so the total cost was about $1.48 billion per year. The cost per job created was therefore a whopping $821,000 per job ($1.48 billion/1,800). Instead of creating jobs by paying more for washers and dryers, U.S. consumers would have been much better off paying each new worker in the laundry industry $100,000 to enjoy a nice vacation!

The Economics and Politics of a Trade War

The most important feature of protectionism that is not taken into account by the supply and demand model is the possibility of a trade war. Protectionism is much more costly if other countries respond to U.S. tariffs with tariffs of their own on U.S. exports. The Trump administration increased tariffs on more than 12,000 products imported from China, Canada, Mexico, and other countries, and most of these tariffs have not been lifted by the Biden administration. These other countries retaliated with tariffs on thousands of U.S. exports. Furthermore, these tariffs are part of a broader pattern of two-way retaliatory interactions, including restrictions on foreign investment, restrictions on foreign market entry (you can't use Facebook in China), restrictions on joint ventures between the firms of the two countries, and new visa restrictions on travel.

Tariffs and other trade restrictions on imports harm U.S. consumers but offer some, less than offsetting, benefits to U.S. producers. Foreign tariffs and other trade restrictions on U.S. exports harm U.S. producers but offer some, less than offsetting, benefits to U.S. consumers. Thus, when U.S. tariffs bring foreign tariffs in retaliation it's likely that U.S. consumers and U.S. producers are both harmed on net. China's retaliatory strike was well targeted to impose economic costs on the United States and also to do maximum political damage to President Trump's political base. Many of China's tariffs and trade restrictions, for example, were placed on goods produced in counties where a majority of voters voted for Republicans in 2016, especially agricultural products.[4] China, for example, abruptly ordered Chinese companies to stop buying American soybeans. U.S. farmers lost sales and billions of pounds of soybeans had to be stored in hopes of finding alternative markets.[5] President Trump authorized over $28 billion in bailouts to compensate farmers for the loss of trade. Thus, instead of Chinese consumers supporting American farmers, American taxpayers ended up supporting American farmers.

China increased its trade restrictions on U.S. soybeans but not on U.S. aircraft. Why the difference? It's much easier to find alternative suppliers of soybeans than aircraft, so China chose to impose trade restrictions that would hurt the United States at least cost to China. Indeed, at the same time as China raised tariffs on U.S. goods, they reduced tariffs on imports from U.S. competitors! China, for example, imposed a tariff of 25% on exports of U.S. lobster and at the same time they reduced the tariff on Canadian exports of lobster. The American lobster industry saw its exports fall by 70%, with most of the loss being made up by increased Canadian exports.

Lobster consumers in China bought more Canadian lobsters to avoid the Chinese tariff on American lobsters. In exactly the same way, American consumers bought more from other countries to avoid American tariffs on Chinese goods. Firms have also been incentivized to move production out of China and into other low-wage countries such as Vietnam and India. Trade networks are costly to set up, so when the trade war ends it is not obvious that either China or the United States will regain the sales they have lost. The worldwide shift in trade networks illustrates how a trade war can increase economic uncertainty and make it harder for businesses to know where to invest. That may stifle investment altogether, which also lowers wages and slows down economic growth.

The lesson is that trade wars are easy to lose.

Nintendo switched production from China to Vietnam to avoid high American tariffs on Chinese imports.

Hugh Threlfall/Alamy Stock Photo

The U.S. Politics of Protectionism

Why does the government sometimes support protectionist tariffs even when U.S. consumers lose more than producers gain? One explanation is that the costs of protectionism are often spread over millions of consumers while the benefits flow to a small number of producers. As a result, the cost to each consumer is small, but the gain to each producer is large. The sugar quota we discussed earlier costs every person in the United States about $8 per year but it benefits a small number of sugar producers by millions of dollars per firm. The small cost per sugar consumer means that it's not worth knowing about, let alone lobbying against, the sugar quota. Similarly, the washing machine tariff raised the price of a washer/dryer combination by $180, which is substantial. But when the Trump tariffs were announced the stock price of Whirlpool jumped by $20, raising Whirlpool's value by about $1.26 billion.[6] It's not surprising, therefore, that producers are more informed and they lobby harder for trade protectionism than consumers lobby against trade protectionism, even when consumers are harmed more in total.

The sugar quota and washer tariffs are classic examples of spreading the costs of a policy and concentrating the benefits. The Trump tariffs, however, were large and they covered thousands of products making this explanation less applicable. Whirlpool, for example, lobbied hard for the washer tariffs, but just weeks after the washer tariffs were announced the Trump administration imposed new tariffs on steel—and Whirlpool uses steel to make washers and dryers! After the steel tariffs were announced, Whirlpool's sales and their stock price decreased. Taking into account both the washer and steel tariffs, it's not obvious that Whirlpool benefited from U.S. protectionism.

To understand wide-scale support for protectionism, we need to recall that the United States has a comparative advantage in goods and services produced by skilled workers and a comparative disadvantage in goods and services produced by unskilled or less-skilled workers. As a result, increased international trade increases the demand for skilled workers and decreases the demand for unskilled workers. Given these dynamics, it's not surprising that more educated workers and their political representatives tend to support free trade more than do less educated workers and their political representatives. Although it is somewhat unclear whether educated workers support free trade because it is in their *interest*, or because education helps workers to understand the benefits of free trade, or because education makes workers more cosmopolitan and more culturally open to international trade—probably a mix of all these motives.[7]

Less-skilled manufacturing workers have been hit in the last several decades by increased international trade and by technological changes such as automation. It's not surprising, therefore, that regions of the country with more unskilled workers were, all else equal, more supportive of the protectionist policies of Donald Trump. It's less clear, however, that less-skilled workers will end up benefitting from the trade war. In theory, greater U.S. protectionism will increase the demand for unskilled workers and reduce the demand for skilled workers. But that only works for certain if there is no retaliation. Unfortunately, everyone can be made worse off by a trade war. As we mentioned earlier, the Chinese retaliatory tariffs were specifically designed to hit Trump voters. When we combine a trade war with the fact that protectionism reduces world income by pushing countries away from their comparative advantage, it's likely that even many low-skilled U.S. workers lose from greater protectionism.

If protectionism isn't the answer, how should we respond to rapid changes in the economy that create losers as well as winners? We should first remember that all change generates losers and winners. Thomas Edison destroyed the whale oil industry with his invention of the electric lightbulb in 1879. That was bad for whalers but good for people who like to read at night (and very good for the whales). Compact discs destroyed jobs in the vinyl record industry and then MP3s destroyed jobs in the CD industry. Music lovers, however, gained access to tens of millions of songs on services like Spotify at a price less than the cost of a dozen Beatles CDs in 2001. In each case, however, these changes were ultimately beneficial to most people.

We shouldn't forget the winners but neither, of course, should we ignore the losers. Unemployment insurance, retraining assistance, and a strong education system can help workers respond to economic shocks. If we want the gains from a growing and dynamic economy, it's better to adjust to shocks than to try to prevent change. Over time, the results of adjusting to change have been a tremendous increase in the U.S. standard of living.

Arguments Against International Trade

It would take several books to analyze all the arguments against international trade. We will take a closer look at three of the most common arguments:

- It's wrong to trade with countries that use child labor.
- We need to keep certain industries at home for reasons of national security.
- We can increase U.S. well-being with strategic trade protectionism.

Child Labor

Is child labor a reason to restrict trade? In part, this is a question of ethics on which reasonable people can disagree, but our belief, for which we will give reasons, is that the answer is no.

In 1992, labor activists discovered that Walmart was selling clothing that had been made in Bangladesh by subcontractors who had employed some child workers. Senator Tom Harkin angrily introduced a bill in Congress to prohibit firms from importing any products made by children under the age of 15.

CHECK YOURSELF

- Who benefits from a tariff? Who loses?
- Why does trade protectionism lead to wasted resources?
- If there are winners and losers from trade restrictions, why do we hear more often from the people who gain from trade restrictions than from the people who lose?
- Identify the lost gains from trade in Figure 9.3 and describe in words what is lost.

Harkin's bill didn't pass, but in a panic the garment industry in Bangladesh dismissed 30,000 to 50,000 child workers. A success? Before we decide, we need to think about what happened to the children who were thrown out of work. Where did these children go? To the playground? To school? To a better job? No. Thrown out of the garment factories, the children went to work elsewhere, many at jobs like prostitution with worse conditions and lower pay.[8]

About 10% of all children aged 5–14 around the world work for a significant number of hours each week. The vast majority of these children work in agriculture, often alongside their parents, and not in export industries. Restrictions on trade, therefore, cannot directly reduce the number of child workers, and by making a poor country poorer, trade restrictions may increase the number of child workers. In fact, studies have shown that more openness to trade increases income and reduces child labor.[9]

Child labor is more common in poor countries and it was common in nineteenth-century Great Britain and the United States when people were much poorer than today. Child labor declined in the developed world as people got richer.

The forces that reduced child labor in the developed world are also at work in the developing world. The vertical axis of Figure 9.5 shows the percentage of child laborers against real GDP per capita on the horizontal axis. The sizes of the circles are proportionate to the total number of child laborers, so although the percentage of child laborers is much higher in Peru (22.55%) than in India (1.7%), there are many more child laborers in India. The lesson of Figure 9.5 is that economic growth reduces child labor.

The pin factory Lewis Hine photograph of bowling alley boys in New Haven, CT. Circa 1910.

FIGURE 9.5

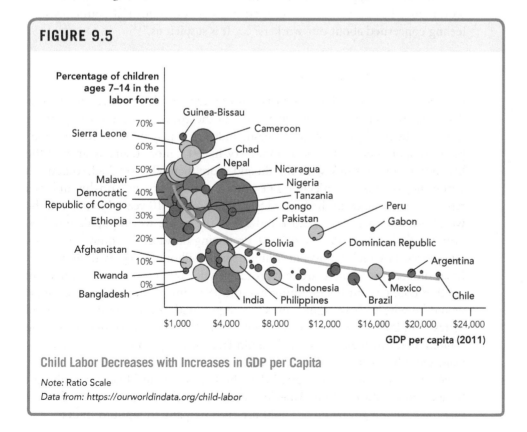

Child Labor Decreases with Increases in GDP per Capita

Note: Ratio Scale

Data from: https://ourworldindata.org/child-labor

Bans on child labor can also backfire. Bans can help in relatively rich countries where child labor is already low and strong enforcement is possible. But the economists Prashant Bharadwaj, Leah Lakdawala, and Nicholas Li studied India's partial ban on child labor in 1986 and what they found was that instead of reducing child labor, the ban increased child labor.[10] How is this possible? The ban reduced child wages because firms that hired children now faced the possibility of fines. Lower child wages meant that poor families became even poorer. To make up for the decline in their income, poorer families were forced to increase the amount of work done by children. It's a sad story of how well-intentioned legislation can sometimes have perverse and unintended consequences.

Rather than pushing them out of work with bans, governments and non-profits can help by pulling children toward education. In Bangladesh, at about the same time that child workers were being thrown out of work by the Harkin bill, the government introduced the Food for Education program. The program provides a free monthly stipend of rice or wheat to poor families who have at least one child attending school that month. The program has been successful at encouraging school attendance. Even more important, increased education of children today means richer parents tomorrow—parents who will have enough wealth to feed their children *and* send them to school.

More generally, it's common for protectionists to lobby under the guise of some other motive. Many people, for example, are concerned about working conditions in developing countries, but does it surprise you that U.S. labor unions are often the biggest lobbyists for bills to restrict trade on behalf of "oppressed foreign workers"? As Youssef Boutros-Ghali, Egypt's former minister for trade, put it, "The question is why all of a sudden, when third world labor has proved to be competitive, why do industrial countries start feeling concerned about our workers? . . . It is suspicious."[11]

Trade and National Security

If a good is vital for national security but domestic producers have higher costs than foreign producers, it can make sense for the government to tax imports or subsidize the production of the domestic industry. It may make sense, for example, to support a domestic vaccine industry. In 1918, more than a quarter of the U.S. population got sick with the flu and more than 500,000 died, sometimes within hours of being infected. The young were especially hard-hit and, as a result, life expectancy in the United States dropped by 10 years. No place in the world was safe, as between 2.5% and 5% of the entire world population died from the flu between 1918 and 1920. Producing flu vaccine requires an elaborate process in which robots inject hundreds of millions of eggs with flu viruses. In an ordinary year, there are few problems with buying vaccine produced in another country, but if something like the 1918 flu swept the world again, it would be wise to have significant vaccine production capacity in the United States.[12] In 2020, the world was struck by the COVID-19 pandemic and the United States struggled to quickly build factories to produce vaccines, masks, vials, and other pandemic fighting tools.

Many people have also argued that the Chinese firm Huawei should not be allowed a critical role in America's communications infrastructure, for fear that the Chinese government could use the company to tap into military and intelligence communications or the corporate transmission of valuable intellectual property. Restrictions on Huawei became one of the major issues in the U.S.-Chinese trade war.

Don't be surprised, however, if every domestic producer in trouble claims that their product is vital for national security. Everything from beeswax to mohair, not to mention steel and computer chips, has been protected in the name of national security.

Strategic Trade Protectionism

In some cases, it's possible for a country to use tariffs and quotas to grab a larger share of the gains from trade than would be possible with pure free trade. A tariff is a tax but it's a special kind of tax because the demanders live in the United States and the suppliers are foreign firms. Now who bears the burden of a tax? Demanders or suppliers? In Chapter 6, we came up with a simple way to remember: Elasticity = escape; that is, the more elastic side of the market can escape (some) of the tax so the more inelastic side of the market bears more of the burden of a tax. See Figure 6.4 for a reminder.

Now let's return to the beginning of this chapter. We assumed that the world supply curve was perfectly elastic. So who bears the burden of a tariff? If the supply curve is perfectly elastic the suppliers escape the tariff/tax so the demanders bear the burden. The assumption that the world supply curve is perfectly elastic makes sense for a small economy in a big world market. A small economy can buy more from the world without pushing up the world price and if it buys less the world price won't fall. Notice from Figure 9.2 that with perfectly elastic supply the price paid by U.S. consumers increases by the full amount of the tariff. The U.S. economy accounts for about 15% of the world economy—pretty big! It's somewhat surprising, therefore, that most empirical studies of tariffs find that tariffs are almost fully passed on to consumers in higher prices. Thus, the small economy assumption is reasonably accurate, even for the United States. Nevertheless, the changes in U.S. demand should be big enough to affect the world price for at least some goods. Figure 9.6 shows what happens in this case.

In Figure 9.6 the foreign supply curve isn't flat but quite inelastic which means that if the foreign suppliers lose the U.S. market they have no other major customers.[13] When the (domestic) demand curve is more elastic than the (foreign) supply curve, a tariff reduces the price received by foreigners much more than it increases the price paid by domestic consumers. Notice that in this case only a fraction of the tariff is passed on to consumers; that is, the price paid by U.S. buyers after the tariff is only slightly higher than price under free trade.

The consumers, of course, still don't like the tariff because it raises prices and it also creates a deadweight loss (i.e., lost gains from trade. Can you find this area?). But there is an offsetting factor. The tariff creates revenues that flow to the U.S. government and notice that most of the revenues are paid by the foreign suppliers. Thus, the tariff creates a small deadweight loss for U.S. consumers but a relatively large increase in government revenues that could be used to reduce other taxes. It's quite possible, therefore, that the net effect of these two factors is positive for the United States.

Taxing foreigners may sound like a great idea but it's trickier than it looks. As the tariff increases so does the deadweight loss and if the tariff gets too large

Norman Eggert/Alamy Stock Photo

Vital for national security?
In 1954 the U.S. government declared that mohair, the fleece of the Angora goat, was vital for national security (it can be used to make military uniforms). For nearly 40 years mohair producers received millions of dollars in annual payments. Finally, after much ridicule, the program was eliminated in 1993 . . . only to be reestablished in 2002. Hard to believe? Yes, but we aren't kidding.

FIGURE 9.6

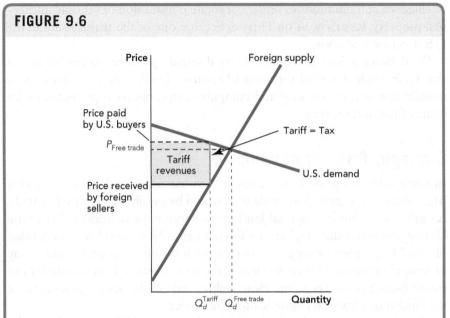

A Tariff Is a Tax When the foreign supply curve is very inelastic relative to the domestic demand curve, most of the burden of the tariff will fall on foreign suppliers. Notice that the price paid by U.S. buyers rises only slightly but the price received by foreign sellers falls a lot. As a result, the tariff revenues that flow to the U.S. government are paid mostly by the foreign sellers, and the net effect of the tariff, even taking into account the deadweight loss on U.S. buyers, could be positive.

CHECK YOURSELF

- Most U.S. garment manufacturing has moved overseas, to places such as India and China, where wages are lower. The result of this shift has been a sizable drop in the number of garment workers in the United States. While bad for these workers, why has this trend been a net benefit for the United States?

- What would happen if the U.S. government decided that computer chip manufacturing was a strategic national industry and provided monetary grants to Silicon Valley companies? Trace the effects of this policy on Silicon Valley companies, foreign competitors, and the cost and benefit to U.S. taxpayers and consumers.

revenues will decline. Thus, there is an optimal tariff that balances the increase in deadweight loss with the increase in revenues. Finding such a tariff may be quite difficult. Moreover, how will other nations feel when we try to tax their citizens? Retaliation may be quite likely and the net effect is then likely to be negative.

Takeaway

We have shown in this chapter how to use demand and supply curves to analyze trade and the costs of trade protectionism. As always, make sure you can read and correctly draw the graphs!

Protectionism wastes resources by transferring production from low-cost foreign producers to high-cost domestic producers. Restrictions on trade also prevent domestic consumers from exploiting gains from trade with foreign producers, creating deadweight losses.

International trade creates jobs in some industries and destroys them in other industries raising wages on average. The United States has an abundance of high-skilled labor relative to much of the rest of the world. As a result, the United States will tend to export goods and services produced by high-skilled labor and import goods and services produced by low-skilled labor. Adjusting to changes in demand from trade, technology, or other sources of disruption can be costly and traumatic and such adjustment costs may generate demands for protectionism. Small-scale protectionism can also persist because the benefits from restrictions are often concentrated on small groups who lobby for protection, while the costs of restrictions are spread over millions of consumers and can be small for each individual.

Protectionism will be especially costly when it leads to retaliation, a trade war. In a trade war, both producers and consumers are likely to lose on net.

We have set out various common arguments for restricting trade. Some of these arguments are valid, but they are usually of limited applicability.

CHAPTER REVIEW

Go online to practice with more examples of these types of problems, including live links to videos, data sources, and feedback.

KEY CONCEPTS

protectionism, p. 167

tariff, p. 167

trade quota, p. 167

FACTS AND TOOLS

1. Both the Trump and the Biden administrations significantly raised the tariff rate on Canadian softwood lumber. If the United States removed its trade barriers so that American consumers could buy lumber at the world price, who would be better off, and who would be worse off: American consumers or American lumber producers? If we added all the gains and losses, would there be a net gain or net loss? Who would make a greater effort lobbying for or against this reduction in trade barriers: American consumers or American lumber producers?

2. The supply curve for lumber in the United States slopes upward, just like any normal supply curve. If the United States eliminated its trade barriers to lumber, what would happen to the number of workers employed in the lumber-producing industry in the United States: Would it rise or fall? What would these workers probably do over the next year or so? Will they ever work again?

3. In Figure 9.3, consider triangles *B* and *C*. One of these could be labeled "Workers and machines who could be better used in another sector of the economy," while the other could be labeled "Consumers who no longer purchase the product because of the higher price." Which is which?

4. In the book *The Choice,* economist Russ Roberts asks how voters would feel about a machine that could convert wheat into automobiles.

   a. Do you think that voters would complain that this machine should be banned, since it would destroy jobs in the auto industry?

   b. Would this machine, *in fact,* destroy jobs in the auto industry? If so, would roughly the same number of jobs eventually be created in other industries?

   c. Here is Roberts's punch line: If voters were told that the wonder machine was in fact just a cargo ship that exported wheat and imported autos from a foreign country, how would voters' attitudes toward this machine change?

5. Spend some time driving in Detroit, Michigan—the Motor City—and you're sure to see bumper stickers with messages like "Buy American" or "Out of a job yet? Keep buying foreign!" or "Hungry? Eat your foreign car!" Explain these bumper stickers in light of what you've learned in this chapter. Who is hurt by imported automobiles? Who benefits?

6. This chapter pointed out that trade restrictions on sugar cause U.S. consumers to pay more than twice the going world price for sugar. However, you are very unlikely to ever encounter bumper stickers that say things like "Out of money yet? Keep taxing foreign sugar!" or "Hungry? It's probably because domestic sugar is so expensive!" Why do you think it is that these bumper stickers are not popular?

7. Of the three conditions that explain why a free market is efficient (from Chapter 4), which

condition or conditions cease to hold in the case of a tariff on imported goods? Which condition or conditions continue to hold even in the case of a tariff on imports?

THINKING AND PROBLEM SOLVING

8. a. Just to review: Back in Chapter 8, we illustrated price ceilings with a horizontal line below the equilibrium price. Did price ceilings create surpluses or shortages?

b. The horizontal line in Figure 9.1 is sort of like a price ceiling, but it doesn't cause a surplus or a shortage. What does it represent and why doesn't it cause a surplus or a shortage?

c. Figure 9.1 considers the case of a country that can buy as many semiconductors as it wants at the same world price. Why do people in this country only buy $Q_d^{\text{Free trade}}$ units? Why don't they buy more of this inexpensive product?

9. Figure 9.1 looks at a case in which the world price is below the domestic no-trade price. Let's look at the case in which the world price is *above* the domestic no-trade price. We'll work with the market for airplanes shown in the following figure.

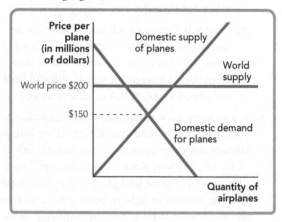

a. In the figure, use the Quantity axis to label $Q_s^{\text{Free trade}}$ and $Q_d^{\text{Free trade}}$. This is somewhat similar to Figure 9.1.

b. What would you call the gap between $Q_s^{\text{Free trade}}$ and $Q_d^{\text{Free trade}}$?

c. Also following Figure 9.1, label "Domestic consumption" and "Domestic production."

d. Will domestic airplane buyers—airlines and delivery companies like FedEx—have to pay a higher or a lower price under free trade compared with the no-trade alternative? Will domestic airplane buyers purchase a higher

or a lower quantity of planes if there's free trade in planes?

e. Based on your answer to part d, would you expect domestic airplane demanders to support free trade in planes or oppose it?

10. In the text, we discuss sugar farmers in Florida who use unusually large amounts of fertilizer to produce their crops; they do so because their land isn't all that great for sugar production. If we translate this into the language of the supply curve, would these Florida sugar farms be those on the lower-left part of a supply curve or those along the upper right of the supply curve? Why?

11. Many people will tell you that, whenever possible, you should always buy U.S.-made goods. Some will go further and tell you to spend your money on goods produced in your own state whenever possible. (Just do a simple Google search for "Buy [any state]" and you'll find a website encouraging this kind of thinking.) The idea is that if you spend money in your state, you help the economy of *your* state, rather than the economy of some other state. By the same logic, shouldn't one buy only goods produced in one's own city? Or on one's own street? Where does this thinking lead to? And how does it relate to Big Idea Five from Chapter 1?

12. Some people argue for protectionism by pointing out that other countries with which we trade engage in "unfair trade practices" and that we should retaliate with our own protectionist measures. One such policy is the policy of some countries to subsidize exporting industries. In fact, the claim that the Canadian government is illegally subsidizing their lumber industry was the primary justification used for the U.S. tariff increases discussed previously. Assuming this claim is true (Canadian lumber producers deny it, and their claim has been held up by the resolution panel of the World Trade Organization), U.S. lumber producers are hurt by this policy and would like to restrict imported lumber from Canada. From an economic perspective, is this a good reason to place tariffs on Canadian lumber? Why or why not?

13. In March 2002, then President George W. Bush put a tariff on imported steel as a means of protecting the domestic steel industry. In February, before the tariff went into effect, the United States produced 7.4 million metric tons of crude steel and imported about 2.8 million metric tons of steel products at an average price of $363 per metric ton. Two months later, after the tariff was in effect, U.S. production increased to 7.9 million metric tons. The volume of imported steel fell to about 1.7 million metric tons, but the price of the imported steel rose to about $448 per metric ton. The following supply and demand diagram shows this situation (along with an estimated no-trade domestic equilibrium at a price of $625 per metric ton and a quantity of 8.9 million metric tons).

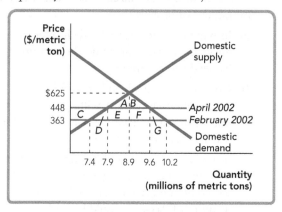

Determine which areas on the graph represent each of the following:

a. The increase in producer surplus gained by U.S. steel producers as a result of the tariff

b. The loss in consumer surplus suffered by U.S. steel consumers as a result of the tariff

c. The revenue earned by the government because of the tariff

d. The wasted resources and lost gains from trade (deadweight loss) created by the tariff

14. For each of the four parts of question 13, calculate the *values* of these areas in dollars. How much of the deadweight loss is due to the overproduction of steel by higher-cost U.S. steel producers, and how much is due to the underconsumption of steel by U.S. steel consumers?

15. A senator finds out about possible opposition party plans to more greatly open the economy to free trade—a move that the senator does not agree with, particularly as the country is facing a global pandemic. The senator takes to television to publicly denounce the plans, stating not only that opening the economy during a pandemic would be a threat to national security but also that domestic jobs would be lost and consumers would be supporting child labor in other countries. Explain why each argument is valid or invalid.

16. When can strategic trade protectionism work to the benefit of the domestic country at the expense of foreign countries?

CHALLENGES

17. In the chapter, we focused on a sugar tariff that eliminated all imports. Let's now take a look at the case where the sugar tariff eliminates some but not all imports. We will also examine the closely related case of a quota on sugar imports. The figure shows a tariff on sugar that raises the U.S. price to 20 cents per pound but at that price some sugar is imported even after the tariff.

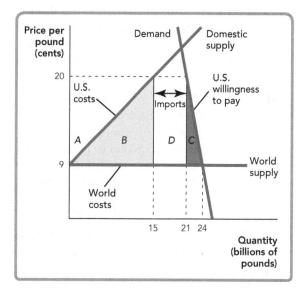

a. Label the free trade equilibrium, the tariff equilibrium, wasted resources, lost gains from trade, and tariff revenues.

b. Now imagine that instead of a tariff, the U.S. government uses a quota that forbids imports of sugar greater than 6 billion pounds. (Equivalently, imagine a tariff that is zero on the first 6 billion pounds of imports but then jumps to a prohibitive level after that quantity of imports—this is closer to how the system works in practice.) Under the quota system, what does area *D* represent? Would importers of sugar prefer a tariff or a quota?

c. The sugar quota is allocated to importing countries based on imports from these countries between 1975 and 1981 (with some subsequent adjustments). For example, in 2016 Australia was given the right to export 87 thousand metric tons of sugar to the United States at a very low tariff rate, and

Belize was given the right to export 11.5 thousand metric tons of sugar to the United States at a very low tariff rate. How do you think these rights are allocated to firms within the sugar-exporting countries?

d. Discuss how the quota and the way it is allocated could create a misallocation of resources that would further reduce efficiency relative to a tariff that resulted in the same quantity of imports.

18. There are estimated to be roughly 12,000 registered lobbyists in Washington, D.C. (https://www.opensecrets.org/federal-lobbying/summary), people whose primary job is asking the federal government for something. A lobbyist who comes with long experience as an aide to a powerful politician will earn at least $200,000 per year, while the median salary of a lobbyist in 2020 was over $115,000. Many lobbyists (not all) are attempting to restrict trade in order to turn consumer surplus into producer surplus.

a. Let's focus just on the lobbyists who are restricting trade. If the United States were to amend the Constitution to permanently ban all tariffs and trade restrictions, these lobbyists would lose their jobs, and they'd have to leave Washington. Would this job change raise U.S. productivity or lower it?

b. Would most of these lobbyists likely earn more after the amendment was enacted or less?

c. How can you reconcile your answers to parts a and b?

19. One of the assumptions made in the chapter was that the U.S. market for sugar was small relative to the overall world market for sugar, so that when the United States entered the world market for sugar, and U.S. buyers began to buy imported sugar, the price did not change. If we relax this assumption, how do you think that would affect Figure 9.1?

a. Draw the world market for sugar. Show on the graph what happens when the United States enters the market, assuming the United States is large enough to impact

market price. What happens to the world price?

b. Show how this changes the U.S. market for sugar, starting with a graph like Figure 9.1, where the world price of sugar is less than the U.S. domestic price. How does this change influence U.S. imports or exports of sugar?

20. The tables that follow show the domestic supply and demand schedules for bushels of flaxseed (used as an edible oil and a nutrition supplement) in the United States and Kazakhstan, with prices measured in U.S. dollars and quantities measured in millions of bushels.

a. In which country is flaxseed cheaper to produce? In which country do the consumers of flaxseed value it more?

b. Complete the blank table that follows by describing each nation's willingness to import or export flaxseed at each price. One row has been done for you as an example.

c. If the United States and Kazakhstan entered into free trade with only one another, what would be the price of flaxseed, and what quantity of flaxseed would be traded?

d. For each of the following four constituent groups, determine whether free trade between the United States and Kazakhstan would help or harm the members of that group relative to the two no-trade domestic equilibriums. Calculate the change in consumer or producer surplus in each country as necessary to support your claim.

 i. The buyers of flaxseed in Kazakhstan

 ii. The sellers of flaxseed in Kazakhstan

 iii. The buyers of flaxseed in the United States

 iv. The sellers of flaxseed in the United States

e. Suppose the sellers of flaxseed in the importing country successfully lobby for protection in the form of a $4 tariff per bushel of flaxseed. Describe the impact of this tariff on flaxseed trade and on the consumer and producer surpluses you calculated in part d. How much deadweight loss does this tariff generate?

	Price	$2	$4	$6	$8	$10	$12	$14	$16	$18	$20
U.S.	Q_D	12	11	10	9	8	7	6	5	4	3
	Q_S	0	1	2	3	4	5	6	7	8	9

	Price	$2	$4	$6	$8	$10	$12	$14	$16	$18	$20
Kz	Q_D	5.5	5	4.5	4	3.5	3	2.5	2	1.5	1
	Q_S	1.5	3	4.5	6	7.5	9	10.5	12	13.5	15

At a price of . . .	the United States would be willing to . . .	and Kazakhstan would be willing to . . .
$2	import 12 million bushels	import 4 million bushels
$4		
$6		
$8		
$10		
$12		
$14		
$16		
$18		
$20		

WORK IT OUT

For interactive, step-by-step help in solving this problem, go online.

According to Chinese government statistics, China imported over 1 million cars in 2012. Let's see what would happen to consumer and producer surplus if China were to ban car imports. To keep things simple, let's assume that if car imports were banned, the equilibrium price of cars (holding quality constant!) would rise by $5,000.

a. In the figure, shade the area that represents the total gains when car imports are allowed into China.

b. Once China bans the import of cars, what is the dollar value of the wasted resources plus the lost gains from trade? (*Hint:* The chapter provides the formula.)

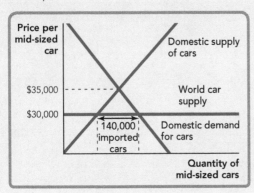

c. If car imports are banned, Chinese car producers will be better off and Chinese car consumers will be worse off. A polygon in the figure shows the surplus that will shift from consumers to producers. Write the word "Transfer" in this polygon. (*Hint:* It's not the area you calculated in part b.)

d. If quality *weren't* held constant, what would you expect to happen to the additional Chinese cars produced after the import ban? Would they be as good as the ones that used to be imported? (*Hint:* Which types of cars do you think that China imports? Low-quality or high-quality? Why?)

10

Externalities: When the Price Is Not Right

On a sunny day in June 1924, a young man developed a blister on his toe after playing a game of tennis. A week later, he was dead from a bacterial infection. The young man had been given the best medical care possible: He was the son of the president of the United States. President Coolidge wept when he learned that all the "power and the glory of the presidency" could not prevent the death of his son from a simple blister.

The president's son, Calvin Jr., was probably killed by a bacterium called *Staphylococcus aureus* or *staph* for short. Penicillin could easily have cured him, but penicillin was not discovered until 1928. When penicillin and other antibiotics became widely available in the 1940s, they were hailed as miracle drugs. Dying from a blister became a thing of the past—until recently.

Staph has evolved. Today it is resistant to penicillin and some "superbug" strains are resistant to almost all antibiotics. The Centers for Disease Control estimate that roughly 20,000 people in the United States are killed every year from staph infections that are resistant to antibiotics. *Staphylococcus aureus* is now spreading around the globe.

Antibiotic resistance is a product of evolution. Any population of bacteria includes some bacteria with unusual traits, such as the ability to resist an antibiotic's attack. When a person takes an antibiotic, the drug kills the defenseless bacteria, leaving the unusually strong bacteria behind. Without competition for resources, these stronger bacteria multiply. When the same antibiotic is applied again and again, the stronger bacteria get even stronger until after many generations of bacteria, the antibiotic loses its power to perform miracles.

Evolution is a powerful force so it was inevitable that staph would grow resistant to penicillin eventually, but staph has grown more resistant more quickly than was necessary. The problem is that antibiotics are overused.

Antibiotic users get all the benefits of antibiotics but they do not bear all of the costs. The person who demands an antibiotic must pay a **private cost** for the antibiotic, the market price. But because bacteria spread widely, each use of an antibiotic creates a small increase in bacterial resistance, which raises the probability that other people could die from a simple infection. For example, when a teenager takes tetracycline for acne, there is an increase in antibiotic-resistant bacteria on the skin of *other* members of their family.

CHAPTER OUTLINE

External Costs, External Benefits, and Efficiency

Private Solutions to Externality Problems

Government Solutions to Externality Problems

Takeaway

A **private cost** is a cost paid by the consumer or the producer.

187

Antimicrobial detergents that are washed down the sink enter into the environment where they increase the proportion of resistant bacteria for us all. Almost half of all antibiotics are used on farm animals, not to treat disease but primarily because they accelerate growth (the FDA has begun to phase out some antibiotic use in animals to help prevent resistance). Bacteria that develop resistance on the farm travel onto and into human beings, where they may cause incurable infections.

In a sense, each use of antibiotics pollutes the environment with more resistant and stronger bacteria. Thus, each use of antibiotics creates an **external cost,** a cost that is paid not by the consumers or producers of antibiotics but by bystanders to the transaction. The **social cost** of antibiotic use is the cost to everyone: the private cost plus the external cost.

Since the external cost is not paid by consumers or producers, it is not built into the price of antibiotics. So when patients or farmers choose whether to use more antibiotics, they compare their private benefits with the market price, but they ignore the external costs just as a factory will ignore the cost of the pollution that it emits into the atmosphere (assuming there are no regulations forbidding this). Since antibiotic users ignore some relevant costs of their actions, antibiotics are overused. Alternatively stated, since the price of antibiotics does not include all the costs of using antibiotics, the price sends an imperfect signal—the price is too low and so antibiotics are overused. Thus, the problem of antibiotic resistance is about evolution *and* economics. Evolution drives antibiotic resistance, but the process is happening faster than we would like because antibiotic users do not take into account the external costs of their choices.

External Costs, External Benefits, and Efficiency

This chapter is about products, like antibiotics, for which some of the costs or benefits of the product fall on bystanders. These costs or benefits are called external costs or external benefits or, for short, **externalities.** (External costs are sometimes also called negative externalities, and external benefits are sometimes also called positive externalities.) When externalities are significant, markets work less well and government action can increase social surplus.

In Chapter 4, we showed that a market equilibrium maximizes consumer plus producer surplus (the gains from trade). But maximizing consumer plus producer surplus isn't so great if bystanders are harmed in the process. Everyone counts, not just the consumers and producers of a particular product. So, when we evaluate how well a market with externalities is working, we want to look at **social surplus,** namely consumer surplus plus producer surplus plus everyone else's surplus.

To show why a market with externalities *does not* maximize *social surplus,* it's useful to briefly review why a market equilibrium *does* maximize *consumer plus producer surplus* (see also Chapter 4). The key is to remember that you can read the value of the *n*th unit of a good from the height of the demand curve and the cost of the *n*th unit of a good from the height of the supply curve. For example, imagine that buyers and sellers are currently exchanging 99 units of a good. What is the value to buyers and the costs to sellers of one additional unit, the 100th unit? In Figure 10.1, you can read the value to buyers from the height of the demand curve at the 100th unit, namely $22. You can

---

An **external cost** is a cost paid by people other than the consumer or the producer trading in the market.

The **social cost** is the cost to everyone: the private cost plus the external cost.

Externalities are external costs or external benefits, that is, costs or benefits, respectively, that fall on bystanders.

Social surplus is consumer surplus plus producer surplus plus everyone else's surplus.

read the cost to sellers from the height of the supply curve at the 100th unit, namely $10. Since the value of the 100th unit exceeds the additional cost of the 100th unit, there is an incentive to trade and thus an opportunity to increase consumer and producer surplus. Following this logic, trade is mutually profitable up until the 210th unit is sold. The value to buyers of the 210th unit is $13 and the cost to sellers of producing that additional unit is $13 so at this point there are no further incentives to trade. If any fewer units were traded, gains from trade would be left on the table. If any more units were traded, the cost of those units would exceed their value. Thus, gains from trade are maximized at the market equilibrium of 210 units.

Let's call the price and quantity that maximize social surplus the **efficient equilibrium.** If there are no significant externalities, the market equilibrium is also the efficient equilibrium (because if there are no significant external costs or benefits, maximizing producer plus consumer surplus is the same as maximizing everyone's surplus). But if there are significant externalities, the market equilibrium is no longer the efficient equilibrium, as we will now show.

External Costs

Panel A of Figure 10.2 on the next page shows the market equilibrium for antibiotics. As usual, the market equilibrium maximizes consumer plus producer surplus. But now the use of antibiotics creates an external cost, a cost to people who are neither buying nor selling antibiotics. At the market equilibrium, the price of a round of antibiotics—such as your doctor would prescribe to cure an infection—is $5 and we will assume that the external cost of antibiotic use is $7, a number that is consistent with one study of the matter.[1] The private cost plus the external cost is the social cost of antibiotic use.

In Panel B of Figure 10.2, we add the external cost to the supply curve to show the social cost curve. Because the social cost curve takes into account *all* of the costs of antibiotic use, we use the social cost curve to figure out the **efficient quantity,** the quantity that maximizes social surplus. The efficient quantity $Q_{Efficient}$ is found where the demand curve intersects the social cost curve.

To see exactly why the market equilibrium is *not* efficient, let's consider the value to buyers and the social costs of the Q_{Market} unit of the good. The height of the demand curve at the Q_{Market} unit (the black arrow labeled "Private value") tells us that this unit has a private value of $5. The height of the social cost curve at Q_{Market} (the green arrow labeled "Social cost") tells us that this unit has a social cost of $12. Thus, producing this unit creates a social loss or deadweight loss of $7. Following this logic, you can see that reducing output increases social surplus so long as the social cost of an additional prescription of antibiotics exceeds the value to buyers, that is, so long as the social cost curve lies above the demand curve. Thus, to maximize social surplus, output should be reduced to $Q_{Efficient}$, the point at which the social cost curve intersects the demand curve and where the social costs of an additional unit just equal the value.

FIGURE 10.1

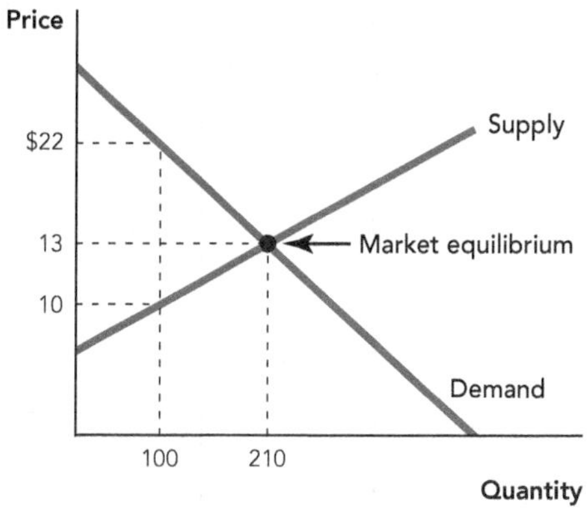

Reviewing Gains from Trade The value of the 100th unit to buyers is $22. The cost of the 100th unit to sellers is $10. At the 100th unit, there is a $12 gain from exchange. Gains from trade are maximized when a total of 210 units are exchanged. Notice that the value of the 210th unit is just equal to the cost of the 210th unit.

The **efficient equilibrium** is the price and quantity that maximize social surplus.

The **efficient quantity** is the quantity that maximizes social surplus.

FIGURE 10.2

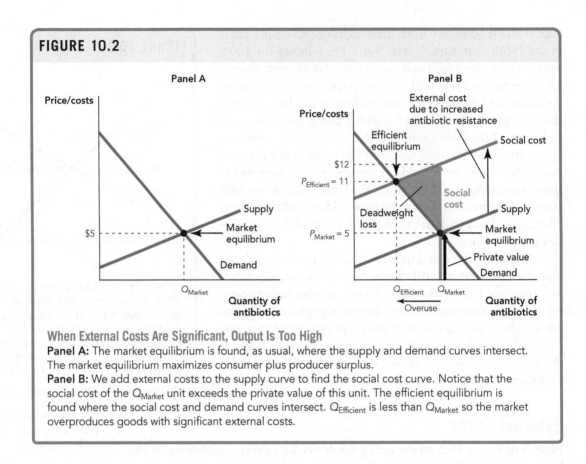

When External Costs Are Significant, Output Is Too High

Panel A: The market equilibrium is found, as usual, where the supply and demand curves intersect. The market equilibrium maximizes consumer plus producer surplus.

Panel B: We add external costs to the supply curve to find the social cost curve. Notice that the social cost of the Q_{Market} unit exceeds the private value of this unit. The efficient equilibrium is found where the social cost and demand curves intersect. $Q_{Efficient}$ is less than Q_{Market} so the market overproduces goods with significant external costs.

A final way of illustrating the overuse of antibiotics is to notice that *if* the users did bear all the costs of antibiotic use, that is, *if* the private cost included the $7 external cost, then the supply curve would shift upward and would be the same as the social cost curve. The market equilibrium would then be the same as the efficient equilibrium; that is, buyers would purchase $Q_{Efficient}$ units. But for determining efficient quantities, who bears the costs is irrelevant—*costs are costs regardless of who bears them.* Thus, $Q_{Efficient}$ is the efficient quantity when antibiotic users pay all of the costs *and* when they pay only some of the costs—the only difference is that when other people bear some of the costs, antibiotic users purchase more antibiotics, so $Q_{Market} > Q_{Efficient}$.

This way of explaining why antibiotics are overused suggests one potential solution to the problem of external costs. If antibiotic users had to pay a tax just equal to the external costs, $7, they would demand only the amount $Q_{Efficient}$. Remember from Chapter 6 that we can analyze a tax by shifting the supply curve up by the amount of the tax. Thus, in Figure 10.2, notice that a tax set equal to the level of the external cost would shift the supply curve up so that it exactly overlays the social cost curve. The market quantity would then fall from Q_{Market} to $Q_{Efficient}$. Thus, a tax set equal to the external cost would once again mean that the market equilibrium was the efficient equilibrium!

A tax on an ordinary good increases deadweight loss, as discussed in Chapter 6, but a tax on a good with an external cost reduces deadweight loss and raises revenue. For these reasons, there is a strong argument for taxing goods with external costs. Such taxes are often called **Pigouvian taxes,** after the economist Arthur C. Pigou (1877–1959) who first focused attention on

A **Pigouvian tax** is a tax on a good with external costs.

externalities and how they might be corrected with taxes. We will return to look at solutions to external cost problems in more detail after we have examined a parallel issue, external benefits.

External Benefits

An **external benefit** is a benefit to people other than the consumers or the producers trading in the market. Consider, for example, another medical good, vaccines. Vaccines benefit the person who is vaccinated but they also create an external benefit for other people because people who have been vaccinated are less likely to harbor and spread disease-causing viruses.[*]

In a typical year, for example, some 36,000 Americans die from the flu, a contagious respiratory disease caused by influenza viruses. Fortunately, millions of Americans get a yearly vaccination—a "flu shot"— that is usually effective at preventing the flu. Flu viruses spread from person to person when someone who *already has the flu* coughs or sneezes. As a result, when one person gets a flu shot, the expected number of people who get the flu falls by more than one. So getting a flu shot is a real public service. Get a flu shot. The life you save may not be your own.

So what's the problem? The problem is not the millions of Americans who get a flu shot—it's the even larger number of Americans who don't get one. When an individual compares the private costs and benefits of getting a flu shot, it may be quite sensible not to get one. It takes time to get a shot, it costs money, and often a slight fever and ache are associated with the vaccine itself. The problem is that the person getting the shot bears all these costs but doesn't receive all the benefits. As a result, fewer people get flu shots than is efficient.

In Figure 10.3 on the next page, for example, we show the demand and supply of vaccines. Demanders compare their private value of vaccines with their private costs and purchase Q_{Market} units at the price P_{Market}. Vaccination, however, reduces the probability that a disease spreads so there are external benefits from vaccination. The social value curve counts *all* the benefits of vaccine use, the private value plus the external benefits, so the efficient quantity is found where the social value curve intersects the supply curve.

To see exactly why the market equilibrium is not efficient, consider in Figure 10.3 the private and social value of the Q_{Market} unit of vaccination. This unit has a private cost of $20 (the black arrow labeled "Private cost"), but it has a social value of $40 (the green arrow labeled "Social value"). Thus, consuming more units would increase social surplus. Following this logic, you can see that increasing output increases social surplus so long as the social value of an additional flu shot exceeds the private cost, that is, so long as the social value curve is above the supply curve. Thus, to maximize social surplus, output should increase to $Q_{Efficient}$, the unit for which social value just equals the costs of production.

A final way of illustrating the underuse of vaccines is to notice that *if* people who got a flu shot did receive all the benefits of vaccination, then their demand

An **external benefit** is a benefit received by people other than the consumers or producers trading in the market.

A private cost and a social benefit

---

[*] An antibiotic could also have an external benefit in the case of infections that can be easily transmitted. Not all infections are easily transmitted, however, and the external costs due to antibiotic resistance appear to be much larger than any external benefits.

FIGURE 10.3

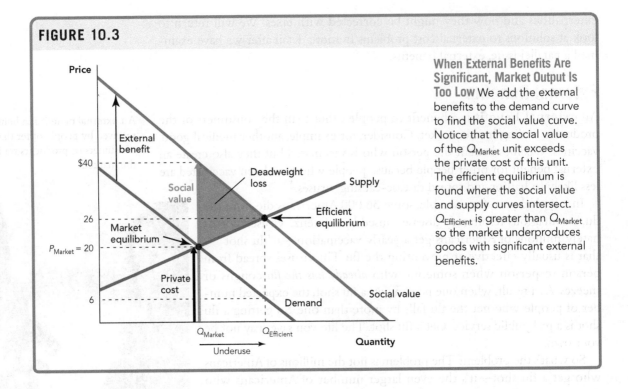

When External Benefits Are Significant, Market Output Is Too Low We add the external benefits to the demand curve to find the social value curve. Notice that the social value of the Q_{Market} unit exceeds the private cost of this unit. The efficient equilibrium is found where the social value and supply curves intersect. $Q_{Efficient}$ is greater than Q_{Market} so the market underproduces goods with significant external benefits.

curve would shift upward by $20 and would be the same as the social value curve. The market equilibrium would then be the same as the efficient equilibrium; that is, buyers would purchase $Q_{Efficient}$ units. But for determining efficiency, *who* receives the benefits is irrelevant—benefits are benefits regardless of who receives them. Thus, $Q_{Efficient}$ is the efficient quantity when vaccine users receive all of the benefits of vaccination *and* when they receive only some of the benefits—the only difference is that when other people receive some of the benefits, fewer people purchase flu shots, so $Q_{Market} < Q_{Efficient}$.

This way of thinking about the problem of external benefits also suggests one potential solution. If every time someone was vaccinated they were given a subsidy of $20, the monetary equivalent of the external benefit, they would demand the amount $Q_{Efficient}$. Recall from Chapter 6 that we can analyze a subsidy by shifting up the demand curve by the amount of the subsidy. Thus, in Figure 10.3, notice that a subsidy set equal to the level of the external benefit would shift the demand curve up and increase the market quantity from Q_{Market} to $Q_{Efficient}$. In other words, if set correctly, a subsidy will make the market equilibrium equal to the efficient equilibrium. In addition, unlike in Chapter 6 where we looked at subsidies on ordinary goods, a subsidy on a good with an external benefit will reduce deadweight loss, thereby increasing social surplus.

A subsidy on a good with an external benefit is often called a **Pigouvian subsidy,** again after Pigou, who first discussed these issues. Another way of thinking about Pigouvian taxes and subsidies is to recall from Chapter 7 that market prices are signals. But when there are external costs or benefits, the market price sends the wrong signal. If there are external costs, the market price is too low, thus resulting in overconsumption. A Pigouvian tax increases the price so that the after-tax price sends the correct signal. Similarly, if there

A **Pigouvian subsidy** is a subsidy on a good with external benefits.

are external benefits, the market price is too high, thus resulting in underconsumption. A Pigouvian subsidy reduces the price paid by buyers so that the after-subsidy price sends the correct signal.

COVID-19 and the External Benefits of Vaccination The COVID-19 pandemic demonstrated that the external benefits of vaccination can be very large. As many as 20 million people around the world were likely killed by the SAR-COV-II virus.[2] Fear of the virus caused governments to lock down cities and regions, greatly reducing GDP. Even without lockdowns, people fled from restaurants, bars, and sports stadiums and started to work from home. Once people were vaccinated, however, death rates fell dramatically, and GDP increased as people started to once again work, travel, and play together. Overall, economists estimated that the external benefits of a course of vaccine were worth $5,800 or more.[3] Vaccines were typically priced at approximately $20 to $40 per course (two doses), so the value of vaccines far exceeded their price.

https://youtu.be/2EFG6dvtQ6M

The Economics of COVID

Governments responded to the external benefits of COVID-19 vaccination in two ways. First, the price of vaccines was subsidized so that consumers paid nothing. Indeed, the external benefits of vaccination were so high that it might have made sense to pay people to get vaccinated. Beyond giving away some lottery tickets or doughnuts, however, few governments paid people to get vaccinated. But some governments did mandate vaccination, especially in certain occupations. Mandates are a type of command and control that we discuss at greater length later in the chapter. Vaccine mandates were controversial, a reminder that what is efficient on paper may not be efficient in practice.

Second, governments subsidized the production of vaccines. The biggest effort came from the United States with Operation Warp Speed (OWS). OWS, for example, paid for the clinical trials of the Moderna vaccine. Clinical trials are the most expensive part of the vaccine development process, and by funding the trials generously, the trials could be made large, which meant that they could be done much more quickly than if Moderna had paid for the trials out of their own pocket. The U.S. government also invested in capacity, helping to build factories for the vaccines and also for the needles, vials, and other necessary inputs, even before any of the vaccines were approved. Ordinarily, a vaccine manufacturer wouldn't build a factory until after its vaccine was approved. By paying to build the factories in advance, OWS ensured that capacity was ready to go the moment a vaccine was approved. Bringing the vaccines to market fast saved hundreds of thousands and perhaps millions of lives worldwide.

Let's look in more detail at how to solve problems caused by external costs or benefits. We will discuss private solutions to problems created by externalities and three types of solutions involving government: taxes and subsidies (which we have mentioned already), command and control, and tradeable permits.

CHECK YOURSELF

- In our discussion of Pigouvian taxes, we assumed that the government set the correct tax to achieve the efficient equilibrium. What if government overshoots and adds a tax that is too high? Will the equilibrium quantity be higher or lower than the efficient equilibrium?

- In our discussion of Pigouvian subsidies, we assumed that government set the correct subsidy amount to achieve the efficient equilibrium. What if the government undershoots and provides a subsidy that is too low? Will the equilibrium quantity be higher or lower than the efficient equilibrium?

Private Solutions to Externality Problems

In a classic paper on externalities, the Nobel Prize–winning economist James Meade wrote that the market for honey was inefficient. As they make honey, bees pollinate fruits and vegetables, which is an important benefit to farmers.

Since pollination is an external benefit of honey production, Meade argued there was too little honey being made.

Meade was right about the bees, but wrong about the market for honey. Bee pollination is a thriving business for which beekeepers are paid. In fact, in the United States, beekeepers manage many billions of bees that they truck around the country to rent out to farmers. Since farmers pay beekeepers to pollinate their crops, the "external benefit" becomes **internalized**—the beekeepers earn money from the pollination of fruits and vegetables and so expand production toward the efficient quantity, the quantity that takes into account the benefits of bees for honey production and for fruit and vegetable production.[4]

Internalizing an externality means adjusting incentives so that decision makers take into account all the benefits and costs of their actions, private and social.

The lesson of the bees is that our earlier story was a bit too pessimistic. The market equilibrium can be efficient even when there are externalities, *if* there is systematic trading in those externalities. To see which externalities the market can handle, let's take a closer look at why the market for pollination works reasonably well.

The market for pollination works because transaction costs are low and property rights are clearly defined. **Transaction costs** are all the costs necessary to reach an agreement. The costs of identifying and bringing buyers and sellers together, bargaining, and drawing up a contract are all transaction costs. Transaction costs are low for beekeepers and farmers because farms are large and bees don't fly that far. So when a beekeeper places bees in the center of a large farm, the beekeeper and the farmer know that the bees will pollinate the crops owned by the farmer who is paying and not pollinate some other farmer's crops. As a result, the externality from bees is limited to one farmer at a time and can be internalized with one transaction.

Transaction costs are all the costs necessary to reach an agreement.

iStock/Getty Images

Bees create external "beenefits."

Property rights over farms and bees are also clearly defined. Everyone knows that the beekeeper has the right to the benefits created by bee pollination, so if the farmer wants bees to pollinate their crops, they must pay the beekeeper. This works for beekeepers and farmers, but as you will see, property rights in other externalities are not as clearly defined and this makes transactions more difficult; you might say that unclear property rights are a type of transaction cost, since they make it harder to trade.

It's not so difficult for beekeepers to trade with farmers, but how many transactions would it take to internalize the external benefit created when someone has a flu shot? When one person is vaccinated, thousands of other people benefit by a small amount, especially if the vaccinated person spends a lot of time in airports. When Alex has the flu and coughs while boarding a plane, he could spread the flu virus to dozens of other people, each of whom could in turn pass it on to many others. If Alex receives a flu shot, all these people are better off. In theory, if each of these people paid Alex a small amount for getting a flu shot, Alex would be more likely to get a flu shot. But the transaction costs of arranging a deal like this are enormous—simply to identify the beneficiaries is difficult and getting thousands of them to send a check to Alex is next to impossible (trust us, we have tried!).

What about property rights? We assumed that other people might be willing to pay Alex to get a flu shot because the flu shot creates an external benefit. But when Alex spreads the flu, he imposes an external cost on other people. Maybe

Alex should have to pay other people when he doesn't get a flu shot! Even when other transaction costs are low, if property rights are not well defined—who should have to pay whom—it will be difficult to solve externality problems with bargaining.

Ronald Coase, another Nobel Prize winner, summarized the situations in which markets alone can solve the externality problems in what has come to be called the **Coase theorem**. The Coase theorem says that if transaction costs are low and property rights are clearly defined, then private bargains will ensure that the market equilibrium is efficient even when there are externalities. In other words, in these cases trading makes sure that just the right amount of the externality is produced. If there were either too little or too much of the externality, trading would push the quantity to the optimum level.

Recall that in a free market, the quantity of goods sold maximizes the sum of consumer and producer surplus. If the conditions of the Coase theorem are met, we can replace this with the even stronger conclusion that in a free market, the quantity of goods sold will maximize social surplus, the sum of consumer, producer, and everyone else's surplus.

But the conditions of the Coase theorem are often *unlikely* to be met. Transaction costs for many externalities are high and property rights are often not clearly defined. Thus, markets alone will *not* solve all externality problems.

The importance of the Coase theorem lies not in suggesting that markets alone might solve externality problems, but in suggesting a solution: the creation of new markets. If property rights can be clearly defined and transaction costs reduced, then a market for externalities might develop. If such a market does develop, we know from the Coase theorem that it will have all the efficiency properties of ordinary markets.

Government can play a role in defining property rights and reducing transaction costs. In fact, governments have helped to create working markets in many externalities, verifying the insights of the Coase theorem. Next, we discuss one of these new markets, a market in the right to emit pollution.

> The **Coase theorem** posits that if transaction costs are low and property rights are clearly defined, private bargains will ensure that the market equilibrium is efficient even when there are externalities.

CHECK YOURSELF

- You want to hold a Saturday night party at your house but are worried that your older neighbors will complain to the police about the noise. Suggest a solution to this problem using what you know about the Coase theorem.

- Consider a factory near you that pollutes. What are the transaction costs involved in you and your neighbors negotiating with the factory to reduce the pollution? Is a private solution possible?

Government Solutions to Externality Problems

We have already discussed one kind of government solution to externality problems, namely taxes and subsidies. Two other solutions are also common: command and control and tradeable allowances for the activity in question. We will look at both of these solutions in the context of another externality, acid rain, and we will also offer some comparisons with taxes and subsidies.

Acid rain damages forests and lakes, it corrodes metal and stone, and in the form of particulates, it creates haze and increases lung diseases such as asthma and bronchitis. Acid rain is caused when sulfur dioxide (SO_2) and nitrogen oxides (NO_x) are released into the atmosphere. A majority of SO_2 and a significant fraction of NO_x are created in the process of generating electricity from coal. Let's look at how the government has reduced the external cost of acid rain.

Command and Control

When external costs are significant, we know that $Q_{Market} > Q_{Efficient}$, so the most obvious (but not necessarily the best) method to reduce the external cost of electricity generation is for the government to order firms to use (or make) less electricity. This is called a command and control method. Command and control methods are not always efficient. The government, for example, issued a command and control regulation in January 2007 that required manufacturers to make clothes washers that use 21% less electricity, yet *Consumer Reports* testing found that traditional top-load washers were having difficulty getting clothes clean with less power. *Consumer Reports* reviewed the clothes washers produced under this new standard and the reviewers were not happy with the results:[5]

> Not so long ago you could count on most washers to get your clothes very clean. Not anymore. Our latest tests found huge performance differences among machines. Some left our stain-soaked swatches nearly as dirty as they were before washing. For best results, you'll have to spend $900 or more.

The problem with command and control is that there are typically many methods to achieve a goal and the government may not have enough information to choose the least costly method. Let's suppose, for example, that the Department of Energy's regulation on clothes washers reduces electricity consumption by 1% (this number is too large but it will do for our purposes). Now let's compare command and control with a tax on electricity consumption that causes people to reduce their electricity consumption by *exactly the same amount*, 1%.[6] Faced with an increase in price, how would people choose to reduce their electricity consumption?

If the price of electricity increased, some people would choose to cut back on electricity by turning their lights off more often or by switching to lower-consumption LED bulbs. Other people would respond by turning down the heat or the air conditioning, or by buying a cover for their pool, or by installing insulation in their attic. The ways in which people would reduce electricity consumption are as different as the people themselves. But notice that probably very few people would respond to an increase in the price of electricity by spending a *lot* more on a clothes washer that saves electricity or by buying a clothes washer that saves electricity but doesn't clean very well. Thus, the government's method of reducing electricity consumption is not the lowest-cost method.

A tax on electricity can reduce the consumption of electricity by exactly the same amount as a regulation on clothes washers but a tax will cost less. The tax costs less because a tax gives people the flexibility to reduce consumption in the way that is least costly to them. Recall from Chapter 7 that prices are signals. A tax on electricity sends a signal to every user of electricity that says "Economize!" But the tax leaves it to each person to use their local knowledge and unique preferences to choose the least costly method of economizing.

It's better to reduce electricity consumption with a tax than with a regulation on clothes washers, but we can do even better. After all, we don't really want to reduce *electricity*—we want to reduce *pollutants* like SO_2 and NO_x. It's true that pollutants are a by-product of electricity generation but there are many ways of reducing SO_2 and NO_x other than by producing less electricity. Thus, monitoring the production of SO_2 and NO_x and taxing the pollutants directly is a better way of creating incentives to reduce pollution than is taxing electricity. Taxing the pollutants directly gives firms the maximum flexibility to adopt the least costly methods of reducing pollution. Remember it's the pollutants that are creating the external cost so taxing the pollutants sends the right signal.

Command and control is not always a bad idea. The advantage of using incentives like taxes to control an externality is flexibility. The government corrects the price with a tax or subsidy so the price sends the right signal and people adapt using their own information and preferences (with all the benefits of the price system that we described in Chapters 4 and 7). But flexibility is not always desirable. Consider, for example, one of the great triumphs of humanity—the eradication of smallpox. Smallpox killed 300–500 million people in the twentieth century alone. As late as 1967, 2 million people died and millions more were scarred and blinded from smallpox, but in that year the World Health Organization (WHO) launched a program of mass vaccination, intensive surveillance, and immediate quarantine. The WHO program relied on command and control because so long as *any* reservoir of smallpox remained anywhere on the planet, the virus could reemerge and spread worldwide. To be successful, the WHO could not rely on taxes because it needed everyone to follow its policies—flexibility was not desirable. Fortunately, the WHO program was successful and by 1978 smallpox was extinct— the first and so far the only human infectious disease to be stopped dead in its tracks.*

Command and control was also used to address the COVID-19 pandemic of 2020. Universities and schools were closed, and many countries around the globe, including regions of Italy, China, and the United States, were locked down. Events with more than a small number of people were banned. Most controversially, governments sometimes mandated that people be vaccinated or else lose their jobs. Requiring people to be vaccinated made sense when focusing on the external benefits of vaccination, but it should not be forgotten that the preferences of the people being vaccinated against their will also count. Command and control works best when it works in the same direction as incentives and social consensus.

The bottom line is that command and control can be useful if the best approach to a problem is well known and if success requires very strong compliance. If it's important to control the externality at the least possible cost and if the government doesn't have full information, then more flexible approaches such as taxes and subsidies are preferable.

Tradeable Allowances

Another type of command and control program is to require that firms reduce pollutants by a specific quantity. In the 1970s, for example, the government limited SO_2 from all generators of electricity to a maximum rate. The problem with this approach is that because of differences in location, fuel, and technology, it's much cheaper to reduce emissions of SO_2 from some firms than from others. By treating all firms the same, the government reduced flexibility and increased the cost of eliminating a given amount of pollution.

A simple example illustrates the problem with quantity restrictions and a potential solution. Suppose that there are two firms. We begin with a command and control regulation that limits each firm to 100 tons of SO_2 emissions in a year. Now imagine that reducing pollution at High-Cost Industries is

---

* Command and control continues to be used today in handling other infectious diseases. Before registering for classes, for example, school-age children and college and university students must show that they have had their MMR vaccine (preventing measles, mumps, rubella).

MRU

mru.org/pollution-permits

Should We Trade the Right to Pollute?

expensive, so High could save $1,100 if it were allowed to produce 101 tons of SO_2 instead of being limited to 100 tons. Low-Cost Industries can control its pollution quite cheaply, so if Low reduces its pollution level even further to 99 tons, its costs increase by only $200.

Now imagine that the CEOs of High and Low approach the head of the Environmental Protection Agency (EPA) with a proposal. The CEOs suggest that High be allowed to increase its pollution level by 1 ton to 101 tons. High will also pay $500 to Low. In return, Low will cut its pollution level by 1 ton to 99 tons. It's clear why High and Low want the deal—it's profitable. High cuts its pollution control costs by $1,100 for which it pays $500 for a net increase in profit of $600. Low increases its pollution control costs by $200, but it receives a $500 payment for a net increase in profit of $300. But should the EPA accept this deal?

Yes, if the EPA cares about social surplus, it should accept the deal. Notice that pollution stays exactly the same, 200 units, so the deal does not harm the environment. The deal, however, does increase profits by $900 ($600 to High and $300 to Low). Should the EPA care about firm profits? Maybe not directly, but notice why profits increase in this example. Profits increase because the costs of reducing pollution fall. By trading, the firms reduce the cost of eliminating the last unit of pollution from $1,100 to just $200—a $900 fall in costs and that represents an increase in resources available to society.

So, let's ask our question in a different way. Should the EPA care about decreasing the costs of reducing pollution? Of course the answer is yes. If we can reduce the same amount of pollution at lower cost, that means more resources are available for other goods. And the lower the costs of eliminating pollution, the more pollution it makes sense to eliminate.

What we have shown is that trading pollution allowances is like a new technology that reduces pollution at lower cost. The EPA should always be in favor of new technologies to reduce pollution and so it should also be in favor of trades in the right to pollute.

Tradeable Allowances in Practice A formal version of the tradeable allowances system that we have just described was created by the Clean Air Act of 1990. Under this reform, the EPA distributes pollution allowances to generators of electricity, and each allowance gives the owner the right to emit 1 ton of SO_2. Firms may trade allowances as they see fit and they have organized sophisticated markets in tradeable allowances. Firms can even bank allowances for future use. The EPA monitors each firm's emissions of SO_2, and it also tracks how many allowances each firm owns so no firm can emit more pollution than it has allowances for. Congress sets the total number of allowances.

The EPA's tradeable allowances program has been very successful, as SO_2 emissions have been reduced, air quality has improved, and illness has been reduced.[7] Remarkably, as shown in Figure 10.4, electricity generation has increased even as SO_2 emissions have decreased.

The EPA's system of tradeable allowances is a successful application of the Coase theorem. Recall that the Coase theorem says that markets can internalize externalities when transaction costs are low and property rights are clearly defined. The Clean Air Act of 1990 clearly defined

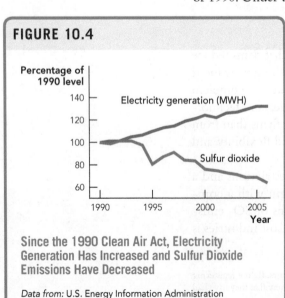

FIGURE 10.4

Percentage of 1990 level

Electricity generation (MWH)

Sulfur dioxide

Since the 1990 Clean Air Act, Electricity Generation Has Increased and Sulfur Dioxide Emissions Have Decreased

Data from: U.S. Energy Information Administration

rights to emit SO_2, and the EPA has reduced transaction costs by distributing the allowances, monitoring emissions, and creating a database that tracks ownership. Trading in markets has then allocated the allowances among firms in the way that minimizes the costs of reducing pollution.

One of the most interesting aspects of the market in rights to emit sulfur dioxide is that anyone can participate, not just generators of electricity. We bought the rights to emit 30 pounds of SO_2. We don't intend to emit any pollutants; rather, we bought the rights and ripped them up in order to create more clean air. Environmentalists and industry often oppose one another, but when markets in externalities are created, environmentalists can buy pollutants and industry is happy to sell—as always, trade makes both parties better off.

An important result of the SO_2 trading program is that firms that generate electricity from relatively clean sources such as solar power can make money by selling their pollution allowances. In contrast, firms that generate electricity from relatively dirty sources must buy allowances. In essence, clean energy is subsidized and dirty energy is taxed—thus, a program of tradeable allowances correctly reflects the fact that clean energy has lower social costs than dirty energy.

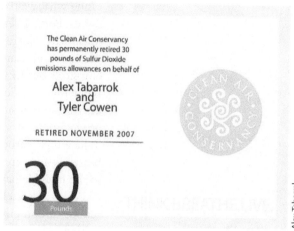

We bought the right to pollute.

Climate Change and the Carbon Tax

In January 2019, thousands of economists including 28 Nobel laureates signed an open letter arguing that the best way to address the problem of climate change was a carbon tax. To quote the letter:

1. A carbon tax offers the most cost-effective lever to reduce carbon emissions at the scale and speed that is necessary. By correcting a well-known market failure, a carbon tax will send a powerful price signal that harnesses the invisible hand of the marketplace to steer economic actors toward a low-carbon future.

2. A carbon tax should increase every year until emissions reductions goals are met and be revenue neutral to avoid debates over the size of government. A consistently rising carbon price will encourage technological innovation and large-scale infrastructure development. It will also accelerate the diffusion of carbon-efficient goods and services.

3. A sufficiently robust and gradually rising carbon tax will replace the need for various carbon regulations that are less efficient. Substituting a price signal for cumbersome regulations will promote economic growth and provide the regulatory certainty that companies need for long-term investment in clean-energy alternatives.

4. To prevent carbon leakage and to protect U.S. competitiveness, a border carbon adjustment system should be established. This system would enhance the competitiveness of American firms that are more energy-efficient than their global competitors. It would also create an incentive for other nations to adopt similar carbon pricing.

5. To maximize the fairness and political viability of a rising carbon tax, all the revenue should be returned directly to U.S. citizens through equal

lump-sum rebates. The majority of American families, including the most vulnerable, will benefit financially by receiving more in "carbon dividends" than they pay in increased energy prices.

Using what we have learned in this chapter, we can now understand each of these points. Point 1 reminds us that carbon released into the atmosphere contributes to climate change and thus imposes an eventual cost on bystanders. But note that the economists argue that the goal of a carbon tax is not to eliminate all carbon emissions but to solve the market failure by correctly pricing carbon emissions. Remember, a price is a signal wrapped up in an incentive. Thus, by correctly pricing carbon emissions the market will send a signal about the true cost of different products and services and that signal will incentivize demanders and suppliers to reduce high-carbon products and develop substitutes. In other words, when carbon emissions are correctly priced, self-interest will align with the social interest so the invisible hand can steer economic actors in the right direction.

Point 1 also tells us that a carbon tax offers the most "cost-effective" lever to reduce carbon emissions. Point 2 explains some of the reasons why. A carbon tax operates on *many margins*. A carbon tax will encourage demanders to switch from higher-priced carbon-intensive goods and services to lower-priced, less-carbon intensive substitutes. At the same time, suppliers will be encouraged to research and develop less carbon-intensive goods and services. Over time a carbon tax will even encourage large-scale changes in how energy is generated, where people work and live and how they transport as well as produce goods and services.

Point 3 says that a carbon tax is better than command and control regulations. Remember the clothes washers that didn't work after command and control regulations on energy efficiency were imposed before the available technology was cost-effective? The same principles apply to a carbon tax. Instead of requiring that every new home install solar panels, a potentially very costly mandate imposed in California, the economists are suggesting that we apply a carbon tax and let people decide how to reduce carbon emissions in the least costly way. Command and control works on only a few margins, whereas a carbon tax works across many margins in ways that are too complex for planners to predict or plan. Recall from Chapter 7 how one response to increased oil prices was to move flower production overseas and how another response was to pave driveways with brick instead of asphalt! A carbon tax uses the forces of creative destruction, which brought us cell phones, online dating, and movies on demand, to address the challenge of climate change.

Point 4 makes an important point that we have not made before. The problem of climate change is especially difficult to solve because the external cost of carbon emissions crosses all borders and boundaries. A carbon tax is unlikely to be effective if it is imposed by the United States alone. Indeed, it could be even counterproductive if relatively low-carbon U.S. producers were taxed but not higher-carbon foreign competitors. Thus, Point 4 suggests a border adjustment scheme so that at least within the United States all producers, foreign and domestic, would be taxed on a level playing field. The United States is one of the world's largest markets, so Point 4 suggests that this will encourage other countries to adopt carbon taxes. Getting both the economics and the politics right is one of the most difficult parts of designing a global carbon tax.

The politics of a carbon tax are also discussed in Points 2 and 5. Point 2 argues that a carbon tax should be "revenue neutral." The signatories to the letter don't necessarily agree on whether the government should spend more or less money on defense or Medicare or the National Institutes of Health. What they do agree on is that a carbon tax is the best way to reduce atmospheric carbon emissions. To get everyone on board, therefore, the economists suggest that all the money raised by the carbon tax should be returned to the residents of the United States. One possibility, for example, is to reduce income taxes by a dollar for every dollar raised by the carbon tax—tax burning not earning. Another possibility is to give each U.S. citizen an equal "carbon dividend." Here the economists' signatories are making a political point. A carbon dividend might be a good way of selling the carbon tax to a large number of voters, especially as the dividend would be more than most voters would pay in tax.

Carbon Taxes Around the World Coal powered the industrial revolution, and for more than 150 years coal was a major source of energy for the United Kingdom. On April 21, 2017, however, the United Kingdom went 24 hours without any electricity generated from coal—the first time this had happened since the 1880s. Coal use had been slowly declining in the United Kingdom since its peak in the 1950s, but as late as 2012, coal still accounted for nearly 20% of U.K. energy use. In 2013, however, the United Kingdom introduced a carbon tax and coal use began a rapid and dramatic decline as shown in Figure 10.5. By 2017, coal accounted for only 5% of energy use. By 2025, it's expected that coal will be phased out entirely.

In 1952 coal smog engulfed London, killing thousands of people.

The United Kingdom's carbon tax raised the price of coal relative to other energy sources such as solar, wind, and natural gas. Natural gas is a carbon-emitting fuel, but it emits carbon at half the rate of coal for the same amount of energy, so switching to natural gas reduced the tax on electricity generators and the tax on the environment.

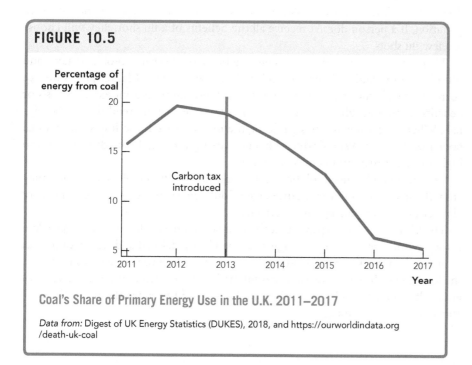

FIGURE 10.5

Percentage of energy from coal

Carbon tax introduced

Coal's Share of Primary Energy Use in the U.K. 2011–2017

Data from: Digest of UK Energy Statistics (DUKES), 2018, and https://ourworldindata.org/death-uk-coal

MRU

mru.org/pollution-health

Pollution Is an Attack on Human Capital

Chess players make worse moves when there is a lot of air pollution.

CHECK YOURSELF

- Government sets a total quantity of tradeable pollution allowances and auctions them off. After the auction, the price for an individual allowance is high. Over time, the price falls dramatically. What does this tell you?

- The local government has decided to set and apportion tradeable allowances for pollution in your neighborhood. Name three groups that would press for a large total quantity of allowances. Name three groups that would press for a smaller total quantity of allowances. Considering these groups, how likely is it that government would set a total quantity of allowances that would achieve an efficient equilibrium?

Other countries around the world have also introduced carbon taxes. Canada has a carbon tax and the revenues from the tax are rebated back to Canadian citizens. Sweden, Argentina, Japan, and Norway also have carbon taxes, and China has introduced the largest tradeable allowance program for carbon (cap and trade) in the world and has slowly been making the cap more binding. Although there is no federal carbon tax in the United States, California has a tradeable allowance program, and there are several regional programs, including the Regional Greenhouse Gas Initiative that covers twelve states.

Phasing out coal will not only reduce carbon emissions but also increase health, as coal-burning emissions are especially toxic. Indeed, some types of pollution are so toxic that they can reduce productivity, meaning that taxing them could result in net gains to production!

Economists have found, for example, that infants exposed to high levels of air pollution are more likely to be born premature or with low birth weight, factors that can reduce productivity and health for a lifetime. Other studies show that air pollution tends to reduce cognitive performance. Chess players, for example, make worse chess moves on high-pollution days, and students who go to schools that are downwind of major highways tend to have lower grades than students who go to schools that are upwind of major sources of air pollution.[8] These studies and many others, which use advanced statistical techniques to eliminate other explanations for these effects (see video), have convinced many economists that reducing air pollution could increase both health and wealth.

Takeaway

In a free market, the quantity of goods sold maximizes consumer plus producer surplus. When the consumers and producers bear all the significant costs and benefits of trading, the market quantity is also the efficient quantity. But when there are external costs or benefits, the market quantity is not the efficient quantity. If it doesn't bear all the costs of pollution, an electricity generator will emit too much pollution. If a person doesn't receive all the benefits of a flu shot, they will choose too few flu shots.

There are three types of government solutions to externality problems: taxes and subsidies, command and control, and tradeable allowances. Market prices do not correctly signal true costs and benefits when there are significant external costs or benefits. Taxes and subsidies can adjust prices so that they do send the correct signals. When external costs are significant, the market price is too low, so an optimal tax raises the price. When external benefits are significant, the market price is too high, so an optimal subsidy lowers the price.

Command and control solutions can work but are often high cost because they are inflexible and do not take advantage of differences in the costs and benefits of eliminating and producing the externality.

The Coase theorem explains that the ultimate source of the externality problem is too few markets. If property rights can be clearly defined and transaction costs reduced, then markets in the externality will solve the problem and will do so at the lowest cost. In recent years, successful markets have been created in the right to emit sulfur dioxide, and new markets are being used to reduce the gases that contribute to global warming.

CHAPTER REVIEW

Go online to practice with more examples of these types of problems, including live links to videos, data sources, and feedback.

KEY CONCEPTS

private cost, p. 187

external cost, p. 188

social cost, p. 188

externalities, p. 188

social surplus, p. 188

efficient equilibrium, p. 189

efficient quantity, p. 189

Pigouvian tax, p. 190

external benefit, p. 191

Pigouvian subsidy, p. 192

internalizing an externality, p. 194

transaction costs, p. 194

Coase theorem, p. 195

FACTS AND TOOLS

1. Let's sort the following eight items into private costs, external costs, private benefits, or external benefits. There's only one correct answer for each of questions a–h.

   a. The price you pay for an iTunes download

   b. The benefit your neighbor receives from hearing you play your pleasant music

   c. The annoyance of your neighbor because they don't appreciate your wonderful taste in music

   d. The pleasure you receive from listening to your iTunes download

   e. The price you pay for a security system for your home

   f. The safety you enjoy as a result of having the security system

   g. The crime that is more likely to occur to your neighbor once a criminal sees a "Protected by alarm" sticker on your window

   h. The extra safety your neighbor might experience because criminals tend to stay away from neighborhoods that have a lot of burglar alarms

2. If the students at your school started saying "thank you" to friends who got COVID-19 vaccines, would this tend to reduce the undersupply of people who get vaccinated? Why or why not?

3. a. Consider a factory, located in the middle of nowhere, producing a nasty smell. As long as no one is around to experience the unpleasant odor, are any externalities produced?

   b. Suppose that a family moves in next door to the smelly factory. Do we now have an externalities problem? If so, who is causing it: the factory by producing the smell, the family by moving in next door, or both?

   c. Suppose that the family clearly possesses the right to a pleasant-smelling environment. Does this mean that the factory will be required to stop producing the bad smell? What could happen instead? There are many right answers. (*Hint:* Think about the Coase theorem. Actually, it's *always* a good idea to think about the Coase theorem, whether the topic is smelly factories, labor–management disputes, international peace negotiations, or divorce settlements.)

4. Considering what we've learned about externalities, should the emissions leading to human-caused global warming be *completely* stopped? Explain, using the language of social benefits and social costs.

5. In the following cases, the markets are in equilibrium, but there are externalities. In each case, determine whether there is an external benefit or cost and estimate its size. Finally, decide between a tax or a subsidy as a simple way to compensate for the externality. Fill out the table that follows with your answers.

   a. In the market for automobiles, the private cost of manufacturing one more small SUV is $20,000, and the social cost of one more small SUV is $30,000.

   b. In the market for fashionable clothes, the marginal social benefit of one more dress per person is $100, and the marginal private benefit is $500. Bonus: Can you tell an externality story that makes sense of these numbers?

Case	External Cost or Benefit?	Size of External Benefit (or Cost If Negative)	Tax It or Subsidize It?
a. SUVs			
b. Fashionable clothes			
c. Ideas			

c. In the market for really good ideas, ideas that will dramatically change the world for the better, the private benefit of one more really good idea (from speaker's fees, book sales, patents, etc.) is $1 million. The marginal social benefit is $1 billion.

6. In which cases are the Coase theorem's assumptions likely to be true? In other words, when will the parties be likely to strike an efficient bargain? How do you know?

a. My neighbor wants me to cut down an ugly shrub in my front yard. The ugly shrub, of course, imposes an external cost on them and on their property value.

b. My neighbors all would love for me to get that broken-down Ford Pinto off my front lawn. It's been years now, after all. And would it be too much for me to paint the house and fill up that 6-foot deep ditch in the front yard? The whole neighborhood is annoyed.

c. A coal-fired electricity plant dumps its leftover hot water into the nearby lake, killing the naturally occurring fish. Thousands of homes line the banks of the lake.

d. A coal-fired electricity plant dumps its leftover hot water into the nearby river, killing the naturally occurring fish downstream. There is one large fishery 1 mile downstream affected by this. After that, the water cools enough so it's not a problem.

7. With electricity, we saw that it was important to tax the pollutant rather than the final product itself. In the following cases, will the proposed taxes actually hit at the source of the external cost, or will it only land an inefficient glancing blow? What kind of tax might be better?

a. Gas-guzzling cars create more pollution, so the government should tax big SUVs at a higher rate.

b. All-night liquor stores seem to generate unruly behavior in nearby neighborhoods, so owners of all-night liquor stores should pay higher property taxes.

c. Mom jeans have recently made a comeback, and their ugliness creates external costs for all who see them. Therefore, mom jeans should be taxed heavily.

d. American parents are worried about their children hearing too much profanity on television. Congress decides to tax TV shows based on the number of profane words used on the shows.

8. When the government expands the number of pollution allowances, does that increase the cost of polluting or cut it? What about when the number of pollution allowances is cut back?

9. Baron Energy is opening a new coal-fired power plant, but the government wants to keep pollution down.

a. Based on what we've seen in this chapter, which is a more efficient way to reduce pollution: commanding Baron Energy to use one particular air-scrubbing technology that will reduce pollution by 25% or commanding Baron Energy to reduce pollution by 25%?

b. If a corrupt government just grants Baron Energy all of the (tradeable) pollution permits in the entire nation (even though there are many energy companies), does this guarantee that Baron Energy will engage in an enormous amount of pollution? Why or why not?

THINKING AND PROBLEM SOLVING

10. When someone is sick, the patient's decision to take an antibiotic imposes costs on others—it helps bacteria evolve resistance faster. But it also gives free benefits to others: It may slow down the spread of infectious disease the same way that vaccinations do (assuming that it is properly being used to treat a bacterial disease). Thus, antibiotics can create external *costs* as well as external *benefits*. In theory, these could cancel each other out, so that just the right amount of antibiotics is being used. But economists think that, on balance, there is overuse of antibiotics,

not underuse. Why? (*Hint:* Think on the margin!)

11. A flu shot typically costs about $20–$75 but some firms offer their workers free flu shots. Why might a firm prefer to offer its workers free flu shots if the alternative is an equally costly wage increase?

12. "The environment is priceless." What evidence do you have that this statement is incorrect?

13. Cultural influences often create externalities, for good and ill. A happy movie might make people smile more, which improves the lives of people who don't see the movie. A fashion trend for tight-fitting clothing might hurt the body image of people who think they won't look good in the trendy clothing.

Let's consider the market for one cultural good that unrealistically raises expectations about the opposite sex: the romance novel. In romance novels, men are dangerous yet safe, they are wealthy yet never at work, they ride high-speed motorcycles yet never get in terrible accidents, they look fantastic even though they never waste endless hours at the gym, and so on. (Of course, advertising that focuses on sexy female models may also unrealistically raise expectations about the opposite sex so feel free to change our example as you see best.)

a. Consider the following market. Romance novels impose an external cost on men, who have to try to live up to these unrealistic expectations. Illustrate the effect of this external cost in the figure.

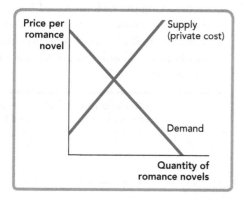

b. Illustrate in the figure the deadweight loss from the externality, before a tax or other solution is imposed.

c. If the government decides to compensate for the externality by imposing a tax on romance novels, should the tax be high

enough to stop everyone from reading the novels? Why or why not?

d. Show graphically how big the tax should be per novel.

e. As long as the government spends the money efficiently, does it matter what the government spends the money from the "romance novel tax" on? In other words, could the government just use the money to pay for necessary roads and bridges, or does it need to spend the money to fix the harmful social effects of romance novels?

14. Neptune 09 Apartments wants to build a playground to increase demand for its larger, high-end, family-friendly apartments but is worried that it will be overcrowded with tenants from the Sunnyvale Mobile Estates and Twin Crests Townhomes developments nearby.

a. What type of externality is the playground: external cost or external benefit?

b. What type of compromise might Neptune 09 be able to make with Sunnyvale and Twin Crests so that all three developments will benefit from the playground? More than one answer is possible, but give just one based on reasoning from this chapter.

15. a. Refer to the figure here. Suppose that the COVID-19 vaccine has just been approved by the U.S. Food and Drug Administration for public use, but due to skepticism surrounding the efficacy of the vaccine, only 5 people have so far been vaccinated. How many units less is this than the socially optimal quantity of vaccinations? What is the total deadweight loss in the market at the current market equilibrium of 5 units?

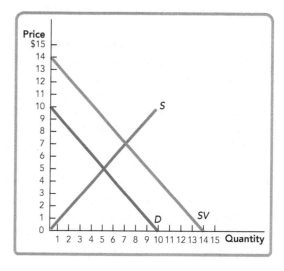

b. Jung is unsure if he wants to get vaccinated against COVID-19, so he decides to consider the social marginal benefit of getting a vaccination to help him make his decision. If Jung is the sixth person to be vaccinated, then what is the social marginal benefit of his vaccination? What is the marginal cost of producing the sixth vaccination? From a societal standpoint, should Jung get vaccinated? State why or why not.

c. What is one way that the government can incentivize people to become vaccinated?

16. In Chapter 6, we said that taxes create deadweight losses. When we tax goods with external costs, should we worry about deadweight losses? Why or why not?

17. Economists have found that increasing the proportion of girls in primary and secondary schools leads to significant improvement in students' cognitive outcomes (Victor Lavy and Analia Schlosser. 2011. Mechanisms and impacts of gender peer effects at school, *American Economic Journal: Applied Economics*.) One key channel seems to be that, on average, boys create more trouble in class, which makes it harder for everyone to learn. In newspaper English, we'd say that "boys are a tax on every child's education."

a. Using the tools of this chapter, do girls in a classroom provide external costs or benefits? What about boys?

b. Just based on this study, if you are a parent of a boy, would you rather your son be in a class with mostly boys or mostly girls? What if you are the parent of a girl?

c. Who should be taxed in this situation? Can you see any problems implementing this tax?

18. In the example of honeybees, we said that the farmers pay the beekeepers for pollination services. But why don't the beekeepers pay the fruit farmers? After all, the beekeepers need the fruit farmers to make honey, so why does the payment go one way and not the other? (*Hint:* What if the honey produced by some fruits and vegetables such as almonds is bitter?)

19. A government is deciding between command and control solutions versus tax and subsidy solutions to solve an externality problem. In each case, explain why you think one is better, using arguments from the chapter.

a. Suppose that whales are threatened with extinction because a large number of people like to eat whale meat. Governments are torn between banning all whaling except for certain religious ceremonies and heavily taxing all whale meat. Assume that only a few countries in the world consume whale meat and that they have fairly efficient governments.

b. Fires create external costs because they spread from one building to another. Should governments encourage subsidies to install sprinklers or should they just mandate that everyone have sprinklers?

c. Pets who procreate can create external costs due to problems with stray animals. Strays are extremely common on the streets of poor countries. Sterilization can solve the problem, but is a tax/subsidy or command and control a better method to encourage sterilization? Does the best solution depend on the sex of the animal?

20. At 5 PM there are 1,000 cars on a highway slowly moving toward home. Adding another car to the highway slows everyone down slightly, increasing the time it takes each person/car to get home by four seconds. How much should the additional car be charged to enter the highway? Assume that people value their time at $15 per hour.

21. Consider a hypothetical nation that provides universal, tax-funded health care to all its citizens. In such a nation, does a positive externality result from citizens eating a healthy diet and regularly exercising? Explain.

22. a. Considering the table provided here, if the federal government required that each firm reduce its pollution by 3 tons, how much would this total pollution reduction of 6 tons cost?

	Firm Pollution (in tons of CO_2)	Cost of removing 1 ton of CO_2
Firm X	25	$400
Firm Y	25	$200

b. Suppose that the federal government decides to issue tradeable permits for CO_2 emissions such that one permit allows the firm to emit 1 ton of CO_2. If the federal government issues 22 CO_2 tradeable permits to Firm X and another 22 CO_2 tradeable permits to Firm Y, describe how the permits will be traded between these two firms. Specifically, identify which firm will purchase permits and which firm will sell permits, how many permits will be traded, and the acceptable trade price range of the permits.

c. If the permits are traded among the firms in the manner you have described, what is the total cost of 6 tons of pollution reduction?

CHALLENGES

23. Before Coase presented his theorem, economists who wanted economic efficiency argued that people should be responsible for the damage they do—they should pay for the social costs of their actions. This advice fits nicely with notions of personal responsibility. Explain how the Coase theorem refutes this older argument.

24. A government is torn between selling annual pollution allowances and setting an annual pollution tax. Unlike in the messy real world, this government is quite certain that it can achieve the same price and quantity either way. It wants to choose the method that will pull in more government tax revenue. Is selling allowances better for revenues or is setting a pollution tax better, or will both raise exactly the same amount of revenue? (*Hint:* Recall that tax revenue is a rectangle. Compare the size of the tax rectangle in Figure 10.5 with the most someone will pay for the right to pollute at the efficient level.)

25. It's common to think that reducing pollution is necessarily costly because to reduce pollution we need to tax firms who will then produce less. But can you think of ways in which pollution might not only be unpleasant but might actually reduce production? Put differently, can you think of ways in which reducing pollution might actually lead to *increases* in worker productivity?

26. Palm Springs, California, was once the playground of the rich and famous—for example, the town has a Frank Sinatra Drive, a Bob Hope Drive, and a Bing Crosby Drive. The city once had a law against building any structure that could cast a shadow on anyone else's property between 9 AM and 3 PM (*Information from:* Alchian, Armen, and William Allen. 1964. *University Economics*, Belmont, CA: Wadsworth). What are some alternatives to this command and control solution? Are they any better than this approach?

WORK IT OUT

For interactive, step-by-step help in solving this problem, go online.

A local town is under pressure from voters to close a polluting factory. The head of the homeowner's organization argues that the pollution is a menace, and if the full external costs of the pollution were included, the factory would be unprofitable. The homeowners calculate that the pollution generates an external cost of $3,000,000 per year in medical bills and $1,000,000 per year in suppressed property values (the difference in home prices with and without the pollution). The factory, on its books, makes a profit of $5,000,000 per year.

a. What is the external cost of the pollution?

b. If the factory is forced to consider the total social costs of pollution, would it be profitable?

c. How much could the town tax the factory before profits became zero?

d. What does the Coase theorem suggest about negotiations between the town and the factory?

11

Costs and Profit Maximization Under Competition

rive through the Texas countryside and standing alone in a field of wheat, you will often see a nodding donkey. In Texas, a nodding donkey isn't an animal but an oil pump. Most oil comes from giant oil fields, but in the United States there are roughly 400,000 "stripper oil wells," oil wells that produce 15 barrels or less per day. That's not much per well, but it adds up to nearly a million barrels of oil a day or over 7% of all U.S. production.[1]

Imagine that you are the owner of a stripper oil well and that you want to maximize your profit. Three questions present themselves:

- What price to set?
- What quantity to produce?
- When to enter and exit the industry?

These three questions are basic to any firm. In this chapter, we will be looking at how to answer these questions in a competitive industry. In later chapters, we will look at these questions for a monopolist.

What Price to Set?

The first of these questions—what price should a firm set?—is the easiest to answer because under some conditions, the firm doesn't set prices; it simply accepts the price that is given by the market. So, let's start with the pricing decision.

If the price of oil is $50 per barrel, will you be able to sell your oil for $100 a barrel? Of course not. Oil is pretty much the same wherever it is found in the world (this is not quite true but it's close enough for our purposes), so even your mother probably won't pay much extra just because it's *your* oil. Thus, you can't charge appreciably more than $50 a barrel. What about charging a lower price? You could charge less, but why would you? The world market for oil is so large that you can easily sell all that you can produce at the market price. Thus, your pricing decision is easy; you can't sell *any* oil at a price above the market price and you can sell *all* your oil at the market price. Thus to maximize profit, you sell at the market price.

A nodding donkey

209

To better understand this result, let's recall an insight about the elasticity of demand from Chapter 5: The more and the better the substitutes, the more elastic the demand. With more than 400,000 oil wells in the United States alone, the substitutes for oil from your well are so plentiful that a useful approximation is to think of the demand for your oil as perfectly elastic (flat) at the world price. In Figure 11.1, we compare the world market for oil on the left with the demand for *your* oil on the right.

The price of oil is determined in the world market, where approximately 100 million barrels are bought and sold every day. Your stripper well, however, can at best produce a tiny fraction of world demand, perhaps 10 barrels of oil per day. As a result, the world price of oil won't change by a noticeable amount whether you produce 2, 7, or 10 barrels of oil a day.* This is why in the right panel of Figure 11.1, we draw the demand curve for your oil as flat at the market price—whether you choose to sell 2, 7, or 10 barrels, the price is the same: $50 per barrel. As a result, we say that the competitive firm is a price taker.

Your job as an entrepreneur is greatly simplified if you don't have to decide on the price, and so is our job as economists trying to understand firm behavior. Thus, in this chapter, we are going to simplify by assuming that the demand for a firm's product is perfectly elastic at the market price.

A stripper well doesn't have much influence on the price of oil because there's nothing special about oil from a particular producer, and there are many

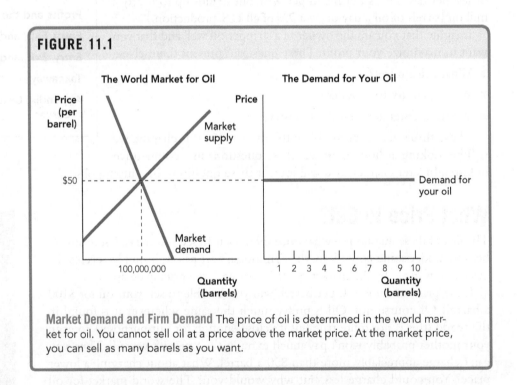

FIGURE 11.1

The World Market for Oil

Price (per barrel)

Market supply

$50

Market demand

100,000,000

Quantity (barrels)

The Demand for Your Oil

Price

Demand for your oil

1 2 3 4 5 6 7 8 9 10

Quantity (barrels)

Market Demand and Firm Demand The price of oil is determined in the world market for oil. You cannot sell oil at a price above the market price. At the market price, you can sell as many barrels as you want.

---

* How much is not a noticeable amount? Recall from Chapter 5 that the elasticity of demand is $E_D = \dfrac{\%\Delta Q}{\%\Delta P}$ or, rearranging, $\%\Delta P = \dfrac{\%\Delta Q}{E_D}$. Suppose that the elasticity of demand for oil is 0.5. This means that a 10% increase in the quantity of oil will reduce price by 20% $= \dfrac{10\%}{0.5}$. An increase in the supply of oil of 10 barrels a day is a percentage increase of $\dfrac{10}{100,000,000} \times 100 = 0.00001\%$, so price falls by $\dfrac{0.00001}{0.5} = 0.00002\%$. At a price of $50 per barrel, this means that an increase in 10 barrels of oil would reduce price to 49.99999; that is, it would not be noticeable.

buyers and sellers of oil, each small relative to the total market. Generalizing, a perfectly elastic demand curve for firm output is a reasonable approximation when the product being sold is similar across different firms and there are many buyers and sellers, each small relative to the total market. The markets for gold, wheat, paper, steel, lumber, cotton, sugar, vinyl, milk, trucking, glass, Internet domain name registration, and many other goods and services satisfy these conditions.

In addition, don't forget another lesson from Chapter 5: Demand curves are more elastic in the long run. We define the **long run** as the time after all exit and entry has occurred, and the **short run** as the period before exit and entry can occur. Imagine that you are the owner of the only grocery store in a small town. Can you raise prices to exorbitant levels, reasoning that everyone needs food and you are the only seller? In the short run, you probably could. But if you raise prices too high, other sellers will set up shop and your business will be wiped out. Thus, even when there aren't many sellers, there are sometimes many *potential sellers* so a perfectly elastic demand curve can be a reasonable assumption even in a market with a few firms, at least in the long run.

Summarizing, economists say that an industry is competitive (or sometimes "perfectly competitive") when firms don't have much influence over the price of their product. This is a reasonable assumption under at least the following conditions:

- The product being sold is similar across sellers.
- There are many buyers and sellers, each small relative to the total market. and/or
- There are many potential sellers.

When *do* firms have a lot of influence on the price of their product? Briefly, for purposes of comparison, a firm selling a product for which there are neither many other sellers nor potential sellers has considerable freedom to choose its price. We will analyze how firms choose price and output under these conditions in Chapters 13 through 17.

A competitive firm will sell its output at the market price, but what quantity will it choose to produce?

> The **long run** is the time after all exit or entry has occurred.
>
> The **short run** is the period before exit or entry can occur.

CHECK YOURSELF
- In a competitive market, what happens when a firm prices its product above the market price? Below the market price?
- What kind of demand elasticity curve does the competitive firm face?
- How can a firm that produces oil face a very elastic demand curve when the demand for oil is inelastic?

Maximizing Profits

Before showing how to find the profit maximizing quantity for a competitive firm, let's look at some general principles. Maximizing profits requires knowing what to ignore and what to consider.

Ignore Sunk Costs and Ignore Fixed Costs in the Short Run

Here's a general principle of rational choice: *Ignore what you can't change.* Focus on what you can change. Suppose you pay $15 for a ticket to the movies and the movie is awful. Should you walk out? The price you paid for the ticket is a sunk cost. Your money is gone, so ignore what you paid for the ticket. Focus on what you can change. Walk out!

Ignoring **sunk cost** can be psychologically difficult. No one likes to admit that they made a mistake. Nevertheless, throwing good money (or time) after bad only makes things worse. By the way, Tyler, at least, practices what he preaches and walks out of movies all the time. Alex finds this harder to do, but he knows he's usually wrong when he continues to watch the movie.

> A **sunk cost** is a cost that cannot be recovered.

Here's a business example. Suppose that you spend $5,000 to drill your oil well. What influence should that cost have on what quantity you produce? Answer: None. The cost to drill the well is a sunk cost (literally in this case). A sunk cost is a nonrecoverable cost, a cost that you cannot change. Since you can't change a sunk cost it should be ignored.

Here's a trickier example. Suppose that you rent the land on which your oil well sits. One day the landlord tells you that your rent has doubled. Do you change the quantity that you produce? Answer: No. It's tempting to think that since the rent has increased you should produce more. But the rent is the same whether you produce more or less. Since your choice to produce more or less can't change the rent, you should ignore the rent *when deciding what quantity to produce*. Ignore what you can't change.

Why is this example tricky? It's tricky because you can't change the rent by changing how much you produce, but you *can* change the rent by exiting the industry. You are not obligated to pay rent forever. If you exit the industry, your rent will fall. So our principle tells us that we should ignore the rent when choosing what quantity to produce but not when choosing whether or not to exit. More generally, **fixed costs** can't be changed in the short run and so should be ignored for short-run decisions like what quantity to produce, but, fixed costs can be changed in the long run so they should be focused on for long-run decisions like entry or exit.

What makes fixed costs different from sunk costs is that sunk costs are *never* relevant because they cannot be changed by *any* choice. Fixed costs can't be changed by short-run choices but they can be changed by long-run choices and so should be ignored in the former case and focused on in the latter case.

Don't Ignore Opportunity Costs

Maximizing profit requires taking into account *explicit costs* and also *implicit costs*, the costs of forgone alternatives. Imagine that Lian runs a flower shop. Each month she spends $10,000 buying flowers from a wholesaler. The cost of flowers is an **explicit cost** of running her shop, like the rent and electricity that she pays out of pocket by writing a check. But these are not her only costs. If Lian weren't selling flowers, let's suppose that she could be working as a patent attorney earning $7,000 a month. Lian is giving up something of value when she works as a florist, namely the opportunity to earn $7,000 a month, which is also a cost of running a flower shop, even though she is not writing anybody a check. It is an **implicit cost**. When deciding whether she would rather be a florist or a patent attorney, for example, Lian needs to take into account *all* her costs, including opportunity costs.

Accountants typically don't take into account all opportunity costs so **accounting profits** are usually more than **economic profits**. Why is the distinction between accounting and economic profit important? Answer: Because firms want to maximize economic profit, not accounting profit.

Suppose, for example, that you inherit a bookshop, including the building where the shop is located so you pay no rent. Each month the bookshop makes enough to pay the employees; in some months it makes a little bit more so your accounting profits are positive. Is your economic profit positive? Probably not. If you closed the bookshop and rented the building to another firm, your profit might be considerably higher. So when calculating your economic profit, you should include the opportunity cost of renting the building to another firm. The easiest way to do this is to pretend that your bookshop has to pay the

A **fixed cost** does not vary with the quantity produced.

An **explicit cost** is a cost that requires a money outlay.

An **implicit cost** is a cost that does not require an outlay of money.

Accounting profit is total revenue minus explicit costs.

Economic profit is total revenue minus total costs, including implicit opportunity costs.

market rate for rent, even if you are paying it to yourself. If your bookshop isn't profitable when it has to pay rent then you should probably sell the bookshop and go into business as a landlord instead.

Calculating economic profit is important for entrepreneurs, who must always think about the future. Entrepreneurs should ask themselves, Is this the best use of our firm's assets? What am I giving up by following this strategy? Could these assets be used to make more profit if I used them in another way?

What Quantity to Produce?

Now that we know what to ignore and what to consider, let's return to the question of what quantity to produce in order to maximize profit. Profit is total revenue minus total cost, so the owner wants to maximize the difference between total revenue and total costs.

Profit = π = Total Revenue − Total Cost

Total revenue is pretty easy to understand. **Total revenues (*TR*)** are simply price times quantity: $(P \times Q)$. If the price of oil is \$50 per barrel, then total revenues are \$50 per day if 1 barrel is produced per day, \$100 if 2 barrels are produced, \$150 if 3 barrels are produced, and so forth.

Total cost is simply the cost of producing a given quantity of output. Let's break total cost into two components, fixed costs and variable costs.

Total Cost (*TC*) = Fixed Costs (*FC*) + Variable Costs (*VC*)

Fixed costs are costs, such as rent, that do not vary with output. Let's assume that the oil well must pay rent of \$30 per day regardless of how many barrels the well produces. **Variable costs** are costs that do vary with output. Pumping more oil will require more electricity and maintenance costs for the pump, for example, and also more transportation costs to deliver the oil, so these are all part of variable cost.

The table in Figure 11.2 shows total revenues (*TR*) and total costs (*TC*) for a typical stripper oil well. Notice that at zero barrels the firm still has total costs of \$30 per day—that's the rent, the fixed cost. Profit is the difference between total revenue and total cost, and it is shown in the fourth column. Thus, to find the maximum profit, one method is to look for the quantity that maximizes *TR* − *TC*. Using the table in Figure 11.2, we can see that the profit-maximizing quantity is 8 barrels of oil per day.

It is helpful, especially in order to create graphs, to use a second method to find the quantity that maximizes profit. Instead of looking at total revenue and total cost, we can compare the increase in revenue from selling an additional barrel of oil, called **marginal revenue**, with the increase in cost from selling an additional barrel, called **marginal cost**. To maximize profit, we will show that the owner wants to keep producing oil so long as Marginal revenue > Marginal cost, which means that the last drop of oil that the firm produces should be the one where Marginal revenue = Marginal cost. Let's step through this argument.

Marginal revenue is the change in total revenue from selling an additional barrel of oil. Suppose that the price of a barrel of oil is \$50. Then what is marginal revenue? If the owner sells an additional barrel of oil, his revenues increase by \$50, so marginal revenue is just equal to \$50, the price. That was easy, because we assumed that the price of oil doesn't change as the firm sells more barrels. In other words we used our assumption that a stripper oil well is in a competitive industry and thus faces a perfectly elastic demand curve at the market price. Thus, we have a simple rule: For a firm in a competitive industry, *MR* = *P*.

Total revenue is price times quantity sold: $TR = P \times Q$

Total cost is the cost of producing a given quantity of output.

Variable costs are costs that do vary with output.

MRU

mru.org/max-profit

How Does a Competitive Firm Maximize Profit?

Marginal revenue, *MR*, is the change in total revenue from selling an additional unit.

$$MR = \frac{\Delta TR}{\Delta Q}$$

For a firm in a competitive industry, *MR* = Price.

Marginal cost, *MC*, is the change in total cost from producing an additional unit.

$$MC = \frac{\Delta TC}{\Delta Q}$$

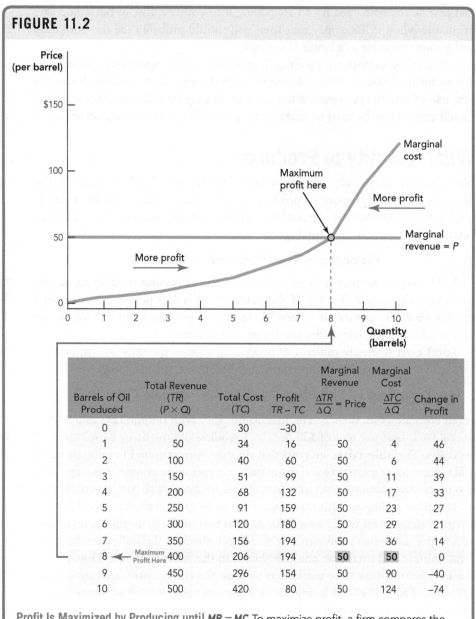

FIGURE 11.2

Barrels of Oil Produced	Total Revenue (TR) (P × Q)	Total Cost (TC)	Profit TR − TC	Marginal Revenue $\frac{\Delta TR}{\Delta Q}$ = Price	Marginal Cost $\frac{\Delta TC}{\Delta Q}$	Change in Profit
0	0	30	−30			
1	50	34	16	50	4	46
2	100	40	60	50	6	44
3	150	51	99	50	11	39
4	200	68	132	50	17	33
5	250	91	159	50	23	27
6	300	120	180	50	29	21
7	350	156	194	50	36	14
8 ← Maximum Profit Here	400	206	194	50	50	0
9	450	296	154	50	90	−40
10	500	420	80	50	124	−74

Profit Is Maximized by Producing until MR = MC To maximize profit, a firm compares the revenue from selling an additional unit, marginal revenue (for a firm in a competitive industry, this is equal to the price), to the costs of selling an additional unit, marginal cost. Profit increases from an additional sale whenever MR > MC so profit is maximized by producing up until the point where MR = MC.

Marginal cost is the change in total cost from producing an additional barrel of oil. The owner of a small oil well has some choice about whether to produce a little bit more or a little bit less. The owner, for example, can increase the pump rate and produce more oil per day but only by spending more on electricity, on maintenance, and on more frequent pickup and shipping of the oil. The extra costs that come with a little additional production are called marginal costs. Notice, for example, that if the well produces 2 barrels of oil per day, Total cost = 40, and if the well produces 3 barrels per day, then Total cost = 51. Thus, producing the third barrel of oil increases costs by $11; that is, the marginal cost of the third barrel of oil is $11.

At some point, marginal costs must increase because you can only get so much blood out of a stone and only so much oil out of rock. The well, for example, cannot be pumped more than 24 hours a day. As the well reaches capacity, the marginal cost of an additional barrel approaches infinity!

We can now use the data in Figure 11.2 to find the profit-maximizing quantity using our second method. The owner should keep producing additional barrels so long as the revenue from producing an additional barrel exceeds the cost of producing an additional barrel. The first barrel of oil that the firm produces adds $50 to revenue and $4 to costs, so $MR > MC$, and by producing that barrel the firm can add $46 to profit. On the second barrel the marginal revenue is $50 and the marginal cost is $6 so producing that barrel adds $44 to profit. Following through on this logic, we can see that each additional barrel of oil adds to profit up until the eighth barrel. If the firm produces the ninth barrel of oil, however, it adds $50 to revenue but $90 to costs, so the firm will not want to produce the ninth barrel. The profit-maximizing quantity is thus 8 barrels of oil. Notice that the profit-maximizing quantity is where $MR = MC$, and since $MR = P$ for a competitive firm, we can also say that the profit-maximizing quantity for a competitive firm is where $P = MC$.

Students are often confused by why economists say that the profit-maximizing output is 8 barrels instead of 7 barrels. Why produce the eighth barrel, where $P = MC$, and thus there is no addition to profit? Consider the graph above the table in Figure 11.2. Notice that wherever $P > MC$, producing additional barrels means more profit, and wherever $MC > P$, producing fewer barrels means more profit. Now think about producing oil not in barrels but in drops. Then the graph says that at 7.9999 barrels you still want to add a drop or two but at 8.0001 barrels you want to take away a drop or two. The reason we say profit is maximized where $P = MC$ is that $P = MC$ is the "just right" point between too little and too much.

As the price changes, so does the profit-maximizing quantity. When the price is $50, the profit-maximizing quantity is 8. If the price of oil rises to $100 per barrel, then the firm will expand production. But by how much? The firm will expand until it is once again maximizing profit when $P = MC$. In Figure 11.3 we show how the firm expands production along its MC curve as the price of oil increases from $50 to $100 per barrel.

To maximize profit a firm in a competitive industry increases output until $P = MC$.

FIGURE 11.3

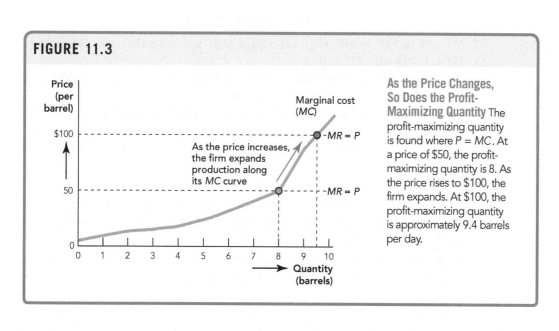

As the Price Changes, So Does the Profit-Maximizing Quantity The profit-maximizing quantity is found where $P = MC$. At a price of $50, the profit-maximizing quantity is 8. As the price rises to $100, the firm expands. At $100, the profit-maximizing quantity is approximately 9.4 barrels per day.

The **average cost** of production is the cost per unit, that is, the total cost of producing Q units divided by Q:

$$AC = \frac{TC}{Q}$$

We have now answered our second question: To maximize profit, the firm should produce the quantity such that $MR = MC$, which for a firm in a competitive industry means produce up until $P = MC$.

By the way, remember that we said that fixed costs should be ignored when deciding how much to produce? Since fixed costs don't change when we increase output, they don't influence marginal costs; thus, our profit-maximizing condition, choose the quantity such that $P = MC$, means that fixed costs are irrelevant. Our $P = MC$ condition will give us the same profit-maximizing quantity whether fixed costs are high or low.⋆

Even though the firm's fixed costs are irrelevant for determining the profit-maximizing quantity, we know that they are relevant for the choice to exit or not. To understand that choice we will now introduce the average cost curve.

Profits and the Average Cost Curve

We have shown that the firm maximizes profits by producing the quantity such that $P = MC$, but a firm can maximize profits and still have low profits or even losses. Just because the firm is doing the best it can doesn't mean that it is doing very well. We would like, therefore, to be able to show profits in a diagram. To do this, we need to introduce the average cost curve.

The **average cost** of production is simply the cost per barrel; that is, the average cost of producing Q barrels of oil is the total cost of producing Q barrels divided by Q: $AC = \frac{TC}{Q}$. For example, in Figure 11.4, we can read from the table within it that the total cost of producing 6 barrels of oil per day is $120; thus, the cost per barrel is $120/6 = $20. Figure 11.4 computes average cost (in the last column) and graphs the average cost curve alongside the price and marginal cost curves.

With a little bit of work, we can now show profit on our graph. Recall that

$$\textbf{Profit = Total revenue – Total cost} = \textbf{\textit{TR}} - \textbf{\textit{TC}}$$

so we can also write

$$\textbf{Profit} = \left(\frac{\textbf{\textit{TR}}}{\textbf{\textit{Q}}} - \frac{\textbf{\textit{TC}}}{\textbf{\textit{Q}}} \right) \times \textbf{\textit{Q}}$$

or

$$\textbf{Profit} = (\textbf{\textit{P}} - \textbf{\textit{AC}}) \times \textbf{\textit{Q}}$$

(To get to the last statement, notice that we used the two definitions, $TR = P \times Q$ and $AC = \frac{TC}{Q}$.)

The last statement says that profit is equal to the average profit per barrel ($P - AC$) times the number of barrels sold, Q.

We already know that 8 barrels is the profit-maximizing quantity when the price is $50, but now we can show profit on our graph. To illustrate profit, begin at a quantity of 8 barrels and move up to find the price of $50 at point *a*.

⋆ If you know calculus, this result is very easy to see: $\pi = TR - TC$. To maximize profit, we take the derivative of the profit function with respect to quantity and set the total equal to zero. Since $\frac{\partial TR}{\partial Q} = MR$ and $\frac{\partial TC}{\partial Q} = MC$ we immediately have our general condition for any firm to maximize profit, $MR - MC = 0$ or $MR = MC$. Notice also that since fixed costs don't vary with Q, $\frac{\partial FC}{\partial Q} = 0$, so fixed costs don't influence marginal cost and thus have no effect on the profit-maximizing quantity.

FIGURE 11.4

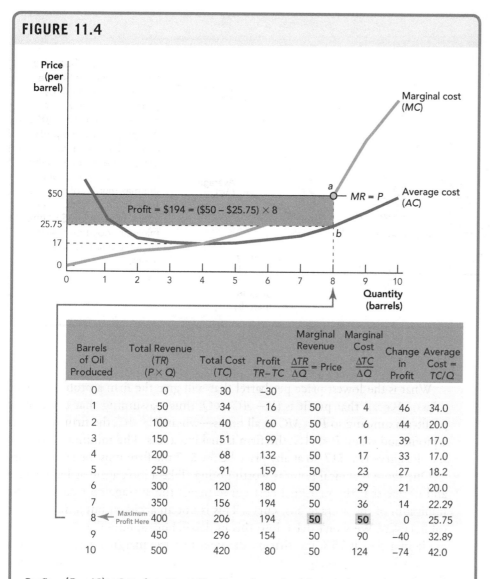

Barrels of Oil Produced	Total Revenue (TR) (P × Q)	Total Cost (TC)	Profit TR−TC	Marginal Revenue $\frac{\Delta TR}{\Delta Q}$ = Price	Marginal Cost $\frac{\Delta TC}{\Delta Q}$	Change in Profit	Average Cost = TC/Q
0	0	30	−30				
1	50	34	16	50	4	46	34.0
2	100	40	60	50	6	44	20.0
3	150	51	99	50	11	39	17.0
4	200	68	132	50	17	33	17.0
5	250	91	159	50	23	27	18.2
6	300	120	180	50	29	21	20.0
7	350	156	194	50	36	14	22.29
8 ← Maximum Profit Here	400	206	194	**50**	**50**	0	25.75
9	450	296	154	50	90	−40	32.89
10	500	420	80	50	124	−74	42.0

Profit = (P − AC) × Q Profit is (P − AC) × Q, profit per barrel times the number of barrels produced. When the price is $50 and 8 barrels of oil are produced, profit is shown on the graph as the shaded area. Notice that the price is the height of point a, AC is the height of point b, so that the area (a − b) × Q is equal to profit or $194 = ($50 − $25.75) × 8.

Now reading down from point *a*, find the average cost from the *AC* curve at point *b*, which is $25.75. (You can also check this by examining the table below the diagram for the *AC* of producing 8 barrels.) The average profit per barrel, *P − AC*, is ($50 − $25.75) or $24.25 per barrel. Finally, since production is 8 barrels, the total profit is (*P − AC*) × Q or $24.25 × 8 = $194 per day, the shaded area in the diagram.

As we said earlier, just because a firm is maximizing profits doesn't mean that it is making profits. If the price of oil were to drop to $4 per barrel, what happens? The best the firm could do is produce at *P = MC*. Looking at the *MC* column in the table, *MC* = $4 at 1 barrel of oil produced. So at a price of $4, the firm produces 1 barrel of oil. But at this price, the firm is taking a loss because *P < AC*. Figure 11.5 illustrates.

FIGURE 11.5

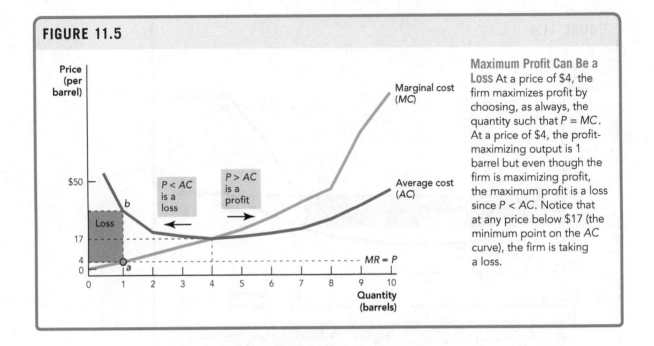

Maximum Profit Can Be a Loss At a price of $4, the firm maximizes profit by choosing, as always, the quantity such that $P = MC$. At a price of $4, the profit-maximizing output is 1 barrel but even though the firm is maximizing profit, the maximum profit is a loss since $P < AC$. Notice that at any price below $17 (the minimum point on the AC curve), the firm is taking a loss.

What is the lowest price per barrel that will give the firm a profit (not take a loss)? Recall that profit is $(P - AC) \times Q$, thus—assuming that the firm is profit-maximizing so $P = MC$ at all times—when $P > AC$, the firm is making a profit, and when $P < AC$, the firm is making a loss. The minimum point of the AC curve is at $17, so at any price below $17 the firm must be taking a loss.

One more technical point is worth noting. Take a look again at Figure 11.5 and notice that the marginal cost curve meets the average cost curve at the minimum of the average cost curve. This is not an accident but a mathematical necessity. We won't delve into this in detail, but suppose that your average grade in a class is 75% and that on the next test, the marginal test, you earn a grade below your average, 60%. What happens to your average grade? It falls. So whenever your marginal grade is below your average grade, your average falls. Now suppose that your average grade is 75% and on the next test, the marginal test, you earn a grade above your average, 80%. What happens to your average? It rises. So whenever your marginal grade is above your average grade, your average rises. What is true for your average and marginal grade is equally true for average and marginal cost. So think about what must happen around the point at which the MC and AC curves meet. When marginal cost is just below average cost, the average cost curve is falling, and when marginal cost is just above average cost, the average cost curve is rising, so AC and MC must meet at the minimum of the AC curve. Thus, on an exam be sure to draw the MC curve rising through the minimum point of the AC curve.

We are now ready to turn to our third question: When should the firm enter or exit the industry?

CHECK YOURSELF

• Use average costs to define profit for the competitive firm.
• Using average cost, describe all the prices at which the firm would make a profit and all the prices at which the firm would make a loss.

Entry, Exit, and Shutdown Decisions

Firms seek profits so in the long run firms will enter an industry when $P > AC$ and exit an industry when $P < AC$. Notice that at the intermediate point, when $P = AC$, profits are zero and there is neither entry nor exit.

In Figure 11.5, we can see that at a price of $4, the firm is taking losses. Thus, in the long run, this firm will exit the industry. In fact, at any price below $17, the firm will be making a loss at any output level. Thus at any price below $17, the firm will exit the industry in the long run. At any price above $17, firms will be making profits and other firms will enter the industry.

Only when $P = AC$, in this case when $P = \$17$, will firms be making zero profits, and there will be no incentive to either enter or exit the industry. Students often wonder why firms would remain in an industry when profits are zero. The problem is the language of economics. By **zero profits**, economists mean what everyone else means by *normal profits*. Remember that average cost includes wages and payments to capital, so even when the firm earns "zero profits," labor and capital are being paid enough to keep them in the industry. Thus, when we say that a firm is earning zero profits, we mean that the price of output is just enough to pay labor and capital their ordinary opportunity costs.

Zero profits, or **normal profits,** occur when $P = AC$. At this price the firm is covering all of its costs, including enough to pay labor and capital their ordinary opportunity costs.

The Short-Run Shutdown Decision

If $P < AC$, the firm is making a loss so it wants to exit the industry but exit typically cannot occur immediately. Remember our stripper oil well and how it rents the land from which it pumps the oil? We said the rent was $30 per day but that doesn't mean the firm can stop paying rent immediately. Rent contracts, for example, often require that the renter give 30 days' notice. So suppose that the firm gives notice to the landowner that in 30 days it will exit and stop paying rent. What does the firm do for the next 30 days? Should it shut down and produce nothing or should it continue to produce something even though it is taking a loss?

If the well shuts down immediately, the firm will lose $30 per day for 30 days. On the other hand, if the price of oil is, say, $11 and if the firm produces 3 barrels of oil (the profit-maximizing amount when $P = \$11$; see the table in Figure 11.4), then the firm will have daily revenues of $33 and daily costs of $51 ($30 rent plus $21 in variable cost; see table in Figure 11.4) for a total daily loss of $18 ($33 − $51). A daily loss of $18 isn't good—that is why the firm wants to exit—but it's better than a daily loss of $30. In other words, by not shutting down, the firm is able to cover all of its variable costs and *some* of its fixed costs (the rent), and that is better than producing nothing and paying the rent.

As usual in economics we can also show this insight with another curve! The firm is taking a loss when

$$TR < TC$$

Recall that when we divide both sides of this equation by Q, we get our condition for long-run exit, $P < AC$. To understand the firm's optimal short-run shutdown decision we are going to do something very similar. Total cost can be broken down into fixed costs and variable costs:

$$TC = FC + VC$$

But in the short run the firm has no choice about its fixed costs; it has to pay the fixed costs no matter how much output the firm produces. Since choice doesn't influence the fixed costs, the fixed costs should not influence choice. In the short run, the fixed costs are an expense but not an economic (opportunity) cost so they should be ignored. Thus, the firm should shut down immediately

FIGURE 11.6

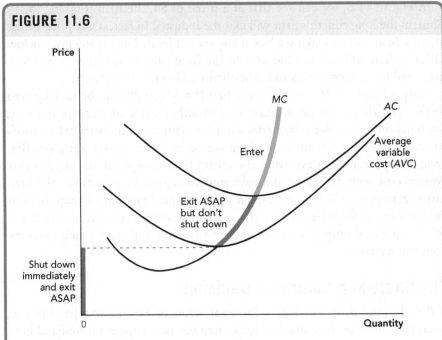

The Firm's Entry, Exit, and Shutdown Decisions If the price is below the minimum of the AVC curve, then the firm should shut down (produce 0 as shown by the red curve) and exit the industry as soon as possible (ASAP). If the price is above the AVC curve but below the AC curve, then the firm should produce the quantity such that P = MC (along the brown curve) but exit ASAP. If the price is at or above the AC curve, the firm should remain within the industry producing where P = MC or enter if it is not already in the industry.

only if $TR < VC$, or dividing both sides by Q as before, the firm should shut down immediately only if

$$P < \frac{VC}{Q} = AVC$$

We call $\frac{VC}{Q}$ the average variable cost or AVC, and give an example in Figure 11.6. The AVC curve has a very similar shape to the AC curve and it gets closer and closer to the AC curve as Q increases. (Why? This is a good question to test your knowledge—see Thinking and Problem Solving problem 24 at the end of this chapter.)

We can summarize, therefore, all of the firm's entry, exit, and shutdown decisions in Figure 11.6. If the price is so low that the firm can't even cover its average variable cost, then the firm should shut down immediately and exit the industry as soon as possible. If the price is high enough to cover the average variable cost but not all of the fixed costs (i.e., above AVC but below AC), then the firm should minimize its losses by producing the quantity such that $P = MC$ (along the brown curve) but exit the industry as soon as possible. If the price is high enough to cover the firm's average costs (at or above the AC curve), then the firm should remain in the industry or enter if it is not already in the industry and, of course, produce where $P = MC$.

By the way, the shutdown rule—shut down if you cannot cover your variable costs—can be applied in instances even when long-run exit is not at issue. Seasonal businesses, such as seaside hotels in the northeast of the United States, make their money during the busy season. What about in the winter when few people want to go to the beach? Do they stay open or close for a few months? It depends on whether these hotels can cover their variable costs in the slow season and contribute something to the paying of their fixed costs. This explains why it can sometimes make sense to run a hotel even when it is mostly empty.

Entry, Exit, and Industry Supply Curves

Now that we have examined the output and entry and exit decisions for firms in a competitive market, we can derive the industry supply curve, which you have been working with since Chapter 3. Industry supply curves can slope upward, be flat, or in rare circumstances even slope downward. We will show that the slope of the supply curve can be explained by how costs change as industry output increases or decreases.

In an **increasing cost industry**, costs increase with greater industry output and this generates an upward-sloping supply curve. In a **constant cost industry**, costs do not change with changes in industry output and this generates a flat supply curve. In a **decreasing cost industry**, costs decrease with greater industry output and this generates a downward-sloping supply curve. Decreasing cost industries are rare.

Let's start with increasing cost industries.

Increasing Cost Industries

In an increasing cost industry, costs rise as industry output increases. The oil industry is an increasing cost industry because greater quantities of oil can be produced only by using more expensive methods such as drilling deeper, drilling in more inhospitable spots, or extracting the oil from tar sands.

To illustrate, let's focus on just two firms. Firm 1 is the firm that we examined earlier. Its oil is located near the surface, so its average costs are low and it enters the industry when the price of oil rises to just $17. Firm 2's oil, however, is located deeper than Firm 1's, and so Firm 2's fixed costs of drilling are higher and its average cost curve is higher than that of Firm 1's. As a result, Firm 2 will not enter the industry until the price of oil reaches $29. We can now build the industry supply curve.

At any price below $17, what is the quantity supplied? Zero. At a price less than $17, both firms are losing money so no firm enters the industry, and the industry supply curve, indicated in the rightmost panel of Figure 11.7 by the red line, shows a quantity supplied of zero. When the price of oil hits $17, Firm 1 enters the industry at its profit-maximizing quantity of 4 barrels and thus industry supply at a price of $17 jumps to 4 barrels. As the price rises, Firm 1 expands along its *MC* curve and so does industry supply. When the price hits $29, Firm 2 enters the industry with its profit-maximizing quantity of 5 barrels of oil. To find the quantity supplied by the industry, we sum the quantity supplied by each firm in the industry. At a price of $29, Firm 1 supplies 6 barrels of oil and Firm 2 supplies 5 barrels of oil, so industry supply is 11 barrels of oil. As the price rises further, both firms now expand along their respective *MC* curves. Once again, industry supply at any price is found by adding up the quantity supplied by each firm at that price. Thus, at a price of $50, Firm 1 produces 8 barrels of oil and Firm 2 produces 7 barrels of oil, so industry supply at a price of $50 is 15 barrels of oil.

Increasing cost industry is an industry in which industry costs increase with greater output; shown with an upward-sloped supply curve.

Constant cost industry is an industry in which industry costs do not change with greater output; shown with a flat supply curve.

Decreasing cost industry is an industry in which industry costs decrease with an increase in output; shown with a downward-sloped supply curve.

FIGURE 11.7

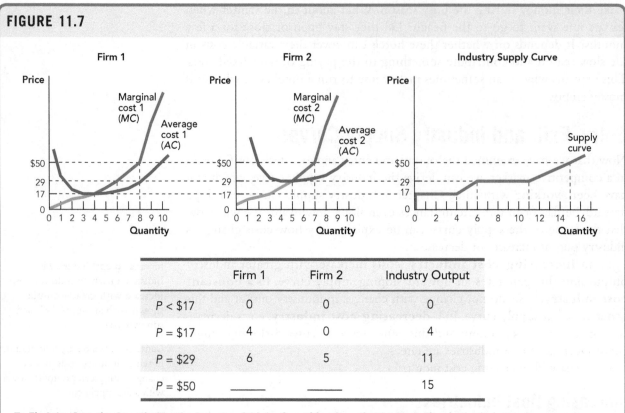

	Firm 1	Firm 2	Industry Output
P < $17	0	0	0
P = $17	4	0	4
P = $29	6	5	11
P = $50	_____	_____	15

To Find the Quantity Supplied by the Industry, Add the Quantities Supplied by Each Firm in the Industry At any price below $17, profits for both Firm 1 and Firm 2 are negative, so industry output is 0. At a price of $17, Firm 1 enters the industry with a profit-maximizing quantity of 4 barrels, so industry output jumps to 4 barrels. As price rises further, Firm 1 expands along its *MC* curve. At a price of $29, Firm 2 enters the industry with a profit-maximizing quantity of 5 barrels, so total industry output is 11 barrels (6 from Firm 1 and 5 from Firm 2). As price rises further, both firms expand along their marginal cost curves. At any price, industry output is the sum of each firm's output. At a price of $50, what quantity does Firm 1 produce? What quantity does Firm 2 produce? Fill in the blanks in the table and check that the production from Firm 1 and Firm 2 add up to industry output.

Our explanation of the supply curve is simply a more detailed version of the account in Chapter 3. At a low price, the only oil that is profitable to exploit is the oil that can be recovered at low cost from places like Saudi Arabia. As the price of oil rises, it becomes profitable to supply oil from the North Sea, the Athabasca tar sands, and other higher-cost sources. The analysis in Chapter 3 focused on how a higher price encourages entry from higher-cost producers. This chapter adds to the entry story the idea that as the price increases, each firm expands output by moving along its marginal cost curve.

More generally, any industry that buys a large fraction of the output of an increasing cost industry will also be an increasing cost industry. The gasoline industry, for example, is an increasing cost industry because greater demand for gas will push up the price of oil, which in turn increases the price of gas. The electricity industry is an increasing cost industry because greater demand for electricity pushes up the price of coal, and coal is an increasing cost industry for the same reasons as oil.

Constant Cost Industries

Consider the industry of domain name registrars. Web pages on the Internet have a conventional name, called a domain name, such as that for the National Bureau of Economic Research, which has the domain name NBER.org. But the conventional names are just masks for more difficult-to-remember numbers called IP (Internet Protocol) addresses. When you type www.NBER.org into a browser, the browser sends a message to the Domain Name System (DNS), which looks up and returns the corresponding IP address, in this case http://23.185.0.2/. The IP address tells your browser where to find the information that is posted by the NBER. So, in order to work, every domain name must be registered with the DNS and assigned an IP address. Domain name registrars are firms that manage and register domain names.

The domain name registration industry has two important characteristics. First, domain name registration satisfies all of the conditions for a competitive industry.

- The product being sold is similar across sellers.
- There are many buyers and sellers, each small relative to the total market.
- There are many potential sellers.

As far as the user is concerned, there is little difference between registering with GoDaddy.com or BigRock.in, so the product is similar across sellers. There are many buyers and many sellers. There are hundreds of registrars in the United States alone. Indeed, GoDaddy.com is based in the United States and BigRock.in is based in India; thus, there is *worldwide* trade in domain name registration. Furthermore, not only are there many competitors in the industry, but just about anyone in the world can become an accredited registrar with an investment of a few thousand dollars, so there are many potential competitors.

The second important characteristic of the domain name industry is that the major input for domain name registration is a bank of computers, but all the computers of all the domain name registrars in all the world don't add up to much compared with the world supply of computers. The domain name industry, therefore, can expand without pushing up the prices of its major inputs and thus without raising its own costs. An industry that can expand or contract without changing the prices of its inputs is called a constant cost industry.

These two characteristics, free entry and the fact that the industry demands only a small share of its major inputs, produce the following properties: (1) The price for domain name registration is quickly driven down to the average cost of managing and assigning a domain name, so profits are quickly driven to normal levels; and (2) because average costs don't change much when the industry expands or contracts, the price of domain name registration doesn't change much when the industry expands or contracts so the long-run supply curve is very elastic (flat).

Let's examine these characteristics in turn. Suppose that GoDaddy.com charges $8.99 to register a domain name for one year. What would happen if it raised its price to $14.95 a year? GoDaddy would quickly lose a significant fraction of its business. New customers would choose other firms, and since domains must be renewed every few years, old customers would soon also switch. As a result of this competition, GoDaddy and every other firm in the industry price their services at near average cost and earn a zero or normal profit.

Now consider what happens when the demand for domain names increases. In 2005, there were more than 60 million domain names. Just one year later, as the Internet exploded in popularity, there were more than 100 million domain names. If the demand for oil nearly doubled, the price of oil would rise dramatically, but despite nearly doubling in size, the price of registering a domain name did not increase. When an increase in demand hits a constant cost industry, the price rises in the short run as each firm moves up its MC curve. But the expansion of old firms and the entry of new firms quickly push the price back down to average cost.

Figure 11.8 on the next page illustrates how a constant cost industry responds to an increase in demand. The figure looks imposing, but if we consider it in steps, the logic of the story will be clear. In the top panel, we have the initial equilibrium. On the left-hand side of the panel, we illustrate the industry. The market price is P_{lr} ($8.99 in the case of domain name registration), the market quantity is Q_{lr}, and the quantity demanded is exactly equal to the quantity supplied so the industry is in equilibrium. On the right-hand side of the panel, we have a typical firm in the industry. The firm is profit-maximizing because $P = MC$ and it is making a zero or normal profit because $P = AC$. Note that the industry output is Q_{lr} but the firm output is q_{lr}, which indicates that each firm in the industry produces only a small share of total industry output.

In the middle panel on the left, we illustrate an increase in demand from Old demand to New demand. In the short run, the increase in demand increases price to P_{sr}, $9.99, where New demand and Short-run supply meet. The industry quantity increases to Q_{sr}. Where does the increase in quantity come from? It comes from many firms in the industry, each of which produces a little bit more by increasing production along its MC curve. In the middle panel on the right, we show that the typical firm in the industry expands to q_{sr}, and since the price is above average cost, the firm earns profits as illustrated by the shaded area $(P - AC) \times q_{sr}$.

Before turning to the bottom panel, let's remember that the short run is the period before entry (or exit) occurs. In the middle panel, we are illustrating the *first* response to an increase in demand, which is that the price rises and every firm in the industry responds by increasing production along its marginal cost curve. (Indeed, the short-run supply curve is simply the sum of the MC curves for each firm in the industry.)

The increase in price generates above-normal profits for each firm in the industry. Notice that above-normal profits attract new investment and entry. Entry is the *second* response to the increase in demand. In some industries, like the domain name registration industry, entry might take a matter of a few months or even as little as a few weeks, while in other industries it could take several years before significant entry occurs.

When entry does occur, the short-run supply curve shifts to the right, and as it does, the price falls and profits are reduced. Entry doesn't stop until profits return to normal levels so entry continues until price is pushed down to AC. In the long run, after all entry and exit have occurred, profits have returned to normal.

Since the prices of the industry inputs don't change when the industry expands, the AC curve of each firm in the industry doesn't change, so in the new industry, equilibrium price is again equal to P_{lr}, $8.99. Although the typical firm produces q_{lr}, just as it did before the increase in demand, the industry quantity has increased to Q_{lr} because there are now more firms in the industry.

FIGURE 11.8

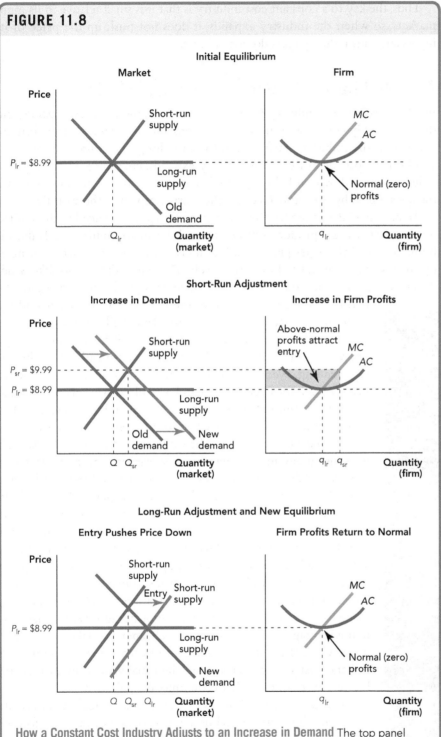

Initial Equilibrium

Market   **Firm**

Price

Short-run supply

$P_{lr} = \$8.99$

Long-run supply

Old demand

Q_{lr} Quantity (market)

MC

AC

Normal (zero) profits

q_{lr} Quantity (firm)

Short-Run Adjustment

Increase in Demand   **Increase in Firm Profits**

Price

Short-run supply

$P_{sr} = \$9.99$
$P_{lr} = \$8.99$

Long-run supply

Old demand   New demand

Q Q_{sr} Quantity (market)

Above-normal profits attract entry

MC
AC

q_{lr} q_{sr} Quantity (firm)

Long-Run Adjustment and New Equilibrium

Entry Pushes Price Down   **Firm Profits Return to Normal**

Price

Short-run supply

Entry   Short-run supply

$P_{lr} = \$8.99$

Long-run supply

New demand

Q Q_{sr} Q_{lr} Quantity (market)

MC
AC

Normal (zero) profits

q_{lr} Quantity (firm)

How a Constant Cost Industry Adjusts to an Increase in Demand The top panel shows the initial industry and firm equilibrium. The market price for domain name registration is $8.99 and each firm is making a normal profit. In the middle panel, the demand for registration increases, which pushes up the market price to $9.99. In the short run, each firm in the industry expands along its MC curve and thus market quantity increases to Q_{sr}. Each firm earns above-normal profits. In the bottom panel, the above-normal profits attract entry. As more firms enter the industry, the short-run supply curve shifts to the right and as it does price falls. Firms continue to enter and the price continues to fall until price returns to $8.99. At that price, firms are once again earning normal (zero) profits, since $P = AC$.

Thus, the key to a constant cost industry is that it is small relative to its input markets, so when the industry expands, it does not push up the price of its inputs and thus industry costs do not increase.

A Special Case: The Decreasing Cost Industry

In an increasing cost industry, firm costs increase as the industry expands, and thus, the supply curve slopes upward. In a constant cost industry, firm costs are constant as the industry expands, and thus, the long-run supply curve is flat. Could firm costs decrease as the industry expands, creating a decreasing cost industry with a downward-sloping supply curve? Yes. To see how, we must ask the question: Why is Dalton, Georgia, the "carpet capital of the world"?

An amazing 72% of the $12 billion worth of carpets produced in the United States every year are produced in Dalton and the surrounding area. Dalton is home to over 150 carpet plants and hundreds of machine shops, cotton mills, dye plants, and other related industries. Why Dalton? Dalton is not like Saudi Arabia, as it has no outstanding natural advantages for producing carpets, so why is Dalton the carpet capital of the world? The answer is nothing more than an accident of history that launched a virtuous circle.

The Dalton carpet industry began in 1895 with one teenage girl who crafted an especially beautiful bedspread for her brother's wedding. Wedding guests saw the bedspread and asked her to make more. To meet the demand, she hired workers and trained them in her innovative techniques. As demand grew even further, these workers and others went into business for themselves, creating a bedspread industry. The skills needed to make bedspreads were also useful for making carpets, so carpet firms began to locate in Dalton. With so many carpet firms located in Dalton, it became profitable to open trade schools to teach carpet-making skills. In turn, the trade schools made it even more cost-efficient for carpet firms to move to Dalton. Similarly, machine shops, cotton mills, and dye plants moved to Dalton to be close to their customers, and the ready access to machine shops, cotton mills, and dye plants made it even less costly for carpet firms to make carpets in Dalton. The resulting virtuous circle made Dalton the cheapest place to make carpets in the United States—not because Dalton had natural advantages but because it was cheaper to make carpets in a place where there already were a lot of carpet makers. Economists call the cost savings that occur when many firms in an industry locate near to one another economies of agglomeration.

What do carpet makers in Dalton, moviemakers in Hollywood, and flower sellers in Aalsmeer have in common? Economies of agglomeration!

Decreasing cost industries or economies of agglomeration are important, but very special because costs cannot decrease forever. Dalton became the cheapest place to produce carpets in the United States many years ago and that is unlikely to change any time soon. But if the demand for carpets were to increase today, the cost of making carpets in Dalton would increase, not fall further. The cost of making carpets in Dalton fell when the local industry expanded from 1 to 50 firms, but they didn't fall by nearly as much when the industry expanded from 50 to 100 firms.

Economists use the idea of a decreasing cost industry to explain the history of industry clusters: not just carpets in Dalton, Georgia, but computer technology in Silicon Valley, movie production in Hollywood, and flower distribution in Aalsmeer, Holland. Once the cluster is established, however, constant or increasing costs are the norm. If the demand for carpet were to increase today, for example, the price of carpets would rise, not fall.

Industry Supply Curves: Summary

In an increasing cost industry, costs increase with industry output and the supply curve slopes upward. If the industry is small relative to its input markets so the industry can expand without pushing up its costs, the supply curve will be flat; we call this a constant cost industry. Industry supply curves can even slope downward but this is rare and temporary, although the idea of a decreasing cost industry is important for explaining the existence of industry clusters. Figure 11.9 illustrates the three possibilities.

Takeaway

We have now answered the three questions with which we opened the chapter. What price to set? Answer: A firm in a competitive industry sets its price at the market price. What quantity to produce? Answer: To maximize profit, a competitive firm should produce the quantity that makes $P = MC$. When to exit and enter an industry? Answer: In the short run, the firm should shut down only if price is less than average variable cost. In the long run, the firm should enter if $P > AC$ and exit if $P < AC$.

A competitive industry is one where the product being sold is similar across sellers; there are many buyers and sellers, each small relative to the total market; and/or there are many potential sellers.

We have also shown how profit maximization and entry and exit decisions are the foundation of supply curves. In an increasing cost industry, costs rise as more firms enter so supply curves are upward sloping. In a constant cost industry, costs remain the same as firms enter so the long-run supply curve is flat. And in the rare case of a decreasing cost industry, costs fall as firms enter so supply curves are downward sloping.

FIGURE 11.9

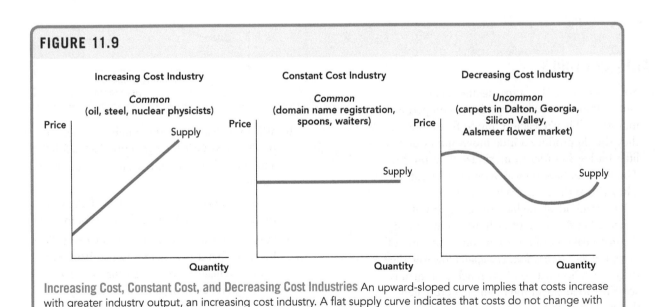

Increasing Cost, Constant Cost, and Decreasing Cost Industries An upward-sloped curve implies that costs increase with greater industry output, an increasing cost industry. A flat supply curve indicates that costs do not change with industry output, a constant cost industry. A downward-sloping curve implies that costs fall with greater industry output, a decreasing cost industry.

CHAPTER REVIEW

Go online to practice with more examples of these types of problems, including live links to videos, data sources, and feedback.

KEY CONCEPTS

long run, p. 211

short run, p. 211

sunk cost, p. 211

fixed cost, p. 212

explicit cost, p. 212

implicit cost, p. 212

accounting profit, p. 212

economic profit, p. 212

total revenue, p. 213

total cost, p. 213

variable costs, p. 213

marginal revenue, MR, p. 213

marginal cost, MC, p. 213

average cost, p. 216

zero (normal) profits, p. 219

increasing cost industry, p. 221

constant cost industry, p. 221

decreasing cost industry, p. 221

FACTS AND TOOLS

1. You've been hired as a management consultant to four different companies in competitive industries. They're each trying to figure out if they should produce a little more output or a little bit less in order to maximize their profits. The firms all have typical marginal cost curves: They rise as the firm produces more.

   Your staff did all the hard work for you of figuring out the price of each firm's output and the marginal cost of producing one more unit of output *at their current level of output*. However, they forgot to collect data on how much each firm is actually producing at the moment. Fortunately, that doesn't matter. In your final report, you need to decide which firms should produce more output, which should produce less, and which are producing just the right amount:

   a. Eleven Waffles, maker of generic-brand frozen waffles. Price = $4 per box, marginal cost = $2 per box.

   b. Rio Blanco, producer of copper. Price = $32 per ounce, marginal cost = $45 per ounce.

   c. Bluehost, domain name registry. Price = $5 per website, marginal cost = $2 per website.

   d. Luke's Lawn Service. Price = $80 per month, marginal cost = $120 per month.

2. In the competitive electrical motor industry, the workers at Galt Inc. threaten to go on strike. To avoid the strike, Galt Inc. agrees to pay its workers more. At all other factories, the wage remains the same.

   a. What does this do to the marginal cost curve at Galt Inc.? Does it rise, does it fall, or is there no change? Illustrate your answer in the figure.

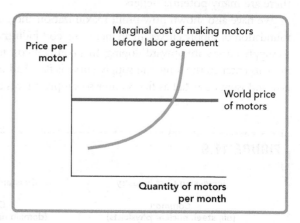

   b. What will happen to the number of motors produced by Galt Inc.? Indicate the "before" and "after" levels of output on the x-axis in the figure.

   c. In this competitive market, what will the Galt Inc. labor agreement do to the price of motors?

   d. Surely, more workers will *want* to work at Galt Inc. now that it pays higher wages. Will more workers *actually* work at Galt Inc. after the labor agreement is struck? Why or why not?

3. In Figure 11.8, you saw what happens in the long run when demand rises in a constant cost industry. Let's see what happens when demand falls in such an industry: For instance, think

about the market for gasoline or pizza in a small city after the city's biggest textile mill shuts down. In the following figure, indicate the price and quantity of output at three points in time:

I. In the long run, before demand falls

II. In the short run, after demand falls

III. In the long run, after demand falls

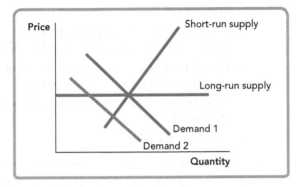

Also, answer the following questions about the market's response to this fall in demand.

a. When will the marginal cost of production be lowest: at stage I, II, or III?

b. When firms cut prices, they often do so in dramatic ways. During which stage will the local pizza shops begin making "Buy one, get one free" offers? During which stage will the local gas station be more likely to offer "Free car wash with fill-up?"

c. When is $P > AC$? $P < AC$? $P = AC$?

d. Restating the previous question: When are profits positive? Negative? Zero?

e. Roughly speaking, will the long-run response mostly involve firms leaving the industry, or will it mostly involve individual firms shrinking? The Firm column of Figure 11.8 should help you with the answer.

4. Suppose that a can of sparkling water costs $1.99. Now imagine that the demand for sparkling water increases dramatically—suddenly everyone wants low-calorie fizzy drinks. What do you think the price of a can of sparkling water will be in, say, 3 years?

5. Arguing about economics late one night in your dorm room, your friend says, "In a free market economy, if people are willing to pay a lot for something, then businesses will charge a lot for it." One way to translate your friend's words into a model is to think of a product with highly inelastic demand: items like life-saving drugs or

basic food items. Let's consider a market where costs are roughly constant: perhaps they rise a little or fall a little as the market grows, but not by much.

a. In the long run, is your friend right?

b. In the long run, what has the biggest effect on the price of a good that people really want: the location of the average cost curve or the location of the demand curve?

6. a. In the highly competitive TV manufacturing industry, a new innovation makes it possible to cut the average cost of a 65-inch LED TV from $1,200 to $500. Most TV manufacturers quickly adopt this new innovation, earning massive short-run profits. In the long run, what will the price of a 65-inch LED TV be?

b. In the highly competitive flash drive industry, a new innovation makes it possible to cut the average cost of a 256-gigabyte flash drive, small enough to fit on your keychain, from $30 to $15. In the long run, what will the price of a 256-gigabyte flash drive be?

c. Assume that the markets in parts a and b are both constant cost industries. If demand rises massively for these two goods, why won't the price of these goods rise in the long run?

d. In constant cost industries, does demand have any effect on price in the long run?

e. When average cost falls in *any* competitive industry, regardless of cost structure, who gets 100% of the benefits of cost cutting in the long run: consumers or producers?

7. On November 5, 2021, the price of Tesla Inc. stock hit an all-time high at $407.36 per share. (Two years prior, in November 2019, Tesla stock was trading for about a *twentieth* of that price.)

a. Suppose that on November 5, 2021, you owned 10,000 shares of Tesla stock (a small fraction of the roughly 3 billion shares). You offered to sell your stock for $407.40 per share, just slightly above the market price. Would you have been successful?

b. What if, on November 5, 2021, you wanted to sell your 10,000 shares of Tesla stock but you reduced your asking price to $407.30 per share? Would you have found a lot of willing buyers?

c. What do your answers for parts a and b tell you about the demand curve that you, as an individual seller of Tesla stock, face?

8. Whenever money is used to purchase capital, interest costs are incurred. Sometimes those costs are explicit—like when Alex borrowed money from the bank—and sometimes those costs are implicit—like when Tyler had to forgo the interest he could have earned had he left his funds in a savings account. If both an economist and an accountant calculated Alex and Tyler's costs, for whom would they have identical numbers and for whom would the numbers differ?

9. Inaya owns a local restaurant that has the following list of costs. She is currently trying to learn how to better budget the restaurant and wants to know what costs may end up varying from month to month. Which of the following are variable costs? Which are fixed costs?

   a. Food ingredients and beverages

   b. Employee hours

   c. Rent and building insurance

   d. Utilities

   e. Liquor license

10. Kendall has always had aspirations to be an entrepreneur. As she will be graduating from college in May, she is trying to decide where she should move postgraduation to start her business. After considering many locations, Kendall chooses Austin, Texas. Kendall loves Austin for its vibrant culture and southern charm. Additionally, she loves the fact that Austin has a large start-up culture, meaning that she would have many opportunities to make connections with and learn from investors and other start-up executives in Austin, all while being able to work for an established start-up while she is getting her business up and running.

    Which agglomeration effects is Kendall taking into consideration when making this decision? Which has she not yet considered? Assuming that Austin's reputation as a hub for tech start-ups continues, should Kendall expect costs in the Austin tech industry to be increasing, constant, or decreasing over time? Why?

THINKING AND PROBLEM SOLVING

11. Suppose Julius sells mangoes picked from his mango tree in a competitive market. Assume all mangoes are equal in quality but grow at different heights on the tree. Julius, being fearful of heights, demands greater compensation the higher he goes: So for him, the cost of grabbing a mango rises higher the higher and higher he must climb, as shown in the total cost column in the following table. The market price of a mango is $0.50.

    a. What is Julius's marginal revenue for selling mangoes?

    b. Which mangoes does Julius pick first: those on the low branches or high branches? Why?

    c. Does this suggest that the marginal cost of mangoes is increasing, decreasing, or staying the same as the quantity of mangoes picked increases? Why?

    d. Complete the table.

Mangoes	Total Cost	Marginal Cost	Marginal Revenue	Change in Profit
1	$0.10	$0.10	$0.50	$0.40
2	$0.22			
3	$0.50			
4	$1.00			
5	$1.73			
6	$2.78			

    e. How many mangoes does Julius pick?

12. How long is the "long run?" It will vary from industry to industry. How long would you estimate the long run is in the following industries?

    a. The market for pretzels and soda sold from street carts in the Wall Street financial district in New York

    b. The market for meals at newly trendy Korean porridge restaurants

    c. The market for electrical engineers

    d. After 2022, the market for movies that are suspiciously similar to *Top Gun: Maverick*

13. In this chapter, we discussed the story of Dalton, Georgia, and its role as the carpet capital of the world. A similar story can be used to explain why some 60% of the motels in the United States are owned by people of Indian origin or why, as of 1995, 80% of doughnut shops in California were owned by Cambodian immigrants. Let's look at the latter case. In the 1970s,

Cambodian immigrant Ted Ngoy began working at a doughnut shop. He then opened his own store (and later, stores).*

Ngoy was drawn to the doughnut industry because it required little English, start-up capital, or special skills. Speaking the same language as your workers, however, helps a lot.

a. As other Cambodian refugees came to Los Angeles fleeing the tyrannical rule of the Khmer Rouge, which group—the refugees or existing residents—was Ngoy more likely to hire from? Why?

b. Did this make it more or less likely that other Cambodian refugees would open doughnut shops? Why?

c. As more refugees arrived, did this encourage a virtuous cycle of Cambodian-owned doughnut shops? Why?

d. At this point in the story, what sort of cost industry (constant, increasing, or decreasing) would you consider doughnut shops owned by Cambodians to be? Why?

e. Why did this cycle not continue forever? What kind of cost structure are Californian doughnut shops probably in now?

14. Sawyer opened a small shop on Etsy selling personalized pet accessories. The price of his most popular item is $5, and the market for Etsy pet accessories is very competitive. Sawyer's cost curves are shown in the figure below.

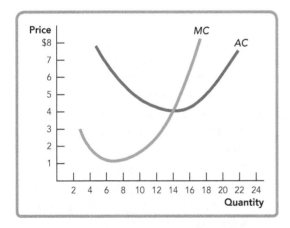

a. At what quantity will Sawyer produce? Why?

b. When the price is $5, shade the area of profit or loss in the graph provided and calculate Sawyer's profit or loss (round up).

c. If all other sellers of pet accessories have the same marginal and average costs as Sawyer, should he expect more or fewer competitors in the future? In the long run, will the price of pet accessories rise or fall? How do you know? What will the price of pet accessories be in the long run?

15. In the competitive hairdressing industry, new government licensing regulations raise the average cost of a haircut by $2.

a. If this is a constant cost industry, then in the long run, what happens to the price of a haircut?

b. If this is an increasing cost industry, will the long-run price of a haircut rise by more than $2 or less? (*Hint:* The long-run supply curve will be shaped just like an ordinary supply curve from the first few chapters. If you treat this like a $2 tax per haircut, you'll get the right answer.)

c. If this is an increasing cost industry, how much will this new regulation change the average hairdresser's profits in the long run?

d. Given your answer to part c, why do businesses in competitive industries often oppose costly new regulations?

16. In the ancient Western world, incense was one of the first commodities transported long distances. It grew only in the south of the Arabian Peninsula (modern-day Yemen, known then as Arabia Felix) and was transported by camel to Alexandria and the Mediterranean civilizations, notably the Roman Republic. As the republic expanded into a richer and larger empire, the demand for incense grew and planters in Arabia added a second and then a third annual crop (though this incense was not as high in quality). Cultivation also crossed to the Horn of Africa even though such fields were farther away from Rome.[2]

a. How does the lower quality of the additional annual crops illustrate incense as an increasing cost industry? (*Hint:* Think in terms of an amount of good crop produced per unit of currency.)

b. How does the added distance of incense grown in the Horn of Africa illustrate incense as an increasing cost industry?

* Not only are 60% of the small motels and hotels in the United States owned by East Indians, nearly a third of these owners have the surname Patel; see http://news.bbc.co.uk/2/hi/south_asia/3177054.stm. The story of Cambodian doughnut shops in Los Angeles is from Postrel, Virginia. 1999. *The Future and Its Enemies*. New York: Touchstone, pp. 49–50.

c. It's more costly to grow incense in Eastern Africa than in Arabia Felix. Which region would you expect to see more incense grown in?

17. You run a small firm. Two management consultants are offering you advice. The first says that your firm is losing money on every unit that you produce. To reduce your losses, the consultant recommends that you cut back production. The second consultant says that if your firm sells another unit, the price will more than cover your increase in costs. In order to reduce losses, the second consultant recommends that you should increase production.

a. As an economist, can you explain why both facts that the consultants rely on could be true?

b. Which consultant is offering the correct advice?

18. Paulette, Camille, and Hortense each own wineries in France. They produce inexpensive, mass-market wines. Over the past few years, such wines sold for 7 euros per bottle; but with a global recession, the price has fallen to 5 euros per bottle. Given the information below, let's find out which of these three winemakers (if any) should shut down temporarily until times get better. *Remember:* Whether or not they shut down, they still have to keep paying fixed costs for at least some time (that's what makes them "fixed").

To keep things simple, let's assume that each winemaker has calculated the optimal quantity to produce if they decide to stay in business; your job is simply to figure out if she should produce that amount or just shut down.

Annual Income Statement When Price = 5 euros				
Winemaker	Fixed Costs	Variable Costs	Recession Revenues	Profits
Paulette	50,000	80,000	120,000	
Camille	100,000	40,000	70,000	
Hortense	200,000	250,000	200,000	

a. First, calculate each winemaker's profit.

b. Which of these women, if any, earned a profit?

c. Who should stay in business in the short run? Who should shut down?

d. Fill in the blank: Even if profit is negative, if revenues are _____ variable costs, then it's best to stay open in the short run.

e. For which of these wineries, if any, is $P > AC$? You don't need to calculate any new numbers to answer this.

19. Let's explore the relationship between marginal and average a little more. Suppose your grade in your economics class is composed of 10 quizzes of equal weight. You start off the semester well, then your grades start to slip a little, but then you get back into the swing of things, your grades pick up, and you finish off the semester with a bang. Your 10 quiz grades, in order, are 82, 74, 68, 72, 77, 83, 86, 88, 90, and 100. Graph your *marginal* grades, along with your *average* grade, after each quiz. What do you notice about the relationship between *marginal* and *averages*? Your grades start improving with your fourth quiz grade; does your average also start increasing with your fourth quiz grade? Why or why not?

20. Given the cost function in the following table for Olivia, a housepainter in a competitive local market, answer the questions that follow. (You may want to calculate average cost.)

Number of Rooms Painted per Week	Total Cost
0	$100
1	$120
2	$125
3	$145
4	$200
5	$300
6	$460

What is the minimum price per room at which Olivia would be earning positive economic profit? At prices below this price, what will Olivia's long-run plan be?

21. Asia owns a firm with annual revenues of $1,000,000. Wages, rent, and other costs are $900,000.

a. Calculate Asia's accounting profit.

b. Suppose that instead of being an entrepreneur, Asia could get a job with one of the following annual salaries (i) $50,000; (ii) $100,000; or (iii) $250,000. Assume that a job would be as satisfying to Asia as being an entrepreneur. Calculate Asia's economic profit under each of these scenarios.

22. You and your roommate are up one night studying microeconomics, and your roommate looks puzzled. You ask what is wrong, and you get this response: "The book says that in the short run fixed costs are an *expense* but not a *cost*—but that doesn't make any sense. How can something be an expense but not a cost?" How do you respond? (*Hint:* Think of Big Idea #3.)

23. Use the variable cost information in the following table to calculate average variable cost and average cost (assume fixed cost is $350), and then use this data to answer the questions that follow. One of them might not have an answer.

Q	FC	VC	AVC	AC
10	$350	$100		
20	$350	$180		
30	$350	$240		
40	$350	$300		
50	$350	$450		
60	$350	$630		
70	$350	$840		

a. Give an example of a price at which this firm would want to produce and sell output in *both* the short run *and* the long run.

b. Give an example of a price at which this firm would want to produce and sell output in *neither* the short run *nor* the long run.

c. Give an example of a price at which this firm would want to produce and sell output in the long run but *not* in the short run.

d. Give an example of a price at which this firm would want to produce and sell output in the short run but *not* in the long run.

24. Look carefully at Figure 11.6. What is represented by the space in between the average cost (*AC*) and average variable cost (*AVC*) curves? Why do they get closer together as quantity increases? Will they ever meet?

25. Iain quit his job as an electrician where he earned $60,000 a year. He took $40,000 out of savings that earned 5% interest annually ($2,000 in interest per year) and invested it in a martial arts school. He has 110 students willing to pay $1,000 a year apiece for martial arts classes at the school. The annual costs for rent, insurance, and equipment for the studio total $50,000. What is Iain's accounting profit or loss from this business venture? What is his economic profit or loss?

If he's indifferent between the two jobs, where should he invest his labor resources?

CHALLENGES

26. The demand for most metals tends to increase over time. Moreover, as we discussed in this chapter and also in Chapter 5, these types of natural resource industries tend to be increasing cost industries. And yet the price of metals compared with other goods has tended to fall slowly over time (albeit with many spikes in between). The following figure, for example, shows an index of prices for aluminum, copper, lead, tin, and zinc from 1900 to 2015 (adjusted for inflation). The trend is downward. Why do you think this is the case?

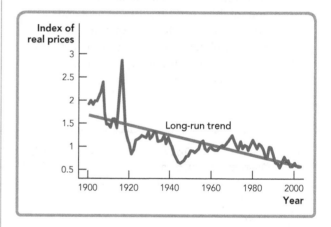

27. Frequent moviegoers often note that movies are rarely based on original ideas. Most of them are based on a television series, a video game, or, most commonly, a book. Why? To help you answer this question, start with the following.

a. Does a movie or a book have a higher fixed cost of production?

b. Hollywood releases about 100 new movies widely every year while just one publisher, Penguin Random House, releases about 15,000 book titles a year in print (and 70,000 digital titles). How does your answer in part a explain such a wide difference? Which is riskier: publishing a book or producing a movie?

c. How does the difference in fixed costs and risk of failure explain why so many movies are based on successful books? As a result, where do you expect to see more innovative plots, dialogues, and characters: in novels or movies?

28. a. In the nineteenth century, economist Alfred Marshall wrote about decreasing cost industries, writing in his *Principles of Economics* (available free online) that "when an industry has thus chosen a locality for itself . . . [t]he mysteries of the trade become no mysteries; but are as it were in the air." In Chapter 10, we had a concept for benefits that are not internal to a firm but are "as it were in the air." What specific concept from Chapter 10 is at work in a business cluster?

b. In the twenty-first century, economist Michael Porter of the Harvard Business School writes about decreasing cost industries, as well: He calls them "business clusters." Porter's work has been very influential among city and town governments that argue that carefully targeted tax breaks and subsidies can attract investment and create a business cluster in their town, which will subsequently reap the benefits of decreasing costs. Is this argument correct? Be careful, it's tricky!

29. In Kolkata, India, it is very common to see beggars on the streets. Imagine that the visitors and residents of Kolkata become more generous in their donations; what will be the effect on the standard of living of beggars in Kolkata? Answer this question using supply and demand, making assumptions as necessary.

30. Just to make sure you've gotten enough practice using the different formulas in this chapter, let's try a challenging exercise with them. Very little information is given in the table below, but surprisingly, there's enough information for you to fill in all of the missing values—if you remember all of the relationships and can think of creative ways to use them.

31. The theologian Reinhold Niebuhr wrote the famous Serenity Prayer that says:

> God, grant me the serenity to accept the things I cannot change,
>
> Courage to change the things I can,
>
> And wisdom to know the difference.

At the risk of ruining a lovely prayer, how would you interpret this in economic terms?

Quantity	Total Costs	Fixed Costs	Variable Cost	Average Cost	Marginal Cost	Total Revenue	Profit
0				—	—		−$80
10					$4		
20	$200						
30			$240			$450	
40							
50				$13.60	$20		

WORK IT OUT

For interactive, step-by-step help in solving this problem, go online.

Suppose Marisa decides to lease a professional color printer and open up a photo and poster service in her dorm room for use by faculty and students. Her total cost, as a function of the number of prints she produces per month, is given in the table:

Number of Prints per Month	Total Costs	Fixed Costs	Variable Cost	Total Revenue	Profit
0	$100				
1,000	$110				
2,000	$125				
3,000	$145				
4,000	$175				
5,000	$215				
6,000	$285				

a. Fill in the missing numbers in the table, assuming that Marisa can charge 6 cents per print.

b. How many prints per month should Marisa sell?

c. If the lease rate on the printer were to increase by $50 per month, how would that impact Marisa's profit-maximizing level of output? How would this $50 increase in the lease rate affect Marisa's profit? What will she do when it is time to renew her lease?

CHAPTER 11 APPENDIX

Using Excel to Graph Cost Curves

We can use a spreadsheet such as Excel to take some of the drudgery out of graphing and calculating things like marginal revenue and marginal cost. In Figure A11.1, we show some of the data from the chapter on revenues and costs for the oil well. Notice that in cell B5 we show the Excel formula "= $A$2*A5", which takes the price from cell A2 and multiplies it by the quantity in cell A5 to produce total revenue. We then copy and paste this formula into the remainder of the column. We use the $ sign in $A$2 to tell Excel not to adjust the cell reference when we copy and paste (A5 doesn't have dollar signs so it is automatically adjusted to A6, A7, etc. when we copy and paste).

FIGURE A11.1

	B5	▼	f_x =$A$2*A5	
	A	B	C	D
1	Price			
2	50			
3				
4	Barrels of Oil Produced	Total Revenue (P * Q)	Total Cost	
5	0	0	30	
6	1	50	34	
7	2	100	40	
8	3	150	51	
9	4	200	68	
10	5	250	91	
11	6	300	120	
12	7	350	156	
13	8	400	206	
14	9	450	296	
15	10	500	420	
16				

With total revenue and total cost input, it's easy to create the other data that we need. Profit is just total revenue minus total cost, which in Figure A11.2 we show in column D. Marginal revenue and marginal cost are defined as $MR = \frac{\Delta TR}{\Delta Q}$ and $MC = \frac{\Delta TC}{\Delta Q}$. We show in cell F4 how to implement these formulas in Excel. The formula "= (C4 − C3)/(A4 − A3)" takes the cost of producing 2 barrels of oil from cell C4 and subtracts the cost of producing 1 barrel of oil from C3; we then divide by the increase in the number of barrels as we move from producing 1 to 2 barrels. In this case, $MC = (40 − 34)/(2 − 1) = 6$. The formula for MR is entered into Excel in a similar manner.

FIGURE A11.2

	F4	▼	f_x =(C4-C3)/(A4-A3)				
	A	B	C	D	E	F	G
1	Barrels of Oil Produced	Total Revenue (P * Q)	Total Cost	Profit	Marginal Revenue (Price)	Marginal Cost	
2	0	0	30	-30			
3	1	50	34	16	50	4	
4	2	100	40	60	50	6	
5	3	150	51	99	50	11	
6	4	200	68	132	50	17	
7	5	250	91	159	50	23	
8	6	300	120	180	50	29	
9	7	350	156	194	50	36	
10	8	400	206	194	50	50	
11	9	450	296	154	50	90	
12	10	500	420	80	50	124	
13							
14							

Average cost is $AC = TC/Q$ and we show this calculation in Figure A11.3.

FIGURE A11.3

	G13	▼	f_x =C13/A13				
	A	B	C	D	E	F	G
1	Price						
2	50						
3							
4	Barrels of Oil Produced	Total Revenue (P * Q)	Total Cost	Profit	Marginal Revenue (Price)	Marginal Cost	Average Cost
5	0	0	30	-30			
6	1	50	34	16	50	4	34
7	2	100	40	60	50	6	20
8	3	150	51	99	50	11	17
9	4	200	68	132	50	17	17
10	5	250	91	159	50	23	18.2
11	6	300	120	180	50	29	20
12	7	350	156	194	50	36	22.28571
13	8	400	206	194	50	50	25.75
14	9	450	296	154	50	90	32.88889
15	10	500	420	80	50	124	42
16							

It's now easy to graph *MR, MC,* and *AC.* By highlighting the Marginal Revenue, Marginal Cost, and Average Cost columns, including the labels, and clicking Insert and then Line Chart, we can produce a graph similar to that shown in Figure A11.4 (to get the exact graph, you must also tell Excel to use the barrel numbers in Column 1 on the *x*-axis—you can do this by clicking on the graph, clicking Select Data, and then Edit, Horizontal [Category] Axis Labels).

Remember that the profit-maximizing quantity is found where $MR = MC$. You can check this by looking at the table. You can see what happens to the profit-maximizing quantity when price changes simply by changing the price in cell A2; the graph will change automatically.

FIGURE A11.4

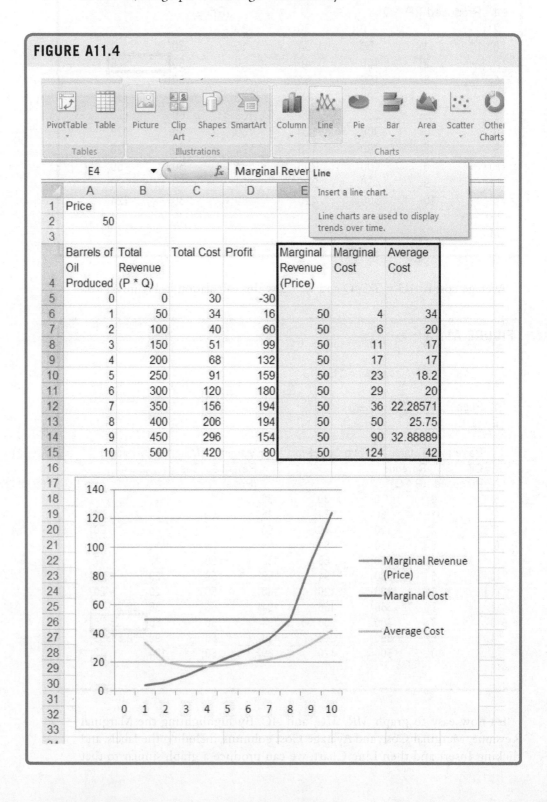

12

Competition and the Invisible Hand

I n Chapter 7, we explained how the price system—the signaling and incentive system—solves the great economic problem of arranging our limited resources to satisfy as many of our wants as possible. We showed how markets connect the world in a great cooperative endeavor, and how price signals and the accompanying profits and losses create incentives for entrepreneurs to direct labor and capital to their highest-value uses. Chapter 7 was a "big picture" view of markets. In Chapter 11, we took a closer look at firms and showed that to maximize profit, a firm wants to (1) produce the quantity such that $P = MC$, (2) enter industries where $P > AC$, and (3) exit industries where $P < AC$. In this chapter, we connect these two perspectives on markets.

We also return in this chapter to the invisible hand. Recall Big Idea Two from Chapter 1, namely the metaphor of the invisible hand. With the right institutions, individuals acting in their self-interest can generate outcomes that are neither part of their intention nor design but that nevertheless have desirable properties. In this chapter, we show exactly this: how the conditions for profit maximization under competition lead entrepreneurs to produce outcomes that they neither intend nor design but that nevertheless have desirable properties.

In particular, we show that the $P = MC$ condition for profit maximization in a competitive market balances production across firms in an industry in just the way that minimizes the total industry costs of production. Second, we show that the entry $(P > AC)$ and exit $(P < AC)$ signals balance production across different industries in just the way that maximizes the total value of production.

Invisible Hand Property 1: The Minimization of Total Industry Costs of Production

We know from the previous chapter that a firm in a competitive industry increases output until $P = MC$. What's even more important is that every firm in the same industry faces the *same* price. Thus, in a competitive market with N firms, the following will be true:

$$P = MC_1 = MC_2 = \ldots = MC_N$$

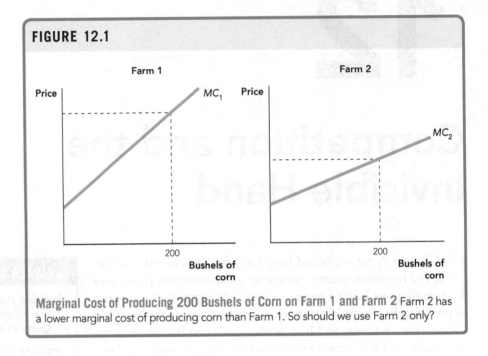

FIGURE 12.1

Marginal Cost of Producing 200 Bushels of Corn on Farm 1 and Farm 2 Farm 2 has a lower marginal cost of producing corn than Farm 1. So should we use Farm 2 only?

MRU

mru.org/cost-production

The Invisible Hand and the Minimization of Total Industry Costs

where MC_1 is the marginal cost of firm 1, MC_2 is the marginal cost of firm 2, and so forth. To understand the importance of this condition, let's briefly consider a seemingly different problem. Suppose that you own two farms on which to grow corn. Farm 1 is in a hilly region that is costly to seed and plow. Farm 2 is on land ideal for growing corn. The marginal cost of growing corn on each of these farms is illustrated in Figure 12.1.

Let's say that you would like to grow 200 bushels. It might seem that the lowest-cost way to produce 200 bushels is to produce all 200 bushels on Farm 2. After all, the marginal costs of production on Farm 2 are lower than on Farm 1 for any level of output.

Assume that you did produce all 200 bushels on Farm 2 and no bushels on Farm 1. Can you see a way of lowering your total costs of production?

Let's think in marginal terms. Instead of producing all 200 bushels on Farm 2, what would happen to your total costs of production if you produced, say, 197 bushels on Farm 2 and 3 bushels on Farm 1? Notice from Figure 12.2 that when you produce less on Farm 2, your costs of production decrease by the shaded area labeled A—this is the marginal cost of producing those last few bushels on Farm 2. By instead producing those bushels on Farm 1, your costs increase by area B, the marginal cost of production on Farm 1. But area B is less than area A, so by switching some production from Farm 2 to Farm 1, your total costs of producing 200 bushels of corn go down.

How far can you extend this logic? Clearly, you should continue producing fewer bushels on Farm 2 and more on Farm 1 if the marginal costs of production on Farm 2 exceed those on Farm 1; that is, produce less on Farm 2 and more on Farm 1 if $MC_2 > MC_1$. By the same logic, you should switch production from Farm 1 to Farm 2 if $MC_1 > MC_2$. Put these two statements together and it follows that the way to minimize the total costs of production is to produce just so much on each farm so that the marginal costs of production are equalized, $MC_1 = MC_2$. In the bottom panel of Figure 12.2, we show that the

FIGURE 12.2

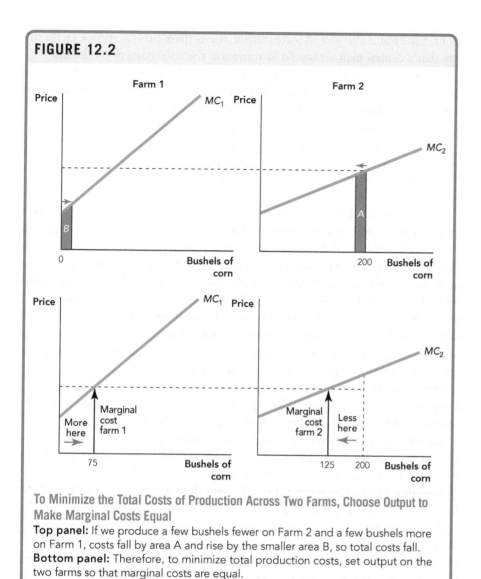

To Minimize the Total Costs of Production Across Two Farms, Choose Output to Make Marginal Costs Equal
Top panel: If we produce a few bushels fewer on Farm 2 and a few bushels more on Farm 1, costs fall by area A and rise by the smaller area B, so total costs fall.
Bottom panel: Therefore, to minimize total production costs, set output on the two farms so that marginal costs are equal.

cost-minimizing way to produce 200 bushels of corn is to produce 75 bushels on Farm 1 and 125 bushels on Farm 2.

Now comes the really important part. If you own both farms, you can act as a "central planner" and allocate production across the two farms so that the marginal costs of production are equal and thus the total costs of production are minimized. But now suppose that Farm 1 is in North Carolina and Farm 2 is in Iowa, and let's say Farm 1 is owned by Sandy and Farm 2 by Pat. Let's further suppose that Sandy and Pat will live their entire lives without ever meeting. Is there any way to organize production so that the output is split in exactly the way that you would split it if you owned both farms? Yes, there is.

Sandy and Pat sell their corn in the same market so each of them sees the same price of corn. How will Sandy maximize profits? How will Pat maximize profits? To maximize profits, Sandy will set $P = MC_1$ and Pat will set $P = MC_2$, but this means that $MC_1 = MC_2$! But we know that if $P = MC_1 = MC_2$, then the total costs of production are minimized. Amazingly, in pursuit of their own profit, Sandy and Pat will allocate output across their two farms in exactly the way that a central planner would to minimize the total costs of production!

It's remarkable that a free market could mimic an ideal central planner. What's even more remarkable is that a free market can allocate production across the two farms to minimize total costs even when an ideal central planner could not! Imagine, for example, that only Sandy knows MC_1 and that only Pat knows MC_2. For a free market, this is no problem, and Sandy and Pat, each acting in their own self-interest, choose the output levels that minimize total costs. But a central planner cannot allocate production correctly if it lacks knowledge of MC_1 or MC_2.

The insight that a free market minimizes the total costs of production is one of the most surprising and deepest in all of economics. In a famous phrase in *The Wealth of Nations*, Adam Smith described a similar situation saying that each individual "in this, as in many other cases, [is] led by an invisible hand to promote an end which was no part of his intention." Sandy and Pat don't intend to minimize the total costs of producing 200 bushels of corn; they intend only to make a profit. But this beneficial outcome is the result of their action. Indeed, until Adam Smith and other economists began to study markets, not only did no one intend to minimize industry costs, no one even *knew* that individuals acting to maximize their own profits would minimize industry costs.

Friedrich Hayek, a Nobel Prize–winning economist we discussed in Chapter 7, said that properties like the minimization of the total costs of production were "products of human action but not of human design."

Invisible Hand Property 1 says that even though no actor in a market economy intends to do so, in a free market $P = MC_1 = MC_2 = \ldots = MC_N$ and, as a result, the total industry costs of production are minimized.

Invisible Hand Property 1 provides another perspective on free trade. In Chapter 9, we explained how free trade increased wealth by letting the United States buy goods from the lowest-cost producers. We can now see this in another way. Remember that costs are minimized when $MC_1 = MC_2$ so costs are *not* minimized when $MC_1 \neq MC_2$. Now imagine that Farm 1 and Farm 2 are in different countries with no free trade between them. Sandy and Pat, therefore, face *different* prices for corn. Since Sandy and Pat face different prices, $MC_1 \neq MC_2$ and thus the total costs of producing corn cannot be at a minimum.

Invisible Hand Property 2: The Balance of Industries

Invisible Hand Property 1 tells us that in a competitive industry, the total industry costs of production are minimized. But we could minimize the total costs of producing corn and still have too much or too little corn. It's good to know that if 20 or 200 million bushels of corn are produced, we get those bushels at the lowest cost, but how many bushels is the right amount? It's the second invisible hand property that ensures the right amount of corn is produced.

Consider two industries, the car industry and the computer industry. Both industries use labor and capital to produce goods. Labor and capital, however, are limited. Recall from Chapter 7 that the great economic problem is to arrange our limited resources to satisfy as many of our wants as possible. So how do we allocate our limited labor and capital across the computer and car industry to satisfy as many of our wants as possible?

CHECK YOURSELF

- If the MC of production on Sandy's farm is higher than on Pat's farm, how should production be rearranged to minimize the total costs of production?

Profit in the computer industry is total revenue minus total cost. Total revenue measures the value of the output of the computer industry, the computers. Total cost measures the value of the inputs to the computer industry, the labor and capital. High profits, therefore, mean that outputs of high value are being created from inputs of low value. Profit is a signal that our limited labor and capital are being used productively in satisfying our wants.

Now suppose that the computer industry is more profitable than the car industry—then a unit of labor and capital in the computer industry is creating more value than in the car industry. What we would like, therefore, is for labor and capital to move from the car industry to the computer industry. Or, in other words, to use our limited resources most effectively, we would like resources to flow from low-profit industries to high-profit industries.

Of course, moving labor and capital from low-profit to high-profit industries is exactly what entrepreneurs would like to do! Recall that our condition to enter an industry is $P > AC$, but as we showed in Chapter 11, that's equivalent to $TR > TC$ (multiply both sides of $P > AC$ by Q). So, in a competitive market, the incentives that entrepreneurs have to seek profit and avoid losses align with the social incentive to move labor and capital out of low-value industries and into high-value industries.

Notice that profits encourage entry, but what happens to price and profits when firms enter an industry? As firms enter, supply increases and the price declines, which reduces profits. Losses encourage exit, but what happens to price and profits when firms exit an industry? As firms exit, supply decreases and the price increases, which increases profit (reduces losses). Thus, there is a tendency for the profit rate in all competitive industries to go to zero (normal profits). Since the profit rate tends to the same level in the car and the computer and all other industries, the marginal value of resources in all industries is the same. That's just another way of saying that the total value of production is maximized because if the profit rate in one industry were greater than in another, total value would increase if resources were to move from the less profitable to the more profitable industry.

The Invisible Hand

Invisible Hand Property 1 showed how self-interest worked to minimize the total costs of, say, corn production. Invisible Hand Property 2 shows how the self-interest of entrepreneurs causes them to enter and exit the car, computer, corn, apple, and other industries in such a way that the total value of all production is maximized. An implication of Invisible Hand Property 2 is that the profit rate in all competitive industries tends toward the same level.

Creative Destruction

Although the profit rate in all competitive industries tends toward the same level, that's just a tendency. Change is constant—tastes change, technologies change, and, in their pursuit of profit, entrepreneurs are always trying to discover new and better products and processes—so some profitable industries are always popping up and some unprofitable industries, as well. So, although the great economic problem is never solved completely, in a dynamic economy, resources are always moving toward an increase in the value of production. In a dynamic economy, entrepreneurs listen to price signals and they move capital and labor from unprofitable industries to profitable industries.

Profits pop up all the time, but in a dynamic economy, the entry of new firms quickly whacks them down again.

According to the **elimination principle**, above-normal profits are eliminated by entry and below-normal profits are eliminated by exit.

These dynamics illustrate a general feature of competitive markets that we call the **elimination principle:** *Above-normal profits are eliminated by entry and below-normal profits are eliminated by exit.*

The elimination principle says that above-normal profits are temporary. Great ideas are soon adopted by others; they diffuse throughout the economy and become commonplace—and no one profits from the commonplace. Since no one profits from the commonplace, *to earn above-normal profits an entrepreneur must innovate.*

The economist Joseph Schumpeter was eloquent on this point. In textbooks, he said, competition is about pushing price down to average cost:

> [But] in capitalist reality as distinguished from its textbook picture, it is not that kind of competition which counts but the competition from the new commodity, the new technology, the new source of supply, the new type of organization . . . competition which commands a decisive cost or quality advantage and which strikes not at the margins of the profits and the outputs of the existing firms but at their foundations and their very lives. . . .

This process of Creative Destruction is the essential fact about capitalism.[1]

Thus, the elimination principle serves as both a warning and an opportunity to entrepreneurs. Stand still and fall behind. Leap ahead and profits may follow. In a dynamic economy, there is a constant dance between elimination and innovation. Above-normal profits are constantly being eliminated by competition, and new sources of profit are constantly being created through innovation.

The Invisible Hand Works with Competitive Markets

We have shown in this chapter that competitive markets have some desirable "invisible hand" properties, but don't forget that the invisible hand works only in certain circumstances. For the competitive process to work, for example, it's important that prices accurately signal costs and benefits. But we already know from Chapter 10 on externalities that prices do not always accurately signal costs and benefits. We can now see from another perspective why this is a problem. If prices don't accurately signal costs and benefits, then Invisible Hand Property 2 won't work perfectly and there will not be an ideal balance between industries. We will get too few resources in some industries and too many resources in other industries.

Similarly, if markets are not competitive, then the invisible hand doesn't work as well. We will be taking up the problem of monopoly in Chapter 13 and oligopoly (a few firms but not many) in Chapter 15, but we can point to the basic issue here. Monopolists and oligopolists earn above-normal profits. We know that if an industry earns above-normal profits, we would like resources to move to that industry, but without the pressure of the competitive process, not enough resources will move and profits will not be eliminated. We can see right away, therefore, that output will be too low in a monopoly or in an oligopoly.

We will also be showing in Chapter 19, Public Goods and the Tragedy of the Commons, that for some types of goods, self-interest either doesn't align with the social interest or sometimes it may align in the wrong direction. All this remind us of the basic point: Good institutions align self-interest with the social interest, but good institutions are sometimes hard to find or create.

CHECK YOURSELF

- In Chapter 7, we saw how prices are signals. In competitive markets, how are profits signals?
- In a competitive market, how does a firm make profits if it has no control over price?

Joseph Schumpeter (1883–1950) In his youth, Schumpeter said he wanted to be "the greatest lover in Vienna, the best horseman in Europe, and the greatest economist in the world." He later claimed to have achieved two of the three, adding that he and horses just didn't get along.

Bettmann/Getty Images

Takeaway

Invisible Hand Property 1 says that by producing where $P = MC$, the self-interested, profit-seeking behavior of entrepreneurs results in the minimization of the total industry costs of production even though no entrepreneur intends this result. Invisible Hand Property 2 says that entry and exit decisions not only work to eliminate profits, they work to ensure that labor and capital move across industries to optimally balance production so that the greatest use is made of our limited resources.

The elimination principle tells us that above-normal profits are eliminated by entry and below-normal profits are eliminated by exit. Perhaps even more importantly, the elimination principle tells us that to earn above-normal profits, a firm must innovate.

Competitive markets do a good job of aligning self-interest with the social interest, but not all markets are competitive.

CHAPTER REVIEW

Go online to practice with more examples of these types of problems, including live links to videos, data sources, and feedback.

KEY CONCEPTS

elimination principle, p. 244

FACTS AND TOOLS

1. Entrepreneurs shift capital and labor across industries in pursuit of profit. Let's look at this a little more closely. Suppose there are two industries: a high-profit industry, Industry H, and a low-profit industry, Industry L. Answer the following questions about these two industries.

    a. If the two industries have similar costs, then what must be true about prices in the two industries?

    b. What does your answer to part a imply about the value of the output in the two industries?

    c. If labor and capital are moved from Industry L to Industry H, what is given up? What is gained?

    d. Suppose instead that the prices in the two industries were identical. In this case, what must be true about the costs in the two industries?

    e. What does your answer to part d imply about the amounts of capital and labor

required to produce one unit of output in each industry?

    f. If labor and capital are moved from Industry L to Industry H, are more units of output lost in Industry L or gained in Industry H?

2. Suppose that two industries, the pizza industry and the calzone industry, are equally risky, but rates of return on capital investments are only 5% in the pizza industry and 8% in the calzone industry.

    Which way will capital flow—from the pizza industry to the calzone industry, or from the calzone industry to the pizza industry?

3. We've claimed that the efficient way to spread out work across firms in the same industry is to set the marginal cost of production to be the same across firms. Let's see if this works in an example.

    Consider a competitive market for rolled steel (measured by the ton) with just two firms: SmallCo and BigCo. If we wanted to be more realistic, we could say there were 100 firms like SmallCo and 100 firms like BigCo, but that would just make the math harder without generating any insight. The two firms have marginal cost schedules like this:

	Marginal Cost	
Quantity	SmallCo	BigCo
1	$10	$10
2	$20	$10
3	$30	$10
4	$40	$10
5	$50	$20
6	$60	$30
7	$70	$40
8	$80	$50

a. We'll ignore the fixed costs of starting up the firms just to make things a little simpler. What is the total cost at each firm of producing each level of output? Fill in the table.

	Total Cost	
Quantity	SmallCo	BigCo
1	$10	$10
2	$30	$20
3	$60	
4		
5		
6		
7		
8		

b. What's the cheapest way to make 11 tons of steel? 5 tons?

c. What would the price have to be in this competitive market for these two firms to produce a total of 11 tons of steel? 5 tons?

d. Suppose that a government agency looked at BigCo and SmallCo's cost curves. Which firm looks like the low-cost producer to a government agency? Would it be a good idea, an efficient policy, for the government to shut down the high-cost producer? In other words, could a government intervention do better than the invisible hand in this case?

e. Let's make part d more concrete: What would the total cost be if BigCo were the only firm in the market, and it had to produce 7 tons of rolled steel? What would marginal and total costs be if SmallCo and BigCo let the invisible hand divvy up the work between them?

4. Let's review the basic mechanism of the elimination principle.

a. When demand rises in Industry X, what happens to profits? Do they rise, fall, or remain unchanged?

b. When that happens, do firms, workers, and capital tend to enter Industry X, or do they tend to leave?

c. Does this tend to increase short-run supply in Industry X or reduce it?

d. In the long run, after this rise in demand, what will profits typically be in Industry X?

THINKING AND PROBLEM SOLVING

5. The elimination principle discussed in this chapter tells us what we can expect in the long run from perfectly competitive markets: zero (normal) profits across industries. If this were the case, and this fate were unavoidable, going into business would seem to be a fairly dismal choice, given that the end result of normal profits is known right out of the gate. Despite this, we constantly see entrepreneurs working hard to earn profits. Is this a waste of time, given what we know about the elimination principle? Is the fate of zero profit unavoidable? What would Joseph Schumpeter say about all of this?

6. How can the market mechanism guarantee that the marginal cost of production will be the same across all firms if those firms have different owners, are in different locations, and have unique cost functions known only to the firms themselves? Why don't these different firms need to have one shared owner or one shared manager to coordinate this "equal marginal cost" condition?

7. We've seen already from this chapter that dividing up output over multiple producers—even

when one has higher costs than the other—can lead to lower industry costs, so long as output is divided up such that $MC_1 = MC_2 = MC_N$. You've already done some practice in Facts and Tools question 3 with cost functions presented as tables. Let's try to see how this works graphically.

Take a look at the following two marginal cost functions:

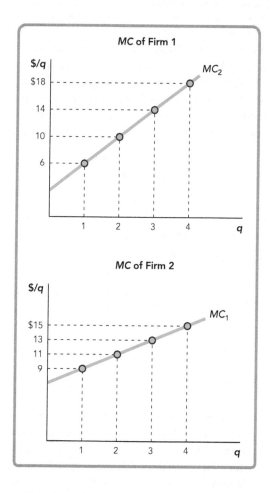

Based on the graphs of these two marginal cost functions, fill in the table for industry-wide marginal cost, assuming that production is divided up among the two firms according to Invisible Hand Property 1. To help you get started, take a look at the table and answer the following questions assuming both firms can produce a maximum of 4 units. Which firm produces the first unit of industry output? Which firm produces the second unit of industry output? Why? Once the table is complete, create a graph of the industry marginal cost curve.

Quantity	Industry-Wide MC
1	$6
2	$9
3	
4	
5	
6	
7	
8	

8. In the process of creative destruction, what gets destroyed?

Firms

Workers

Machines

Buildings

Business plans

Valuable relationships

Or some combination of these? The chapter itself contains quite a few ideas about how to answer this question, but you'll have to think hard about the "opportunity cost" for each item on the list.

9. Every year, American television introduces many new shows, only about one-third of which survive past their first season.[2] The few shows that last, however, prove to be very profitable.

a. How does creative destruction explain why studios bother to make new shows if most of them will fail?

b. In the summer of 2010, *The Great British Bake Off* (known as *The Great British Baking Show* in the United States due to trademark issues) premiered on television and became immensely popular, eventually coming to the United States on PBS in 2014 and really breaking through Stateside on Netflix in 2018. How did Netflix and other television producers respond to this surprise hit? (Interestingly, the show itself can be seen as a more recent offshoot of the reality show boom that began with *American Idol* in 2002.)

c. What happened over the next several years to profits from *The Great British Bake Off*?

You don't need to check Love Production's financial statements to get the answer; use the elimination principle!

10. Let's suppose that the demand for allergists increases in California. How does the invisible hand respond to this demand? There is more than one correct answer to this question: Try to come up with two or three.

11. Suppose a friend approaches you with a business proposition. Noticing the high current price for cage-free eggs, your friend has created a spreadsheet that incorporates production costs and calculates high profits for years to come in this industry. The calculations estimate that you will both be millionaires in just several years' time. Should you invest based on these calculations?

CHALLENGES

12. Let's take a look at Invisible Hand Property 2 in action using a mathematical example. Suppose an industry is characterized by the equations in the following table. (We're going to assume that all individual firms are identical to make this problem a little simpler.)

Demand	$Q_D = 100 - 2P$
Individual firm's supply	$q_S = 0.5 + 0.1P$
Market supply with n firms	$Q_S = n \times q_S = 0.5n + 0.1nP$
Individual firm's average cost	$AC = 5q_S - 5 + (24.2/q_S)$

a. Suppose 24 firms are in this industry. What is the equation for market supply? What are the equilibrium price and quantity (this can be found by setting $Q_D = Q_S$)? How much profit is each firm earning? According to the elimination principle, what should occur in this industry over time?

b. Suppose 35 firms are in this industry. Answer the same questions from part a.

c. The elimination principle says that profits will be eliminated in the long run, which means that $AC = P$. Using that fact, figure out how many firms will be in this industry in the long run (solve for n).

WORK IT OUT

For interactive, step-by-step help in solving this problem, go online.

Now let's take a look at the equations for the marginal cost functions that are graphed in Thinking and Problem Solving question 7, and see if we can combine them into one equation for industry-wide marginal cost. This is what the two equations for the graphs in the question look like:

$$MC_1 = 2 + 4q_1$$
$$MC_2 = 7 + 2q_2$$

Can you create an industry marginal cost equation that shows MC_{Total} as a function of q_{Total} instead of just q_1 or q_2?

a. First, solve both equations for q.

b. Now, replace MC_1 and MC_2 with MC_{Total}, since Invisible Hand Property 1 tells us that marginal cost will be equal for all of the firms in the industry.

c. Next, write an equation for q_{Total}, which is just $q_1 + q_2$.

d. Finally, solve the equation for MC_{Total}. Now you have created an industry marginal cost function from the cost functions of two different firms in the industry. (If you compare this equation with your answers for Thinking and Problem Solving question 7, you'll see that the marginal cost is a little different when you use the equation. This is, in part, because this equation assumes you can produce *partial* units at either firm, whereas your graph was based on the assumption that only *whole* units were produced.)

13

Monopoly

On June 5, 1981, the Centers for Disease Control and Prevention reported that a strange outbreak of pneumonia was killing young, healthy, homosexual men in Los Angeles. Alarm spread as similar reports streamed in from San Francisco, New York, and Boston. What had at first looked like a disease peculiar to homosexual men turned out to be a worldwide killer caused by HIV (the human immunodeficiency virus). Since 1981, AIDS (acquired immune deficiency syndrome) has killed more than 40 million people.

There is no known cure for AIDS, but progress has been made in treating the disease. In the United States, deaths from AIDS dropped by approximately 50% between 1995 and 1997. The major cause of the falling death rate was the development of new drugs called combination antiretrovirals, such as Combivir.[1] The drugs, however, were expensive. A single pill of Combivir cost about $12.50—at two per day, every day, that's nearly $10,000 per year.[2] If you had the money, $10,000 a year was a small price to pay for life, but millions of people with AIDS could not afford $10,000 annually.[3]

If HIV drugs were expensive because production costs were high, economists would have little to say about drug pricing. But it cost about 50 cents to produce a pill of Combivir—thus, the price of one pill was about 25 times higher than the cost.[4] In earlier chapters, we emphasized how competitive markets drive the price of a good down to marginal cost. Why didn't that process work here? There are three reasons why HIV drugs were priced well above cost.

1. Market power
2. The "you can't take it with you" effect
3. The "other people's money" effect

The primary reason that AIDS drugs were priced well above cost was monopoly or market power, the subject of this chapter. The "you can't take it with you" and "other people's money" effects, which we will also discuss in this chapter, make market power especially strong in the pricing of pharmaceuticals.

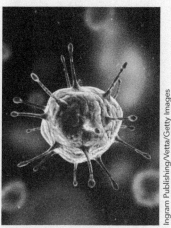

The cause of AIDS, the human immunodeficiency virus (HIV)

Market Power

GlaxoSmithKline (GSK), one of the world's largest producers of AIDS drugs, owned the patent on Combivir. A patent is a government grant that gives the owner the exclusive rights to make, use, or sell the patented product.

GlaxoSmithKline, for example, was the only legal seller of Combivir. Even though the formula to manufacture was well-known and easily duplicated, competitors who tried to make Combivir or its equivalent would be jailed, at least in the United States and other countries where the patent is enforced.

GSK's patent on Combivir gives GSK **market power**, the power to raise price above marginal cost without fear that other competitors will enter the market. A **monopoly** is simply a firm with market power.

India, however, did not recognize the Combivir patent, so in that country competition prevailed and an equivalent drug sold for just 50 cents per pill.[5] Thus, economics correctly predicted that competition will drive price down to marginal cost; it's just that GSK's patent prevented competition from operating.

Patents are not the only source of market power. Government regulations other than patents, as well as economies of scale, exclusive access to an important input, and technological innovation can all create firms with market power. We discuss the sources of market power and appropriate responses at greater length later on in this chapter. For now, we want to ask how a firm will use its market power to maximize profit.

How a Firm Uses Market Power to Maximize Profit

We know that a firm with market power will price above cost—but how much above cost? Even a firm with no competitors faces a demand curve, so as it raises its price, it will sell fewer units. Higher prices, therefore, are not always better for a seller—raise the price too much and profits will fall. Lower the price and profits can increase. What is the profit-maximizing price?

To maximize profit, a firm should produce until the revenue from an additional sale is equal to the cost of an additional sale. This is the same condition that we discovered in Chapter 11: produce until **marginal revenue** equals **marginal cost** ($MR = MC$). In Chapter 11, however, calculating marginal revenue was easy because even if a small oil well increases production significantly, the effect on the world price of oil is so small it can be ignored. For a small firm, therefore, the revenue from the sale of an additional unit is the market price (MR = Price). But when a firm's output of a product is large relative to the entire market's output of that product (or very close substitutes), a significant increase in the firm's output will cause the market price of that product to fall. When GSK produces and sells more Combivir, for example, it pushes the price of Combivir down. Thus, for a firm that produces a large share of the market's total output of a product, the revenue from the sale of an additional unit is less than the current market price (MR < Price). In Chapter 11, we said that the competitive firm was a price taker. In contrast, a firm with monopoly power is a price maker; when this firm changes the quantity it produces, it also changes the price at which it can sell.

To understand how a firm with market power will choose what quantity to produce and thus the price at which it sells its product, we need to calculate marginal revenue for a firm that is large enough to influence the price of its product.

We show how to calculate marginal revenue in the table in the left panel of Figure 13.1. Suppose that at a price of $16 the quantity demanded is 2 units, so that total revenue is $32 ($2 \times \$16$). If the monopolist reduces the price to $14, it can sell 3 units for a total revenue of $42 ($3 \times \$14$). Marginal revenue, the

Market power is the power to raise price above marginal cost without fear that other firms will enter the market.

A **monopoly** is a firm with market power.

Marginal revenue, MR, is the change in total revenue from selling an additional unit.

Marginal cost, MC, is the change in total cost from producing an additional unit.

To maximize profit, a firm increases output until $MR = MC$.

FIGURE 13.1

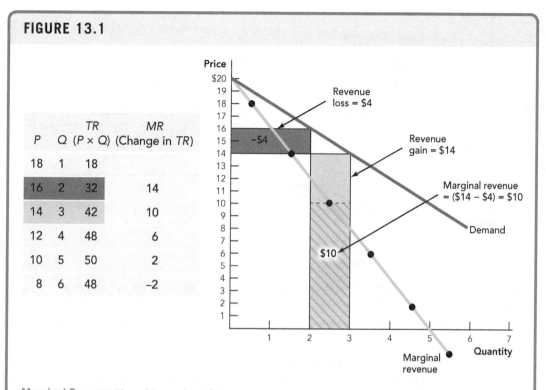

		TR	MR
P	Q	(P × Q)	(Change in TR)
18	1	18	
16	2	32	14
14	3	42	10
12	4	48	6
10	5	50	2
8	6	48	−2

Marginal Revenue The table on the left shows that marginal revenue is the change in total revenue when quantity sold increases by 1 unit. When the quantity sold increases from 2 units to 3 units, for example, total revenue increases from $32 to $42 so marginal revenue, the change in total revenue, is $10. The figure on the right shows how we can break down the change in total revenue into two parts. When the firm lowers the price from $16 to $14, it sells one more unit and so there is a gain in revenue of $14, the price of that unit, but since to sell that additional unit the firm had to lower the price, it loses $2 on each of its two previous sales so there is a revenue loss of $4. Thus, marginal revenue is the revenue gain on new sales plus the revenue loss on previous sales.

change in revenue from selling an additional unit, is therefore $10 ($42 − $32). Thus, we can always calculate *MR* by looking at the change in total revenue when production changes by 1 unit.

The right panel of Figure 13.1 shows another way of thinking about marginal revenue. When the monopolist lowers its price from $16 to $14, it makes one additional sale, which increases revenues by the price of 1 unit, $14—the green area. But to make that additional sale, the monopolist had to lower its price by $2, so it loses $2 on *each* of the 2 units that it was selling at the higher price for a revenue loss of $4—the red area. Marginal revenue is the revenue gain (green, $14) plus the revenue loss (red, −$4) or $10 (green striped area). Notice that *MR* ($10) is less than price ($14)—once again, this is because to sell more units, the monopolist must lower the price so there is a loss of revenue on sales the firm would have made at the higher price.

Now that you understand the idea of marginal revenue, here's a shortcut for finding it. If the demand curve is a straight line, then the marginal revenue curve is a straight line that begins at the same point on the vertical axis as the demand curve but with twice the slope.[6] Figure 13.2 shows three demand curves and their associated marginal revenue curves. Notice that if the demand curve cuts the horizontal axis at, say, *Z*, then the marginal revenue curve will always cut the horizontal axis at half that amount, *Z*/2.

FIGURE 13.2

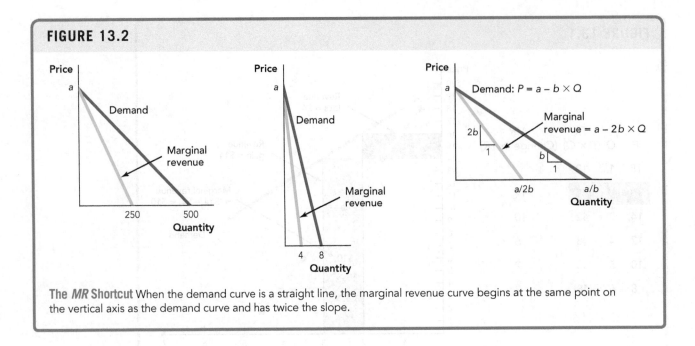

The *MR* Shortcut When the demand curve is a straight line, the marginal revenue curve begins at the same point on the vertical axis as the demand curve and has twice the slope.

Figure 13.3 sketches the demand, marginal revenue, marginal cost, and average cost curve for a firm with market power, like GlaxoSmithKline. GSK maximizes profit by producing the quantity where $MR = MC$. In Figure 13.3, this is at point a, a quantity of 80 million units. What is the maximum price

FIGURE 13.3

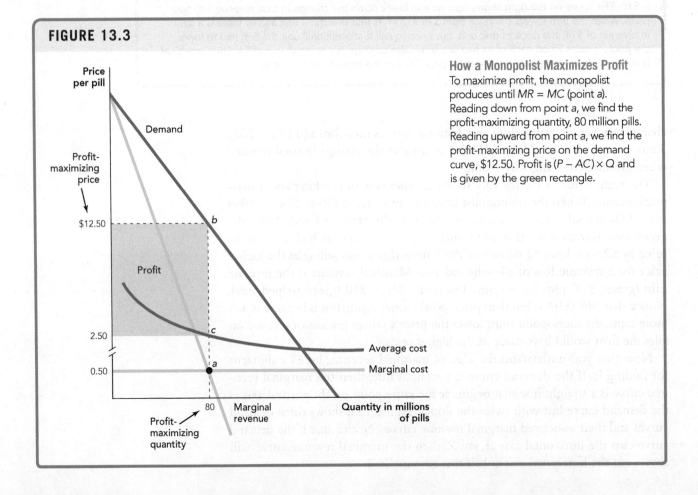

How a Monopolist Maximizes Profit
To maximize profit, the monopolist produces until $MR = MC$ (point a). Reading down from point a, we find the profit-maximizing quantity, 80 million pills. Reading upward from point a, we find the profit-maximizing price on the demand curve, $12.50. Profit is $(P - AC) \times Q$ and is given by the green rectangle.

at which the monopolist can sell 80 million units? To find the maximum that consumers will pay for 80 million units, remember that we read up from the quantity supplied of 80 million units to the *demand curve* at point *b*. Consumers are willing to pay as much as $12.50 per pill when the quantity supplied is 80 million pills, so the profit-maximizing price is $12.50.

We can also use Figure 13.3 to illustrate the monopolist's profit. Remember from Chapter 11 that profit can be calculated as $(P - AC) \times Q$. At a quantity of 80 million units, the price is $12.50 (point *b*), the average cost (*AC*) is $2.50 (point *c*), and thus profit is $(\$12.50 - \$2.50) \times 80$ million units or $800 million, as illustrated by the green rectangle. (By the way, the fixed costs of producing a new pharmaceutical are very large so the minimum point of the *AC* curve occurs far to the right of the diagram.) Recall that a competitive firm earns zero or normal profits but a monopolist uses its market power to earn positive or *above-normal* profits.

The Elasticity of Demand and the Monopoly Markup

Market power for pharmaceuticals can be especially powerful because of the two other effects we mentioned earlier: the "you can't take it with you" effect and the "other people's money" effect. If you are dying of disease, what better use of your money do you have than spending it on medicine that might prolong your life? If you can't take it with you, then you may as well spend your money trying to stick around a bit longer. Consumers with serious diseases, therefore, are *relatively insensitive to the price of life-saving pharmaceuticals*.

Moreover, if you are willing to spend *your* money on pharmaceuticals, how do you feel about spending *other people's money*? Most patients in the United States have access to public or private health insurance, so pharmaceuticals and other medical treatments are often paid by someone other than the patient. Thus, both the "you can't take it with you" and the "other people's money" effects make consumers with serious diseases relatively insensitive to the price of life-saving pharmaceuticals—that is, they will continue to buy in large quantities even when the price increases.

If GlaxoSmithKline knows that consumers will continue to buy Combivir even when it increases the price, how do you think it will respond? Yes, it will increase the price! When consumers are relatively insensitive to the price, what sort of demand curve do we say consumers have? An inelastic demand curve. The "you can't take it with you" effect and the "other people's money" effect make the demand curve more *inelastic*. Thus, we say that the more inelastic the demand curve, the more a monopolist will raise its price above marginal cost.

Is it ethically wrong for GSK to raise its price above marginal cost? Perhaps, but keep in mind that in the United States, it costs nearly a billion dollars to research and develop the average new drug. Once we better understand how monopolies price, we will return to the question of what, if anything, should be done about market power.

Figure 13.4 illustrates that the more inelastic the demand curve, the more a monopolist will raise its price above marginal cost. On the left side of the figure, the monopolist faces a relatively elastic demand curve, and on the right side a relatively inelastic demand curve. As usual, the monopolist maximizes profit by choosing the quantity at which $MR = MC$ and the highest price that consumers will pay for that quantity. Notice that even though the marginal cost curve is identical in the two panels, the markup of price over marginal cost is much higher when the demand curve is relatively inelastic.

mru.org/monopoly-markup

Monopoly Markup

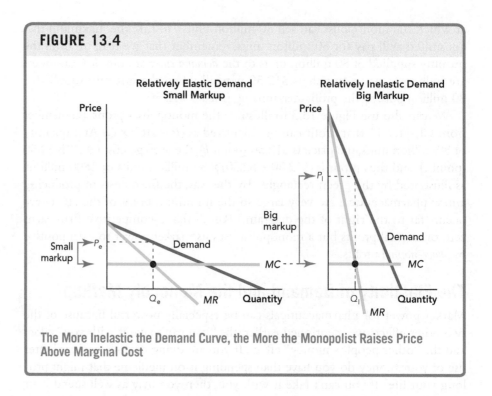

FIGURE 13.4

The More Inelastic the Demand Curve, the More the Monopolist Raises Price Above Marginal Cost

Remember from Chapter 5 that the fewer substitutes that exist for a good, the more inelastic the demand curve. With that in mind, consider the following puzzle. Recently, American Airlines was selling a flight from Washington, D.C., to Dallas for $772. On the same day, it was selling a flight from Washington to San Francisco for $322. That's a little puzzling. You would expect the shorter flight to have lower costs, and Washington is much closer to Dallas than to San Francisco. The puzzle, however, is even deeper. The flight from Washington to San Francisco stopped in Dallas. In fact, the Washington-to-Dallas leg of the journey was on exactly the same flight![7]

Thus, a traveler going from Washington to Dallas was being charged nearly $450 *more* than a traveler going from Washington to Dallas and then on to San Francisco even though both were flying to Dallas on the same plane. Why?

Here's a hint. Each of the major airlines flies most of its cross-country traffic into a hub, an airport that serves as a busy "node" in an airline's network of flights, and most hubs are located near the center of the country. Delta's hub, for example, is in Atlanta. So if you fly cross-country on Delta, you will probably travel through Atlanta. United's hub is in Chicago and American Airlines has its hub in Dallas. Have you solved the puzzle yet?

Of the flights into the Dallas-Fort Worth airport, 84% are on American Airlines, so if you want to fly from Washington to Dallas at a convenient time, you have few choices of airline. But if you want to fly from Washington to San Francisco, you have many choices. In addition to flying on American Airlines, you can fly Delta, United, or Jet Blue. Since travelers flying from Washington to Dallas have few substitutes, their demand curve is inelastic, like the demand curve in the right panel of Figure 13.4. Since travelers flying from Washington to San Francisco have many substitutes, their demand curve is more elastic, like the one in the left panel of Figure 13.4. As a result, travelers flying from Washington to Dallas (inelastic demand) are charged more than those flying from Washington to San Francisco (elastic demand).

You are probably asking yourself why someone wanting to go from Washington to Dallas doesn't book the cheaper flight to San Francisco and then exit in Dallas? In fact, clever people try to game the system all the time—but don't try to do this with a round-trip ticket or the airline will cancel your return flight. As a matter of contract, most airlines prohibit this and similar practices—their profit is at stake!

The Costs of Monopoly: Deadweight Loss

What's wrong with monopoly? The question may seem absurd—isn't it the high prices? Not so fast. The high price is bad for consumers, but it's good for the monopolist. And what's so special about consumers? Monopolists are people, too. So if we want to discover whether monopoly is good or bad, we need to count the gains to the monopolist equally with the losses to consumers. It turns out, however, that the monopolist gains less from monopoly pricing than the consumer loses. So monopolies are bad—they are bad because, compared with competition, monopolies reduce *total surplus*, the total gains from trade (consumer surplus plus producer surplus).

In Figure 13.5, we compare total surplus under competition with total surplus under monopoly. In the left panel, the competitive equilibrium price and quantity are P_c and Q_c. We also label Q_c the optimal quantity because it is the quantity that maximizes total surplus (recall from Chapter 4 that a competitive market maximizes total surplus). For simplicity, we assume a constant cost industry so the supply curve is flat ($MC = AC$) and producer surplus is zero. Total surplus is thus the same as consumer surplus and is shown by the blue triangle.

The right panel shows how a monopolist with the same costs would behave. Setting $MR = MC$, the monopolist produces Q_m, which is much less than Q_c, and prices at P_m. Consumer surplus is now the much smaller blue triangle. Now here is the key point: *Some* of the consumer surplus has been transferred to the

CHECK YOURSELF

- As a firm with market power moves down the demand curve to sell more units, what happens to the price it can charge on all units?
- What type of demand curve does a firm with market power prefer to face for its products: relatively elastic or inelastic? Why?

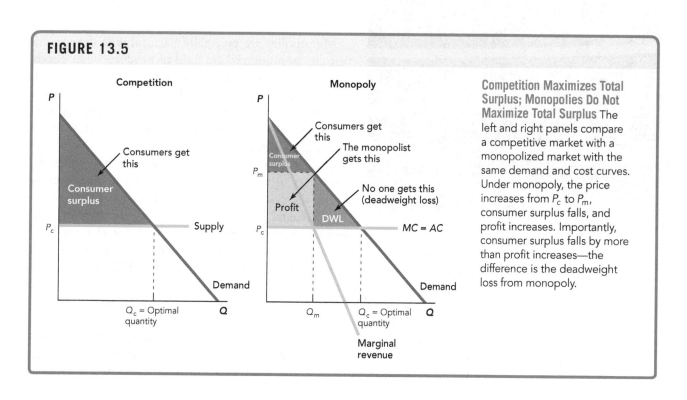

FIGURE 13.5

Competition Maximizes Total Surplus; Monopolies Do Not Maximize Total Surplus The left and right panels compare a competitive market with a monopolized market with the same demand and cost curves. Under monopoly, the price increases from P_c to P_m, consumer surplus falls, and profit increases. Importantly, consumer surplus falls by more than profit increases—the difference is the deadweight loss from monopoly.

monopolist as profit, the green area. But some of the consumer surplus is not transferred; it goes to neither the consumers nor the monopolist; it goes to no one and is lost. We call the lost consumer surplus *deadweight loss*.

To better understand deadweight loss, remember that the height of the demand curve tells you how much consumers are willing to pay for the good, and the height of the marginal cost curve tells you the cost of producing the good. Now notice that in between the amount that the monopolist produces, Q_m, and the amount that would be produced under competition, Q_c, the demand curve is above the marginal cost curve. In other words, consumers value the units between Q_m and Q_c more than their cost; so if these units were produced, total surplus would increase. But the monopolist does not produce these units. Why not? Because to sell these units, the monopolist would have to lower its price; and if it did so, the increase in revenue would not cover the increase in costs; that is, MR would be less than MC, so the monopolist's profit would decrease.

Let's look at deadweight loss in practice. GlaxoSmithKline prices Combivir at $12.50 a pill, the profit-maximizing price. There are plenty of consumers who can't pay $12.50 a pill but would gladly pay more than the marginal cost of 50 cents a pill. Deadweight loss is the value of the Combivir sales that do not occur because the monopoly price is above the competitive price.

CHECK YOURSELF
- Does the monopolist price its product above or below the price of a competitive firm?
- Does the monopolist produce more or less than competitive firms? Why?

The Costs of Monopoly: Corruption and Inefficiency

Sadly, around the world today, many monopolies are government-created and born of corruption. Indonesian President Suharto (in office from 1967 to 1998), for example, gave the lucrative clove monopoly to his playboy son, Tommy Suharto. Cloves may sound inconsequential, but they are a key ingredient in Indonesian cigarettes, and the monopoly funneled hundreds of millions of dollars to Tommy. A lot of rich playboys buy Lamborghinis—Tommy bought the entire company.

Monopolies are especially harmful when the goods that are monopolized are used to produce other goods. In Algeria, for example, a dozen or so army generals each control a key good. Indeed, the public ironically refers to each general by the major commodity that they monopolize—General Steel, General Wheat, General Tire, and so forth.

Steel is an input into automobiles, so when General Steel tries to take advantage of their market power by raising the price of steel, this increases costs for General Auto. General Auto responds by raising the price of automobiles even more than they would if steel were competitively produced. Similarly, General Steel raises the price of steel even more than they would if automobiles were competitively produced. Throw in a General Tire, a General Computer, and, let's say, a General Electric and we have a recipe for economic disaster. Each general tries to grab a larger share of the pie, but the combined result is that the pie gets much, much smaller.

Compare a competitive market economy with a monopolized economy: Competitive producers of steel work to reduce prices so they can sell more. Reduced prices of steel result in reduced prices of automobiles. Cost savings in

Peter Harholdt/Superstock

Monopoly profit

one sector are spread throughout the economy, resulting in economic growth. In a monopolized economy, in contrast, the entire process is thrown into reverse. Each firm wants to raise its prices, and the resulting cost increases are spread throughout the economy, resulting in poverty and stagnation.

One of the great lessons of economics is to show that good institutions channel self-interest toward social prosperity, whereas poor institutions channel self-interest toward social destruction. Business leaders in the United States are no less self-interested than generals in Algeria. So why are the former a mostly positive force, while the latter are a mostly negative force? It's because competitive markets channel the self-interest of business leaders toward social prosperity, whereas the political structure of Algeria channels self-interest toward social destruction.

The Benefits of Monopoly: Incentives for Research and Development

Let's return to GlaxoSmithKline's (GSK's) patent monopoly on Combivir. If GSK didn't have a monopoly, competition would have pushed prices down, more people could have afforded to buy Combivir, and total surplus would have been larger (i.e., deadweight loss would decline). So isn't the solution to the monopoly problem obvious? Open up the industry to competition by refusing to enforce the firm's patent or force GSK to lower its price.

In fact, many countries pursue one or the other of these policies. India, for example, has traditionally not offered strong patent protection, and Canada controls pharmaceutical prices. India's and Canada's policies have successfully kept pharmaceutical prices low in those countries. Many people argue that the United States should also control pharmaceutical prices. Unfortunately, the story is not so simple. We need to revisit our question: What's wrong with monopoly?

In the United States, researching, developing, and successfully testing the average new drug costs over $1 billion.[8] Firms must be compensated for these expenses if people expect them to invest in the discovery process. But if competition pushes the price of a pill down to the marginal cost, nothing will be left over for the cost of invention. And those who have no hope of reaping will not sow.

Patents are one way of rewarding research and development. Look again at Figure 13.3, which shows the green rectangle of monopoly profit. It's precisely the expectation (and hope) of enjoying that monopoly profit that encourages firms to research and develop new drugs.

If pharmaceutical patents are not enforced, the number of new drugs will decrease. India is poor and Canada is small, so neither contributes much to the global profit of pharmaceutical firms. But if the United States were to limit pharmaceutical patents significantly or to control pharmaceutical prices, the number of new drugs would decrease significantly.[9] But new drugs save lives. As noted in the introduction, antiretrovirals like Combivir were the major cause of the 50% decrease in AIDS deaths in the United States in the mid-1990s. We should be careful that in pushing prices closer to marginal cost, we do not lose the new drug entirely.

In evaluating pharmaceutical patents, you should keep in mind that patents don't last forever. A patent lasts for at most 20 years, and by the time a new drug is FDA-approved, its effective life is typically only 12–14 years. In fact, GSK's patent on Combivir ended in 2012, and generic competitors quickly entered the market, pushing prices down. Today, generic Combivir can be bought for

Don Farrall/Photodisc/Getty Images

Thomas Edison spent years experimenting with thousands of materials before he discovered that carbonized bamboo filament would make a long-lasting lightbulb. If anyone could have capitalized on his idea, Edison would not have been able to profit from his laborious research and development and perhaps he would not have done the necessary research in the first place.

Profit fuels the fire of invention.

Eyes on the prize Prizes are another way of rewarding research and development without creating monopolies. SpaceShipOne, pictured here, won the $10 million Ansari X Prize for being the first privately developed manned rocket capable of reaching space and returning in a short time. Netflix, the DVD distribution firm, offered and paid a $1 million prize for improvements to its movie recommendation system. The Department of Defense has sponsored prizes for driverless vehicles and Congress established the L-Prize for advances in lightbulb technology.

less than $1 per pill. Thus, high prices were a temporary price to pay for increased innovation.

Pharmaceuticals are not the only goods with high development costs and low marginal costs. Information goods of all kinds often have the same cost structure. Big-budget AAA video games like Fortnite, Call of Duty, and Overwatch have typical development costs of $60 to $80 million; Grand Theft Auto V cost more than $130 million to develop. Once the code has been written, however, the marginal cost of distributing on the Internet is close to zero. Prices, typically $40–$60, are therefore well above marginal costs. Since prices exceed marginal costs, there is a deadweight loss, which in theory could be reduced by a price control. Reducing prices, however, would reduce the incentive to research and develop new games. What would you rather have: Pong at $2, or, for $50 a game, a constant stream of new and better games?

Video games may seem trivial, but the trade-off between lower prices today at the expense of fewer new ideas in the future is a central one in modern economies. In fact, modern theories of economic growth emphasize that monopoly—*when it increases innovation*—may increase economic growth.

Nobel Prize–winning economic historian Douglass North argues that economic growth was slow and sporadic until laws, including patent laws, were created to protect innovation:

> [T]hroughout man's past he has continually developed new techniques, but the pace has been slow and intermittent. The primary reason has been that the incentives for developing new techniques have occurred only sporadically. Typically, innovations could be copied at no cost by others and without any reward to the inventor or innovator. The failure to develop systematic property rights in innovation up until fairly modern times was a major source of the slow pace of technological change.[10]

Patent Buyouts—A Potential Solution?

Is there a way to eliminate the deadweight loss without reducing the incentive to innovate? Nobel Prize–winning economist Michael Kremer has offered one speculative idea.[11] Take a look again at Figure 13.3. The green profit rectangle is the value of the patent to the patent owner, $800 million. Suppose that the government were to offer to buy the rights to the patent at, say, $850 million. The monopolist would be eager to sell at this price. What would the government do with the patent? Rip it up! If the government ripped up the patent, competitors would enter the field, drive the price down to the marginal cost of production, and eliminate the deadweight loss. In other words, Combivir would fall from $12.50 a pill to 50 cents a pill, and more of the world's poor could afford to be treated for AIDS.

The great virtue of Kremer's proposal is that it reduces the price of new drugs without reducing the incentive to develop more new drugs. Indeed, by offering more than the potential profit, the government could even increase the incentive to innovate! As usual, however, there is no such thing as a free lunch. To buy the patent, the government must raise taxes, and we know from Chapter 6 that taxes, just like monopolies, create deadweight losses.

MRU

mru.org/patents

Patents, Prizes, and Subsidies

Also, determining the right price to buy the patent is not easy and some people worry that corruption could be a problem.

Kremer's idea has never been tried on a widespread basis, but despite these problems, economists are becoming increasingly interested in patent buyouts and the closely related idea of prizes as a way to encourage innovation without creating too much deadweight loss.

Sources of Market Power

Patents and government regulation are not the only source of market power. Monopolies may be created by economies of scale, significant barriers to entry, network effects, or innovation. Let's give some examples of each case.

Economies of scale are the advantages of large-scale production that reduce average cost as quantity increases. Toyota's factory in Kentucky, for example, produces over 500,000 cars a year. Toyota's costs would be much higher if it produced 500 cars in 1,000 factories. By concentrating production, Toyota can invest in specialized equipment, such as robots, that lower their costs. If economies of scale are large relative to the size of the market, then *one* large firm can produce at lower cost than many small firms. When a single firm can supply the entire market at lower cost than two or more firms, we say that the industry is a **natural monopoly**.

A subway is a natural monopoly because one subway system could serve the entire market at a lower cost than two systems. Why build two parallel subway tunnels when one is enough? Utilities such as water, natural gas, and cable television are typically natural monopolies because in each case it's much cheaper to run one pipe or cable than to run multiple pipes or cables to the same set of homes. Auto firms are not natural monopolies because the size of the market is larger than are the economies of scale so no single firm dominates the market. Economies of scale, however, do explain why there are a dozen or so major auto manufacturers rather than hundreds. See Chapter 15 for more on oligopolies, industries with a small number of firms.

In Figure 13.5, we compared competitive firms with an *equal cost* monopoly and showed that total surplus was higher under competition. The comparison between competitive firms and natural monopoly is more difficult. Even though natural monopolies produce less than the optimal quantity, competitive firms would also produce less than the optimal quantity because they could not take advantage of economies of scale.

If the economies of scale are large enough, it's even possible for price to be lower under a natural monopoly than it would be under competition. Figure 13.6 shows just such a situation. Notice that the average cost curve for the monopoly is so far below the average cost curves of the competitive firms that the monopoly price is below the competitive price. It's possible, for example, for every home to produce its own electric power with a small generator or solar panel, but the costs of producing electricity in this way would typically be higher than buying electricity produced from a dam, even if the dam charged the monopoly price.

More generally, however, when economies of scale are important we have a trade-off—costs are lower with one or a handful of firms but market power and prices are greater. We will later discuss that trade-off after discussing other causes of monopoly power.

Barriers to entry can also generate monopoly power. One firm, for example, might own an input that is difficult to duplicate. Oil is found in large

Economies of scale are the advantages of large-scale production that reduce average cost as quantity increases.

A **natural monopoly** is said to exist when a single firm can supply the entire market at a lower cost than two or more firms.

Barriers to entry are factors that increase the cost to new firms of entering an industry.

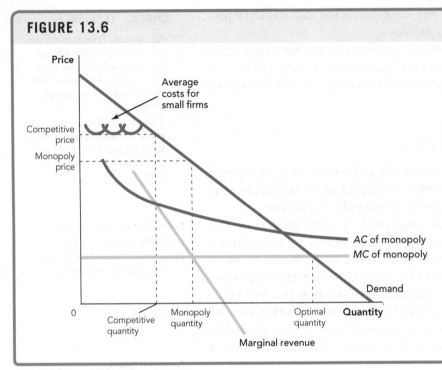

FIGURE 13.6

A Monopoly with Large Economies of Scale Can Have a Lower Price Than Competitive Firms Economies of scale mean that a monopoly producer can have lower costs of production than competitive firms. It's cheaper to produce electricity for 100,000 homes with one large dam, for example, than with a solar panel for each home. If economies of scale are large enough, the monopoly price can be lower than the competitive price and the monopoly output can be higher than the competitive output.

quantities in only a few places in the world, so a single firm in the right place can monopolize a significant share of the total supply. Saudi Arabia is one of those places, so it has some market power in the oil market. Its market power is enhanced when, instead of competing with other suppliers, it joins with them to form a cartel, a group of firms that acts in concert to maximize total profits. We analyze cartels at greater length in Chapter 15.

Barriers to entry can also be more subtle. Remember the TI–84 Plus graphing calculator that you probably used in high school? The TI–84 hasn't changed much in over a dozen years; it still has a tiny black and white screen and just 24k of memory. Yet, despite being less powerful and more expensive than other graphing calculators, more TI–84s are sold than any other graphing calculator. Why? Texas Instruments (TI), the maker of the TI–84 Plus, spent a lot of time and effort training high-school teachers to use their calculator and many math textbooks even include exact instructions for solving problems using the TI–84. So teachers assign the TI–84 for their classes. And since the parents, not the teachers, are paying, the teachers don't care much about the price. As a result, the graphing calculator division of TI is very profitable. Market entry will eventually break down TI's barrier to entry but sometimes small advantages can mean big profits.

Brands and trademarks can also give a firm market power because the prestige of owning the real thing cannot be easily duplicated. Timex watches tell the time as well as a Rolex, but only the Rolex signals wealth and status.

Network effects are another source of monopoly power. Because everyone wants to be on the site that everyone else is on, there is a tendency for people to gravitate toward the same site. Thus, Twitter does not have many direct competitors. Similarly, there are only a handful of credit card companies (MasterCard, Visa, American Express). Customers want to have a card that is widely accepted and firms want to accept cards that are widely used, so there is

A calculating monopoly

a tendency to gravitate toward one or a handful of credit card companies. We take up the economics of network goods in Chapter 16.

Copyrights are another kind of barrier to entry. Does the picture at right look a little familiar? It's the cover from a Russian series of books about Tanya Grotter, an orphan with magical powers, a strange mark on her face, and an evil nemesis called Chuma-del-Tort. The Tanya Grotter series sold well in Russia but is not available in English because J. K. Rowling and the other copyright holders to the Harry Potter series successfully sued for copyright infringement. In the information age, copyrights are becoming an important source of monopoly power.

Tanya Grotter and the copyright infringement lawsuit

Finally, monopolies may also arise when a firm innovates, producing a product that no other firm can immediately duplicate. In recent years, Apple has sold over 50% of all smartphones in the United States, even though Apple has many competitors. Why? People simply like iPhones. Apple's high market share, however, isn't guaranteed and has come under increasing threat as other firms improve their products. As with patent monopolies, monopolies produced by innovation involve a trade-off: iPhones are priced higher than they would be if Apple had better competitors, but Apple would have less incentive to innovate if it didn't expect to earn some monopoly profits.

Table 13.1 summarizes common sources of market power.

TABLE 13.1 SOME SOURCES OF MARKET POWER

Sources of Market Power	Example
Patents	GSK's patent on Combivir
Laws preventing entry of competitors	Indonesian clove monopoly, Algerian wheat monopoly, U.S. Postal Service
Economies of scale	Subways, cable TV, electricity transmission, major highways
Hard-to-duplicate inputs	Oil, diamonds, Rolex watches
Innovation	Apple's iPhone, Wolfram's Mathematica software, Amazon
Copyright	Novels, movies, musical compositions, computer software
Network effects	Twitter, Amazon, credit cards

Regulating Monopoly

The government has many tools to regulate monopolies. We will examine price controls, government ownership, and antitrust law.

Price Controls

In Chapter 8, we showed that a price control set below the market price would create a shortage. But surprisingly, when the market price is set by a monopolist, a price control can increase output. Let's see how.

If there is no regulation, then the monopolist in Figure 13.7 will choose the usual monopoly price and quantity: P_m, Q_m. But suppose that the government imposes

FIGURE 13.7

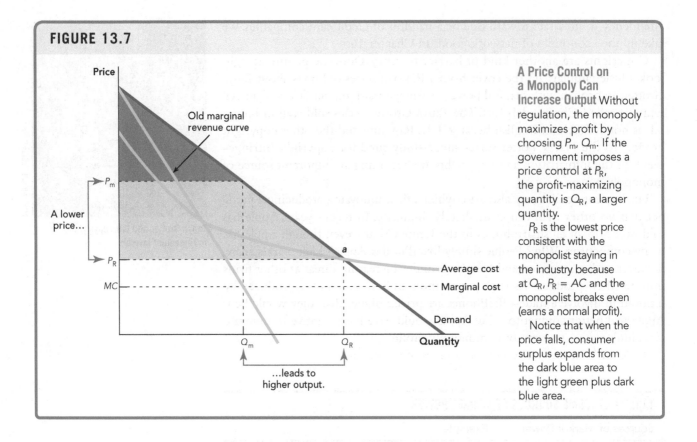

A Price Control on a Monopoly Can Increase Output Without regulation, the monopoly maximizes profit by choosing P_m, Q_m. If the government imposes a price control at P_R, the profit-maximizing quantity is Q_R, a larger quantity.

P_R is the lowest price consistent with the monopolist staying in the industry because at Q_R, $P_R = AC$ and the monopolist breaks even (earns a normal profit).

Notice that when the price falls, consumer surplus expands from the dark blue area to the light green plus dark blue area.

a price control at level P_R. To avoid a loss, the monopolist must charge a price greater than or equal to average cost. But at the price P_R, the only quantity that lets the monopolist avoid a loss is Q_R. Thus, if the government sets $P_R = AC$ at point *a,* where the *AC* curve intersects the demand curve, the monopolist chooses Q_R and just breaks even. Most importantly, notice that when the government lowers the price from P_m to P_R, output increases from Q_m to Q_R and consumer surplus increases from the dark blue area to the light green plus dark blue area.

Reducing monopoly prices to the level of average cost seems like a promising policy, but there are problems. When a monopolist's profits are regulated, it doesn't have much incentive to increase quality with innovative new products or to lower costs. Recall our discussion of pharmaceuticals. A price control on pharmaceutical monopolies could lower prices and increase the output of *currently existing drugs*. But reduced profits mean a reduced incentive to invest in research and development, and *that* would result in fewer new drugs. Over time, the net result could be great harm to patients. A price control is equivalent, in this context, to reducing the power of patents and, as we discussed earlier, this could end up harming patients through reduced innovation.

Let's also examine cable TV and electricity regulation before turning to another way to regulate monopolies, merger policy.

I Want My HBO Cable TV is a natural monopoly—at least it was in its early years, before satellite and streaming media—and it has long been regulated in the United States. Regulating retail subscription rates for cable TV seemed to keep prices low early on, when there were basically only three channels, ABC, CBS, and NBC. Beginning in the 1970s, however, new technology made it possible for cable operators to offer 10, 20, or even 30 channels. But if subscription

Watching the good stuff comes at a price

rates were fixed at the low levels, thereby limiting profit rates, the cable operators would have little incentive to add channels. Recognizing this, Congress lifted caps on pay TV rates in 1979 and on all cable television in 1984. (Cable TV remains largely unregulated today, although there was some further regulation and deregulation in 1992 and 1996, respectively.)

Deregulation of cable TV rates led to higher prices, just as the theory of natural monopoly predicts, but something else happened—the number of television stations and the quality of programming increased dramatically. And, contrary to natural monopoly theory, consumers seemed to appreciate the new channels more than they disliked the higher prices: Even as prices rose, more people signed up for cable television.

Although there were just a few new and excellent shows at first, the number of quality productions has continued to grow. When the only way to pay for TV was advertising, it paid a producer to appeal to mass taste—the more eyes the better, even if the eyes were a little bored. First with cable and subscription television and now with services such as Netflix and Hulu, it can pay to produce shows that appeal to a smaller number of people, so long as enough of them are willing to pay the subscription fee to support the show. As a result, writers and directors are given much more room to experiment, and they have come up with outstanding entries in drama (*Succession*), fantasy (*Game of Thrones*), historical drama (*Bridgerton*), and whatever genre *The Rehearsal* falls under, among others.

The bottom line is that despite increases in prices and in part *because of* the increase in prices, the deregulation of cable TV appears to have created a much more dynamic and exciting market in entertainment. Deregulation of electricity, on the other hand, has proved shocking.

Government Ownership

Electric Shock Government ownership is another potential solution to the natural monopoly problem. In the United States, there are some 3,000 electric utilities, and two-thirds of them are government-owned (the remainder are heavily regulated). Government ownership of utilities began early in the twentieth century when municipalities began owning local distribution companies. In the 1930s, the federal government became a major generator of electricity when it constructed the then largest man-made structures ever built, the Hoover Dam in 1936 and the even larger Grand Coulee Dam in 1941.

The system of government ownership and regulation of electricity worked reasonably well for several decades in providing the United States with cheap power. Without the discipline of competition or a profit motive, however, there is a tendency for a government-run or government-regulated monopoly to become inefficient. Why reduce costs when costs can be passed on to customers? As the price of power in the 1960s and 1970s increased, multibillion-dollar cost overruns for the construction of nuclear power plants drew attention to industry inefficiencies.

Historically, a single firm handled the generation, long-distance transmission, and local distribution of electricity. In the 1970s, however, new technologies reduced the average cost of generating electricity at small scales (in Figure 13.6 you can think of the curves

The Hoover Dam The natural monopoly that lights Las Vegas.

labeled "Average costs for small firms" as moving down). Although the transmission and distribution of electricity remained natural monopolies, the new technologies meant that the *generation* of electricity was no longer a natural monopoly. Economists began to argue that unbundling generation from transmission and distribution could open up electricity generation to competitive forces, thereby reducing costs.

California's Perfect Storm Hoping to benefit from lower costs and greater innovation, California deregulated wholesale electricity prices in 1998. All appeared well in the first two years after deregulation. Then in 2000, a hot summer and an earlier dry winter (low snowfall meant low lake levels and less opportunity for hydroelectric power) led to massive increases in the price of electricity. For example, in April of that year electricity was selling for $26 per megawatt hour (MWh), but by December prices had reached $377 per MWh. For brief periods it had even been as high as $3,900 per MWh. Worse yet, when not enough power was available to meet the demand, blackouts threw more than 1 million Californians off the grid and into the dark.

Mother Nature was not the only one to blame for California's troubles, however. The combination of increased demand, reduced supply, and a poorly designed deregulation plan had created the perfect opportunity for electricity generators to exploit market power. When the demand for electricity is well below capacity, each generator has very little market power. If a few generators had shut down in 1999, for example, the effect on the price would have been minimal because the power from those generators could easily have been replaced with imports or power from other generators. In 1999, then, each generator faced an elastic demand curve. In 2000, however, every generator was critical because nearly every generator needed to be up and running just to keep up with demand. Electricity is an unusual commodity because it is expensive to store; and, if demand and supply are ever out of equilibrium, the result can be catastrophic blackouts. Thus, when demand is near capacity, a small decline in supply leads to much higher prices as utilities desperately try to buy enough power to keep the electric grid up and running. Thus, in early 2000, the demand curve facing each generator was becoming very inelastic. And what happens to the incentive to increase price when demand becomes inelastic? Do you remember the lesson of Figure 13.4, also pictured at left in Figure 13.8?

In the summer and winter of 2000, demand was near capacity and *every* generator was facing an inelastic demand curve. A firm that owned only one generator couldn't do much to exploit its market power: If it shut down, the price of electricity would rise but the firm wouldn't have any power to sell! Because many firms owned more than one generator, however, a terrible incentive was created in 2000. A firm with four generators could shut down one generator, say, for "maintenance and repair," and the price of electricity would rise by so much that the firm could make more money selling the power produced by its three operating generators than it could if it ran all four! Suspiciously, far more generators were taken off-line for "maintenance and repair" in 2000 and early 2001 than in 1999.[12]

California was not the only state to restructure its electricity market in the late 1990s. Texas and Pennsylvania had opened up generation to competition and both have seen modestly lower electricity prices. Restructuring

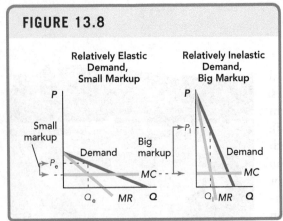

FIGURE 13.8

Relatively Elastic Demand, Small Markup

Relatively Inelastic Demand, Big Markup

CHECK YOURSELF

• Telephone service used to be a natural monopoly. Why? Is it a natural monopoly today? Discuss how technology can change what is and isn't a natural monopoly.

has also occurred in Great Britain, New Zealand, Canada, and elsewhere, but California's experience has demonstrated that unbundling generation from transmission and distribution, which remain natural monopolies, is tricky.

Antitrust Law and Merger Policy

Two of the most important U.S. **antitrust laws** are the Sherman Act, passed in 1890, and the Clayton Act, passed in 1914. (The word "trust" can be thought of as another term for monopoly, so the antitrust laws are antimonopoly laws.) Together, these two acts give the federal government legal authority to prosecute monopolies or firms' attempts to monopolize. For example, the government can break up a monopoly, prohibit a merger, and prevent various acts that might reduce competition, such as collusion, predatory pricing (pricing below cost to drive a competitor out of business), and exclusive dealing (requiring that a buyer deal with only one seller).

The **antitrust laws** give the federal government legal authority to prosecute monopolies or attempts to monopolize.

It's important to understand that most of these acts are not illegal in every circumstance. It's not illegal to be a monopolist, for example; it's only illegal to become a monopoly using illegal means. Mergers can be legal, even if they reduce competition. Predatory pricing is always illegal—if proven, but it is difficult to prove. It is not obvious, for example, how to define "below cost" (marginal cost? average cost?); moreover, however defined, pricing below cost can be legal if it's not intended to drive a competitor out of business (think, for example, of sharp discounts on clothing that is no longer in fashion). What all of this means is that the government cannot simply declare that an action is illegal—it must prove it in a court of law. The government wins some antitrust cases and it loses others. In 1984, for example, the government was allowed to break AT&T into eight smaller companies, but in 2001 the courts ruled against breaking Microsoft into two companies, as the government had wanted.

Let's now take a closer look at mergers. In a dynamic, capitalist economy, firms grow, shrink, split, and merge all the time. Prices, technology, and market conditions are constantly changing, and firms must adjust to remain competitive. A firm that sells accounting services on the East Coast, for example, may merge with a firm that sells accounting services on the West Coast; this creates a national firm that can better serve both markets. Or a firm that sells fishing rods may merge with a firm that sells outdoor clothing. Together, the two firms can reduce costs and better serve both markets. When two small firms merge, there is little chance that they will gain market power and be able to significantly raise prices. But, when two large firms merge, there is a potential trade-off between increased market power (and thus higher prices) and lower costs.

When a merger is likely to increase market power but also to increase efficiency, the antitrust authorities must try to balance higher prices with lower costs. In 2015, for example, Staples, the office supply store, offered to buy one of its rivals, Office Depot. The two companies argued that competition from Costco, Amazon, and Walmart had cut into their traditional market and made it difficult for both firms to survive. By merging, the companies hoped to close some stores that were too close to one another and reduce their input costs by buying even more paper and pens in bulk. The firms argued that their costs would fall but competition would still be fierce because of all the other firms in the industry. The government, however, disagreed and argued that the merger would increase market power and increase prices by too much to be justified. A federal judge agreed with the government and blocked the merger.

Was the judge correct? It's hard to know for certain. If Staples and Office Depot slowly close some stores over the next few years, then we will have fewer firms, as the antitrust authorities feared, but without the cost savings that might have come with a merger. On the other hand, if both firms continue to compete vigorously, then the government's position is more likely to be vindicated.

Antitrust law is a very contested area of law and it is not uncommon to find economists testifying on both sides of an antitrust trial. Merger or no merger, therefore, the economists usually end up profiting from hefty consulting fees—another reason why it's good to be an economist.

Takeaway

After reading this chapter, you should be able to find marginal revenue given either a demand curve or a table of prices and quantities (as in Figure 13.1). Given a demand and marginal cost curve, you should be able to find and label the monopoly price, the monopoly quantity, and deadweight loss. With the addition of an average cost curve, you should be able to find and label monopoly profit. You should also be able to demonstrate why the markup of price over marginal cost is larger the more inelastic the demand—this relationship will also be useful in the next chapter.

What makes monopoly theory interesting and a subject of debate among economists is that it's not always obvious whether monopolies are good or bad. Instead, we are faced with a series of trade-offs. Patent monopolies, such as the one on Combivir, create a trade-off between deadweight loss and innovation. The monopolist prices its product above marginal cost, but without the prospect of monopoly profits, there might be no product at all.

Natural monopolies also involve trade-offs, this time between deadweight loss and economies of scale. Deadweight loss means that monopoly is not optimal, but when economies of scale are large, competitive outcomes aren't optimal either. Regulating monopoly seems to offer an escape from this trade-off, but as we saw in our analysis of cable TV and electricity regulation, the practice of regulation is much more complicated than the theory. Cable TV regulation kept prices low but it kept quality low as well. Overall, deregulation of cable television rates worked surprisingly well, at least according to the consumers who flocked to cable even as rates rose. In contrast, electricity deregulation left California at the mercy of firms wielding market power.

Antitrust laws like the Sherman Act and the Clayton Act give the U.S. government the legal authority to prosecute monopolies or attempts to monopolize. Mergers between large firms are often challenged by the government, and they typically create a difficult trade-off between increases in market power and reductions in cost.

Economists don't always agree on the best way to navigate the trade-offs between market power, innovation, and efficiency. Many monopolies, however, perhaps most on a world scale, are "unnatural"—they neither support innovation nor efficiency. They are instead created to transfer wealth to politically powerful elites. For these monopolies, economics does offer guidance—open the field to competition! Alas, economics offers less clear guidance about how to convince the elites to follow the advice of economists.

CHAPTER REVIEW

Go online to practice with more examples of these types of problems, including live links to videos, data sources, and feedback.

KEY CONCEPTS

market power, p. 250

monopoly, p. 250

marginal revenue, *MR*, p. 250

marginal cost, *MC*, p. 250

economies of scale, p. 259

natural monopoly, p. 259

barriers to entry, p. 259

antitrust laws, p. 265

FACTS AND TOOLS

1. For each of the following, state the source of the firm's market power.

   a. Marty McFly invents a time machine and gets legal protection from competition.

   b. One electric company can operate at a lower cost per unit than multiple electric companies.

   c. The author of *Economics for N00bs* is given exclusive rights to produce and sell the book.

   d. Only the U.S. Postal Service can deliver first-class mail by law.

   e. DeBeers Jewelers owns 80% of the world's diamond mines.

2. A monopolist invents stain-resistant basketball shoes that increase your vertical leap by five inches. At a price of $100 each, it can sell 20 pairs of shoes. At a price of $98 each, it can sell 21 pairs of shoes. Assume the monopolist cannot price discriminate.

   a. At a price of $100, what is the monopolist's total revenue?

   b. At a price of $98, what is the monopolist's total revenue?

   c. What is the marginal revenue of the twenty-first pair of shoes? Is it more or less than the price?

3. In the following diagram, label the marginal revenue curve, the profit-maximizing price, the profit-maximizing quantity, the profit, and the deadweight loss.

4. **a.** Consider a market like the one illustrated in Figure 13.5, where all firms have the same average cost curve. If a competitive firm in this market tried to set a price above the minimum point on its average cost curve, how many units would it sell?

   b. If a monopoly did the same thing, raising its price above average cost, what would happen to the number of units it sells: Does it rise, fall, or remain unchanged?

   c. What accounts for the difference between your answers to parts a and b?

5. **a.** In the textbook *The Applied Theory of Price,* D. N. McCloskey refers to the equation *MR* = *MC* as the rule of rational life. Who follows this rule: monopolies, competitive firms, or both?

   b. Victory, the shoe company, is so popular that it has monopoly power. It's selling 20 million shoes per year, and it's highly profitable. The marginal cost of making extra shoes is quite low, and it doesn't change much if the company produces more shoes. Victory's marketing experts tell the CEO of Victory that if it *decreased* prices by 20%, it would sell so many more shoes that profits would rise. If the expert is correct, at its current output, is $MC > MR$, is $MC = MR$, or is $MR > MC$?

c. If Victory's CEO follows the expert's advice, what will this do to marginal revenue: Will it rise, fall, or be unchanged? Will Victory's total revenue rise, fall, or be unchanged?

d. Tres Rayas, another highly profitable shoe company, also has market power. It's selling 15 million shoes per year, and it faces marginal costs quite similar to Victory's. Tres Rayas's marketing experts conclude that if the company *increased* prices by 20%, profits would rise. For Tres Rayas, is $MC > MR$, is $MC = MR$, or is $MR > MC$?

6. a. When selling e-books, music on iTunes, and downloadable software, the marginal cost of producing and selling one more unit of output is essentially zero: $MC = 0$. Let's think about a monopoly in this kind of market. If the monopolist is doing its best to maximize profits, what will marginal revenue equal at a firm like this?

b. All firms are trying to maximize their profits $(TR - TC)$. The rule from part a tells us that in the special case in which marginal cost is zero, "profit maximization" is equivalent to which of the following statements?

"Maximize total revenue."

"Minimize total cost."

"Minimize average cost."

"Maximize average revenue."

7. a. What's the rule: Monopolists charge a higher markup when demand is highly elastic or when it's highly inelastic?

b. What's the rule: Monopolists charge a higher markup when customers have many good substitutes or when they have few good substitutes?

c. For the following pairs of goods, which producer is more likely to charge a bigger markup? Why?

   i. Someone selling new trendy shoes or someone selling ordinary tennis shoes?

   ii. A movie theater selling popcorn or a New York City street vendor selling popcorn?

   iii. A pharmaceutical company selling a new powerful antibiotic or a firm selling a new powerful cure for dandruff?

8. In 1996, the X Prize Foundation created what became known as the Ansari X Prize—a $10 million prize for the first nongovernment group to send a reusable manned spacecraft into space twice within two weeks. In 2004, it was won by the Tier One project, financed by Microsoft cofounder Paul Allen.

a. An answer you can find on the Internet: How high did *SpaceShipOne* fly when it won the Ansari X Prize?

b. How much did it cost to develop *SpaceShipOne*? Was the $10 million prize enough to cover the costs? Why do you think Microsoft cofounder Paul Allen invested so much money to win the prize? Do Allen's motivations show up in our monopoly model?

9. Which of the following is true when a monopoly is producing the profit-maximizing quantity of output? More than one may be true.

Marginal revenue = Average cost

Total cost = Total revenue

Price = Marginal cost

Marginal revenue = Marginal cost

10. a. Draw the graph of a monopoly, showing demand, marginal revenue, and marginal cost. Show what happens when the monopolist finds a way to lower marginal cost. Indicate on the graph the new equilibrium price and quantity.

b. Draw a graph of a perfectly competitive industry and show on it a decrease in costs. What happens to equilibrium price and quantity for this industry?

11. a. The figure A shows the firm that has a patent on drug A:

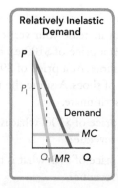

Indicate on the graph the firm's markup. Is demand for drug A elastic or inelastic?

b. The figure B shows the firm that has a patent on drug B:

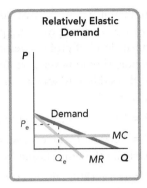

Relatively Elastic Demand

Indicate on the graph the firm's markup. Is demand for drug B elastic or inelastic?

c. Which of those two drugs is more likely to be "important?" Why?

d. Now, consider the lure of profits: If a pharmaceutical company is trying to decide what kind of drugs to research, will it be lured toward inventing drugs with few good substitutes or drugs with many good substitutes?

e. Is your answer to part d similar to what an all-wise, benevolent government agency would do, or is it roughly the opposite of what an all-wise, benevolent government agency would do?

12. True or False?

a. When a monopoly is maximizing its profits, price is greater than marginal cost.

b. For a monopoly producing a certain amount of output, price is less than marginal revenue.

c. When a monopoly is maximizing its profits, marginal revenue equals marginal cost.

d. Ironically, if a government regulator sets a fixed price for a monopoly *lower* than the unregulated price, it is typically *raising* the marginal revenue of selling more output.

e. In the United States, government regulation of cable TV cut down the price of premium channels to average cost.

f. When consumers have many options, monopoly markup is lower.

g. A patent is a government-created monopoly.

THINKING AND PROBLEM SOLVING

13. In addition to the clove monopoly discussed in this chapter, Tommy Suharto, the son of Indonesian President Suharto (in office from 1967 to 1998), owned a media conglomerate, Bimantara Citra. In their entertaining book, *Economic Gangsters* (Princeton University Press, 2008), economists Raymond Fisman and Edward Miguel compared the stock price of Bimantara Citra with that of other firms on Indonesia's stock exchange around July 4, 1996, when the government announced that President Suharto was traveling to Germany for a health checkup. What do you think happened to the price of Bimantara Citra shares relative to other shares on the Indonesian stock exchange? Why? What does this tell us about corruption and monopoly power in Indonesia?

14. a. Sometimes, our discussion of marginal cost and marginal revenue unintentionally hides the real issue: the entrepreneur's quest to maximize total profits. Here is information on a firm:

Demand: $P = 50 - Q$ Fixed cost = 100
Marginal cost = 10

Using this information, calculate total profit for each of the values in the following table, and then plot total profit in the figure. Clearly label the amount of maximum profit and the quantity that produces this level of profit.

Quantity	Total Revenue	Total Cost	Total Profit
18			
19			
20			
21			
22			
23			

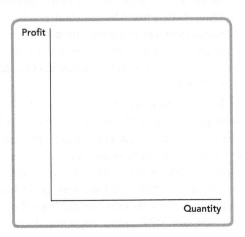

b. If the fixed cost increased from 100 to 200, would that change the shape of this curve at all? If so, would it shift the location of the curve to the left or right? Up or down? How does this explain why you can ignore fixed costs most of the time when thinking about a monopoly's decision-making process?

15. When a sports team signs an expensive new player or builds a new stadium, you often hear claims that ticket prices have to rise to cover the new, higher cost. Let's see what monopoly theory says about that. It's safe to treat these new expenses as fixed costs: something that doesn't change if the number of customers rises or falls. You have to pay Juan Soto the same salary whether people show up or not; you have to make the interest payments on Globe Life Field whether the seats are filled or not. Treat the local sports team as a monopoly in this question, and to keep it simple, let's assume there is only one ticket price.

    a. As long as the sports team is profitable, will a rise in fixed costs raise the equilibrium ticket price, lower the equilibrium ticket price, or have no effect whatsoever on the equilibrium ticket price? Why? Hint: Draw a monopoly diagram. Which curve shifts? Which remains constant?

    b. In fact, it seems common in real life for ticket prices to rise after a team raises its fixed costs by building a fancy new stadium or hiring a superstar player. Draw a graph showing a team that increased its fixed costs *and* raised its ticket price. Two curves must shift to make this happen.

    c. So, do sports teams spend a lot of money on superstars so that they can pass along the costs to the fans? Why *do* they spend a lot on superstars, according to monopoly theory? (*Note:* Books like *Moneyball* and *The Baseball Economist* apply economic models to the national pastime, and it's common for sports managers to have solid training in economic methods.)

16. Earlier we mentioned the special case of a monopoly where $MC = 0$. Let's find the firm's best choice when more goods can be produced at no extra cost. Since so much e-commerce is close to this model—where the fixed cost of inventing the product and satisfying government regulators is the only cost that matters—the $MC = 0$ case will be more important in the future than it was in the past. In each case, be sure to see whether profits are positive! If the "optimal" level of profit is negative, then the monopoly should never start up in the first place; that's the only way it can avoid paying the fixed cost.

    a. $P = 100 - Q$ Fixed cost = 1,000

    b. $P = 2,000 - Q$ Fixed cost = 900,000 (Driving the point home from part a.)

    c. $P = 120 - 12Q$ Fixed cost = 1,000

17. **a.** Just based on self-interest, who is more likely to support strong patents on pharmaceuticals: young people or old people? Why?

    b. Who is more likely to support strong patent and copyright protection on video games: people who really like old-fashioned video games or people who want to play the best, most advanced video games?

    c. How are parts a and b really the same question?

18. Common sense might say that a monopolist would produce more output than a competitive industry facing the same marginal costs. After all, if you're making a profit, you want to sell as much as you can, don't you? What's wrong with this line of reasoning? Why do monopolistic industries sell less than competitive industries?

19. In the early part of the twentieth century, it was cheaper to travel by rail from New York to San Francisco than it was to travel from New York to Denver, even though the train to San Francisco would stop in Denver on the way.

    a. Denver is a city in the mountains. Suggest alternate ways to get there from New York without taking the train.

    b. San Francisco is a city on the Pacific Ocean. Suggest alternate ways to get there from New York without taking the train.

    c. Why was San Francisco cheaper?

    d. How is this story similar to the one told in this chapter about prices for flights from Washington, D.C., to either Dallas or San Francisco?

20. This chapter told the story of how the 2000 California energy shortage was aggravated by price deregulation.

    a. Suppose you are an entrepreneur who is interested in building a power plant to take advantage of the high prices for energy.

Seeing rising energy prices, would price deregulation make it more or less likely you would build a new power plant? Why?

b. It's very difficult to build and operate a new power plant, at least partially because new plants have to comply with a long list of environmental and safety regulations. Compared with a world with fewer such regulations, how do these rules change the average cost of building and operating a power plant? Why?

c. Do these regulations make it more or less likely that you will build a new power plant? Why?

d. Do these regulations increase or decrease the market power of power plants that already exist?

21. The lure of spices during the medieval period wasn't driven merely by the desire to improve the taste of food (Europe produced saffron, thyme, bay leaves, oregano, and other spices for that). The lure of nutmeg, mace, and cloves came from their mystique. Spices became a symbol of prestige (just as Louis Vuitton and Ferrari are today). Most Europeans didn't even know that they grew in the tiny chain of islands that is called the Spice Islands today.

a. Suppose you grow much of the spices in the Spice Islands. Knowing that few people could compete with you, how would you adjust your production to maximize your profits?

b. Suppose you heard rumors that the Europeans to whom you often sell are also becoming fascinated by the mechanical clock, a new invention that was spreading across Europe as a new novelty and as yet another symbol of prestige. How would this change your optimal production? Why?

c. Once Europeans made contact with the Americas, a new, high-status novelty arose: chocolate. Was this good news or bad news for you, the monopolist in the Spice Islands?

22. China developed gunpowder, paper, the compass, water-driven spinning machines, and many other inventions long before its European counterparts. Yet the Chinese did not adopt cannons, industrialization, and many other applications until *after* the West did.

a. Suppose you are an inventor in ancient China and suddenly realize that the fireworks used for celebration could be enlarged into a functioning weapon. It would take time and money to develop, but you could easily sell the cutting-edge result to the government. If there is a strong patent system, would you put a big investment into developing this technology? Why or why not?

b. Suppose there was no patent system, but you could still sell your inventions to the government. Compared with a world with a good patent law, would you be more inclined, less inclined, or about equally inclined to invest in technological development? Why?

CHALLENGES

23. a. For the following three cases, calculate

i. The marginal revenue curve

ii. The level of output where $MR = MC$ (i.e., set the equation from item i equal to marginal cost and solve for Q)

iii. The profit-maximizing price (i.e., plug your answer from equation ii into the demand curve)

iv. Total revenue and total cost at this level of output (something you learned in Chapter 11)

v. What entrepreneurs really care about—total profit

vi. The markup measured in dollars, as price minus marginal cost

vii. The markup measured as a percentage markup ($[100 \times (P - MC)/MC$, reported as a percent])

Case A: Demand: $P = 50 - Q$
Fixed cost = 100   Marginal cost = 10

Case B: Demand: $P = 100 - 2Q$
Fixed cost = 100   Marginal cost = 10

Case C: Demand: $P = 100 - 2Q$
Fixed cost = 100   Marginal cost = 20

b. If you solved part a correctly, you found that when costs rose from case B to case C, the monopolist's optimal price increased. Why didn't the monopolist charge that same higher price when costs were lower? After all, it's a monopolist, so it can charge what price they want. Explain in language that your grandmother could understand.

24. In Challenges question 23, what was the deadweight loss of monopoly in each of the three cases? (*Hint:* Where does the marginal cost curve cross the demand curve? The same place it does under competition. Also keep in mind that marginal cost is considered constant in each of these examples and that demand is linear in each case. Drawing a picture can help with this problem. What you really need to solve this question is the price markup and the difference in quantity between a monopolist and a competitive market.) Is this number measured in dollars, in units of the good, or in some other way?

25. **a.** In 2006, Medicare Part D was created to subsidize spending on prescription drugs. What effect would you expect this expansion to have on pharmaceutical prices? What principle in the chapter would explain this result?

b. Given your answer in part a, what effect on pharmaceutical research and development would you predict?

c. Whatever answer you gave in part a, can you think of an argument for the opposite prediction? (*Hint:* In writing the Part D law, Congress said that subsidized drug plans must cover all pharmaceuticals in some "protected" classes, such as AIDS drugs, but that in other areas subsidized plans could pick and choose which drugs to offer. Understanding this difference may lead to different predictions.)

26. In 1983, Congress passed the Orphan Drug Act, which gave firms that developed pharmaceuticals to treat rare diseases (diseases with U.S. patient populations of 200,000 people or fewer) the exclusive rights to sell their pharmaceutical for seven years, basically an extended patent life. In other words, the act gave greater market power to pharmaceutical firms who developed drugs for rare diseases. Perhaps surprisingly, a patient organization, the National Organization for Rare Disorders (NORD), lobbied for the act. Why would a patient group lobby for an act that would increase the price of pharmaceuticals to its members? Why do you think the act was specifically for rare diseases?

27. For Kremer's patent buyout proposal (mentioned in the chapter) to work, the government needs to pay a price that's high enough to encourage pharmaceutical companies to develop new drugs. How can the government find out the right price? Through an auction, of course. In Kremer's plan, it works roughly like this: The government announces that it will hold an auction the next time that a

company invents a powerful anti-AIDS drug. Once the drug has been invented and thoroughly tested, the government holds the auction. Many firms compete in the auction—just like on eBay—and the highest bid wins. Now comes the twist: After the auction ends, a government employee rolls a 20-sided die. If it comes up "1," then the highest bidder gets the patent, it pays off the inventor, and it's free to charge the monopoly price. If the die comes up "2" through "20," then the government pays the inventor whatever the highest bid was, and then it tears up the patent. The auction had to be held to figure out how much to pay, but most of the time it's the government that does the paying. Similarly, most of the time, citizens get to pay marginal cost for the drug, but one-twentieth of all new drugs will still charge the monopoly price.

a. In your opinion, would taxpayers be willing to pay for this?

b. Using Figure 13.5 to guide your answer, what polygon(s) would these firms' bid be equal to (in expectation)?

c. If the government wins the die roll, what net benefits do consumers get, using Figure 13.5's polygons as your answer? (Be sure to subtract the cost of the auction!)

28. **a.** Let's imagine that the firm with cost curves illustrated in the left panel of the following figure is a large Internet provider. Assuming that the firm is free to maximize profit, label the profit-maximizing price, quantity, and the firm's profit.

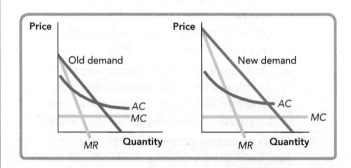

b. Now assume that the firm is regulated and that the regulator sets the price so that the firm earns a normal (zero) profit. What price does the regulator set and what quantity does the firm sell? (Label this price and quantity on the diagram.)

c. Which price and quantity pair do consumers prefer: that in part a or in part b? Do consumers benefit from price regulation?

d. Imagine that the Internet provider can invest in fiber-optic cable, faster and more reliable servers, or some other service that increases the demand for the product, as shown in the right panel. If the firm were regulated as in part b, do you think it would be more or less likely to make these investments?

e. Given your answer in part d, revisit the question of price regulation and make an argument that price regulation could harm consumers once you take into account dynamic factors. Would this argument apply to all consumers or just some? If so, which ones?

WORK IT OUT

For interactive, step-by-step help in solving this problem, go online.

Earlier we mentioned the special case of a monopoly in which $MC = 0$. Let's find the firm's best choice when more goods can be produced at no extra cost. Since so much e-commerce is close to this model—where the fixed cost of inventing the product and satisfying government regulators is the only cost that matters—the $MC = 0$ case will be more important in the future than it was in the past. In each case, be sure to see whether profits are positive! If the "optimal" level of profit is negative, then the monopoly should never start up in the first place; that's the only way it can avoid paying the fixed cost.

a. $P = 200 - Q$ Fixed cost = 1,000

b. $P = 4,000 - Q$ Fixed cost = 900,000 (Driving the point home from part a.)

c. $P = 120 - 12Q$ Fixed cost = 1,000

14

Price Discrimination and Pricing Strategy

After months of investigation, police from Interpol swooped down on an international drug syndicate operating out of Antwerp, Belgium. The syndicate had been smuggling drugs from Kenya, Uganda, and Tanzania into the port of Antwerp for distribution throughout Europe. Smuggling had netted the syndicate millions of dollars in profit. The drug being smuggled? Heroin? Cocaine? No, something more valuable: Combivir. Why was Combivir, the anti-AIDS drug we introduced in Chapter 13, being illegally smuggled from Africa to Europe when Combivir was manufactured in Europe and could be bought there legally?[1]

The answer is that Combivir was priced at $12.50 per pill in Europe and, much closer to cost, about 50 cents per pill in Africa. Smugglers who bought Combivir in Africa and sold it in Europe could make approximately $12 per pill, and they were smuggling millions of pills. But this raises another question. Why was GlaxoSmithKline (GSK) selling Combivir at a much lower price in Africa than in Europe? Remember from Chapter 13 that GSK owned the patent on Combivir and thus has some market power over pricing. In part, GSK reduced the price of Combivir in Africa for humanitarian reasons, but lowering prices in poor countries can also increase profit. In this chapter, we explain how a firm with market power can use **price discrimination**—selling the same product at different prices to different customers—to increase profit.

> **Price discrimination** is selling the same product at different prices to different customers.

Price Discrimination

Figure 14.1 shows how price discrimination can increase profit. In the left panel we show the market for Combivir in Europe and in the right panel the market in Africa. The demand curve in Africa is much lower and more elastic (price sensitive) than in Europe because, on average, Africans are poorer than Europeans.

Now let's suppose for the moment that Europe is the only market. What price should GSK set? We know from Chapter 13 that the profit-maximizing quantity is found where marginal revenue equals marginal cost. From $MR = MC$ in the left panel, we find that the profit-maximizing quantity is Q_{Europe}. The profit-maximizing price is the highest price that consumers will pay to purchase Q_{Europe} units, which we label P_{Europe}. Profit is given by the green area labeled $Profit_{Europe}$.

FIGURE 14.1

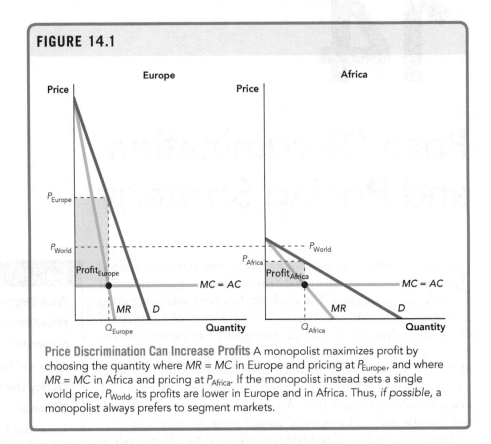

Price Discrimination Can Increase Profits A monopolist maximizes profit by choosing the quantity where $MR = MC$ in Europe and pricing at P_{Europe}, and where $MR = MC$ in Africa and pricing at P_{Africa}. If the monopolist instead sets a single world price, P_{World}, its profits are lower in Europe and in Africa. Thus, *if possible*, a monopolist always prefers to segment markets.

Similarly, if Africa were the only market, GSK would choose the profit-maximizing quantity Q_{Africa} and the profit-maximizing price P_{Africa}, which would generate profit in the amount $Profit_{Africa}$.

But what price should GSK set if it wants to have a single "world price" for both Europe and Africa? If GSK wants a single world price, it should lower the price in Europe and raise the price in Africa, setting a price somewhere between P_{Europe} and P_{Africa}, say, at P_{World}. (In a more advanced class, we would solve for the exact profit-maximizing world price, but that level of detail is not necessary here.)

But remember that P_{Europe} is the profit-maximizing price in Europe and P_{Africa} is the profit-maximizing price in Africa, so by lowering the price in Europe, GSK must be reducing profit in Europe. Similarly, by raising the price in Africa, GSK must be reducing profit in Africa. Thus, profit at the single price P_{World} must be less than when GSK sets two different prices earning the combined profit: $Profit_{Europe} + Profit_{Africa}$.

We have now arrived at the first principle of price discrimination: *(1a) If the demand curves are different, it is more profitable to set different prices in different markets than a single price that covers all markets.*

We also know from Chapter 13 and from Figure 14.1 how a monopolist should set prices. Recall that the more inelastic the demand curve, the higher the profit-maximizing price. In this case, the demand for Combivir is more inelastic (less sensitive to price) in the European market than in the African market, so the price is higher in Europe. This really isn't an independent principle; it's an implication of profit maximization, as we showed in Chapter 13. But it's a useful reminder, so we will add to our first principle:

(1b) To maximize profit, the monopolist should set a higher price in markets with more inelastic demand.

The first principle of price discrimination tells us that GSK wants to set a higher price for Combivir in Europe than in Africa. But we also know from the introduction that setting two different prices for Combivir encourages drug smuggling. Smugglers buy Combivir at P_{Africa} and sell at P_{Europe}, which leaves fewer sales for GSK. A smuggler's profit comes out of GSK's pocket.

If smuggling is extensive, GSK will end up selling most of its output at P_{Africa}, which is less profitable than if GSK set a single world price. Thus, if GSK can't stop the drug smugglers, it will abandon its attempt at price discrimination and will instead set a single price—perhaps a single world price such as P_{World} or, if the African market is small, GSK may abandon Africa altogether and set a single price of P_{Europe}.

Smuggling is a special example of a more general (and legal) process that economists call **arbitrage**—buying low in one market and selling high in another market. Thus, we arrive at the second principle of price discrimination: *(2) Arbitrage makes it difficult for a firm to set different prices in different markets, thereby reducing the profit from price discrimination.*

Let's summarize the principles of price discrimination.

> **Arbitrage** is taking advantage of price differences for the same good in different markets by buying low in one market and selling high in another market.

The Principles of Price Discrimination

1a. If the demand curves are different, it is more profitable to set different prices in different markets than a single price that covers all markets.

1b. To maximize profit, the firm should set a higher price in markets with more inelastic demand.

2. Arbitrage makes it difficult for a firm to set different prices in different markets, thereby reducing the profit from price discrimination.

The first principle tells us that a firm *wants* to set different prices in different markets. The second principle tells us that a firm may not be *able* to set different prices in different markets. To succeed at price discrimination, the monopolist must prevent arbitrage.

Preventing Arbitrage

If it wants to profit from price discrimination, GSK must prevent the Combivir that it sends to Africa from being resold in Europe. GSK has a number of tools to discourage smuggling. GSK, for example, sends red Combivir pills to Africa and sells white Combivir in Europe. If GSK detectives find red Combivir in Europe, they know that a GSK distributor has broken its agreement. Using special bar codes on each package, GSK can then track the smuggled pills back to the distributor who was supposed to distribute them in Africa. Interpol is called in to make arrests.

Markets can differ in more ways than geography. Rohm and Haas is a producer of plastics. One of its plastics, methyl methacrylate (MM), was used in industry and also in dentistry as a material for dentures. MM had lots of substitutes as an industrial plastic but few as a denture material, so Rohm and Haas sold MM for industrial uses at 85 cents per pound and sold a slightly different

Preventing arbitrage Animals are often prescribed exactly the same pharmaceuticals as humans. The pharmaceutical firms know that people won't pay as much to save Oscar (elastic demand) as to save Uncle Oscar (inelastic demand) so they set low prices for the veterinary market and high prices for the human market even when the same drug is being sold. Arbitrage is sometimes reduced by making the animal product in inconvenient dosages or forms (do you really want an injectable or suppository designed for a horse?). Most fundamentally, vets cannot legally write prescriptions for humans so the pharmaceutical firms are able to set different prices in the two markets without fear of much arbitrage.

version designed for dentures at $22 per pound. At these prices, it wasn't long before enterprising individuals started buying industrial MM and converting it to denture MM. Just like GSK, Rohm and Haas needed a way to prevent arbitrage between the two markets.

One bold thinker came up with what Rohm and Haas internal documents called "a very fine method of controlling the bootleg situation." The innovator suggested that Rohm and Haas should mix industrial MM with arsenic. This wouldn't reduce the value of MM in industry, but it would surely deter people from making it into dentures! Rohm and Haas's legal department rejected this plan, but the company came up with an idea nearly as good: They planted a *rumor* that industrial MM was mixed with arsenic![2]

Although Rohm and Haas never implemented the poisoning idea, the U.S. government has. The government taxes alcohol but subsidizes ethanol fuel. To prevent arbitrage, that is, to prevent entrepreneurs from buying ethanol fuel and converting it to drinkable alcohol, the government requires that ethanol fuel be poisoned!

It's easier to prevent arbitrage of some products than of others. Someone who gives massages, for example, may easily set different prices for different customers because it's difficult for a customer who buys a massage at the low price to resell it to another customer at the higher price. Services, in general, are difficult to arbitrage.

Price Discrimination Is Common

Once you know the signs, price discrimination is easy to see. Movie theaters, for example, often charge less for seniors than for younger adults. Is this because theater owners have a special respect for the elderly? Probably not. More likely it's that theater owners realize that young people have a more inelastic demand for movies than seniors. Thus, theater owners charge a high price to young people and a low price to seniors. It would probably be even more profitable if theater owners could charge people who are on a date more than married people (no one likes to look cheap on a date). But it's easy for theater owners to judge age and not so easy for them to figure out who is on a date and who is married.

Students don't always pay higher prices, however. Stata is a well-known statistical software package. It costs a business $840 per year to buy Stata/SE, but registered students pay only $179. Thus, it's not about age—the young sometimes pay more and sometimes pay less—it's about how age correlates with what businesses really care about, which is how much the customer is willing to pay.

Here's another example. Airlines know that businesspeople are typically less sensitive to the price of an airline ticket than are vacationers (i.e., businesspeople have more inelastic demand curves). An airline would like, therefore, to set a high price for businesspeople and a low price for vacationers, as illustrated in Figure 14.2.

But airlines can't very well say to their customers, "Are you flying on business? Okay, the price is $600. Going on a vacation? The price is $200." So how can airlines segment the market?

Airlines set different prices according to characteristics that are correlated with the willingness to pay. Vacationers, for example, can easily plan their trips weeks or months in advance. Businesspeople, however, may discover that they need to fly tomorrow. Thus, if a customer wants to fly to Tampa, Florida, in two weeks' time, they are probably a vacationer and the airline will charge that person a low price, but if the customer wants to fly tomorrow, the price will be higher. On the day these words were written, United was charging $448 to fly

CHECK YOURSELF

- Why does a monopolist want to segment a market?
- Would a price-discriminating firm set higher or lower prices for a market segment with more inelastic demand?
- What is arbitrage? How does arbitrage affect the ability of a monopolist to price-discriminate?

FIGURE 14.2

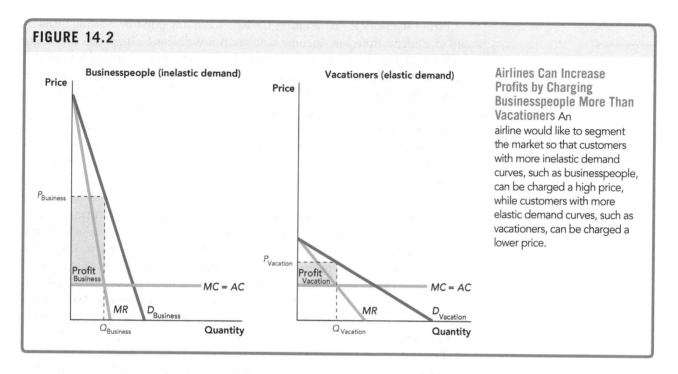

Airlines Can Increase Profits by Charging Businesspeople More Than Vacationers An airline would like to segment the market so that customers with more inelastic demand curves, such as businesspeople, can be charged a high price, while customers with more elastic demand curves, such as vacationers, can be charged a lower price.

from Washington, D.C., to Chicago with two weeks' notice but more than 70% more, $773, to fly tomorrow. Except for the dates, the flights were identical. Figure 14.3 illustrates how one airline charged many different prices for the same flight.

Similarly, publishers knew that hard-core fans were willing to pay a high price for the latest Colleen Hoover book, while others would buy only if the price was low. Publishers would like to charge the hard-core fans a high price and the less devoted a low price. How can they do this? One way is to start with a high price and then lower it once the hard-core fans have bought their fill. Thus, when *Verity* hit the shelves, it retailed at $29 in hardback, but when the paperback was released about a year later, it sold for just $11.99. Does it cost more to produce a hardback? Yes, but not much more, maybe a dollar or two. The hard-core fans pay a higher price not because costs are higher, but because the publisher knows that they are willing to pay a higher price.

Universities and Perfect Price Discrimination

Universities are one of the biggest practitioners of price discrimination, although they hide this practice under the blanket of "student aid." Student aid is a way of charging different students different prices for the same good. Consider Williams College, a small, prestigious liberal arts college. In 2020, some students at Williams paid the sticker price of $66,540, while others paid just $5,480 for exactly the same education. Why the big difference in price?

FIGURE 14.3

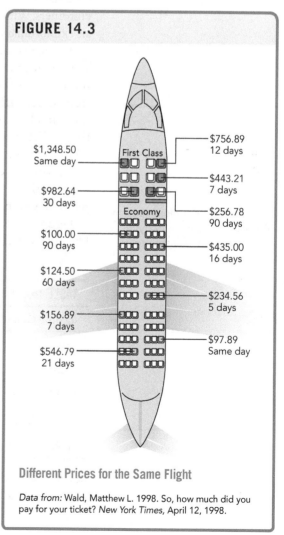

$1,348.50
Same day

$982.64
30 days

$100.00
90 days

$124.50
60 days

$156.89
7 days

$546.79
21 days

$756.89
12 days

$443.21
7 days

$256.78
90 days

$435.00
16 days

$234.56
5 days

$97.89
Same day

First Class

Economy

Different Prices for the Same Flight

Data from: Wald, Matthew L. 1998. So, how much did you pay for your ticket? *New York Times,* April 12, 1998.

Part of the story is that Williams College was doing good by offering financial aid to students from low-income families. But Williams College was also doing well. To see why, notice that Williams College is a lot like an airline. If United is going to fly an airplane from New York to Los Angeles anyway, then United can increase its profits by filling extra seats so long as its customers are willing to pay the marginal costs of flying (say, the extra fuel costs). Of course, if a customer is willing to pay $800 to fly to L.A., then United wants to charge that customer $800 and not less. But if the marginal cost of flying is $100, then United can increase its profits by filling an empty seat so long as the customer is willing to pay at least $101.

Williams College is a lot like an airline because if Ancient Greek History 101 is going to be taught anyway, then Williams can increase its profits by filling extra seats so long as its students are willing to pay the marginal costs of teaching. Of course, if a student is willing to pay $66,540 for a year of education at Williams, then Williams wants to charge that student $66,540 and not less. But if the marginal costs of teaching are $5,480 a year, then Williams can increase its profits by filling an empty seat so long as the student is willing to pay at least $5,480.

About half the students at Williams paid the full sticker price of $66,540, but half did not. Table 14.1 shows the average price paid by students in five different income classes, low to high, after taking into account "financial aid."

The difference in price is extreme. Even the airlines, masters of price discrimination, can rarely charge some customers 20 times what they charge other customers. Williams has a big advantage over the airlines, however. Williams has an extraordinary amount of information about its customers.

To receive financial aid, Williams requires that students and their parents submit their tax returns to Williams. Williams, therefore, has very detailed information about the income of its customers, and it uses that information to set different prices. Table 14.1 shows *average* prices within each income class, but, in fact, Williams divided prices even more finely, setting a different price, for example, to a student with family income of $35,000 than one with family income of $38,000. In theory, Williams could offer a different price to each one of its students, charging each student their maximum willingness to pay. This is what economists call **perfect price discrimination**.

Under **perfect price discrimination (PPD)**, each customer is charged their maximum willingness to pay.

Figure 14.4 shows how perfect price discrimination works in a market like education, where each customer buys one unit of the good. Alex values

TABLE 14.1 PRICE DISCRIMINATION AT WILLIAMS COLLEGE, 2020

Income Quintile	Family Income	Average Net Price
Low	$0–$30,000	$1,451
Lower Middle	$30,001–$48,000	$5,480
Middle	$48,001–$75,000	$5,576
Upper Middle	$75,001–$110,000	$14,702
High	$110,001+	$43,967

Note: Students who did not apply for financial aid, about half the student body, paid $66,540.

Data from: CollegeCalc.org, using data from the United States Department of Education.

FIGURE 14.4

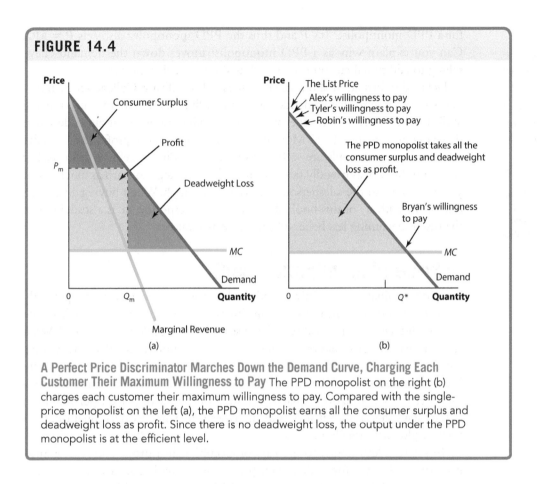

A Perfect Price Discriminator Marches Down the Demand Curve, Charging Each Customer Their Maximum Willingness to Pay The PPD monopolist on the right (b) charges each customer their maximum willingness to pay. Compared with the single-price monopolist on the left (a), the PPD monopolist earns all the consumer surplus and deadweight loss as profit. Since there is no deadweight loss, the output under the PPD monopolist is at the efficient level.

education the highest, Tyler the second highest, Robin the third highest, all the way down to Bryan who thinks that education has very little value. A firm that has a lot of information about Alex, Tyler, Robin, and Bryan can set four different prices, charging each of them their maximum willingness to pay (or, if you like, a penny less than their maximum willingness to pay). Thus, Alex is charged the most and Bryan the least.

Since a perfectly price-discriminating (PPD) monopolist charges each consumer their maximum willingness to pay, consumers end up with zero consumer surplus. All of the gains from trade go to the monopolist. This is bad for consumers but does have a beneficial side effect: Since the PPD monopolist gets all the gains from trade, the PPD monopolist has an incentive to maximize the gains from trade, and maximizing the gains from trade means no deadweight loss.

In Chapter 13, we showed that a single-price monopoly creates a dead-weight loss, but this is not true for a perfectly price-discriminating monopoly. In Figure 14.4, notice that whenever a consumer's willingness to pay is higher than marginal cost, then that consumer is sold a unit of the good—but this means that the PPD monopoly produces the efficient quantity! In fact, the perfectly price-discriminating monopolist produces until $P = MC$ (i.e., $Q^\star$ units), exactly as does a competitive firm!

Another way of seeing why the perfectly price-discriminating monopolist produces the efficient quantity is to remember that all firms want to produce until $MR = MC$. For a competitive firm, $MR = P$, so the competitive firm produces until $P = MC$. For a single-price monopolist, $MR < P$, so the single-price monopolist produces less than the competitive firm. But what is MR

CHECK YOURSELF

- Is the early bird special (eating dinner at a restaurant before 6:00 PM or 6:30 PM) a form of price discrimination? If so, what are the market segments? Can you think of another explanation for this type of pricing?
- Why is it much more expensive to see a movie in a theater than to wait a few months and see it at home on demand? Can you give an explanation based on price discrimination?

for a PPD monopolist? It's P and thus the PPD monopolist also sets $P = MC$. Can you explain why as a PPD monopolist moves down the demand curve selling to additional customers, its MR is always equal to price?

Detailed information about its customers helps Williams College set each student's price close to that student's maximum willingness to pay, thus maximizing Williams's revenue. Ever wonder why many retailers ask for your zip code when they ring up your purchase? More information means more profit. Ever wonder why used car salespeople are so friendly? Sure, friendliness helps to sell cars, but what you think of as friendly talk is really a clever strategy to learn as much about you as possible so the salesperson can price accordingly. When buying a new car, one of the authors of this book always tells the salesperson he is a student. Alas, the ruse is becoming less believable as the years wear on.

Is Price Discrimination Bad?

Price discrimination certainly sounds bad, but we just showed that a perfectly price-discriminating monopolist produces more output than a single-price monopolist, and this is good so price discrimination can't always be bad. What about if price discrimination is imperfect? Does a monopolist that sets two (or a handful of) prices raise or lower total surplus? The answer is subtle, but there is a similar intuition to the case of the perfectly price-discriminating monopolist. Price discrimination is bad if the total output with price discrimination falls or stays the same, but if output increases under price discrimination, then total surplus will usually increase.

To see this, let's return to the case of Combivir in Europe and Africa. Suppose that GSK was forbidden from price discriminating so it had to set one world price. What world price would GSK set, and would this increase or decrease total surplus?

One possibility is that if forced to set a single price, GSK would lower the price enough so that some Africans could buy Combivir—for example, a price like P_{World} in Figure 14.1. A single price of P_{World} is better for Europeans since $P_{World} < P_{Europe}$, but it is worse for Africans since $P_{World} > P_{Africa}$. Thus, depending on exactly how much better off Europeans are and how much worse off Africans are at P_{World}, price discrimination could be better or worse than single pricing.

How likely is it, however, that GSK would lower the price to P_{World}? Roughly one-third of the 1.2 billion people living in sub-Saharan Africa live in extreme poverty, which is defined as less than \$2.15 per day. Thus, even when GSK sells Combivir at close to its cost of 50 cents a pill, most Africans with AIDS cannot afford Combivir. GSK, therefore, cannot make up for a low price by selling large volumes of Combivir to Africans. Thus, if GSK cannot set two different prices, it will probably abandon the African market altogether and sell to the world at P_{Europe}. At P_{Europe}, only Europeans can afford to buy Combivir.

At the single price of P_{Europe}, are Europeans better off than with price discrimination? No, the price to Europeans hasn't changed and thus the quantity of Combivir consumed by Europeans is the same under both pricing systems. What about Africans? At the single price of P_{Europe}, Africans pay more for Combivir than with price discrimination and they consume less. Thus, in the most plausible case, forcing GSK to set a single price doesn't help Europeans but does hurt Africans. Alternatively stated, price discrimination in this case increases total surplus because price discrimination increases output—with price discrimination, Europeans consume as much Combivir as with a single price, but Africans increase their consumption from what it would be with a high single price.

Why Misery Loves Company and How Price Discrimination Helps to Cover Fixed Costs

In industries with high fixed costs, price discrimination has another benefit. To explain why, we ask a strange question. Imagine that there are two diseases that if left untreated are equally deadly. One of the diseases is rare, the other is common. If you had to choose, would you rather be afflicted with the rare disease or the common disease? Take a moment to think about this question because there is a definite answer.

It's much better to have the common disease because there are more drugs to treat common diseases than to treat rare diseases, and more drugs means greater life expectancy. Patients diagnosed with a rare disease are 45% more likely to die before the age of 55 than patients diagnosed with a more common disease.[*]

The reason there are more drugs to treat common diseases is the market is larger. Simply put, it costs about the same to develop a drug for a rare or a common disease but the revenues are much greater for a drug that treats a common disease. Thus, the larger the market, the more profitable it is to develop a drug for that market.

The fact that profits increase with market size explains why price discrimination can benefit *Europeans*, as well as Africans. We have already shown that Africans benefit from price discrimination because of lower prices. Europeans benefit because price discrimination increases the profit from producing pharmaceuticals, and more profit means more research and development, more new drugs, and greater life expectancy.

Pharmaceuticals are not the only industry with high fixed costs—airlines, chemicals, universities, software, and movies all have a similar cost structure. Low prices for vacationers, for example, can benefit business travelers because the extra profit that airlines earn from selling to vacationers encourages airlines to offer more flights to more places at more times. The synthetic fabric Kevlar is five times stronger by weight than steel and is used to make bulletproof vests as well as auto tires. As a bulletproof vest, Kevlar has few substitutes, but as tire belting, it has many. As a result, DuPont charges more for Kevlar used in vests than for Kevlar used in belting. If DuPont had to charge the same price in all markets, Kevlar might not be used for belting at all, and DuPont would have lower profits and less incentive to innovate.

Tying and Bundling

Everyone knows that airlines charge different prices to different customers for the same flight. Senior citizen and student discounts are obvious. Universities advertise their scholarship policies—even if they don't always advertise that this is a way of increasing profit! But other types of price discrimination are more subtle and difficult to see. Let's take a look at tying and bundling, two types of price discrimination that are hidden to the untrained observer.

> **CHECK YOURSELF**
> - When is price discrimination likely to increase total surplus?
> - How does price discrimination help industries with high fixed costs? Use universities as an example.

---

[*] "Rare" is defined as a disease in the bottom quarter of incidence in the United States in 1998; "common" is defined as a disease in the top quarter of incidence. See Lichtenberg, Frank R., and Joel Waldfogel, June 2003, *Does Misery Love Company? Evidence from Pharmaceutical Markets Before and After the Orphan Drug Act*. NBER Working Paper No. W9750. Available at http://www.ssrn.com/abstract=414248.

JoKMedia/E+/Getty Images

Brian Hagiwara/The Image Bank/Getty Images

Printer ink is more expensive than champagne by the ounce. Someone is celebrating.

Tying occurs when to use one good, the consumer must use a second good that is sold (only) by the same firm. A firm can price-discriminate by tying two goods and carefully setting their prices.

Tying

Why are printers so cheap and ink so expensive? As we write this chapter, one remarkable Hewlett-Packard (HP) photo printer/scanner/copier sells for just $69. A full set of color ink cartridges, however, will set you back $44. At that price, it almost pays to buy a new printer (which comes with a cartridge) every time you run out of ink! Clearly, HP is pricing its printers low and making its profit from selling ink. HP is not alone in pursuing this strategy. Xbox game consoles are priced below cost, and Xbox games are priced above cost. Cell phones are priced below cost and phone plans are priced above cost. Why?

Think of HP as selling not printers and ink, but the package good, "ability to print color photos." HP wants to charge a high price to consumers with a high willingness to pay and a low price to consumers with a low willingness to pay. Consumers with a high willingness to pay for the "ability to print color photos" probably want to print a lot of color photos. Consumers with a low willingness to pay probably want to print only the occasional color photo. By charging a high price for ink, HP is charging high-willingness-to-pay consumers a high price. Yet, because the price of printers is low, consumers who have only a low willingness to pay are charged a low price.

HP's pricing scheme is especially brilliant because the price is so flexible. Instead of two prices, there are many: one for a consumer who prints 10 photos a month, another for a consumer who prints 15 photos a month, and yet another for a consumer who prints 100 photos a month.

For HP's scheme to work, it's critical that no one else but HP be allowed to sell ink for HP printers—HP must *tie* its printers to HP ink cartridges, which is why this form of price discrimination is called **tying**. If competitors could easily enter the market for ink, the price of ink would fall to marginal cost and HP's pricing scheme would fall apart. HP manages to keep competitors out of the market for ink in a clever way—the HP ink cartridge contains not just ink, but also a crucial and patented component of the printer head. Since other firms are forbidden by law from manufacturing the printer head, and since the head and the ink must be packaged together, HP manages to keep competitors out of the market for ink. Well, almost. There is an active market in *refilling* HP printer heads, which is much cheaper than buying them new.

HP's strategy illustrates both the benefits and costs of price discrimination. Price discrimination, as usual, may increase output by lowering the price to users who only want to print the occasional photo. Price discrimination also spreads the fixed costs of research and development—which are extensive for color photo printers—over more users, thus encouraging more innovation. But putting printer heads in the ink cartridge rather than in the printer probably raises the total cost of printing. Although there are some advantages to disposable printer heads, HP is spending the extra money not to benefit consumers but to keep competitors out of the ink business. Since the extra costs of production don't benefit consumers, they are a cost of price discrimination.

By the way, in addition to price discrimination, HP is probably also taking advantage of a bit of consumer irrationality. When comparing printers, consumers *should* look at the total price, printer plus ink, over the entire lifetime of the printer. But it takes some work to estimate the total price, and consumers who are shortsighted may focus on amazingly cheap printers rather than astonishingly expensive ink.

Bundling

Goods are **bundled** when they must be bought in a package. Nike doesn't sell right and left shoes individually; Nike sells shoes only in a right-and-left bundle.* Toyota doesn't sell engines, steering columns, and wheels. It sells a bundle called a car. As the examples suggest, most bundling is easily explained as a way to reduce costs. But why does Microsoft sell Word, Excel, Outlook, Teams, and PowerPoint in a bundle called Microsoft Office?

Bundling is requiring that products be bought together in a bundle or package.

Unlike buying a car piece by piece, it would not be difficult for consumers to buy the Office products individually and assemble them as they wanted. Almost every car buyer wants an engine and four wheels, but not every Office buyer wants Microsoft Teams. So why does Microsoft bundle? Note that Microsoft does sell most Office products individually, but the sum of the individual prices far exceeds the price of the bundle, so most consumers buy Office.

Bundling is a type of price discrimination. Suppose that we have two consumers, Amanda and Yvonne, whose maximum willingness to pay for Word and Excel is as given in Table 14.2.

Microsoft can sell each product individually or it can sell Word and Excel together as a bundle. Let's calculate profit for each possibility. To make our lives simple, we will assume that the marginal costs of production are zero (which is approximately true—it costs very little to download Word).

TABLE 14.2 MAXIMUM WILLINGNESS TO PAY FOR WORD AND EXCEL

	Amanda	Yvonne
Word	$100	$40
Excel	$20	$90

If Microsoft sets prices individually, there are two sensible choices for the price of Word: $40 or $100. If Microsoft sets a price of $40 for Word, both Amanda and Yvonne will buy, and profit will be $80. If Microsoft sets a price of $100, Amanda alone will buy, but profit will be higher, $100. Similarly, Microsoft can sensibly sell Excel for $20 or $90. Profit is higher at a price of $90 because $2 \times \$20 = \$40 < \$90$. If Microsoft sets prices individually, therefore, it will charge $100 for Word and $90 for Excel for a total profit of $190 = $100 + $90.

Now consider bundling Word and Excel and selling them as Office. What price to set? To calculate this, we need to know the maximum amount that Amanda and Yvonne will pay for Word plus Excel. We calculate this in Table 14.3.

Amanda is willing to pay up to $120 for the Office bundle and Yvonne is willing to pay up to $130. What is the profit-maximizing price for the Office bundle? Microsoft will set the bundle price at $120 and sell two Office bundles for a total profit of $240. What has happened to Microsoft's profit compared with when it set prices individually? When Microsoft priced Word and Excel individually, its profit was just $190. When Microsoft sells Word and Excel in a bundle called Office, its profits increase by $50, or 26%. Why?

Notice that in this example bundling is equivalent to a sophisticated scheme of (almost) perfect price discrimination. At a bundle price of $120, we can think of Amanda as being charged $100 for Word and $20 for Excel, and Yvonne as being charged $40 for Word and $80 for Excel. But in order to implement this price discrimination scheme directly, Microsoft would have to know a lot about Amanda's and Yvonne's willingness to pay for Word and Excel and Microsoft would have

Textbooks are bundles of chapters.

TABLE 14.3 MAXIMUM WILLINGNESS TO PAY FOR OFFICE

	Amanda	Yvonne
Word	$100	$40
Excel	$20	$90
Office = Word + Excel	$120	$130

---

* The difference between tying and bundling is that bundled goods are sold one to one. Every right shoe comes with a left shoe. Tied goods are sold one to many. Every HP printer is tied to a variable number of ink cartridges, depending on consumer demand.

mru.org/bundling

Should Cable Companies Be Required to Sell by the Channel?

Mario Tama/ Getty Images

Why does FedEx sometimes delay its own packages?

to prevent Yvonne from buying Word at $40 and reselling it to Amanda (and similarly keep Amanda from reselling Excel to Yvonne). When Microsoft bundles, however, it's easier to price-discriminate because although Amanda and Yvonne place very different values on Word and Excel, they have similar values for Office. Microsoft, therefore, knows more about the demand for Office than about the demand for Word or Excel, and the more Microsoft knows about demand, the easier it is for Microsoft to price-discriminate.

As with other forms of price discrimination, bundling can increase efficiency, especially when fixed costs are high and marginal costs are low. In our example, when Microsoft set prices individually, only Amanda bought Word and only Yvonne bought Excel. This is inefficient because Amanda values Excel at $20 and the costs of providing Excel are zero (and similarly for Yvonne and Word). When Microsoft bundles, Amanda and Yvonne buy both Word and Excel, which increases total surplus.

Total surplus without bundling is $190. What is total surplus with bundling? It's $250. Check that you understand where this number came from.

Furthermore, the costs of producing software are primarily the fixed costs of research and development. Bundling means that these fixed costs are spread across more consumers, which raises the incentive to innovate.

Quality Discrimination or Versioning

A subtle form of price discrimination occurs when firms offer different versions or different quality levels of a product in order to segment customers and charge different prices. IBM, for example, offered one of its laser printers in two models: the regular version and the Series E (E for economy). The regular version printed at 10 pages per minute, and the Series E printed at 5 pages per minute. The regular version was much more expensive than the Series E. What's surprising is that the only difference between the regular and the Series E was that the Series E printer contained an extra chip that slowed the printer down! IBM wasn't charging more for the regular printer because that printer cost more to produce; it was charging more because it knew that the demand for speed was correlated with willingness to pay.

We see the same idea with FedEx deliveries. FedEx offers three options for delivery of an overnight package from Washington to Los Angeles, a first-class delivery by 8 AM for approximately $120, a second-class delivery at 10:30 AM for about half that price, and a third-class option for delivery at 4:30 PM at an even lower price. Now think about FedEx's delivery methods. Do you think that three planes fly from Washington to Los Angeles (via FedEx's hub in Memphis) with the first plane leaving earlier or flying faster to get the first-class package delivered by 8 AM instead of by 4:30 PM? Of course not. In fact, all three packages travel on the same plane and are delivered to FedEx trucks at the same time. The only difference is that FedEx delays the second and third packages.

Why would FedEx delay its own packages?! FedEx delays its second- and third-class packages so it can charge a higher price for first class. Remember, price discrimination is all about separating customers according to their willingness to pay, and a customer who wants their package delivered overnight by 8 AM is probably willing to pay substantially more than a customer who is willing to have their package delivered at 4:30 PM. But if FedEx promised to deliver all its packages by 8 AM—which it could do—it would have to either charge a high price to everyone and lose all those customers who aren't willing to pay for 8 AM delivery or charge a low price to everyone but lose the extra revenue from charging more to high-willingness-to-pay customers.

Is quality discrimination bad? Once again, there are trade-offs. In theory, it wouldn't cost FedEx more to deliver everyone's packages at 8 AM. It might even cost less; FedEx will sometimes deliver to the same address three times, once at 8 AM, once at 10:30 AM, and once at 4:30 PM even though every package could have been delivered at 8 AM. If all else remained the same, faster package delivery would be great! But if it couldn't charge different customers different prices, FedEx's profits would be lower, and that means FedEx would be less willing to invest in the fixed costs of setting up a worldwide network. In fact, if FedEx could offer only one level of service at one price, it might not offer any services at all on some routes. It's the same story with airlines. Charging first-class passengers more means the airlines can afford to offer more flights to different destinations, which also benefits second- and third-class passengers, even if they do complain about the lack of legroom.

Takeaway

Price discrimination—selling the same good to different customers at different prices—is a common feature of many markets. The most obvious form of price discrimination is when a firm sets different prices in different markets—as, for example, when GSK sells Combivir for a high price in Europe and a low price in Africa. Firms also price goods based on characteristics that are correlated with willingness to pay so student and senior discounts are a form of price discrimination, as are the different prices that airlines set for the same flight depending on how far in advance the flight is booked.

Price discrimination isn't always easy. To price-discriminate, the firm must prevent consumers who are charged a low price from reselling to consumers who would be charged a high price, that is, prevent arbitrage. Price discrimination also requires that the firm know a lot about its customers. The more the firm knows, the better it can price-discriminate. If the firm knew exactly how much each of its customers valued its product and it could prevent arbitrage, the firm could charge each customer that customer's maximum willingness to pay—this is called perfect price discrimination. Universities come closest to practicing perfect price discrimination because to provide scholarships, the university can demand a lot of information about the income of its students and their families and it's hard to resell an education.

Tying and bundling are less obvious forms of price discrimination. By setting a low price for printers and a high price for ink, HP is setting different prices for the "ability to print color photos"—a low price for those who print only occasionally and a high price for those who print often. Cell phones are priced below cost and cell phone plans are priced above cost for the same reason.

Bundling goods in a package can also be a form of price discrimination. When consumers place very different values on package components but similar values on the package, bundling can increase profits.

Firms want to price-discriminate because price discrimination increases profits. Price discrimination may also increase total surplus. Price discrimination is most likely to increase total surplus when it increases output and when there are large fixed costs of development. Price discrimination for pharmaceuticals, for example, lowers the price for consumers in poor countries (thus increasing output) and, by increasing profits, price discrimination increases the incentive to research and develop new drugs.

CHAPTER REVIEW

Go online to practice with more examples of these types of problems, including live links to videos, data sources, and feedback.

KEY CONCEPTS

price discrimination, p. 275

arbitrage, p. 277

perfect price discrimination, p. 280

tying, p. 284

bundling, p. 285

FACTS AND TOOLS

1. True or false? A business that price-discriminates will generally charge some customers more than marginal cost, and it will generally charge other customers less than marginal cost.

2. Two customers, Fred and Lamont, walk into Grady's Used Pickups. Who probably has a more inelastic demand for one of Grady's pickups: people like Lamont, who are good at shopping around, or people like Fred, who know what they like and just buy it?

3. Who probably has more elastic demand for a Hertz rental car: someone who reserves a car online weeks before a trip, or someone who walks up to a Hertz counter without a reservation after he walks off an airplane following a 4-hour flight? Who probably gets charged more?

4. When arbitrage is easy in a market of would-be price discriminators, who is more likely to get priced out of the market: those with elastic demand or those with inelastic demand?

5. There are people who absolutely must have the latest fashions. Can you classify them as probably having elastic or inelastic demand?

6. Why would a firm hand out coupons for its products rather than just lowering the price? (*Hint:* At your school, what kind of students use coupons to buy their pizza? What kind of students *never* use coupons to buy their pizza?)

7. Where will you see more price discrimination: in monopoly-type markets with just a few firms or in competitive markets with many firms? Why?

8. When will a monopoly create more output: when it is allowed to and can perfectly price-discriminate or when the government bans price discrimination?

9. Some razors, like Gillette's Fusion and Venus razors, have disposable heads. The razor comes with an initial pack with a razor handle plus three or four heads; after that, you need to buy refills separately.

   a. Where do you think Gillette gets more revenue: by selling the initial pack or by selling the refills?

   b. The next time you buy a new razor, are you going to spend more time looking at the price of the razor or at the price of the refills?

THINKING AND PROBLEM SOLVING

10. Consider the figure here when answering the following questions.

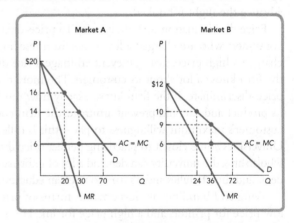

   a. How many units of output will the firm produce in Market A? What price will the monopolist charge in Market A?

   b. How many units of output will the firm produce in Market B? What price will the monopolist charge in Market B?

   c. How much consumer surplus is earned in Market A? How much profit is earned in Market A?

   d. How much consumer surplus is earned in Market B? How much profit is earned in Market B?

e. In which market does the monopolist make the most profit? How much profit do they make in this market? In which market is there the most deadweight loss? How much deadweight loss is created in this market?

f. Suppose that due to some technological innovation, the monopolist is now able to gather perfect data on all of its customers. How would total profit, consumer surplus, and deadweight loss change if the monopolist begins to practice perfect price discrimination?

11. Subway, the fast-food chain, sells foot-long sandwiches at a lower price than it costs to purchase two six-inch versions of the same sandwich. For example, a six-inch Italian BMT might be priced at $6.39, while a foot-long Italian BMT might cost only $9.79.

a. Can you think of a way that in theory you could make money from Subway's pricing practices? Would this method work in practice? What does this tell you about the limits of arbitrage?

b. In many of our price discrimination examples, we think that businesses try to break customers into two groups: more price-sensitive and less price-sensitive. What kinds of Subway customers fit into the first group? Into the second?

- Busy lawyers with 20-minute lunches
- College students
- Health-conscious soccer moms
- Long-haul truck drivers

12. A dry cleaner has a sign in its window: "Free Internet Coupons." The dry cleaner lists its website, and indeed there are good discounts available with the coupons. However, most customers don't use the coupons.

a. What probably would be the main difference between customers who use the coupons and those who don't?

b. Some people might think "The dry cleaner offers the coupons to get people in the door to try the place out, but then the customers will pay the normal high price afterward." But the coupons are always there, so even repeat customers can keep using the coupons. Is this a mistake on the business owner's part? (*Hint:* Think about marginal cost.)

13. **a.** When will a firm find it easier to price-discriminate: before the existence of eBay or afterward?

b. Which of the two "principles of price discrimination" does this invoke?

14. As we saw in this chapter, drug companies often charge much more for the same drug in the United States than in other countries. Congress often considers passing laws to make it *easier* to import drugs from these low-price countries (it also considers passing laws to make it illegal to import these drugs, but that's another story).

If one of these laws passes, and it becomes effortless to buy AIDS drugs from Africa or antibiotics from Latin America—drugs that are made by the same companies and have essentially the same quality controls as the drugs here in the United States—how will drug companies change the prices they charge in Latin America and Africa? Why?

15. Some people think that *businesses* create monopolies by destroying their competition, and there is certainly some truth to that. But as we learned from Obi-Wan Kenobi, "You will find that many of the truths we cling to depend greatly on our own point of view." For instance, some people (Convenience Shoppers) love shopping at one particular store and will switch stores only when a product is outrageously expensive, while other people (Bargain Shoppers) will gladly spend hours looking through newspaper advertisements searching for the best deal.

a. When both kinds of people, the Convenience Shoppers and the Bargain Shoppers, are shopping at the same Walmart, who is more likely to stick to their prearranged shopping list, and who is more likely to splurge on a little something?

b. Which group does Walmart have monopoly power over? Which group does Walmart have little to no monopoly power over?

c. Does this mean that the same shop can simultaneously be a "monopolist" to some customers and a "competitive firm" to other customers? Why or why not?

d. Does this mean that Darth Vader really *did* kill Anakin Skywalker?

16. Where are you more likely to see businesses "bundling" a lot of goods into one package: in industries with high fixed costs and low

marginal costs (like computer games or moviemaking), or in industries with low fixed costs and high marginal costs (like doctor visits, where the doctor's time is expensive)?

17. Isn't it surprising that movies, with tickets that cost around $10, often use vastly more economic resources than stage plays, where tickets can easily cost $100?

    Compare, for example, a live stage performance of Shakespeare's *Hamlet* with a movie of *Hamlet*.

    a. In which field is the marginal cost of one more showing lower: on stage or on screen?

    b. "Bundling" in a movie or stage performance might show up in the form of adding special effects, expensive actors, or fancy costumes: Some customers might not be too interested in an Elizabethan revenge drama, but they show up to see Liam Neeson waving an authentic medieval dagger. Is it better to think of these extra expenses as "fixed costs" or "marginal costs"?

    c. In which setting will it be easier for a business to cover its total costs: in a "bundled" stage production or in a "bundled" movie production?

18. When is a pharmaceutical company more likely to spend $100 million to research a new drug: when it knows it will be able to charge different prices in different countries or when it knows that it will be required to charge the same price in different countries? Why?

19. True or false? A price-discriminating business will sometimes be willing to spend money to make a product worse.

20. Let's calculate the profit from price discrimination. The average daily demand for dinners at Sycamore, an upscale new American restaurant known for their lunchtime pork sandwiches and gourmet salads, is as follows:

    Demand for dinners by senior citizens:

    $P = 50 - 0.5Q, \quad MR = 50 - Q$

    Demand for dinners by others:

    $P = 100 - Q, \quad MR = 100 - 2Q$

    Marginal cost = 10 in both cases.

    a. What is the profit-maximizing price for each group?

    b. Translate this into real-world jargon: If you owned this restaurant, what "senior citizen discount" would you offer, in percent?

    c. Ignoring fixed costs, how much profit would Sycamore make if it did this?

d. If it became illegal to discriminate on the basis of age, you would face only one demand curve. Adding up these two demand curves turns out to yield

$$P = 67 - \left(\frac{1}{3}\right)Q, \quad MR = 67 - \left(\frac{2}{3}\right)Q$$

What are the optimal price and quantity in this unified market? Are the total meals sold in this discrimination-free market higher or lower than in part a?

e. What is the profit in this discrimination-free market?

21. At the Kennedy Center for the Performing Arts in Washington, D.C., if you make a $120 donation per year, you are allowed to go to a small room before the concert and drink free coffee and eat free cookies. If you make a donation of $1,200 per year, you are allowed to go to a *different* small room before the concert and drink the *same* free coffee and eat the *same* free cookies. There are always a lot of people in both rooms before the concert: Why doesn't everybody just pay the $120 instead of the higher price?

22. Consider the market for Ironman triathlons. An Ironman triathlon is a long-distance triathlon where athletes complete a 2.4-mile swim (3.9K), 112-mile bike (180.2K), and 26.2-mile run. These races take place throughout the United States and world, often occurring in destination locations like Kona, Hawaii, where the Ironman world championships are held each year. Many are drawn to Ironman races for the challenge and are dedicated triathletes. Many are not as serious, though, and are not as willing to travel so far out of their way to compete in the race, though they might participate if it was held at a location close to them or was not so expensive.

    In what ways could the World Triathlon Corporation (which is the company responsible for holding all Ironman races) practice price discrimination to maximize its profits? (*Hint:* Think about timing and location.)

23. In an age where smartphones and devices rule our lives, there is a lot of pressure on companies to continue improving and innovating their products, and there is a lot of pressure on consumers to be up to date with the latest technology. Many companies have been accused of practicing planned obsolescence,

which is a tactic used in product planning wherein a product is intentionally designed to have an artificially limited life span or a purposely frail design so that it becomes obsolete after a certain period of time. How could this be useful for a profit-maximizing monopolist?

CHALLENGES

24. In the following table, we consider how Alex, Tyler, and Monique would fare under à la carte pricing and under bundling for a streaming TV service (like Hulu+live TV or YouTube TV) when there are two channels: Bravo and the Food Network.

Alex and Tyler like to watch *Project Runway* so they each place a higher value on Bravo than on the Food Network. Monique is practicing to be an Iron Chef in her second life and so she places a higher value on the Food Network than on Bravo.

Maximum Willingness to Pay for Cable TV			
	Alex	Tyler	Monique
Bravo	10	15	3
The Food Network	7	4	9
The Bundle	17	19	12

a. If the channels are priced individually, the most profitable prices for the streaming TV operator turn out to be 10 for Bravo and 7 for the Food Network. At these prices, who buys what channel and how much profit is there?

b. Let's just check to see if these prices really are profit-maximizing. What would profit be if the streaming TV company raised Bravo to a price of 11 and Food Network to a price of 8?

c. At the profit-maximizing prices, how much total consumer surplus would there be for the three of them? (Recall that consumer surplus is just each customer's willingness to pay minus the amount each person actually paid.)

d. Now consider what happens under bundling: Customers get a take-it-or-leave-it offer of both channels or nothing at all. The profit-maximizing bundle price turns out to be 12, and at that price, Alex, Tyler, and Monique all subscribe. How much consumer surplus is there at this price? How much profit? And, most

important, what would profit equal if the cable company raised the price to 13 instead?

25. The French economist and engineer Jules Dupuit (1804–1866) was puzzled by why third-class rail service in nineteenth-century France was so bad. At the time, the third-class compartments didn't even have roofs. It seemed to Dupuit that adding a roof wouldn't cost much and would surely benefit third-class passengers. How would you explain why nineteenth-century French railroads treated their third-class passengers so poorly?

26. Consider the following seating arrangement for a concert hall:

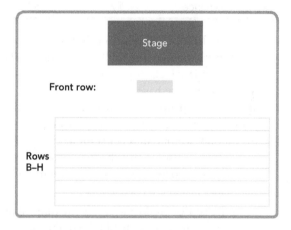

The front row seats only two people. Rows B–H, about 50 feet back from the front row, seat 20 people per row.

a. Would these front-row seats sell for more or for less than the front-row seats at a typical concert hall? Why?

b. Why don't we see concert halls set up like this?

27. a. In competitive markets in the long run, if there are two kinds of steaks, "regular" and "high-quality Angus beef," and the regular beef sells at a lower price, is this an example of price discrimination? (*Hint:* Think of the long-run pricing outcome in a competitive market.)

b. How is this different from the HP printer story in this chapter?

28. Amanda and Yvonne are thinking of going out to the movies. Amanda likes action flicks more, but Yvonne likes a little bit of romance. Warner Bros. is trying to decide what kind of movies to make this year. Should it make one movie for release this summer, an action flick with a romantic subplot, or should it make two movies for release this summer, an action flick and a romantic drama?

Here's the two friends' willingness to pay for the separate kinds of movies. As you can see, both Amanda and Yvonne are annoyed by the idea of a hybrid movie: Each would rather see their favorite kind of movie.

Maximum Willingness to Pay for a Movie Ticket		
	Amanda	Yvonne
Pure action	$10	$2
Pure romance	$2	$10
Action + romance	$9	$9

Now, let's look at this from Warner Bros.' point of view. You're the midlevel executive who has to decide which project to green light. Your marketing people have figured out that there are 5 million people like Amanda and 5 million people like Yvonne in the United States, and they'll only see one film per summer. To make things simple, assume that the marginal cost of showing the movie one more time is zero, and that ticket prices are fixed at $8.

a. If the cost of producing any of the three films is $30 million, what should the studio do: make the two films or just the one hybrid film? Of course, the right way to find the answer is to figure out which choice would generate the most profit for Warner Bros.

b. Of course, the hybrid might cost a bit more to make. What if the hybrid costs $40 million to make, the pure action flick $30 million, and the romance a mere $15 million? What's the best choice now: one hybrid or two pure films?

c. Let's see how much costs would have to change for the answer to this question to change. Holding all else equal, how low would the cost of the pure romance film have to fall before the two-movie deal would get the green light?

d. (Hard) There's an underlying principle here: The "unbundled" two-movie deal won't get the green light unless its total cost is less than what? The answer is not a number—it's an idea. Is this likely to happen in the real world? Why or why not?

29. Think about the kind of 40-year-old who pulls out a faded, obviously expired student ID to get a discount ticket at a movie theater: What can you predict about their willingness to pay for a full-price movie? Is the movie theater making a mistake when it lets them pay the student price?

30. We mentioned that airlines charge much more for flights booked at the last minute than for flights booked well in advance, even for exactly the same flight. This is because people who tend to book at the last minute tend to have inelastic demand. Think of other characteristics that airlines use to vary their pricing: Do you think these characteristics are correlated with business travel or any other sort of inelastic demand? (If you don't fly too often, just ask someone who does: "What's the key to getting the lowest possible airfare?")

31. Apple's iTunes music service sells music by the song. Other services, such as Spotify and Pandora, sell subscriptions to a library of music. Using the material in this chapter, which type of service do you think is most likely to succeed in the marketplace and why?

32. It's very common for products to come in different quality levels. You can buy beef for $5 per pound or Grade A certified Wagyu beef raised in Japan for $100 per pound or more. How do these ordinary differences in quality differ from the type of "quality discrimination" examples discussed, such as when FedEx offers its customers different delivery speeds?

Japanese Wagyu beef can cost $100 per pound or more. Is this an example of quality discrimination or just delicious beef?

sutiporn somnam/Moment/Getty Images

WORK IT OUT

For interactive, step-by-step help in solving the following problem, go online.

If Congress passed a privacy law making it illegal for colleges to ask for parents' tax returns, would that tend to help students from high-income families or students from low-income families?

CHAPTER 14 **APPENDIX**

Solving Price Discrimination Problems with Excel (Advanced Section)

Excel's Solver tool can be used to solve difficult price discrimination problems. Imagine that there are two groups of customers with the following demand curves:

$$Q_1^D = 330 - 2 \times P_1$$
$$Q_2^D = 510 - 4 \times P_2$$

where Q_1^D is the quantity demanded by Group 1 when it faces price P_1 and Q_2^D is the quantity demanded by Group 2 when it faces price P_2. We could think of these markets as Europe and Africa or as business travelers and vacationers, similar to the way we did earlier in the chapter. The monopolist has the following costs:

$$\text{Costs} = 1,000 + Q^2$$

where Q is the quantity produced by the monopolist.

The monopolist's goal is simple: It wants to choose prices P_1 and P_2 in order to maximize its profits. We will assume that the two markets are distinct, so arbitrage is not possible. Although the goal is simple, the solution is difficult. In fact, this problem is considerably more difficult than any of the problems we dealt with in the text. In the text, we assumed that marginal cost was constant (a flat MC curve). Assuming constant marginal costs simplified the problem because it meant that when the monopolist produced more in Market 1, the costs of producing another unit in Market 2 didn't change. In our problem here, marginal cost is increasing—which means that when the monopolist produces more in Market 1, its cost of producing an additional unit in Market 2 also increases. In an intermediate or graduate economics class, you would use calculus to solve a problem like this.

In the real world, business managers and entrepreneurs must solve problems like this every day and they don't all know calculus, so we will show you how to solve the problem using Excel. First, let's write down what we know. In Figure A14.1, we highlight the equation for Q_1^D, which we enter as "$= 330 - 2 * B2$". We put the price for Group 1 in cell B2. We want to find the profit-maximizing price for Group 1 but we don't know what it is, so for now we just put a zero in cell B2. The equation and price for Group 2 are entered similarly.

FIGURE A14.1

B3		f_x	=330-2*B2	
	A	B	C	
1		Group 1	Group 2	
2	Price	$0.00	$0.00	
3	Quantity Demanded	330.00	510.00	
4				

Now we enter the formula for the monopolist's cost. The total quantity produced by the monopolist is simply the quantity produced for Group 1 plus the quantity produced for Group 2. Thus, we can rewrite the monopolist's costs as

$$\text{Costs} = 1,000 + (Q_1^D + Q_2^D)^2$$

In Figure A14.2, we have entered the monopolist's costs in cell B5 as "= 1000 + (B3 + C3)^2".

FIGURE A14.2

	B5	f_x =1000+(B3+C3)^2	
	A	B	C
1		Group 1	Group 2
2	Price	$0.00	$0.00
3	Quantity Demanded	330.00	510.00
4			
5	Monopoly Cost	$706,600.00	
6			

It is important to see that what matters here is the formula for costs; the number in the picture, $706,600.00, is simply the monopolist's costs if the monopolist set P_1 and P_2 at zero and produced everything its customers demanded at those prices!

Finally, we enter the formula for profits, as shown in Figure A14.3.

FIGURE A14.3

	B6	f_x =B2*B3+C2*C3-B5	
	A	B	C
1		Group 1	Group 2
2	Price	$0.00	$0.00
3	Quantity Demanded	330.00	510.00
4			
5	Monopoly Cost	$706,600.00	
6	Monopoly Profit	-$706,600.00	
7			

Profits are revenues minus costs so we enter into Excel "= B2 ⋆ B3 + C2 ⋆ C3 − B5", which is price times the quantity demanded for Group 1 plus price times quantity demanded for Group 2 minus total costs. Excel now has enough information to solve this problem. In Excel 365, the Solver function is found in the Analyze group under the Data tab (but you may first have to add-in the Solver application—see Excel help for instructions on how to do this). Clicking the Solver button produces Figure A14.4.

FIGURE A14.4

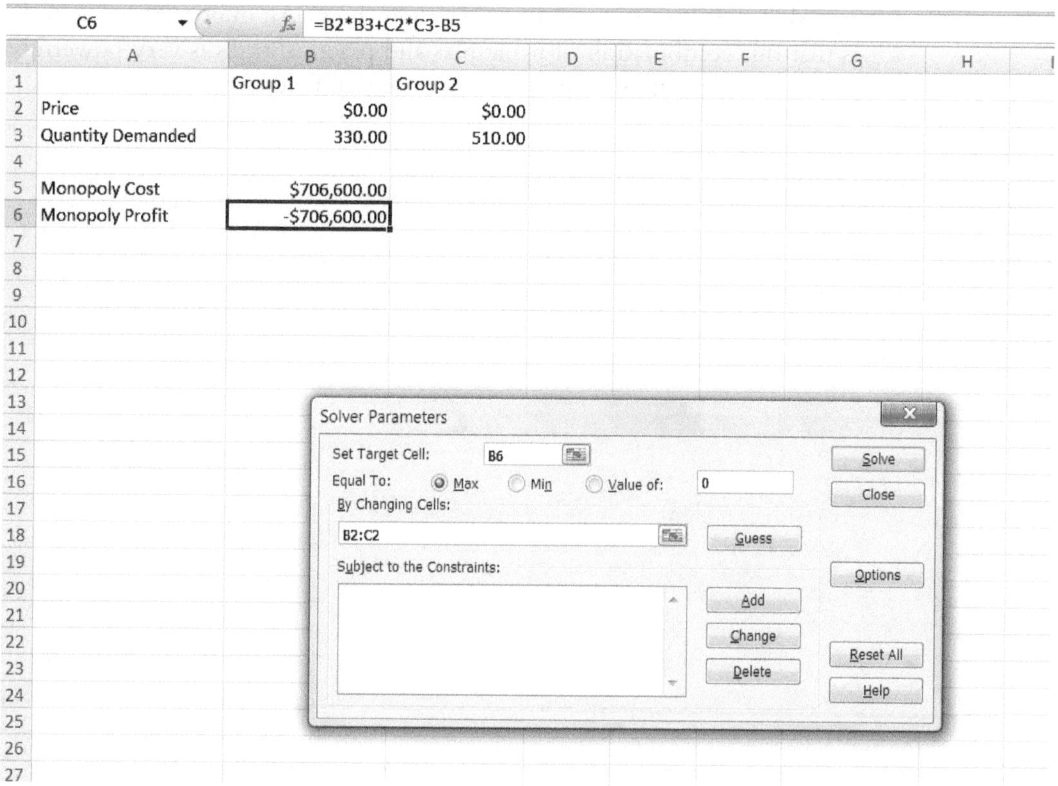

	C6		f_x =B2*B3+C2*C3-B5						
	A	B	C	D	E	F	G	H	I
1		Group 1	Group 2						
2	Price	$0.00	$0.00						
3	Quantity Demanded	330.00	510.00						
4									
5	Monopoly Cost	$706,600.00							
6	Monopoly Profit	-$706,600.00							
7									
8									
9									
10									
11									
12									
13									

Solver Parameters

Set Target Cell: B6

Equal To: ● Max ○ Min ○ Value of: 0

By Changing Cells:

B2:C2

Subject to the Constraints:

[Solve] [Close] [Guess] [Options] [Add] [Change] [Delete] [Reset All] [Help]

Our target is profits so in the Solver box next to "Set Target Cell", we enter B6. We want a maximum of profits, so make sure the "Equal to" button is filled in on Max. Finally, we are going to maximize profits by changing prices, so in the box for "By Changing Cells", we enter "B2:C2". Now we click Solve and Excel finds the answer shown in Figure A14.5.

FIGURE A14.5

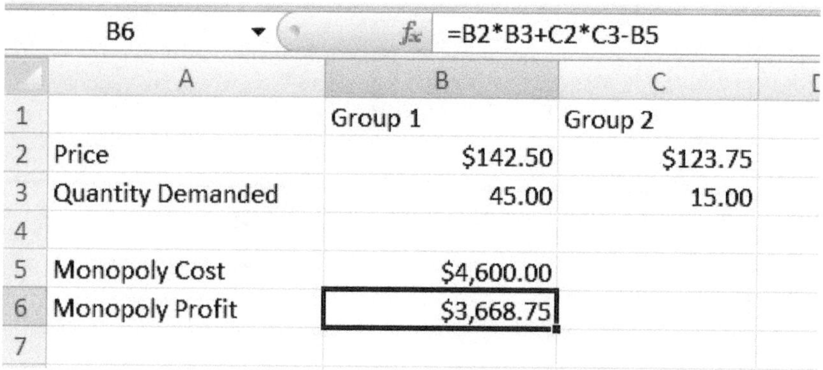

	B6		f_x =B2*B3+C2*C3-B5	
	A	B	C	D
1		Group 1	Group 2	
2	Price	$142.50	$123.75	
3	Quantity Demanded	45.00	15.00	
4				
5	Monopoly Cost	$4,600.00		
6	Monopoly Profit	$3,668.75		
7				

Excel tells us that the profit-maximizing prices are $142.50 for Group 1 and $123.75 for Group 2. At these prices, Group 1 customers buy 45 units, Group 2 customers buy 15 units, and monopoly profits are $3,668.75.

Once you understand the basic ideas, it's easy to make these models even more realistic by adding additional details, such as more groups. Notice that we have solved this problem with a combination of economic principles and practical skills (in this case, a bit of Excel know-how). An important lesson to learn is that this combination of principles and practical skills is very powerful and eagerly sought out by employers in a variety of fields.

15

Oligopoly and Game Theory

As oil prices neared a historic high in July 1979, President Jimmy Carter spoke to the nation. Quoting a concerned American, Carter said, "Our neck is stretched over the fence and OPEC has a knife." What is OPEC and what power did OPEC have to control the price of oil?

OPEC, which is short for the Organization of the Petroleum Exporting Countries, is a **cartel**, a group of suppliers who try to act together to reduce supply, raise prices, and increase profits. In other words, a cartel is a group of suppliers who try to act as if they were a monopolist.

We analyzed monopoly in Chapter 13 so we have a good understanding of what cartels are *trying* to achieve, but the question we address in this chapter is, when will cartels be *able* to achieve their goals? As we will see, it's not easy for a group of firms to act as if they were a monopolist. But even when a group of firms is not able to coordinate or collude to act like a monopolist, prices are likely to be higher in an industry with a small number of firms than in a highly competitive market. We call an industry that is dominated by a small number of firms an **oligopoly**. Thus, we begin our chapter by discussing cartels, an oligopoly that acts like a monopolist, and then move to a more general discussion of oligopoly.

In this chapter, we also introduce a new tool: game theory. Game theory is the study of **strategic decision making**. An example illustrates what we mean. In Las Vegas, craps players make decisions, but poker players make strategic decisions. Craps is a dice game and deciding when and how much to bet can be complicated, but the outcome depends only on the dice and the bet and not on how other people bet. In contrast, poker is a game of strategy because a good poker player must forecast the decisions of other players, knowing that they in turn are trying to forecast their decisions. Game theory is used to model decisions in situations in which the players interact.

Although we introduced game theory with an example from poker, a game in the usual sense of the word, game theory is used to study decision making in any situation that is interactive in a significant way. Game theory has also been used to study war, romance, business decisions of all kinds, evolution, voting, and many other situations involving interaction.

In this chapter, we use game theory to look at the economics of oligopoly.

A **cartel** is a group of suppliers who try to act *as if* they were a monopoly.

An **oligopoly** is a market that is dominated by a small number of firms.

Strategic decision making is decision making in situations that are interactive.

Cartels

Figure 15.1 shows the price for a barrel of oil from 1960 to 2020. We will focus in this chapter on the dramatic increase in the price of oil in the early 1970s and on the almost equally dramatic fall in the early 1980s. Between December 1973 and January 1974, the price of oil more than doubled! What happened? The answer is simple: Led by Saudi Arabia, a cartel of oil-exporting countries cut back on their production of oil.[*]

The left panel of Figure 15.2 shows a competitive market in a constant-cost industry so the supply curve is flat (the constant-cost assumption makes the analysis simpler but is not necessary); remember that in a competitive market each supplier earns zero economic profit. The right panel shows the *same market* but now run *as if* it were controlled by a monopolist; profits, shown in green, are maximized. A cartel is not a monopolist, but if all the firms in a market

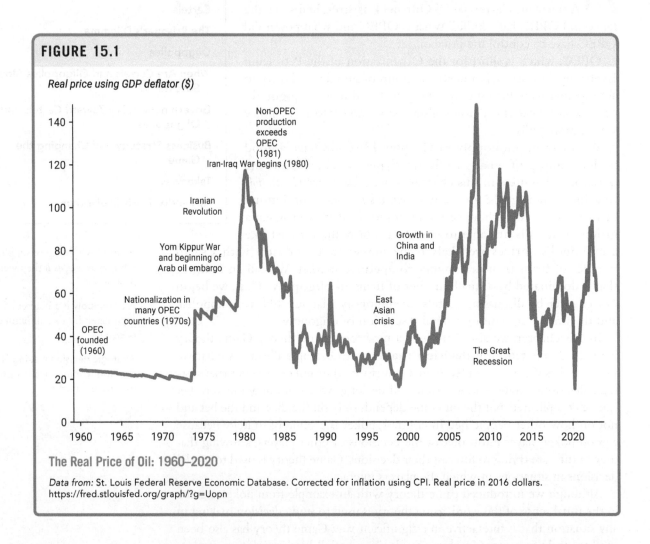

FIGURE 15.1

Real price using GDP deflator ($)

The Real Price of Oil: 1960–2020

Data from: St. Louis Federal Reserve Economic Database. Corrected for inflation using CPI. Real price in 2016 dollars. https://fred.stlouisfed.org/graph/?g=Uopn

[*] OPEC began in 1960 with five founding members—Iran, Iraq, Kuwait, Saudi Arabia, and Venezuela—and was initially not very powerful. But as more countries joined and nationalized their oil fields, it grew in power. The original five were joined by Qatar (1961–2019), Indonesia (1962–2009, 2016), Libya (1962), United Arab Emirates (1967), Algeria (1969), Nigeria (1971), Ecuador (1973–1992, 2007–2020), Gabon (1975–1995, 2016), Angola (2007), Equatorial Guinea (2017), and Republic of Congo (2018).

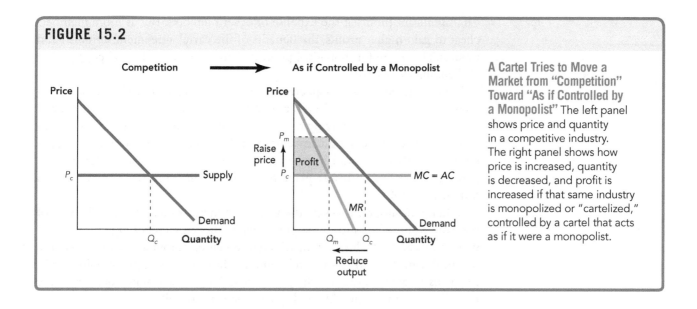

FIGURE 15.2

Competition ──────▶ As if Controlled by a Monopolist

A Cartel Tries to Move a Market from "Competition" Toward "As if Controlled by a Monopolist" The left panel shows price and quantity in a competitive industry. The right panel shows how price is increased, quantity is decreased, and profit is increased if that same industry is monopolized or "cartelized," controlled by a cartel that acts as if it were a monopolist.

could be convinced to cut supply so that total supply fell from Q_c to Q_m, then each firm could share in the "monopoly" profits. Thus, a cartel is an organization of suppliers who try to move the market from the left panel of Figure 15.2 to the right panel, that is, from "Competition" toward "As if Controlled by a Monopolist."

Very few cartels can move an industry from competition to pure monopoly, but Figure 15.2 shows the basic tendency of cartels to reduce output and raise price.

It might seem from this short look at OPEC that cartels are all-powerful. But in reality few cartels—unless they have strong government support—have much control over market price for very long. A cartel is a deal in which businesspeople promise: "I will raise my price and cut back my production if you promise to do the same." But will the promise be kept?

Cartels tend to collapse and lose their power for three reasons:

1. Cheating by the cartel members
2. New entrants and demand response
3. Government prosecution and regulation

OPEC, although a relatively successful cartel by historical standards, could not keep the price of oil high for very long. In 1980, oil prices were more than five times higher than they had been in late 1973, but by 1986 they had fallen again to near 1973 levels. OPEC nations were unhappy, but there was little they could do to keep oil prices high.

How did this happen? To understand, let's turn to the first reason why cartels collapse, namely cheating by the cartel members.

The Incentive to Cheat

Cartels aim to maximize profits for their members by coordinating to reduce supply and increase prices, but the inherent greed and self-interest of members often prove to be a cartel's undoing. As cartel members benefit from higher oil prices due to reduced production, they are incentivized to cheat by producing more than their allotted quota. If only a few members cheat, they can gain significant profits at the expense of other members. But as more members cheat to gain higher profits, the benefits of the cartel agreement diminish and unravel. The desire for individual profit thus makes sustained cartel cooperation challenging to achieve.

We can get another perspective on the incentive to cheat by comparing a monopolist with a cartel member. When a monopolist increases quantity beyond the profit-maximizing quantity, the monopolist hurts itself. But when a cartel cheater increases quantity beyond the profit-maximizing quantity, the cheater benefits itself and hurts *other cartel members*. In Figure 15.3, we compare the incentive to lower price for a monopolist and for a member of a four-firm cartel.

When a monopolist lowers the price and increases its sales, it enjoys all of the gains from selling more (the green area in the left panel of Figure 15.3), but it also bears all of the losses from selling its previous output at a lower price (the red area). But if a four-firm cartel member cheats on the cartel, it enjoys all of the gains from selling more (the green area), but it bears only a quarter of the losses from a lower price (the red area in the right panel).

If a cheater hurts the other cartel members, not so many tears will be shed by the cheater. This is especially true for the OPEC cartel. Iran and Iraq, for example, fought a major war from 1980 to 1988, with more than 800,000 people killed. The war saw the use of poison gas, chemical weapons, and child soldiers as advance scouts to trigger land mines. While this war was going on,

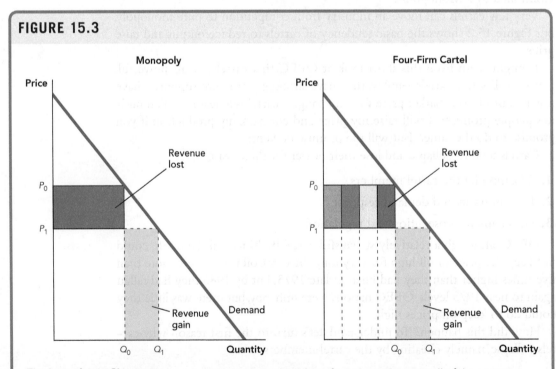

FIGURE 15.3

Monopoly

Four-Firm Cartel

The Incentive to Cheat When a monopolist increases quantity from Q_0 to Q_1 it gets all of the revenues from the new sales (the green area) but it also bears all of the losses from the lower price on old sales (the red area). The red plus green area is equal to marginal revenue (see Chapter 11).

When a single firm in a four-firm cartel increases quantity from Q_0 to Q_1 it gets all of the revenues from the new sales (the green area), but the fall in price is spread across all firms in the industry in proportion to their sales, so the cartel member loses only the much smaller red area. The cartel member, therefore, has a much larger incentive to increase output than does the monopolist.

Iran and Iraq were both in OPEC. Each nation, in effect, was promising it would not undercut the other when it came to selling more oil at a lower price. Do you really think they felt obliged to keep their word?

And so have most cartels ended. The more successful the cartel is in raising member profits, the greater the incentive to cheat. And once a cartel falls apart, it is difficult to put it back together again. Everyone correctly expects cheating to be the norm.

No One Wins the Cheating Game

It's useful to show the incentive to cheat in another way, using what is called a payoff table. With more than two firms, the payoff table would be quite complicated and hard to draw in two dimensions, but the same logic of cheating applies if there are just two firms. So imagine that the oil market is dominated by two large firms, Saudi Arabia and Russia.

Saudi Arabia has two choices, or strategies, Cooperate (by cutting back production) or Cheat. These strategies are shown in Figure 15.4 by the rows of the payoff table. Russia also has the same two strategies, shown as the columns of the payoff table.

I promise never to cheat on you. Venezuelan President Hugo Chavez (left) hugs Saudi Crown Prince Abdullah bin Abdul Aziz Al Saud during an OPEC summit in 2000.

The two numbers in each box of the table are the payoffs to the players; the first number is the payoff to Saudi Arabia, the second to Russia. For instance, if both Saudi Arabia and Russia choose to cooperate by cutting back production, the payoff is $400 (million per day) to Saudi Arabia and $400 (million per day) to Russia. If Saudi Arabia cheats and Russia cooperates, then the payoff to Saudi Arabia is $500 and the payoff to Russia is $200.

Now let's see what the "players" will do in this "game." Consider the incentives faced by Saudi Arabia. If Russia cooperates, then Saudi Arabia can choose Cooperate and receive a payoff of $400 or choose Cheat and receive a payoff of $500. Since $500 is more than $400, Saudi Arabia's best strategy *if Russia cooperates* is to cheat.

FIGURE 15.4

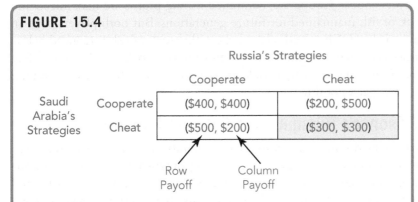

		Russia's Strategies	
		Cooperate	Cheat
Saudi Arabia's Strategies	Cooperate	($400, $400)	($200, $500)
	Cheat	($500, $200)	($300, $300)

Row Payoff   Column Payoff

The Cheating Dilemma The numbers are the payoffs, in millions of dollars per day, that each player receives given the combination of strategies played. If Russia plays Cooperate and Saudi Arabia plays Cheat, the payoff to Saudi Arabia is $500 and the payoff to Russia is $200. In this game, Cheat is a better strategy for each player no matter what the other player's strategy. Thus, the equilibrium of this game (shaded) is (Cheat, Cheat).

A **dominant strategy** is a strategy that has a higher payoff than any other strategy no matter what the other player does.

What is Saudi Arabia's best strategy if Russia cheats? If Russia cheats, Saudi Arabia can cooperate and earn a payoff of $200 or Saudi Arabia can cheat and earn a payoff of $300. Cheat is again the more profitable strategy. A strategy that has a higher payoff than any other strategy, no matter what the other player does, is called a **dominant strategy**. In this setup, cheating is a dominant strategy for Saudi Arabia.

Cheating is also a dominant strategy for Russia. If Saudi Arabia cooperates, Russia earns $500 by choosing Cheat and $400 by choosing Cooperate. If Saudi Arabia cheats, Russia earns $300 by choosing Cheat and $200 by choosing Cooperate. Thus, both Saudi Arabia and Russia will cheat and we shade (Cheat, Cheat) to show that this is the equilibrium outcome of the game.

The logic is compelling but also surprising. When Saudi Arabia and Russia each follow their individually sensible strategy of Cheat, each receives a payoff of $300. If Saudi Arabia and Russia instead both chose to cooperate, a strategy that is not individually sensible, they will receive a higher payoff of $400. Thus, when Saudi Arabia acts in its interest and Russia acts in its interest, the result is an outcome that is in the interest of neither. That is a dilemma well verified by both theory and evidence.

The Prisoner's Dilemma

The **prisoner's dilemma** is the negative counterpart to the invisible hand, in which the pursuit of self-interest leads to a group or social outcome that is in the interest of no one.

The analysis we have just given of cartel cheating is one version of a very famous game called the **prisoner's dilemma**. The prisoner's dilemma describes situations where the pursuit of self-interest leads to a group or social outcome that is in the interest of no one. The prisoner's dilemma is the negative counterpart to the invisible hand. The pursuit of self-interest can, with the right rules, lead to the social interest—that's the invisible hand. The pursuit of self-interest can also lead, with the wrong rules, to an outcome that no one intends and no one wants.

To give another example of this phenomenon, the world's stock of fish is rapidly being depleted. To understand why, replace Saudi Arabia and Russia in Figure 15.4 with two large fishing firms or countries, say the United States and Japan. Cooperate now means "produce less fish" (instead of less oil). If both players choose Cooperate, combined fishing profits are maximized and the stock of fish maintained for future generations. But both players have an incentive to cheat! When both players cheat, the stock of fish is reduced below the profit-maximizing optimum and eventually the stock may be completely depleted. That's why so many people are concerned that the world is running out of many species of fish.

CHECK YOURSELF

- When Great Britain discovered large oil deposits in the North Sea, why didn't it immediately join OPEC?
- What is the surprising conclusion of the prisoner's dilemma?

The Prisoner's Dilemma and Repeated Interaction

The prisoner's dilemma suggests that cooperation is difficult to maintain both when cooperation is good (preventing overfishing) and when cooperation is bad (maintaining a cartel). The situation is more optimistic and more pessimistic with repeated interactions! If the same players engage with one another repeatedly, they are more likely to cooperate than if they meet and play the prisoner's dilemma just once. The political scientist Elinor Ostrom, who was awarded the Nobel Prize in economics in 2009, has shown, for example, that fishermen do not invariably overfish common fishing grounds. In small communities with repeated interaction, people generally find rules or norms, such as limits on how much it is okay to take, that lead to greater cooperation and that limit the prisoner's dilemmas. We will have more to say about overfishing in Chapter 19.

For the same reasons, however, cheating does not always break down cartels when a small number of players interact repeatedly. The asphalt industry, for example, is notorious for cartel-like behavior (asphalt is the tar-like material used for paving roads). Thousands of firms produce asphalt so you might think that cartels wouldn't work. The problem is that asphalt is costly to transport and it has to be kept hot, so a firm can't deliver asphalt at a reasonable price anywhere more than an hour or so away from its place of production. In rural regions, that limits the number of bidders on a road contract to just a handful of firms.

When only a handful of firms can realistically bid on a road contract, it becomes profitable to collude. For instance, the firms could secretly agree to all submit high bids, while agreeing that on each bid cycle one firm will be the "low" bidder, and then rotating the identity of this firm over time so that each firm shares in the profits. In the 1980s, the government prosecuted more than 600 bid-rigging cases in the asphalt industry. What's most interesting, however, is that there is evidence that the cartels did not disappear, even after this prosecution.

Government prosecution eliminated explicit agreements to rig bids but it didn't solve the underlying problem. In many parts of the country, there are still only a handful of firms that can realistically bid on a contract. Moreover, the same firms face each other repeatedly and each firm understands that if they bid aggressively on every contract, then no one will ever profit very much. In this situation, strategies often evolve that can duplicate collusive outcomes even without explicit agreement. If Firm A bids low today, for example, Firm B can punish them by bidding low on the next contract. But if Firm A cooperates by submitting a high bid today, then Firm B can cooperate by submitting a high bid tomorrow. This strategy—do whatever your partner did the last period—is called "tit for tat" and it can be very effective at developing **tacit collusion**, collusion without explicit agreement or communication.

Another strategy is for firms to tacitly agree on territories—"I won't underbid you in this area if you don't underbid me in this other area." Between 2005 and 2007, for example, more than 1,000 road contracts were put up for bid by the Kentucky government and a stunning 64% had only one bidder! Moreover, two economists, David Barrus and Frank Scott, discovered that the pattern of bids wasn't random.[1] Remember that asphalt firms have to deliver their product within about an hour of production. What Barrus and Scott discovered is that the firms weren't bidding for every potential contract within their one-hour radius. Instead, the firms more often made bids just within the county in which the firm had its production plant. A firm might bid on a contract 40 miles away in the same county, for example, but not bid on a contract just 10 miles away but in another county. Even though county lines are irrelevant to the economics of asphalt production, they had become a focal point for firms to tacitly collude.

Most importantly, notice that it's much harder to prosecute collusion when the colluding firms never meet or discuss an agreement and the only signal of collusion is not bidding!

Tacit collusion occurs when firms limit competition with one another but they do so without explicit agreement or communication.

The Prisoner's Dilemma Has Many Applications

The prisoner's dilemma has a remarkable number of applications throughout economics and the social sciences and even in biology, computer science, and philosophy. We show a few examples in Figure 15.5.

FIGURE 15.5

The Arms Race Few people wanted to develop the hydrogen bomb but no one wanted the other side to develop it first so we ended up in a very dangerous world.

There Is Trouble with the Trees Each tree grows tall to try to grab up all the light. But when all the trees do, none gain an advantage and all expend resources in fruitless competition.

Standing Room Only At the concert everyone stands to get a better view but no one gets it (unless you have a very good friend).

Battle of the Brands Coke and Pepsi have spent billions trying to convince buyers that their brand is better. The war has been profitable . . . for the advertising agencies.

Oligopolies

Cartels are difficult to form and maintain, but a small number of firms, an oligopoly, that fail to form a cartel are still very likely to maintain prices above competitive levels. In Figure 15.3, we showed how a cartel member has an incentive to cheat on the agreement by lowering price and producing more than the assigned quota. Exactly the same diagram shows why the price in an oligopoly is likely to be below the monopoly price. A firm in an oligopoly that produces more and cuts price earns all the gains for itself, but bears only a fraction of the costs. Thus, prices in an oligopoly are likely to be below monopoly levels, but how will prices in an oligopoly compare with competitive levels?

In Figure 15.6, we show how an oligopolist has an incentive to raise prices above competitive levels. Imagine first that the oligopolistic market is producing at competitive levels. Recall from Chapter 11 that this means the price is equal to marginal cost and no firm is making an above-normal profit. In Figure 15.6, the competitive price and quantity are $P_0 (= MC)$ and Q_0. Now suppose that one firm in, say, a four-firm oligopoly were to cut output by $Q_0 - Q_1$, thus raising the price to P_1. At P_1, every firm in the industry is making a profit since $P_1 > MC$. In particular, even the firm that cut its output increased its profits since before it was making zero profits and now it is making positive profits, as shown by the green area.

In a competitive industry, no firm is able to influence the price, so a competitive firm has no incentive to reduce output. In an oligopoly, each firm is large relative to the total size of the market. Thus, a firm in an oligopoly has some influence over the price and therefore has an incentive to reduce output and increase price from the competitive level.

Figures 15.3 and 15.6 tell us that price in an oligopoly is likely to be below monopoly levels but above competitive levels. Moreover, we can also see that the more firms in the oligopoly, the greater the incentive to cut price from monopoly levels and the smaller the incentive to increase price above competitive levels. Thus, we can also predict that the more firms in an industry, the closer price will be to competitive levels.

Can we be more precise about pricing in an oligopolistic market? Economists have developed many models of oligopolistic pricing. Famous models in this literature include those by Bertrand, Cournot, Nash, and Stackelberg. Each

---

FIGURE 15.6

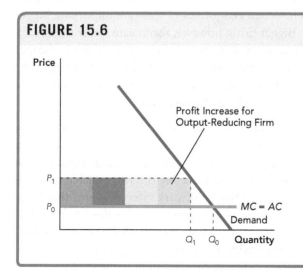

The Incentive to Raise Price Above Competitive Levels in an Oligopoly The competitive equilibrium is shown at P_0, Q_0. In the competitive equilibrium no firm makes an above-normal profit since $P = MC$. Even though no firm makes an above-normal profit, a competitive firm has no control over the price and thus cannot increase its profits by reducing output. But a firm in a four-firm oligopoly who reduces quantity by the amount $Q_0 - Q_1$ increases the market price to P_1 which is greater than MC. The increase in price increases the profits of the firm that cuts output (the green area), as well as increasing the profits of the other firms in the industry.

Barriers to entry are factors that increase the cost to new firms of entering an industry.

TABLE 15.1 SOME BARRIERS TO ENTRY
Control over a key resource or input
Economies of scale
Network effects
Government barriers

Maciej Frolow/Getty Images

Is the diamond cartel forever? Diamonds are found in only a few places in the world. As a result, for decades the DeBeers cartel has been able to keep prices high. This diamond, however, was not mined—it was *printed*. Human-made diamonds are as beautiful as natural diamonds—even an expert jeweler cannot tell them apart. Human-made diamonds could break the DeBeers cartel.

of these models has its uses, but it's difficult to say that one model is best for all purposes. A lot depends on factors specific to the industry; the right model for the auto industry might not be the right model for the soft-drink industry or the aircraft industry. The field of industrial organization has a lot more to say about the specifics of oligopoly.

When Are Cartels and Oligopolies Most Successful?

As with monopolies, cartels and oligopolies tend to be most successful when there are significant **barriers to entry**, that is, factors that increase the cost to new firms of entering an industry. Table 15.1 lists some important barriers to entry.

Control over a Key Resource or Input Oil and diamonds are two goods in which cartels have been partially successful because these natural resources are found in only a few places in the world (but see the sidebar on diamonds!). As a result, it's possible for a few firms or countries to control a significant share of the world's output. Similarly, Indonesia and Grenada tried to create a nutmeg cartel in the late 1980s when they controlled 98% of the world's supply. The nutmeg cartel had the support of the Indonesian and Grenadian governments and it had some success. Within a few years, however, the cartel broke down as higher prices increased entry and Indonesian farmers started to smuggle nutmeg out of the country! The copper cartel (Intergovernmental Council of Copper Exporting Countries, CIPEC) tried to follow OPEC's model starting in 1967, but they never controlled more than one-third of the world's copper supply. There are also good substitutes for copper in most uses, including plastic, aluminum, and recycled copper. The copper cartel was never terribly successful and dissolved in the 1990s.

Economies of Scale The advantages of large-scale production mean that it is much cheaper for five car manufactures to make 3 million cars each than for 500 manufacturers to make 30,000 cars each. When economies of scale are important, bigger means cheaper. Bigger firms, however, also means fewer firms, each with potentially more market power. Since people want cheaper cars more than they want extreme variety, it is never going to be optimal to have 500 car manufacturers in the United States so the market will remain something of an oligopoly.

Network Effects Some goods are more valuable the more people use them. Instagram, for example, is more valuable to you when your friends also use Instagram. eBay is more valuable to buyers when there are more sellers on eBay, and eBay is more valuable to sellers the more buyers are on eBay. "Network effects" means that firms can snowball in size as each new customer makes the firm's product more valuable to the next customer. As a result, goods with significant network effects tend to be sold by monopolies or oligopolies. We discuss network goods at greater length in the next chapter.

Government Barriers Governments sometimes try to combat monopolies and oligopolies with antitrust law. At other times, governments create barriers to entry with licenses or other regulations that limit entry. Let's take a closer look at both situations.

Government Policy Toward Cartels and Oligopolies

Most cartels have been illegal in the United States since the Sherman Antitrust Act of 1890. ("Trust" is simply an old word for monopoly. The antitrust laws give the government the power to prohibit or regulate business practices that may be anticompetitive.) In the early 1990s, for example, four firms controlled 95% of the world market for lysine, an amino acid used to promote growth in pigs, chickens, and cattle. The firms—Archer Daniels Midland (USA), Ajinomoto (Japan), Kyowa Hakko Kogyo (Japan), and Sewon America Inc. (South Korea)—held secret meetings around the world at which they agreed to act in unison to reduce quantity and raise prices.

What the conspirators didn't know was that one of them was a mole. A high-ranking executive at ADM informed the FBI of the cartel. Working with FBI equipment, the mole videotaped meetings at which the conspirators discussed how to split the market and keep prices high.

With the evidence in hand, the FBI and the Department of Justice put the conspirators on trial. Three executives of Archer Daniels Midland, including the vice president, Michael D. Andreas, were fined and imprisoned. One of the Japanese executives was also sentenced to prison, but fled the country and is currently a fugitive from U.S. law.

More generally, the antitrust laws in the United States and similar laws in Europe can be used to block mergers or even to break up very large firms. In the 1970s, for example, AT&T was the sole provider of telephone service throughout the United States. That particular monopoly was legally sanctioned but in due time the government changed its mind, and in 1974 the antitrust division of the Department of Justice sued AT&T. The lawsuit led to the breakup of AT&T into eight independent companies in 1984. The breakup of AT&T increased the number of new entrants into the industry, providing a spur to companies such as Sprint and MCI. The Department of Justice continues to regulate the phone industry. In 2011, for example, the division blocked a proposed merger between AT&T and T-Mobile out of fear that such a merger would diminish competitive pressure.

youtube.com/watch?v=E21YYoxRs5g

United States Department of Justice Antitrust Division

Watch the FBI's secret video of the lysine cartel meeting to fix prices.

Government-Supported Cartels

Governments don't always prosecute cartels or break down barriers to entry. In fact, sometimes governments reduce competition and create barriers to entry. OPEC, for example, is a cartel of oil-exporting *governments*. In fact, most successful cartels operate with clear legal and governmental backing. Governments are the ultimate cartel enforcers because they can throw cheaters in jail. In the United States, government-controlled milk cartels combine with subsidies and quotas to raise the price of milk. This cartel is extremely stable. Any seller who breaks it is fined or sent to jail. In the past, the U.S. government has supported cartels in coal mining, agriculture, medicine, and other areas; some but not all of these restrictions have been lifted.

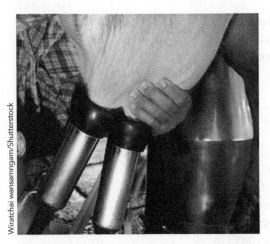

Who is being milked? The government-enforced milk cartel increases the price of milk.

Government-enforced monopolies and cartels are a serious problem facing poor nations today. They plague Mexico, Russia, Indonesia, most of the poor nations in Africa, and many other locales.

A government-supported cartel usually means higher prices, lower-quality service, and less innovation. People with new ideas find it harder or impossible to enter the market. Furthermore, people spend their energies trying to get monopoly or cartel privileges from governments, rather than innovating or finding new ways to service consumers. Governments become more corrupt. For these reasons, most economists generally oppose government-enforced cartels. Those cartels are put in place to serve special interests—usually the politically connected cartel members—rather than consumers or the general citizenry.

Business Strategy and Changing the Game

The prisoner's dilemma game suggests that collusion is difficult (although as we also saw there are more possibilities for collusion/cooperation with repeated interactions). Every firm wants market power, however, so what can firms do? One possibility is to change the game! Let's take a look at two strategies that on the surface seem competitive and proconsumer but that may also have hidden and less beneficial consequences: price match guarantees and loyalty programs such as frequent flyer points.

The Danger of Price Matching Guarantees

What's not to like when a firm guarantees that it will match the price of any competitor and even pay the consumer 10% of the difference? Isn't this a great example of competition at its finest? Not so fast. To evaluate the effects of these policies, we need some game theory.

Suppose that Lowe's and Home Depot are locked into a price war over refrigerator sales. Each firm could set a high price of $1,000 or a low price of $800. Let's also assume that costs are zero (this is convenient but doesn't affect the results) and that there are 1,000 consumers. If both firms set a high price, each gets 500 consumers and makes a profit of $500,000 ($1,000 × 500). If one firm sets a low price ($800) while the other firm continues to set a high price, then the low-price firm gets all the customers (1,000) and makes more money, $800,000. If both firms set a low price, then they again split the market and each makes $400,000. The payoffs are shown in Figure 15.7.

Notice that this is just another version of the prisoner's dilemma. No matter what strategy Lowe's chooses, it's best for Home Depot to choose Low Price, and no matter what strategy Home Depot chooses, it's best for Lowe's to choose Low Price. Thus each firm chooses its dominant strategy and the equilibrium outcome is Low Price, Low Price.

But now let's imagine that each firm offers to match any competitor's price plus give the consumer 10% of the difference. Assume, for example, that Home Depot posts a price of $800. Which firm gets the sales? If Home Depot posts a price of $800 but Lowe's guarantees to match the price and give the consumer 10% of the difference, then a consumer can, in effect, buy the refrigerator from

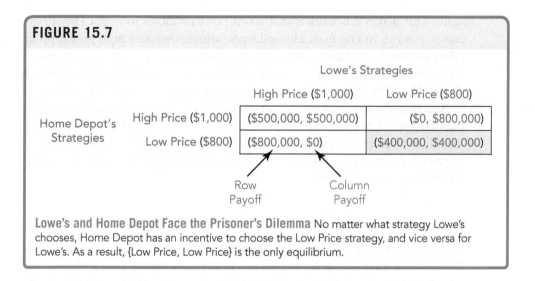

FIGURE 15.7

		Lowe's Strategies	
		High Price ($1,000)	Low Price ($800)
Home Depot's Strategies	High Price ($1,000)	($500,000, $500,000)	($0, $800,000)
	Low Price ($800)	($800,000, $0)	($400,000, $400,000)

Row Payoff   Column Payoff

Lowe's and Home Depot Face the Prisoner's Dilemma No matter what strategy Lowe's chooses, Home Depot has an incentive to choose the Low Price strategy, and vice versa for Lowe's. As a result, {Low Price, Low Price} is the only equilibrium.

Lowe's for $780 ($800 minus 10% of the $200 difference in posted price). By lowering its price, Home Depot ensures that Lowe's sells all the refrigerators and makes $780,000 in profit. Notice that it's Lowe's, the firm with the *high posted price*, that makes the profits! Similarly, if Lowe's posts a Low Price while Home Depot posts a High Price, Home Depot gets all the sales and the profits! Cutting prices no longer looks like a good idea. As before, if both firms choose High Price, they split the market and make $500,000 each, and if both choose Low Price, they make $400,000 each. The new payoffs are shown in Figure 15.8.

The price match guarantee changes the payoffs and that changes the game. In the new game, the dominant strategy is to choose High Price. Once again, let's look at Lowe's incentives. If Home Depot chooses High Price, then Lowe's earns $500,000 by choosing High Price and $0 by choosing Low Price. If Home Depot chooses Low Price, then Lowe's earns $780,000 by choosing High Price and only $400,000 by choosing Low Price. Thus, whatever choice Home Depot makes, it's better for Lowe's to choose High Price! Once

FIGURE 15.8

		Lowe's Strategies	
		High Price ($1,000)	Low Price ($800)
Home Depot's Strategies	High Price ($1,000)	($500,000, $500,000)	($780,000, $0)
	Low Price ($800)	($0, $780,000)	($400,000, $400,000)

The Price Match Game Each firm promises to match any competitor's posted price and give customers 10% of the difference in posted prices. If Home Depot posts a Low Price of $800 and Lowe's posts a High Price of $1,000, then customers are better off buying from Lowe's because Lowe's matches Home Depot's posted price and gives customers 10% of the difference. Thus, when Home Depot lowers its price, Lowe's will get all of the customers and the profits! Similarly, if Lowe's lowers its price and Home Depot does not, Home Depot gets all the profits. In this game, posting a High Price is always more profitable than posting a Low Price! Thus, High Price is a dominant strategy and the equilibrium is {High Price, High Price}.

again what makes this work is that when Lowe's chooses to post a Low Price, consumers run to buy from Home Depot, which, despite a high posted price, offers to match the Lowe's price and give consumers 10% of the difference. The game is symmetric so for the same reasons that Lowe's has an incentive to choose High Price, Home Depot also has an incentive to choose High Price.

Amazingly, a price match guarantee that looks proconsumer changes the equilibrium strategies from {Low Price, Low Price} to {High Price, High Price}. A price match guarantee and a promise to pay 10% of the difference in price turns out to be a clever strategy that reduces the incentive of firms to compete with lower prices!

The High Price of Loyalty

In addition to price guarantees, businesses can also reduce their incentives to lower prices by using loyalty plans. A customer loyalty plan gives regular customers special treatment or a better price. The best-known customer loyalty plans are probably frequent flyer miles on airlines, but you will find customer loyalty plans at Barnes & Noble, Starbucks, and your local Giant and Safeway supermarkets.

Let's take a look at frequent flyer plans. If you join a frequent flyer plan, you get points every time you fly, points that can be used to get a free plane ticket once you have accumulated enough. Alex and Tyler are both members of the United frequent flyer plan because United has the most flights out of Washington, D.C., our usual takeoff point. Now when we book travel we are slightly more likely to book a United flight so that we can accumulate points toward a free trip. So what's not to like?

The trick is this: Suppose United, Delta, and the other major airlines all offer frequent flyer plans. Loyal customers of each of these companies feel good that they are getting points toward a free trip, but once customers are loyal—that is, once they are a bit locked in—the different airlines don't have to compete with each other quite as much. United realizes that if it raises its prices a little, its customers will remain loyal, and if it lowers its prices a little, the customers of the other airlines will also remain loyal! Thus, United has more incentive to raise its prices and less incentive to lower its prices. Loyalty increases monopoly power, and each airline, facing a more inelastic demand curve, will raise prices. See Figure 15.9. As a result, the net effect of more points is higher prices! A cynic might say that exploitation is the price of loyalty.

When you get your free flight, you feel like a winner, but the reality is that you are being conned just a little. It does you no good, however, to stay out of the plans and refuse to use the points. If you refuse to join the loyalty plan, you lose the points. Furthermore, your refusal won't increase competition in the airline market enough to get airlines to lower their prices across the board. Customers are better off refusing to join the loyalty plan only if all or most of them refuse, in which case each airline will face a more elastic demand curve and prices will fall for

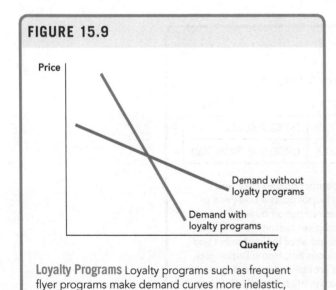

FIGURE 15.9

Price

Demand without loyalty programs

Demand with loyalty programs

Quantity

Loyalty Programs Loyalty programs such as frequent flyer programs make demand curves more inelastic, that is, less sensitive to price.

everyone. Loyalty plans put customers in a type of prisoner's dilemma—it's good for a single customer to join the loyalty plan, but if all the customers join, the result is bad for them as a whole. As you know from the analysis of the prisoner's dilemma, it's going to be difficult to organize a mass boycott of loyalty plans.

By the way, limiting competitive pressure is not the only motivation for customer loyalty plans like frequent flyer programs. Frequent flyer programs also are a form of price discrimination (Chapter 14), as perhaps only the more budget-conscious travelers take the trouble to sign up for miles and cash them in, sometimes altering their flight plans to save the money. Over time, the budget-conscious travelers, who redeem their miles conscientiously and thus get some free flights, pay lower average prices for flying than do the non-budget-conscious travelers. Frequent flyer programs also encourage business travelers to sometimes take the more expensive flight; the traveler will get miles on the preferred airline but the employer will pay the higher price; the airline is indirectly "bribing" the employee to take advantage of the employer. Finally, firms may deliberately let employees keep their frequent flyer miles, even if it means paying for higher ticket prices come reimbursement time. It's one way of rewarding employees while skirting taxes (legally) because the use of fre-quent flyer miles is not considered taxable income or a reward. If you really value the extra flights, you can save up to 40% in value by avoiding the taxation of ordinary monetary income and by taking your marginal compensation in the form of miles. Frequent flyer miles are a good example of how, if you look closely, you will see economics everywhere.

Other Ways of Changing the Game

Firms want market power and sometimes that can be at the expense of con-sumers, but keep in mind that the pursuit of market power can often lead to the social good! One reason that firms innovate, for example, is that by doing so they can produce a good with fewer substitutes. Fewer substitutes means a more inelastic demand curve and that means that firms can charge a higher price and earn a higher profit (all else being equal). Similarly, firms also try to reduce the number of substitutes for their product by differentiating their prod-uct with different styles or varieties. Apple, Samsung, and Google all produce cell phones but by differentiating the features, looks, and capabilities, they com-pete with one another less than if the phones were more similar.

Innovation and product differentiation, however, are usually good things so the pursuit of market power is part of what makes for a competitive, dynamic economy. Less competition is good for firms but at the same time we want firms to have an incentive to innovate. The market is not just a process for reducing price to marginal cost—it's also a discovery process, a way of figuring out what products and features consumers really want. We will discuss product differentiation and competing for market (monopoly) power at greater length in Chapters 16 and 17.

Takeaway

An oligopoly is a market dominated by a small number of firms. A cartel is an oligopoly that is able to maximize its joint profits by limiting competition and producing the monopoly quantity.

The OPEC cartel remains important but its influence on the price of oil has diminished due to cheating, new entrants—especially the massive increase in the U.S. supply of oil from fracking—and substitute products such as electric cars. Most market cartels are not stable. When a cartel successfully raises prices, that increases the incentive of cartel members to cheat on the cartel agreement and new competitors to enter the market. Governments break up some cartels, but they also enforce others. When you observe a harmful cartel, you should ask whether some governmental rule or regulation might be at fault.

Oligopolies form when there are significant barriers to entry, such as control of a key resource or input, economies of scale, network effects, or government barriers. Although firms in an oligopoly are unlikely to be able to produce the joint profit-maximizing quantity, neither are they likely to produce as much as in a highly competitive market. Prices in an oligopoly, therefore, tend to be below monopoly prices but above competitive prices.

Game theory is the study of strategic interaction. A dominant strategy is a strategy that has a higher payoff no matter what the other player(s) do.

The prisoner's dilemma game explains why cheating is common in cartels and more generally how individual interest can make cooperation difficult even when cooperation is better for everyone in the group than noncooperation. Firms use a variety of strategies to reduce competitive pressures. An analysis of price matching guarantees and customer loyalty programs shows that they can reduce competition and raise prices. Innovation and product differentiation can also reduce competitive pressures but at the same time are part of a dynamic economy that discovers valuable new goods and services.

CHAPTER REVIEW

Go online to practice with more examples of these types of problems, including live links to videos, data sources, and feedback.

KEY CONCEPTS

cartel, p. 297

oligopoly, p. 297

strategic decision making, p. 297

dominant strategy, p. 302

prisoner's dilemma, p. 302

tacit collusion, p. 303

barriers to entry, p. 306

Nash equilibrium, p. 319

FACTS AND TOOLS

1. Let's start off by working out a few examples to illustrate the lure of the cartel. To keep it simple on the supply side, we'll assume that fixed costs are zero so marginal cost equals average cost. We'll compare the competitive outcome ($P = MC$) to what you'd get if the firms all

agreed to act "as if" they were a monopoly. In all cases, we'll use terms from the following diagram:

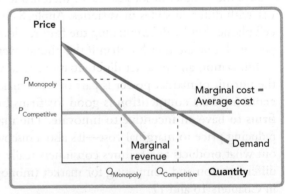

a. First, let's see where the profits are. Comparing this figure with Figure 15.2, shade the rectangle that corresponds to monopoly profit.

b. What is the formula for this rectangle in terms of price, cost, and quantity?

c. Let's look at the market for maple syrup. Assume that there are 7,000 producers of maple syrup and that $MC = AC = \$12$ per gallon. In a competitive market, price will be driven down to marginal cost. Let's assume that when $P = MC$, each maple syrup producer produces 4,000 gallons of maple syrup for a total market production of 28 million gallons. Now imagine that the maple syrup producers form a cartel (this actually exists in Canada!) and each agrees to cut production to 2,000 gallons of syrup, which drives the price up to $35 per gallon. Calculate profit per gallon and total industry profit if the maple syrup producers behave "as if" they were a monopoly and are able to produce according to the following table:

$P_{Monopoly}$	$Q_{Monopoly}$
$35/gallon	14 million gallons
Profit per pound$_{Monopoly}$	Total industry Profit$_{Monopoly}$
_____	_____

d. If a single maple syrup producer broke from the cartel and produced an extra 2,000 gallons of maple syrup, how much additional profit (approximately) would this syrup producer make? As mentioned, there actually is a maple syrup cartel in Canada as well as individual producers who try to produce more than their production quotas.

2. Take a look at the reasons presented in the chapter for why cartels collapse. For each of the following pairs, choose the case in which the cartel is more likely to stick together.

a. An industry where it's easy for new firms to enter vs. an industry where the same firms stick around for decades.

b. When the government makes it legal for all the firms to agree on prices vs. when the government makes it illegal for all firms in an industry to agree on prices. (*Note:* The Sherman Antitrust Act made the latter generally illegal in 1890, but President Franklin Roosevelt's National Industrial Recovery Act temporarily legalized price-setting cartels during the Great Depression.)

c. Cartels in which all the industry leaders went to the same schools and live in the same neighborhood vs. cartels where the industry leaders don't really know or trust each other. (*Hint:* As Adam Smith said in *The Wealth of Nations,* "People of the same trade seldom meet together, even for merriment and diversion, but the conversation ends in a conspiracy against the public, or in some contrivance to raise prices.")

d. An industry in which it's easy for a firm to sell a little extra product without anyone knowing (e.g., music downloads) vs. an industry where all sales are public and visible (e.g., concert tickets).

3. The prisoner's dilemma game is one of the most important models in all of social science: Most games of trust can be thought of as some kind of prisoner's dilemma. Here's the classic game: Two people rob a bank and are quickly arrested. The police do not have an airtight case; they have just enough evidence to put each person in prison for one year, a slap on the wrist for a serious crime.

If the police had more evidence, they could put them away for longer. To get more evidence, they put each person in separate interrogation rooms and offer each of them the same deal: If you testify against your accomplice, we will drop all the charges against you (and convict the other person of the full penalty of 10 years of prison time). Of course, if both prisoners take the deal, the police will have enough evidence to put both prisoners away, and they will each get 6 years. And, as noted, if neither testifies, both will get just 1 year of prison time. What's the best thing for each person to do?

In each cell in the following table, the first number is the number of years Butch will spend in prison, and the second is the number that Sundance will spend in prison given the strategies chosen by Butch and Sundance. If years in prison are minuses, then we can write up the problem as in the following table:

		Sundance	
		Keep quiet	Testify
Butch	Keep quiet	(−1, −1)	(−10, 0)
	Testify	(0, −10)	(−6, −6)

a. If Sundance keeps quiet, what's the best choice (highest payoff) for Butch: keep quiet or testify?

b. If Sundance chooses testify, what's the best choice for Butch: keep quiet or testify?

c. What's the best choice for Butch? What's the best choice for Sundance?

d. Using the definition in this chapter, does Butch have a "dominant strategy"? If so, what is it?

e. What is your prediction about what will happen?

f. How does this help explain why the police never put two suspects in the same interrogation room? (Note the similarity between this question and the earlier Adam Smith quote.)

4. Your professor probably grades on a curve, implicitly if not explicitly. This means that you and your classmates could each agree to study half as much, and you would all earn the same grade you would have earned without the agreement. What do you think would happen if you tried to enact this agreement? Why? Which model in this chapter is most similar to this conspiracy?

5. In many college towns, rumors abound that the gas stations in town collude to keep prices high. If this were true, where would you expect this conspiracy against the public to work best? Why?

a. In towns with dozens of gas stations or in towns with fewer than 10?

b. In towns where the city council has many environmental and zoning regulations, making it difficult to open a new gas station, or in towns where there is a lot of open land for development?

c. In towns where all the gas stations are about equally busy or in towns where half the gas stations are always busy and half tend to be empty?

6. Suppose you have clothes that need altering, and you take them to three different tailors in the same business district to get an estimate of the cost of the alterations. All three tailors give you the exact same estimate of $25. What are two different explanations for the similarity of the price quotes? (*Hint:* One is consistent with competition and one is not.)

THINKING AND PROBLEM SOLVING

7. Usually, we think of cheating as a bad thing. But in this chapter, cheating turns out to be a very good thing in some important cases.

a. Who gets the benefit when a cartel collapses through cheating: consumers or producers?

b. Does this benefit usually show up in a lower price, a higher quantity, or both?

c. Does cheating increase consumer surplus, producer surplus, or both?

d. So, is cheating good for the cheaters or good for other people?

8. Firms in a cartel each have an incentive individually to lower the prices they charge.

a. Suppose there was a government regulation that set minimum prices. Would this regulation tend to strengthen cartels, weaken them, or have no effect?

b. Another way that one firm can cheat on a cartel is to offer a higher-quality product to consumers. Suppose there was a government regulation that standardized the quality of a good. Would this regulation tend to strengthen cartels, weaken them, or have no effect?

9. In the late fifteenth century, Europe consumed about 2 million pounds of pepper per year. At this time, Venice (ruled by a small, tightly knit group of merchants) was the major player in the pepper trade. But after Portuguese explorer Vasco da Gama blazed a path around Africa into the Indian Ocean in 1498, Venice found itself competing with Portugal's trade route. By the mid-sixteenth century, Europeans consumed 6 to 7 million pounds per year, much of it through Lisbon. After da Gama's success, the price of pepper fell.

a. During the fifteenth century, was it likely that a cartel was restricting pepper imports? Why or why not?

b. If the price of pepper before 1498 had been lower, would da Gama have been more willing or less willing to sail around South Africa's Cape of Good Hope? Why?

c. What happened in 1498 that turned a successful cartel into a less successful cartel?

d. The ruling merchants of Venice had no political power in other parts of Europe. Why is that important in understanding how European pepper consumption more than tripled in a little more than half a century?

10. In 1890, Senator Sherman (of the Sherman Antitrust Act mentioned earlier) pushed through the legislation that bears his name, which gave the government significant power to "bust up" cartels, presumably in order to increase output.

More than a century later, economist Thomas J. DiLorenzo examined the industries commonly accused of being cartels and found those industries increased output by an average of 175% from 1880 to 1890—seven times the growth rate of the economy at the time.

Suppose the industries were conspiring. Indeed, let's suppose that these cartels grew ever stronger in the decade before the Sherman Act became law. If that were true, would we expect output in these industries to grow by so much? In other words, is DiLorenzo's evidence consistent with the standard story of the Sherman Antitrust Act?

11. In 2005, economist Thomas Schelling won the Nobel Prize in economics, in part for his development of the concept of the "focal point" in game theory. Focal points are a way to solve a coordination game. If two people both benefit by choosing the same option but cannot communicate, they will choose the most obvious option, called the focal point. Of course, what's obvious will vary from culture to culture: whether to wear business attire or just shorts and a T-shirt, whether to use Apple or Microsoft products, whether to arrive at meetings on time or late. In all these cases, having a group agree on one focal point is more important than which particular focal point you all agree on. Therefore, people will look for cultural clues so that they can find the focal point. (*Note:* Schelling wrote two highly readable books that won him the Nobel Prize: *Micromotives and Macrobehavior* and *The Strategy of Conflict.*)

a. Suppose you are playing a game in which you and another player have to choose one of three boxes. You can't communicate with the other player until the game is over. One box is blue and the other two are red. If the two of you choose the same box, you win $50; otherwise, you get nothing. Which box do you choose: the blue box or one of the red boxes? Why?

b. Suppose that you and another player have to write down on a slip of paper *any* price in dollars and cents between $90.01 and $109.83. If you both write down the same price, you'll each win that amount of money. If your numbers don't match, you get nothing. Again, you can't communicate with the other player until the game is over. What number will both of you probably choose?

c. Many "slippery slope" arguments are really stories about focal points. In the United States during debates over banning guns or restricting speech, people will argue that *any* limitation follows a "slippery slope." What do they mean by that? (*Hint:* Attorneys often worry about "gray areas" and they prefer "bright line tests.")

d. Schelling used the idea of the focal point to explain implicit agreements on the limits to war. Poison gas, for example, was not used in World War II and the agreement was largely implicit. Since focal points have to be obvious, explain why there was no implicit agreement that "some" poison gas would be allowed, but "a lot" of poison gas would not be allowed.

12. Suppose the five landscapers in your neighborhood form a cartel and decide to restrict output to 16 lawns each per week (for a total of 80 lawns in the entire market) to keep prices high. The weekly demand curve for lawn-mowing services is shown in the following figure. Assume that the marginal cost of mowing a lawn is a constant $10 per lawn.

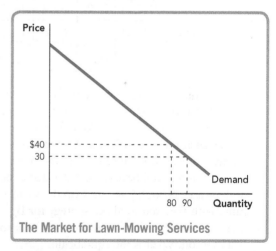

The Market for Lawn-Mowing Services

a. What is the market price under the cartel's arrangement? How much profit is each landscaper earning per week under this arrangement?

b. Suppose one untrustworthy landscaper decides to cheat and increase their own output by an additional 10 lawns. For this landscaper, what is the total increase in revenue from such behavior? What is the marginal revenue per lawn from cheating? Which is higher: the marginal revenue from the extra lawns or the marginal cost?

c. Is it a good idea for the untrustworthy landscaper to cheat? What considerations, other than weekly profit, might enter into the landscaper's decision about whether to cheat?

13. Looking for dominant strategies is a great way to find an equilibrium in many games. However, there are also a lot of games in which this won't work because not all players have dominant strategies. If one player has a dominant strategy but the other doesn't, game theorists remove the first player's dominated strategies (the strategies that are always worse than some other strategy) and then continue to work toward solving the game with what's left. Let's take a look at an example of this. Consider the following payoff table, where the outcomes are written in the form (A's payoff, B's payoff). Each player has four choices, which might make this game seem intimidating, but it's not.

		B's Strategies		
	Red	Blue	Green	Yellow
Red	(1, 3)	(2, 7)	(3, 5)	(4, 6)
Blue	(2, 2)	(3, 2)	(6, 3)	(4, 4)
Green	(3, 2)	(6, 1)	(1, 3)	(3, 2)
Yellow	(4, 0)	(4, 0)	(5, 0)	(5, 1)

A's Strategies (left label)

Start off by trying to figure out whether any player has a strategy that is never best, and then eliminate it. The first one is done for you; no matter what move A makes, B's best response is never to play Red. Since B will never play Red, we don't even have to consider that as part of the game. Next, figure out if (in the smaller game with Red removed as a strategy for B) there's a move A will never make, then back to B, and so on. What is the equilibrium?

		B's Strategies		
	~~Red~~	Blue	Green	Yellow
Red	~~(1, 3)~~	(2, 7)	(3, 5)	(4, 6)
Blue	~~(2, 2)~~	(3, 2)	(6, 3)	(4, 4)
Green	~~(3, 2)~~	(6, 1)	(1, 3)	(3, 2)
Yellow	~~(4, 0)~~	(4, 0)	(5, 0)	(5, 1)

A's Strategies (left label)

CHALLENGES

14. The French economist Antoine Cournot developed an interesting model of competition in an oligopoly that now bears his name. In a Cournot oligopoly, all of the firms know that the total output from all firms will determine the price (based on the downward-sloping market demand curve), but they make independent and simultaneous decisions about how much output to produce. Cournot developed this model after observing how a spring water duopoly (two firms) behaved. So let's look at a duopoly example.

For each firm to decide how much to produce, it must make a guess about how much the other firm is going to produce. Also, the firms basically assume that once the other firm has decided how much to produce, it can't really change its decision.

Here's an example. Suppose the market demand curve for gallons of fresh spring water looks like the one in the next table and, to keep things simple, the marginal cost of spring water is zero. If Firm X believes that Firm Y is going to produce 100 gallons of spring water, for example, then Firm X knows that if it produces 0 gallons, the price will be $2.75; if it produces 100 gallons, the price will be $2.50, and so on. Basically, Firm X will face the market demand curve where all of the quantities are lower by 100.

Market Demand	
Price	Quantity Demanded (gal)
$3.00	0
$2.75	100
$2.50	200
$2.25	300
$2.00	400
$1.75	500
$1.50	600
$1.25	700
$1.00	800
$0.75	900
$0.50	1,000

Based on this demand schedule, calculate the demand schedule that Firm X would face if it suspected Firm Y was going to produce 0, 200, 400, or 600 gallons of spring water. Then, figure out the profit-maximizing amount of spring water for Firm X to produce in response. Fill in the table.

If Firm Y produces . . .	. . . then Firm X should produce . . .
0 gal	
200 gal	
400 gal	
600 gal	

What you have just constructed is what economists would call Firm X's *reaction function.* Even though Firm X thought about the different choices Firm Y could make, Firm Y is not actually going to choose just any random level of output. In fact, Firm Y has its own reaction function, where it considers how best to respond to what it thinks Firm X is doing. Because both firms have the same zero marginal cost, the two reaction functions are symmetrical. (Thus, Firm Y's reaction function looks the same, only with "X" and "Y" switched.)

Graph the two reaction functions. Do you notice any points that stand out? Describe why this point represents an equilibrium for both firms.

15. The following diagram shows the monthly demand for hot dogs in a large city. The marginal cost (and average cost) is a constant $2 per hot dog.

The Market for Hot Dogs

a. If the market for hot dogs is perfectly competitive, how many hot dogs will be sold per month, and at what price? Suppose there are 100 identical firms in this perfectly competitive market. How many hot dogs is each firm selling, and what are the profits for each firm?

b. Suppose the market was almost perfectly competitive, so that each firm has *some* very limited ability to change the price. What would happen if one of the firms in this market reduced its output by one half, and no other firm changed its output? What would happen to the price of a hot dog? How much profit would the firm earn as a result? (*Hint:* You will need to use some of the formulas from Chapter 5 to answer this question.)

c. Discuss the ability of one firm to reduce output and raise the market price if the market for hot dogs was instead an oligopoly made up of four firms, each initially producing 25,000 hot dogs per month. If only one firm reduced its output by half, what would happen to the price of a hot dog? How much profit could this firm potentially earn?

d. Compare your answers for parts b and c. What does this tell you about the ability to earn profits in perfect competition vs. oligopoly?

16. In Chapter 12, we quoted the Austrian economist Joseph Schumpeter, who said that in textbooks the most important fact about competition is that competition pushes price down to marginal cost. However, Schumpeter goes on to say:

> . . . . in capitalist reality as distinguished from its textbook picture, it is not this competition which counts but the competition from the new commodity, the new technology, the new source of supply, the new type of organization . . . competition which commands a decisive cost or quality advantage and which strikes not at the margins of the profits and the outputs of the existing firms but at their foundations and their very lives. This kind of competition is more effective than the other as a bombardment is in comparison with forcing a door, and so much more important that it becomes a matter of

ullstein bild/Getty Images

Joseph Schumpeter (1883–1950) wrote that what was most important in a capitalist economy were the gales of "creative destruction."

comparative indifference whether competition in the ordinary sense functions more or less promptly. . . .

a. Relate Schumpeter's statement to the models of monopoly and oligopoly discussed in this and earlier chapters. In what ways are these market forms inefficient? In what ways might they be efficient or beneficial?

b. The terms *static efficiency* and *dynamic efficiency* are sometimes used in economics. Is there a trade-off between the two types of efficiency? How might we evaluate this trade-off?

WORK IT OUT

For interactive, step-by-step help in solving this problem, go online.

Consider the following demand schedule for Rainbow Looms. Assume that the marginal cost of producing a Rainbow Loom is a constant $2.50.

Price ($/Rainbow Loom)	Quantity Demanded (Rainbow Loom)
$17.50	0
$15.00	12
$12.50	24
$10.00	36
$7.50	48
$5.00	60

a. How many Rainbow Looms would be produced under a Rainbow Loom monopoly?

b. If instead of a monopoly, a two-firm cartel controlled the Rainbow Loom market, how many packs of Rainbow Looms would each firm want to produce in order to maximize industry profits?

c. Determine whether it would be possible for one of the two firms in the cartel to earn higher profits by producing more than the industry profit-maximizing quantity you calculated in part b.

CHAPTER 15 APPENDIX

Nash Equilibrium

The games examples in this chapter can be solved by looking for a dominant strategy, a strategy that is best regardless of what the other player does. Even in simple games, however, there often isn't a dominant strategy. Consider a simple game called the Left, Right game. Olaf and Frida must decide whether to drive their cars on the left side of the road or on the right. The payoff for each combination of choices is illustrated in the payoff matrix in Figure A15-1.

The key point, of course, is that Olaf and Frida have positive payoffs when they both choose Left or when they both choose Right, but it's a disaster when Olaf chooses Left and Frida chooses Right or vice versa. When Olaf and Frida both choose Left, the payoffs are 2,2, and when Olaf and Frida both choose Right, the payoffs are 5,5. But when Olaf and Frida choose different strategies, either {Left, Right} or {Right, Left}, they end up crashing their cars and the payoffs are −10, −10. So what is the equilibrium to this game?

Unlike in the prisoner's dilemma, there is no dominant strategy in this game, no strategy that is best for each player regardless of what the other player does. We can still look for equilibria, however, by drawing on the ideas of John Nash. Nash, who was awarded a Nobel Prize for his contributions to game theory and whose life was featured in the movie *A Beautiful Mind*, defined an equilibrium as a situation in which no player has an incentive to change strategy unilaterally. That is now called a **Nash equilibrium**.

In the Left, Right game, there are two Nash equilibria. Let's start by examining the paired strategies {Left, Left}. Is this a Nash equilibrium? If Frida chooses Left, does Olaf have an incentive to change strategy? No. Olaf earns 2 by choosing Left and −10 by switching to Right, so if Frida chooses Left, then

A **Nash equilibrium** is a situation such that no player has an incentive to change strategy unilaterally.

FIGURE A15.1

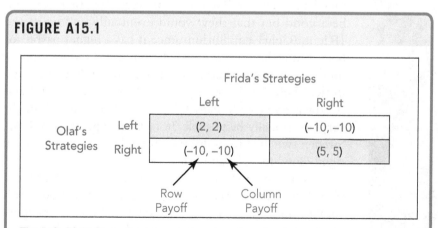

The Left, Right Game Driving on either the left or the right is okay so long as everyone makes the same choice. There are two Nash equilibria in this game: {Left, Left} or {Right, Right}.

Olaf does not have an incentive to change strategy. If Olaf chooses Left, does Frida have an incentive to change strategy? No. Frida earns 2 by choosing Left and −10 by choosing Right, so if Olaf chooses Left, Frida does not have an incentive to switch. Since neither player has an incentive to unilaterally change strategy, {Left, Left} is a Nash equilibrium. By similar reasoning, you should be able to show that {Right, Right} is also a Nash equilibrium.

Is {Right, Left} a Nash equilibrium? If Frida chooses Left, does Olaf have an incentive to change strategy? Yes. Olaf earns −10 by choosing Right and 2 by switching to Left, so if Frida chooses Left then Olaf would have an incentive to change strategy to Left. Since at least one of the parties has an incentive to change strategy, {Right, Left} cannot be a Nash equilibrium (in fact, Olaf and Frida both have an incentive to change but we need show only that one of them has an incentive to change to show that a situation is not a Nash equilibrium). By similar reasoning you should be able to show that {Left, Right} is also not a Nash equilibrium.

If a player can increase their payoff by changing strategy, they probably will change it. So game theory predicts that the outcome of a game will be a Nash equilibrium. If there is more than one equilibrium, however, game theory alone doesn't tell us which equilibrium will be the outcome. In the Left, Right game, {Left, Left} is a Nash equilibrium and so is {Right, Right}, and indeed when we look around the world we see people in some countries driving on the right and in other countries such as Great Britain and Australia driving on the left. Why the difference? Probably nothing more than accidents of history or other random factors.

Coordination On September 3, 1967, the entire country of Sweden switched from driving on the left to driving on the right!

According to the payoff matrix, Olaf and Frida earn 2,2 in the {Left, Left} equilibrium and 5,5 in the {Right, Right} equilibrium. In our world, it is in fact better to drive on the right since more countries drive on the right and more cars are built for driving on the right. If Olaf and Frida were the only two players and if they played this game repeatedly (say they had to choose Right or Left every day), then it would be a good bet that they would eventually end up at the {Right, Right} equilibrium since it has a higher payoff for both. But if there are many Olafs and Fridas and less opportunity for experimentation, the players might become stuck in the {Left, Left} equilibrium, as have Great Britain and Australia. Even with many Olafs and Fridas, a switch might very occasionally be possible. In fact, on September 3, 1967, Sweden switched from driving on the left to driving on the right! Good for Olaf and Frida.

In addition to defining the concept of a Nash equilibrium, John Nash proved that all games have at least one Nash equilibrium (sometimes in what are called mixed strategies, strategies requiring randomization). Thus, the Nash equilibrium concept greatly expanded the number of games that economists could analyze and it has become a standard tool in economics.

Chapter 15 Appendix Questions

1. Cat and mouse is a simple game in which each player can choose either Right or Left. If the cat and mouse both choose Right or both choose Left, however, that is very bad for the mouse but good for the cat. If the cat and mouse choose different strategies, that is good for the mouse but not good for the cat.

   Can you find a Nash equilibrium in this game?

2. Val and Shin are prestigious rival magicians who have developed a new trick that is very popular. If both magicians perform five times a week, each will earn a profit of $6,000. If one magician does a single show while the other does five shows, the former gets a profit of $1,000, and the latter gets a profit of $15,000. If both magicians perform only one show a week, each will earn $10,000.

   a. Use this information to complete the table. (*Hint:* It'll look a lot like Figure 15.4.)

		Shin	
		1 Show	5 Shows
Val	1 Show	,	,
	5 Shows	,	,

   b. Suppose Shin does one show. What is Val's preferred strategy?

   c. Suppose Shin does five shows. What is Val's preferred strategy?

   d. What is Val's dominant strategy?

   e. Suppose Val does one show. What is Shin's preferred strategy?

   f. Suppose Val does five shows. What is Shin's preferred strategy?

   g. What is Shin's dominant strategy?

   h. What is the Nash equilibrium?

   i. Magicians are famously hesitant to reveal the secrets behind their magic, even to other magicians. Based on what you've learned in this question, why do they act like this? Is letting other magicians in on your secrets an optimal strategy?

3. Imagine that two players are competing over a valuable resource. Each player has two options. They can either be aggressive and demand the entire resource, or the player can offer to split the resource equally. The literature uses the word "Hawk" to describe the aggressive behavior and the word "Dove" to describe the sharing behavior. If two Hawks meet, then both will demand the resource, neither will give in, and there will be a fight. If a Hawk meets a Dove, the Hawk will take the resource and the Dove will get nothing. If two Doves meet, the resource will be shared equally.

   Assume that the value of the resource is 60, the cost of losing a fight is 100, and if two Hawks fight, each of them has a 50% chance of losing.

   Here's the payoff matrix:

		B's Strategies	
		Hawk	Dove
A's Strategies	Hawk	,	,
	Dove	,	,

   a. Oops! The payoffs are missing. You'll have to fill them in. Remember, if there's a fight, there is a 50% chance of winning 60 but also a 50% chance of losing the fight, which has a payoff −100. What's the expected outcome? If both animals choose Dove, assume that they peacefully split the resource. If one is a Hawk and the other is the Dove, the Hawk gets the resource, and the Dove receives nothing.

   b. Explain why {Hawk-Dove} and {Dove-Hawk} are both Nash equilibriums.

   c. The Hawk-Dove game is often used to discuss international relations. Can you explain why a country might like to be perceived as a Hawk? What are the dangers of being a Hawk? What are the dangers of being a Dove?

   d. Biologists also use game theory to understand animal behavior, but they interpret the strategies a little differently. Instead of allowing an animal to choose a strategy, they assume that x percent of animals in a population will always play Hawk and $100 - x$ percent of animals in a population will always play Dove, and they also assume that animals will meet randomly.

Biologists argue that if Hawk has an expected higher payoff than Dove, then Hawks will outcompete Doves so that over time, evolution will increase the percentage of animals playing Hawk. Similarly, if Dove has a higher payoff, then over time, evolution will increase the percentage of animals playing Dove.

Can you find a strategy that is *evolutionarily stable*; that is, can you find a strategy where the percentages of animals playing Hawk and Dove are stable over time?

Here are two hints: Let x be the percentage of animals playing Hawk. If 0% of animals play Hawk ($x = 0\%$) and thus all play Dove, is that evolutionarily stable? If all animals play Hawk ($x = 100\%$), is that evolutionarily stable?

16

Networks, Platforms, and the Economics of "Free Goods"

The supply and demand model can explain a tremendous amount of economic activity but it does have difficulty explaining free goods. The monopoly model has even more difficulty explaining free goods since it always predicts a price higher than the competitive market price! Yet, in the modern world, there are many "free" goods such as Facebook, Gmail, and Twitter not to mention some older free goods such as radio and broadcast television. Facebook is a for-profit firm not a charity so we need to understand why a for-profit firm might increase its profits by offering some of its goods and services for free. Fortunately, we have already covered two ideas, externalities and elasticity, which can be used to explain free goods. We will also use these ideas to explain how some types of goods, network goods, naturally tend to result in oligopolies and monopolies and how competition in these markets moves from being "in the market" to being "for the market."

Let's begin with network goods. Tyler likes dark chocolate. Alex likes milk chocolate. If Tyler switches to milk chocolate that doesn't make Alex like or dislike milk chocolate any more than before. But if Tyler switched from Microsoft Word to Google Docs, Alex would be upset. Alex uses Word and likes to write papers with Tyler. If Tyler uses Google Docs that makes it harder for Alex and Tyler to write papers together. Tyler's choice has an external effect on Alex (and vice versa!).

A **network good** is a good that increases in value to a given person the more other people use the good. Word is a network good because the more people use Word, the more valuable Word becomes to other users. Similarly, the more people use WhatsApp or a dating app such as Tinder or OkCupid, the more valuable these services become to other users. If you want to find a date, for example, you probably want to use the dating service that gives you the most choice.

These examples hint at some of the interesting features of network goods that we will be exploring in this chapter. When networks are important, we typically see the following:

Features of Markets for Network Goods

1. Network goods are usually sold by monopolies or oligopolies.
2. When networks are important, the "best" product may not always win.
3. Competition in the market for network goods is "for the market" instead of "in the market."

A **network good** is a good that increases in value to a given person the more other people use the good.

By the way, did you notice the tension between features 1 and 3? Network goods are often sold by monopolies or oligopolies (feature 1), but competition for these markets can be intense (feature 3). In fact, the tension between these features of network-good markets has led to a debate about when the antitrust laws should be applied to network markets and when potential competition alone is enough to discipline monopolies. We will be looking at this debate at greater length in this chapter. Let's look at each of these features in turn.

Network Goods Are Usually Sold by Monopolies or Oligopolies

Microsoft is one of the most profitable corporations on Earth. Most of its profit comes from selling its operating system and software at prices above marginal cost. Microsoft can price above marginal cost not because its products are necessarily the best in some absolute sense but because most people want to use the same software as most other people. Microsoft products are, in most cases, the most likely to be compatible with other products and other readers, writers, and publishers.

The power of coordination in "Office-like" software is so strong that Microsoft can sell millions of Office subscriptions even though there are *free* alternatives such as OpenOffice, Think Free Office, and Google Docs, all of which are roughly similar in quality to Office. But don't make the mistake of thinking that if one of these products became the dominant standard, we would all enjoy free software. The only reason these products are given away for free is that the owners hope to become the dominant standard so that they can charge a high price! Thus, one reason that firms offer products for free is that they want to build up a large user base that increases the value of their product due to network effects. Facebook is already the dominant firm in its industry and it's not likely to start charging anytime soon, however, so this doesn't explain all free goods. We will come back to this point later in the chapter.

Sometimes the pressures for coordination are strong, but other factors mean that more than one firm can compete in the market. eBay is the market leader in online auctions and it uses its market power to charge higher prices than would occur in a standard competitive market. But a handful of other firms in the industry offer slightly different features. Craigslist, for example, is able to compete with eBay because it offers buyers and sellers a way to buy and sell locally, which is especially useful for products that are expensive to ship. As we saw in the previous chapter, a market dominated by a small number of firms is called an oligopoly.

The market for Internet dating is an oligopoly simply because most people want to join large networks with many other people. But it's not a monopoly because Tinder, Bumble, and eHarmony compete with the market leader Match.com by offering different matching algorithms. In addition, there are competing niche services, such as JDate.com (for those looking for a Jewish partner), but notice that JDate dominates its competitors within that niche.

The "Best" Product May Not Always Win

In markets with network goods, it's possible for the market to "lock in" to the "wrong" product or network. We can illustrate using a coordination game as shown in Figure 16.1, similar in structure to the prisoner's dilemma we showed in the previous chapter. Alex and Tyler are choosing whether to use Word or Google Docs to write their textbook. Alex's choices or strategies are the rows, Tyler's are the columns. What Alex and Tyler most want to avoid is making different choices. If Alex chooses Word and Tyler chooses Google Docs, it will be difficult for them to work together so their payoffs will be low, just (3,3). And the same thing is true if Alex chooses Google Docs and Tyler chooses Word. Alex and Tyler receive the highest payoffs if both are using the same software. So, if Alex chooses Google Docs, it will make sense for Tyler to choose Google Docs, and vice versa. In other words, if Alex and Tyler both choose Google Docs, then neither will have an incentive to change their strategy.

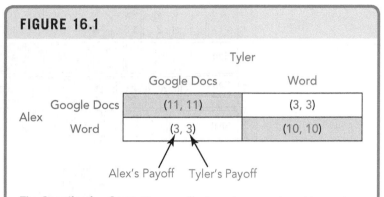

FIGURE 16.1

The Coordination Game The payoffs show the rewards to Alex and Tyler given the combination of strategies that are played. If both Tyler and Alex play Google Docs, neither has an incentive to change strategy. If both Tyler and Alex play Word, neither has an incentive to change strategy. Thus, (Google Docs, Google Docs) and (Word, Word) are both Nash equilibria.

More formally, economists say a situation is an equilibrium if no player in the game has an incentive to change their strategy unilaterally. This is also called a **Nash equilibrium** after John Nash, the mathematician. The outcome (Google Docs, Google Docs) is an equilibrium because neither Alex nor Tyler has an incentive to change their strategy unilaterally, that is, given that Tyler chooses Google Docs, Alex wants to choose Google Docs and vice versa.

But notice that (Google Docs, Google Docs) is not the only equilibrium in this **coordination game**. If Alex chooses Word, then Tyler will also want to choose Word, and vice versa. Thus, (Word, Word) is also an equilibrium strategy. The payoffs to the (Word, Word) equilibrium are slightly lower than the payoffs to the (Google Docs, Google Docs) equilibrium. Nevertheless, (Word, Word) is still an equilibrium because if Alex and Tyler do choose Word, neither will have an incentive to switch. So which equilibrium, (Google Docs, Google Docs) or (Word, Word), will Alex and Tyler end up at?

If Alex and Tyler really are the only players in this game, they could probably talk to each other and coordinate on the best equilibrium, which is (Google Docs, Google Docs). But in reality the coordination game is between Alex, Tyler, and many other people. Coordinating on the best equilibrium is not so easy when many people are involved and when they do not all agree about whether Google Docs really is better than Word. So what will determine the final equilibrium? The classic answer is "accidents of history."

It's an accident of history that computer keyboards are laid out according to the QWERTY design (so named for the keys on the top left side). But is QWERTY the best possible layout for keyboards? According to some studies, a different layout of the keys called the Dvorak design allows for faster and easier typing. So why is the QWERTY design dominant? QWERTY came first, and once people learned to type on a QWERTY keyboard, typewriter manufacturers had an incentive to sell QWERTY typewriters. And, of course, once most manufacturers were selling QWERTY typewriters, it made sense to learn how to type on the QWERTY keyboard. Thus, the QWERTY design became "locked in." If you're wondering, QWERTY is the only way that your authors know how to type.

A **Nash equilibrium** is a situation in which no player has an incentive to change strategy unilaterally.

A **coordination game** is one in which the players are better off if they choose the same strategies than if they choose different strategies, and there is more than one strategy on which to potentially coordinate.

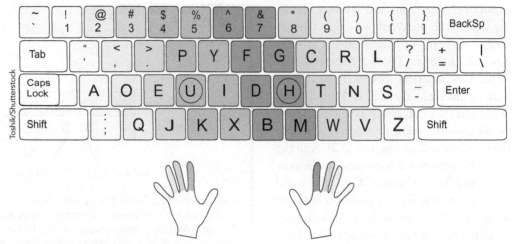

The Dvorak keyboard Would you type faster?

The QWERTY story needs to be taken with a grain of salt, however. The first study showing that the Dvorak layout was better than QWERTY was a 1944 study by the U.S. Navy. But who authored the 1944 study? None other than Lieutenant-Commander August Dvorak. Any guesses as to who created the Dvorak keyboard? Later studies have failed to show big advantages to either keyboard. Thus, it makes sense that few people bother to learn Dvorak even though it's now easy to reprogram a computer keyboard according to any design.*

Competition Is "For the Market" Instead of "In the Market"

Network goods are usually sold by monopolies or oligopolies, but what makes these markets different from standard monopolies and oligopolies is the ease and speed by which the monopoly can change hands. Currently, Facebook is the dominant social network, but not long ago, it was not clear whether MySpace, Friendster, or Facebook would become Number 1. Will Facebook continue its dominance, or will it be supplanted by TikTok, Reddit, or some as yet unknown social media site perhaps operating on a blockchain?

Google looks dominant in search, but many people think that Google results are becoming less useful over time, and they may be vulnerable to competition from search engines with built-in artificial intelligence. Maybe today's dominant firm will be dethroned, maybe not, but it's a mistake to think that a large market share, taken alone, implies that competition is absent. Competition for the market can dethrone market leaders very quickly.

Since Facebook and other network firms could be dethroned by a new entrant, these firms must make choices in light of *potential* competition. Markets in which potential competition disciplines firms are called "contestable." A market is **contestable** if a competitor could credibly enter and take away

> A market is **contestable** if despite the presence of only a few firms the threat of potential competition is enough to make the market behave competitively.

* The QWERTY story was made prominent by David, Paul A. 1985. Clio and the economics of QWERTY. *American Economic Review* 75: 332–337 and is criticized in Liebowitz, Stan J., and Stephen E. Margolis. 1990. The fable of the keys. *Journal of Law & Economics* 33(1): 1–25.

business from the incumbent. Contestability does not require that such entry actually occurs, only that it can potentially occur.

Contestability disciplines an incumbent firm even if the incumbent has a large market share because the mere threat of entry acts as a competitive force. For instance, fear of potential competitors motivates Facebook to keep its prices low (free!) and to keep advertising relatively unobtrusive. To the extent a market, even a network market, is contestable, it is hard for everyone to get locked into the wrong network, as explained previously.

Limiting Contestability with Switching Costs

Facebook, of course, doesn't want its market to be contested. They remember what happened to earlier social network sites like Friendster and MySpace, even if no one else does. So, incumbent firms often try to limit the contestability of the markets they operate in. Facebook, for instance, encourages its users to load as many photos onto the site as possible. The company doesn't charge you for adding more photos, even though the viewing of those photos increases their server costs. Why does Facebook allow so many free photos? In part, they want to attract more users, but it's not just that. Facebook knows that if you load a lot of your photos onto their site, it will be more costly for you to switch to another networking site.

If a new social networking site came along that was 3% better than Facebook, but all your photos were loaded onto your Facebook profile, would you switch? Maybe not. If you haven't kept copies of all those old photos, in a neat and organized way, you are especially unlikely to switch (recall that we gave some other examples of how firms increase switching costs to increase market power in Chapter 15).

Music Is a Network Good

Finally, network products aren't found just in high tech. Most people want to listen to popular music, so music is a network good. If you listen to music that is popular, you can swap songs with your friends, go to concerts together, and talk about the same artists. Thus, popular music is a more valuable good; namely, it offers more benefits to the listener than does obscure music.

In fact, an ingenious experiment by Duncan J. Watts, a sociologist at Columbia University, demonstrated that tastes in music have a strong social component.[1] Watts asked thousands of people to listen to and rate some bands that they had never heard of. If they liked a song, participants could download it for free. The trick was that some of the participants saw only the names of the songs and bands, but others also saw how many times the songs had previously been downloaded by other participants. If tastes in music are independent of what other people are listening to, knowing how many people had previously downloaded a song should be irrelevant. You should just download the songs you like, right?

But Watts discovered that the more downloads a song had, the more people wanted to download the song! So if a few early participants happened to like and download a song, that song got even more downloads. As a result, when participants saw previous downloads, accidents of history turned some songs and bands into big hits, while others languished. Even more surprisingly, when

CHECK YOURSELF

- You change your cell phone provider and get a new cell phone. Why can't you easily move your address list from your old cell phone to your new cell phone?
- Just about everyone uses Google for online searches, so how can we say that Google is in a contestable market?

Watts ran his experiment again and again, the songs that turned into hits were different every time!

So what does this mean? Well, look at two of the principles we outlined for network industries, namely that the best product may not always win and that *potential* competition is often important. You'll find both of those phenomena in music markets. Some bands catch a lucky break and become popular quickly. That popularity feeds on itself so a small head start is turned into a big market advantage even if the band is not necessarily the "best." Was Britney Spears ever that good an entertainer? At the same time there are lots of different entertainers and potential entertainers that compete to be seen as the market leader. Stars can rise or fall quickly depending on public perceptions of popularity. As with other network goods, at any one point in time a handful of entertainers dominate the airwaves and make the most revenues. But a large market share today is no guarantee of popularity in the future, so older stars fear being dethroned by hot, young new stars.

A **platform firm** helps two (or more) sides of a market to connect with one another for mutual gain.

Platform Firms

Facebook's services are free to consumers. So who does pay? Advertisers! Facebook, therefore, really has two types of customers, the readers and the advertisers. To be successful, Facebook must help to connect readers and advertisers for mutual gain. We call a firm that profits by connecting two (or more) sides of a market a **platform firm**. Notice that to succeed Facebook must compete on at least two sides—it must produce a product that appeals to consumers and to advertisers. More generally, a platform firm must compete on more than one side.

Uber is another example of a platform firm because it connects riders and drivers for mutual gain. Similarly, eBay connects buyers and sellers and Airbnb connects renters and homeowners. Older firms such as the *New York Times*, radio stations, and broadcast television also profit by connecting two sides of a market. More examples are given in Figure 16.2.

Platform firms take a cut of the value they create by connecting two sides of a market, so they want to maximize the value of mutually profitable exchanges. OkCupid, for example, profits when it connects people who want to date. OkCupid wouldn't last very long, however, if it connected random people. OkCupid provides value by lowering the transaction cost of finding a *mutually compatible* date. Similarly, Airbnb lowers the transaction cost of connecting people with underused housing with other people who want housing in a specific place at a specific time. Connecting people means lowering the cost of search and can also mean providing each side of the transaction with assurances and guarantees. Airbnb, for example, gives every homeowner who rents through its service a million dollars of homeowner's liability insurance and three million dollars of damage protection insurance, and it gives renters information through photographs, maps, ratings, and reviews.

In a similar way, Uber reduces the transaction costs of connecting drivers to riders. To see the importance of transactions costs, remember that someone wanting a ride could

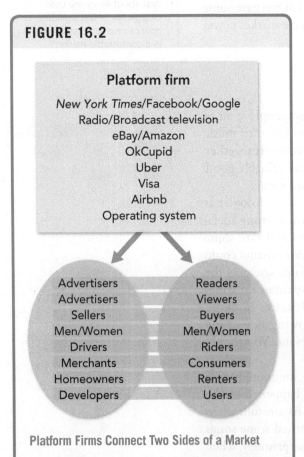

FIGURE 16.2

Platform firm

New York Times/Facebook/Google
Radio/Broadcast television
eBay/Amazon
OkCupid
Uber
Visa
Airbnb
Operating system

Advertisers	Readers
Advertisers	Viewers
Sellers	Buyers
Men/Women	Men/Women
Drivers	Riders
Merchants	Consumers
Homeowners	Renters
Developers	Users

Platform Firms Connect Two Sides of a Market

always flag down a car and try to make a deal with the driver, but before Uber few people did! Uber also offers drivers flexible hours and quick payment while it offers riders a convenient and easy-to-use interface.

Value is created when resources move from low-valued uses to high-valued uses. Airbnb and Uber have created value by reducing transaction costs so that resources such as vacation homes can move from low-value uses (lying empty most of the year) to high-value uses (renting to visitors when the owner isn't in town).

Externalities and Elasticities

To explain platform pricing in more detail let's return to our discussion of externalities. Earlier in this chapter, we discussed consumer-to-consumer externalities. Co-authors want to use the same word processing software. People want to be on the same social media platform as their friends. Consumers want to consume the same music and television shows at the same time so they can be part of the social conversation and so forth. Platform firms have special pricing structures because with two sides of a market, *cross-externalities*, externalities from one side of the market to the other, become important.

A classic example of an externality is getting a flu shot. Getting a flu shot protects you against getting the flu but it also makes it less likely that you will transmit the flu to someone else. Thus, getting a flu shot has a private benefit and a social benefit. The main lesson of Chapter 10 on externalities was that people typically only take into account the private benefit of a flu shot and ignore the social benefit. As a result, there will be too few flu shots. But we also wrote: "A flu shot typically costs about $25–$50 but some firms offer their workers free flu shots." Why might a firm offer their workers free flu shots? Or, to be more pointed, why might a firm that is solely interested in maximizing profit offer its workers a free flu shot?

A worker who gets a flu shot benefits the firm in two ways. First, it makes it less likely that the worker gets sick and that helps the firm avoid medical costs and lost workdays. Second, when a worker gets a flu shot, that makes it less likely that *other* workers get the flu, again saving the firm medical costs and lost workdays. This second advantage could be quite large.

Let's suppose that a worker who gets the flu shot is less likely to get sick and that has an expected savings to the firm of $10. Let's also suppose that by getting the flu shot the worker reduces every other worker's chance of getting the flu by 1/10th as much, so the expected savings to the firm for each *other* worker are $1. Finally, let's assume that there the firm has 100 workers. When a worker gets a flu shot, therefore, the firm benefits by $110 in expectation. Even if the flu shot costs $25, it pays the firm to offer flu shots for free!

The firm is able to increase its profits by offering flu shots for free because it extracts value from the other side of the market—namely, all the other employees who benefit when one worker gets a flu shot. In theory, the worker who gets the flu shot could make a bargain with every other worker and in this way solve the externality problem. But we know from the Coase theorem (Chapter 10) that this will only work when transactions costs are low. The transaction costs of workers bargaining with one another, however, are high. In contrast, the firm is already involved in transactions with all the workers so it can "internalize the externality" at relatively low transaction cost. Figure 16.3 illustrates the basic ideas.

Now let's imagine that one year the flu is especially contagious so that the expected benefit to other employees when one worker gets a flu shot rises from $1 to $1.50. The total benefit to the firm when an employee gets a flu

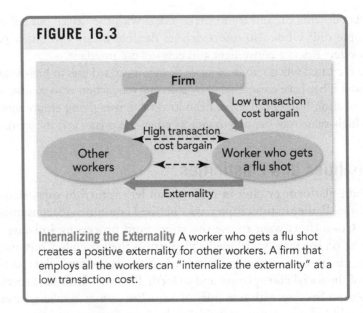

FIGURE 16.3

Internalizing the Externality A worker who gets a flu shot creates a positive externality for other workers. A firm that employs all the workers can "internalize the externality" at a low transaction cost.

shot is now $160 so the firm has an even bigger incentive to subsidize flu shots. Similarly, let's imagine that the firm increases its employees from 100 to 200 (all in the same building). How much does the firm now benefit from an additional employee getting a flu shot? $210. In this case, the firm might even be willing to *pay* its employees a bonus to get a flu shot!

The lesson so far is that the firm will be more willing to subsidize flu shots the greater the total externality to other employees (including both the externality per employee and the number of employees). But how large a subsidy does the firm *have* to give to get an employee to get a flu shot? If employees don't mind getting flu shots, then even a small reduction in the price could be enough to incentivize most employees to get a flu shot. In other words, if the number of flu shots is very elastic with respect to the price, the employer need only offer a small reduction in the price and many more people will get a flu shot. On the other hand, if most employees don't like flu shots, then the demand for flu shots will be inelastic with respect to the price, and the firm will have to reduce the price a lot to get most employees to get a flu shot. Thus, the exact pricing structure that maximizes the employer's profits will depend on the size of the externality and also the elasticity of flu shot demand.

In the next section, we will generalize our example beyond flu shots to platform firms such as Facebook. To give a taste of where we are going, think of the two sides of the market as advertisers and users. Making Facebook free increases the number of users. The users watch ads. Watching ads is like getting a flu shot; it might not be pleasant but it generates value to other people, namely the advertisers. Facebook can extract some of this value by charging the advertisers high prices. As a result, the total Facebook package can be very profitable even when Facebook gives away its consumer product.

Why Platform Firms (Sometimes) Give Services Away for Free

A platform firm chooses its pricing structure to internalize externalities across two sides of a market in a way that maximizes profit. The main difference between platform firms and the flu shot example is that we assumed that the

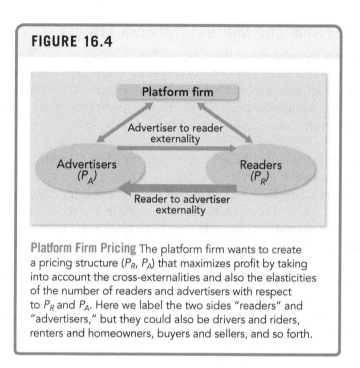

FIGURE 16.4

Platform Firm Pricing The platform firm wants to create a pricing structure (P_R, P_A) that maximizes profit by taking into account the cross-externalities and also the elasticities of the number of readers and advertisers with respect to P_R and P_A. Here we label the two sides "readers" and "advertisers," but they could also be drivers and riders, renters and homeowners, buyers and sellers, and so forth.

employer already has employees whereas the platform firm must bring both sides of the market onboard.

Let's call the two sides a platform must bring onboard advertisers and readers as shown in Figure 16.4. The platform firm lowers transaction costs, allowing the two sides to connect and trade. To maximize its profits, the platform firm sets prices taking into account the cross-externalities (from readers to advertisers and from advertisers to readers) and at the same time, the elasticities of readers and advertisers with respect to their prices, P_R and P_A, respectively. Notice that we have drawn one of the externality arrows larger than the other. This reminds us that the problem is not necessarily symmetric and, of course, the elasticities can be different as well.

Let's give a practical example. Imagine that Facebook begins with a positive price for both readers and advertisers ($P_R > 0$ and $P_A > 0$). Readers, however, are likely to be sensitive to the price so a small decrease in price will cause a large increase in readers (very elastic demand). Thus, imagine that Facebook lowers the price to readers and thus increases the number of readers. With more readers, Facebook can charge its advertisers more, so P_A increases. Indeed, if the demand for advertisers increases enough, it can even pay Facebook to lower the price to readers to zero! Thus, the key to Facebook's decision is how many more readers it will get when it lowers the price (the reader elasticity), how much those readers are worth to advertisers (the externality of readers to advertisers), and how high can it increase the price to advertisers (the advertiser elasticity).

Google, Twitter, and radio and broadcast television all have similar pricing structures to Facebook (free to users and high prices to advertisers) because they face similar externalities and elasticities. Credit cards often involve a similar pricing structure to advertising platforms. Merchants get a bigger externality (sales) from credit card users than vice versa. As a result, credit card users typically get credit cards for free or for a small annual fee and the platform firm (e.g., Visa) makes the bulk of its profits by charging merchants a significant portion of any sale.

Platform Firms and Indirect Network Effects

A **direct network effect** occurs when more side-one users increase the value of the good to other side-one users (Grandma wants to be on Facebook if you are on Facebook).

An **indirect network effect** occurs when more side-one users increase the value of the good to side-two users and more side-two users increase the value of the good to side-one users. (More riders increases the value to drivers, which increases the value to riders.)

Let's conclude by bringing all the topics of this chapter together. We can think of the cross-externalities between the two sides of a platform market as paths that create cross-side network effects. A new Facebook user, for example, increases the value of Facebook to other users (**direct network effect**) and increases the value of Facebook to advertisers (cross-side network effect). If the cross-side network effects are strong in both directions, then new users can even increase the value of the good to other new users *indirectly,* thus creating an **indirect network effect**. Let's explain.

Suppose, for example, that Uber lowers the price of rides. A lower price for rides increases the number of Uber riders, which increases the value of being an Uber driver, since drivers can find fares more quickly the more riders use the system. But more Uber drivers increase the value of Uber to riders, who can now find rides more quickly. Thus, when the price of rides falls the number of riders increases and that increases the number of drivers and that makes Uber more useful, which increases the number of riders! In other words, the fall in the price of rides creates an indirect network effect—from riders to drivers and then from drivers to riders. As with direct network effects, indirect network effects mean that firms such as Uber can grow very rapidly and quickly come to dominate a market.

If this all sounds complicated, that's because it is! Maximizing profits at a platform firm is much more difficult than producing until $P = MC$. The platform firm must bring both sides of the market on board and make it easy for the sides to connect in mutually profitable ways.

A key tool for the platform is its pricing structure. The platform firm chooses a *pricing structure*, in which one side of the market pays higher prices and the other side pays lower prices, prices that may even be lower than costs. The pricing structure depends in a complicated way on the size of the externalities and the relative size of the price elasticities and these in turn depend on the size of direct and indirect network effects. We put it all together in Figure 16.5.

Antitrust and Regulation of Platform Firms

In 2019, the U.S. Federal Trade Commission and Department of Justice—the nation's federal antitrust authorities—announced they would begin an investigation into possible anticompetitive practices at major tech companies, including Facebook, Google, Amazon, and Apple. These have been some of the most successful and most innovative U.S. companies, but some critics charge they have become too large and that they are stifling American privacy and also innovation.

As we are writing this book, the investigation has just begun, but one possible issue is horizontal acquisitions. Facebook is the leading site for social networking. In 2012 Facebook acquired Instagram, which is the leading site for photo-based social networking, and in 2014 Facebook acquired WhatsApp, one of the leading personal messaging services, which you can think of as another form of social networking. The critics charge that Facebook is buying up potential competitors to maintain its dominant position in the market, and some individuals have argued that Facebook should be forced to divest both Instagram and WhatsApp.

It is not obvious how strong this antitrust case will be. Facebook gives away social networking services, and rather than restricting output it tries to get as many people on its platform as possible. Furthermore, Instagram and WhatsApp are also free access services, and Facebook has invested a good deal of money to make those services work better and with greater security. At least as of this

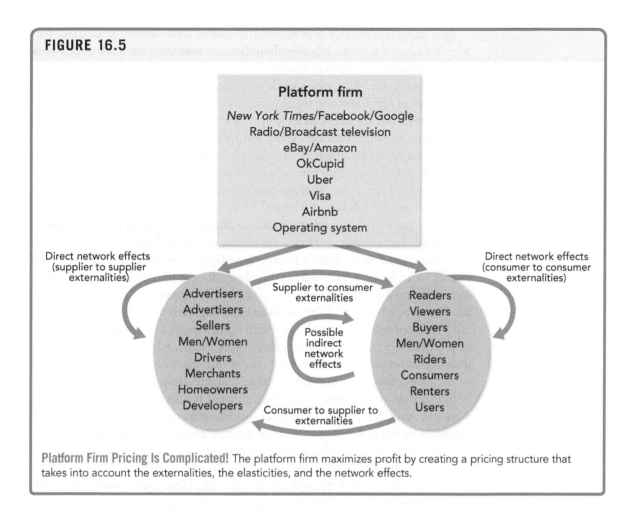

FIGURE 16.5

Platform firm

New York Times/Facebook/Google
Radio/Broadcast television
eBay/Amazon
OkCupid
Uber
Visa
Airbnb
Operating system

Direct network effects
(supplier to supplier
externalities)

Supplier to consumer
externalities

Direct network effects
(consumer to consumer
externalities)

Advertisers
Advertisers
Sellers
Men/Women
Drivers
Merchants
Homeowners
Developers

Possible
indirect
network
effects

Readers
Viewers
Buyers
Men/Women
Riders
Consumers
Renters
Users

Consumer to supplier to
externalities

Platform Firm Pricing Is Complicated! The platform firm maximizes profit by creating a pricing structure that takes into account the externalities, the elasticities, and the network effects.

writing, there are no advertisements on WhatsApp, as in essence the quality of that service is cross-subsidized through the advertisements sold and placed on Facebook and Instagram.

Critics, on the other hand, charge that if Facebook had to compete with independently owned Instagram and WhatsApp services, the market would be more dynamic and innovative. That is a judgment that will likely prove difficult to assess, but the regulators will be considering it. Splitting up Facebook also might increase the number of significant participants in online advertising markets, where currently Facebook and Google are larger than all other outlets.

One dilemma facing the antitrust authorities is that we know the market for network goods will be dominated by a handful of firms. Thus, the question is not monopoly versus competition (in the sense of competition from many firms in the market), but rather it is one dominant firm (or perhaps two or three) versus another. It's not obvious that consumers are worse off when Facebook is the big player compared with an independent Instagram or some other company being the big player.

What is important is that competition *for the market* is not impeded. There are in fact other social networking services ready to expand their market share if Facebook falters, and those include various gaming sites, Snapchat, Twitter, and simply texting people through your phone, not to mention making phone calls and simply hanging out with your friends. How dominant a position you ascribe to Facebook, and indeed significant firms in many other contexts, will depend on how broadly you understand the relevant market.

As a general rule, U.S. regulatory authorities have distrusted bigness. But whether large, dominant firms—when they are supplying network goods—are bad for consumers is another matter.

Although price regulation can be difficult, platform firms sometimes make other types of regulation and social policy easier. It's long been known, for example, that taxis are less likely to pick up Blacks than whites and are less likely to serve minority neighborhoods. Uber and Lyft drivers, however, don't know the race of their passenger until they have agreed to the pickup. Moreover, the fear that both drivers and riders may have when a stranger offers another stranger a ride is greatly diminished using a rideshare app because the app knows who the passenger and driver are and when and where they are picked up. As a result, ride-sharing firms have greatly reduced discrimination in this part of the transportation market.[2]

Similarly, homeowners renting their homes on Airbnb have a legitimate reason to be concerned about who is renting their homes. No one wants a guest who doesn't clean up or who conducts illegal activities. Unfortunately, homeowners sometimes used profile photographs of prospective guests to discriminate against Black renters, which is a violation of the Civil Rights Act of 1964. To combat this kind of discrimination, Airbnb prevented homeowners from seeing photographs of prospective renters until after a booking is confirmed. The solution reduced discrimination although, to be clear, it did not eliminate discrimination. One study, for example, sent out thousands of rental requests and found that people with Black-sounding names were discriminated against even when photographs were not available.[3] People with Black-sounding names were not discriminated against, however, if they had at least one positive review from a previous rental.

The point is not that platforms are necessarily less discriminatory. The point is that by centralizing exchange on a single platform there is a much greater ability to enforce equal treatment through code. Uber and Airbnb have much greater opportunities to reduce ride and rental discrimination than was possible when taxis and homeowners made millions of individual decisions to pick up passengers or rent their homes. It's also true, of course, that firms like Uber and Airbnb could enforce discriminatory policies. Uber, for example, could prevent anyone from using its services anywhere in the world just by flagging an account in its database. That would have been basically impossible in the era of cash payment and taxis.

Indeed, for better or worse, one trend in modern life is that regulation is becoming less a product of government and more a product of platform firms. Uber and Airbnb policies toward discrimination will often be more powerful than governmental policies. Similarly, Facebook has more users than any country has citizens. Thus, debates about Facebook's policies on say pornography or Twitter's policies on free speech are replacing debates that used to occur in the Supreme Court.

Takeaway

Network goods exist when a good increases in value to a given person the more other people use the good; Microsoft Word and Facebook are examples. In these markets, we usually find monopolies or oligopolies because services with lots of users attract even more users. Since networks often grow rapidly and offer significant revenue potential, many entrepreneurs will try to be the dominant seller. Thus, competition switches from being in the market to being for the market.

Sometimes customers will end up "locked in" to the wrong network, or at least users will disagree as to whether the better network has won out. There is a coordination problem involved in switching from one network to another, since virtually everyone must make a coordinated change. Businesses often take actions to deliberately increase switching costs. The end result is that often not everyone is happy with the dominant network.

Still, network markets often are highly competitive, as different firms compete to be the dominant player. This competition induces them to upgrade their products, make them more convenient, and introduce innovations. It is common that a new market leader will leapfrog the old leader and replace it. The more contestable the market, the greater the incentive for product improvement and the less likely that customers will be locked into the wrong network.

Platform firms reduce transaction costs, making it easier for two sides of a market to find mutually profitable transactions. Platform firms profit by taking a cut of the transaction value that they help to create. Platform firms often have interesting pricing structures because they can use their pricing structure to internalize externalities. A platform firm, for example, may offer one side of the market free goods and earn profit with a higher price on the other side of the market. The profit-maximizing pricing structure will depend in a complicated way on the externalities and elasticities that exist across all sides of the market. When the cross-externalities are strong in both directions, an indirect network effect may be created.

CHAPTER REVIEW

Go online to practice with more examples of these types of problems, including live links to videos, data sources, and feedback.

KEY CONCEPTS

network good, p. 323

Nash equilibrium, p. 325

coordination game, p. 325

contestable markets, p. 326

platform firm, p. 328

direct network effect, p. 332

indirect network effect, p. 332

FACTS AND TOOLS

1. Antitrust laws make certain "anticompetitive" practices illegal because these practices raise prices and reduce output, which reduces the total amount of consumer surplus. Explain why antitrust action may not be helpful or necessary in markets that are:

   a. Characterized by network goods

   b. Highly contestable

2. Explain the difference between competition "in the market" and competition "for the market." What impact does each kind of competition have on prices and output in a market? Is one better

than the other? How does the distinction make the application of antitrust laws more complicated?

3. LinkedIn is an online professional networking site, much like Facebook, except that it's for connecting with classmates and colleagues to create networks that may be helpful in, among other things, finding job opportunities. The site boasts approximately half a billion members and claims to be the "world's largest professional network on the Internet." What made LinkedIn the largest professional network site? Since it is already the largest, does that mean LinkedIn will always be the largest? Why or why not?

4. For each of the following pairs, determine which business is more likely to operate in a contestable market, and explain why.

   a. The only clothing store in a small town vs. the only natural gas provider in a small town

   b. The only clothing store in a small town vs. the only cable TV provider in a small town (What recent technologies make part b different from part a?)

   c. De Beers diamond mining vs. Intuit TurboTax tax preparation services

5. In the following three games, is each a coordination game or a prisoner's dilemma?

The best way to check is to see if there is exactly one Nash equilibrium; another way is to see if there is a dominant strategy for each player. To keep it a little challenging, we won't give the actions obvious labels that might give away the answer. Higher numbers are always better:

a.

		Player B	
		Left	Right
Player A	Up	(3, 3)	(5, 5)
	Down	(5, 5)	(1, 1)

b.

		Player B	
		Left	Right
Player A	Up	(100, 100)	(600, 50)
	Down	(50, 600)	(500, 500)

c.

		Player B	
		Left	Right
Player A	Up	(8, 6)	(7, 5)
	Down	(3, 0)	(9, 9)

6. The mantra of Amazon.com CEO Jeff Bezos is "Get big fast." As we saw in Chapter 13 on monopoly, one reason to "get big fast" is because in some industries the firm's average cost will plummet as the firm expands—so size helps on the supply side. In this chapter, network effects illustrated how size helps on the demand side. With this in mind, explain the following real-world drives to get big fast: Do you think it's mostly about increasing returns or mostly about network effects? Explain why:

   a. Second Life, an online virtual world, lets people use many of its features for free. To use the best features, you have to pay.

   b. Likewise, Tinder, the dating app, is free to download and use. However, you can pay for additional features, such as "Super Likes" and Boosts and the ability to message users before matching with them.

   c. Adobe Acrobat Reader is free, but the software to create sophisticated Adobe documents is not.

   d. King Gillette (real name) gave away his first disposable razor blades in 1885. They came free with the purchase of a box of Cuban cigars.

   e. Amazon.com itself.

7. State whether each of the following events will increase or decrease the contestability of a market:

   a. New legal restrictions are placed on entering a market.

   b. The number of food trailer permits increases.

   c. A student posts open-source code—allowing anyone full access—for a project.

   d. A brand starts to reward consumers for loyalty.

   e. Multiple firms are allowed to use the same distribution network.

THINKING AND PROBLEM SOLVING

8. If you get a crack in your windshield, you can take your car to an auto glass repair shop where they will gladly try to repair your windshield, so you can avoid having to replace it. They guarantee their work, too; if the repair is not successful, they will allow you to apply the money you already paid for the unsuccessful repair toward the purchase of a new windshield. Sounds terrific, but how does this strategy relate to the material in the chapter? If all auto glass repair shops employ this strategy, what impact do you think this has on the price of a new windshield?

9. Every so often, rumors float around claiming that Facebook is going to begin charging its users a small monthly fee. So far, those rumors have always turned out to be false.

   a. Do you have a Facebook account? If so, how much would you be willing to pay per month for access to Facebook? (If you don't use Facebook, how much do you imagine the typical user would be willing to pay to use it? Or how much would you be willing to pay to use your preferred social media app?)

   b. Besides the price itself, what else would determine whether it was worth it to you to pay for Facebook? Is your response independent of others' responses?

   c. Do you think Facebook ever will charge users a fee? What are some reasons Facebook might do this? What are some arguments against this idea?

10. Deciding which side of the road to drive on is a kind of coordination game. In some countries, people drive on the right side of the road, and in other countries (notably the United Kingdom and some of its former colonies, as well as Japan), they drive on the left. These customs developed hundreds of years ago. If there were a single world standard, car companies could save some money by not having to produce both left and right types, and cars would be a little bit cheaper. Why do you think it is that these customs persist? In other words, what keeps the world "locked in" to two separate kinds of cars? (Interestingly, there is some research suggesting that driving on the left side is slightly safer than driving on the right. Now that you know this, will you start driving on the left the next time you drive? Why not? This example helps provide some nice intuition to the mechanics of the coordination game.)

11. Consider the shipping container (the large box that stacks on cargo ships and attaches to trucks). If all containers are the same size and design, then the container can pass seamlessly between ships, trains, trucks, and cranes along the way. Today, the standard dimensions are 8 feet wide, 8.5 feet tall, and 40 feet long. (The 2008 book *The Box* by Marc Levinson tells the surprisingly gripping tale of how this size came to be the standard and how it has cut the cost of shipping worldwide.) Let's see how this standard dimension illustrates the meaning of "Nash equilibrium."

    a. Suppose an inventor created a new shipping container that was slightly cheaper to make, as well as stronger, but it *had* to be 41 feet long. Keeping the idea of standardization in mind, would this inventor be successful? Why or why not?

    b. Suppose a container manufacturer reduced the strength of the end walls of their containers (saving $100 per container made). Although this makes no difference to containers on a ship, containers on a train are at risk as the container bumps against the flatcar when the train hits the brakes. Who would tend to oppose these weaker, cheaper containers: the company whose products are stored in the container, the train companies who transport the goods, or both?

    c. Why does Federal Express, the overnight delivery company, require everyone to use FedEx packaging for most shipments?

12. Suppose a friend is taking an economics course at another college or university, and their professor uses a different textbook. Your friend, after learning about monopolies and the lost gains from trade that result from monopolies, becomes very agitated about firms with market power and makes this statement: "It should be strictly forbidden for any company, in any market, to have more than 50% market share—market power like this always leads to higher prices, deadweight loss, and inefficiency!" After you calm your friend down, how would you respond to this statement? Is your friend right?

13. Mall developers charge rent to the retailers who sell in the mall. The largest stores often receive the *lowest* rental price per square foot. Why might a mall developer set rental prices in this way? (*Hint:* Think of the mall developer as a platform firm that connects retailers and consumers.)

14. It's always been possible to flag down a car and try to make a mutually profitable deal for a ride, but before Uber this didn't happen very often. Why not? Describe some of the methods Uber uses to make these transactions possible and how this unlocks value.

15. Suppose that Uber created a way to advertise to riders. For example, riders might watch an advertisement as their car approaches. What do you predict would be the impact on the price of an Uber ride. Why?

CHALLENGES

16. Why doesn't everyone just switch to one language?

17. Nobel Laureate Paul Krugman once asked, "Who would enter a demolition derby without the incentive of a prize?" (Source: Krugman, Paul. 1998. Soft microeconomics: The squishy case against you-know-who. *Slate*. www.slate .com/id/1933/. Posted April 24, 1998.) (And for those who don't know, a demolition derby is a competition where drivers deliberately crash into the competing vehicles with the goal of making the vehicles inoperable. The last car left moving is the winner. Search for "demolition derby" on YouTube for plenty of fun examples.)

    a. The "demolition derby" he was talking about was the battle over Internet browsers: Many enter the battle, but only one (or two) survive. But let's take his story literally: If there were

MySpace?

Mindy Schauer/ZUMApress/Newscom

two cars in a demolition derby, each car costs $20,000 to build, and one car will be totally destroyed, how big will the prize probably have to be to get two people to enter if there's a 50–50 chance of losing all your investment?

b. What if we want a really good demolition derby: one where 10 of these cars compete but only one survives. About how big will the prize have to be now?

c. Let's draw the lesson for network goods: Since competition in network good markets is competition "for the market," then it's like winning a prize in a demolition derby. If there's a fixed price of starting up a new social network (you need so many computers, so many nerds, so many advertisers), then when would you see a lot of firms competing for the prize: when the prize is large or when the

prize is small? Thus, if we want a lot of competition *for the market,* do we necessarily want to restrict the profits of the winner?

18. The market for college textbooks is an interesting one. One thing that makes it unique is that the person who chooses the textbook (the professor) is not the person who purchases the textbook (the student). Therefore, much of a textbook publishing company's marketing is geared toward college professors. Most publishers of economics textbooks have developed (or have partnered with other companies to provide) online course-management systems. This textbook has one, as you may already know if your professor is using it. Explain how a course-management system might benefit a professor. What impact might a course-management system have on switching costs?

19. Bars and clubs sometimes offer "ladies' nights" where women are allowed in for free or given discounted drinks. Is this practice unfair to men? Can you think of an economic explanation for this practice?

20. Imagine that there are two television networks, the Wolf network and the Peacock network. At first, their audiences are similar and many people switch between networks depending on what's on that evening. Over time, however, the networks begin to differentiate so that some people watch only the Wolf network and other people watch only the Peacock network. In other words, each network develops a monopoly on its audience. As the networks differentiate, describe what happens to the prices charged to advertisers and viewers of the two networks.

WORK IT OUT

For interactive, step-by-step help in solving this problem, go online.

Prisoner's dilemmas are common in real life, but not all real-life games are as dismal as the prisoner's dilemma. One game, known as "stag hunt," describes situations where cooperation is possible but fragile. The philosopher Jean-Jacques Rousseau described the game. He said that a lot of social situations are like going hunting with a friend: If you both agree to hunt for a large male deer (a stag), then you each have to hold your positions near each end of a valley so that the animal can't escape. If you both hold to your positions, then you will almost surely get your kill. If one hunter wanders off to hunt the easier-to-find rabbit, however, then the stag will almost surely get away. Rabbit hunting works fine as a solo sport, but to catch a deer, you need a team effort. This is the usual way of writing the game:

		Hume	
		Hunt Stag	Hunt Rabbit
Rousseau	Hunt Stag	(5, 5)	(0, 3)
	Hunt Rabbit	(3, 0)	(3, 3)

a. If Rousseau is quite sure that Hume will hunt stag, will he also hunt stag?

b. If Rousseau is quite sure that Hume will hunt rabbit, will Rousseau still hunt stag?

c. There are two Nash equilibria here: What are they? (Check by looking in each box and asking, "Would one player unilaterally change their choice between rabbit and stag?" If so, this isn't an equilibrium.)

d. Of these two equilibria, economists call one the "payoff-dominant equilibrium" and the other the "risk-dominant equilibrium." You can figure out which is which by the process of elimination. What do you think is the biggest risk that might push someone to choose the "risk-dominant equilibrium"?

e. Is this a coordination game or is there a dominant strategy?

f. In the coordination games we looked at in previous questions, if you failed to coordinate, things turned out badly. Is that the case here?

g. Anytime someone says, "I'll do it as long as I'm not the only one," they're probably describing a stag hunt. Wearing a cocktail dress to a dinner party, making a solid team effort, keeping your lawn mowed—all might be examples of stag hunts. In a stag hunt, if you think the other players are nice, then you'll want to be nice yourself. But if you suspect they're not nice, you'll probably just be a "rugged individualist" and go hunt the rabbit on your own. With this in mind, think of two more examples of stag hunt situations on your own.

(For an excellent, somewhat technical treatment of how people might agree to hunt stag across many areas of life, see Skyrms, Brian. 2004. *The Stag Hunt and the Evolution of Social Structure*. Cambridge, UK: Cambridge University Press. Skyrms is a philosopher who uses the tools of game theory to investigate important social questions.)

17

Monopolistic Competition and Advertising

You can find a mystery at Amazon.com. In fact, you can find thousands of mysteries, including novels by Colleen Hoover, Stephen King, and George R. R. Martin. What we have in mind, however, is a different but closely related economic puzzle or mystery.

In some ways, the market for books appears to be very competitive. There are lots of choices and very few barriers to entry. Authors today, for example, don't even need access to an expensive printing press because they can "print" their books electronically and sell them on Amazon alongside books from established publishers like HarperCollins. Yet even though the market appears competitive, prices are above marginal cost. It doesn't cost $18 to print the latest Stephen King novel, even including delivery, and it certainly doesn't cost $11.99 to deliver the book electronically to a Kindle or iPad. Why are prices higher than marginal cost in a market with lots of choices and few barriers to entry?

In other ways, however, the market for books looks like a monopoly. Anyone can sell mysteries but only Stephen King can sell Stephen King novels. In fact, copyright law makes it a crime for anyone else to sell a Stephen King novel until 70 years after his death! Thus, there is a significant barrier to entry for selling Stephen King novels. True, it is legal to write and sell mysteries in the style of Stephen King but many readers find that Stephen King substitutes are just not as horrifying as the real thing. As a result, Stephen King faces a downward-sloping demand curve and he is not forced to price at marginal cost.

In this chapter, we will be looking at a type of market structure that combines some features of competitive markets with some features of monopoly, namely **monopolistic competition**. Monopolistic competition describes a market with the following features:

- *Many sellers:* There are lots of firms in the market and lots of potential firms.
- *Free entry:* Firms can enter or exit the market without restriction. As a result, firms will enter when $P > AC$ and exit when $P < AC$ so, just as with competitive markets, in the long run profits are driven to zero (normal profits) with $P = AC$.
- *Product differentiation:* Each firm produces a product that is somewhat different from its competitors. Thus, each firm faces a downward-sloped demand curve.

Monopolistic competition is a market with a large number of firms selling similar but not identical products.

341

Perfectly competitive markets also feature many sellers and free entry so what makes monopolistic competition different is the final feature, product differentiation. Recall our example of a perfectly competitive market, the market for oil. If you owned a small oil well, you would face a perfectly elastic demand curve because one seller's oil is pretty much the same as another seller's oil. As we said in Chapter 11, even your mother probably wouldn't pay extra for your oil.

But instead of owning a small oil well, suppose you owned a small restaurant. There are many sellers in the restaurant business and there is free entry, but the food in your restaurant will probably be a little bit different from the food in other restaurants. Indeed, some of your customers might be willing to pay a bit extra to eat in your restaurant compared with the next best substitute. As a small restaurant owner, if you raise your prices a little, you will lose some but not all of your customers, and if you lower prices a little, you will sell more but you won't suddenly find yourself with lines out the door. In other words, unlike the owner of a small oil well, as a small restaurant owner, you would face a downward-sloping demand curve.

Sources of Product Differentiation

Products can be differentiated along any dimension that people care about, such as taste, style, features, or location.

Taste is one obvious source of product differentiation. McDonald's, Burger King, and Wendy's all sell hamburgers but most people have a favorite among the three. Coca-Cola and Pepsi both produce cola but if Coca-Cola raised its prices by 5 cents it wouldn't lose all of its customers. Style is also a source of product differentiation. Levi's, 7 For All Mankind, and American Eagle all produce denim jeans but some people do not regard these products as close substitutes. Apple, Motorola, and Samsung all produce cell phones with different styles and also a range of slightly different features, and most people are not indifferent to all the choices. Even when consumers are indifferent about the brand, such as Shell versus Chevron gasoline, they might prefer one gasoline station simply because it is closer or more convenient.

Products can also be differentiated by location or by ease of purchase. The milk at 7-Eleven, for example, is the same milk as at your local grocery store but usually it's a bit more expensive. Why? Although the milk is identical, it can be more convenient to buy it at 7-Eleven (hence the name "convenience store"), especially if you are already buying gas. The different location and the bundling of milk and gas make milk at 7-Eleven a slightly different product from milk at the grocery store, so prices can be slightly different.

Ease of purchase can also make a surprisingly big difference in how willing people are to buy. Your authors buy a lot of books, but we don't always search to find the lowest price. Instead, we are more likely to find something on Amazon and hit "Buy now with 1-Click." We could save some money by searching Barnes & Noble, Walmart, and other stores but we are willing to pay a little bit extra for the convenience.

You might also have noticed one other feature about differentiated products—they are often highly advertised. Firms want consumers to perceive their products as different and better because that increases their market power. Advertising, therefore, isn't just about informing consumers about price and availability. It can also be used to increase perceptions of product differentiation. We will say much more about advertising later in this chapter.

The Monopolistic Competition Model

Monopolistic competition takes the standard model of monopoly but allows for the free entry of competing business firms. To see how this works, let's imagine the economic situation for the very first Chinese restaurant in our town of Fairfax, Virginia. In the short run, the first Chinese restaurant would use its market power to make profits, much like a monopoly. Unlike a monopoly, however, those profits would attract more entrants.

As more restaurants open, the demand curve facing the former monopolist shifts down and to the left, as some of the previous customers start patronizing other restaurants. In Figure 17.1 we show this process.

We begin on the left when the first Chinese restaurant in Fairfax has a monopoly. As you know, a monopoly maximizes profit by producing the quantity such that $MR = MC$. Profit is given by $(P - AC) \times Q$ and is shown by the green rectangle. All of this is exactly the same as for monopoly discussed in Chapter 13. The difference comes in the long run. No barriers to entry prevent an entrepreneur from starting a new Chinese restaurant in Fairfax so monopoly profits attract entry. Entry reduces the demand for the original restaurant. The firm continues to make profits so long as price is greater than average cost, $P > AC$, but that means entry occurs so long as $P > AC$. The end result is that the demand curve is driven to the left and down until it becomes tangent to (just touching) the average cost (AC) curve. At this point, $P = AC$ and each firm in the industry is earning zero economic profits.

It's the entry of competing business firms that drives the move from the left side of Figure 17.1 to the right side. Indeed, Google lists hundreds of restaurants in or near Fairfax as serving some form of Chinese food.

FIGURE 17.1

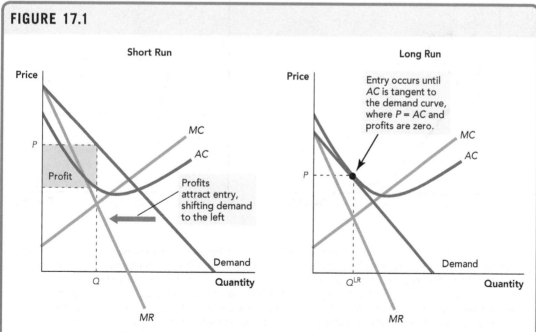

Monopolistic Competition In the short run, a firm in monopolistic competition can make profits exactly like a monopolist. In the long run, however, entry occurs, shifting the demand curve to the left/down until the demand curve is tangent to the AC curve. At this point the firm produces Q^{LR} and makes zero profits but $P > MC$.

Although producers under monopolistic competition don't earn above-normal profits, they still are charging prices above marginal cost, $P > MC$, as you can see in the right panel of Figure 17.1. When $P > MC$, output is not at the efficient level. Remember that the price P measures the value to consumers of one additional meal, and the MC curve at Q^{LR} tells us the cost of producing one additional meal. Thus, when $P > MC$, the value of an additional meal exceeds the cost of an additional meal and social surplus would be higher if the firm produced more. Production under monopolistic competition, just as with monopoly, is not perfectly efficient.

A monopolistic competitive firm is able to charge $P > MC$ because its product is slightly different from the product of other firms. Your authors have a favorite Chinese restaurant in Fairfax—China Star. It's where we take visitors to the university for lunch. The food there is spicier and the menu has some tasty dishes, such as scallion fried fish, that you can't find elsewhere. Call us fussy if you like, but such features are specific examples of what is called product differentiation. Since there are no perfect substitutes for China Star, it can price its scallion fried fish above marginal cost and yet not lose us as customers. Product differentiation also means that under monopolistic competition, a firm does not produce at the minimum of its AC curve. To see this in a picture, Figure 17.2 compares long-run output under monopolistic competition (on the left) with that under competition (on the right).

FIGURE 17.2

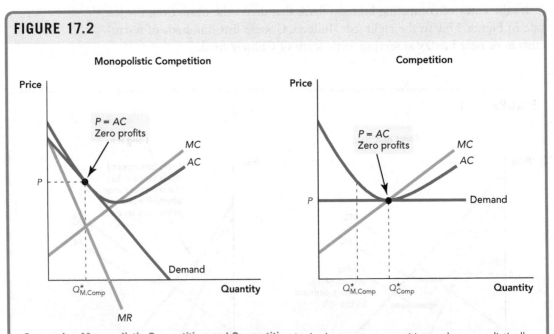

Comparing Monopolistic Competition and Competition In the long run, competitive and monopolistically competitive firms produce where $P = AC$ and earn zero profits. Each firm in monopolistic competition offers a slightly different product and so each firm faces a downward-sloping demand curve. As a result, firms under monopolistic competition charge prices above marginal cost, they produce a smaller quantity compared with competitive firms, and $Q^*_{M.Comp}$ is not at minimum average cost. In the case of competitive firms, each firm produces exactly the same product so there are perfect substitutes for each firm's products. As a result, the demand curve is perfectly elastic, production quantity is higher than under monopolistic competition, and output is at the point that minimizes average costs.

Note that for comparison we show the monopolistic competition output level, $Q^*_{M.Comp}$, and the competitive output level, Q^*_{Comp}, in the right panel.

A competitive firm, sometimes also called a perfectly competitive firm, produces a product like oil that has perfect substitutes. As a result, the firm can't control the price of its product, and just to earn zero profits, it must produce at the output level that minimizes average costs. A monopolistic competitive firm produces a slightly different product than its competitors, and so it can reduce output and raise the price without losing all of its customers. But when a monopolistic competitive firm reduces output, it no longer produces at the minimum of its average cost curve.

Is Monopolistic Competition Inefficient?

Although monopolistic competitive firms don't produce at the minimum of their average cost curves, an offsetting advantage is the possibility of greater dynamism and product variety. If a restaurant comes up with a new recipe, for example, or some new and interesting décor, the demand curve for that restaurant's product will shift up and to the right and that restaurant will enjoy higher profits. Or consider the market for books introduced at the beginning of the chapter. Books are priced at higher than marginal cost but there is a continual stream of authors who are trying to innovate and become the next Stephen King or J. K. Rowling. Although monopolistic competitive industries feature some market power, usually in the longer run, consumers are better off from the new products and the better matching of products to tastes.

We can see both the benefits and the costs of monopolistic competition in the market for drinking water. Water is simple: It's uniform, and it's often available for free. So who would imagine that you could sell water by the bottle for billions of dollars? And yet bottled water products like Dasani, Fiji, and Voss sell more than $100 billion worth worldwide. The fact that there are many producers of bottled water means that the average costs of production is not minimized—bottled water would be cheaper if we could consolidate production in just a few firms, each of which would produce more. (And it would be even cheaper if we just used tap water.) On the other hand, many people do have a favorite brand of water so the product variety and experimentation of the industry does create value. Yes, sometimes we think this is a bit absurd—we have seen people buy bottled water at a restaurant instead of tap water even when the bottled water comes from exactly the same source! On the other hand, mineral water, sparkling water, and flavored waters, not to mention soft drinks, coffee, and tea (all mostly water), are different and it's hard to say how different is different enough to justify the extra costs.

Keep in mind also that the market is a discovery process. Consumers may not even know that they want a product until entrepreneurs test the market and make new discoveries. Who knew that consumers would love milk shakes blended with coffee? Starbucks, however, has made millions selling Frappuccinos.

As inefficiencies go, the fact that average cost is not minimized under monopolistic competition is typically considered fairly minor, but it is one way of understanding how monopolistic competition differs from competition.

The Economics of Advertising

Firms that sell undifferentiated goods don't advertise very much because any benefits from advertising would flow mostly to other firms in the same industry. If a carrot farmer, for example, advertised how delicious carrots

CHECK YOURSELF

- McDonald's, Burger King, and Wendy's are monopolistic competitors. What does this categorization tell you about each company's long-term profits? Long-term costs?
- Why do we classify McDonald's and Burger King as monopolistic competitors rather than as pure competitors? Isn't a hamburger just a hamburger?

were, most of any additional sales would go to other carrot farmers—unless the farmer could somehow convince consumers that their carrots were different and better. Firms will only pay for advertising if they sell a differentiated good.

Perhaps you are wondering about some counterexamples. You may have seen advertisements for Milk ("Got Milk?"), Pork ("The Other White Meat"), or Cotton ("The Fabric of Our Lives"). Each of these goods is undifferentiated so who is paying for the commercials? These examples are the exceptions that prove the rule because the advertising campaigns for these products are funded through special programs run by the Agricultural Marketing Service, a division of the U.S. Department of Agriculture. Since firms in these industries won't pay for advertising themselves (even if the industry as a whole would benefit from the advertising—an example of a prisoner's dilemma), the government requires that any firm in the industry pay a special tax earmarked for advertising. The industry as a whole benefits from the advertising, although individual farmers sometimes gripe about the special taxes.

Monopolies are also less likely to advertise since they aren't worried about a competitor gaining market share. The U.S. Postal Service (USPS), for example, doesn't advertise first-class mail very much since no other firm is allowed to compete in that market. The USPS, however, does advertise its parcel delivery services, since it competes in that market with FedEx and UPS.

Firms with differentiated products are the most likely to advertise because (1) unlike carrot farmers, they can advertise their specific product rather than the industry category and (2) they want more customers since $P > MC$ (unlike in a perfectly competitive industry). But why does advertising increase sales?

Informative Advertising

One reason that advertising increases sales is that it informs consumers about price, quality, and availability. Supermarkets, for example, send out newspaper supplements boasting of low prices for ground meat, apples, and milk. Price advertising is part of the competitive process, and there is good evidence for how advertising lowers prices and improves consumer welfare. In some states, for example, it used to be illegal for optometrists to advertise prices for eyeglasses; this restriction allowed economists to test the effect of advertising on prices. Would the states with advertising restrictions have lower prices for eyeglasses, on the theory that optometrists would save money if they didn't advertise and would pass on these lower costs to consumers? Or would states with restrictions on advertising have higher prices, on the theory that without advertising there would be less competition? The states that allowed price advertising for eyeglasses had systematically lower eyeglass prices; in other words, advertising improves the competitive process. The same pattern—lower prices where advertising is allowed—has been true for prescription drugs, retail gasoline prices, eye exams, and legal services.[1]

Other times, advertising promotes messages of quality, thereby informing consumers and also giving suppliers a better incentive to meet quality standards. Once it was discovered that high-fiber cereals may help prevent cancer, and such advertising was allowed by law, companies had (1) a greater incentive to produce and advertise high-fiber cereals and (2) consumers became better

MRU
mru.org/econ-advertising

Is Advertising Good?

informed about the benefits of high-fiber cereals and they ate more of the healthier cereals.[2] These two processes were mutually reinforcing.

Advertising as Signaling

Sometimes advertising doesn't appear to be about price, quality, or availability but the ad itself could be informative. If a new product debuts with a lot of accompanying advertising, consumers might infer that the seller expects the product to make a big splash. The biggest piece of information is the ad itself. Consumers see all the ads and think implicitly or explicitly, "If they're spending so much advertising on this new product, they must expect it to have a long and profitable life." That makes potential customers more interested in buying or at least sampling the product. Similarly, if a new movie or musical release is accompanied by a lot of ads, consumers will rationally infer that the producers expect the new product to hit it big; for a while, it seemed that Amazon's *House of the Dragon* commercials were everywhere—you might even find some in this book! It might seem that the advertising creates the demand, but we also have to take into account that the firms who believe that their products are likely to be hits are the ones who have the biggest incentive to advertise.

Advertising Changes Our Tastes

It's obvious that a lot of advertising is simply about trying to change our minds and not about information at all. You can watch a Coca-Cola ad on YouTube that has no words, catchy music, lots of beautiful images, including tumbling snowmen, no information about price, a cool dude pulling a Coke out of a vending machine, and at the end you see on the screen the simple words, "The Coke side of life."[3] Coke ads have been, well, vague for many years. Previous slogans include "The pause that refreshes," "Thirst knows no season," "Things go better with Coke," and "The real thing."[4] It's not so well-known that Coca-Cola publicized the idea, through its ads, of Santa as an old man in a red suit, but that shows how central Coke ads have been to the U.S. national consciousness.[5] It's not obvious how these messages have anything to do with informing buyers about Coca-Cola, if only because just about everyone already has heard of Coke. Worldwide, for all brands, Coca-Cola spends several billion dollars a year on advertising. Through advertising, Coca-Cola is trying to make the demand for Coca-Cola more inelastic. By persuading us that Pepsi is *not* a close substitute, Coca-Cola reduces the elasticity of demand and nudges the market in the direction of monopoly.

Can you tell the difference?

Yet is persuasion through advertising always such a bad thing? Persuasion can give us tastes that appear silly or unjustified to outside observers, such as when we believe that drinking a particular beer will make us more suave or more attractive to potential dates. Nonetheless, persuasion also can deepen our enjoyments and our memories.

Here's an example of how advertising gives us richer memories. In a blind taste test performed by researchers, the subjects reported roughly equal preferences for Coke and Pepsi. As part of the same test, the subjects were given one cup labeled as "Coke" and another cup, also containing Coke, but unlabeled. The subjects reported greater enjoyment from drinking the labeled cup, and brain scans showed that they were activating the memory regions of their brain when they offered these reports. The researchers suspected that the subjects

How about now?

Constantin Iosif/Shutterstock

were associating Coke with fond images from ads or from earlier moments in their lives. It was not possible to replicate the same effect of "enhanced enjoyment from memory" when labeled and unlabeled Pepsi were put in the cups and sampled by subjects. In other words, the very act of thinking about the Coke brand has resonance with a lot of customers.[6]

It's possible to read this story in two differing ways. Are the people who enjoy the Coke being "manipulated" or "tricked" by the advertisers? (If so, do your friends ever manipulate or trick you in the same way? Do you ever manipulate or trick them?) Or do the Coke ads mean many of us enjoy the Coca-Cola product more? Do the ads themselves enhance consumer welfare by turning a sweet, fizzy drink into something more? It's common that people bring their value judgments to bear on advertising, as some will condemn and others will praise persuasive ads; economic science itself does not give us a means of deciding which ads are good and which are bad, all things considered. What we do know is that persuasive advertising can create some market power by brand differentiation, but at the same time advertising also helps people enjoy a lot of products.

Advertising Lowers the Price of Many Products

Advertising, whether informative or persuasive, also helps finance many useful goods and services. Why is Google available for free? Because the company earns income by selling click-through ads and thus doesn't need to charge users of a web search. In fact, Google has an incentive to provide search services for free in order to maximize the number of people who will see the ads that it sells. We analyze these types of "platform markets" at greater length in Chapter 16. Facebook, Instagram, and Twitter are all free to consumers because of advertising. Advertising also makes newspapers, magazines, and radio much cheaper than otherwise would be the case. For instance, many newspapers earn more from their ads than from subscription revenue. In this sense, you, as a reader, benefit from ads even if you don't care about the advertised products. Not everyone enjoys every ad but advertising is an important part of what makes business work—at the most fundamental level, advertising is about bringing businesses and customers together.

Takeaway

A monopolistically competitive industry features many sellers, free entry, and differentiated products.

Since products are differentiated, each firm retains a downward-sloped demand curve and P remains above MC. Free entry, however, means that in the long run price is driven down until $P = AC$ and each firm earns a zero economic profit. Monopolistically competitive industries have lots of variety but products are not produced at minimum average cost.

Advertising can be informative as in advertising about price, quality, and availability. Advertising can also increase perceptions of product differentiation, which allows firms to increase prices. Put differently, advertising can add to consumers' understanding and enjoyment of a product by changing what the product means to them.

CHAPTER REVIEW

Go online to practice with more examples of these types of problems, including live links to videos, data sources, and feedback.

KEY CONCEPTS

monopolistic competition, p. 341

FACTS AND TOOLS

1. Though its name can sometimes cause confusion for students, the market structure we call "monopolistic competition" is so named because it has some features of monopoly and some features of competition.

   a. In what ways is a monopolistically competitive market like a monopoly? In what ways is it like competition?

   b. Which of the outcomes of monopolistically competitive markets is a direct result of its monopoly-like features? Which outcome is a result of its competitive features? Can you summarize these results, so that they can be applied to product markets in general?

2. In a city like New York, the market for stand-up comedians is likely to be monopolistically competitive. Explain why this is so. If the market is monopolistically competitive, then what can be said about prices, output, and profits in this market?

3. Shakespeare's Pizza is a very popular pizza place in Columbia, Missouri, that won *Good Morning America*'s "Best Bites: College Edition" prize in 2015. However, it faces plenty of competition from other pizzerias in town, such as Pizza Tree, Gumby's, other local pizza places, and the big national chains. If Shakespeare's Pizza slightly raised the price of its pizzas, would it lose all its customers to these other pizza places?

4. Fill in the blanks with "=," "<," or ">" as appropriate to describe the long-run outcome in a monopolistically competitive market.

   a. MC ___ AC

   b. P ___ AC

   c. MR ___ MC

   d. P ___ MC

5. The figure here represents the market for a monopolistically competitive firm. Use the figure to answer the following questions. Assume the firm's fixed costs are such that it chooses to operate in the short run.

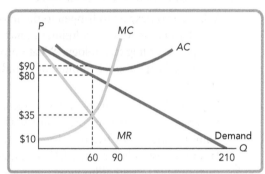

   a. What quantity will the monopolistically competitive firm sell? What price will they charge?

   b. What will be the firm's profit?

   c. Should this firm continue to operate? Why or why not?

   d. Assume that the cost structure in the figure represents a typical firm in this monopolistically competitive market. What would you expect to happen in the long run?

6. For each of the following items, describe how the market that these sellers participate in resembles monopolistic competition. For bonus points (if your instructor agrees), describe briefly the strategies that sellers in the market use in order to differentiate their products.

   a. New car dealerships

   b. Real estate agents

   c. College bars

THINKING AND PROBLEM SOLVING

7. As you read in the chapter, the requirements for an industry to be considered monopolistically competitive are that there are many firms and those firms are producing unique, or differentiated, products. One industry in which we find differentiated products is the recording industry. Not only are there many genres of music

(iTunes lists around 50), but within each genre there are countless artists as well.

Over the past few decades, technology has reduced the fixed costs of recording and the marginal costs of distributing music. In 1979, for example, the average studio bill for an album was more than $30,000 ($120,000 in today's dollars). Nowadays, with digital recording technology, an artist or band can record an entire album for a few thousand dollars and the album can be distributed at low cost as MP3s on the Internet, with no record store involved.

a. What do you expect to happen to the music industry because of the evolution of much cheaper recording technology? What do you expect to happen to the number of recording artists?

b. Suppose there are initially only two recording artists in all of the record industry: The Shins (an indie rock band) and Yo-Yo Ma (a famous cellist). How many MP3s will they each be able to sell? Who would buy MP3s from The Shins? What about from Yo-Yo Ma? Will anybody buy MP3s from both?

c. Now suppose that another artist joins the industry: Isobel Campbell (an indie rock cellist!). What will happen to the demand curves for MP3s that The Shins and Yo-Yo Ma face? Will they keep all of their fans? Will they keep *any* of their fans? What do you think will happen to the total number of MP3s sold in the industry?

d. Generally speaking, as technology makes it cheaper and cheaper to produce MP3s, and as more and more bands join the music industry, what will happen to the total number of MP3s downloaded by music fans? What will happen to the MP3s sold by each individual band? What will happen to the profits of each band?

8. In a famous article on advertising,[7] Gary Becker and Kevin Murphy wrote about advertisements that run during television programs: "One can say either that advertising pays for the programming—the usual interpretation—or that programming compensates for the advertising, which is our preferred interpretation." Viewing ads during a television program (or hearing them during a radio broadcast) makes consumers worse off, so they must be compensated (with programming) for having experienced the ads. On the other hand, print ads in newspapers and magazines can be avoided by consumers, so these ads must make consumers better off; otherwise, no one would ever read them. Use this theory to answer the following questions:

a. Think about the different types of advertisements discussed in the chapter (informative, signaling, part of the product). Which type is more likely to appear on TV? Which type is more likely to appear in a newspaper or magazine? Often you'll see television commercials, especially for pharmaceuticals, that say: "See our ad in *such-and-such* magazine." What does this say about the difference between television and print ads?

b. Becker and Murphy wrote their article before online streaming became popular. Nowadays, ads on television are avoidable (to a degree), just like ads in a newspaper. What impact do you think this new technology has on the types of ads you see?

9. Why do you think chain restaurants like Chili's, Applebee's, and TGI Fridays are always changing their menus—introducing new appetizers, new entrees, and new cocktails? Are they all just trying to find the perfect menu, or is there something else going on?

10. Red Bull is estimated to spend around $1 billion each year on marketing. In addition to its "Red Bull gives you wings" advertising spots, they also generate awareness for their product by sponsoring extreme sports events and an F1 racing team. Clearly, these marketing activities do not provide much information on Red Bull to consumers. So what is the point of the advertising? How would an economist view this type of advertising? How do you view it? Would it be better to have a perfectly competitive market in energy drinks?

11. Many restaurants are not 100% full all day long, especially in the late morning and during the afternoon. Economists call this "excess capacity" and it is a characteristic result of monopolistic competition. What would restaurants have to do in order to be closer to 100% full all of the time? Why won't they do this?

WORK IT OUT

For interactive, step-by-step help in solving this problem, go online.

Let's compare monopolistic competition with perfect competition.

a. Do competitive firms make profits in the short run? How about in the long run?

b. Do monopolistically competitive firms make profits in the short run? How about in the long run?

c. Is there a difference in profits between competition and monopolistic competition? If so, what accounts for it?

d. Examine Figure 17.2. In the figure, what are the differences between monopolistic competition and competition?

e. In Figure 17.2, which point represents the price we pay for product differentiation?

18

Labor Markets

A janitor in the United States earns about $15 an hour; a typical janitor in India earns less than $2 an hour. Why is there such a difference? Why does one person earn so much more than the other? After all, janitors in both countries do many of the same things: they clean windows and floors, scrub toilets, remove trash, and so forth.

If you think the differences in wages have to do with supply and demand, you are on the right track.

Wages are determined in the market for labor just like other prices are determined.

In this chapter, we look more deeply at the factors underlying the demand for labor and the supply of labor. A deeper understanding explains how wages are determined at a fundamental level, why most Americans earn so much by global standards, why education raises wages, whether and how much labor unions help workers, and how discrimination still shapes labor markets today.

The Demand for Labor and the Marginal Product of Labor

A firm is willing to hire a worker when the worker increases the firm's revenues more than the firm's costs. Economists call the increase in revenue created by hiring an additional worker the **marginal product of labor (MPL)**. The increase in costs created by hiring an additional worker is, for a competitive firm, simply the worker's wage (including the cost of other compensation like health benefits). Thus, we can say that a firm is willing to hire a worker when the marginal product of labor is greater than the wage.

When the Cleveland Cavaliers signed (in fact, re-signed) star player LeBron James in 2014, they went from having the third-worst record in the NBA to four straight appearances in the NBA Finals, including a championship in 2016. Not only did the Cavaliers win more games when they hired LeBron, their attendance increased and they sold more merchandise. In the long run, the value of their TV contract was higher too. When the Cavaliers hired LeBron, their revenues increased by a lot. That's why the Cavaliers were willing to pay him $100 million over three years. LeBron's salary may seem high but so was LeBron's marginal product.

McDonald's considers marginal product when the company hires people to keep its restaurants clean and in good running order. No one wants to eat in a

The **marginal product of labor (MPL)** is the increase in a firm's revenues created by hiring an additional laborer.

TABLE 18.1 THE MARGINAL PRODUCT OF LABOR

Number of Janitors	Task	Marginal Product of Labor (MPL per hour)
One	Clean restrooms, once a day.	$35
Two	Empty trash.	$30
Three	Clean restrooms, second time in a day.	$24
Four	Wash floors.	$20
Five	Pick up outside trash.	$16
Six	Clean restrooms, third time in a day.	$12
Seven	Clean windows.	$11
Eight	Remove gum from the bottom of tables.	$8

restaurant that looks unclean, so a cleaner restaurant increases profit. But how clean is clean enough? At some point, additional cleanliness costs more than it's worth. Thus, to maximize profit, *McDonald's will hire janitors so long as the increase in revenue from hiring an additional janitor exceeds the janitor's wage.*

To make that more concrete, let's consider the marginal product of labor as we vary the number of janitors, as in Table 18.1.

You'll notice a few things about these numbers. First, the marginal product of labor generally declines as more labor is hired. If there is one janitor, they will focus on the most important tasks so the marginal product of labor is high. As McDonald's adds janitors, each subsequent janitor is assigned to a less important task so the marginal product of labor falls.

We can see from Table 18.1 that if McDonald's hires three janitors, then the marginal product of labor (per hour) is $24. If McDonald's hires four janitors, the marginal product of labor is $20, and so forth. But how many janitors will McDonald's hire? That depends on the wage.

If a janitor's wage is above $35 an hour, then McDonald's will hire zero janitors. If the wage falls to, say, $32 an hour, McDonald's will compare the additional revenues from hiring a janitor (the MPL), $35 an hour, with the cost of hiring the janitor, $32 an hour. Since the MPL is greater than the wage W, McDonald's will make the hire. If the wage falls to $28, McDonald's will hire a second janitor. If the wage falls to $22, McDonald's will hire a third janitor and so forth.

Notice that when the wage falls, McDonald's hires more janitors and assigns them to less important tasks, so as the wage falls, so does the MPL. The wage and the marginal product of labor will always be very close together since McDonald's will keep hiring workers so long as the MPL is greater than W.

If we know the marginal product of labor, we can derive the demand curve for labor. In Figure 18.1, for example, we show McDonald's demand curve for janitors. From the figure and from Table 18.1, you can see that if the wage is $10, then McDonald's will hire seven janitors.

Of course, we still have not explained what determines the wage. To do that, we need to remember that many firms demand janitors, so the wage of

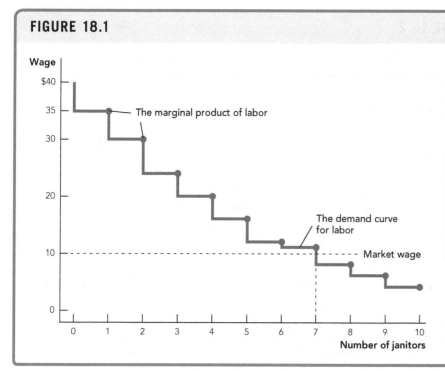

FIGURE 18.1

The marginal product of labor

The demand curve for labor

Market wage

The Marginal Product of Labor Determines a Firm's Demand Curve for Labor The marginal product of the first janitor is $35. If the wage is above $35, McDonald's will hire no janitors. If the wage falls to just below $35, McDonald's will find it profitable to hire one janitor. The marginal product of the second janitor is $30. If the wage falls below $30, McDonald's will hire its second janitor. If the wage falls below $24, McDonald's will find it profitable to add a third janitor, and so forth.

janitors will be determined by the *market* demand and supply of janitors. But don't worry, the market demand for janitors is very similar to McDonald's demand for janitors. At a high wage, only some firms (and some individual consumers, such as the very wealthy) will demand janitors. As the wage falls, more and more firms will demand janitors and each firm will demand more janitors, as we saw with McDonald's. Thus, the market demand for janitors is downward-sloping, as usual.

CHECK YOURSELF

• Why does the marginal product of labor fall as more workers are hired?

Supply of Labor

The market supply curve for labor will be upward-sloping, again as usual. In other words, high wages encourage a greater supply of labor. That's intuitive but we do have to take into account one complication. An *individual's* labor supply curve need not slope upward at all wages. When Rihanna started out, she was happy to tour more when her concerts began to sell out. Now that she is a billionaire, the same increase in wage doesn't cause her to tour more often. If his wage is already high, even Joe the janitor might decide that he would prefer spending more time with his family to working more hours at an even higher wage rate.

Figure 18.2 illustrates. In panel A, if the wage is between $7 and $16 an hour, Joe works 40 hours a week, so over this range Joe's supply curve for labor is vertical. If the wage rises to $20 an hour, Joe is willing to work overtime and he puts in 50 hours a week (a positively sloped labor supply curve). At $20 an hour, Joe is making a comfortable income—enough so that if his wage rises even further, Joe would prefer to work fewer hours and instead enjoy the money he is making by taking more leisure time. Thus, it is quite plausible that as the wage rises to $28 an hour, Joe asks his bosses for less overtime (a negatively sloped, or backward-bending, labor supply curve).

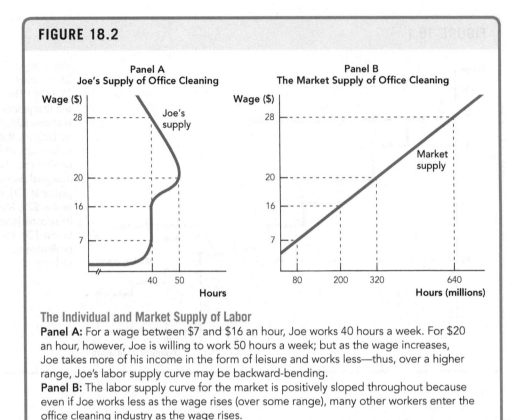

FIGURE 18.2

Panel A
Joe's Supply of Office Cleaning

Panel B
The Market Supply of Office Cleaning

The Individual and Market Supply of Labor

Panel A: For a wage between $7 and $16 an hour, Joe works 40 hours a week. For $20 an hour, however, Joe is willing to work 50 hours a week; but as the wage increases, Joe takes more of his income in the form of leisure and works less—thus, over a higher range, Joe's labor supply curve may be backward-bending.

Panel B: The labor supply curve for the market is positively sloped throughout because even if Joe works less as the wage rises (over some range), many other workers enter the office cleaning industry as the wage rises.

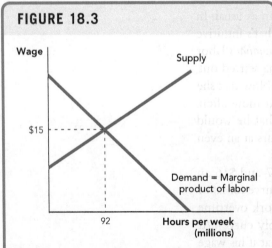

FIGURE 18.3

Market Demand for Janitors The price of labor (wage) is determined in the market for labor. In this case, the wage of janitors is determined by the demand and supply of janitors.

Although Joe's supply curve for labor could have a positive or negative slope, the market supply curve for labor is very likely to be positively sloped. Why? Let's go back to when Joe was earning $7 an hour and putting in 40 hours a week. When the wage rises to $16 an hour, Joe doesn't work more hours; but, at a higher wage, Mary, who was working in the restaurant business, is likely to switch to office cleaning. Thus, in panel B, we show the market supply of janitors. When the wage increases, the market supply increases for two reasons: first, some workers—although not all—are likely to work more as the wage increases. Second, and more important, when the wages of janitors increase, that attracts workers from other industries. Together, these two factors mean that even if some individuals supply less labor at a higher wage, a higher wage increases the quantity of labor supplied overall.

Thus, an upward-sloping *market* supply curve is the normal situation.

We can now put together the supply and demand for janitors in the usual fashion to represent the market for janitors.

In the United States, there are about 2.3 million janitors, each working about 40 hours a week (92 million hours a week in total) and earning an average wage of $15 an hour. Thus, the market for janitors can be represented in Figure 18.3. As usual, the price (wage) is found at the intersection of the demand for janitors and the supply of janitors.

By the way, recall that we said earlier that the wage and the marginal product of labor will always be very close together. That is because a firm will keep hiring workers so long as MPL is greater than W. When we think about many firms and many workers, it often simplifies things to say that the MPL = W. Thus, we know that in the United States, the marginal product of a janitor is about $15 an hour.

CHECK YOURSELF

• Why might an individual's supply of labor curve be backward-bending? Explain.

Labor Market Issues

Now that we know the basic principles underlying the demand and supply of labor, let's turn to some specific questions and issues that our principles can help us to understand.

Why Do Janitors in the United States Earn More Than Janitors in India Even When They Do the Same Job?

The short answer for why janitors in the United States earn more than janitors in India—even though janitors in India work as hard or harder—is that janitors in the United States have a higher marginal product. Janitors in the United States have a higher marginal product for two reasons, demand and supply. The demand or willingness to pay for janitors in the United States is higher than in India not because U.S. janitors clean more offices per hour but because the price that people are prepared to pay for a clean office is higher in the United States. Janitors in the United States work for productive firms like McDonald's or in office buildings producing valuable products and that raises the demand for their cleaning work.

To put it in a single sentence, the U.S. janitor gets the benefit of productivity in many other sectors of the U.S. economy. A typical janitor in India might earn less than $1,000 per year. That same worker, if they win the green card lottery and come to the United States, might instead earn around $30,000 in a similar job or even up to $40,000, depending on location and hours. It's not that they have suddenly learned new cleaning techniques but rather that they are working in a more productive economy.

Let's look a little more closely at the differences between the typical U.S. and Indian office building. The U.S. office building has more and better equipment such as more and better printers, copiers, and computers. Overall, there is more capital invested in the U.S. workplace, and that makes the U.S. office building more productive. That building also has a better marketing department, longer global reach for its sales force, and greater investment in building up the brand name of the product. Most importantly, the U.S. office is producing a more valuable product.

Since it's more valuable to keep a productive workplace clean than to keep a less productive workplace clean, the wages of U.S. janitors are higher than those in India.

There is no doubt that you are a very productive person—perhaps you know how to use a computer, have some artistic talents, and write well. Now look around the world—how much would these skills earn you in another country? Your skills are yours alone, but your wage is determined not by your skills alone but by the productivity of the entire economy.

The second reason that janitors in the United States have a higher marginal product than janitors in India is that the supply of janitors is lower in the United States than in India. Or to put it another way India has many more janitors than does the United States. Of course, India has more workers than the United States, but what's more important than India's total population is that India has many low-skilled workers who eagerly compete for the job of janitor. A much greater proportion of Indians than Americans, for example, would

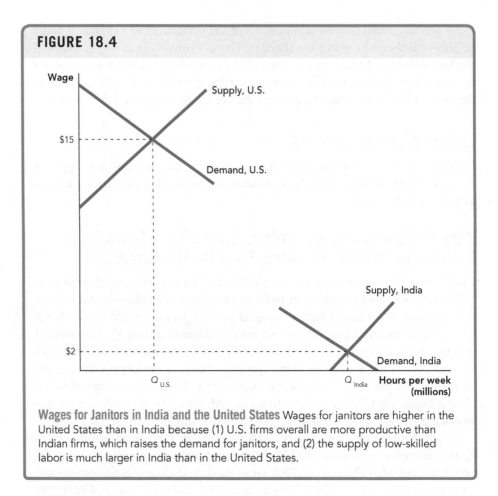

FIGURE 18.4

Wages for Janitors in India and the United States Wages for janitors are higher in the United States than in India because (1) U.S. firms overall are more productive than Indian firms, which raises the demand for janitors, and (2) the supply of low-skilled labor is much larger in India than in the United States.

Human capital is tools of the mind, the stuff in people's heads that makes them productive.

consider a cleaning job in a modern office building to be a very attractive job. Since many Indians compete for the job of janitor, the wages of janitors are pushed down and since their wages are low they are assigned to low marginal product tasks.

Figure 18.4 shows the two reasons why the wages of janitors are lower in India than in the United States. First, the demand for janitors is higher in the United States, and second, the supply of relatively low-skill workers is much higher in India than in the United States.

Human Capital

Americans are fortunate to work in a productive economy. But high wages are not just the result of fortunes of birth. Wages within America differ greatly from worker to worker so let's look at some of the reasons why.

Some workers have higher wages than others because they have more human capital. Physical capital is tools like computers, bulldozers, and 3D printers. **Human capital** is tools of the mind, the stuff in people's heads that makes them productive. Human capital is not something we are born with—it is produced by investing time and other resources in education, training, and experience.

Of course, investing in human capital usually costs money; it costs not just what a doctor spends on medical school tuition but what they could have earned during those eight years in medical school and residency, namely

FIGURE 18.5

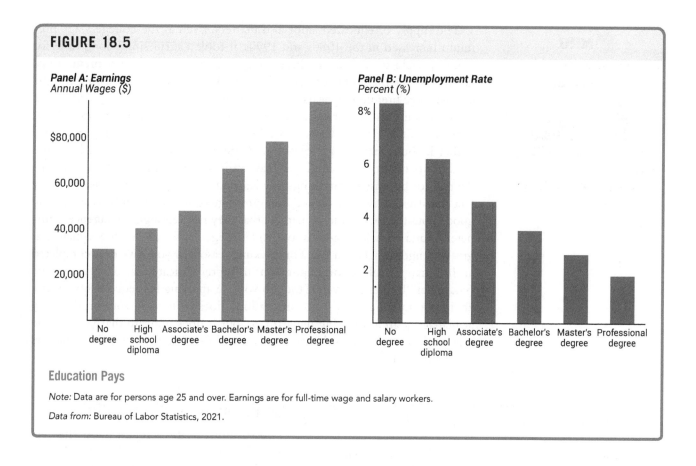

Panel A: Earnings
Annual Wages ($)

Panel B: Unemployment Rate
Percent (%)

Education Pays

Note: Data are for persons age 25 and over. Earnings are for full-time wage and salary workers.

Data from: Bureau of Labor Statistics, 2021.

opportunity cost. But, in general, investments in human capital bring a good return in the United States. In recent years, college graduates have made almost twice as much as high school graduates.

Panel A of Figure 18.5 shows annual wages by education level. Clearly more education, on average, brings a higher wage. Panel B shows unemployment levels by education. The exact numbers will change year by year, but the pattern—higher education results in lower unemployment rates—is remarkably consistent.

College pays off more now than ever before. From the 1960s to the 1980s, wages for people with a college degree were approximately 1.5 times higher than the wages of a high school graduate. Today, however, wages for people with a college degree are almost double the wages of a high school graduate, in part because wages for those with college degrees have been going up and also in part because wages for those with just a high school degree have been going down in inflation-adjusted terms.

Why has the return to human capital increased so dramatically? Demand and supply. Today's labor market is demanding and rewarding workers who have numeracy, communication skills, creativity, and technical knowledge. Many of these skills are taught or demonstrated by having a college education. At the same time, the demand for less-skilled labor has been decreasing, in part due to changes in technology such as automation, and in part due to increased trade with countries like China with a large supply of low-skilled labor. The net effect has been an increase in the college wage premium.

mru.org/duel-education

Econ Duel: Is Education Signaling or Skill Building?

The supply of educated labor also matters. Even as the college wage premium increased in the 1980s and 1990s, it took a surprisingly long time for young people to respond by increasing their educational attainment. Since 2004, however, the supply of new college graduates has been increasing and the college wage premium appears to have stabilized.

We should also mention that the return to education is not just about human capital. Have you ever wondered why an art history major earns a higher income than a high school graduate even when neither works in the field of art history? An employer may want to hire someone with a college degree not because of anything they learned at college but because the very fact that this individual earned a degree signals to the employer something good about the job candidate, namely that they have enough intelligence, competence, and conscientiousness to earn a college degree (we discuss signaling at greater length in Chapter 24). For the same reasons, if you have ever completed an Ironman triathlon, you might want to subtly indicate that on your résumé (say, under "Interests") even if the job you are applying for requires no athletic ability. Competing in an Ironman triathlon doesn't increase your productivity at managing an advertising department, but it does indicate that you are the type of person who doesn't give up easily and that is a characteristic employers frequently seek.

Compensating Differentials

The supply of labor depends on the real wage, but the real wage of a job includes not just the monetary pay but also how much fun the job is. Some people work for nice bosses; others work for tyrants. Some jobs are dangerous; others are very safe. Some jobs are interesting; others are a bore.

Right now being a fisherman is one of the most dangerous jobs in the United States, more dangerous than being a police officer or a firefighter. There are a lot of accidents out on the water. Most of all, a lot of people just slip and fall overboard. Being a truck driver is dangerous, too, mostly because of road accidents. That's why those professions earn relatively high wages, especially given that they do not demand a college degree.[1]

It's simple supply and demand. The danger of a dangerous job reduces the supply of labor, pushing the supply curve for labor to the left and up, as shown in Figure 18.6.

FIGURE 18.6

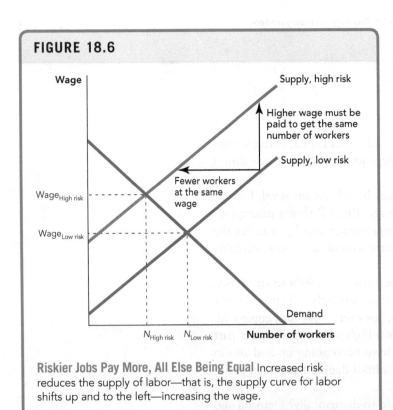

Riskier Jobs Pay More, All Else Being Equal Increased risk reduces the supply of labor—that is, the supply curve for labor shifts up and to the left—increasing the wage.

A **compensating differential** is a difference in wages that offsets differences in working conditions.

The resulting wage is higher than it otherwise would be, and that is what economists call a compensating differential. It is called a **compensating differential** because a difference in wages compensates for the difference in working conditions.

There's a lesson here. People talk all the time about wanting interesting, fun, and rewarding jobs but *beware*: being an accountant might be boring, but all else being equal, that's a sign of higher wages. Being a musician is fun but most musicians don't make a lot of money. The higher wage of accountants compensates for the lack of fun or, equivalently, the greater fun of being an artist compensates for the lack of money.

To see this in more detail, consider the following principle: *Similar jobs must have similar compensation packages.* Imagine that being an accountant or a musician requires similar amounts of skill, education, training, and so forth. Now what would happen if musicians were paid higher wages than accountants? Higher wages *and* more fun can't be beat so the supply of musicians will increase and the supply of accountants will decrease. But the increased supply of musicians will drive down the wages of musicians and the decreased supply of accountants will drive up the wages of accountants. In fact, musician wages will fall and accountant wages will rise until a typical young person deciding on a career will be more or less indifferent: Higher wages and less fun equal lower wages and more fun. Figure 18.7 illustrates the main idea.

Every job has a different combination of wages, benefits, fun, risk, and other conditions. Some workers will choose jobs with less risk but lower wages, while others will prefer jobs with more risk but higher wages. In fact, workers who choose the less risky jobs are "buying" safety with a reduction in their wages. Now consider who is more likely to buy safety, a rich worker or a poor worker?

The rich buy more safety for the same reason they buy more BMWs—buying safety is one of the things that money is good for! We've already noted that being a fisherman is a dangerous job. It should come as no surprise that many of these fishermen are recent immigrants to the United States. But it's not

mru.org/tradeoff

The Tradeoff Between Fun and Wages

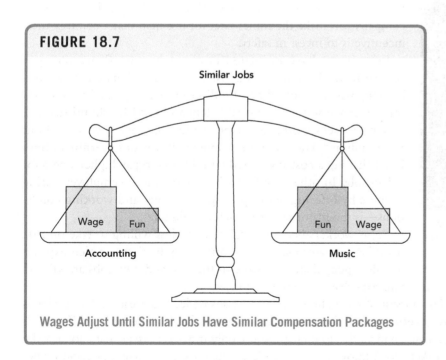

FIGURE 18.7

Wages Adjust Until Similar Jobs Have Similar Compensation Packages

the immigrants from wealthy Sweden who take the fishing jobs. Instead, it's poor immigrants from Honduras who concentrate in the fishing trade. These poorer immigrants need the money the most and are less willing to buy safety by taking jobs with lower wages.

The same reasoning explains why jobs in the United States are much safer than similar jobs in poorer countries. Workers in the United States use their wealth to buy more smoke detectors, fire extinguishers, and airbags on their cars and they also "buy" more job safety. Thus, one of the most important reasons why job safety increases over time is economic growth.

In other words, workers become less willing to accept risk as economic growth makes them wealthier. You might take a dangerous job if you need the money to feed your family, but not if you need the money to feed your family at The French Laundry, one of the most expensive restaurants in the United States.

Government regulation has improved the quality of American jobs, as well (see below), but increasing wealth and the profit incentive are the main drivers behind this process. Are you surprised that the pursuit of profit leads to *greater* job safety? Remember that firms must pay workers to take on higher risks, the compensating differentials we talked about earlier. But the process works the other way just as well—when firms make jobs safer, they can pay lower wages, thus increasing their profits.

Coal mining is a tough job anywhere, but in China the death rate per ton of coal is more than 100 times higher than in the United States.

Reinhard Krause/Newscom

Take a job like coal mining. An American coal miner will earn between $50,000 and $80,000 annually—let's say $70,000.[2] If that sounds like a pretty good wage to you, it is because coal mining is not especially fun. But how much would wages have to be if coal mining in the United States were as dangerous as in China, where the mortality rate per ton of coal is more than 100 times higher? Coal miners might demand $100,000 to take on the extra risk. That's an extra $30,000 per coal miner per year that firms would have to pay because of riskier working conditions. If the mining company can make the mines safer for less than that, obviously their incentive is to invest in safety.

Economists have estimated how much more firms must pay American workers to take on risk and the numbers are very large, by one estimate around $150 billion in recent years. In comparison, OSHA (the Occupational Safety and Health Administration), which oversees workplace safety, levies fines every year of about $150 million.[3] These numbers imply that fear of government fines is not that big a cost, compared with having to pay higher wages for riskier jobs. In other words, market competition—employers luring laborers by offering better packages of wages and working conditions—is the major factor in making jobs safer.

So, as workers become wealthier and less willing to take on risk, firms have greater incentives to increase job safety—which explains why jobs are safer today than they were in the past and why jobs are safer in wealthier countries than in poorer countries.

The pursuit of profit, however, doesn't always lead to greater safety, which is why government regulation also has a role to play. Compensating differentials give firms an incentive to increase safety only if workers *know* that a job is risky. If workers don't know about or underestimate risk, they won't demand higher wages. A government agency like OSHA can help to ensure that firms do not hide job risks. Even more important, in the United States, firms are required to buy workers' compensation insurance—which pays workers for on-the-job injuries. Crucially, the premiums that firms must pay to buy this insurance are *experienced-based*, which means that the more injuries a firm has, the more it must pay for insurance. Thus, workers' compensation programs give firms an incentive to reduce risk so they can save money on insurance. Since the insurance premiums a firm must pay are based on actual injuries, this incentive works even when workers do not know or underestimate risk.

Do Unions Raise Wages?

It is commonly suggested that unions are a fundamental reason why wages are so high in some countries and so low in other countries. Yet the evidence does not bear out this view. The more unionized countries do not obviously have higher levels of wages. For instance, the United States and Switzerland have much lower levels of unionization (10% and 15%, respectively, in recent years) than does most of Western Europe, where unionization rates can run between 20% and 80%. Yet the United States and Switzerland have equally high or higher wage levels.

It is true that wages in unionized jobs tend to be higher than in nonunionized jobs for similar workers. Studies that compare the wages of unionized electricians with the wages of nonunionized electricians, for example, typically find that unionized electricians have wages about 10% to 15% higher than nonunionized electricians. But this doesn't mean that unions could raise wages in all jobs because the primary method that unions use to raise wages is to reduce industry employment.[4]

If you are wondering how unions raise wages and reduce employment, it is easy to see on a supply and demand graph. By restricting their membership and threatening to strike unless employers hire union labor, unions reduce the supply of labor to an industry. The reduction in labor supply shifts the supply curve for labor to the left and up, as shown in Figure 18.8. Notice that the reduction in the supply of labor increases wages but reduces employment from $N_{\text{Without union}}$ to $N_{\text{With union}}$.

Unions can be beneficial in ensuring that employees are treated fairly and by improving labor/management relations, but the main reason that unions raise wages is through restricting the supply of labor. In this respect, a union is quite similar to a cartel, like those we discussed in Chapter 15. The OPEC oil cartel raises the price of oil by restricting the supply of oil and unions raise the wages of labor by restricting the supply of labor.

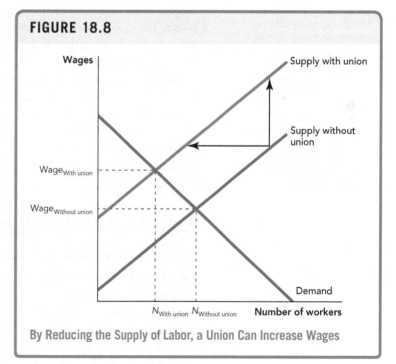

FIGURE 18.8

By Reducing the Supply of Labor, a Union Can Increase Wages

Unions also can lower wages, although this effect is more difficult to see. First, consider what happens to the workers who are not hired in the unionized industry—these workers must seek employment in other industries, which increases the supply of labor to those other industries and drives wages down. Second, unions sometimes bring strikes and work stoppages, which can slow down an entire economy. For instance, the British economy was highly unionized from 1970 to 1982; this coincided with Britain's period of long economic decline relative to other nations. In 1970, dockworkers were on strike for so long that it shut down almost all of Britain's main ports. Coal miners went on strike in 1972, which led to a shortage of electricity. A three-day workweek was implemented for a short time to save power. In 1974, the miners went on strike again and a shortened workweek was implemented again. Ten years later, the British experienced another strike that lasted for almost one year. Prime Minister Margaret Thatcher limited the government-supplied privileges of the British unions during the 1980s. At the height of the strikes, Britain was losing more than a 1,000 days of work for every 1,000 workers. By the mid-1990s, however, Britain was losing just 22 days of work to strikes for every 1,000 workers, a remarkable change that increased productivity.[5]

When people think of unions, the longshoreman's union or a union of electricians often comes to mind, but it's important to remember that doctors, lawyers, dentists, accountants, and other professionals have their own type of union, called a professional association. The American Medical Association (AMA), for example, works to restrict the supply of physicians for the same reason that an electrician's union works to reduce the supply of electricians. It's very difficult to get into a medical school, for example. The AMA says that restricting the supply of physicians is necessary to maintain high standards. Maybe that is true, but restricting the supply of physicians also maintains high wages. The AMA lobbies for laws that make competing against physicians more difficult; for instance, they restrict the procedures that can be legally performed by nurse practitioners, midwives, chiropractors, and pharmacists, and they make it more difficult for foreign-educated physicians to practice in the United States. As noted, the AMA says that restrictions are necessary to maintain quality; there is some truth to this claim, but, as always, you should be somewhat skeptical when members of a group claim that their high wages are good for you!

The bottom line is this: Unions can raise the wages of particular classes of workers, but unions are not the fundamental reason why wages are high in the wealthy countries.

How Bad Is Labor Market Discrimination, or Can Lakisha Catch a Break?

We all think we know what discrimination is. Discrimination is *bad*. Discrimination is what racists and bigots do. And, yes, that is partly right: Discrimination often is morally objectionable. It's also true that there are different types of discrimination and not all discrimination is motivated by prejudice. Let's take a closer look at two major types of discrimination, statistical discrimination and preference-based discrimination.

Statistical Discrimination

Let's say you are walking down a dark alley, late at night, in the warehouse district of your city. Suddenly, you hear footsteps behind you. You turn around and you see an old lady walking her dachshund. Do you breathe a sigh of relief? Probably. Would you breathe the same sigh of relief if you saw an angry young man in a dark leather jacket, muttering to himself? What if he was holding a knife? What if he was walking with his two-year-old daughter in a baby stroller?

One way of reading this story is to claim that you are discriminating against young men, relative to old ladies, or relative to young men with baby girls at their side. Another way of describing this story is that you are using information rationally. A mugger is far more likely to be an angry young man in a leather jacket than an old lady walking her dachshund. Maybe both descriptions capture some aspect of the reality, but suddenly discrimination isn't so simple a concept anymore.

Statistical discrimination is using information about group averages to make conclusions about individuals. Not every young man in a leather jacket walking the warehouse district late at night is a mugger and not every young man with a baby girl at his side is safe, but that's the way to bet. Although statistical discrimination is a useful shorthand for making some decisions, it also causes people to make errors. They refuse to deal with some people they really ought to. They may refuse to hire some people who deserve the job. We gave one example of this earlier—employers may not look carefully at workers without college degrees, even though some of these workers are just as intelligent and industrious as those with college degrees. It is called statistical discrimination because, in essence, the employer is treating the worker as an abstract statistic. Even though statistical discrimination is not motivated by malice, its long-run consequences can be harmful to the penalized groups.

Over time, markets tend to develop more subtle and more finely grained ways of judging people and judging job candidates. An employer can give prospective employees multiple interviews and psychological tests, Google previous histories or writings, look up people on social media, ask for more references, and so on, all to get an accurate picture of the person. Eventually, these practices break down the crudest methods of statistical discrimination but, of course, some statistical discrimination always remains.

Public policies that do not take into account the possibility of statistical discrimination can backfire. Many states and localities, for example, have passed "Ban the Box" policies—these policies forbid employers from asking about a job applicant's criminal record early in the application process. The idea of banning the box (the checkbox where a candidate would indicate that they have a criminal record) was to make it a bit easier for workers with a criminal record, especially Black workers, to get jobs. A noble goal, but economists Amanda Agan and Sonja Starr sent out thousands of fictitious job applications before and after "Ban the Box" was introduced into New Jersey and New York.[6] What they found was that after "Ban the Box" went into effect, Black applicants were much less likely than white applicants to get a callback, compared with before "Ban the Box" went into effect. In other words, when employers were forbidden from making the fine-grained distinction between workers with and without a criminal record they relied on the coarser and less accurate distinction between Black and white workers.

Statistical discrimination tends to be most persistent when people meet in purely casual settings with no repeat interactions. Profit-seeking employers, who make money from finding and keeping the best workers, have significant incentives to overcome unfairness.

Statistical discrimination is using information about group averages to make conclusions about individuals.

How many times a day do you discriminate?

Preference-Based Discrimination

A second kind of discrimination—preference-based discrimination—is based on a plain, flat-out dislike of some group of people, such as a race, religion, or gender. We're going to lay out three different kinds of preference-based discrimination: discrimination by employers, discrimination by customers, and discrimination by employees. The first of these is easiest for a market economy to overcome whereas the last is the most difficult to solve.

Discrimination by Employers

When most people think of discrimination, they think of an employer with bigoted tastes. Some employers just don't want to hire people of a particular race, ethnicity, religion, or gender. If this discrimination is widespread, the wages of people who are discriminated against will fall since the demand for their labor falls. But fortunately, this kind of discrimination, if taken alone, tends to break down for two reasons: Employer discrimination is expensive to the employer and it leaves the bigot open to being outcompeted.

Imagine, for example, that Black workers are widely discriminated against and thus that their wages are lower than those of white workers. Say that a firm can hire white workers for $10 an hour or equally productive Black workers for $8 an hour. Imagine that the firm needs 100 workers. If it hires Black workers instead of white workers, the firm can increase its profits by $2 per hour per worker. Thus, by hiring Black workers, the firm can increase its profits by $1,600 per day ($2 saving per hour for 100 workers for 8 hours a day), $8,000 per week (5 days a week), or $400,000 in a year (50 working weeks). Even a prejudiced employer will likely think twice about discriminating when it costs $400,000 a year just to indulge the prejudice.

In fact, the profit-hungry firm could earn *more than* $400,000 by hiring Black workers because it could also take advantage of its lower costs to reduce prices and thus sell more output. So, profit-hungry firms benefit discriminated-against workers in two ways. First, they increase the demand for discriminated-against workers, thereby increasing their wages. Second, those firms tend to drive firms that irrationally discriminate out of business.

The logic of profit-maximization implies that employer discrimination is costly, especially in the long run, not that it never happens. Consider, for example, two studies of the job market for low-wage labor in New York City. In 2004, researchers sent paired individuals to apply for jobs—the pairs had equivalent résumés and similar demographics but one person in the pair was Black and the other was white. The Black applicants received significantly fewer callbacks than the equivalent white applicants. Six years later, the same researchers went back to their data and found that many of the firms that they had studied had gone out of business. But remarkably, 36% of the firms that had discriminated had gone out of business, but only 17% of the nondiscriminating firms had failed. Whether the discriminators failed because they discriminated or because the discriminating firms were simply less well run is unclear, but in either case the market tended to reward the firms that hired rationally and without prejudice. Bigotry is bad for business.[*]

In 1947, Brooklyn Dodgers General Manager Branch Rickey hired Jackie Robinson to be the first Black player in modern major league baseball.

---

[*] The two studies are: Pager, Devah, Bruce Western, and Bart Bonikowski. 2009. Discrimination in a low-wage labor market: A field experiment. *American Sociological Review* 74(5): 777–799; and Pager, Devah. 2016. Are firms that discriminate more likely to go out of business? *Sociological Science* 3: 849–859.

Robinson already had extensive experience in what were then called the "Negro leagues," and he proved to be an immediate star. Robinson won the Rookie of the Year award and then in his third season he won the MVP award. The second Black player in major league baseball, Larry Doby, proved to be a star for the Cleveland Indians. The baseball teams that moved first to hire Black players had a competitive advantage and eventually all teams had to follow, whether or not they were run by bigots.

Of course, that story is about baseball, but it applies to the broader world of business, as well. If employer-driven discrimination is depressing the wages of a group of people, you can make money by hiring them.

If the pursuit of profit raises wages so that all workers earn their marginal product, why do women earn less than men? It's often said, for example, that women earn about 80 cents per the dollar earned by men. The trouble with this widely reported statistic, however, is that it compares the wages of all women with those of all men—the statistic does not mean that a woman with the same qualifications earns less than a man for doing the same job.

Jackie Robinson, the first Black baseball player in modern major league baseball Robinson faced great discrimination but he was a profitable hire for the Brooklyn Dodgers.

One factor lowering wages for women as a group is that women tend to have less job experience than men of the same age because they sometimes leave the job force, typically to take care of children. In fact, if we compare the wages of single men and single women, single women earn just as much as single men. Married women without children also earn about as much as married men without children.

Men may have specialized in higher-paying fields and they also take more dangerous jobs. Remember those coal miners we discussed earlier with an average wage of $70,000? Most of them are men, perhaps because women prefer jobs with lower wages but less risk.

Over time, women have moved toward higher-paying sectors (more lawyers and economists, for instance) and there has been a long decline in the birth rate. Since women are having fewer children and they are having their children at later ages, that is helping women earn higher wages.

Nevertheless, some discrimination against women may yet remain, but it is probably more subtle than employer discrimination. We need to look at the roles of customers and employees to better understand other forms of discrimination.

Discrimination by Customers When the customers drive discrimination, owners are not always so keen to hire undervalued, victimized workers. If employing underpaid Black workers upsets the customers, it's not a surefire way for an employer to earn more money.

Let's revisit the story of Jackie Robinson and Branch Rickey. You might wonder why Branch Rickey hired Robinson in 1947 but not 1946. It's not that one day Rickey stopped being prejudiced against Blacks; he may not have been prejudiced in the first place. Rather, in 1947, Rickey sensed that his ticket-buying customers were ready for the idea of watching a Black man play baseball in a Brooklyn Dodgers uniform. The lesson is that sometimes discrimination comes from the customers of a business, not always from the owners or managers.

Or let's consider a lunch counter or hamburger joint in the Deep South in 1957, before the civil rights movement had much influence. Part of the problem

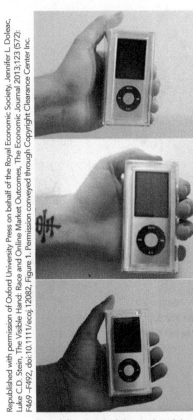

The visible hand of the market Ads to sell iPod Nanos illustrated with tattooed and also Black hands received fewer responses and lower offers.

was that state laws did not allow mixed-race establishments. But part of the problem came from customers, as well. At that time, many white customers didn't like the idea of eating a hamburger while sitting next to a Black person. These white customers demanded separate facilities, so usually there were separate lunch counters and separate restaurants for white and Black people in many parts of the United States. The entrepreneur running the lunch counter may or may not have been racist, but in any case the preferences of their customers encouraged them to discriminate and to keep out Black patrons.

Don't make the mistake of thinking customer-based discrimination has vanished from modern America. Economists Jennifer Doleac and Luke Stein came up with a clever method for measuring customer discrimination.[7] They placed ads to sell iPod Nanos on local classified websites across the country. The ads were similar except for one small detail—a photograph showed the iPod being held by one of three hands: a white hand, a white hand with a tattoo, or a Black hand (as shown in the images here).

Doleac and Stein found that ads illustrated with a Black hand had 13% fewer responses and average offers that were 11% lower than ads illustrated with a white hand. Interestingly, ads illustrated with a tattooed white hand also had fewer and lower offers, which suggests that customers may have been engaging in statistical discrimination rather than racial animus. It's clear, however, that discrimination whether statistical or driven by animus can reduce the opportunities available to minorities. One positive note is that Doleac and Stein found that discrimination was less in markets with more buyers.

By the way, the decline of employer-based discrimination, through market forces, also tends to weaken customer-based discrimination. Marketplace transactions bring different groups into regular contact with each other. Many white people who started listening to Black music on the jukebox in the 1950s, or who saw Jackie Robinson play baseball, started asking themselves what was so wrong with integrated lunch counters. Discrimination is also weakened by economic growth more generally. For instance, declining costs of production make it possible for businesses to take more chances. If a small town has only two lunch counters, maybe neither will take a chance with integration. If the town grows and also the costs of starting a new business fall, suddenly there are seven lunch counters. Maybe one will experiment with integration. In the long run, no successful market economy has succeeded in maintaining widespread formal segregation.

Discrimination by Employees Customers and employers aren't the only possible sources of discrimination. Sometimes workers don't want to mix with people from different groups. In India, many workers don't want to work alongside Dalits, workers from a low caste who are considered impure. In the United States, some firefighters—rightly or wrongly—don't want women to have equal status in the firehouse. Similarly, some men in the armed forces don't think that women or gay men should serve in combat and some men are looked at with suspicion if they want to work as nurses or at a day care center.

The profit incentive doesn't necessarily break down discrimination of this kind. An employer in India who hires Dalits, for example, may find that they have to pay other workers a higher wage to compensate them for the negative experience of working with Dalits. As a result, it's cheaper to discriminate than to hire everyone equally. Similarly, if you hire a woman into an all-male firehouse that doesn't want women, morale may fall and some men may leave for other jobs.

As a result, employers are less likely to hire a person, even a productive person, from the victimized group.

Of course, an employer might hire only Dalits, or if women are not welcome in firehouses, an employer may set up an entirely new firehouse, one equipped with women and nonprejudiced men, but starting from scratch in this fashion isn't always so easy to do.

Discrimination of this kind can be self-reinforcing and difficult to identify. If it's unpleasant for women to work in firehouses, then many women who want to be firefighters won't want to work in firehouses. Few women are hired but employers might say that's because few women are applying. Maybe it won't look like discrimination at all, but discrimination will still be a force at work.

Discrimination by Government

So far we've been talking about discrimination in markets but it's important to remember that governments discriminate, too. Government is sometimes part of the problem rather than part of the solution. We've already mentioned that prosegregation policies in the American South, before the civil rights movement, often came from governments. Governments required separate hospitals for Black and white patients, separate public and private schools, separate churches, separate cemeteries, separate public restrooms, and separate restaurants, hotels, and train service. Before prosegregation laws were passed after the Civil War, many parts of the South were moving (albeit sometimes hesitantly) toward more integration.

Government discrimination didn't just occur in the U.S. South. The federal government also routinely discriminated against Blacks. The Federal Housing Administration (FHA), for example, was set up during the Great Depression to insure home mortgages thereby encouraging more mortgage lending. But, until 1968, the FHA restricted its subsidies to all-white neighborhoods and refused to insure loans to Blacks or even to whites in integrated neighborhoods. This practice of "redlining" made it more difficult and expensive for Blacks to obtain mortgages and it encouraged segregated neighborhoods.

The best known example of widespread government segregation was the apartheid system of South Africa, which was enforced from 1948 until the early 1990s. ("Apartheid" is a word in the Afrikaans language that translates literally as "apartness.") Under this arrangement, Black people had to live in special areas and could not compete with white workers for many jobs. But this highly unjust situation was enforced by government laws, and enacted by white minority governments (Black citizens also couldn't vote). Once those laws were removed, Black people moved into many jobs and received higher wages. Many forms of implicit segregation continue in South Africa, but some of the most egregious examples of discrimination have fallen away. Many employers are happy to hire the most productive workers they can find, regardless of the skin color or ethnic background of those workers.

Why Discrimination Isn't Always Easy to Identify

Two economists had a neat idea. They sent around two sets of identical résumés. On one set of résumés, the names were quite traditional and did not identify the background of the person applying. An applicant named "John Smith," for instance, could be either white or Black. The second set of résumés had more unusual names on them—names like "Lakisha Washington" or "Jamal Jones." As you may know, those are names closely associated with Blacks. Names can tell you a lot about who a person is. In recent years, more than 40% of the Black girls born in California were given names that, in those same years, not one of the roughly 100,000 white newly born California girls was given.[*]

The result was striking: the resumes with the Black names received many fewer interview requests. The job applicants with the "whiter" names received 50% more calls.

But that is not the end of the story. Steven Levitt (of *Freakonomics* fame) and Roland Fryer (a Harvard professor and a Black man) set out to test how much Black names really mattered in the long run for earnings. It seems that having a "Black name" does not appear to hurt a person's chances in life, once the neighborhood that person comes from is controlled for. In other words, the number of interviews a person gets at first may not matter so much in the long run. Levitt and Fryer consider two possibilities. It may be that the so-called Black names get fewer interviews, but they end up with jobs of equal quality. Alternatively, people with Black-sounding names may have fewer chances in white communities but greater chances in Black communities; the two tendencies might balance each other out.

One point to note is that in the résumé experiment, by far the most common outcome of submitting a résumé, for both the white and Black candidates and regardless of name, was not receiving any interview requests at all. The lesson is that just about everyone can expect a lot of rejection before they find the job that is right for them.

Did you know that good-looking people earn more, even if they have the same job credentials? That's right, good-looking people earn about 5% more. Tall people earn more, too, again if they are compared with shorter people with the same paper credentials. Under one account, an extra inch in height translates into a 1.8% increase in wages.[**]

But these studies also show just how difficult it is to identify true discrimination. For instance, maybe tall people are paid more because they are more self-confident and not because anyone discriminates against shorter people. One study found that what best predicts wages, in this context, is *the height a man had at the time of high school* and not the height he ends up with as an adult. So if you were a tall person in high school, maybe that built up your self-confidence and makes you a better leader today, even if you stopped growing while your friends kept on getting taller.[†]

One question is why employers might prefer to hire tall people and to pay them more. One possibility is simply that the employer has an unreasonable preference against shorter people. Another possibility is that the employer is subconsciously tricked into thinking the taller leader is better, without ever realizing it. Yet another option is that the taller leader really is better (for the firm) because subordinates are

Did the man on the left get the better deal?

Radius Images/Getty Images

* That is from Bertrand, Marianne, and Sendhil Mullainathan. 2004. Are Emily and Greg more employable than Lakisha and Jamal? A field experiment on labor market discrimination. *American Economic Review* 94(4): 991–1013. For the earnings study, see Fryer Jr., Roland G., and Steven D. Levitt. 2002. The causes and consequences of distinctively black names. *Quarterly Journal of Economics* 119(3): 767–805.

** To survey this literature, see Engemann, Kristie M., and Michael T. Owyang. April, 2005. So much for that merit raise: The link between wages and appearance. *The Regional Economist*. https://www.stlouisfed.org/publications /regional-economist/april-2005/so-much-for-that-merit-raise-the-link-between-wages-and-appearance

† Persico, Nicola, Andrew Postlewaite, and Dan Silverman. 2004. The effect of adolescent experience on labor market outcomes: The case of height. *Journal of Political Economy* 112(5): 1019–1053.

more likely to pay that person respect. Again, we don't know the right answer, and this illustrates just how difficult it is to estimate the scope of labor market discrimination.

In many cases, market forces have succeeded in making some discrimination go away, or at least markets have minimized some of the bad effects of discrimination. But few people doubt that discrimination remains a feature of our world today.

Takeaway

It is no accident that workers in some countries earn much more than workers in other countries. Workers in wealthy, high-wage countries work with more physical capital, they have more education and training (human capital), and they work in a more efficient and flexible setting. Those are the fundamental reasons why wages are high.

The theory of compensating differentials explains why fun jobs pay less and dangerous jobs pay more. As wealth increases, workers become more willing to give up money for safety and so job safety increases over time and is higher in wealthier countries than in poorer countries.

Unions can raise some workers' wages, often at the expense of other workers, but unions are not a fundamental reason why wages are high in wealthy countries.

At least two kinds of discrimination occur in labor markets, statistical discrimination and preference-based discrimination. Markets tend to break down discrimination over time, because profit-seeking employers are looking to hire the most productive workers. Nonetheless, this force is imperfect and some discrimination persists.

CHECK YOURSELF

- From a profit-making perspective, why is employer discrimination just plain dumb?
- Of the three types of discrimination—employer, customer, employee—which has been affected most by market economies? Which has been affected least? Why?

CHAPTER REVIEW

Go online to practice with more examples of these types of problems, including live links to videos, data sources, and feedback.

KEY CONCEPTS

marginal product of labor (MPL), p. 353

human capital, p. 358

compensating differential, p. 360

statistical discrimination, p. 365

FACTS AND TOOLS

1. In Chapter 3, we listed six important demand shifters. Since the demand for labor is like the demand for any other good, those same factors apply here. Let's look at factors that might shift the demand for janitors at the McDonald's we discussed. For each of the following cases, state whether labor demand will rise or fall, and also state which of the six factors seems to be causing the shift in demand.

    a. A new junior high school opens up across the street from the McDonald's.

    b. Customers become much more concerned about clean restaurants: They'll walk out if there's dirt on the floor.

    c. As robots like the Roomba vacuum cleaner become cheaper, the McDonald's buys some robots to do half of the janitors' work.

2. Now let's do the same with shifts in Joe's labor supply from Figure 18.2. We listed five important supply shifters in Chapter 3. For each example, state whether you think Joe's labor supply will tend to increase or decrease as a result of the change, and state which of the five factors seem to cause the supply shift.

   a. The government raises Joe's income tax rate, so now he pays 20% of his wages to the government instead of the old 10%.

   b. The price of comfortable work shoes falls dramatically. Now, his feet won't ache nearly as much after a full day of work.

   c. While in Las Vegas for the weekend, Joe wins a $1 million jackpot.

3. True or false: Since an individual's labor supply curve can be backward-bending and a market's labor supply is just the summation of individual labor supply curves, then it is likely the case that the market's labor supply curve is also backward-bending.

4. Let's apply the idea of compensating differentials to janitorial jobs. Suppose there are two quite similar restaurants in the same town, Cafe Tropical and JJ's Diner. Both have the same demand for janitorial labor. But all the janitors in town know that it's much more fun to work at JJ's Diner.

   a. Which restaurant will pay a higher wage for janitors? Why?

   b. Which restaurant will hire more janitors? Why?

5. According to the theory of compensating differentials, which low-skilled jobs in the United States will tend to pay the most:

   a. The safe jobs or the dangerous jobs?

   b. The fun jobs or the boring jobs?

   c. The dead-end jobs or the first-rung-on-the-ladder jobs?

6. As mentioned in the chapter, OSHA fines companies for unsafe workplaces. At the same time, the labor market also "fines" companies that give their workers dangerous jobs. The fines of the marketplace are larger than the U.S. government's fines by about what factor: a factor of 10, of 100, of 1,000, or of 10,000?

7. The director of human resources at Wernham Hogg Paper Merchants is hiring new engineers. The director has a stack of 250 applications and is going to do a little research. With a little cyber-snooping on all 250, the director finds the following:

   i. Of the 150 who have Facebook pages, 50 are holding a bottle of beer in their profile photo, and 100 aren't.

   ii. Of the 100 who have their own websites, 20 have more than two typos.

   iii. Of the 150 who have Facebook pages, 25 have at least two friends who have apparently spent time in prison, according to a quick check of public records.

   a. Each of these are cases of sending bad signals. In each case, describe what you think these might be signals of.

   b. In each case, is the bad signal 100% correct? For example, is every applicant with three or four typos on their personal website worse than every applicant with an error-free page?

   c. In each case, is the bad signal probably better or probably worse than having no signal at all? In other words, should the bad signal get at least a little bit of weight in the balance if the HR director's only goal is to hire the best workers?

8. It is commonly said that women earn roughly 80 cents for every dollar that a man earns, even when doing the same job. Let's assume this is literally true in order to see how an entrepreneur would respond to this fact.

   a. Exetek, a battery manufacturer, has an all-male workforce. It pays $10 million per year in salary to these men, and has annual profits of $1 million. You've just been hired as an outside consultant to help Exetek raise its profits. Your advice is to fire all the men and replace them with women. If Exetek followed your advice, what would Exetek's salary costs fall to? How much would this decision raise Exetek's profits?

   b. After your success at Exetek, you start getting a lot more consulting jobs. You give the same advice to all the companies looking to boost profits: Fire your men and hire an all-female workforce for 20% less. What will this do to the demand for female labor? And what will this tend to do to women's wages?

9. Michael Lynn, a social psychologist in Cornell's School of Hotel Administration, has spent years studying tipping (his homepage has well tested

advice on how to increase your tips). He finds that men tip more when they have a female server, while women tend to tip more when they have a male server. This sounds a lot like discrimination by customers.

a. If this is a fact, who will tend to apply for jobs waiting tables at truck stops: mostly men or mostly women?

b. If this is a fact, who will tend to apply for jobs waiting tables at steakhouses: mostly men or mostly women?

c. If this is a fact, who will tend to apply for jobs waiting tables at vegetarian restaurants: mostly men or mostly women?

d. In these three cases, does your experience match up with what this simple theory predicts? If there's a contradiction, what do you think the simple model is missing?

10. True or false?

a. The marginal product of labor is the amount of extra profit that a firm will earn if it hires one more worker.

b. The benefit of having a college education has increased since the 1960s.

c. The wage gap between high school graduates and high school dropouts is insignificant.

d. By definition, a labor supply curve cannot have a negative slope.

e. Compensating differentials is a government program that pays injured workers.

f. The main reason that an immigrant earns more when they move from Algeria to France is because the French have strong labor unions.

g. If customers are racist and sexist, then self-interest will tend to push entrepreneurs to engage in racist and sexist hiring.

h. If some employers are bigots but others are not, the bigoted employers will be able to hire good workers for less money and will tend to drive the fair-minded employers out of business.

THINKING AND PROBLEM SOLVING

11. Construction jobs in Mumbai pay roughly $1 to $3 per hour. The job isn't that safe:

a lot of sharp objects, a lot of ways to fall off a building. The city council of Mumbai decides to set some job safety regulations for the construction industry. Let's assume that the government enforces these new regulations effectively and fairly, so that half as many workers get hurt on the job. Let's also assume that the city council makes the taxpayers pay the cost of making these jobs safer, so there's no noticeable shift in the labor demand curve.

a. After these new job safety regulations come into effect, will workers be more willing to take these jobs than before or less willing than before?

b. Is that like a rise in the supply of labor or like a fall in the supply of labor?

c. Let's put it all together: What will these job safety regulations do to the wage for construction jobs in Mumbai?

d. What principle from this chapter does this illustrate?

e. In the United States, OSHA doesn't make taxpayers pay the cost of making jobs safer. Instead, OSHA requires employers to spend the money themselves to make their firm's jobs safer. Thus, OSHA requirements work like a tax on labor demand. What would this probably do to the demand curve for construction labor: Would it increase or decrease construction labor demand?

12. We've seen what happens when job safety regulations are imposed. Now let's see what happens when they're taken away.

a. If a radical free-market, antiregulation government comes to power in the land of Randonia, and it begins dismantling job safety regulations, what will this tend to do to the supply of labor for dangerous jobs in Randonia: Will it increase or decrease?

b. Will that push wages in dangerous jobs up or down?

c. What will this do to the supply of labor in safer jobs? And to the number of people working in safer jobs?

d. Overall, will employers have to pay for their decision to offer dangerous jobs, or will they have a free lunch handed to them by the new government?

13. As we saw, unions can raise wages in a sector of the economy by restricting the number of workers in that sector. Let's see what tends to happen to the workers who don't get jobs in those favored unionized sectors. We'll use the computer programmer data from the Work It Out problem to illustrate:

Number of Programmers per Firm	Robotron's MPL ($)	Korrexia's MPL ($)
10	200	110
20	150	80
30	120	60
40	110	50
50	80	40
60	60	20
70	50	10
80	40	0
90	20	0
100	10	0

a. As in the Work It Out problem, there are 100 workers. In 2084, after decades of complaining about low wages, the programmers at Robotron have a secret-ballot vote and form a union. Their new union bargains for a wage of $80 per hour, and the newly unionized programmers are very excited. How many workers will Robotron hire at the new, higher wage?

b. How many Robotron workers just got laid off? Compare your answer to part a against the answer to part c of the Work It Out problem to find out.

c. A natural choice for the other programmers is to look for work at Korrexia: As before, the remaining workers have perfectly inelastic labor supply, so all 100 workers are going to work at one of the two firms. What's the wage for the nonunion Korrexia workers? How many programmers work for Korrexia?

d. You might think that one solution is to unionize both firms and lift wages for all the programmers. If the unions negotiate a high-wage contract and unionized wages rise to $110 at both firms, how many of the 100 workers will have jobs?

14. Suppose that we tax CEO salaries very highly, as some are proposing in the United States. What is your prediction about CEO perks such as jets and in-house chefs?

15. a. The average person doesn't like working the night shift. According to the theory of compensating differentials, are night-shift wages probably higher or lower than day-shift wages?

b. Most companies do their high-skilled work during the day shift: The big meetings, the major deliveries, the crucial repair work—all get done during the day. As a result, firms prefer to hire workers with more human capital during day-shift work, and they prefer to hire less-skilled workers at night. According to the theory of human capital, are night-shift wages probably higher or lower than day-shift wages?

c. Just based on these two theories, will night-shift work pay more than day-shift work on average, will it pay less on average, or can't you tell with the information given?

d. Economist Peter Kostiuk, in a 1990 article in the *Journal of Political Economy*, wanted to see whether the theory of compensating differentials was true for U.S. workers. He had information on the wages, education backgrounds, and work experience of U.S. workers, and he knew whether they worked the day shift or the night shift. On average, those who worked the night shift actually earned about 4% *less* than workers on the day shift. Is this probably because of compensating differentials, or is it probably because of human capital differences?

e. Kostiuk then used statistical techniques to simulate how much a typical worker in a low-skilled job would earn if they switched from the day shift to the night shift. The answer? The worker would earn 44% *more* money, on average. Is this 44% wage increase caused by a lower supply of night-shift labor, or is it caused by a higher demand for night-shift labor?

16. True or false? Morticians are paid lower wages than other workers because very few people want to work with dead bodies.

17. One way that Jim Crow segregation laws operated was by providing worse government schools for Black students. This widened the human capital gap between Black workers and white workers (this human capital gap has narrowed dramatically since the successes of the 1960s Civil Rights Movement). Would this form of government segregation tend to increase statistical discrimination on the basis of race or lower it? How can you tell?

18. In the United States, it's legal to work for free: We call this an "unpaid internship."

    a. Why will college students take these zero-wage jobs when they could get a minimum-wage job instead?

    b. Which idea in this chapter does this sound like?

    c. Just for thought: Why do you think federal law allows people to work for free, but not for $1 per hour? Is it just an oversight on the part of government, or do you think there's some grand design at work?

CHALLENGES

19. Explain how wage differentials caused by discrimination by employees could appear to be driven by human capital differences.

20. In the decades after the Civil War, most streetcar companies in the South discriminated against one class of citizens: smokers. Customers who wanted to smoke had to ride in the back of the car. Around 1900, many governments in the South passed laws mandating segregation by race instead. As Jennifer Roback documented in the *Journal of Economic History* in 1986, many streetcar operators protested against this new form of segregation. Assuming that these entrepreneurs were driven by self-interest alone rather than a desire for equality, why would they do that?

21. We mentioned that "a [college] degree signals . . . something good about the job candidate, namely that they have enough intelligence, competence, and conscientiousness to earn a college degree." This view, put forward by Nobel laureate Michael Spence, is unsurprisingly known as the signaling theory of education. Taken to the extreme, signaling theorists say that you suffer through college not because you get valuable job skills, but only because it's a good way to prove that you were *already* smart and capable before you started college.

    a. Suppose you want to prove this theory wrong: You want to show that college courses really do make you a better worker, just like the human capital theorists say. How would you go about proving that? Remember, just showing that college graduates earn more isn't evidence!

    b. If that's too difficult, at least explain why the following plausible-sounding tests of human capital vs. signaling aren't very good tests at all:

        i. Looking at wages of people with degrees compared with people without degrees

        ii. Comparing wages for people whose parents can afford college with wages for people whose parents can't afford college

22. In a market economy, firms with more workers can make and sell more output—that goes without saying. The marginal product of labor tells you how much extra revenue each extra worker generates. Economists often tend to use one particular equation to sum up the link between workers, revenue, and the marginal product of labor: We call it the production function. Let's practice with it just a little here.

    a. At Dunder Mifflin, the hourly revenue production function works like this:

$$\text{Revenue} = 100 \times \sqrt{(\text{Number of semiskilled workers})}$$

    This is a way of saying that in order to sell product, you actually need workers to do work. Use this formula to fill out the "Total Revenue" column in the next table.

Number of Workers	Total Revenue ($)	Marginal Product of Labor ($)
0	0	N/A
1	100	100
2	141	41
3		
4		
5		

    b. As we mentioned in the chapter, the marginal product of labor is the extra revenue that's generated by each extra worker. It's the change in revenue from adding one more worker. Fill out that column, as well.

c. If the market wage for semiskilled workers is $25 per hour, how many workers should Dunder Mifflin hire?

23. In Chapter 8, we analyzed a minimum wage in the usual way, as a price floor, and we showed that a minimum wage creates unemployment. Now suppose that firms must pay the minimum wage but they can adjust the working conditions, such as increasing the pace of work, reducing lunch breaks, cutting back on employee discounts, and so forth. Will the minimum wage create (as much) unemployment if firms adjust in this way? (*Hint:* Think of the balance in Figure 18.7.)

Discovering DATA

24. Using the FRED Economic database (https://fred.stlouisfed.org/), find the median weekly earnings of high school graduates (no college) who are 25 years of age or over. Click Edit Graph, then Add Line, and add the median weekly earnings of people with a bachelor's degree or higher who are 25 years of age or older.

a. In the second quarter of 2022, what were the weekly earnings of high school graduates without a college degree? What were the weekly earnings of college graduates?

b. What accounts for the different weekly earnings?

WORK IT OUT

For interactive, step-by-step help in solving this problem, go online.

One way to think about wages for different jobs is to see it as another application of the law of one price. We came across this law when we discussed speculation in Chapter 7, and it came up again when we discussed international trade in Chapter 9. The basic idea is that the supply of workers will keep adjusting until jobs that need the same kinds of workers earn the same wage. If *similar* workers earned *different* wages, then the workers in the low-paid jobs would reduce their labor supply, and the workers in the high-paid jobs would face more competition from those low-paid workers.

Let's look at 100 computer programmers who are trying to decide whether to work for one of two companies: Robotron or Korrexia. To keep things simple, assume that both companies are equally fun to work for, so you don't need to worry about compensating differentials here. The marginal product of labor (per additional hour of work) is in the following table:

Number of Programmers per Firm	Robotron's MPL ($)	Korrexia's MPL ($)
10	100	55
20	75	40
30	60	30
40	55	25
50	40	20
60	30	10
70	25	5
80	20	0
90	10	0
100	5	0

a. These two firms are the whole market for programmer labor. In the next table, estimate the programmer demand curve by adding up the quantity of programmers demanded at each wage. For example, at a wage of $40 per hour, Robotron would hire 50 workers (since the first 50 workers have a MPL ≥ 40) and Korrexia 20, so the total demand is 70 workers.

Wage ($)	Number of Programmers Demanded
100	10
75	
60	
55	
40	50 + 20 = 70
30	
25	
20	
10	
5	

b. The programmers in this town are going to work at one of these two places for sure: Their labor supply is vertical, or in other words, perfectly inelastic, with **supply** = 100. So, what will the equilibrium wage be? Just as in Figure 18.1, the numbers may not work out exactly—so use your judgment to come up with a good answer.

c. Now, head back to the first table: About how many programmers will work at Robotron and how many at Korrexia? Again, use your judgment to come up with a good answer.

d. Suppose 50 more programmers come to town. What will the wage be now? And how many will work at each firm?

19

Public Goods and the Tragedy of the Commons

Sixty-six million years ago Chicxulub, a 7-mile-wide asteroid, smashed into the Earth near the coast of modern-day Mexico. The impact unleashed the energy of a billion Hiroshima bombs and threw a jet of molten rock and dust into the sky that reached halfway to the moon. The debris was hotter than the surface of the sun and, as it descended, it set everything on fire. As the Earth turned, the fire spread until the entire Indian subcontinent was burning. The dust and soot soon blocked out the sun, plunging the Earth into darkness and cold. As you probably know, the asteroid wiped out the dinosaurs. It also killed more than 99.9999% of all living organisms.[1]

The probability of death by asteroid is remarkably high—by some calculations about the same as death by passenger aircraft crash. How can this be? Although the probability of an asteroid hitting Earth is very small, a lot of people would be killed if one did hit, so the probability of death by asteroid is much larger than most people imagine. It doesn't happen very often, but watch out when it does.[*]

Let's assume that we have convinced you that the danger from an asteroid collision is real and thus that asteroid deflection would be a valuable good to have. Markets provide us with all kinds of valuable goods like food, clothing, and cell phones, but you can't buy asteroid deflection in the market. Even if everyone were to become convinced of the benefits of asteroid deflection, you probably will *never* be able to buy asteroid deflection in the market. To see why, we need to take a closer look at some of the common properties of ordinary goods and some of the special properties of asteroid deflection.

When you spend $100 on a new pair of jeans, you get the exclusive use of a new pair of jeans. If you don't spend $100 on a new pair of jeans, you are excluded from using the jeans. In other words, the $100 makes a big difference in whether or not you get the jeans. That's obvious.

CHAPTER OUTLINE

Four Types of Goods

Private Goods and Public Goods

Club Goods

Common Resources and the Tragedy of the Commons

Takeaway

Appendix: The Tragedy of the Commons: How Fast?

MRU

mru.org/public-goods

Public Goods and Asteroid Defense

---

[*] Everyone dies from something. In the United States, the probability of death by car crash is about 1 in 100 and the probability of death by commercial airplane crash is about 1 in 20,000. Chapman and Morrison (1994) estimate that the probability of death by asteroid collision is also about 1 in 20,000. See Chapman, Clark and David Morrison. 1994. Impacts on the earth by asteroids and comets: Assessing the hazard. *Nature* 367: 33–40.

Now consider paying $100 toward asteroid deflection. What do you get for your $100? There are really only two situations to consider: Either enough people pay for asteroid deflection so that the asteroid will be deflected even without your $100 or so few people pay that the asteroid will not be deflected even with your $100.* Either way, your $100 makes no appreciable difference in the amount of asteroid deflection that you will receive. In other words, you get the same amount of asteroid deflection whether you pay or don't pay.

Since your $100 doesn't get you more asteroid deflection but it does get you a new pair of jeans, most people will buy the jeans rather than the asteroid deflection. As a result, we see a lot of firms selling jeans and none selling asteroid deflection. That's a problem because asteroids are a threat to everyone.

Jeans are an example of a private good. Asteroid deflection is an example of what economists call a public good, a good that markets are unlikely to produce in efficient quantities. Let's look more closely at these terms and the differences between jeans and asteroid deflection.

Four Types of Goods

Jeans are different from asteroid deflection for two reasons. First, as we said, people are willing to pay for jeans because paying makes the difference between getting the jeans or not—nonpayers can be cheaply excluded or prevented from consuming jeans. But people aren't willing to pay for asteroid deflection because paying makes no appreciable difference in how much asteroid deflection they consume—nonpayers cannot be excluded from consuming the benefits of asteroid deflection. When a person can easily be prevented from using a good, economists say the good is excludable. When a person cannot be easily prevented from using a good, economists say the good is **nonexcludable**. Jeans are excludable; asteroid deflection is nonexcludable.

> A good is **nonexcludable** if people who don't pay cannot be easily prevented from using the good.

The second reason why asteroid deflection is different from jeans is that when one person is wearing a pair of jeans, it's not easy for a second person to wear the same jeans. But two people can enjoy the benefits of the same asteroid deflection. In fact, billions of people can enjoy the benefits of the same asteroid deflection. But don't try fitting a billion people into the same pair of jeans!

When one person's use of a good reduces the ability of another person to use the same good, economists say the good is rival. When one person's use of a good does not reduce the ability of another person to use the same good, economists say the good is **nonrival**. Jeans are rival; asteroid deflection is nonrival.

> A good is **nonrival** if one person's use of the good does not reduce the ability of another person to use the same good.

These two factors, whether a good is excludable or nonexcludable and whether it is rival or nonrival, can be used to divide goods into four types, as in Table 19.1. We have already given an example of a private good, a good that is excludable and rival. Jeans are a private good; hamburgers and contact lenses are other familiar examples. We have also given one example of a public good, a good that is nonexcludable and nonrival. Asteroid deflection is nonexcludable and nonrival. National defense is another example. Let's take a closer look at the differences between private and public goods and then we will examine the other two categories of goods, club goods and common resources.

---

* The probability that your $100 makes the difference between a successful asteroid deflection and an unsuccessful asteroid deflection is so small that we can ignore it.

TABLE 19.1 FOUR TYPES OF GOODS

	Excludable	Nonexcludable
Rival	**Private Goods** Jeans Hamburgers Contact lenses	**Common Resources** Tuna in the ocean The environment Public roads
Nonrival	**Club Goods** Video streaming Wi-Fi Digital music	**Public Goods** Asteroid deflection National defense Mosquito control

Private Goods and Public Goods

Private goods are excludable and rival. Since private goods are excludable, they can be provided by markets—someone who doesn't pay, doesn't get; so there is an incentive to pay for and thus to produce these goods. Furthermore, since the goods are rival, excludability doesn't result in inefficiency—in a competitive market the only people who will be excluded from consuming a private good are the people who are not willing to pay what it costs to produce the good, and that's efficient.

Public goods are nonexcludable and nonrival. Since public goods are nonexcludable, it's difficult to get people to pay for them voluntarily. Markets, therefore, will tend to underprovide public goods.

Public goods are also nonrival, which means that one person's use doesn't reduce the ability of another person to use the good. As a result, 8 billion people can be protected from an asteroid strike for the same cost as protecting 1 million people. Since public goods are nonrival, the losses from the failure to provide these goods can be especially large.

Let's look at another public good, mosquito control. Mosquitoes are annoying insects. With the spread of the West Nile virus in the United States, they are also dangerous. Mosquitoes can be killed by spraying, but spraying just one house won't do much good for its owners because mosquitoes from other areas will quickly repopulate any small region, so you have to spray a city or neighborhood. But who will pay to spray a city or neighborhood? If some people do pay, then many others are likely to **free ride**, sit back and enjoy the benefits without contributing to their share of the costs. Fewer mosquitoes mean fewer mosquitoes for everyone, not just those who pay for mosquito control. If a lot of people free ride, then mosquito control will be underprovided by the market even though it is a valuable good.

The benefits of public goods provide an argument for taxation and government provision. By taxing everyone and producing the public good, government can make people better off. Many cities and counties, for example, pay for mosquito control from government tax revenues. National defense is another example of a public good that would be difficult to provide voluntarily but is provided by government.

It may seem paradoxical that people can be made better off by requiring them to do something that they would not choose to do voluntarily, but

Private goods are excludable and rival.

Public goods are nonexcludable and nonrival.

A **free rider** enjoys the benefits of a public good without paying a share of the costs.

The English philosopher Thomas Hobbes (1588–1679) explained under what conditions individuals might voluntarily give up their rights.

I authorise and give up my right of governing myself to this man, or to this assembly of men, on this condition; that thou give up, thy right to him, and authorise all his actions in like manner.

— *Leviathan*, Chapter 17

A **forced rider** is someone who pays a share of the costs of a public good but who does not enjoy the benefits.

the paradox can be resolved. Imagine that there are a million people, all of whom want national defense, but none of whom chooses to voluntarily contribute to national defense because of the incentive to free ride. Now imagine that this group is offered the following plan: "The government will tax each of you and use the proceeds to pay for national defense but only if you all agree to the plan." It's quite possible that even though none contribute voluntarily, all will agree to be taxed, *so long as everyone else is also taxed.*

Of course, just because everyone *can* be made better off by taxation does not mean that everyone *will* be made better off. Some people want more national defense, some people want less, pacifists want none. So, taxation means that some people will be turned into **forced riders**, people who must contribute to the public good even though their benefits from the public good are low or even negative.

What quantity of the public good should the government produce? In principle, the government should produce the amount that maximizes consumer plus producer surplus or the total benefits of the public good minus the total costs. But, in practice, figuring this out is very difficult. The total benefit of a public good, for example, is the sum of the benefits to each individual. But some individuals value the public good more than others and there is no easy way to find out exactly how much each person values the good.

We showed in Chapter 4 that (under certain conditions) a market automatically produces the quantity of a good that maximizes consumer plus producer surplus. We now know that one of the required conditions is that the good be a private good, a good that is rival and excludable. Unfortunately, no one has yet discovered a workable process that, as if guided by an "invisible hand," produces optimal amounts of public goods.

Voting and other democratic procedures can help to produce information about the demand for public goods, but these processes are unlikely to work as well at providing the optimal amounts of public goods as do markets at providing the optimal amounts of private goods (see Chapter 20 for more). Thus, we have more confidence that the optimal amount of toothpaste is purchased every year ($2.3 billion worth in recent years) than the optimal amount of defense spending ($773 billion) or the optimal amount of asteroid deflection (less than $1 billion). In some cases, we could get too much of the public good with many people being forced riders, and in other cases, we could get too little of the public good. Nevertheless, since markets are challenged to provide public goods, we are probably fortunate that government can provide public goods even if the method is imperfect.

One final point about public goods: A public good is *not* defined as a good produced in the public sector. If the government started to produce jeans, for example, that does not make jeans a public good. The government does produce mail delivery even though mail delivery is not a public good. Similarly, asteroid deflection is a public good even though, as of yet, the government does not produce very much asteroid deflection.

CHECK YOURSELF

- What happens if government provides more of a public good than is efficient? Who is hurt? Who benefits? Use national defense as an example.

Club Goods

Club goods are goods that are excludable but nonrival. A television show like *Succession*, for example, is excludable—you must buy HBO to watch the show, at least in its first run—but it's also nonrival because when one person watches, this does not reduce the ability of another person to watch. Clearly, markets can provide goods that are excludable but nonrival, but they do so at the price of some efficiency. HBO prohibits some people from watching *Succession*, for example, even though they would be willing to pay the cost (close to zero for an additional viewer) but not the price (say, $9.99 for HBO Max per month).

In practice, the inefficiency from the underprovision of most nonrival private goods like television, music, and software is not that big a deal. The fixed costs of producing these goods must be paid somehow and we do not want to lose the diversity, creativity, and responsiveness provided by markets.

Entrepreneurs are constantly looking for ways to turn nonexcludable, nonrival goods, such as broadcast television, into club goods (nonrival but excludable), such as video streaming services, so that they can be provided at a profit. Furthermore, entrepreneurs can sometimes find clever ways of profiting from nonrival goods *even without relying on exclusion.*

Club goods are goods that are excludable but nonrival.

The Peculiar Case of Advertising

Radio and broadcast television are peculiar goods because although they are public goods, nonrival *and* nonexcludable, they are provided in large quantities by markets. How is this possible? When radio first appeared, no one could figure out how to make a profit from it and most people thought that government provision would be necessary if people were to benefit from this amazing discovery. After much experimentation, however, entrepreneurs did discover how to give radio away for free (the efficient solution) and yet still make a profit—they discovered advertising. Advertisers pay for the costs of programming that is then given away for free.

Advertising, of course, is not a perfect solution to the problem of nonexcludability and nonrivalry, but for radio and broadcast television, it has worked fairly well. Advertising works so well that some nonrival goods are provided without exclusion even when exclusion would be cheap. Google, for example, spends billions of dollars indexing the Web and developing search algorithms and then it offers its product to anyone in the world for free. Google could exclude people who don't pay for its service, but Google has discovered that selling advertising while providing its services for free is more profitable.

Finally, Wi-Fi is an interesting example of a nonrival but potentially excludable good because it is currently provided in just about every possible manner. Wi-Fi is sold by private firms like Sprint who exclude nonpayers by requiring security codes. Other firms offer Wi-Fi for free but only if you watch advertising. Cafés such as Panera Bread offer free Wi-Fi to help attract customers. Wi-Fi is also given away by people who choose not to close their access points. In Houston, the government taxes citizens to pay for the network and then offers free access. Each of these methods has its advantages and disadvantages.

CHECK YOURSELF

• Could advertising be used to pay for the upkeep of public parks? Where would the advertising be seen?

Common Resources and the Tragedy of the Commons

Common resources are goods that are nonexcludable but rival.

Common resources are goods that are nonexcludable but rival. An example is tuna in the ocean. Until they are caught, the tuna are unowned—hence nonexcludable—and it's difficult to prevent anyone from fishing for tuna. But tuna are not public goods since when one person catches and consumes a tuna, that leaves fewer tuna for other people. The result of nonexcludability and rivalry is often the **tragedy of the commons**, overexploitation and undermaintenance of the common resource. As a result of the tragedy of the commons, tuna are being driven toward extinction.

The **tragedy of the commons** is the tendency of any resource that is unowned and hence nonexcludable to be overused and undermaintained.

Since 1960, the tuna catch has decreased by 75% (see Figure 19.1). The southern bluefin is highly prized as sushi and demand has increased as sushi has become more trendy. The increase in demand and the decrease in the catch have driven up prices so much that a single choice tuna can now fetch $200,000 or more at the Tokyo fish market. As a result of the high price, corporations hunt tuna across the oceans in fast ships using satellites, sophisticated radar, and onboard helicopters. The sad truth is that because so many fish are caught, various types of sushi may soon become a thing of the past.

Tuna aren't the only fish headed toward extinction. A 2006 paper in *Science* estimated that if the long-term trend continues, *all* of the world's major seafood stocks will collapse by 2048. Already nearly 30% of seafood species have collapsed (defined as a decline in the catch of 90%). As seafood species decline so do all the species that depend on them in the food chain. Overfishing is draining the oceans of fish.

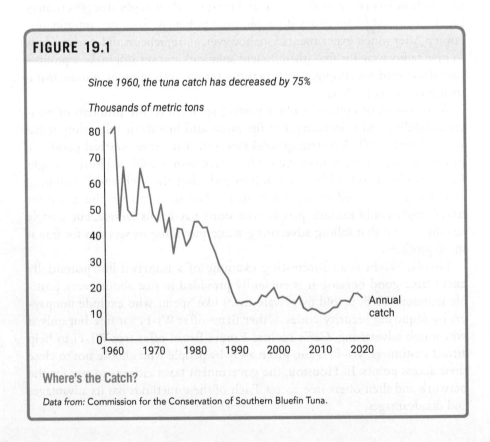

FIGURE 19.1

Since 1960, the tuna catch has decreased by 75%

Thousands of metric tons

Where's the Catch?

Data from: **Commission for the Conservation of Southern Bluefin Tuna.**

Overfishing, however, is not primarily caused by increased demand. People like to eat chickens even more than they like to eat tuna but chickens are not going extinct. Why not? The difference is that chickens are owned and tuna, "chickens of the sea," are unowned.

To see why ownership means that chickens are plentiful and tuna are scarce, let's take a closer look at the incentives of fishermen and chicken ranchers.

Everyone, including the fishermen whose livelihoods depend on tuna, knows that tuna are being fished to extinction. So, you might think that the logical thing for a tuna fisherman to do is to fish less. But that's not correct. If Haru, a Japanese tuna fisherman, fishes less, will there be more tuna for him to catch in the future? No; if Haru fishes less, that just leaves more tuna for other fishermen to catch—fishing less doesn't help Haru because he doesn't own the tuna until it's in the hold of his ship. Since Haru doesn't own the tuna in the ocean, he has no way of securing the fruits of his restraint.

Compare the incentives facing Haru with those facing Frank Perdue, the legendary chicken entrepreneur. Will Frank Perdue ever let his chickens go extinct? Of course not. Perdue makes money from his chickens, so to maximize profits, he will keep his stock of chickens healthy and growing. If Perdue "overfishes" his chickens, he pays the price. If Perdue exercises restraint and grows his flock, he gets the benefit. In short, Frank Perdue will never kill the chicken that lays his golden eggs.

The difference is ownership. Chickens (owned, not endangered)

"Chickens of the Sea" (unowned, endangered)

The problem of overfishing is one example of the *tragedy of the commons*, the tendency for any resource that is unowned to be overused and undermaintained. The theory goes back at least to Aristotle, who in criticizing Plato's idea of raising children in common said, "that which is common to the greatest number has the least care bestowed upon it."[2]

Do you live with other students? Take a look at your kitchen—that's the tragedy of the commons. Other examples of the tragedy of the commons include the slaughter of the open-range buffalo during the nineteenth century, deforestation in the African Sahel region, and the hunting of elephants to near extinction.

The tragedy of the commons applies especially strongly to resources like fish, forests, and agricultural land because these resources must be carefully maintained to remain useful. But when resources are unowned, the users do not have strong incentives to invest in maintenance because maintenance mostly creates an external benefit, not a private benefit. In other words, the fisherman who throws the small fish back mostly increases other people's future catch, not his own. The tragedy of the commons is thus a type of externality problem like those we examined in Chapter 10.

We typically call something a *tragedy* of the commons when the lack of maintenance is so severe that exploitation is pushed beyond the point where the resource can reproduce itself. To maintain a healthy stock of fish, for example, the yearly catch of fish must be no more than the yearly increase in fish population. If a population of 100 fish grows by 10% every year, then fishermen can catch 10 fish *forever*. But if the fishermen catch just one more

The tragedy of the commons

fish, 11 fish per year, the stock of fish will be extinct in just 26 years. (See the chapter appendix for a proof.) So, the fishermen who overfish are not just driving the fish into extinction, they are driving *their own way of life* into extinction—that's a tragedy.

Happy Solutions to the Tragedy of the Commons

The tragedy of the commons can sometimes be averted in small groups. Elinor Ostrom, the first woman to win a Nobel Prize in economics, found that all over the world, small villages and tribes have avoided the tragedy of overfishing a lake or overgrazing a pasture through the enforcement of norms. A tribe member who takes too many fish from the common lake will be shunned, like someone who litters in a public park. A tribe member who exercises restraint and throws the small fish back will be respected. Tragedy of the commons problems, however, are more difficult to solve when a lot of unrelated people have access to the common good.

Command and control and, more recently, tradable allowances have been used to solve tragedy of the commons problems, just as they have been used to solve other externality problems, as discussed in Chapter 10. When fishing stocks have neared depletion, for example, governments have tried command and control solutions like limiting the number of fishing boats. To protect their salmon fishery, British Columbia limited the number of boats in 1968. Unfortunately, the scheme did not work well because the fishermen installed more powerful engines and better electronics for finding fish—this is often called "capital stuffing" because the fishermen stuffed their boats with expensive capital so those boats could be more effective. As a result of capital stuffing, the value of the typical fishing boat tripled in just 10 years; not surprisingly, the salmon fishery continued to decline. Similar problems have occurred when governments have restricted the number of days that fishing is allowed.

New Zealand pioneered an alternative approach in 1986 with individual transferable quotas (ITQs). ITQs are similar to the pollution allowances that we looked at in Chapter 10; the owner of an ITQ has the right to catch a certain share of the total allowable catch of fish. The total allowable catch is set by the government. If the fishing stock increases then the government can increase the total allowable catch, which means that each fisherman can catch more.[3] ITQs can be bought and sold and the government does not restrict the types of boats or equipment that the fishermen use so resources are not wasted by capital stuffing.

The ITQ system has been very successful. Figure 19.2 shows that after the ITQ system was put into place, the fish catch in New Zealand increased—in other words, preventing the fishermen from overfishing *increased* the amount of fish that they caught! This may seem paradoxical but it's just a reminder of why the tragedy of the commons is a tragedy—when each fisherman chooses to fish rather than show restraint, the net result is less fish for everyone.* The same logic works in reverse—when each fisherman shows restraint the net result is a growing fish population, a higher total allowable catch and more fish for everyone.

New Zealand was able to create an ITQ system and rescue its fishery because most of the New Zealand fish live and spawn within 230 miles of New Zealand's shore—the economic zone that international law assigns

MRU

mru.org/ostrom

Women in Economics: Elinor Ostrom

---

* Thus, the tragedy of the commons can also be understood as a prisoner's dilemma, which we introduced in Chapter 15.

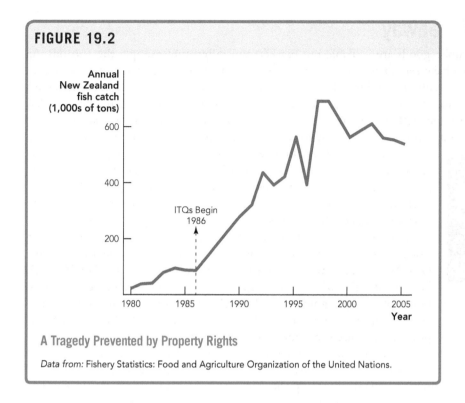

FIGURE 19.2

A Tragedy Prevented by Property Rights

Data from: Fishery Statistics: Food and Agriculture Organization of the United Nations.

https://www.youtube.com/
watch?v=MI8OVVpTGkQ

exclusively to New Zealand. Thus, the New Zealand government was able to create property rights and exclude anyone who didn't have the right to fish (i.e., an ITQ) from catching fish within its waters. Property rights in other common resources such as African elephants have also been created and have resulted in substantial improvements.

Unfortunately, it's not easy to create property rights in all common resources. Southern bluefin tuna, for example, migrate throughout the Pacific and Indian Oceans, and some have been tagged and tracked across thousands of miles of ocean. So any solution to the tragedy of the tuna commons will require a multi-country agreement. That's not impossible. In the 1970s, scientists discovered that certain chemicals commonly used in aerosols could disrupt the ozone layer, which protects the earth from UV-B radiation. Protecting the ozone layer is a public good since it is nonexcludable and nonrival. Fortunately, an international treaty called the Montreal Protocol has been signed by 197 countries, making it the first treaty in the history of the United Nations to be universally ratified, and it restricts the use of chemicals that damage the ozone layer. The treaty is widely regarded as the most successful environmental treaty since emissions of ozone-depleting chemicals have declined and the ozone layer is recovering.[4]

Similarly, if there were world agreement, technology could be used to tag tuna and create property rights, but as we know from our discussion of the Coase theorem in Chapter 10, the more parties required to make an agreement, the greater the transactions costs and the less likely a solution. Moreover, rather than working to create property rights or restrict fishing to sustainable levels, most major governments today subsidize fishing extensively, which is making the tragedy of the commons worse. Thus, the tragedy of the tuna commons may not have a happy solution any time soon, either for sushi lovers or for tuna.

CHECK YOURSELF

- Why do small communities find it easier to deal with common resource problems than a state or a country?

- Why is the establishment of property rights a key way to solve the problem of some common resources?

Takeaway

Public goods are valuable but markets will often undersupply these goods. As we have seen, *nonexcludability* and *nonrivalry* are important qualities of public goods, but nonexcludability is usually the more important problem. Nonrival but excludable goods such as video streaming or digital music can often be provided privately. Although there may be some inefficiency when nonpayers are excluded, private provision does allow for entrepreneurship and market discovery. When a good is nonexcludable, however, demanders don't have an incentive to pay for the good and, as a result, suppliers don't have an incentive to supply the good. That's why, for instance, markets don't sell protection against asteroid strikes. The benefit of providing public goods is an argument for government taxation and supply. Governments can produce public goods, but just because they can doesn't mean they will. Asteroid protection, for example, is a public good, but it isn't produced very much by anyone. Give NASA credit where credit is due, however. On September 26, 2022, NASA intentionally crashed a spacecraft into the asteroid Dimorphos. Dimorphos wasn't going to hit Earth, but NASA proved that it could successfully hit an asteroid and deflect it onto a new path, thus proving that planetary defense is possible. Three cheers for NASA!

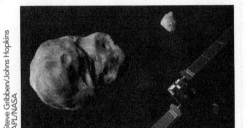

In a test run, NASA successfully altered the path of an asteroid and thus has begun the era of planetary defense!

A resource that is nonexcludable but rival will tend to be overused and undermaintained. The tragedy of the commons explains many of the major environmental problems facing the world today. Sometimes there are creative solutions to the tragedy of the commons, such as instituting new property rights. Unfortunately, creating property rights is not automatic and may require extensive understanding of economic principles and agreement among many of the world's governments.

In short, many of the world's problems arise when property rights to goods are either not possible, not protected, or not easily implemented.

CHAPTER REVIEW

Go online to practice with more examples of these types of problems, including live links to videos, data sources, and feedback.

KEY CONCEPTS

nonexcludable, p. 380

nonrival, p. 380

private good, p. 381

public good, p. 381

free rider, p. 381

forced rider, p. 382

club goods, p. 383

common resources, p. 384

tragedy of the commons, p. 384

FACTS AND TOOLS

1. Take a look at the following list of goods and services:

iPhones

Open-heart surgery

Streaming television services (e.g., Netflix)

Farm-raised salmon

Yosemite National Park

Central Park, New York City

The Chinese language

The idea of calculus

a. Is each item on the list excludable or nonex-cludable? Sometimes the border is a little fuzzy, but justify your answer if you think there's any ambiguity. (*Hint:* To categorize the two parks, it is useful to do a bit of research about their geography. More on this in part d.)

b. Rival or nonrival?

c. Based on your answers to parts a and b, sort each good or service into one of the four categories from Table 19.1.

d. How do you exclude people from a park?

2. Which of the following are free riders, which are forced riders, and which are just people paying for public goods?

a. In Britain, Alistair pays a tax to support the British Broadcasting Corporation. He doesn't own a radio or TV.

b. Monica pays her local property taxes and state income taxes. Police patrol her neighborhood regularly.

c. Miles, a young boy in 1940s Los Angeles, jumps on board the streetcar without paying.

d. In the United States, Monique pays taxes to fund children's immunizations. She lives out in the forest, has no family, and rarely sees other people.

e. In Japan, Dave, a tourist from the United States, enjoys the public parks.

3. a. Is education—a college course, for instance—excludable?

b. Is education a rival good? That is, if your class has more students, do you get a worse education on average? Do students (and parents) typically prefer smaller class sizes? Do professors typically prefer smaller classes? Does it usually cost more for a school to educate more students?

c. According to the standard economists' definition of a public good—the definition we use in this chapter—is education a public good?

d. Into which of the four categories from Table 19.1 does education seem to fit best?

4. Emeril says, "In my economics class, I learned that the only way to fund public goods was to have the government tax citizens to pay for those goods. Is that what you learned?"

Lupe responds, "Actually, in my class, we used *Modern Principles*, and we learned that there are other ways to fund public goods, like _____." Complete Lupe's statement.

5. The Patagonian toothfish is a large, ugly fish that can weigh 200 pounds. In the 1990s, it became very popular when it was rebranded as the Chilean sea bass. Soon, it almost became extinct. (Rebranding fish to make them more palatable to consumers is not uncommon. The orange roughy was originally known as the slimehead, which doesn't sound very appetizing.)

a. Why was the Chilean sea bass almost driven to extinction?

b. Some top chefs boycotted the Chilean sea bass in the hope of increasing the stock. Why was this unsuccessful?

c. Australia now enforces limits on the catch. Why would this tend to be more successful than the boycott?

Angelafoto/E+/Getty Images

6. a. The nation of Bumpo has been hunting its deer population to extinction. The government decrees strict limits on the number of hunters and on the number of rounds of ammunition that each hunter can take into the hunt. Hunters, like fishermen, are a creative lot: What will "capital stuffing" look like in this case?

b. What would an individual transferable quotas (ITQ) system look like in this case?

c. Do real governments use quotas like this to control deer populations? If you don't know the answer, just ask your classmates: There's probably a hunter or two in your course.

7. This chapter noted that chickens and the "chicken of the sea" (tuna) are fundamentally different in terms of population though they are both food. Indeed, chickens are eaten far more than tuna, and chickens are abundant compared with their ocean-living cousins.

a. What difference between these two species does this chapter identify as the explanation for this seemingly strange puzzle?

b. As population and prosperity have increased, the demand for chicken has increased. What happens to the price of chickens as a result? Why?

c. Because of the rules humans have concerning chickens, what happens to the number of people raising chickens as a result of the price change? Why? What happens to the number of chickens? Why?

d. What happens to the price of tuna as population and prosperity increase? Why?

e. Because of the rules humans have concerning tuna (as well as practical limitations that limit the ability to institute policies like ITQs on tuna catches), what happens to the number of people harvesting tuna as a result of the price change? Why?

8. a. Why did the fish catch *increase* in New Zealand after the amount that each fisherman could catch was *limited* by a quota?

b. Given your answer to part a, would an individual fisherman in New Zealand want to catch more fish than they are allowed if they knew no one would ever catch them?

c. So given your answer to part b, does the New Zealand system depend on government enforcement to work, or will individual fishermen agree out of self-interest to abide by the ITQ?

THINKING AND PROBLEM SOLVING

9. In 2008, Jean Nouvel won the Pritzker Architecture Prize (the highest prize in architecture). One of his most notable works is the Torre Agbar (pictured), a breakthrough skyscraper that lights up each night thanks to more than 4,000 LED devices—a pricey but purely cosmetic feature.

Atlantide Phototravel/Getty Images

a. Many people enjoy looking at the Torre Agbar. Just considering that enjoyment, how would you classify the Torre Agbar: rival or nonrival? Why?

b. The Torre Agbar is the third-tallest building in Barcelona. For the purposes of enjoying its illuminated façade, would you classify the building as an excludable or nonexcludable good? Why?

c. Based on your answers, is the LED façade a public good?

d. Companies often hire architects like Nouvel to create beautiful buildings that are expensive to design, build, and maintain, yet they cannot charge people to look at them. This chapter offered one possible explanation for this puzzle. What's the explanation and how does it help justify the construction of a widely enjoyed building? (*Hint:* The building is the headquarters for Grupo Agbar, a company dedicated to the distribution and treatment of water in countries all over the world. For most of you, this is the first time you've heard of this company.)

10. a. "A public good is just a good that provides large external benefits." Discuss.

b. "A tragedy of the commons occurs when using a good causes massive negative external costs." Discuss. In parts a and b, compare the definitions from Chapter 10 with those from this chapter.

11. a. Has the rise of the Internet and file sharing turned media such as movies and music into public goods? Why?

b. Taking your answer in part a into account, would government taxation and funding of music improve social welfare? In your answer, at least *mention* some of the practical difficulties of doing this.

12. We mentioned that the tragedy of the commons is a form of prisoner's dilemma, something we saw back in Chapter 15. As is so often the case in economics, the same model can apply to many different settings. Let's recycle Facts and Tools question 5b from Chapter 16 just to emphasize the point:

		Player B	
		Left	Right
Player A	Up	(100, 100)	(600, 50)
	Down	(50, 600)	(500, 500)

a. We have given you very generic strategies: up, down, left, and right. Relabel the matrix so the game applies to farmers deciding how much water to pull from the river for irrigation.

b. Which set of strategies would give the farmers the highest joint payoff?

c. Which set of actions would be equivalent to the following choice: One farmer decided not to conserve and instead to use more water than their fair share. (There are two right answers here.)

d. Which set of actions is the one and only Nash equilibrium? How would you describe it in terms of these two farmers? As a hint to this question, do an Internet search to see if the Colorado River reaches the ocean.

13. As already mentioned, the line between "public good" and "private good" is genuinely blurry. Electronic tolls on roadways are making excludability a little bit easier every year. In your view, should we continue to think of roads as public goods? (To be more accurate, we really should say, "Should we continue to think of *travel* on uncongested roads as public goods?")

14. The massive stone faces that pepper Easter Island puzzled people for centuries. What happened to the civilization that erected these faces? A clue is that the island currently has no trees. Trees would have been necessary to make the boats to bring the stones to the island and to then roll those stones into place. Archeological digs have discovered the island *did* have trees very long ago, but it's believed that the natives used up all the trees until they had no choice but to leave. Can you think of an explanation for why people would behave in this way? The following questions may suggest an answer.

James L. Amos/Getty Images

a. Who bore the cost of planting new trees? Who benefited from planting new trees?

b. As the population of the island grew, what happened to the number of trees? Why?

c. Biologist Jared Diamond, writing on the subject of trees in Easter Island, asked, "What were they thinking when they cut down the last palm tree?"[5] What do you think the person who cut down that last palm tree was thinking if they acted like a person facing a tragedy of the commons?

15. Economists typically remind people to weigh the costs of an action against the benefits of that action. Let's invent some examples where it's just too expensive or too risky to solve the very real problems discussed in this chapter.

a. It's possible that it would just cost too much to defend the earth from asteroids, where the best option, all things considered, is just to hope for the best. Invent an extreme example where this is the case—your example might take place in a world with different technology, different type of government, and so forth.

b. What about saving the tuna? Invent an example where the best option is to just let the fishermen do what they want, even if tuna go extinct.

16. A new type of entertainment has seen a large growth in demand over roughly the past decade. Individuals "stream" themselves playing video games over the Internet in front of a live audience. Typically, the streamer can directly communicate with their viewers through a text window. People cannot be prevented from watching the stream, making it impossible to charge an admission fee. How could it possibly be profitable to provide this service?

CHALLENGES

17. a. Two girls are sharing a cold chocolate milk, as in the picture. How long do you think it will take them to drink all the milk? How long would it take if each girl had her own glass and half the milk? Can you see a problem when the girls drink from a common glass?

Sean Justice/Corbis

b. What is going on in this picture of an East Texas oil field in 1919? Can you see the problem?

Bygone Collection/Alamy Stock Photo

c. Why did we put these two questions together? (*Hint:* A speech from the movie *There Will Be Blood* gets at the same question—it's based on a 1924 speech by U.S. Senator Albert Fall of New Mexico.)

18. If greenhouse gas emissions are not cut, climate change could have very large future costs. Let's assume that there are 100 equally sized countries in the world and that cutting greenhouse gas emissions will cost each country 10 but each cut will create much larger world benefits of 500. Since the benefits of cutting greenhouse gas emissions far exceed the costs, why isn't climate change in this scenario an easy problem to solve?

a. If a country cuts its greenhouse gas emissions, what are the costs to that country?

b. If a country cuts its greenhouse gas emissions, what are the benefits to that country?

c. Since the costs are _____ [greater than/smaller than/equal to] the benefits, a country has an incentive to _____ [cut emissions/free ride].

d. Cutting greenhouse gas emissions is difficult because it is a global _____ because benefits are _____ and _____.

19. The economic theory of public goods makes a very clear prediction: If the benefits of some action go to strangers, not to yourself, then you won't do that action. Economists have run dozens of experiments testing out this prediction. (You can find a readable article by Nobel laureate Elinor Ostrom summarizing the results in the summer 2000 issue of the *Journal of Economic Perspectives*.)

A typical "public goods game" is quite simple: Everyone in the experiment is given, say, $5 each, theirs to take home if they like. They're told that if they donate money to the common pool, all the money in the pool will then be doubled. The money in the pool will then be divided equally among all players, whether they contributed to the pool or not. That's the whole game. Let's see what a purely self-interested person would do in this setting. (*Hint:* A public goods game is just like a prisoner's dilemma, only with more people.)

a. If 10 people are playing the game, and they all chip in their $5 to the pool, how much will be in the pool *after* it doubles?

b. So how much money does each person get to take home if everyone puts the money into the pool?

c. Now, suppose that you are one of the players, and you've seen that all nine other players have put in all their money. If you keep your $5, and the pool money gets divided up equally among all 10 of you, how much will you have in total?

d. So are you better or worse off if you keep your money?

e. What if none of the nine had put money into the pot: If you were the only one to put your money in, how much would you have afterward? Is this better or worse than if you'd just kept the money yourself?

f. So if you were a purely self-interested individual, what's the best thing to do regardless of what the other players are doing: put all the money in, put some of it in, or put none of it in? (Answer in percent.) Do the benefits of donating go to you or to other people?

g. If people just cared about "the group," they'd surely donate 100%. In part f, you just said what a purely self-interested person would do. In the dozens of studies that Ostrom summarizes, people give an average of 30% to the common pool. So, are the people in these studies closer to the pure self-interest model from part f, or are they closer to the pure altruist model of human behavior?

20. Canada's Labrador Peninsula (which includes modern-day Newfoundland and most of modern-day Quebec) was once home to an indigenous group, the Montagnes, who, in contrast to their counterparts in the American Southwest, established property rights over land. This institutional change was a direct result of the increase in the fur trade after European traders arrived.[6]

a. Before European traders came, the amount of land in the Labrador Peninsula far exceeded the indigenous people's needs. Hunting animals specifically for fur was not yet widely practiced. What can you conclude about the relative scarcity of land or animals? Why?

b. Before the European arrival, land was commonly held. Given your answer in part a, did the tragedy of the commons play out for the indigenous Montagnes? (Remember, air is also commonly held.)

c. Once the European traders came, the demand for fur increased. Do you expect the tragedy of the commons to play out under these circumstances? Why or why not?

d. The Montagnes established property rights over the fur trade, allocating families' hunting territory. This led to rules ranging from when an animal is accidentally killed in a neighbor's territory to laws governing inheritance. Why did the Montagnes create property rights only after the European traders came?

21. It's one of the ironies of American history that when the pilgrims first arrived at Plymouth Rock, they promptly set about creating a communal society in which all shared equally in the produce of their land. As a result, the pilgrims were soon starving to death.

Fortunately, "after much debate of things," Governor William Bradford ended the corn commons, decreeing that each family should keep the corn that it produced. In one of the most insightful statements of political economy ever written, Bradford described the results of the new and old systems.

[Ending the corn commons] had very good success, for it made all hands very industrious, so as much more corn was planted than otherwise would have been by any means the Governor or any other could use, and saved him a great deal of trouble, and gave far better content. The women now went willingly into the field, and took their little ones with them to set corn; which before would allege weakness and inability; whom to have compelled would have been thought great tyranny and oppression.

The experience that was had in this common course and condition, tried sundry years and that amongst godly and sober men, may well evince the vanity of that conceit of Plato's and other ancients applauded by some of later times; that the taking away of property and bringing in community into a commonwealth would make them happy and flourishing; as if they were wiser than God. For this community (so far as it was) was found to breed much confusion and discontent and retard much employment that would have been to their benefit and comfort. For the young men, that were most able and fit for labour and service, did repine that they should spend their time and strength to work for other men's wives and children without any recompense. The strong, or man of parts, had no more in division of victuals and clothes than he that was weak and not able to do a quarter the other could; this was thought injustice. The aged and graver men to be ranked and equalized in labours and victuals, clothes, etc., with the meaner and younger sort, thought it some indignity and disrespect unto them. And for men's wives to be commanded to do service for other men, as dressing their meat, washing their clothes, etc., they deemed it a kind of slavery, neither could many husbands well brook it. Upon the point all being to have alike, and all to do alike, they thought themselves in the like condition, and one as good as another; and so, if it did not cut off those relations that God hath set amongst men, yet it did at least much diminish and take off the mutual respects that should be preserved amongst them. And would have been worse if they had been men of another condition. Let none object this is men's corruption, and nothing to the course itself. I answer, seeing all men have this corruption in them, God in His wisdom saw another course fitter for them.

(*Information from:* Bradford, William. *Of Plymouth Plantation, 1620–1647.* Edited by Samuel Eliot Morison. New York: Modern Library, 1967.)

a. Imagine yourself a pilgrim under the communal (commons) system. If you worked hard all day in the fields, would that increase your share of the food by a lot or a little? Describe the incentive to work under the communal system.

b. Under this system, what type of good was the pilgrims' harvest?

c. According to Bradford, the communal system "retard[ed] much employment that would have been to their benefit and comfort." Why would the communal system reduce something that would have been to the pilgrims' benefit? How would you describe this using the tools of economics?

d. According to Bradford, what happened to the amount of food produced and the amount of labor after the communal system was abolished and workers got to keep a larger share of what they produced?

e. Read Bradford's statement carefully. What other effects did the communal system create? (Note that economists typically ignore these kinds of effects.)

22. A small town consists of three families who live in an area with lots of mosquitoes. The town is considering a spraying program to control the mosquito population. The marginal benefits of the spraying program are provided for each family, along with the marginal costs of the spraying program. Refer to the table here. How many times should the town spray for mosquitoes?

| | Family A | Family B | Family C | |
Number of sprayings	Marginal benefit	Marginal benefit	Marginal benefit	Marginal cost of spraying
1	$50	$80	$30	$80
2	$40	$60	$10	$100
3	$20	$40	$5	$135
4	$10	$20	$1	$147

WORK IT OUT

For interactive, step-by-step help in solving this problem, go online.

a. American bison once freely roamed the Great Plains. In the 1820s, there were some 30 million bison in the United States but a survey in 1889 counted just 1,091. Why were the bison driven to near extinction? How were the bison like tuna?

b. At some restaurants and grocery stores, you can buy bison burgers, made from farm-raised bison. Is this good news or bad news if we want more bison around?

CHAPTER 19 APPENDIX

The Tragedy of the Commons: How Fast?

We can use a simple spreadsheet to see how quickly common resources can become tragically overexploited and ruined. Suppose that we start with a stock of 100. This could be 100 million fish, 100 thousand elephants, or 100 units of agricultural quality or other common resource. Let's suppose that this resource grows or reproduces itself by 10% every year. We can then set up our spreadsheet as shown in Figure A19.1. The key cell is Cell B3, which contains the formula =B2*(1+$C$2)−$D$2. This formula takes the stock of fish in the previous year from Cell B2, multiplies it by 1 plus the growth rate in Cell C2 (using the dollar signs to make sure that this cell reference stays the same when we copy it elsewhere), and then subtracts the annual catch or usage in Cell D2 (which we initially set at 10) to get the stock in this year.

FIGURE A19.1

		B3	▾	f_x	=B2*(1+$C$2)-$D$2	
	A	B	C		D	E
1	Year	Stock	Natural Growth Rate		Annual Catch	
2	1	100		0.10	10	
3	2	100				
4	3	100				
5	4	100				
6	5	100				
7	6	100				
8	⋮	⋮				
9						
10						

We now copy and paste Cell B3 into Cells B4 onward. It's fairly obvious that if a stock of 100 fish grows by 10% every year, then a catch of 10 is sustainable forever and this is what our spreadsheet indicates.

What is more surprising is how quickly an increase in the catch can drive a stock to extinction. If we change the annual catch in Cell D2 to 11, for example, we get the result in Figure A19.2.

FIGURE A19.2

	A	B	C	D
1	Year	Stock	Natural Growth Rate	Annual Catch
2	1	100	0.10	11
3	2	99		
4	3	97.9		
5	4	96.69		
6	5	95.359		
7	6	93.8949		
8	7	92.28439		
9	8	90.51283		
10	9	88.56411		
11	10	86.42052		
12	11	84.06258		
13	12	81.46883		
14	13	78.61572		
15	14	75.47729		
16	15	72.02502		
17	16	68.22752		
18	17	64.05027		
19	18	59.4553		
20	19	54.40083		
21	20	48.84091		
22	21	42.725		
23	22	35.9975		
24	23	28.59725		
25	24	20.45698		
26	25	11.50267		
27	26	1.652941		
28	27	-9.18177		
29				

Notice that the decline starts slowly, but by year 27 the stock of fish has gone negative; that is, the fish are extinct. You can experiment with different assumptions about growth rates and catches to see how long stocks can be sustained under different scenarios.

20

Political Economy and Public Choice

I f you have read this far, you may now be asking, "What's wrong with the world?" Economists tend to favor free and competitive markets and to be skeptical about policies like price controls, tariffs, command and control regulation, and high inflation rates. Yet around the world, markets are often suppressed, monopolies are supported, and harmful policies, such as those just listed, are quite common. Why do the arguments of economists fall on deaf ears?

One possible answer is that politicians are right to reject mainstream economics. As we explore in Chapter 21, some people do argue that mainstream economics ignores important ethical values. Or perhaps mainstream economics is simply wrong about economics. Of course, that is not our view, so you will have to seek other books to judge that question for yourself. A third answer to what's wrong with the world and the one we will explore in this chapter is . . . can you guess? Bad incentives.

A good incentive system aligns self-interest with the social interest. In Chapters 7 and 10, we explored the conditions under which markets do and do not align self-interest with the social interest. It's now time to turn to government. The critical question is this: When does the self-interest of politicians and voters align with the social interest and when do these interests collide? This question is at the heart of political economy, or **public choice**, which is the study of political behavior using the tools of economics.

We just made an important but implicit assumption that is worth emphasizing. We assumed that self-interest is as important in politics as in economics.[*] Economists call this the assumption of behavioral symmetry—we assume that institutions differ but people are the same. Comparative institutional analysis is all about analyzing the incentive issues associated with alternative institutional arrangements.

This is exactly what political economists such as James Madison, Alexander Hamilton, Thomas Jefferson, and George Mason were doing when they

Public choice is the study of political behavior using the tools of economics.

---

[*] Note that we are not assuming that self-interest is the only important motivator, only that self-interest is equally important across different institutions.

debated the design of the U.S. Constitution. As James Madison put it famously in Federalist 51:

> *Ambition must be made to counteract ambition . . . In framing a government which is to be administered by men over men, the great difficulty lies in this: you must first enable the government to control the governed; and in the next place oblige it to control itself.*

> *Federalist 51*

Ambition is another word for self-interest, and framing is another word for designing, so Madison was trying to design a constitution that channeled the self-interest of political actors towards the social good.

We will begin this chapter looking at some of the major institutions and incentives that govern the behavior of voters and politicians in a democracy. As we will see, democracies have many problems, including voter ignorance, control of politics by special interests, and political business cycles. Yet, to quote Winston Churchill, "No one pretends that democracy is perfect or all-wise. Indeed, it has been said that democracy is the worst form of government except all those other forms that have been tried from time to time."[1] Thus, in the latter half of the chapter, we look at nondemocracies and some of the reasons why nondemocracies have typically failed to produce either wealth or political or economic liberty for their citizens.

Let's begin with voters and the question: "Do voters have an incentive to be well informed about politics?"

https://youtu.be/HRUOdjNrODM

What Is Public Choice?

Voters and the Incentive to Be Ignorant

Knowledge is a good thing, but sometimes the price of knowledge is too high. Imagine that your professor changed the grading scheme. Instead of awarding grades based on individual performance, your professor averages test scores and assigns the same grade to everyone. Will you study more or less under this new grading scheme? We think that most people would study less because studying now has a lower payoff. Let's say that before the change an extra few hours of studying would raise your grade by 10 points. What is the payoff to studying under the new system? Imagine that there are 100 people in your class. The same hours of studying will now raise your grade by just 10/100 or 0.1 points.[*] Studying doesn't pay under the second system because your grade is mostly determined by what other people do, not by what you do.

Now let's apply the same idea to politics. When you choose a politician, does studying their record have a high payoff? No. Studying position papers, examining voting histories, and listening to political speeches is sometimes entertaining, but it doesn't offer much concrete return. Even when studying changes your vote, your vote is very unlikely to change the outcome of the election. Studying politics doesn't pay because the outcome of an election is mostly determined by what other people do, not by what you do.

Economists say that voters are **rationally ignorant** about politics because the incentives to be informed are low.

Rational ignorance occurs when the benefits of being informed are less than the costs of becoming informed.

---

[*] It's possible that some people could study more under the new system. Under the old system, studying only raises an individual's grade, but under the new system, it raises everyone's grades! Thus, if there are some super-altruistic students, they might study more under the new system. We have not met many such students. Have you?

It's not hard to find evidence that Americans are uninformed about politics. Consider the following questions. Who is the speaker of the U.S. House of Representatives? Who sings "Bad Guy"? Be honest. Which question was it easier for you to answer? And which question is more important? (At the time of writing, Kevin McCarthy is speaker of the House. "Bad Guy" is a Billie Eilish hit.)

Rational Ignorance

Not knowing who the speaker of the House is might not be critical, but Americans are equally uninformed or worse—misinformed—about important political questions. For example, in one survey Americans were asked to name the two largest sources of government spending out of the following six choices.

- Welfare
- Interest on the federal debt
- Defense
- Foreign aid
- Social Security
- Health care

Amazingly, 41% named foreign aid as one of the two biggest programs. But foreign aid is by far the smallest program of the six listed. Do you know the correct answers? The two biggest programs are defense and Social Security. Americans were not even close to the correct answers; for instance, the second most popular choice was welfare, which, though a large program, is still much smaller than defense and Social Security.[2]

Similarly, by their own admission, most Americans know "not much" or "nothing" about important pieces of legislation such as the USA Patriot Act. Most Americans cannot estimate the inflation rate or the unemployment rate to within five percentage points. Hundreds of surveys over many decades have shown that most Americans know little about political matters. Of course, we'd all like to change that—we are glad you are reading this book!—but in the meantime it is simply a fact. And it appears to be a fact that is not easily changed.

Andrew Harnik/Getty Images

Rational ignorance Do you recognize this man?

Why Rational Ignorance Matters

Ignorance about political matters is important for at least three reasons. First, if voters don't know what the USA Patriot Act says or what the unemployment rate is, then it's difficult to make informed choices. Moreover, voters who think that the unemployment rate or the crime rate is much higher than it actually is are likely to make quite different choices than if they knew the true rate. The difficulty is compounded if voters don't know the positions that politicians take on the issues, and it is worse yet if voters don't know much about possible solutions to problems such as unemployment. Voters are supposed to be the drivers in a democracy, but if the drivers don't know where they are or where they want to go or how to get there, they are unlikely to arrive at a desirable destination.

Second, voters who are rationally ignorant will often make decisions on the basis of low-quality, unreliable, or potentially biased information. Not everyone has read a good principles of economics textbook and those who

CHECK YOURSELF

- Would you expect more rational ignorance about national issues among national voters or about local issues among local voters? Make an argument for both possibilities.

haven't are likely to vote in ways that are quite different from someone who is better informed.[*] It's not really surprising, for example, that better-looking politicians get more votes even if good looks have nothing to do with policy. Once again, we should not expect too much in the way of wise government policy when voters are rationally ignorant.

The third reason that rational ignorance matters is that not everyone is rationally ignorant. Let's look at this in more detail.

Special Interests and the Incentive to Be Informed

Let's return to the sugar quota discussed in Chapter 9. As you may recall, the government restricts how much sugar can be imported into the United States. As a result, the U.S. price of sugar is about double the world price. American consumers of candy, soda, and other sweet goods pay more for these goods than they would if the quota was lifted. Why does the government harm sugar consumers, many of whom are voters?

Although sugar consumers are harmed by the quota, few of them even know of the quota's existence. That's rational because even though the quota costs consumers more than a billion dollars, the costs are diffused over millions of consumers, costing each person about $5 or $6 per year. Even if sugar consumers did know about the quota, they probably wouldn't spend much time or effort to oppose it. Will you? After all, just writing an email to your Congressperson opposing the quota might cost $5 or $6 in time and trouble, and what's the probability that your email will change the policy?

Sugar consumers, therefore, won't do much to oppose the quota but what about U.S. sugar producers? U.S. sugar producers benefit enormously from the quota. As we saw in Chapter 9, if the quota were lifted, most sugar producers in Florida would be outcompeted by producers in Brazil where better weather makes sugar cheaper to produce. But with the quota, U.S. producers are shielded from competition and sugar farming in Florida becomes very profitable. Moreover, although there are millions of sugar consumers, sugar production is concentrated among a small number of producers. Each producer benefits from the quota by hundreds of thousands or even millions of dollars.

Sugar producers, unlike sugar consumers, have a lot of money at stake so they have a strong incentive to be *rationally informed*. The sugar producers know when the sugar quota comes up for a vote, they know who is pictured on the previous page, they know who is on the House and Senate agricultural committees that largely decide on the quota, they know which politicians are running for reelection and in need of campaign funds, and they act accordingly. Table 20.1, for example, lists the members of the Senate Agricultural Committee in 2020 and the amount of money from 2018 to 2022 that they received from the American Crystal Sugar Political Action Committee (PAC), an industry lobby group in favor of the sugar quota.

As you can see, 14 of the 22 senators on the Agricultural Committee (perhaps not coincidentally just over a majority!) received money from the American Crystal Sugar PAC. Many senators on the committee *also* received money from the American Sugar Cane League, the Florida Sugar Cane League, the

---

[*] For a superb treatment of this issue, see Caplan, Bryan. 2007. *The Myth of the Rational Voter: Why Democracies Choose Bad Policies*. Princeton, NJ: Princeton University Press.

American Sugarbeet Growers Association, and the U.S. Beet Sugar Association! But that isn't even the end of the story. The owners and executives of the major players in the sugar industry also donate campaign funds as individuals. The "sugar barons" José and Alfonso Fanjul, for example, head Florida Crystals Corporation, which is one of the country's largest sugarcane growers. The Fanjuls donate money to the Florida Sugar Cane League and give money to politicians in their own names. Interestingly, José directs most of his support to Republicans, while his brother Alfonso supports Democrats. Do you think there is a difference of political opinion between the two brothers? Or can you think of another explanation for their pattern of donations? Other Fanjul family members, including brothers, wives, daughters, sons, and even sisters-in-law, are also active political contributors.

A Formula for Political Success: Diffuse Costs, Concentrate Benefits

The politics behind the sugar quota illustrate a formula for political success: Diffuse costs and concentrate benefits. The costs of the sugar quota are diffused over millions of consumers, so no consumer has much of an incentive to oppose the quota. But the benefits of the quota are concentrated on a handful of producers; they have strong incentives to support the quota. So, the sugar quota is a winning policy for politicians. The people who are harmed are rationally ignorant and have little incentive to oppose the policy, while the people who benefit are rationally informed and have strong incentives to support the policy. Thus, we can see one reason why the self-interest of politicians does not always align with the social interest.

The formula for political success works for many types of public policies, not just trade quotas and tariffs. Agricultural subsidies and price supports, for example, fit the diffused costs and concentrated benefits story. It's interesting that the political power of farmers has *increased* as the share of farmers in the population has *decreased*. The reason? When farmers decline in population, the benefits of, for example, a price support become more concentrated (on farmers) and the costs become more diffused (on nonfarmers).

The benefits of many government projects such as roads, bridges, dams, and parks are concentrated on local residents and producers, while the costs of these projects can be diffused over all federal taxpayers. As a result, politicians have an incentive to lobby for these projects even when the benefits are smaller than the costs.

TABLE 20.1 SPECIAL INTERESTS ARE RATIONALLY INFORMED

Senators on the Agriculture Committee, 2020	Donations from the American Crystal Sugar PAC (2018–2022)
Cindy Hyde-Smith (R-MS)	$15,000
Chuck Grassley (R-IA)	$10,000
Debbie Stabenow (D-MI)	$10,000
John Boozman (R-AR)	$10,000
John Hoeven (R-ND)	$10,000
Raphael Warnock (D-GA)	$10,000
Tina Smith (D-MN)	$10,000
Amy Klobuchar (D-MN)	$7,500
Deb Fischer (R-NE)	$7,500
Michael Bennet (D-CO)	$7,500
Ben Ray Lujan (D-NM)	$5,000
John Thune (R-SD)	$5,000
Joni Ernst (R-IA)	$5,000
Patrick Leahy (D-VT)	$5,000
Cory Booker (D-NJ)	$0
Dick Durbin (D-IL)	$0
Kirsten Gillibrand (D-NY)	$0
Mike Braun (R-IN)	$0
Mitch McConnell (R-KY)	$0
Roger Marshall (R-KS)	$0
Sherrod Brown (D-OH)	$0
Tommy Tuberville (R-AL)	$0

Data from: Federal Election Commission data compiled by OpenSecrets.org.

▶▶ **SEARCH ENGINE**

Extensive information on campaign contributions can be found at www.OpenSecrets.org.

Concentrated Benefits and Dispersed Costs

https://youtu.be/UCQkCyCvk9M

Consider the infamous "Bridge to Nowhere," a proposed bridge in Alaska that would connect the town of Ketchikan (population 8,200) with its airport on Gravina Island (population 50) at a cost to federal taxpayers of $398 million. At present, a ferry service runs to the island but some people in the town complain that it costs too much ($7 per car). If the town's residents had to pay the $398 million cost of the bridge themselves—that's $48,536 each!—do you think they would want the bridge? Of course not, but the residents will be happy to have the bridge if most of the costs are paid by other taxpayers.

As far as the residents of Ketchikan are concerned, the costs of the bridge are *external costs*. Recall from Chapter 10 that when the costs of a good are paid for by other people—rather than the consumers or producers of the good—we get an inefficiently large quantity of the good. In Chapter 10, we gave the example of a firm that pollutes—since the firm doesn't pay all the costs of its production, it produces too much. The same thing is true here, except the external cost is created by government. When government makes it possible to push the costs of a good onto other people—to *externalize the cost*—we get too much of the good. In this case, we get too many bridges to nowhere.

The formula for political success works for tax credits and deductions, as well as for spending. The federal tax code, including various regulations and rulings, is more than 70,000 pages long and it grows every year as politicians add special interest provisions. Tax breaks for various manufacturing industries, for example, have long been common, but in 2004, the term "manufacturing" was significantly expanded so that oil and gas drilling as well as mining and timber could be included as manufacturing industries. The new tax breaks were worth some $76 billion to the firms involved. One last-minute provision even defined "coffee roasting" as a form of manufacturing. That provision was worth a lot of *bucks* to one famous corporation.[3]

Every year Congress inserts many thousands of special spending projects, exemptions, regulations, and tax breaks into major bills. A multibillion-dollar lobbying industry works the system on behalf of their clients, and it is not unusual for those lobbies, in essence, to propose and even write up the details of the forthcoming legislation. Many lobbyists are former politicians who find that lobbying their friends can be very profitable.

When benefits are concentrated and costs are diffuse, resources can be wasted on projects with low benefits and high costs. Consider a special interest group representing 1% of society that proposes a simple policy that benefits the special interest by $100 and costs society $100. Thus, the policy benefits the special interest by $100 and it costs the *special interest* just $1 (if you are wondering where that came from, $1 is 1% of the total cost to society). The special interest group will certainly lobby for a policy like this.

But now imagine that the policy benefits the special interest by $100 but costs society twice as much, $200. The policy is very bad for society, but it's still good for the special interest, which gets a benefit of $100 at a cost (to the lobby) of only $2 ($2 is 1% of the total social costs of $200). Indeed, a special interest representing 1% of the

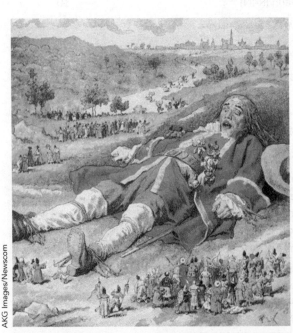

Many small distortions can tie a giant down.

AKG Images/Newscom

population will benefit from any policy that transfers $100 in its favor, even if the costs to society are nearly 100 times as much!

If each policy, taken on its own, wastes a few million or billion dollars' worth of resources, the country will be much poorer. A country with many inefficient policies will have less wealth and slower economic growth. No society can get rich by passing policies with benefits that are less than costs.

In extreme situations, an economy can falter or even collapse when fighting over the division of the pie becomes more profitable than making the pie grow larger. The fall of the Roman Empire, for instance, was caused in part by bad political institutions. As the Roman Empire grew, courting politicians in Rome became a more secure path to riches than starting a new business. Toward the end of the empire, the emperors taxed peasant farmers heavily. Rather than spending the money on roads or valuable infrastructure, the activities that had made Rome powerful and rich, tax revenues were used to pay off privileged insiders and to placate the public in the city of Rome with "bread and circuses." When the empire finally collapsed in 476 CE, the tax collector was a hated figure and the government enjoyed little respect.[4]

Another Formula: Concentrated Costs, Diffuse Benefits We have just seen an example of government failure: policies with concentrated benefits and diffuse costs can win in a democratic process even when the benefits are less than the costs. When *costs* are concentrated and benefits are diffuse another government failure can happen—policies with concentrated costs and diffuse benefits can lose in a democratic system even when the benefits are *more* than the costs. The logic is similar. Concentrated benefits or costs concentrate the mind and lead to lobbying and political action, while diffuse benefits or costs are often too small to motivate awareness or action.

Concentrated costs can sometimes overrule much larger diffuse benefits.

In Chapter 5 we noted that many cities make it costly and difficult to build new housing. In part, this may be due to preferences held by a majority of voters but it's also a consequence of the decentralized permit and approval process. In a typical process, even when land is zoned for construction, a builder must also get approval from a neighborhood review board which holds hearings. Who shows up and speaks to the neighborhood review board?

The next-door neighbor worried about parking might show up to argue against the project. As might the older resident concerned about new people moving into "their" neighborhood. The costs of the project, whether real or imagined, are concentrated on a small number of people who will likely be vocal about their opposition. The benefits, however, are diffuse.

The developer will benefit and will speak in favor, but what about the future residents of the apartment building? The future residents are probably unknown, even to themselves. As a result, it's not surprising that one careful survey in Massachusetts found that at local review boards, opposition to new housing proposals always far exceeded support. The surprise is that at the same time, voters in Massachusetts passed legislation favoring more building. Why the difference? Diffuse beneficiaries are more likely to vote about general rules (a relatively low cost activity) than they are to attend and speak at a review board about a specific proposal (a relatively high cost activity). Thus, the power of local review boards magnifies the power of interest groups with concentrated costs and, as a result of this political structure, small groups with concentrated costs can often veto projects with large benefits.[5]

CHECK YOURSELF

- President Ronald Reagan set up a commission to examine government spending and cut waste. It had some limited success. If special interest spending is such a problem, why don't we set up another federal commission to examine government waste? Who would push for such a commission? Who would resist it? What will be its prospects for success?

- A local library expanded into a new building to establish a local history collection. The state senator found some state money and had that contributed to the library. Who benefits from this? Who ultimately pays for it?

Voter Myopia and Political Business Cycles

We turn now from the microeconomics of political economy to an application in macroeconomics. Rational ignorance and another factor, voter myopia, can encourage politicians to boost the economy before an election to increase their chances of reelection.

Presidential elections appear to be fought on many fronts. Candidates battle over education, war, health care, the environment, and the economy. Pundits scrutinize the daily chronicle of events to divine how the candidates advance and retreat in public opinion. Personalities and "leadership" loom large and are reckoned to swing voters one way or another. When the battle is done, historians mark one personality and set of issues as having won the day and as reflecting the "will of the voters."

But economists and political scientists have been surprised to discover that a simpler logic underlies this apparent chaos of seemingly unique and momentous events. Over the past 100 years, the American voter has voted for the party of the incumbent when the economy is doing well and voted against the incumbent when the economy is doing poorly. Voters are so responsive to economic conditions that the winner of a presidential election can be predicted with considerable accuracy, even if one knows nothing about the personalities, issues, or events that seem, on the surface, to matter so much.

The green line in Figure 20.1 shows, for presidential elections since 1948, the share of the two-party vote won by the party of the incumbent (that is, a share greater than 50% usually means the presidency stayed with the incumbent party and a share less than 50% usually means the presidency switched party). The blue line is the share of the two-party vote predicted by just three variables: growth in personal disposable income (per capita) in the year of the election, the inflation rate in the year of the election, and a simple measure of how long the incumbent party has been in power. Notice that these three variables alone give us great power to predict election results.

More specifically, the incumbent party wins elections when personal disposable income is growing, when the inflation rate in the election year is low, and

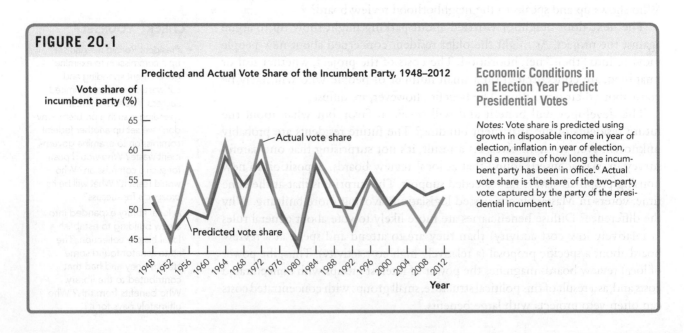

FIGURE 20.1

Predicted and Actual Vote Share of the Incumbent Party, 1948–2012

Vote share of incumbent party (%)

Actual vote share

Predicted vote share

Year

Economic Conditions in an Election Year Predict Presidential Votes

Notes: Vote share is predicted using growth in disposable income in year of election, inflation in year of election, and a measure of how long the incumbent party has been in office.[6] Actual vote share is the share of the two-party vote captured by the party of the presidential incumbent.

when the incumbent party has not been in power for too many terms in a row. Personal disposable income is the amount of income a person has after taxes. It includes income from wages, dividends, and interest but also income from welfare payments, unemployment insurance, and Social Security payments. The inflation rate is the general increase in prices. The last variable, a measure of how long the incumbent party has been in power, reduces a party's vote share. Voters seem to get tired or disillusioned with a party the longer it has been in power, so there is a natural tendency for the presidency to switch parties even if all else remains the same.

https://youtu.be/Aldi4n7S78Q

Short-Sightedness in Government

Figure 20.1 tells us that voters are responsive to economic conditions, but more deeply it tells us that voters are surprisingly responsive to economic conditions *in the year of an election*. Voters are myopic—they don't look at economic conditions over a president's entire term. Instead, they focus on what is close at hand, namely economic conditions in the year of an election. Politicians who want to be reelected, therefore, are wise to do whatever they can to increase personal disposable income and reduce inflation in the year of an election even if this means decreases in income and increases in inflation at other times. Is there evidence that politicians behave in this way? Yes.

One of the most brazen examples comes from President Richard Nixon. Just two weeks before the 1972 election, he sent a letter to more than 24 million recipients of Social Security benefits. President Nixon's letter read:

Higher Social Security Payments

Your social security payment has been increased by 20 percent, starting with this month's check, by a new statute enacted by Congress and signed into law by President Richard Nixon on July 1, 1972.

The President also signed into law a provision that will allow your social security benefits to increase automatically if the cost of living goes up. Automatic benefit increases will be added to your check in future years according to the conditions set out in the law.

Of course, higher Social Security payments must be funded with higher taxes, but Nixon timed things so that the increase in payments started in October but the increase in taxes didn't begin until January, that is, not until after the election! Nixon was thus able to shift benefits and costs so that the benefits hit before the election and the costs hit after the election.

To be fair, President Nixon's policies were not unique or even unusual. Government benefits of all kinds typically increase before an election while taxes hardly ever do—taxes increase only after an election!

Using 60 years of U.S. data, Figure 20.2 shows the growth rate in personal disposable income in each quarter of a president's 16-quarter term. Growth is much higher in the year before an election than at any other time in a president's term. In fact, in an election year personal disposable income grows on average by 3.01% compared with 1.79% in a nonelection year. The difference is probably not due to chance.

Inflation also follows a cyclical pattern, but since voters dislike inflation, it tends to decrease in the year of an election and increase after the election. These patterns have been observed in many other countries, not just the United States. We also see political patterns at lower levels of politics. Mayors and governors, for example, try to increase the number of police on the streets in an election year, so that crime will fall and people will feel safer.[7]

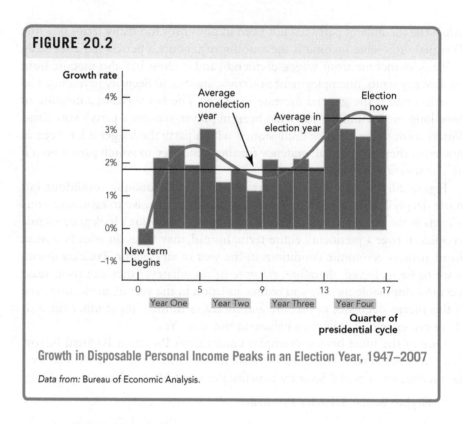

FIGURE 20.2

Growth in Disposable Personal Income Peaks in an Election Year, 1947–2007

Data from: Bureau of Economic Analysis.

There are a limited number of things that a president can do to influence the economy, so presidents do not always succeed in increasing income during an election year. Presidents can influence transfers and taxes much more readily than they can influence pure economic growth. This is one reason why cyclical patterns are more difficult to see in GDP statistics than they are in personal disposable income.

Two Cheers for Democracy

You might be wondering by now: Why isn't everything from the federal government handed out to special interest groups, and why aren't politicians always reelected? Do the voters ever get their way? In fact, voters in a democracy can be very powerful. If you want to think about when voters matter most and when lobbies and special interests matter most, turn to the idea of incentives.

When a policy is specialized in its impact, difficult to understand, and affects a small part of the economy, it is likely that special interests get their way. Let's say the question is whether the depreciation deduction in the investment tax credit should be accelerated or decelerated. This issue is important to many powerful corporations, but you can expect that most voters have never heard of the issue and so it will be settled behind closed doors by a relatively small number of people.

But when a policy is highly visible, appears often in the news and on social media, and has a major effect on the lives of millions of Americans, the voters are likely to have an opinion. The point isn't that voter opinions are always well informed or rational, but that voters do care about some of the biggest issues such as Social Security, Medicare, and taxes and when they do care, politicians have an incentive to serve them. But how exactly does voter opinion translate into policy? After all, opinions are divided, so which voters will get their way in a democracy?

The Median Voter Theorem

To answer this question, we develop a model of voting called the "median voter model." Imagine that there are five voters, each of whom has an opinion about the ideal amount of spending on Social Security. Max wants the least spending, followed by Sofia, Inez, Peter, and finally Alex, who wants the most spending. In Figure 20.3, we plot each voter's ideal policy along a line from least to most spending. We also assume that each voter will vote for the candidate whose policy position is closest to their ideal point.

The median voter is defined as the voter such that half of the other voters want more spending and half want less spending. In this case, the median voter is Inez, since compared with Inez, half of the voters (Peter and Alex) want more spending and half the voters (Max and Sofia) want less spending.

The **median voter theorem** says that under these conditions, the median voter rules! Or more formally, the median voter theorem says that when voters vote for the policy that is closest to their ideal point on a line, then the ideal point of the median voter will beat any other policy in a majority rule election.

Let's see why this is true and, as a result, how democracy will tend to push politicians toward the ideal point of the median voter. First, consider any two policies such as those adopted by Candidate D and Candidate R. Which policy will win in a majority rule election? Max and Sofia will vote for Candidate D since D's policy is closer to their ideal point than R's policy. But Inez, Peter, and Alex will vote for Candidate R. By majority rule, Candidate R will win the election. Notice that, of the two policies offered, the policy closest to that of the median voter's ideal policy won the election.

Most politicians don't like to lose. So in the next election Candidate D may shift their position, becoming Candidate D′. By exactly the same reasoning as before, Candidate D′ will now win the election. If we repeat this process, the

> The **median voter theorem** says that when voters vote for the policy that is closest to their ideal point on a line, then the ideal point of the median voter will beat any other policy in a majority rule election.

FIGURE 20.3

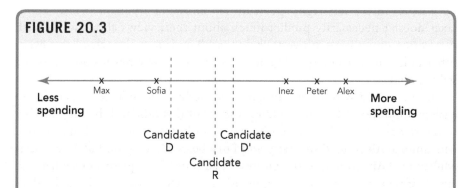

The Median Voter Theorem Each voter has an ideal policy, marked by an x, on the less-to-more spending line. Voters will vote for the candidate whose policy is closest to their ideal. The median voter is the voter such that half of the other voters want more spending and half of the other voters want less spending—Inez is the median voter. Under majority rule, the ideal policy of the median voter will beat any other policy. Consider any two candidate policies, such as those of Candidate D and Candidate R. Candidate D will receive two votes (Max and Sofia) and Candidate R will receive three votes (Inez, Peter, and Alex). But Candidate R's position can be beaten by a policy even closer to the ideal policy of the median voter, such as that of Candidate D′. Over time, competition pushes both candidates toward the ideal policy of the median voter, which is the only policy that cannot be beaten.

only policy that is not a *sure loser* is the ideal point of the median voter (Inez). As Candidates D and R converge on the ideal point of the median voter, there will be little difference between them and each will have a 50% chance of winning the election.[*]

The median voter theorem can be interpreted quite generally. Instead of thinking about less spending and more spending on Social Security, we can interpret the line as the standard political spectrum of left to right. In this case, the median voter theorem can be interpreted as a theory of democracy in a country such as the United States where there are just two major parties.

The median voter theorem tells us that in a democracy, what counts are noses—the number of voters—and not their positions per se. Imagine, for example, that Max decided he wanted even less spending or that Alex decided he wanted even more spending. Would the political outcome change? No. According to the median voter theorem, the median voter rules, and if the median voter doesn't change, then neither does policy. Thus, under the conditions given by the median voter theorem, democracy does not seek out consensus or compromise or a policy that maximizes voter preferences, on average—it seeks out a policy that cannot be beaten in a majority rule election.

The median voter theorem does not always apply. The most important assumption we made was that voters will vote for the policy that is closest to their ideal point. That's not necessarily true. If no candidate offers a policy close to Max's ideal point, he may refuse to vote for anyone, not even the candidate whose policy is (slightly) closer to his own ideal. In this case, a candidate who moves too far away from the voters on their wing may lose votes even if their position moves closer to that of the median voter. As a result, this type of voter behavior means that candidates do not necessarily converge on the ideal point of the median voter.

We have also assumed that there is just one major dimension over which voting takes place. That's not necessarily true either. Suppose that voters care about two issues, such as taxes and war, and assume that we cannot force both issues into a left–right spectrum (so knowing a person's views about taxes doesn't necessarily predict much about their views about war). With two voting dimensions, it's very likely that there is *no* policy that beats every other policy in a majority rule contest, so politics may never converge on a stable policy.

To understand why a winning policy sometimes doesn't exist, consider an analogy from sports. Imagine holding a series of (hypothetical) boxing matches to figure out who is the greatest heavyweight boxer of all time. Suppose that Muhammad Ali beats Tyson Fury and Fury beats Mike Tyson but Tyson beats Muhammad Ali. So who is the greatest of all time? The question may have no answer if there is more than one dimension to boxing skill, so Ali has the skills needed to beat Fury and Fury has the skills needed to beat Tyson, but Tyson has the skills to beat Ali. In a similar way, when there is more than one dimension to politics, no policy may exist that beats every other policy. In terms of politics, the result may be that every vote or election brings a new winner, or alternatively, constitutions and procedural restrictions may slow down the rate of political change. The U.S. Constitution, for example, requires that new

---

[*] In terms of the game theory discussed in Chapters 15 and 16, the ideal policy of the median voter is the only policy that cannot be beaten by another policy and thus the only Nash equilibrium of a two-candidate game is for both candidates to choose this policy.

legislation must pass two houses of Congress and evade the president's veto, which is more difficult than passing a simple majority rule vote.

As a predictive theory of politics, the median voter theorem is applicable in some but not all circumstances. The theorem, however, does remind us that politicians have substantial incentives to listen to voters on issues that the voters care about. This is a powerful feature of democracy, although the quality of the democracy you get will depend on the wisdom of the voters behind it.

Democracy and Nondemocracy

Our picture of democracy so far has been a little disillusioning, at least compared with what you might have learned in high school civics. Yet when we look around the world, democracies tend to be the wealthiest countries, and despite the power of special interests, they also tend to be the countries with the best record of supporting markets, property rights, the rule of law, fair government, and other institutions that support economic growth.

Figure 20.4 graphs an index meant to capture good economic policy, called the economic freedom index (with higher numbers indicating greater economic freedom), on the horizontal axis against a measure of the standard of living on the vertical axis. The figure shows two things. First, there is a strong correlation between economic freedom and a higher standard of living. Second, the countries that are most democratic (strong democracies are shown in red) are among the wealthiest counties in the world and the countries with the most economic freedom. The only interesting exceptions to this rule are Singapore and Hong Kong; both score very highly on economic freedom and the standard of living, but are not quite strong democracies (Hong Kong even less now that it is under Chinese rule.)

Notice, however, that in part there is an association between democracy and the standard of living because greater wealth creates a greater demand for democracy. When citizens have satisfied their basic needs for food, shelter, and security, they demand more cerebral goods, such as the right to participate in the political process. This is exactly what happened in South Korea and Taiwan,

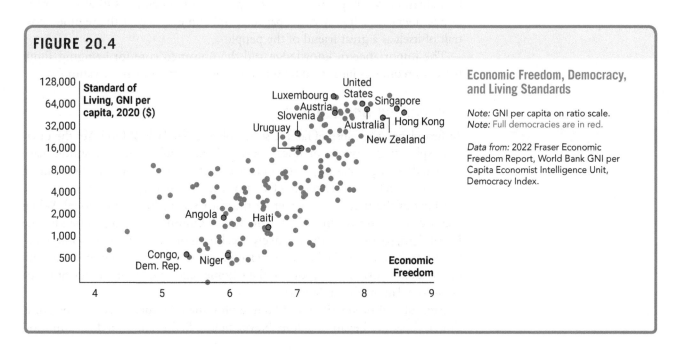

FIGURE 20.4

Economic Freedom, Democracy, and Living Standards

Note: GNI per capita on ratio scale.
Note: Full democracies are in red.

Data from: 2022 Fraser Economic Freedom Report, World Bank GNI per Capita Economist Intelligence Unit, Democracy Index.

two countries that became more democratic as they grew wealthier. Many people predicted that China would become a more democratic country as it grew wealthier; so far that does not seem to be the case. But it's not just that wealth brings democracy. Democracy also seems to bring wealth and favorable institutions. Democracies must be doing something right. We therefore need to examine some of the benefits of democratic decision making.

We've already discussed rational ignorance under democracy, but keep in mind that public ignorance is often worse in nondemocracies.[8] In many quasi democracies and in nondemocracies, the public is not well informed because the media are controlled or censored by the government.

In Africa, for example, most countries have traditionally banned private television stations. In fact, African countries typically have state-controlled television stations and newspapers. Indeed, by one measure, there are no fully independent private media in all of Africa.[9] Government ownership and control of the media are also common in most Middle Eastern countries and, of course, the former Communist countries controlled the media extensively.

Control of the media has exactly the effects that we would expect from our study of rational ignorance in democracies—it enables special interests to control the government for their own ends. Greater government ownership of the press, for example, is associated with lower levels of political rights and civil liberties, worse regulation (more policies like price controls that economists think are ineffective and wasteful), higher levels of corruption, and a greater risk of property confiscation. The authors of an important study of media ownership conclude that "government ownership of the press restricts information flows to the public, which reduces the quality of the government."[10]

Citizens in democracies may be "rationally ignorant," but on the whole they are much better informed about their governments than citizens in quasi democracies and nondemocracies. Moreover, in a democracy, citizens can use their knowledge to influence public policy at low cost by voting. In a democracy, knowledge is power. In nondemocracies, knowledge alone is not enough because intimidation and government violence create steep barriers to political participation. Many people just give up or become cynical. Other citizens in nondemocracies fall prey to propaganda and come to accept the regime's portrait of itself as a great friend of the people.

The importance of knowledge and the power to vote for bringing about better outcomes is illustrated by the shocking history of mass starvation.

Democracy and Famine

At first glance, the cause of famine seems obvious—a lack of food. Yet the obvious explanation is wrong or at least drastically incomplete. Mass starvations have occurred during times of plenty, and even when lack of food is a contributing factor, it is rarely the determining factor of whether mass starvation occurs.

Many of the famines in recent world history have been intentional. When Stalin came to power in 1924 in the Soviet Union, for example, he saw the Ukrainians, particularly the relatively wealthy independent farmers known as kulaks, to be a threat. Stalin collectivized the farms and expropriated the land of the kulaks, turning them out of their homes and sending hundreds of thousands to gulag prisons in Siberia.

Agricultural productivity in Ukraine plummeted under forced collectivization and people began to starve. Nevertheless, Stalin continued to ship food out of Ukraine. Peasants who tried to escape starving regions were arrested or turned back at the border by Stalin's secret police. Desperate Ukrainians ate dogs, cats, and even tree bark. Millions died.[11]

The starvation of Ukraine was intentional and it's clear that it would not have happened in a democracy. Stalin did not need the votes of the Ukrainians and thus they had little power to influence policy. Democratically elected politicians will not ignore the votes of millions of people.

Even unintentional mass starvations can be avoided in democracies. It's estimated that during the 1974 famine in Bangladesh, a hundred thousand people may have died from mass starvation and many more from related causes. It was probably the first televised starvation, and it illustrates some important themes in the relationship between economics and politics.

Floods destroyed much of the rice crop of 1974 at the same time as world rice prices were increasing for other reasons. The flood meant that there was no work for landless rural laborers who in ordinary years would have been employed harvesting the rice.

The lower income from work and the higher rice prices, taken together, led to starvations. Yet in 1974, Bangladesh in the aggregate did not lack for food. In fact, food per capita in 1974 was at an all-time high, as shown in Figure 20.5.

Mass starvation occurred not because of a lack of food per se, but because a poor group of laborers lacked both economic and political power. Lack of economic power meant they could not purchase food. Lack of political power meant that the elites then running Bangladesh were not compelled to avert the famine. Bangladesh continued to pursue bad economic policies; for instance, government regulations made it very difficult to purchase foreign exchange so it wasn't easy for capitalists to import rice from nearby Thailand or India. In fact, rice was even being smuggled out of Bangladesh and into India to avoid price controls and other regulations.

Amartya Sen, the Nobel Prize–winning economist and philosopher, has argued that "no famine has taken place in the history of the world in a functioning democracy." The precise claim can be disputed depending on how one defines "functioning democracy" but the lesson Sen draws is correct:

> Perhaps the most important reform that can contribute to the elimination of famines, in Africa as well as in Asia, is the enhancement of democratic practice, unfettered newspapers and—more generally—adversarial politics.[12]

Economists Timothy Besley and Robin Burgess have tested Sen's theory of democracy, newspapers, and famine relief in India.[13] India is a federal democracy. The Indian states vary considerably in their susceptibility to food crises, newspaper circulation, education, political competition, and other factors.

Besley and Burgess ask whether state governments are more responsive to food crises when there is more political competition and more newspapers. Note that both of these factors are important. Newspapers won't work without political competition and political competition won't work without newspapers. Knowledge and power together make the difference.

MRU

mru.org/seniii-democracy-and-famines

Democracy and Famines

Chaideer Mahyuddin/AFP/Getty Images

FIGURE 20.5

Food Availability per Head in Bangladesh

Data from: Sen, Amartya. 1990. Public Action to Remedy Hunger. Arturo Tanco Memorial Lecture given in London on August 25, 1990.

Democracy plus newspapers equals famine relief.

Besley and Burgess find that greater political competition is associated with higher levels of public food distribution. Public food distribution is especially responsive in election and preelection years. In addition, as Sen's theory predicts, government is more responsive to a crisis in food availability when newspaper circulation is higher. That is, when food production falls or flood damage occurs, governments increase food distribution and calamity relief more in states where newspaper circulation is higher. Newspapers and free media inform the public and spur politicians to action.

Notice that there is nothing special about democratic politicians. Democratic politicians may also ignore the public. It's only when democratic politicians face the right incentives due to competitive elections and good information that their incentives become more aligned with the social good.

Democracy and Growth

Democracies have a good record of not killing their own citizens or letting them starve to death. Not killing your own citizens or letting them starve may seem like rather a low standard, but many governments have failed to meet this standard so we count this accomplishment as a serious one favoring democracies. Democracies also have a relatively good record of supporting markets, property rights, the rule of law, fair government, and other institutions that promote economic growth, as shown in Figure 20.4.

One reason for the good record of democracies on economic growth may be that the *only* way the public as a whole can become rich is by supporting efficient policies that generate economic growth. In contrast, small (nondemocratic) elites can become rich by dividing the pie in their favor even if it means making the pie smaller.

Recall the special interest group that we discussed earlier that made up 1% of the population. Consider a policy that transfers $100 to the special interest group at a cost of $4,000 to society. Will the group lobby for the policy? Yes, because the group gets $100 in benefits but it bears only $40 of the costs (1% of $4,000).

By definition, oligarchies or quasi democracies are ruled by small groups. Thus, the rulers in these countries don't have much incentive to pay attention to the larger costs of their policies as borne by the broader public. The ruling elites may even have incentives to promote and maintain policies that keep their nations poor. An entrenched, nondemocratic elite, for example, might not want to support mass education. Not only would a more educated populace compete with the elite, but an informed people might decide that they don't need the elite and, of course, the elite know this. As a result, the elites will often want to keep the masses weak and uninformed, neither of which is good for economic growth or, for that matter, preventing starvation.

But now let's think about a special interest group that represents 20% of society. Will this special interest favor a policy that transfers $100 to it at a cost of $4,000 to society? No. The special interest group receives $100 in benefits from the transfer but its share of the costs is now $800 (20% of $4,000), so the policy is a net loser even for the special interest. Thus, the larger the group, the greater the group's incentives to take into account the social costs of inefficient policies.

Large groups are more concerned about the cost to society of their policies simply because they make up a large fraction of society. Thus, large groups tend to favor more efficient policies. In addition, the more numerous the group in charge, the less lucrative transfers are as a way to get rich. A small group has a big incentive to take $1 from 300 million people and transfer it to themselves. But a group of 100 million that takes $1 from each of the remaining 200 million gets only $2 per person. Even if the large group took 100 times as much as the small group, $100, from each of the 200 million people, that's only $200 each. Pretty small pickings. It's usually better for a large group to focus on policies that increase the total size of the pie.

In other words, the greater the share of the population that is brought into power, the more likely that policies will offer something for virtually everybody, and not just riches for a small elite.

The tendency for larger groups to favor economic growth is no guarantee of perfect or ideal policies, of course. As we have seen, rational ignorance can cause trouble. But on the big questions, a democratic leader simply will not want to let things become too bad. That's a big reason why democracies tend to be pretty good—although not perfect—for economic growth.

CHECK YOURSELF

• The free flow of ideas helps markets to function. How does the free flow of ideas help democracies to function?

Takeaway

Incentives matter, so a good institution aligns self-interest with the social interest. Does democracy align self-interest with the social interest? Sometimes. On the negative side, voters in a democracy have too little incentive to be informed about political matters. Voters are rationally ignorant because the benefits of being informed are small—if you are informed, you are more likely to choose wisely at the polls, but your vote doesn't appreciably increase the probability that society will choose wisely, so why bother to be informed? Being informed creates an external benefit because your informed vote benefits everyone, but we know from Chapter 10 that goods with external benefits are underprovided.

Rational ignorance means that special interests can dominate parts of the political process. By concentrating benefits and diffusing costs, politicians can often build political support for themselves even when their policies generate more costs than benefits. And special interests can also block good policies when costs are concentrated and benefits diffused.

Incumbent politicians can use their control of the government to increase the probability that they will be reelected. Politicians typically increase spending before an election and increase taxes only after the election. Voters pay attention to current economic conditions even when the prosperity is temporarily and artificially enhanced at the expense of future economic conditions.

Our study of political economy can usefully be considered a study of government failure that complements the theory of market failure presented in Chapter 10 on externalities and Chapter 13 on monopoly. When markets fail to align self-interest with the social interest, we get market failure. When the institutions of government fail to align self-interest with the social interest, we get government failure. No institutions are perfect and trade-offs are everywhere—this is a key lesson when thinking about markets and government.

A close look at democracy can be disillusioning, but the record of democracies on some of the big issues is quite good. It's hard for politicians in a democracy to ignore the major interests of voters. And if things do go wrong, voters in a democracy can always "throw the bums out" and start again with new ideas. Partially as a result, democracies have a good record on averting mass famines, maintaining civil liberties like free speech, and supporting economic growth. Most of all, democracies tend not to kill their own citizens, who after all are potential voters.

CHAPTER REVIEW

Go online to practice with more examples of these types of problems, including live links to videos, data sources, and feedback.

KEY CONCEPTS

public choice, p. 397

rational ignorance, p. 398

median voter theorem, p. 407

FACTS AND TOOLS

1. Which of the following is the smallest fraction of the U.S. federal budget? Which are the two largest categories of federal spending?

   Welfare

   Interest on the federal debt

   Defense

   Foreign aid

   Social Security

   Health care

2. Do you believe that public school teachers in the United States should be paid higher salaries? Without searching online, what do you believe is the average annual salary of public school teachers in the United States?

3. **a.** How many famines have occurred in functioning democracies?

   b. What percentage of famines occurred in countries without functioning democracies?

4. Around 155 million voters participated in the 2020 U.S. presidential election. Imagine that you are deciding whether to vote in the next presidential election. What do you think is the probability that your vote will determine the outcome of the election? Is it greater than 1%, between 1% and 0.1%, between 0.1% and 0.01%, or less than 0.01% (i.e., less than 1 in 10,000)?

5. If a particular government policy—like a decision to go to war or to raise taxes—works only when citizens are informed, is that an argument for that policy or against that policy?

6. True or false?

a. During Bangladesh's worst famine, average food availability per person was much lower than usual.

b. Democracies are less likely to kill their own citizens than other kinds of governments.

c. Surprisingly, newspapers aren't that important for informing voters about hungry citizens.

d. Compared with a dictatorship or oligarchy, democracies have a stronger incentive to make the economic pie bigger.

e. Compared with most other countries, full democracies tend to put a lot of restrictions on markets and property rights.

f. When it comes to disposable income, American presidents seem to prefer "making a good first impression" rather than "going out with a bang."

g. When the government owns most of the TV and radio stations, it's motivated to serve the public interest, so voters tend to get better, less biased information.

7. The median voter theorem is sometimes called the "pivotal voter theorem." This is actually a fairly good way to think of the theorem. Why?

8. Perhaps it was in elementary school that you first realized that if everyone in the world gave you a penny, you'd become fantastically rich. This insight is at the core of modern politics. Sort the following government policies into "concentrated benefits" and "diffuse benefits."

a. Social Security

b. Tax cuts for families

c. Social Security Disability Insurance for the severely disabled

d. National Park Service spending for remote trails

e. National Park Service spending on the National Mall in Washington, D.C.

f. Tax cuts for people making more than $250,000 per year

g. Sugar quotas

THINKING AND PROBLEM SOLVING

9. David Mayhew's classic book *Congress: The Electoral Connection* argued that members of Congress face strong incentives to put most of their efforts into highly visible activities like foreign travel and ribbon-cutting ceremonies, instead of actually running the government. How does the rational ignorance of *voters*

explain why *politicians* put so much effort into these highly visible activities?

10. Several cities have experimented with using lottery-based financial incentives to increase voter turnout. For example, a voter in Philadelphia won a $10,000 prize after voting in a local election. A "Voteria" (which rhymes with the Spanish *loteria*) of $25,000 was run as part of a school board election in Los Angeles. People enter the lottery by voting in the given election, and a random voter is drawn to win the prize. These types of incentives have been shown to modestly increase voter turnout (e.g., see LaRaja, R. J. and Schaffner, B. F. [2022]. A cash lottery increases voter turnout. *PLoS One*; and John, P. [2015]. Targeting voter registration with incentives. *Electoral Studies*). But how do you think a lottery like this might influence voter ignorance?

11. We mentioned that voters are myopic, mostly paying attention to how the economy is doing in the few months before a presidential election. If they want to be rational, what should they do instead? In particular, should they pay attention to all four years of the economy, just the first year, just the last two years, or some other combination?

12. In the book *The Myth of the Rational Voter*, our GMU colleague Bryan Caplan argues that not only can voters be rationally ignorant, they can even be rationally irrational. People in general seem to *enjoy* believing in some types of false ideas. If this is true, then they won't challenge their own beliefs unless the cost of holding these beliefs is high. Instead, they'll enjoy their delusion.

Let's consider two examples:

a. John has watched a lot of Bruce Lee movies and likes to think that he is a champion of the martial arts who can whip any other man in a fight. One night, John is in a bar and he gets into a dispute with another man. Will John act on his beliefs and act aggressively, or do you think he is more likely to rationally calculate the probability of injury and seek to avoid confrontation?

b. John has watched a lot of war movies and likes to think that his country is a champion of the military arts that can whip any other country in a fight. John's country gets into a dispute with another country. John and everyone else in his country go to the polls to vote on war. Will John act on his beliefs and vote for aggression, or do you think he is more likely to rationally calculate the probability of defeat and seek to avoid confrontation?

13. In the television show *Scrubs* (well worth diving into your Amazon Prime video subscription to watch), the main character J. D. is a competent and knowledgeable doctor. He also has very little information outside of the field of medicine, admitting he doesn't know the difference between a senator and a representative and believes New Zealand is near "Old Zealand."

   a. Suppose J. D. spends some time learning some of these common facts. What benefits would he receive as a result? (Assume there are no benefits for the sake of knowledge itself.)

   b. Suppose instead J. D. spends that time learning how to diagnose a rare disease that has a slight possibility of showing up in one of his patients. What benefits would he receive as a result? (Again, assume there are no benefits for the sake of knowledge itself.)

   c. Make an *economic* argument that, even given your answer to part b, voters have too little incentive to be informed about political matters.

14. In a small city, a proposed change to trash collection policies would result in 250 people receiving a benefit equivalent to $800 each, but it would also result in 200,000 people bearing a cost equivalent to $3 each. The net benefit/loss to society of the policy change is $_____. Is this policy likely to be enacted? Why or why not?

15. Driving along America's interstates, you'll notice that few rest areas have commercial businesses. Vending machines are the only reliable source of food or drink, much to the annoyance of the weary traveler looking for a hot meal. Thank the National Association of Truck Stop Operators (NATSO), who consistently lobby the U.S. government to deny commercialization. They argue:

   > Interchange businesses cannot compete with commercialized rest areas, which are conveniently located on the highway right-of-way ... Rest area commercialization results in an unfair competitive environment for privately-operated interchange businesses and will ultimately destroy a successful economic business model that has proven beneficial for both consumers and businesses.[14]

Steve Craft

The sorrow of a land without burgers

   a. How does NATSO make travel more expensive for consumers?

   b. Do you think most Americans have heard of NATSO and the legislation to commercialize rest stops? How does your answer illustrate rational ignorance? Do you think that the owners of interchange businesses (i.e., restaurants, gas stations, and other businesses located near but not on highways) have heard of NATSO?

   c. Why does NATSO often succeed in its lobbying efforts despite your answer to part a? (*Hint:* What is the concentrated benefit in this story? What is the diffused cost?)

16. The following figure shows the political leanings of 101 voters. Voters will vote for the candidate who is closest to them on the spectrum, as in the typical median voter story. Again as usual, politicians compete against each other, entering the "political market" just as freely as firms enter the economic market back in Chapter 11.

   a. Which group of voters will get their exact wish: the group on the left, the center-left, the center-right, or the right?

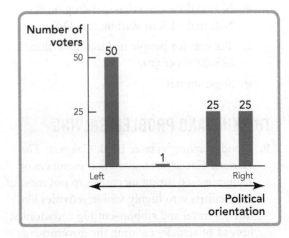

b. Now, four years later, it's time for a new election. Suppose that in the meantime, the two right-leaning groups of voters have merged: The 25 center-right voters move to the far right, forming a far-right coalition. In the new election, whose position will win now?

c. As you've just seen, there's a "pivotal voter" in this model. Who is it?

17. Let's rewrite a sentence from the chapter concerning the Roman Empire: "As the American Empire grew, courting politicians in Washington became a more secure path to riches than starting a new business." Does this seem true today? If it started happening, how would you be able to tell? In your answer, put some emphasis on market signals that could point in favor of or against the "decadent empire" theory. (*Hint:* Moscow is known as a city with high real estate prices, especially compared to the overall income level in the country, and it's probably not due to low housing supply.)

CHALLENGES

18. Is rational ignorance the whole explanation for why voters allow programs like the sugar quota to persist? Perhaps not. In the early 1900s, the government of New York City was controlled by a Democratic Party organization known as Tammany Hall. In a delightful essay entitled "Honest Graft and Dishonest Graft" by George Plunkitt, one of the most successful politicians from the Tammany machine, Plunkitt argued that voters actually approve of these kinds of government-granted favors. (The essay and the entire book, *Plunkitt of Tammany Hall: A Series of Very Plain Talks on Very Practical Politics*, are available for free online.)

For example, Plunkitt said that ordinary voters like it when government workers get paid more than the market wage: "The Wall Street banker thinks it is shameful to raise a [government] clerk's salary from $1,500 to $1,800, but every man who draws a salary himself says, 'That's all right. I wish it was me.' And he feels very much like votin' the Tammany ticket on election day, just out of sympathy."

a. Plunkitt said this in the early 1900s. Do you think this is more true today than it was back then, or less true? Why?

b. If more Americans knew about the sugar quota, do you think they would be outraged?

Or would they approve, saying, "That's all right, I wish it was me"? Why?

c. Overall, do you think that real-world voters prefer a party that gives special favors to narrow groups, even if those voters aren't in the favored group? Why?

19. a. When a drought hits a country, and a famine is possible, what probably falls more: the demand for food or the demand for haircuts? Why?

b. Who probably suffers more from a deep drought: people who own farms or people who own barbershops? (*Note:* The answer is on page 164 of economist Amartya Sen's summary of his life's work, *Development as Freedom*, 1999.)

c. Sen emphasizes that "lack of buying power" is more important during a famine than "lack of food." How does Sen's barber story illustrate this?

20. Political scientist Jeffrey Friedman and law professor Ilya Somin say that since voters are largely ignorant, that is an argument for keeping government simple. Government, they say, should stick to a few basic tasks. That way, rationally ignorant voters can keep track of their government by simply catching a few bits of the news between reruns of *The Big Bang Theory* and *The Office*.

a. What might such a government look like? In particular, what policies and programs are too complicated for today's voters to easily monitor? Just consider the U.S. federal government in your answer.

b. Which current government programs and policies are fairly easy for modern voters to monitor? What programs do you think that you and your family have a good handle on?

c. Can you think of easy replacements for the too complex programs in part a? For instance, cutting one check per farmer and posting the amount on a website might be easier to monitor than the hundreds of farm subsidies and low-interest farm loans that exist today.

21. We mentioned that the median voter theorem doesn't always work, and sometimes a winning policy doesn't exist. This fact has driven economists and political scientists to write thousands of papers and books, both proving that fact and trying to find good workarounds. The most famous theoretical example of how voting doesn't work is the Condorcet paradox. The Marquis de Condorcet, a French nobleman in the 1700s, wondered what would happen if three voters had the preferences like the ones in the following table. Three friends are holding a vote to see which French economist they should read in their study group. Here are their preferences:

	Jean	Marie	Claude
1st Choice	Walras	Bastiat	Say
2nd Choice	Bastiat	Say	Walras
3rd Choice	Say	Walras	Bastiat

a. They vote by majority rule. If the vote is Walras vs. Say, who will win? Say vs. Bastiat? Bastiat vs. Walras?

b. They decide to vote in a single-elimination tournament: Two votes and the winner of the first round proceeds on to the final round. This is the way many sporting events and legislatures work. Now, suppose that Jean is in charge of deciding in which order to hold the votes. He wants to make sure that his favorite, Walras, wins the final vote. How should he stack the order of voting to make sure Walras wins?

c. Now, suppose that Claude is in charge instead: How would Claude stack the votes?

d. And Marie? Comment on the importance of being the agenda setter.

(In case you think these examples are unusual, they're not. Any kind of voting that involves dividing a fixed number of dollars can easily wind up the same way—check for yourself! Condorcet himself experienced another form of democratic failure: He died in prison, a victim of the French Revolution that he supported.)

22. In the previous question, you showed that sometimes there may be no policy that beats every other policy in a majority rule election and, as a result, the agenda can determine the outcome. In the previous question, all of the policy choices on the agenda were as good as any other, but this is not always the case. Imagine that three voters, L, M, and R, are choosing among seven candidates. The preferences of the voters are given in the following table. Voter M, for example, likes Grumpy the best and Doc the least.

Preferences for President of Voters L, M, R			
	Voter L	Voter M	Voter R
1st Choice	Happy	Grumpy	Dopey
2nd Choice	Sneezy	Dopey	Happy
3rd Choice	Grumpy	Happy	Sleepy
4th Choice	Dopey	Bashful	Sneezy
5th Choice	Doc	Sleepy	Grumpy
6th Choice	Bashful	Sneezy	Doc
7th Choice	Sleepy	Doc	Bashful

a. Imagine that we vote according to a given agenda starting with Happy vs. Dopey. Who wins? We will help you with this one. Voter L ranks Happy above Dopey, so voter L will vote for Happy. Voter M prefers Dopey to Happy, so voter M will vote for Dopey. Voter R ranks Dopey above Happy, so voter R will vote for Dopey. So _____ wins.

b. Now take the winner from part a and match him against Grumpy. Who wins?

c. Now take the winner from part b and match him against Sneezy. Who wins?

d. Now take the winner from part c and match him against Sleepy. Who wins?

e. Now take the winner from part d and match him against Bashful. Who wins?

f. Finally, take the winner from part e and match him against Doc. Who wins?

g. We have now run through the entire agenda so the winner from part f is the final winner. Here is the point. Look carefully at the preferences of the three voters. Compare the preferences of each voter for Happy (or Grumpy or Dopey or Sneezy) with the final winner. How many of the voters would prefer Happy (or Grumpy or Dopey or Sneezy) to Doc? The answer to this question should shock you.

(This question is drawn from the classic and highly recommended introduction to game theory, *Thinking Strategically* by Avinash K. Dixit and Barry J. Nalebuff [New York: Norton, 1993].)

23. In the 1998 Minnesota gubernatorial election, there were three main candidates: Norm Coleman (the Republican), Jesse "The Body" Ventura (an Independent), and Hubert Humphrey III (the

Democrat). Although we can't know for certain, the voters probably ranked the candidates in a way similar to that found in the following table. The table tells us, for example, that 35% of the voters ranked Coleman first, Humphrey second, and Ventura third; and 20% of the voters ranked Ventura first, Coleman second, and Humphrey third; and so forth.

Minnesota Gubernatorial Election, 1998				
Rank	35%	28%	20%	17%
1	Coleman	Humphrey	Ventura	Ventura
2	Humphrey	Coleman	Coleman	Humphrey
3	Ventura	Ventura	Humphrey	Coleman

a. Suppose the election is by plurality rule, which means that the candidate with the most first-place votes wins the election. Who wins in this case?

b. In Challenges question 21, you were introduced to the Marquis de Condorcet. Today, voting theorists call a candidate a Condorcet *winner* if they can beat every other candidate in a series of 1:1 or *"face-off"* elections. Question 21 showed you that in some cases, there is no Condorcet winner. What about in the Minnesota gubernatorial election of 1998?

c. A Condorcet winner beats every other candidate in a face-off. A Condorcet loser loses to every other candidate in a face-off. Was there a Condorcet loser in the 1998 Minnesota gubernatorial election (given the preferences we have estimated)?

Jesse "The Body" Ventura
Who are you calling a loser?

WORK IT OUT

For interactive, step-by-step help in solving this problem, go online.

Let's walk through the median voter theorem in a little more detail. Consider a town with three voters, Enrique, Nandini, and Torsten. The big issue in the upcoming election is how high the sales tax rate should be. As you'll learn in macroeconomics (and in real life), on average, a government that wants to do more spending has to bring in more taxes, so "higher permanent taxes" is the same as "higher government spending." Enrique wants low taxes and small government, Nandini is in the middle, and Torsten wants the biggest town government of the three. Each one is a stubborn person, and their favorite position—what economic theorists call the "ideal point"—never changes in this problem. Their preferences can be summed up like this, with the x denoting each person's favorite tax rate:

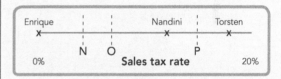

a. Suppose there are two politicians running for office, N and O. Who will vote for N? Who will vote for O? Which candidate will win the election?

b. O drops out of the campaign after the local paper reports that he hasn't paid his sales taxes in years. P enters the race, pushing for higher taxes, so it's N vs. P. Voters prefer the candidate who is closest to them, as in the text. Who will vote for N? Who will vote for P? Who will win? Who will lose?

c. In part b, you decided who was heading for a loss. You get a job as the campaign manager for this candidate just a month before election day. You advise her to retool her campaign and come up with a new position on the sales tax. Of course, in politics as in life, there's more than one way to win, so give your boss a choice: Provide her with two different positions on the sales tax, both of which would beat the would-be winner from part b. She'll make the final pick herself.

d. Are the two options you recommended in part c closer to the median voter's preferred option than the loser's old position, or are they further away? So in this case, is the median voter theorem roughly true or roughly false?

21

Economics, Ethics, and Public Policy

I s it okay to export pollution from rich to poor countries? Larry Summers said not only that it was, but also that exporting pollution should be encouraged. Summers, if you don't already recognize the name, is one of the best economists of his generation, and a former president of Harvard, secretary of the Treasury, and lead advisor to President Obama. In a memo to some of his colleagues when he was chief economist at the World Bank, Summers wrote:

> Just between you and me, shouldn't the World Bank be encouraging *more* migration of the dirty industries to the LDCs [Less Developed Countries]? . . .

> The measurements of the costs of health impairing pollution depend on the foregone earnings from increased morbidity and mortality. From this point of view a given amount of health impairing pollution should be done in the country with the lowest cost, which will be the country with the lowest wages. I think the economic logic behind dumping a load of toxic waste in the lowest wage country is impeccable and we should face up to that.*

Unfortunately for Summers, his memo didn't remain "just between you and me." When it was leaked to the press, there was a firestorm of controversy, not just against Summers but against economics and the type of "impeccable" economic reasoning that Summers found convincing.

If you found Summers's memo disturbing, what about some of the ideas of Nobel prize–winning economist Gary Becker? Becker said that we should legalize the trade in human kidneys. In fact, in a survey, Robert Whaples found that 70% of the economists he surveyed (128 members of the American Economic Association) agreed or strongly agreed with this idea.[1] Right now around 90,000 Americans are waiting for kidney transplants. Many of them will die; others will undergo painful and exhausting dialysis for four hours a day, three days a week. The hospital waiting lists run for five years or more to get a kidney from a willing donor. In case you didn't know, the law won't allow kidneys to be bought and sold, so at a price of zero we have a severe kidney shortage (see Chapter 8 for a discussion of how price controls work).

---

*The Summers memo can be widely found online.

Becker said that to alleviate the shortage, we should allow people to sell their kidneys (you only need one of the two you have). Many citizens of poorer countries would be willing to sell their kidneys for a few thousand dollars or less; in fact, some of these people are selling their kidneys on the black market right now.

Thus, we have two outstanding economists, one of whom said we should export pollution *to* poor countries, while the other said we should import kidneys *from* poor countries. No doubt, these two economists would probably also agree with each other!

Economists sometimes draw a distinction between positive economics and normative economics. **Positive economics** is about describing, explaining, or predicting economic events. For instance, if a quota restricts imports of sugar, the price of sugar will increase and people will buy less sugar. That's true whether or not we think that sugar is good for people. **Normative economics** is about making recommendations on what economic policy should be. Is a sugar quota a good policy? That depends on what we think is good and who we think counts most when we measure benefits and costs.

> **Positive economics** is describing, explaining, or predicting economic events.
>
> **Normative economics** is recommendations or arguments about what economic policy should be.

Not all of this chapter is economics—much of it touches on ethics and morals—but it is still important material for understanding economics as a broader approach to the world. First, economics has limitations and you need to know what they are. It helps to know which ethical values are left out of economic theory. Second, sometimes you will hear bad or misleading arguments against economics, and you need to know those, too, and where they fall short.

We warn you, however, that in this chapter our primary goal is to raise questions rather than provide answers. And we try not to present our own normative claims. Instead, we consider the normative claims made by other people, especially critics of economics, and how they intersect with the positive economics that you have learned already.

The Case for Exporting Pollution and Importing Kidneys

The case for exporting pollution and importing kidneys is actually a familiar one: trade makes people better off. One person wants the kidney more than the money; the other wants the money more than the kidney. Both people can be made better off by trade.

Similarly, it's not surprising that the rich are willing to pay the poor to take some of their pollution. On the margin, the rich value health more than money and the poor value money more than health, so both can be made better off by trade.

What's wrong with these trades? Plenty, according to many people who argue that economic reasoning ignores important values. Economists, it has been said, know the price of everything and the value of nothing.

Some of the objections to standard economic reasoning that we will examine are:

1. The problem of exploitation.

2. Meddlesome preferences.

3. Fair and equal treatment.

4. Cultural goods and paternalism.

5. Poverty, inequality, and the distribution of income.

6. Who counts? Should some count for more?

Let's consider each in turn. You can think of these as the major reasons why not everyone thinks that voluntary exchanges are, in every case, a good idea.

Exploitation

Is the seller of a kidney being exploited? To focus on the difficult issues, let's assume that the seller is of good mind and fully informed about all the risks of donating a kidney. Even in this situation, many people argue that someone selling a kidney is being exploited. Dr. Francis Delmonico, a transplant surgeon and prominent opponent of kidney sales, argues that "payments eventually result in the exploitation of the individual. It's the poor person who sells."[2]

https://youtu.be/QHwDeCBlqqY

Kidneys for Sale?

Delmonico is correct that a poor person is more likely to sell a kidney than a rich person. But does this mean that the poor person who sells a kidney is being exploited? Let's consider three cases.

- Case 1: Alex buys a kidney from Ajay.
- Case 2: Alex pays Ajay to clean his house.
- Case 3: George Mason University pays Alex to grade exams.

In all three cases, the seller would not sell if they were wealthier. So are the sellers (Ajay in the first two cases and Alex in the third) being exploited? We may feel that there is something different about selling a kidney, but it's difficult to see the dividing line that separates exploitation from exchange. Many people in rich and poor countries alike take jobs that involve significant risks. The yearly mortality rate for logging workers in the United States, for example, is nearly three times higher than the mortality rate for donating a kidney—so why is donating a kidney different from logging in the United States?[3]

One response is that for a poor person the money is exploitative because the circumstances of poor people give them little choice but to sell things they would rather keep. But consider which of the three following cases is most exploitative:

- Case 1: Someone asks you to donate a kidney but offers you nothing in return.
- Case 2: Someone offers you $5,000 to donate a kidney.
- Case 3: Someone offers you $500,000 to donate a kidney.

Few people would say that case 1 involves exploitation. But what about case 2 and case 3? If case 2 is exploitative, then case 3 must be even more exploitative—after all, the temptation to sell is many times greater. In fact, many more people, including a great many people in rich countries, would accept an offer of $500,000 to sell one of their kidneys. But it seems odd to say that case 3 is the *most* exploitative case. The usual story is that buyers exploit sellers by offering them too little, not too much! But if bigger offers are less exploitive, then case 2 can't be exploitative either because case 2 is case 1 plus some money and how can offering someone more be a way to exploit them?

If someone offered *you* $500,000 to sell your kidney, would you feel exploited? Probably not. After all, you could always say no. But if case 3 doesn't exploit you, it's hard to see how case 2 exploits Ajay. Maybe Ajay needs the money more than you but imagine, for example, that 10% of the people in India would accept $5,000 for a kidney and 12% of people in the United States would accept $500,000 for a kidney. Does this make the larger offer more exploitive?

Keep in mind that everyone agrees that abject poverty is itself a problem. Overall, it would be better if people had access to clean water, good health care, and more wealth. The issue is whether it's wrong to offer to buy things from the poor just because they are poor. We will be returning to the issue of poverty and the distribution of income later in the chapter.

One more point: we assumed for the sake of argument that the seller of the kidney was of good mind and understood all the risks. One possible response is to say that no one ever understands the risks well enough to make trades like this. If that is the case, however, then we ought to ban gifts of kidneys as well as sales. In fact, thousands of people voluntarily give one of their kidneys away every year and we generally regard such people as heroes. But we don't allow anyone to buy or sell a kidney, despite the fact that doing so could save many thousands of lives.

By the way, although it is illegal to compensate someone for donating a kidney, it is legal in the United States to compensate someone for giving blood plasma, a critical ingredient in blood used to treat trauma victims. In much of the rest of the world, however, it is illegal to compensate plasma donors, and, perhaps not surprisingly, these countries have a shortage of domestic plasma. This has resulted in a peculiar situation: The United States exports a lot of plasma from compensated donors to countries where it is illegal to compensate donors!

The United States exports a lot of blood plasma. Can you guess why?

Meddlesome Preferences

Even if exploitation isn't an issue, many people have a gut feeling that trading kidneys for money is just wrong. How much should this gut feeling count when thinking about justice?

Consider this: Is it okay to eat a horse? Not in California. Millions of Californians voted for a law that says, "No restaurant, cafe, or other public eating place may offer horsemeat for human consumption." The market in horsemeat is open, however, in Europe and Japan where you'll find horse on the menu at many restaurants. In Japan, it's even common to find raw horsemeat for sale as a kind of sushi. But in the United States, the National Horse Protection League doesn't want anyone eating horses—especially foreigners—so it took out full-page ads in the *New York Times* to lobby for a ban on the export of horses to save them from a "brutal fate designed to feed foreign coffers."

In America the horse is, so to speak, a sacred cow (unlike in India where the cow is a sacred cow). So should horsemeat be banned? And if horsemeat is banned because people don't like the idea of someone eating horses, should kidney sales be banned because some people don't like the idea of someone trading kidneys? And what about homosexuality, interracial dating, or various religious practices that do not meet with anything close to universal approval? Often these practices offend someone, so how much should these meddlesome preferences count?

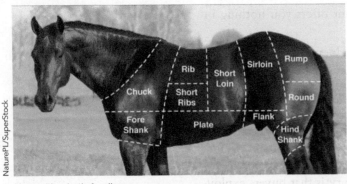

Horse: it's what's for dinner.

Preferences about what other people do, even when those other people don't interfere in any direct way with what you do, are sometimes called meddlesome preferences. It's often difficult to resolve meddlesome preferences with other values that are considered important, such as liberty, rights, or religious freedom.

We—Alex and Tyler—don't usually put much normative weight on meddlesome preferences (we think that "live and let live" should be more popular), but that's one of our value judgments, not anything intrinsic to being economists.

Fair and Equal Treatment

The notion of fair and equal treatment also can run up against the value of trade and efficiency. Consider some of the programs to make mass transit accessible to passengers who are disabled. In New York City, it has long been the case that buses are capable of accepting passengers in wheelchairs. In essence, the bus "kneels down" until the wheelchair can board and then the bus elevates again.

Taxis would be cheaper but would they be equal?

Equipping buses in this fashion was very costly. A study commissioned by Ed Koch, the mayor of New York City at the time of bus conversion, estimated that it would have been cheaper for each wheelchair user or severely handicapped person to take a taxi than refit all buses. Not only would it have cost less, but it would have been more convenient, as well. But would that have been the right thing to do? On one side of the equation stands the virtue of efficiency. Taxpayers would have saved money and people with disabilities, if they took taxis, would have had easier and more luxurious transport options. But defenders of the bus investments claimed that the principle of "equal treatment" was more important than buying each person with a disability free taxi trips for life. Even if the taxpayers and people with disabilities both agreed that taxis were preferable, the critics were saying that more is involved in mass transit than getting a person from place A to place B. Mass transit was, in part, about the sacred value of equal treatment and not making people feel different or disadvantaged.

Economics does not make distinctions between the sacred and the profane, but these issues underlie many arguments about public policy. When thinking about trade-offs, we need to be aware of the resulting tensions and subtleties, many of which are ethical in nature.

Cultural Goods and Paternalism

A closely related issue is whether governments should support some goods even when the public isn't willing to pay for them. The French government, for example, spends billions subsidizing culture and related "higher values."[4] The implicit judgment is that culture is "more valuable" than what people will otherwise spend their money on, and that government is a better judge of "what is best" than are private individuals, at least for these particular sums of money.

The French also place a minimum quota on how many French-language movies must be shown on TV, specifically 40% of the total. For a while, there was even a French minister of rock 'n' roll, to support the production of French-language popular music. The government tried to give the French people French rock 'n' roll instead of the American and British rock music that the French people were buying. Supporters of the policy say that subsidizing French culture is valuable in its own right, and that the aesthetic judgments of the marketplace should not be the final ones.

The French government sees a dark side to American culture, but when it premiered in Paris, the French public made the opening day revenues of *Spiderman 3* the highest in French history.

The pragmatic criticism of French policy argues that these subsidy schemes tend to be counterproductive and wasteful. Maybe French movies would be more successful if they had to appeal to French consumers rather than to the French bureaucrats who hand out the subsidies. The more philosophical criticism is that people should be allowed to spend their money as they choose. In the latter view, freely chosen values have a moral worth of their own that is to be respected.

Of course, it is not just the French who give special support to some cultures and not others. The American government exempts the Amish, a small religious community living predominantly in Ohio, Pennsylvania, and Indiana, from many forms of taxation and compulsory education. America's approximately 300 Indian reservations have a special legal status, in part because the U.S. government takes special care to preserve those cultures. The U.S. federal government also spends money supporting the arts (though the American government spends less than does the French government), in part, because some people want to encourage a higher quality of art than they think will arise through the marketplace and voluntary charity. In fiscal year 2022, the U.S. budget for the National Endowment for the Arts was just $180 million.

Poverty, Inequality, and the Distribution of Income

Perhaps the problem with kidney sales and exporting pollution to poor countries is not trade per se, but the poverty and inequality that make the trade happen. We might accept that when a poor person sells a kidney to a rich person, both are made better off, but still rue the fact that the poor person is poor. In earlier chapters, we emphasized that under certain conditions, markets maximize consumer plus producer surplus—that is an important virtue—but as the kidney example illustrates, in addition to efficiency, we may also have concerns about justice or equity. With a different distribution of income, the demand and supply curves would shift and the poor might not want to sell their kidneys at a price that the rich could afford—that too would be efficient and it might also be more just.

But what is a just distribution of income? How much is owed to the poor? How much is owed to the rich? Questions like these are at the heart of many debates about foreign aid, trade, taxation, health care, and immigration, to name just a few controversial areas.

Many economists have turned to moral philosophy to seek support for their normative policy judgments, and three views have proven especially influential: John Rawls's maximin principle, utilitarianism, and Robert Nozick's entitlement theory of justice. These three views have very different implications for how we, as citizens, should judge the distribution of income and the status of voluntary marketplace transactions.

Rawls's Maximin Principle

John Rawls's *A Theory of Justice*, published in 1971, argued that questions of income and wealth distribution are keys for evaluating social policy. Rawls, a Harvard philosopher, laid out the **maximin principle**, namely that a government should (without violating people's basic rights) maximize the benefits going to society's most disadvantaged group. The notion of "maximizing the

Rawls's maximin principle says that justice requires maximizing the benefits going to society's most disadvantaged group.

minimum" led to the phrase "maximin." For Rawls, doing well by the worst-off group is more important than improving the lot of better-off groups. Rawls deliberately rejects the economist's idea of trade-offs, instead concluding that the worst-off group should be the clear first priority.

Rawls's argument for making the worst-off the first priority is that if no one knew what position they held in society, that is, if people were behind a "veil of ignorance," then they would want a rule that maximized the position of the worst-off, just in case they turned out to be the worst-off! In economic terms, Rawls believed that people were extremely risk-averse.

To see how maximin works in practice, consider a simple example with three people, Red, Blue, and Green.

Now let's compare Society A where Red, Blue, and Green have equal incomes of 100 to Society B where the respective incomes are 150, 100, and 50. Rawls's maximin principle implies that Society A is better or more just than Society B because the worst-off person in Society B, Green, has more income in Society A. Notice that the only difference between Society A and B is that income is more equally distributed in A than in B; average income is identical so it doesn't seem unreasonable to prefer Society A to Society B.

Society	Red	Blue	Green	Average Income
A	100	100	100	100
B	150	100	50	100
C	600	600	99	433
D	1,096	102	101	433

But now let's compare Society A with Society C. In Society C, Red and Blue are much better off than in Society A and Green is slightly worse off. Notice that average income in Society C is more than four times as high as in Society A. Which society would you rank as the better society? Which society does maximin rank more highly? The maximin principle says that Society A is better than Society C because the worst-off person in Society C, Green, is better off in Society A. The maximin principle says that the extra income of Red and Blue counts for nothing; only the income of the least well-off person counts.

It's sometimes said that the maximin principle favors societies with more equal division of incomes but that is not necessarily true. Let's compare Society A with Society D. Even though income is perfectly egalitarian in Society A, the maximin principle says that Society D is better because, once again, the income of the least well-off person is higher. The maximin principle even prefers Society D to Society C, even though Society C has a more equal division of the same average income.

The maximin principle is influential among philosophers but less so among economists who, as you know, tend to think in terms of trade-offs between values. A little bit less income for the worst-off might be acceptable if it comes with a big enough gain to others. Lower average income might be acceptable if income is a little bit more equally divided, and so forth.

Utilitarianism

Under **utilitarianism**, we try to implement the outcome that brings the greatest sum of utility or "happiness" to society. The best-known utilitarian philosopher today is Peter Singer, whom you also may know as an advocate of animal rights.

When it comes to redistribution, a utilitarian approach tries to determine which people have the greatest need for some additional income. For instance, an extra dollar for a poor person may go toward a doctor's visit, but an extra dollar for a rich person may just go toward buying an extra silk tie. The poor person probably gets greater happiness from the extra dollar. The utilitarian is

Utilitarianism is the idea that the best society maximizes the sum of utility.

likely to suggest that some amount of money be redistributed from rich people toward poor people. Unlike Rawls, however, utilitarians are not always trying to make the poorest people as well off as possible. Utilitarians advocate redistributing income only up to the point where the marginal change in utility created from the redistribution is positive. They try to maximize the total sum of utility, not the utility of the worst-off person. So, in principle, utilitarianism (unlike maximin) allows the poor to undergo some extra suffering, provided that suffering is outweighed by enough gains elsewhere in the economy.

What might limit the amount of wealth a utilitarian would redistribute from rich to poor? Incentives! Taking money away from richer people decreases their incentive to earn, so more redistribution could reduce overall wealth by enough to reduce total utility. A utilitarian recipe therefore might involve only a modest amount of redistribution, especially if people are very responsive to incentives. Utilitarianism will also take into account the incentive effects of redistribution on the poor. Giving dollars to poor people is not always the best way to improve their welfare. As Milton Friedman once said, if you pay people to be poor, you're going to have a lot of poor people.

Uncle Scrooge has a high and very slowly diminishing marginal utility of wealth. Uncle Scrooge loves wealth so much that a consistent utilitarian would endorse increasing total utility by taking a dollar from a poor duck like Donald and giving it to rich Uncle Scrooge. Are you a consistent utilitarian? Or an inconsistent utilitarian?

Walt Disney Pictures/Photofest

Notice that the usual assumption in economics is that a dollar is a dollar no matter who gets the dollar, so utilitarianism needs to make assumptions that extend beyond those of economic theory. Economic theory does not assume that a dollar is worth more to a poor person than to a rich person and standard economic tools don't give us any easy way to measure happiness or utility. In fact, many economists believe that comparing the happiness of two people is not very scientific. We might think that the poor person gets more happiness than the rich person from an extra dollar of wealth, but perhaps the poor person is a monk who neither needs nor wants money, while the rich person really does desire another silk tie. Maybe the rich person is rich precisely because he loves money and worked very hard to get it. We aren't saying that this is the case; we are only pointing out that there is no natural unit of measurement of utility, and human beings have very different preferences.

Most economists do believe in a safety net and a welfare state to take care of the poor people in a wealthy society. But this belief doesn't have to be rooted in any very strict comparison of utilities between rich people and poor people. Economists frequently portray the social safety net as a way of obtaining insurance against bankruptcy, major health-care problems, and other bad outcomes. If you think that insurance has value, and that private markets might not provide this insurance on their own (see Chapter 24 for a discussion), that provides some case for a social safety net. Utilitarians go further, however, and try to offer very specific recipes for just how much money should be transferred from the rich to the poor.

Robert Nozick's Entitlement Theory

Whether we accept Rawls's maximin principle or prefer utilitarianism or choose almost any other theory of justice, one thing is clear. There is no guarantee that the distribution of income generated by market forces will be anything like what these theories describe as the just distribution. Most theories of justice, therefore, will call for some amount of taxation and redistribution, using the force of government. One of the few exceptions is Robert **Nozick's entitlement theory of justice**, which is also known as a libertarian theory of justice.

Robert Nozick, another Harvard philosopher, laid out a moral system very different from that of Rawls. Nozick was far more sympathetic to the market economy than was Rawls, and he outlined a defense of the market in a 1974 book called *Anarchy, State, and Utopia*. Nozick argued that the pattern of the distribution of income was irrelevant. What mattered was whether income differences were *justly acquired* and thus Nozick focused on the process by which income is distributed.

Nozick argued that if John wishes to trade with Mary, that decision should be up to John and Mary alone, provided they do not infringe on the rights of others. In the words of Nozick, all capitalist acts between consenting adults should be allowed. Nozick admitted and indeed emphasized that such trades, performed on a cumulative basis, would result in different and indeed unequal outcomes and opportunities for people, but he saw nothing wrong with those inequalities. Nozick went further and positively endorsed those inequalities that resulted from freely chosen market transactions, devoid of coercive force or fraud.

Nozick offered a classic rebuttal to Rawlsian and other theories of justice. Nozick said let's imagine that one day we create a world in which the distribution of wealth is exactly as described by some theory of justice. Let's say the distribution of wealth is exactly like that described by *your* theory of justice. Now, Nozick said, imagine someone like J. K. Rowling, the author of the Harry Potter book series (Nozick actually used the example of Wilt Chamberlain, the basketball star of the 1960s and 1970s).

Rowling, let us say, writes another Harry Potter book and she offers to sell a copy to anyone who is willing to buy. Of course, many people are very willing to buy Rowling's book, and so person by person money is transferred from book buyers to Rowling. Rowling becomes very rich, so at the end of the day, the distribution of wealth will be very different than at the beginning of the day, when by assumption all was just. Yet how can the new distribution of wealth, the one with a very rich J. K. Rowling, be unjust? No one's rights were violated in the process and indeed everyone, including both the fans and Rowling, was made better off every time Rowling sold a book. All that has happened has been voluntary, peaceful trade. A just and rightful trade, Nozick's theory would imply. So why should any outsider disapprove of the resulting pattern of wealth?

Note that this example is not fanciful: When she wrote her first book, J. K. Rowling was an unemployed single mother living on welfare. Yet Rowling became the first author ever to become a billionaire solely through her written works and today her income is thousands of times higher than that of her average fan.

Nozick's example is a direct criticism of the view that equality of outcome is important. Nozick argues that what we should care about is the justness of the process that leads to differences in wealth—theft is bad and should be condemned and rectified, but voluntary, peaceful trade should not be condemned even when it leads to large differences in wealth.

In the libertarian account, what is just is to respect an individual's rights. One way to think of libertarian rights is that they are "side constraints" on possible government actions. The libertarian view corresponds to some common intuitions. For instance, as discussed, many people in the world need kidneys;

Nozick's entitlement theory of justice says that the distribution of income in a society is just if property is justly acquired and voluntarily exchanged.

otherwise, they will die or require dialysis. You have two good kidneys and need only one to live. Is it okay to take a kidney from you against your will? Is it okay to draft your kidney for the greater good? Is it okay to redistribute kidneys?

If you believe the answer to that question is no, you have taken one big step toward the libertarian theory of justice. If you want to think about the next step, a libertarian would ask, if it's not okay to draft your kidney, why is it okay to draft your whole body? And if redistributing kidneys is wrong, isn't redistributing income wrong for similar reasons?

Philosophers continue to debate the relevance of the perspectives of Rawls, utilitarianism, and Nozick, among other ideas. One contribution of the economist is simply to insist that people should be more focused on producing rather than redistributing wealth. Moral philosophers sometimes write as if all the goods were just sitting there on the table ready to be divvied up, but economists know this isn't true. Economists usually stress the importance of producing the wealth in the first place.

Who Counts? Immigration

When economists evaluate a public policy like trade or immigration, they tend to count the benefits and costs to all individuals equally, regardless of where they live. But this isn't always how politics works. Usually, national governments weigh the welfare of their citizens more heavily—usually much more heavily—than the welfare of foreigners.

Immigration is the most salient current issue where the welfare of citizens is counted much more than the welfare of foreigners. Some people argue that immigration hurts U.S. citizens because low-skilled immigrants reduce the wages of low-skilled Americans. Other people argue that immigrants add to the U.S. economy through their entrepreneurship and their willingness to work at very tough jobs.

On net, careful studies indicate that immigration has some positive and some negative effects, but the U.S. economy is so large that overall immigration is not such a big issue—economists who support and oppose immigration agree on this conclusion. People debate the pluses and minuses of additional immigration, and often this is an emotional issue, but again, no matter what your view, the net cost or benefit is likely small relative to the entire U.S. economy.

So let's assume that immigration is either a small benefit or a small cost to U.S. citizens. Everyone agrees, however, that immigration is a huge benefit to the immigrants. The typical Mexican immigrant today comes from a small village in Chiapas, Guerrero, Oaxaca, or some other very poor part of Mexico. People in those villages usually earn ten dollars a day or less. If they come to the United States, they can earn $10 an hour or more. Of course, they send a lot of this money home to their families. Remittances, most of which come from the United States, are Mexico's number one leading "import" industry. Remittances often make the difference between hunger and plenty, or between a collapsing village and a revitalized one. Immigration matters a great deal to the many thousands of Mexicans who cross the border every year and to those who would come if it were easier to do so.

CHECK YOURSELF

• The libertarian theory rejects kidney redistribution as unjust. What about the utilitarian theory or Rawl's maximin principle?

Fred Greaves/Reuters/Newscom

Does this person's well-being count?

So, if the United States is making decisions about its immigration policy, how much should it weigh the benefits accruing to Mexicans from immigration? We're talking not just about the Mexicans who arrive in this country (some of whom may become citizens), but also the Mexicans back home receiving the remittances. Economics tends to be cosmopolitan in its implications since it treats all people equally, no matter where those people live. If the gains to foreigners are counted as much as the gains to nationals, then Mexican immigration into the United States will look especially beneficial. But again, not everyone buys the presumption that the welfare of foreigners should count for as much as the welfare of U.S. citizens. A presidential candidate who held that assumption as a campaign platform would be unlikely to win election.

Foreign aid is another policy issue where we must ask whether our government should be looking after American citizens or people in other countries. In reality, the amount of money the American government spends on foreign aid is very low. The exact sum is difficult to determine, because in the government budget, "foreign aid" and "military assistance" are not completely distinct categories. But, by standard accounts, formal measures of foreign aid amount to around $40 billion per year, or less than 1% of the federal budget. Of course, simply sending money to other countries does not always make them better off; some foreign aid is captured by corrupt elites or used for bad ends. Still you could say the same about some of the money the U.S. government spends at home! The point is this: It remains within the voters' power to have the federal government spend less money on American citizens and more money on needy people overseas. If you are worried about corruption, why not just drop some dollar bills from a helicopter flying over a poor country?

Whether we should do this will depend, in part, on your views as to "who counts?" and "how much?"

CHECK YOURSELF
• How would the libertarian, utilitarian, and maximin theories treat immigration?

Economic Ethics

When economists recommend ideas like exporting pollution or paying for kidneys, they are often said to be ignoring ethics. Economists sometimes agree, perhaps with a bit of pride! But a closer look shows that this is not true. Even though the predictions of economics are independent of any ethical theory, there are ethical ideas behind normative economic reasoning. An economist who rejects the idea of exploitation in kidney purchases, for example, is treating the seller of kidneys with respect—as a person who is capable of choosing for themselves even in difficult circumstances.

Similarly, economists don't second-guess people's preferences very much. If people like wrestling more than opera, then so be it; the economist, acting as an economist, does not regard some preferences as better than others. In normative terms, economists once again tend to respect people's choices.

Respect for people's preferences and choices leads naturally to respect for trade—a key action that people take to make themselves better off. As we saw in Chapter 10 on externalities, economists recognize that trade can sometimes make the people who do not trade worse off. Nonetheless, the basic idea that people can make decisions and know their own preferences leads economists to be very sympathetic to the idea of noncoercive trade.

Economists also tend to treat all market demands equally, no matter which person they come from. Whether you are white or black, male or female, quiet

MRU

mru.org/dismal

How the Dismal Science Got Its Name

or talkative, American or Belgian, your consumer and producer surplus count for the same in an economic assessment of a policy choice.

None of this is to say that economists are always right in their ethical assumptions. As we warned you in the beginning, this chapter has more questions than answers. But the ethical views of economists—respect for individual choice and preference, support for voluntary trade, and equality of treatment—are all ethical views with considerable grounding and support in a wide variety of ethical and religious traditions. Perhaps you have heard that Thomas Carlyle, the Victorian-era writer, called economics the "dismal science." What you may not know is that Carlyle was a defender of slavery and when he made that statement he was attacking the ethical views of economics. Economists like John Stuart Mill believed that all people were able to make rational choices; that trade, not coercion, was the best route to wealth; and that everyone should be counted equally, regardless of race. As a result, Mill and the laissez-faire economists of the nineteenth century opposed slavery, believing that everyone was entitled to liberty. It was these ethical views that Carlyle found dismal.* We beg to differ.

Takeaway

Economics stresses the core idea of gains from trade. Yet in many circumstances, not everyone approves of gains from trade, mostly for ethical reasons. Not everyone thinks that kidneys should be bought and sold and not everyone thinks that pollution should be exported to poor countries. Intuitions about fairness, equitable treatment, distribution, and other matters often clash with the economic notion of increasing gains from trade.

We respect the distinction between positive economics—predicting what will happen—and normative judgments—what should be done. So we haven't tried to answer these ethical dilemmas or give you our sense of the best possible ethical theory. But we do know that if you want to understand and participate in debates about economic policy in the real world, then you must also have some understanding of different ethical theories and their foundations.

---

* "The Secret History of the Dismal Science" is discussed in an excellent article of that title by David M. Levy and Sandra J. Peart, available online at http://www.econlib.org/library/Columns/LevyPeartdismal.html#.

CHAPTER REVIEW

Go online to practice with more examples of these types of problems, including live links to videos, data sources, and feedback.

KEY CONCEPTS

positive economics, p. 422

normative economics, p. 422

Rawls's maximin principle, p. 426

utilitarianism, p. 427

Nozick's entitlement theory of justice, p. 429

FACTS AND TOOLS

1. a. In this chapter, we never actually defined "exploitation." What is one dictionary definition of the word?

b. Decide whether the six cases of alleged exploitation we discussed earlier in the chapter fit your dictionary's definition. Yes, this will involve quite a bit of personal judgment, as will most of this chapter's questions.

   c. In your opinion, does the dictionary definition go too far or not far enough when it comes to labeling some voluntary exchanges as exploitation?

2. Of the three ethical theories we discuss (Rawlsian, utilitarian, and Nozickian), which two are most different from the third? In what way are the two different from the third?

3. One of Nozick's arguments against utilitarianism was the "utility monster": a person who *always* gets enormous happiness from every extra dollar, more happiness than anyone else in society. If such a person existed, the utilitarian solution would be to give all the wealth in society to Nozick's utility monster; any other income distribution would needlessly waste resources. This possibility was appalling to Nozick. Nozick's argument is intentionally extreme, but we can use it as a metaphor to think about the ethics of real-world income redistribution.

   a. Do you know any utility monsters in your own life: people who get absurdly large amounts of happiness from buying things, owning things, going places? Perhaps a family member or someone from high school?

   b. Do you know any utility misers? That would be people who don't get much pleasure from anything they do or anything they own, even though they probably have enough money to buy what they want.

   c. In your view, would it be ethical for the government to distribute income from real-world utility misers to real-world utility monsters? Why or why not?

4. **a.** Just thinking about yourself, if you did not know in advance whether you were a Red, Blue, or Green person, would you rather live in Society A, B, C, or D, discussed in the Rawls's section of the chapter? Why?

   b. Which society would you like least? Why?

5. Rawlsians support government income redistribution to the worst-off members of society. If "society" means the whole world, how much redistribution might be involved? In other words, what fraction of people in the rich countries might have to give most of their income to people in the poorest countries? Keep in mind that the poorest Americans have clean water, guaranteed food assistance (SNAP benefits), and free health care (Medicaid), while billions of people around the world lack such guarantees.

6. Would a "global utilitarian" (someone who values the utility of everyone in the world equally, without giving more weight to people in their own country) who lives in America want more immigrants from poor countries or more immigrants from rich countries? Why?

7. In some parts of the United States it's illegal to buy or sell alcohol on Sundays. In Maine and Illinois it's illegal to buy or sell a car on Sundays. These are examples of what this chapter calls what type of preference? Would a complete ban on alcohol or a ban on sales of all goods on Sundays necessarily be an example of the same types of preference?

8. Select the correct answers to these statements: Economists tends to put (more/less/equal) weight on immigrants' preferences compared to citizens, while politicians tend to put (more/less/equal) weight on immigrants' preferences compared to citizens. This is because economists generally focus on maximizing (equality/efficiency/liberty), while politicians are focused on representing the view of the citizens and getting reelected.

THINKING AND PROBLEM SOLVING

9. To a Rawlsian, would the world be better off without the Harry Potter novels and one additional billionaire?

10. Some people say that the right to equal treatment has no price. But it seems that most people don't really believe that: Those are just polite words that we tell one another. Consider the following cases:

   a. What if it costs $10 million per kneeling bus?

   b. What if it costs $10,000 to hire translators to translate ballots into a rare language spoken by fewer than 10 voters?

   c. What if it costs the lives of hundreds of government officials, police officers, and perhaps even members of the armed forces, such as the National Guard, to ensure the right of a persecuted minority to vote?

   d. At these prices, is the right to equal treatment too expensive for society to buy it? In each case, describe what you think the exact price cutoff should be (in dollars or lives), and briefly explain how you came to that decision. Why not twice the price? Why not half?

11. The line between "having a meddlesome preference" and "recognizing an externality" is not always clear. Both are ways of saying, "What you're doing bothers me." As we used it in this chapter, a "meddlesome preference" is something that reasonable people should just not worry about so much. By contrast, "recognizing an externality" is a way of advancing the subject for public discussion and perhaps even for a vote. In the town you grew up in, which of the following issues were considered things that should be left to individuals and which were things that should be put up for a vote? Is there a good way of distinguishing between the two?

    a. The amount of pollution emitted by a local factory

    b. How much noise would be allowed after 11 PM

    c. Whether siblings should be allowed to marry, even if it is consensual

    d. Where liquor stores could be located

    e. How people should dress in public

    f. How many children someone should have

12. Let's see how a utilitarian dictator would arrange things for Adam, Eve, and Lilith. One heroic assumption that utilitarians make is that you can actually compare happiness and misery across different people: In reality, brain scans are making this easier to do, but it's still a lot of guesswork. Let's suppose that this utilitarian dictator, let's call him Nahash, has eight apples to distribute: The table shows the utility that each person receives from their first apple (a lot), but extra apples give less extra happiness (apples give "diminishing marginal utility," in economic jargon).

Utility per Apple	Adam	Eve	Lilith
1st	1,000	600	1,200
2nd	140	500	200
3rd	20	400	100
4th	1	300	50

    a. So, if the dictator wants to maximize the sum of Adam, Eve, and Lilith's utility, how many apples does each person get?

    b. If, instead, Lilith received 2,000 units of utility from the first apple, how would this change the optimal utilitarian distribution?

13. a. The "trolley problem" is a famous ethical puzzle created by Philippa Foot: You are the conductor of a trolley (or subway or streetcar or train) that is heading out of control down a track. Five innocent people are tied to the track ahead of you: If you run over them, they will surely die. If you push a lever on your trolley, it will shift onto another track, where one unfortunate person is tied up. Either you *let* five people die or you *choose* to kill one person: Those are your only choices. Which will you choose and why? Which ethical view from this chapter best fits your reasoning? (If you Google "trolley problem," you will find many other interesting ethical dilemmas to debate with your friends.)

    b. Another ethical dilemma sounds quite different: You are a medical doctor trying to find five organ donors to save the lives of five people. A new patient comes in for a checkup, and you find that this patient has five organs exactly compatible with the five people. Do you kill the one patient to save the lives of five? Suppose you will never get caught: Perhaps you live in a country where people don't care about such things. Is this the same dilemma? Is it the same dilemma from a utilitarian perspective?

14. What do you think best describes the reason that trade in recreational drugs is illegal: fear of exploitation, meddlesome preferences, notions of fairness, paternalism, concerns about equality, or some other factor?

15. Based on the tools from this chapter, how could a person reasonably justify a ban on gambling?

16. Compare a Rawlsian view with a utilitarian view on the question of whether it should be legal to copy movies and music freely.

17. Consider four societies (A, B, C, and D), each of which has only three citizens. Refer to the table below, which gives each citizen's income, for parts a through d. Assume that each citizen's utility function is the natural log of their income, so the societal utility function for

each society equals ln(Citizen 1's income) + ln(Citizen 2's income) + ln(Citizen 3's income).

Society	Citizen 1	Citizen 2	Citizen 3
A	90	90	90
B	125	200	80
C	85	400	85
D	250	185	75

a. Rank the societies from most just to least just based on Rawls's maximin principle.

b. How could income be redistributed in Society D to create a more just society according to Rawls's maximin principle?

c. Rank the societies from most just to least just using utilitarianism. Does the society with the highest total income rank the highest?

d. Under utilitarianism, what rule should Society B's government follow when redistributing income in order to create a more just society?

CHALLENGES

18. Should responsible adults be allowed to sell a kidney? Why or why not? If so, what restrictions would you place on such sales, if any? (For more on this issue, see the Kidneys for Sale? video in the chapter.)

19. a. In your view, when should governments enforce a "live and let live" rule: on issues that matter most to people (e.g., matters of life and death, matters of how much income to give to the government, matters of religion, matters of sexuality) or on the issues that matter least to people (e.g., what flavors of spices are permitted at the dinner table, what kind of clothing is acceptable in public)?

b. Europeans fought a lot of wars in the 1500s over the right to meddlesome preferences. Thinking back on your history courses, what preferences did Europeans want to meddle with? And if you haven't taken a European history class (or don't remember what you learned), you can do some online research on the French Wars of Religion, Ottoman conflicts in Europe, German Peasant Wars, the War of the League of Cambrai (also known as the War of the Holy League), the Tudor Rebellions, and the Italian Wars (also known as the Habsburg-Valois Wars). You may also want to do some research on the Protestant Reformation. And, by now, you may have already guessed what the Europeans were wanting to meddle with simply from some of the names listed above.

c. What was the usual argument given in the 1500s for why it was right to meddle with other people's preferences?

20. As noted in the chapter, the French government spends billions each year supporting French culture. In the United States, the budget of the National Endowment of the Arts is orders of magnitude smaller. Is there any economic justification for these types of subsidies? What are some of the difficulties in turning the economic theory into practice?

21. Philosopher Alastair Norcross poses the following question. Suppose that 1 billion people are suffering from a moderately severe headache that will last a few hours. The only way to alleviate their headache is for one person to die a horrible death. Can the death of this one person ever be justified in a cost-benefit sense?

22. If the rich countries were able to send individual cash payments to people in poor countries, bypassing possibly corrupt governments, would you let rich countries pay people in poor countries to take their high-polluting factories? If so, how high would the annual payment have to be per family? If not, why not?

23. You would probably sacrifice yourself to save all of humanity, but you probably wouldn't sacrifice yourself to save the life of one random stranger. What number is your cutoff: How many lives would you have to save for you to voluntarily face sure death?

24. Some people feel inequality is justified if the people with unequal outcomes accepted risks voluntarily; it was simply the case that some won and some lost. Imagine two people, each spending $10,000 on lottery tickets, but only one of them wins. We end up with one poor person and one multimillionaire.

Is this inequality better or worse than if one person is born into a rich family and the other is born into a poor family? What exactly is the difference and why?

25. Sometimes poor countries have a lot of people; India has more than 1 billion residents. Indians are relatively poor, and we know that as families become wealthy, they tend to limit their number of children. So, a much wealthier India, over time, would probably have many fewer than 1 billion inhabitants. Would this make for a better India or a worse India? Although each Indian would have much more, there would be fewer Indians. As a result, is there any argument for keeping India poor, so as to have a higher number of people? If not, why not? In general, what can economics tell us about the ideal number of people in a society? Anything at all?

26. Let's say that Tom, who is 25 years old, wants to smoke a cigarette. Consider the following two situations.

    a. Tom is smoking. Suddenly, the government comes along and tells Tom that he cannot do this. The government claims that Tom is inflicting an "external cost" on other human beings. Is this a good policy or bad policy?

    b. Tom is smoking a cigarette at home with no one else around. Suddenly, the government comes along and tells Tom that he cannot do this. The government claims that Tom is inflicting an "external cost" on another human being. Tom asks who this might be? The government says that the 65-year-old Tom will be harmed by the smoking-today-Tom. The government claims that today-Tom isn't doing enough to look out for the well-being of future-Tom. Does this argument make any sense? Is it ethically correct? If so, can and should we trust our government to make these decisions for our future selves?

WORK IT OUT

For interactive, step-by-step help in solving this problem, go online.

Let's see how a utilitarian dictator would arrange things for Charles, Elizabeth, and Mary. One heroic assumption that utilitarians make is that you can actually compare happiness and misery across different people. In reality, brain scans are making this easier to do but it's still a lot of guess-work. Let's suppose that this utilitarian dictator has eight oranges to distribute: The table shows the utility that each person receives from their first orange (a lot), but extra oranges give less extra happiness (oranges give "diminishing marginal utility," in economic jargon).

Utility per Orange	Charles	Elizabeth	Mary
1st	2,000	1,200	2,400
2nd	280	1,000	400
3rd	40	800	200
4th	2	600	100

a. So, if the dictator wants to maximize the sum of Charles's, Elizabeth's, and Mary's utilities, how many oranges does each person get?

b. If, instead, Mary received 4,000 units of utility from the first orange, how would this change the optimal utilitarian distribution?

22

Managing Incentives

A good social system aligns self-interest with the social interest. A successful organization aligns self-interest with the organization's interest.

Organizations—businesses, governments, teams—whose interests conflict with the interests of their members don't last very long. It's often not easy, however, to align everyone's incentives. Incentives matter—this is one of the key lessons of this book—but getting the incentives right is not always easy. Managers of businesses and sports teams, voters, politicians, and parents must all think about and choose incentives. This chapter is about getting the incentives right and what happens when we get the incentives wrong.

Lesson One: You Get What You Pay For

Every May, Chicago public school students take a standardized test. Students are used to being tested, graded, and rewarded accordingly, but beginning in May 1996, teachers and principals had a lot more than usual on the line: Schools with low scores would be closed, teachers reassigned, and principals fired. The idea, of course, was to give educators stronger incentives to work harder and better. If grading was good for the students, why not for the teachers?

Stronger incentives do give teachers and principals an incentive to put in extra hours and search for better teaching methods. But how else can teachers raise the grades of their students? Here's a hint: Some students also use this method. That's right—they cheat. Indeed, teachers can cheat a lot better than students because they know which answers are correct! Two economists who understand incentives, Brian Jacob and Steven Levitt (the latter of *Freakonomics* fame), started to look carefully at test data and asked: Would teachers really cheat to raise student grades?[1] Sure enough, Jacob and Levitt found odd patterns in the data—students who got easy answers wrong and difficult answers right, groups of students who had exactly the same right and wrong answers, and students who received high grades during a test year but low grades the year after. Most telling for an economist was that the indicators of cheating were much stronger after the penalty for low-performing schools went into effect than before!

Perhaps you think that teachers' cheating to raise student grades is a good idea! But it wasn't what the proponents of strong incentives for teachers had in mind. Not all teachers cheated, but cheating was surprisingly common. Jacob and Levitt estimated that cheating occurred in at least 4% to 5% of classrooms.

Other researchers have found that after the introduction of strong incentives, a lot more students are declared learning disabled.[2] Why? Test scores of students called "learning disabled" are usually not counted when it comes to rewarding teachers and principals.

Does all this mean that strong incentives for teachers are a bad idea? Not necessarily. Students who learn more, earn more. If strong incentives for teachers do increase true scores, even by a small amount, maybe it's a good idea even if some of the better scores are due to cheating.[3]

A similar example of incentives for cheating comes from corporate finance. In the 1980s, chief executive officers (CEOs) were given much stronger incentives to increase their firm's stock price. Instead of being paid a straight salary, they were awarded stock options. These are complicated financial instruments, but what you need to know is that they pay off only if the stock rises above a certain price. As with strong incentives for teaching, strong incentives encouraged CEOs to work harder and smarter. It also encouraged them to cheat by manipulating earnings reports to make their firms appear more profitable than they really were. Enron and the other scandals of the 1990s and first decade of the 2000s were, in part, the result. Were strong incentives worth it? If the shareholders believed that on average the costs of cheating exceeded the benefits of encouraging harder work, they would offer their CEOs fewer options and other strong incentives. But so far most of these incentives have stayed in place, albeit with more monitoring of potentially bad behavior.

Shareholders, however, are not the only ones who can be harmed when a company like Enron or Lehman Brothers collapses, so their choice of CEO incentive scheme may not reflect everyone's interests and may not be best for society as a whole. (Recall our discussion of externalities in Chapter 10.) Incentive schemes, for example, that give executives big bonuses for very good performance but don't penalize them very much for very bad performance can encourage executives to take on too much risk. In part for this reason, investment banks such as Bear Stearns and Lehman Brothers took on lots of risk in mortgage securities, and their collapses helped lead to the financial crisis of 2008. Executive compensation, therefore, has become a subject of political controversy. We will return to executive compensation later on in this chapter.

When designing an incentive scheme, remember this: You get what you pay for. That sounds good but there is a problem. What if what you pay for is not exactly what you want? If you pay for higher test scores, you will get higher test scores. But test scores are an imperfect measure of what you really want—more productive teachers and more knowledgeable students. What you pay for is higher stock prices, but what you really want is a more profitable firm. Usually, stock prices reflect a firm's fundamental value, but even the market can be fooled sometimes!

The closer "what you pay for" is to "what you want," then the more you can rely on strong incentives. Careful design of an incentive scheme can narrow the gap between what you want and what you can pay for. After Jacob and Levitt published their results, the administrators of Chicago Public Schools, to their credit, fired some teachers, and instituted new procedures to make cheating more difficult. After the Enron scandal, investors demanded more independent financial audits. The stronger the incentives, the more it pays to invest in careful measurement and auditing, and vice versa.

If you can't bridge the gap between "what you pay for" and "what you want," then weak incentive schemes can be better than strong incentive schemes.

Prisons for Profit?

Should the management of prisons be contracted out to the private sector? The owners of a private firm have a strong incentive to cut costs and improve productivity because they get to keep the resulting profits. If a public prison cuts costs, there is more money in the public treasury but no one gets to buy a yacht, so the incentive to cut costs is much weaker.

In 1986, Kentucky became the first state to contract out a prison to a for-profit firm. Private prisons in the United States today hold about 100,000 prisoners, about 8% of all prisoners in the country. Should efficient private prisons replace inefficient public prisons? Economists Oliver Hart, Andrei Shleifer, and Robert Vishny (collectively known as HSV) say no. HSV don't question that the profit motive gives private prisons stronger incentives than public prisons to cut costs—HSV say that's the problem! Suppose that we care about costs but we also care about prisoner rehabilitation, civil rights, and low levels of inmate and guard violence. What we pay for is cheap prisons, but what we want is cheap but high-quality prisons. If we can't measure and pay for quality, then strong incentives could encourage cost cutting at the expense of quality.

Prisons for Profit? Private prisons in the United States hold about 8% of all prisoners. England and Wales (18%) and Australia (18%) also use private prisons.

The principle is a general one, a strong incentive scheme that incentivizes the wrong thing can be worse than a weak incentive scheme. Suppose a car dealer advertises that its sales staff is not paid on commission. Why would a store advertise that its sales staff do not have strong incentives to help you? The answer is clear to anyone who has tried to buy a car. High-pressure dealers who pounce on you the moment you enter the showroom and bombard you with high-pressure sales tactics ("I can get you 15% off the sticker, but you have to act NOW!") may sell cars to first-time buyers, but the strategy is too unpleasant to win many repeat customers. Car dealers who rely on repeat business usually prefer a low-pressure, informative sales staff.

In theory, a car dealer could have strong incentives *and* repeat business by paying its sales staff based on their "nice" sales tactics, but in practice, it's too expensive to monitor how salespeople interact with clients. Cheating by the sales staff would be difficult to detect and thus would be common. Paying the sales staff a salary instead of a commission calms them down a bit. Of course, there is a price to be paid for weak incentives. Imagine that Joe's Honda pays its sales staff on commission, while Pete's Subaru pays its staff a straight salary. Which dealership do you expect to be open late at night and on Sundays?

What about prisons? Are HSV correct that weak-incentive public prisons are better than strong-incentive private prisons? Not necessarily. HSV assume that cutting quality is the way to cut cost. But sometimes higher quality is also a path to lower costs. Low levels of inmate and guard violence, for example, are likely to reduce costs. And respect for prisoner's civil rights? That can save on legal bills. When quality and cost cutting go together, a private firm has a strong incentive to increase quality.

HSV may also underestimate how well quality can be measured. Measuring intensively pays off more when incentives are strong. Unsurprisingly, therefore, private prison companies and government purchasers have made extensive efforts to measure the quality of private prisons.

Finally, don't forget that weak incentives reduce the incentive to cut costs but they don't increase the incentive to produce high quality! Public prisons might use their slack budget constraints to offer high-quality rehabilitation programs, or they might instead offer prison guards above-market wages. Which do you think is more likely?

Nevertheless, whether HSV are right or wrong about private prisons, their argument is clever. The usual argument against government bureaucracy is that without the profit incentive, public bureaucracies won't have an incentive to cut costs. HSV suggest this is exactly why public bureaucracies may sometimes be better than private firms.[4]

Piece Rates vs. Hourly Wages

A majority of workers are paid by the hour but a significant number are paid by the piece. An hourly wage pays workers for their inputs (of time); a **piece rate** pays workers for their output. Agricultural workers, for example, are often paid by the number of pieces of fruit or vegetable that they pick. Garment workers are often paid per item completed. Salespeople are often paid, in part, by the number of sales that they make. When should workers be paid by the hour and when should they be paid by the piece?

A **piece rate** is any payment system that pays workers directly for their output.

Piece rates increase the incentive to work hard and can work well when output is easy to measure so "what you pay for" is close to "what you want." Piece rates are common in agricultural work because it's easy to measure the number of apples picked and this is close to what the employer wants. Even in agricultural work, however, the employer wants not just apples but ripe and unbruised apples so piece rates usually require some form of quality control. Piece rates do not work well when quality is important but quality control is expensive.

In the early days of computing, IBM paid its programmers per line of code. Can you see the problem? When IBM paid by the line, IBM programmers produced lots of code, but in their rush to earn more money, the programmers often wrote low-quality code. IBM's incentive scheme rewarded what was measurable—lines of code—at the expense of what IBM really wanted but what was difficult to measure, high-quality code. IBM quickly stopped paying its workers by the line and switched to hourly wages. Hourly wages reduced the incentive to work hard but also reduced the incentive to rush the work before it was ready.

The advantage of piece rates is that, if used properly, they can greatly increase productivity. The auto-glass installer Safelite Glass Corporation switched from an hourly wage system to a piece rate. Safelite was able to handle the quality control issue by linking every job with a worker so that if a quality problem arose, the worker who was responsible for that windshield installation had to fix it on their own time. Productivity quickly improved by an astonishing 44%.[5] About half of the increase in productivity was due to the same workers working harder, including lower absenteeism and fewer sick days, but the other half of the productivity increase was due to another important effect of piece rates. A piece rate system attracts more productive workers.

Consider two firms, one of which pays workers by the piece and the other pays workers by the hour. Now consider two workers, one of whom can install five windshields a day, the other just three. Which worker will be attracted to which firm? The piece rate firm will attract the more productive worker because piece rates give productive workers a chance to earn more money. The hourly wage plan will attract workers who are relatively less productive or even "lazy."

The differences between workers in productivity can be surprisingly large. One California wine grower switched from paying grape pickers by the hour to paying by the pound. Previously, the firm had paid its workers $6.20 per hour. Under piece rates the average pay was effectively $6.84 per hour, about the same as before, but some workers were making as much as $24.85 an hour.[6]

When some workers are more productive than other workers, piece rates will tend to increase inequality in earnings. Under the hourly wage, every grape picker earned $6.20 an hour. Under the piece rate, some earned $6.84, while others earned $24.85. Information technology is making it easier to measure the output of all kinds of workers, not just grape pickers. As a result, performance pay (piece rates, commissions, bonuses, and other rewards tied directly to output) is becoming more common in the U.S. economy and this is one reason why the inequality of earnings has increased.[7]

The increase in effective pay under piece rates explains why both firms and employees can benefit from piece rates. Under hourly wages, workers don't have an incentive to work harder even when they can do so at low cost. Piece rates benefit productive workers by giving them an opportunity to use their skills to make more money. Piece rates also benefit firms by increasing productivity more than wages.

Even though firms and workers can both benefit from piece rates, piece rates are sometimes not implemented because of distrust. Workers fear that if they respond to a new piece rate plan by increasing productivity (and thus wages), the firm will respond by reducing the piece rate in the next period (e.g., paying less per pound of grapes picked). In the old Soviet Union, factory managers who increased productivity in response to new incentives were often denounced because their increased performance proved that they had previously been lazy! Of course, this greatly reduced the incentive to increase productivity. Similarly, workers won't work harder if they expect that higher productivity will be punished with lower piece rates. Firms that want to introduce piece rates must build trust with their workers.

Lesson Two: Tie Pay to Performance to Reduce Risk

Consider an auto dealer who wants to motivate their sales staff. Let's assume that all the auto dealer cares about is sales, so they are not worried that strong incentives will make the sales staff too pushy. Are strong incentives now the best? Maybe not.

Auto sales depend on more than hard work. Sales also depend on factors the staff has no control over, such as the price and quality of the car, the price of gas, and the state of the economy. If incentives tie earnings directly to sales, the sales staff are going to do great when the economy is booming but poorly when the economy is in a recession.

When sales vary for reasons having little to do with hard work, strong incentives may be more expensive than they are worth. Most people don't like risk.

CHECK YOURSELF

- Lincoln Electric is a firm famous for using piece rates. Lincoln Electric also has a policy of guaranteed employment. How are these two policies related?
- In the United States, restaurant customers have the option of adding a tip to the restaurant bill. In much of Europe, a "tip" is added on automatically. Where would you expect waiters to be more attentive?

Which would you prefer, $100 for sure or a gamble that pays $200 with probability $\frac{1}{2}$ and $0 with probability $\frac{1}{2}$? Gambling in Las Vegas can be fun but most people will prefer $100 for certain over a gamble with the same expected payoff. Similarly, suppose that there are two jobs: job 1 pays $100,000 a year for sure, job 2 pays $200,000 in a good year but $0 in a bad year. Suppose also that good and bad years are equally likely, so, on average, job 2 also pays $100,000 a year. Which job would you prefer? If the wages are the same on average, most people will prefer job 1, the less risky job. How high would the average wage have to be for you to prefer job 2? $110,000, $150,000, $175,000? The precise number is less important than the principle: The riskier payments are to workers, the more a firm must pay on average. Thus, if the sales staff has to bear the risk of a bad economy or a low-quality car, they will demand a big bonus for every sale. But if the sales staff demand a big bonus, what is left over for the owner? If the sales staff is sufficiently afraid to face these risks, the owner and the staff might not be able to agree on a mutually profitable strong incentive plan.[*]

Weak incentives insulate the sales staff from risk. If the owner is better able than the sales staff to bear the risk of a recession (perhaps because they are wealthier), weak incentives may be mutually profitable. In essence, the owner can sell the staff "recession insurance" by paying them with a fixed or nearly fixed salary. The sales staff "buy" the insurance by accepting smaller bonuses but, of course, their pay is more stable.

Bearing the risk of a recession might be worth it if hard work from the sales force is also the critical factor in sales. But if the state of the economy is a significant determinant of sales, then strong incentives have created risk with very little motivational advantage. Imagine if rewards were based solely on luck—what incentive would there be to exert effort? Similarly, if rewards are mostly based on luck, the incentive to exert effort will be low and many potential employees won't want to face those risks at a price the owner is willing to pay.

Tournament Theory

When sales depend heavily on outside factors such as the state of the economy, tying bonuses directly to sales will reward or penalize agents for outcomes that are often beyond their control—thus shifting risk to the agent but giving the agent little incentive to exert effort. One way a manager can reduce an agent's risk is to tie rewards more closely to actions that a sales agent does control. A surprising way to do this is to pay bonuses based not on a sales agent's absolute number of sales but on their sales relative to other agents—for example, giving a bonus to the sales agents with the highest, second-highest, and third-highest sales. For obvious reasons, economists call a compensation scheme in which pay is based on relative performance, a **tournament**.

A **tournament** is a compensation scheme in which payment is based on relative performance.

If they are used cleverly, tournaments can tie rewards more closely to actions that an agent controls, thereby improving productivity and pay and reducing risk. To see how a tournament works in the business world, let's start with sports, an area where we are all used to thinking about tournaments.

Imagine a golf game in which players are paid based on the total number of strokes to finish the course (by the nature of golf, fewer strokes mean better

---

[*] Or worse, the sales staff may be eager to sell cars when the economy is good but may quit the day the economy turns sour.

play and thus higher payments). If the weather is bad, scores will be high and players won't earn very much even if they work hard. If the weather is good (clear day, no wind), scores will be low and players will earn a lot even if they don't work very hard. Either way, when players are paid based on their absolute scores, random forces—such as the weather—will influence how much the players earn.

Now imagine that players are playing in a tournament with a fixed number of prizes, which of course is usually the case. The fixed number of prizes means that the players are competing *against one another* rather than against some external standard of achievement. Since every player plays with the same weather, the weather no longer influences rewards. Thus, a tournament limits the amount of risk from the external environment. A lot of sporting events, not just golf, are organized in the form of tournaments. Tournaments are also common in the business world.

For instance, paying sales agents based on relative sales will reduce environment risk, risk from external factors that are common to all the agents. When sales agents are paid based on relative sales, factors that the agents do not control such as the state of the economy, the quality of the product, and the price of competing products will no longer influence agent rewards. *Here is the key*: when factors that an agent doesn't control no longer influence rewards, then factors that an agent does control—factors like effort—become more important determinants of rewards. Thus, pay for relative performance such as that used in a tournament can reduce risk and tie rewards more closely to actions that an agent controls. This will mean harder work, less risk, more output, and higher pay.

Improving Executive Compensation with Pay for Relative Performance

A good compensation scheme ties rewards to actions that an agent controls. How would you use the idea of *pay for relative performance* to tie executive pay more closely to actions that executives control?

Today, a large fraction of an executive's pay is tied to the stock price of their firm. When the value of the firm rises, executives are often able to cash in stock options at profitable prices. But many factors other than executive effort or ability influence the price of a stock. When the economy does well, for example, the price of most stocks goes up. Similarly, when the price of oil goes up, the stock price of firms in the oil industry tends to go up—and surprisingly, so does the pay of executives in the oil industry, despite the fact that these executives have no control over the price of oil.[8] Of course, when the price of oil falls, these executives are paid less, despite the fact that they may be working as hard as, or harder than, ever. The bottom line is that quite a bit of executive pay appears to be based on luck. But payment based on luck is not a good compensation scheme on either the upside or downside.

Is there a better way to pay executives? Instead of paying based on how well their stock performs, how about paying executives based on how well their stock performs *relative to other firms in the same industry*? If executives were paid based on relative performance, they wouldn't reap big windfall profits when the industry boomed (due to no virtue of their own) but neither would they necessarily be paid less when the industry declined (due to no fault of their own).

Pay for relative performance seems to make a lot of sense but it has not been widely adopted. As a result, some observers suspect that the complicated stock option schemes currently used to reward executives are less about creating incentives than about creative accounting that takes advantage of shareholders who do not closely monitor how much the executives are being paid. Interestingly, firms that have at least one very large shareholder—and thus at least one shareholder with an incentive to monitor the firm closely—do appear to base more executive pay on relative performance.[9]

In recent times, the American economy has experienced another problem with compensating senior managers, especially in banking and finance: Sometimes the incentive is to take too many "long tail" risks, namely risks that rarely go bad, but when they do, they go very, very bad. Let's say a bank manager encourages their staff to make risky mortgage loans that go bad only once every 30 years, but when they do, they endanger the very existence of the bank and perhaps even the banking system. Most of the time the risks pay off, the bank prospers, and the managers get a nice bonus. Sooner or later, however, the mortgages go bad and the bank ends up insolvent or in need of a government bailout. How much do the managers suffer? Usually, they don't have to give back their old bonuses and often the worst thing that happens—if that—is they are fired. In 2008, two investment banks, Bear Stearns and Lehman Brothers, went bankrupt. This wasn't good for their managers, but over the 2000–2008 period, they had already pulled out about $1.4 billion (Bear Stearns) and $1 billion (Lehman Brothers) in cash bonuses and equity sales.[10] Thus, even though these managers took on huge risks, they still profited handsomely. Many of them found other jobs or retired on their previous bonuses, so the penalties to discourage excess risk-taking aren't so strong. Prior to the financial crisis of 2007–2009, the U.S. financial system took too many risks of this nature. It remains to be seen whether better incentives can be designed to overcome this problem.

In his prime, Tiger Woods was so good that other players slacked off knowing they had little chance of beating him.

Environment Risk and Ability Risk

A tournament insulates rewards from *environment risk* due to outside factors that are common to all the players, but it adds another type of risk called *ability risk*. Imagine that you had to compete in a golf game against Tiger Woods. Would you put in more effort if you were paid based on the number of strokes or if you were paid based on who wins the game? The probability that you could beat Tiger Woods at golf is so low that if all you cared about was money, it would make sense to give up right away—why exert effort in a hopeless cause? Of course, for the same reason, Tiger Woods won't need to try very hard either!

In fact, the logic applies to professional golfers as well as to amateurs. The economist Jennifer Brown found that professional golfers had worse scores when Tiger Woods was also playing than when Tiger Woods wasn't playing, even when competing on the same course in the same weather conditions. The professional golfers probably realized that it doesn't pay to exert a lot of effort in a tournament with a superstar.[11] Remember, an ideal incentive scheme ties rewards to factors that an agent controls, such as effort. But a golf tournament between players with highly unequal abilities doesn't tie rewards to effort; it ties rewards to ability and that often causes people to shirk and slack. Thus, tournaments work best when the risk from the outside environment is more important than ability risk.

Tournaments can be structured to reduce ability risk. At a professional golf tournament, for example, players play in rounds with the weakest players being eliminated in early rounds, so when the final and most important round is played, the players have similar abilities. Similarly, tournaments are often split into age classes or experience classes (beginner, intermediate, expert) so that abilities are similar and each player has a strong incentive to work hard. In amateur but serious golf games, when players of differ- ent ability compete together, the high-ability players will often be handicapped, which makes competition more intense for all the players. A manager who wants a lot of effort will also structure tournaments so that rewards are closely tied to effort. A manager, for example, might create junior and senior sales positions with tournaments played within each class of employee.

Tournaments can encourage too much competition.

Tournaments in business might seem a bit unusual but they are quite common. About one-third of U.S. corporations eval- uate employees based on relative performance.[12] Under the hard-nosed CEO Jeff Bezos, employees at Amazon must com- pete against one another for a limited number of promotions, and employees ranked in the bottom 10% are often shown the door (a so-called rank-and-yank system). Even when employees are not explicitly rewarded based on relative performance, tournaments are often implicit. Lawyers, for example, compete to earn the prize of becoming a partner. Becoming the president of a corporation is a lot like winning a tournament. Imagine that a corporation has eight vice presidents and one president—the vice presidents compete to become the next president. The fact that moving up the corporate ladder is like competing in a tournament may also shed some light on the large salaries and perks of many corporate presidents. Personal chefs, corporate jets, and lavish parties might be a sign of an abuse of power but the perks of presidency may also motivate the eight vice presidents. In part, the high salaries and perks of corporate presidents are intended as motivation for those beneath them.

Tournaments are wonderful at encouraging competition but sometimes competition can be too fierce. In a tournament, when one player falters, the others gain, so tournaments can discourage cooperation. One corporate vice president might be unwilling to mentor another if they see a competitor waiting to take away their job. Thus, as usual, compensation schemes must be carefully designed to balance a variety of goals.

Tournaments and Grades

Let's apply some of the insights from tournament theory to a competition that you are very familiar with: the competition for grades. Some professors grade on a curve, while others use an absolute scale. When a professor "grades on a curve," there are a fixed number of "prizes"—A's, B's, C's—for each class. The competition for grades becomes a tournament.

The costs and benefits of being graded on a curve are just like the more general analysis of tournaments. Grading on a curve reduces environment risk but increases ability risk. Can you think of some examples of environment risk? Suppose that your professor is hard to understand—perhaps the professor has an accent or teaches the material too quickly or is simply not a good teacher (unlike us!). Fortunately, if the professor grades on a curve, their bad performance doesn't mean you have to fail. Bad teaching will reduce how much you learn but bad teaching harms everyone's performance. If the professor grades on a curve, bad teaching need not reduce your grade or reduce your incentive to study.

A bad teacher who grades on an absolute scale, however, is double trouble. First, bad teaching means that you won't learn much. Second, if the grading is on an absolute scale, not learning much means that even if you work hard, you will get a low grade. There isn't much incentive to work hard in that case.

Grading on a curve, however, does have disadvantages—grading on a curve means that you will be competing directly with the other students in the class. If you happen to be in a class with a handful of super-brilliant students, it's like golfing against Tiger Woods (unless *you* are the academic Tiger Woods). Even if you learn a lot and work hard, you won't get a high grade and that reduces your incentive to study.

Grading on a curve, therefore, creates better incentives to study when the big risk is that the professor will be bad (an environment risk), but it reduces the incentive to study when students are of very different abilities (ability risk). Grading on an absolute scale creates better incentives to study when students are of very different abilities (ability risk), but reduces the incentive to study when the big risk is that professors will be bad (environment risk).

What are some other effects of grading on a curve? Remember, tournaments tend to reduce cooperation. If your professor grades on a curve, other students might be less willing to help you with your homework (or you might be less willing to help them!). Study groups will probably be less common. Some students might even try to sabotage other students. Tournaments can also encourage the wrong kinds of cooperation. If a professor grades on a curve, in theory all the students could get together and agree not to study very much. This probably wouldn't happen in a large class, but if two sales agents regularly compete for the "salesperson of the month" award, they could collude to reduce effort and rotate the prize between them.

Here's another problem for you to think about. Suppose that the environment risk is not bad professors but rather difficult material. Imagine, for example, that some classes are more difficult than other classes (quantum physics 101 vs. handball 101). If you really wanted to learn a little about quantum physics, but you were afraid of reducing your GPA, what type of grading system would you prefer? And to ask the classic economist's question: under what conditions? See Thinking and Problem Solving question 17 for further discussion of this question.

Lesson Three: Money Isn't Everything

Incentives are powerful, but not all powerful incentives are for money. If you want to keep meetings short, make everyone stand until the meeting is over. All of a sudden the cost of talking is higher so people have an incentive to talk less.

Other powerful rewards include the feeling of identification and belonging that comes from being part of a team, the joy that comes from a job well done, and the status that comes from success on one's own terms. Intrinsic motivation

CHECK YOURSELF

- At one prominent university, a professor's first name and middle initial are "Harvey C." Undergraduates refer to him as "Harvey C-minus" because he is a notoriously hard grader. What are this professor's incentives to be known as a hard grader? What type of students does he attract? Whom does he encourage to stay away? Why might this professor not want to grade on a curve?

- How can a tournament create too much competition? Isn't competition a good thing?

is when you want to do something simply for feelings of enjoyment and pride. Ideally, firms would like their employees to be motivated by intrinsic rewards like pride in a job well done, as well as extrinsic rewards like money.

A good manager will get workers to enjoy doing what the manager wants. One way of doing this is to encourage workers to identify with the corporation and its goals in the same way that sports fans identify with their team. Many workers, for example, are given shares of stock in the company they work in. Currently, about 34 million American employees own a part of their employers.[13] Since most workers don't have much control over the value of the entire company, this doesn't make sense as a monetary incentive. But workers are more likely to identify with their company if they are also part owners of their company. Workers who identify with their company see corporate success as their success. Sports fans celebrate when their teams win championships even though the fans didn't receive any monetary rewards. In a company with strong worker identification, high profits are a cause for celebration even if the workers don't receive raises. Workers who identify with their company are more likely to see themselves in the same boat as other workers and to think and act more like a team or sometimes even like a family. This is also why many companies run staff retreats or invest in softball teams.

Successful businesses take great care to create the right **corporate culture**. Corporate culture is the shared collection of values and norms that govern how people interact in an organization or firm. Sometimes it is said that corporate culture is "how things get done around here."

> **Corporate culture** is the shared collection of values and norms that govern how people interact in an organization or firm.

The American military is one of the most successful creators of a powerful "corporate culture." In the military, a team member may sacrifice their life for the sake of the team. Business corporations can rarely rely on this intensity of identification, but a strong corporate culture can help align incentives. Recall that one of the big problems with monetary incentives is that the firm can't always measure what it wants. A firm that can't measure quality, for example, may be worried about creating strong incentives for quantity. But a firm with workers who value high quality for its own sake can have the best of both worlds—high quality and high quantity. Corporate culture helps firms incentivize what is difficult to measure.

The importance of morale and good relations extends beyond the business corporation. You can see these same principles at work in your everyday life.

Intrinsic and extrinsic motivation can work together but not always. When intrinsic motivation is strong, people are sometimes insulted by offers of money. If you ask a friend to give you a ride to the airport, the friend would probably say yes (well, *some* friends . . . maybe not all friends). Offer your friend $20 for a ride and all of a sudden the friend feels like a taxi driver, not a friend. The friend who might have done it for free will turn down the job for $20. In one advice column, a woman complained that her husband promised to "pay her by the pound" to lose weight (the advice column did not say whether the husband was an economist). This marriage probably was not a happy one, and we should not expect this proposed transaction to succeed.

Similarly, it is not always possible to pay your teenager to do the dirty dishes. Nagging doesn't always work well either but paying money can be worse. When the parents pay money, the child feels less familial obligation. Once they say to themselves, "Doing the dishes is a job for money," the child is no more obligated to do their parents' dishes than they are to get a job at a restaurant to do other people's dishes.

In these cases, payment causes external motivation to replace internal motivation. Yet for some tasks, internal motivation is what gets the job done; payment can be counterproductive.

Note that payment from a restaurant will get the same child to show up for work on time. Having their own job—which is a signal of adulthood and independence—is "cool" and makes the child feel like a grown-up. Money from parents, which feels like an allowance for tots or like a means of parental control, will not boost the child's internal motivation to do the dishes.

The lesson is this: Monetary rewards are most effective when they are supported by intrinsic motivation and measures of social status. Good entrepreneurs understand these connections, and they design their workplaces so that money, intrinsic motivation, and status incentives work together. Money can't buy you love, however, and sometimes love is the incentive that makes family and personal relationships work well. Money can't buy you duty or honor either, so even within firms and other organizations such as the military, monetary incentives must be used with care. Understanding when extrinsic and intrinsic rewards complement one another and when they are at odds is today more of an art than a science. Questions like these are on the cutting edge of social psychology and behavioral economics.

Lesson Four: Nudges Can Work

Incentives, whether intrinsic or extrinsic, are not the only thing that can change behavior. Sometimes small changes in how a choice is presented, or "framed," can matter a great deal. Do you prefer beef that is 80% lean or beef that is 20% fat? Of course, those are just two different ways of presenting the same choice but supermarkets know that advertising 80% lean sells better. And have you noticed that supermarkets place the attractive candy and gossip magazines next to the checkout line rather than beside the dishwasher detergent in Aisle 7? Someone who needs detergent is going to buy detergent regardless of what aisle it's in but most of us feel a bit guilty about candy and gossip. We enjoy these items even if we also think we consume too much of them. Putting the candy and gossip at the checkout turns it into an "impulse buy": Just one moment of weakness and the salesclerk has already rung the item up. And where do supermarkets put the boring but often purchased items like milk? At the back of the store so you have to walk past the cookies and other temptations to get what you want.

Planning where, when, and how choices are made is sometimes called "choice architecture," and in the case of a supermarket the choice architecture is geared toward getting us to spend more. In contrast, some employers now put healthier foods in especially visible spots in their work cafeterias, so as to encourage healthy eating (and lower health insurance costs) among their employees. For much the same reason, one of your authors bought a refrigerator with clear fruit and vegetable drawers placed at eye level.

Cass Sunstein and Richard Thaler, a lawyer and an economist, have written a best-selling book called *Nudge*, which considers a variety of ways that governments and other organizations can use small changes in the choice architecture—what they call "nudges"—to change or improve decisions.

Most people, for example, don't like to deviate too much from the norm, so in some cases just telling people what is normal or average can change their behavior. In San Marcos, California, the local utility company told people whether they were using more or less energy compared with the average in their neighborhood. People who learned that they were using more electricity than average lowered their consumption in future periods even though the price of electricity didn't change. The change was especially large when people with above-average consumption also received a frowning emoticon on their bill while people with below average consumption earned a smiley face.[14] By the way, good job on studying so hard. ☺

In Chapter 21 on ethics, we discussed how some economists propose to increase the supply of transplant organs by paying donors for their kidneys. Of course, that's a controversial option. A nudge might be less controversial. For instance, in the United States a person must choose to become an organ donor by signing a donor card. In Austria, everyone is automatically considered to be an organ donor unless they have signed a *nondonor* card. Either option is pretty easy but in the United States only 60% of potential donors have signed donor cards while in Austria only 1% have signed nondonor cards. As a result, 99% of Austrians are potential organ donors, more than the U.S. percentage. Maybe Austrians are just more willing to be organ donors, but Sunstein and Thaler argue that more Americans would be willing donors if the choice to do so was made just a little bit easier.[15]

Inspired by Sunstein and Thaler, the British government has created a Behavioral Insights Team, popularly called the "nudge unit," to try to find small nudges to get people to do things the government wants, such as pay their taxes on time, insulate their attics, sign up for organ donation, and stop smoking during pregnancy.

From these examples, perhaps you can see both the potential of the nudge concept but also why it is not popular with everyone. Sometimes nudging is considered a form of manipulation or a step toward controlling more of our choices. Some individuals object to nudges all the more when they are performed by governments because of the fear that this represents a Big Brother paternalistic relationship. Advocates of nudging techniques stress their noncoercive nature, how they are based on freedom of choice, and the potential for better outcomes.

The general lesson is this. Economists usually think that what matters for choice are preferences and constraints such as prices and income. And, of course, incentives do matter. But other things matter too and sometimes how choices are presented can change which choices are made, even without changing more fundamental factors. Smiley faces won't solve the problem of climate change. For that we probably do need changes in the price of greenhouse gas emissions. But if a nudge can moderately improve outcomes at very low cost, why not nudge?

Takeaway

Incentives are a double-edged sword. When aligned with the social interest, incentives can be powerful forces for good but misaligned incentives can be equally powerful forces for bad. One of the goals of economics is to understand which institutions generate good incentives.

On a less grand level, getting the incentives right is an important goal of managers who want to motivate employees, stockholders who want to motivate managers, parents who want to motivate children, and consumers who want to motivate real estate agents, physicians, or lawyers among many others.

CHECK YOURSELF

- Is Christmas wasteful? Instead of presents, wouldn't it be more efficient to give cash that can be used to buy what the recipient really wants? Why don't we see cash gifts more often?

- Some parents and increasingly some schools are using cash to pay students for good grades. Good idea or not?

In this chapter, we discussed four lessons to help get the incentives right. Lesson one: You get what you pay for, but what you pay for is not always what you want. Sometimes the gap between what you pay for and what you want arises because the incentive plan is badly designed. More often the gap arises because measuring exactly what you want is difficult, so you must pay for something that is more easily measurable but is not exactly what you want. When the gap between what you pay for and what you want is large, strong incentives can be worse than weak incentives. As it becomes easier to measure things like quality, however, strong incentive plans are becoming more common.

Lesson two: Tying pay to performance reduces risk. Strong incentives put more risk on agents from factors beyond their control, and to bear this risk, the agents will demand greater compensation. Sales agents on commission, for example, bear the risk that the economy goes into a downturn or that the product they sell is of low quality. As a result of this increased financial risk, sales agents on commission must be paid higher average wages than sales agents on salary. A firm must ask whether the strong incentives created by commissions increase sales enough to justify the higher average wages.

A good incentive plan will reduce unnecessary risk by tying rewards to actions that an agent controls and that are effective in increasing output. Different incentive plans like commissions, bonuses, and tournaments impose different types of risks on agents. Which incentive plan is best will depend on which risks are most important.

Lesson three: Money isn't everything. In addition to earning money, workers want to enjoy their work, identify with a team, and be respected. Successful corporations provide these rewards, as well as monetary rewards. Monetary rewards can be paid only for what is measurable, but a successful corporate culture can help firms incentivize what is difficult to measure. Monetary rewards are most effective when they are supported by intrinsic motivation and measures of social status.

Lesson four: Nudges can work. Sometimes small differences in how a choice is presented or framed can make surprisingly large differences in what people choose. Time, effort, and attention are all scarce so if a choice can be presented in a way that is quick, easy, and obvious, people are more likely to make that choice.

Successful leaders will draw on all four lessons of this chapter to design and frame incentives that align the interests of their employees, agents, and followers with their own interests.

CHAPTER REVIEW

Go online to practice with more examples of these types of problems, including live links to videos, data sources, and feedback.

KEY CONCEPTS

piece rate, p. 440

tournament, p. 442

corporate culture, p. 447

FACTS AND TOOLS

1. This chapter had four big lessons. Each of the following situations illustrates one and (we think) only one of those lessons. Which one?

   a. Militaries throughout the world give medals, citations, and other public honors to members of the military who excel in their duties.

b. People tip for good service after their meal is concluded.

c. Real estate agents work on commission, but office managers at a real estate office are paid a straight salary.

d. In 2016, it was discovered that Wells Fargo (a bank) had fraudulently opened 1.5 million new checking and savings accounts for existing clients without their clients' permission. This behavior was caused by an incentive program that paid account representatives for each new account opened with the intention of increasing the number of new customers. (For a nice rundown of the story, check out the Planet Money episode "The Walls Fargo Hustle," https://www.npr.org/sections/money /2016/10/07/497084491/episode-728-the -wells-fargo-hustle.)

e. Studies have shown that when employers initially enroll all workers in a retirement plan, the workers save more than when they must ask to join the retirement plan, even when in both cases workers can quit or join the plan at any time.

f. Teacher salaries are based primarily on years of service and the teacher's highest degree level attained (bachelor's, master's, etc.) or number of graduate hours. As a result, teachers often pursue higher degrees despite the fact that research has shown that the attainment of higher degrees does not increase teacher performance levels. In fact, some teachers will take graduate classes that have nothing to do with the subject they teach, such as a math teacher taking graduate courses in local history.

2. An American church sends 10 missionaries to Panama for three years to find new converts. Every six months, the missionary with the most new converts gets to be the supervising missionary for the next six months. This basically means that they get to drive a car, while the other nine have to walk or ride bicycles. Clearly, this is a tournament. Now consider the following two cases. For which case will the church's incentive plan work better? (*Hint:* Think about ability risk vs. environment risk.)

Case 1: Missionaries specialize in different regions: Some stay in rich neighborhoods for the whole six months, others stay in poor neighborhoods for the whole six months.

Case 2: Missionaries move from region to region every few weeks, so that all missionaries spend a little time in every kind of Panamanian neighborhood.

3. Clever marketers understand choice architecture. Why are clearance racks in clothing stores usually located in the back of the store rather than in the front?

4. During the 2016–2017 NBA season, Portland Trailblazers player Maurice Harkless had a clause in his contract that stated he would earn a $500,000 bonus if he shot 35% or better from the three-point line over the course of the season. Going into the final four games of the season, his three-point shooting percentage was 35.1%. How many three-point shots do you think he took over the last four games? Is this necessarily good for team performance? Can you think of any problems that such an incentive scheme might cause? Many professional athletes get a bonus if they win a championship. Is this kind of incentive better or worse than a basketball player's bonus for three-point shooting percentage? Why?

5. Let's return to Big Idea Four (thinking on the margin) back in Chapter 1. Why are calls to give harsher penalties to drug dealers and kidnappers often met with warnings by economists?

6. Why are salespeople so much more likely than other kinds of workers to be paid on a "piece rate" (i.e., on commission)? What is it about the kind of work they do that makes the high-commission + low-base-salary combination the equilibrium outcome?

7. Unlike in the previous question, sometimes piece rates don't work so well. Why might the following incentive mechanisms turn out to be more trouble than they're worth?

a. An industrial materials company pays welders by the number of welds per hour. Of course, the company pays only for necessary welds.

b. A magazine publisher pays its authors to write "serial novels" one chapter at a time. The authors are paid by the word (common in the nineteenth century and how Dickens and Dostoyevsky made their livings).

8. If is considering two different job offers. At the first job, she would make a consistent $60,000 salary every year. At the second job, she would be paid a guaranteed salary of $30,000, with a 50% chance to earn an additional $60,000 in sales commissions. What is the expected payout from each job offer? Assuming Ife is risk averse, which job will she choose and why?

9. Mateo, despite being a salaried employee whose income does not depend on how many hours he works, chooses to come into work 30 minutes early every day in order to catch up on e-mails and start his day in a positive manner. Are his actions intrinsically or extrinsically motivated? Seeing this pattern of behavior, his employer offers to pay him a higher yearly salary as long as he continues to come in early. How does this change his motivation?

10. Suppose that you are a janitor who works in a large corporate office building. One of your responsibilities is to take out the garbage for the various cubicles in the building. In an effort to improve productivity, management implements a piece rate pay system for throwing away garbage: For every bag of garbage you throw away, you earn additional pay on top of your hourly wage. How might you exploit this new policy to make more money?

11. The typical corporate executive's incentive package offers higher pay when the company's stock does well. One proposal for such executive merit pay is to instead pay executives based on whether their firm's stock price does better or worse than the stock price of the average firm in their own industry. Does this proposal solve an environment risk problem or an ability risk problem? How can you tell?

THINKING AND PROBLEM SOLVING

12. In 1975, economist Sam Peltzman published a study of the effects of recent safety regulations for automobiles. His results were surprising: Increased safety standards for automobiles had no measurable effect on passenger fatalities. Pedestrian fatalities in automobile accidents, however, increased. (This is now known as the Peltzman effect and has been tested repeatedly over the decades.)

   a. Why might more *pedestrians* be killed when a car has *more* safety features?

   b. Economists have looked for ways out of Peltzman's dilemma. Here's one possible solution: Gordon Tullock, our colleague at George Mason, has argued that cars could have long spikes jutting out of the steering column pointed directly at the driver's heart. Keeping Peltzman's paper and the role of incentives in mind, would you expect this safety mechanism to result in an increase, decrease, or no change in automobile accident fatalities? Why?

   c. Would a pedestrian who never drives or rides in cars tend to favor Tullock's solution? Why or why not?

13. One reason it's difficult for a manager to set up good incentives is because it's easy for employees to lie about how they'll respond to incentives. For example, Simple Books pays Mary Sue to proofread chapters of new books. After an author writes a draft of a book, Simple sends chapters out to proofreaders like Mary Sue to make sure that spelling, punctuation, and basic facts are correct.

   As you can imagine, some books are easy to proofread (perhaps Westerns and romances), while others are hard to proofread (perhaps engineering textbooks). But what's difficult or easy is often in the eye of the beholder: Simple can't tell which books are particularly easy for Mary Sue to proof, so they have to take her word for it. Let's see how this fact influences the publishing industry.

   In the following figure, Q^* is the number of chapters in the new book *Burned: The Secret History of Toast*. It's a strange mix of chemistry and history, so Simple isn't sure how Mary Sue will feel about proofing it. The marginal cost curve shows Mary Sue's true willingness to work: The more chapters she has to read, the more you have to pay her. If Simple offers to pay her $50 per chapter, as shown, she'll actually finish the job.

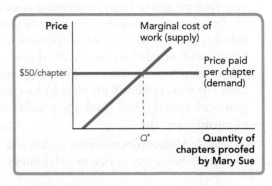

a. If Mary Sue wants to bluff, claiming that the book is painful to read, what is that equivalent to?

> Supply curve shifting left
> Supply curve shifting right
> Demand curve shifting down
> Demand curve shifting up

Once you decide, make the appropriate shift in the figure.

b. The publisher just *has* to have Mary Sue proof all Q^* chapters of *Burned*: All its other proofreaders are busy. The publisher will pay what it needs to for her to finish the book. This is the same as another curve shift in a certain direction: Draw this shift in the figure.

c. What did Mary Sue's complaining do to her price per chapter? What did it do to her workload?

d. (Bonus) You've seen how Mary Sue's bluffing influenced the outcome. What are some things that Simple might do to keep this from happening?

14. Who do you think is in favor of forbidding baseball player contracts from including bonuses based on playing skill? Owners or players? Why?

15. In the short, readable classic *Congress: The Electoral Connection,* David Mayhew uses the basic ideas of incentives and information as a pair of lenses through which to view members of Congress. What he saw was quite simple: The urge for reelection drives everything. Thus, members are driven by self-interest to give the voters in their home district as much as possible. Of course, voters face the same problem in judging members of Congress that any manager faces when evaluating an employee: Some outputs are harder to measure than others, so voters focus on measurable outputs. With that in mind, what will voters be most likely to care about? Choose one from each pair and briefly explain why you made that choice.

a. How many dollars come to the district for new hospitals and highways vs. how many dollars are spent on top-secret military research.

b. How well the member behaved in private meetings with Chinese leaders vs. how the member sounded on *Meet the Press*.

c. How well the member did in reforming the Justice Department vs. how well the member did at the Turkey Toss back in the district last Thanksgiving.

(As you've seen, voters' focus on the visible can easily drive the member's entire career. Mayhew's book was an important early work in "public choice," the use of basic microeconomic ideas like self-interest and strategy to study political behavior. For more on the topic, Kenneth Shepsle and Mark Bonchek's short textbook *Analyzing Politics* is highly recommended. See also Chapter 20 of this textbook.)

16. In the movie business, character actors are typically paid a fixed fee, while movie "stars" are typically paid a share of the box office revenues. Why the difference? Try to give two explanations based on the ideas in this chapter.

17. Let's return to the question we posed in the chapter: Suppose that the big environment risk is not bad professors but rather hard material. Imagine, for example, that some classes are more difficult than other classes (quantum physics 101 vs. handball 101). If you really wanted to learn a little about quantum physics but you were afraid of reducing your GPA, you'd face a tough choice. A curve is better for you than an absolute scale, but even if your professor grades on a curve, you're probably still sitting in a class with other well-trained physics majors. Let's see if we can find a work-around.

a. At your school, are there certain times of the day when the less serious, more fun-loving students tend to take their classes? If so, what time is that? If you sign up for a section scheduled then, you might look better on the curve.

b. Some schools offer simplified (we won't say "dumbed down") versions of some hard courses. Does your school offer anything like this? If so, does it allow majors to take the same sections as the nonmajors? How is this sorting related to tournament theory?

c. If you were a professor, which teaching schedule would you rather have: two sections where the majors and nonmajors are mixed together or one section with the majors and one with the nonmajors?

18. When an accused defendant is brought before a judge to schedule a trial, the judge may release the defendant on their "own recognizance" or the judge may demand that the defendant post bail, an amount of cash that the defendant must give to the court and that will be forfeited if the defendant fails to appear. Many defendants don't have the cash, so they borrow the money from a bail bondsperson. Then, if the defendant fails to appear, the bail bondsperson is out the money, unless the defendant is recaptured within 90–180 days. To recover their money, a bail bondsperson will hire bail enforcement agents, also known as bounty hunters, to track down the missing defendant. If the bounty hunters don't find the defendant, they don't get paid.

David Howells/Getty Images

This Dog knows how to hunt.

   a. If defendants released on their own recognizance fail to appear, they are pursued by the police, but if they are released on bail borrowed from a bondsperson and they fail to appear, they will be pursued by bounty hunters. Which type of defendant do you think is more likely to fail to appear, and which type is more likely to be recaptured if they do fail to appear? Why?

   b. Perhaps surprisingly, bounty hunters tend to be quite courteous and respectful even to defendants who have tried to skip town. Can you think of one reason why?

19. a. Why do so many charitable activities like marathons, walks, and 5K runs give the participants "free" T-shirts, wristbands, hats, bumper stickers, and so forth?

   b. Charitable organizations could probably make a lot of money for their cause by selling these items on their websites, but you usually have to actually attend the "2022 Cancer Run" to get the "2022 Cancer Run" T-shirt. Why?

20. Waiters and waitresses in the United States are generally paid very low hourly wages and receive most of their compensation from customer tips.

   a. As the owner of a restaurant, what do you want from your waitstaff?

   b. Which element of a waiter's or waitress's compensation—the hourly wage or the tips—represents a method of "tying pay to performance"?

   c. Which element of a waiter's or waitress's compensation—the hourly wage or the tips—plays the role of "insurance" that the restaurant owner provides for the waitstaff? Against what are the waiters and waitresses being insured?

   d. Theoretically, a restaurant owner could pay workers a higher wage, raise menu prices, and make the restaurant strictly tip-free. Or, the owner could eliminate the wage, reduce menu prices, and encourage greater tipping by alerting customers to the fact that the waitstaff do not earn an hourly wage. What are the potential pros and cons (from the point of view of the restaurant owner) of each system?

21. In the long-running reality competition show *Hell's Kitchen*, Gordon Ramsay takes the idea of using a tournament for hiring executive chefs to a whole new level. On the show, a group of contestants compete for the opportunity to become the head or executive chef at a restaurant of Ramsay's choosing and a cash prize of $250,000. At the beginning of each season, the contestants are divided up into two teams who, in each episode, compete in a challenge and dinner service, with one or sometimes multiple chefs eliminated at the end of each episode.

   a. For the most part, contestants for *Hell's Kitchen* are auditioned and screened to make sure that each contestant has the skills necessary to do well on the show (or, at least, most of them; a few extremely poor contestants can add entertainment value to the early episodes). Why do you think this screening is done? What kind of risk is being eliminated by this audition process? What would happen if there were one contestant who, right from the beginning, demonstrated more potential and greater capabilities than the other contestants?

b. Though only one contestant will end up becoming a head chef at the end of the show, each must try to prove their worth to Ramsay by performing well in the team challenges. What impact do you think the tournament structure of this show has on these team challenges?

c. Some of the challenges, as well as the dinner service, can be quite demanding, and the contestants often work very hard. Wouldn't it be easier if they all shirked rather than working hard? Ramsay would still (presumably) have to choose one of them as the winner, and chances are that it would be the same person whether everybody worked hard or not. Why are the contestants not likely to all agree to stop trying so hard?

22. Suppose a CEO wanted more of their employees to get flu shots or COVID vaccines. How many of the four big lessons in this chapter can you employ to come up with different solutions? (Don't worry if they're not all feasible or practical—that's the reason there are four big lessons in this chapter, not just one.)

23. An anticorruption campaign in India (5th Pillar) uses a clever tool: a zero-rupee note. The impressive note looks just like a 50-rupee note, but is clearly marked as being worthless and contains anticorruption messages. Indians are encouraged to give these notes to public officials who demand or expect bribes. Millions of the notes have been distributed since 2007, and in 2015, 5th Pillar extended the concept to other countries. A Twitter user tweeted economist Richard Thaler (of *Nudge* fame) to ask whether this counted as a nudge. What do you think his answer was, and why?

24. Researchers seem to have a lot of fun testing different nudges to see how well they work. In one experiment, they placed mirrors in shopping carts so customers at a grocery store were forced to look at themselves while they shopped. How would you expect this kind of nudge would impact shoppers' behavior? (PS: It worked!)

CHALLENGES

25. Let's tie together this chapter's story on incentives with Chapter 15's story about cartels. Suppose your economics professor grades on a curve: The average score on each test becomes a B−. If all of the students in your class form a conspiracy to cut back on studying, point out how this cartel might break down just like OPEC's cartel breaks down during some decades.

26. What type of systems in the United States help overcome the incentives of physicians to order medically unnecessary tests?

27. In his path-breaking book *Managerial Dilemmas*, political scientist Gary Miller says that a good corporate culture is one that gets workers to work together even when they face prisoner's dilemmas (we discussed the prisoner's dilemma in detail in Chapter 15). In a healthy corporate culture, you feel guilty if you're being lazy while your buddy is working. Let's sum up "guilt" as simply as possible: It's some number "X" that represents how you feel. These figures are adapted from Figure 15.4.

		Stan	
		Work	Shirk
Kyle	Work	(4, 4)	(2, X)
	Shirk	(X, 2)	(3, 3)

a. What does X have to be to keep this from being a prisoner's dilemma? Answer with a range (e.g., greater than 12.5, less than −2).

b. Now, there are two Nash equilibria in this problem. What are they? Using the language of Chapters 15 and 16, what kind of game has this just become?

c. There's an idea buried in the questions from Chapter 16 that will "point" Stan and Kyle toward the best possible outcome. What is it? (Keep in mind that a good corporate culture can help with this part, too.)

28. a. Many HMOs pay their doctors based, in part, on how many patients the doctor sees in a day. What problems does this incentive system create?

b. If HMOs pay their doctors a fixed salary, what problems does this incentive system create?

c. Ideally, we would like to pay doctors based on how healthy their patients are! What problems exist in implementing this type of system?

29. In most big cities, taxicab fares are fairly standardized, and they are regulated by local governments. For the sake of simplicity, assume that a cab driver works for a licensed taxicab company, and they pay a fixed daily fee for the use of the taxi; all fares and tips go to the driver.

  a. In Atlanta, Georgia, meter rates are $2.50 for the first 1/8 mile and $0.25 for each additional 1/8 mile. What are the benefits of allowing cab drivers to charge fares based on the number of miles driven? In other words, what good behavior is encouraged—or what bad behavior is discouraged—by this? What are the possible drawbacks?

  b. In addition to the meter rates, there is a $21 per hour waiting fee. Why do you think there is a waiting fee? If cab drivers could not charge a waiting fee, how might that change their behavior? What if cab drivers were always just paid an hourly wage of $21 per hour? What would be the benefits and drawbacks of this payment scheme?

  c. For some fairly standard trips in Atlanta, there are flat fees. A trip from the airport to anywhere downtown, for example, is always $30 (plus $2 for each additional person). What are the potential benefits and drawbacks of this kind of compensation scheme? Why might a city require this payment scheme for trips from the airport?

  d. In the chapter, we talked about the importance of the gap between *what you pay for* and *what you want*. What is it that Atlanta's City Council and taxi customers *want* from the cab drivers in Atlanta? Which basis for cab fares (miles, hours, trips) comes closest to closing the gap between what is *wanted* and what is *paid for*?

  e. Over the last decade, Uber and Lyft have entered this market and disrupted the industry. Thinking back to the previous question, how are these apps better able to close the gap between what is wanted and what is paid for (or incentivized)?

WORK IT OUT

For interactive, step-by-step help in solving this problem, go online.

Punishments, and not just rewards, can also be used as incentives. Consider an assembly line. Why wouldn't you necessarily want to reward the fastest worker on the assembly line? What other incentive system might work?

23

Stock Markets and Personal Finance

Television reporter John Stossel decided to challenge the experts of Wall Street. As a student, Stossel had taken classes from economist Burton Malkiel whose book *A Random Walk Down Wall Street* claimed that the money and fame that went to stock-picking gurus were a sham and a waste. According to Malkiel: "A blindfolded monkey throwing darts at a newspaper's financial pages could select a portfolio that would do just as well as one carefully selected by experts."[1]

Instead of using a monkey, Stossel himself threw darts at a giant wall-sized version of the stock pages of the Wall Street Journal. Stossel followed his portfolio for nearly a year and compared the return with the portfolios picked by major Wall Street experts. Stossel's portfolio beat 90% of the experts! Not surprisingly, none of the experts would speak to him on camera about their humiliating loss. The lesson, according to Stossel, is that if you are paying an expert a lot of money to pick your stocks, it is probably you who are the monkey.

In this chapter, we explain why Stossel's amusing experiment is backed up by economic theory and by many careful empirical studies. We will also be giving you some investment advice in this chapter. No, we can't promise you the secret to get rich. Most of the get-rich-quick schemes sold in books, investment seminars, and newsletters are scams. Economics, however, does provide some important lessons for investing wisely. We can't tell you how to get rich quick, but we can perhaps help you to get rich slowly.

Throughout this chapter, we emphasize a core principle of economics: There's no such thing as a free lunch. That's just another way of saying that you shouldn't expect something for nothing, or that trade-offs are everywhere. Let's see how the principle applies to personal finance.

Passive vs. Active Investing

Many people invest in the stock market through a mutual fund. A mutual fund pools money from many customers and invests the money in many firms, in return, of course, for a management fee. Some of these mutual funds, called "active funds," are run by managers who try to pick stocks—these mutual funds

FIGURE 23.1

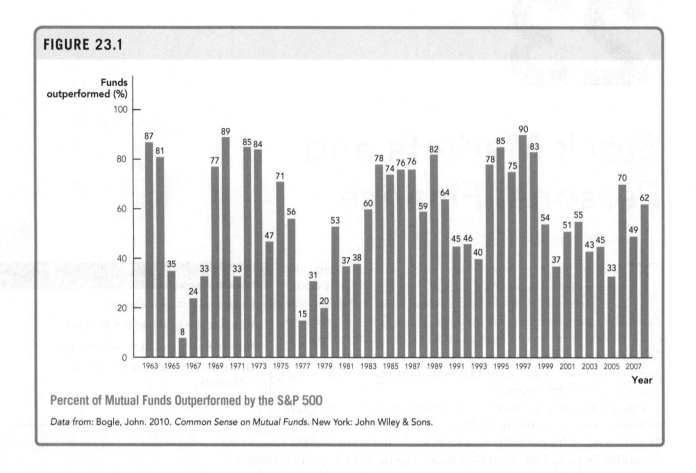

Percent of Mutual Funds Outperformed by the S&P 500

Data from: Bogle, John. 2010. *Common Sense on Mutual Funds.* New York: John Wiley & Sons.

often charge higher than average fees. Other mutual funds are called "passive funds" because they simply attempt to mimic a broad stock market index such as Standard and Poor's 500 (S&P 500), a basket of 500 large firms broadly representative of the U.S. economy.

Figure 23.1 shows that in a typical year passive investing in the S&P 500 Index beats about 60% of all mutual funds. In any given year, some mutual funds beat the index, but what is telling is that the funds that beat the index are different nearly every year! In other words, the funds that beat the index in one year probably just got lucky that year. One study that looked over 10 years found that passive investing beat 97.6% of all mutual funds![2] Overall, it is clear that very few mutual fund managers can consistently beat the market averages.

It is possible that a very small number of experts can systematically beat the stock market. Sometimes Warren Buffett, who promotes long-term investing for value, is cited as an example of a person who sees farther than the rest of the market. He started out as a paperboy and worked his way up to an over $100 billion fortune by purchasing undervalued stocks.

Some economists even think that Buffett, and a few others like him, just got lucky. If enough people are out there trying to pick stocks, you're going to have a few who get lucky many times in a row. Take a look at Figure 23.2. At the top of the figure, we start out with 1,000 experts, each of whom flips a coin to predict whether the market will go up or down in the following year. After one year, 500 of the experts will turn out to be right. After two years, 250 experts will have been right two years in a row. At the end of five

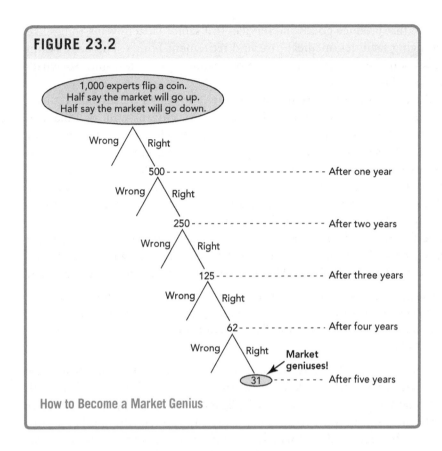

FIGURE 23.2

How to Become a Market Genius

years, just 31 out of 1,000 experts will have been right five years in a row. The experts who get it correct every time will be lauded as geniuses on CNBC and their advice will be eagerly sought. But the reality is that they just got lucky.

Is Buffett skilled or lucky? We're not so sure, but we do know this: Right now there is a small industry of people following the moves of Warren Buffett, trying to guess what he will say and do next. It is harder and harder for Buffett to get a big jump on the rest of the stock market. Even if Buffett could beat the market at first, it is not so clear he can beat the market any longer.

Why Is It Hard to Beat the Market?

These results aren't just an accident. Nor is it a statement about the stupidity of mutual fund managers. We know a few of these managers and most of them are pretty smart. Rather, the difficulty of beating the stock market is a tribute to the power of markets and the ability of market prices to reflect information.

Think about it this way: For every buyer of a stock, there is a seller. The buyer thinks the price is going up, the seller thinks the price is going down. There is a disagreement. On average, who do you think is more likely to be correct, the buyer or the seller? Of course, the answer is neither. But if on average buyers and sellers have about the same amount of information, stock picking can't work very well.

Consider the following bit of pseudo investment advice. The number of senior citizens will double by 2050. So the way to make money is to invest in

mru.org/pick-stocks

Should You Listen to the Expert Stock Pickers?

companies that produce goods and services that senior citizens want, things like assisted living facilities, medical care, and retirement homes. The baby boom can be a boom for you, If You Invest Now! Sounds plausible, right? So, what's wrong with this argument?

All the premises in the argument are true: The baby boomers are retiring and the demand for goods and services that senior citizens want will increase in the future. But investing in firms that produce goods and services for senior citizens is not a sure road to riches. Why not? If it were, why would anyone sell their stock in these firms? Remember, for every buyer there is a seller. If you think the stock is a good buy, why is the seller selling? It's not a secret that the baby boomers are retiring so the stock price of firms that are likely to do well in the future *already* reflects this information.

Since for every buyer there is a seller, you can't get rich by buying and selling on *public information*. This idea is the foundation of what is called the **efficient markets hypothesis.** The best-known form of this hypothesis states:

> The prices of traded assets, such as stocks and bonds, reflect all publicly available information. Unless an investor is trading on inside information, they will not systematically outperform the market as a whole over time.

Let's be clear on what this means. It doesn't mean that market prices are always right, that markets are all powerful, or that traders are calm, cool, and rational people. It just means it is difficult for ordinary investors (that probably means you, too!) to systematically outperform the market, again, unless a trader has inside information—information that no one else has. It's restating our point that you might as well throw darts at the stock pages and try to figure out which companies will beat the market. The efficient markets hypothesis is just another way of saying there is no such thing as a free lunch.

So if you do have some information that no one else has, can you make money in the stock market? Yes, but you have to act very quickly. Within *minutes* of the news that the Russian nuclear power plant at Chernobyl had melted down, shares in U.S. nuclear power plant companies tumbled, the price of oil jumped, as did the price of potatoes. Why potatoes? Clever traders on Wall Street figured out that the disaster at Chernobyl meant that the Ukrainian potato crop would be contaminated, so they bought American potato futures to profit from the coming rise in prices. The traders who acted quickly made a lot of money, but as they bought and sold, prices changed and signaled to other people that something was going on. Quite quickly, the inside information became public information and the opportunities for profit evaporated.

The only way you can take advantage of information that other people don't have is to start buying or selling large numbers of shares. But once you start the buying or selling, the rest of the market knows something is up. That is why secrets do not last very long in the stock market and that is another reason why it is so hard to beat the market as a whole.

Some people believe that they have found exceptions to the efficient markets hypothesis. For instance, it is commonly believed that you can make more money by buying stocks when prices are low, or by buying right after prices have fallen. That sounds good, doesn't it? Buying at lower prices.

The **efficient markets hypothesis** says that the prices of traded assets reflect all publicly available information.

MRU

mru.org/beat-market

The Efficient Market Hypothesis

It feels like what you do when you go to Walmart. But buying a stock isn't like buying a lawn chair or a banana. The value of a stock is simply what its price will be in future periods of time. The banana, in contrast, you can simply eat for pleasure, no matter what the future price of bananas. Often lower prices mean that prices are going to stay low or fall even more and that means lower returns on owning stocks. Some studies find that you can do slightly better with your investments by buying right after prices have fallen. But do you know what? If you adjust those higher returns to account for the broker commissions that you have to pay for the extra trading, the higher returns pretty much go away.

A field of study known as "technical analysis" looks for deep patterns in stock and asset prices. Maybe you've heard on the financial news that stocks have "broken through a key support point" or "moved into a new trading range." If you dig deeper, you will find a claim that stock prices exhibit predictable mathematical patterns. For instance, if a stock hovers in the range of $100 a share but does not exceed that level, and one day goes above $100, it might be claimed that the stock is now expected to skyrocket to a much higher level. Hardly. One nice thing about studying the stock market is that there is a lot of very good data. One team of economists studied 7,846 different strategies of technical analysis. Their conclusion was that none of them systematically beat the market over time.[3]

For most investors, the efficient markets hypothesis looks like a pretty good description of reality.

How to Really Pick Stocks, Seriously

Ok, you probably can't beat the market without a lot of luck on your side. But we do still have four pieces of important advice. *Very* important advice. If you apply this advice over the course of your life, you will probably save thousands of dollars, and if you become rich, you may save millions of dollars. (Suddenly, this textbook seems like a real bargain!) No, we don't have a get-rich-quick formula for you, but there are a few simple mistakes you can avoid to your benefit and at no real cost, other than a bit of time and attention. Let's go through each piece of advice in turn.

Diversify

The first secret to picking stocks is to pick lots of them! Since picking stocks doesn't work well, the "secret" to wise investing is to invest in a large basket of stocks—to diversify. Diversification lowers the risk of your portfolio, how much your portfolio fluctuates in value over time.

By picking a lot of stocks, you limit your overall exposure to things going wrong in any particular company. When the energy company Enron went bankrupt in 2001, many Enron employees had put most of their life's wealth in . . . can you guess? . . . Enron stock. That's a huge mistake, whether you work at the company or not. If you put all your eggs in one basket, it is a disaster if the handle on that basket breaks. Instead, you should buy many different stocks, in many different sectors of the economy, and, yes, in many countries, too. You'll end up with some Enrons, but you'll also have some big winners, such as Google and Apple. And if Google and Apple have become Enrons and gone under

CHECK YOURSELF

- Is it better to invest in a mutual fund that has performed well for five years in a row or one that has performed poorly for five years in a row? Use the efficient markets hypothesis to justify your answer.

since this book was published, well, that is just further reason why you should diversify!

Modern financial markets have made diversification easy. Mutual funds let you invest in hundreds of stocks with just one purchase. And since stock picking doesn't work well, diversification has no downside—it reduces risk without reducing your expected return.

We are focusing on diversification across stocks but there are all kinds of risks in the world and you should diversify across as many of those risks as possible. U.S. stocks, for example, tend to fluctuate in value along with the growth rate of the U.S. economy. You can reduce this source of risk by including a large number of international firms in your portfolio. Bonds, art, housing, and human capital (your knowledge and skills) all have associated returns and risks, and for a given amount of return, you minimize your risk by diversifying across many assets.

If you accept the efficient markets hypothesis, and you accept the value of diversification, your best trading strategy can be summed up very simply. It is called **buy and hold**. That's right, buy a large bundle of stocks and just hold them. You don't have to do anything more. You will be diversified, you will not be trying to beat the market, and you can live a peaceful, quiet life.

Some of the simplest ways to buy and hold mean that you replicate the well-known stock indexes. Just for your knowledge, here are a few of those indexes:

The *Dow Jones Industrial Average* (or the Dow for short) is the most famous stock price index. The Dow is composed of 30 leading American stocks, each of these counted equally, whether the company is large or small. The Dow is not a very diversified index.

The *Standard and Poor's 500* (S&P 500) is a much broader index of stocks than the Dow; as the name indicates, it consists of the prices of 500 different stocks. Unlike in the Dow, the larger companies receive greater weight in the index than the smaller companies. The S&P 500 is a better indicator of the market as a whole than the Dow.

The *NASDAQ Composite Index* averages the prices of all the companies traded on NASDAQ, or National Association of Securities Dealers Automated Quotations, more than 3,000 securities. The NASDAQ index contains more small stocks and high-tech stocks relative to the Dow or the S&P 500.

Notice that diversification changes our understanding of what makes a stock risky, or not risky. You might at first think that a risky stock is one whose price moves up and down a lot. Not exactly. If investors are diversified, and indeed most of them are, their risk depends on how much their portfolio moves up and down, not on how much a single stock moves up and down. A single stock might move up and down all the time but still an overall diversified portfolio won't change in value much if some of your stocks are moving up while others are moving down.

According to finance economists, the riskiest stocks are those that move up and down in harmony with the market. For instance, many real estate stocks are risky because they are highly cyclical. They move up a lot when times are good (and the rest of the market is high) and they move down a lot when times are bad. When a recession comes, a lot of people just can't afford to buy

To **buy and hold** is to buy stocks and then hold them for the long run, regardless of what prices do in the short run.

mru.org/stock-diversify

Diversify, Diversify, Diversify!

a new house. In contrast, for an example of a relatively safe stock, consider Walmart. When bad times come, yes, Walmart loses some business. But Walmart also gains some business because people who used to shop at Nordstrom now have less money and some of them will now shop at Walmart. In this regard, Walmart is partly protected from business downturns.[4] Many health-care stocks are safe in a similar way. Even if times are bad, you're probably not going to postpone that triple bypass operation; if you do, you won't be around to see when times are good again. In other words, if you care about the risk of a stock, don't just look at how the price of that stock moves. Look at how the price varies with the rest of the market. In the language of finance economists or statisticians, the riskiest stocks are those with the highest *covariance* with the market as a whole.

The lesson here is that if you are worried about risk, think about your portfolio as a whole, rather than obsessing over any single stock. Or let's be more specific: If you are going to become an aerospace engineer, don't buy a lot of stock in aerospace companies. The value of your human capital—which is worth a lot—is already tied up in that industry. Don't make your overall portfolio riskier by putting more eggs in that basket. If anything, buy stocks that do well when aerospace does poorly. More generally, finance theorists say that the least risky assets *for you* are assets that are *negatively correlated* with *your portfolio*. What this means is that you should try to buy assets that rise in value when the rest of your portfolio is falling in value. Are you afraid that high energy prices will cripple the prospects for your career? Buy stock in a company that builds roads in Saudi Arabia. If oil prices stay high, the gains of that road-building company will partially offset your other losses. The lesson applies to more than stocks. If you become a dentist, you run the risk that a new technology will eliminate cavities. So try to limit your risk by diversifying your portfolio: Marry an optician or an engineer, not another dentist!

Avoid High Fees

We have some other advice for picking stocks. Avoid investments and mutual funds that have high fees or "loads," as they are sometimes called. It simply isn't worth it.

Let's say for instance that you wish to invest in the S&P 500. Some funds charge management and administrative fees of 0.05% of your investment, but other funds can charge up to 10 or 20 times as much for investing in exactly the same basket of stocks.

The funds with the higher fees don't give you much of value in return. The lesson is simple: Don't pay the higher fees!

Even small fees can add up to large differences in returns over time. Let's say you are investing $10,000 over 30 years. If you invest with a firm that charges 0.10% a year in fees and the stock market gives a real return of 7% a year, then in 30 years you will have earned $74,016. If you invest in a firm that charges 1% a year, then in 30 years you will have about $57,434. The higher fees cost you $16,582 and, as we have shown, you probably got nothing for your extra fees. Small differences in growth or loss rates, when compounded over time, make for a big difference. The same is true for your portfolio.

That brings us to a corollary principle, to which we now turn.

What are the Wolf's incentives? Jordan Belfort, the New York stockbroker whose life was chronicled in Martin Scorsese's movie *The Wolf of Wall Street,* made millions by charging small investors high fees to buy dubious investments.

Moviestore/REX/Shutterstock

Compound Returns Build Wealth

If one investment earns a higher rate of return each year than another investment, in the long run that makes a big difference. Imagine you buy a well-diversified portfolio of stocks and every year you reinvest all of your dividends. A simple approximation, called the rule of 70, explains how long it will take for your investment to double in value given a specified rate of return.

Rule of 70: If the rate of return (annual percent increase in value including dividends) of an investment is $x\%$, then the doubling time is $70/x$ years.

Table 23.1 illustrates the rule of 70 by showing how long it takes for an investment to double in value given different returns. With a return of 1%, an investment will double approximately every 70 years ($70/1 = 70$). If returns increase to 2%, the value of your investment will double every 35 years ($70/2 = 35$). Consider the impact of a 4% return. If this rate of return is sustained, then the value of an investment doubles every 17.5 years ($70/4 = 17.5$). In 70 years, the value doubles 4 times, reaching a level 16 times its starting value!

The rule of 70 is just a mathematical approximation but it bears out the key concept that when compounded, small differences in investment returns can have a large effect. To make this more concrete, if you have a long time horizon, you probably should invest in (diversified) stocks rather than bonds.

TABLE 23.1 **YEARS TO DOUBLE USING THE RULE OF 70**

Annual Return (%)	Years to Double
0	Never
1	70
2	35
3	23.3
4	17.5

In the long run, stocks offer higher returns than bonds. Since 1802, for example, stocks have had an average real rate of return of about 7% per year, while bonds have paid closer to 3% per year.[5] Using our now familiar rule of 70, we know that money that grows at 7% a year will double in 10 years, but money that grows at 3% a year won't double for 23 years. Alternatively, growing at 7% a year, $10,000 will return $81,667 in 30 years, but if that investment grows at 3% a year, the return over that same period of time will be only $24,596.

Stocks, however, have the potential for greater losses than do bonds because bond holders and other creditors are always paid before shareholders. You are unlikely to lose much money if you buy high-grade corporate or government bonds, but the stock market is highly volatile and it does periodically crash. Nonetheless, in American history, stocks almost always outperform bonds over any 20-year time period you care to examine, including the period of the Great Depression and World War II. Stocks are usually the better long-term investment.

Of course, that doesn't mean that everyone should invest so heavily in stocks. In any particular year, or even over the course of a month, week, or day, stocks can go down in value quite a bit. If you are 80 years old and managing your retirement income, you probably shouldn't invest much in stocks. If you have to send your twins to college in two years' time, you might want some safer investments, as well. Nor does the past necessarily predict the future—just because stocks outperformed bonds in the past doesn't mean that will continue to happen. Remember to diversify!

mru.org/rule-70

The Rule of 70

The No-Free-Lunch Principle, or No Return Without Risk

The differences between stocks and bonds, as investment vehicles, reflect a more general principle. There is a systematic **trade-off between return and risk**. Figure 23.3, for example, shows the trade-off between return and risk on four asset classes. U.S. T-bills are safe but have low returns. You can get a higher return by buying stock in a group of large firms such as in the S&P 500, but the value of those firms fluctuates a lot more than the value of T-bills, so to get the higher return, you need to bear higher risk.[*]

The **risk–return trade-off** means higher returns come at the price of higher risk.

If you want even more risk than an investment in the stock market, numerous schemes give you a chance of making a killing. The simplest of such strategies is to take all your money, fly to Las Vegas, and bet on "black" for a spin of the roulette wheel. Yes, there is a 47.37% chance that you double your wealth. That's a high return, sort of. Sadly, there is also a 52.63% chance that you will lose everything you have, including your credit rating and the trust of your spouse and children. That's what we call high risk.

Remember this story when you hear about a high-flying "hedge fund" or other fancy investment device. It's easy to generate high returns for a few years by getting lucky and doubling down (betting all your winnings again). Take a look again at Figure 23.3. Higher returns come at the expense of higher risk.

This no-free-lunch principle can help you evaluate some other investments, as well. Let's say you come into a tidy sum of money and you start wondering

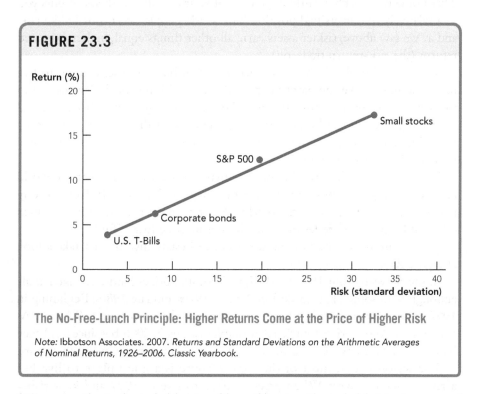

FIGURE 23.3

Return (%)

The No-Free-Lunch Principle: Higher Returns Come at the Price of Higher Risk

Note: Ibbotson Associates. 2007. *Returns and Standard Deviations on the Arithmetic Averages of Nominal Returns, 1926–2006. Classic Yearbook.*

[*] We measure risk using the standard deviation of the portfolio return. The standard deviation is a measure of how much the return tends to fluctuate from its average level; thus, the larger the standard deviation, the greater the risk. A rule of thumb is that there is a 68% probability of being within ±1 standard deviation of the mean return. For the S&P 500, for example, the mean return is about 12% and the standard deviation is about 20% so in any given year, there is a 68% probability that the return will be between −8% and 32%. Of course, there is a 32% probability that something else could happen! But beware! The rule of thumb is only an approximation. Risk in the real world can rarely be modeled with perfect mathematical accuracy. In particular, the normal distribution from which our rule of thumb is derived under-predicts very big events such as booms or crashes. Stock market distributions are sometimes said to be "fat-tailed" to reflect the greater probability of these tail events.

whether you should invest in art. Overall, should you expect art to be a better or inferior financial investment, compared with the market as a whole?

A lot of people—probably most people—buy art because they want to look at it. They enjoy hanging it on their walls. In the language of economics, art yields "a nonmonetary return," which is just our way of saying it is fun to look at. Now suppose that investments in art earned just as high a return as investments in stocks. In that case, art would be fun to have on the wall *and* would be an excellent investment. But wait, that sounds like a free lunch doesn't it? So what does the no-free-lunch principle predict?

We know that the expected returns on different assets, adjusted for risk, should be equal. So if some asset yields a higher "fun" return, those assets should, on average, yield a lower financial return. And that is exactly what we find with art. On average, art underperforms the stock market by a few percentage points a year. You can think of the lower returns as the price of having some beautiful art on your wall. Again, it's the no-free-lunch principle in action.

This kind of analysis applies not just to art but also to real estate. Let's say you want to buy a home. Can you expect superior or inferior financial returns over time? This question is a little trickier than the art question because two different and opposing forces operate. Let's look at each in turn.

First, a home tends to be a risky asset for most purchasers. Let's say you buy a $300,000 home by putting down $200,000 and borrowing the remainder. That home is probably a fairly big chunk of your overall wealth and it puts you in a relatively nondiversified position. That's risk, people don't usually like risk, and as we saw above, riskier assets earn, all other things equal, higher expected returns (the risk-return trade-off).

Second, and probably more important, if you buy a house, you get to live in it. The house, like the painting, provides you with personal services and in this case those services are valuable. Many people enjoy their backyard and the feeling of owning a home and being able to paint the walls any color they want. These nonmonetary returns mean that houses can be expected to pay a relatively low financial return.

Indeed, if we look at the financial returns on real estate all over the world and over a long time horizon, it turns out they are fairly low. In fact, for long periods of time, the average financial rate of return on real estate is not much different from zero. One lesson is that houses must be lots of fun!

If you want to see the ups and downs of real estate investments, take a look at Figure 23.4.

In the 50 years from 1947 to 1997, real housing prices hardly changed at all, although with some blips upward in the late 1970s and late 1980s. Beginning in 1997, a housing boom pushed prices well above any before seen in U.S. history. As you probably know, prices tumbled dramatically starting in 2006, but since 2011 they have risen and are now once again higher than at any time in the twentieth century.

The lesson is that most of the time a house is a good place to live but a risky place to invest. When prices started to rise in 1997 and kept rising year after year, many people thought that real estate was the investment of the century—"they ain't making any more," people said. But the no-free-lunch principle tells us that precisely because houses are a good place to live, we should not also expect them to be a good investment. All other things equal, fun activities yield lower financial returns than nonfun activities.

When prices rose, some people got lucky and made a killing, but other people tried to do the same and ended up bankrupt. So don't expect to make a killing in the real estate market, and remember to diversify! One more point.

FIGURE 23.4

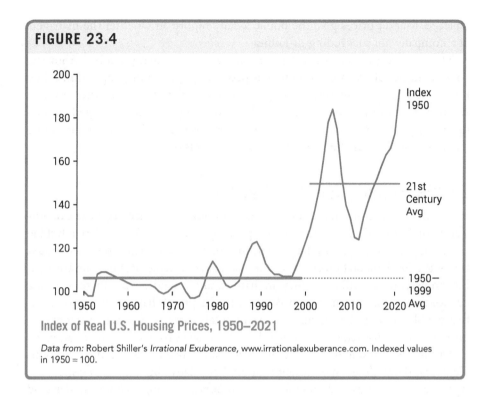

Index of Real U.S. Housing Prices, 1950–2021

Data from: Robert Shiller's *Irrational Exuberance*, www.irrationalexuberance.com. Indexed values in 1950 = 100.

Are you one of those people who doesn't like to mow the lawn? Do you dread the notion of choosing homeowner's insurance or worrying about when your roof will fall in? The lesson is simple: Don't buy a house, you won't have fun, and the financial returns won't make it worth your while.

Other Benefits and Costs of Stock Markets

Throughout this chapter, we've recommended against gambling with all or most of your money. We've recommended buy and hold, based on a diversified portfolio. But hey, maybe some of you are into gambling. You know what? If you want to take risk for the sake of risk alone, the U.S. stock market offers the best odds in the world, better than Las Vegas and better than your local bookie. People on average make money in the U.S. stock market and that is because the productive capacity of the U.S. economy is expanding through economic growth. There is more profit to go around and that means you have a good chance of making some really lucrative investments.

Stock markets have uses beyond investment. First, new stock and bond issues are important to a company as a means of raising capital for new investment (investment now in the economic sense of increasing the capital stock). Stock markets also reward successful entrepreneurs and thus encourage people to start companies and look around for new ideas. The founders of Google are now very rich and selling company shares to the stock market helped make them so. A well-functioning stock market helps companies such as Google get going or expand.

Second, the stock market gives us a better idea of how well firms are run. The stock price is a signal about the value of the firm. When the stock price is increasing, especially when it is increasing relative to other stocks, this is a signal that the firm is making the right investments for future profits. When the stock is declining, especially when it is declining relative to other stocks, this is a signal that something has gone wrong and perhaps management needs to be

CHECK YOURSELF

- How does investing in stocks of other countries help to diversify your investments?
- Many people dream of owning a football or baseball team. Would you expect the return on these assets to be relatively high or low?

replaced. Market prices give the public a daily report on whether the managers of a company are succeeding or failing.

Third, stock markets are a way of transferring company control from less competent people to more competent people. If a group of people think they know the right way to run a company, they can buy it and put their money where their mouth is, so to speak. Maybe a company should be merged, broken up, or simply taken in a new direction. The stock market is the ultimate venue where people bid for the right to make these decisions.

Bubble, Bubble, Toil, and Trouble

It's worth pointing out that stock markets (and other asset markets) have a downside, namely that they can encourage speculative bubbles. A speculative bubble arises when stock prices rise far higher, and more rapidly, than can be accounted for by the fundamental prospects of the companies at hand. Bubbles are based in human psychology and often they are hard to understand. Nobel Prize–winning economist Vernon Smith, whom you met in Chapter 4, has found that speculative bubbles and crashes occur in experimental markets, even when traders are given enough information to easily calculate an asset's true value.[6] Inexperienced traders are more prone to bubbles, but even experienced traders can fall for bubbles when the trading environment changes. Speculative bubbles and crashes have significant costs, as we will discuss, so economists are trying to better understand bubbles and how market institutions can be designed to help avoid them.

During the dot-com era, circa 2000, many Internet or dot-com stocks had very high prices even though many of these companies had never earned a dime of profit or for that matter any revenue. Many of the tech stocks were listed on the NASDAQ stock exchange. As you can see in Figure 23.5, in the space of five years the NASDAQ Composite Index more than tripled from a

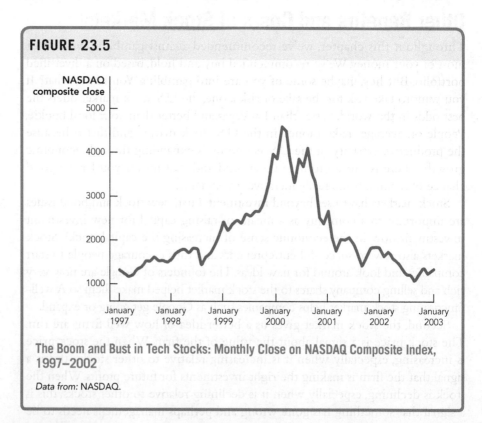

FIGURE 23.5

NASDAQ composite close

The Boom and Bust in Tech Stocks: Monthly Close on NASDAQ Composite Index, 1997–2002

Data from: NASDAQ.

monthly average of about 1,200 to more than 4,000 before falling back down again. Many people made a lot of money on the ride up and many people—maybe the same people, maybe others—lost a lot of money on the ride down.

If you can spot speculative bubbles on a consistent basis, yes, you can become very wealthy. But, of course, a speculative bubble is usually easier to detect with hindsight than at the time. Apple and Google might have looked like speculative bubbles, too; the only problem is that they never burst. Betting too soon that high prices will end is also one way to go bankrupt.

Speculative bubbles, and their bursting, can hurt an economy. During the rise of the bubble, capital is invested in areas where it is not actually very valuable. A second wave of problems comes when the bubble crashes. Lower stock prices (or lower home prices) mean that people feel poorer and so they will spend less. The collapse of the bubble also means that workers must move from one sector to another, such as from high tech to retailing, or from real estate to export industries. Shifting labor from one sector of an economy to another creates labor adjustment costs.

We saw both of these problems with the dot-com bubble and the real estate bubble leading up to the crash of housing prices in 2007–2008. During the dot-com boom years, for example, we invested too much in stringing fiber-optic cable across the world's oceans—cable that later proved to be unprofitable. Similarly, during the housing boom we invested too much in houses that later were abandoned. In addition, the boom in housing prices led banks to be much too lax about the value of financial assets backed by portfolios of mortgages. When housing prices started to fall and people began to default on their mortgages, the value of these asset-backed securities plummeted and banks found themselves nearing bankruptcy. To stave off bankruptcy, these banks cut back on lending, transmitting problems in the housing markets to the wider economy and helping to generate the lengthy recession beginning in late 2007.

Finally, we offer a bit of a warning. Bubbles are more likely to happen in stocks that are traded by inexperienced investors. In recent years, for example, apps like Robinhood have made trading cheaper, easier, and more fun ("gamified" is the industry jargon). The apps have attracted many inexperienced investors. Instead of carefully investigating the fundamentals, inexperienced investors tend to herd: they buy when others are buying and sell when others are selling. The result of herding can be big increases in stock prices. Does that sound great? The problem is that big decreases often follow. In fact, intense buying by Robinhood users tends to forecast negative returns! Could you ride the wave on the way up and then sell at the top? Maybe, but that's what every member of the herd thinks. When it comes to long-term investing, our advice is to buy and hold a well-diversified basket of stocks with low fees. Day trading can be fun, but don't bet your life savings![7]

Robin Hood says he robs the rich and gives to the poor, but be careful; you can't always believe mythical figures.

IanDagnall Computing/Alamy Stock Photo

CHECK YOURSELF

• The Federal Reserve was criticized for not stepping in and bursting the housing bubble, which would have prevented the housing collapse. Do you think this criticism is valid, based on what you read in this section?

Takeaway

We have stressed some simple and practical points. It is difficult for an investor to consistently beat the market over long periods. You are well-advised to diversify your investments. Avoid fees and try to generate a high compound return over time. Understand that the promise of higher returns is often accompanied by higher risk.

Viewed as a whole, stock markets and other trading markets give investors a chance to earn money, diversify their holdings, express opinions on the course of the market, and hedge risks. Stock markets also play a role in financing innovative new firms. Stock markets appear to be subject to speculative bubbles, but active stock markets are an important part of a healthy growing economy.

CHAPTER REVIEW

Go online to practice with more examples of these types of problems, including live links to videos, data sources, and feedback.

KEY CONCEPTS

efficient markets hypothesis, p. 460

buy and hold, p. 462

risk-return trade-off, p. 465

FACTS AND TOOLS

1. Before we plunge into the world of finance, let's review the rule of 70. Suppose your rich relative hands you a $3,000 check at the end of the school year. They tell you it's for your education. But what should you *really* do with that extra money? Let's see how much it would be worth if you saved it for a while.

   a. If you put it in a bank account earning 2% real annual return on average, how many years would it take before it was worth $6,000? Until it was worth $12,000?

   b. If you put it in a Standard and Poor's 500 (S&P 500) mutual fund earning an average 7% real return every year, how many years would it take before it was worth $6,000? Until it was worth $12,000?

   c. Suppose you invest a little less than half your money in the bank and a little more than half in a mutual fund, just to play it somewhat safe, so that you can expect a 5% real return on average. How many years now until you reach $6,000 and $12,000?

2. Let's do something boring just to drive home a point: Count up the number of years in Figure 23.1 in which more than half of the mutual funds managed to beat the S&P 500 index. (Recall that the Standard and Poor's 500 is just a list of 500 large U.S. corporations—it's a list that overlaps a lot with the Fortune 500.) What percentage of the time did the experts actually beat the S&P 500?

3. Consider the supply and demand for oranges. Orange crops can be destroyed by below-freezing temperatures.

   a. If a weather report states that oranges are likely to freeze in a storm later this week,

   what probably happens to the demand for oranges *today*, before the storm comes?

   b. According to a simple supply and demand model, what happens to the price of oranges today given your answer to part a.

   c. How does this illustrate the idea that stock prices *today* "bake in" information about *future* events? In other words, how is a share of Amazon like an orange? (*Note:* Wall Street people often use the expression, "That news is already baked into the price," when they talk about the efficient markets hypothesis.)

4. In the United States, high-level corporate officials have to publicly state when they buy or sell a large number of shares in their own company. They have to make these statements a few days after their purchase or sale. What do you think probably happens (choose a, b, c, or d) when newspapers report these true "insider trades"? (*Note:* The right answer according to theory is actually true in practice.)

   a. When insiders sell, prices rise, since investors increase their demand for the company's shares.

   b. When insiders sell, prices fall, since investors increase their demand for the company's shares.

   c. When insiders sell, prices fall, since investors decrease their demand for the company's shares.

   d. When insiders sell, prices rise, since investors decrease their demand for the company's shares.

5. Let's see how fees can hurt your investment strategy. Let's assume that your mutual fund grows at an average rate of 7% per year—before subtracting the fees. Using the rule of 70:

   a. How many years will it take for your money to double if fees are 0.5% per year?

   b. How many years will it take for your money to double if fees are 1.5% per year (not uncommon in the mutual fund industry)?

   c. How many years to double if fees are 2.5% per year?

6. a. If you talk to a broker selling a high-fee mutual fund, what will they probably tell you when you ask them, "Am I getting my money's worth when I pay your high fees?"

b. According to Figure 23.1, is your broker's answer likely to be right most of the time?

7. In addition to providing a place for people to invest their money, what are three other important functions of financial markets?

THINKING AND PROBLEM SOLVING

8. Your brother calls you on the phone telling you that Meta's share price has fallen by about 25% over the past few days. Now you can own one small slice of Meta for only $130 a share (the price on the day this question was written). Your brother says he is pretty sure the stock is going to head back up to $300 very soon and you should buy. Should you believe your brother? (*Hint:* Remember someone is selling shares whenever someone else is buying.)

9. In most of your financial decisions early in life, you'll be a buyer, but let's think about the incentives of people who sell stocks, bonds, bank accounts, and other financial products.

a. Walking in the shopping mall one day, you see a new store: the Dollar Store. Of course, you've seen plenty of dollar stores before, but none like this one: The sign in the window says, "Dollars for sale: Fifty cents each." Why will this store be out of business soon?

b. If business owners are self-interested and fairly rational people, will they ever open up this dollar store in the first place? Why or why not?

c. This dollar store is similar to stories people tell about "cheap stocks" that you might hear of on the news. Fill in the blank with any prices that make sense: "If the shares of this company were really worth _____, no one would really sell it for _____."

10. How is "stock market diversification" like putting money in a bank account?

11. Warren Buffett often says that he doesn't want a lot of diversification in his portfolio. He says that diversification means buying stocks that go up along with stocks that go down; but he only wants to buy the stocks that go up! From the point of view of the typical investor, what is wrong with this reasoning?

12. There are three stocks available: a solar energy firm, an oil firm, and an airline. You can invest in two. Which two?

13. In early 2021, GameStop achieved meme stock status behind strong backing from r/wallstreetbets and a famous tweet from Elon Musk. Let's consider some key moments in the GameStop saga. You may want to visit https://finance.yahoo.com and look at the historical data for GameStop stock (GME) to help answer these questions.

a. Suppose that you were an early passenger on the GameStop bandwagon and decided to purchase shares of their stock on January 11, 2021, the day they announced three new directors: Alan Attal, Ryan Cohen, and Jim Grube. Has this turned out to be a wise investment?

b. What if you first became aware of GameStop on January 19, 2021, when a well-known stock research firm, Citron Research, called GameStop buyers "suckers"?

c. What about if you did not jump into the fray until January 26, 2021, when Elon Musk tweeted "Gamestonk!!" with a link to r/wallstreetbets?

14. Why do we generally expect stocks to earn higher average rates of return on investment than Magic: The Gathering cards?

Discovering DATA

15. How easy is it to spot a bubble? Go to the FRED economic database (https://fred.stlouisfed.org/) and search for NASDAQ. You should find the NASDAQ Composite Index. Graph it and click "Max" to show all the data available.

a. What happened to the index between November of 1998 and February of 2000? Then what happened?

b. What happened to the index between October of 2009 and October of 2014? Then what happened?

c. What happened to the index between December of 2018 and December of 2021? Then what happened?

d. Are you willing to make a bet about the future direction of the NASDAQ?

CHALLENGES

16. What is so bad about bubbles? If the price of Internet stocks or housing rises and then falls, is that such a big problem? After all, some people say, most of the gains going up are "paper gains" and most of the losses going down are "paper losses." Comment on this view.

17. Mr. Wolf calls you with what he says is a tremendous opportunity in the stock market. He has inside knowledge about a pharmaceutical company and he says that the price will go up tomorrow. Of course, you are skeptical and decline his offer. The next day the price does go up. Mr. Wolf calls again and says not to worry, tomorrow the price will go down and that will be a good time to buy. Again, you decline. The next day the price does go down. Mr. Wolf calls you over the next several weeks and every time he calls his predictions about the stock price prove to be amazingly accurate. Finally, he calls to tell you that tomorrow is the big one, the day the price will skyrocket. Mr. Wolf has been accurate many times in a row so you empty your bank account to buy as much stock as possible. The next day the price of the stock goes nowhere. What happened? (*Hint:* Take another look at Figure 23.2.)

WORK IT OUT

For interactive, step-by-step help in solving this problem, go online.

Let's see how fees can hurt your investment strategy. Let's assume that your mutual fund grows at an average rate of 5% per year—before subtracting the fees. Using the rule of 70:

a. How many years will it take for your money to double if fees are 0.5% per year?

b. How many years will it take for your money to double if fees are 1.5% per year (not uncommon in the mutual fund industry)?

c. How many years to double if fees are 2.5% per year?

24

Asymmetric Information: Moral Hazard and Adverse Selection

I magine that you take your automobile to a mechanic and the mechanic tells you that you need a Johnson rod. Maybe you do, and maybe you don't—it's hard for a nonexpert to tell. In many markets, the seller of a service is also the expert who diagnoses how much service is needed. We rely, for example, on auto mechanics, dentists, and physicians not only to fix problems but also to tell us what the problem is in the first place. When consumers can't tell whether a service is needed, they may be overtreated, undertreated, or overcharged.

One economist, for example, took his aging Subaru to 40 repair shops in Connecticut. In each case, the Subaru was prepped with five problems, including a loose battery cable that caused intermittent starting problems. The okay news is that in 31 of the 40 visits (78%), the intermittent starting problem was solved (which means that 22% of the time, even a simple problem was not solved). The bad news is that for four of the 31 fixes (13%), the mechanic replaced the battery or starter motor! These repairs were completely unnecessary and fixed the problem, a loose battery cable, only by accident. The very bad news is that mechanics often failed to discover necessary repairs (such as a broken tail-light) while at the same time recommending unnecessary repairs.[1]

These types of problems are not limited to auto mechanics. In another study, a brave patient was sent to see 180 dentists—50 of the 180 dentists recommended unnecessary treatment.[2] More generally, economists call these problems **principal–agent problems**. How can a principal incentivize an agent to work in the principal's interest even when the agent has information that the principal does not? The problem applies not only to buyers and sellers but also to employers and employees (see more in Chapter 18), to voters and politicians (Chapter 20), and even to dating and the animal kingdom (this chapter).

Markets work best when traders know exactly what is being traded. When that is the case, markets will attract both buyers and sellers because each side expects trade to be *mutually* profitable. But when one party to a (potential) trade has more or better information than the other party, we say that the market exhibits **asymmetric information**. When there is asymmetric

The **principal–agent problem:** How can a principal incentivize an agent to work in the principal's interest even when the agent has information that the principal does not?

Asymmetric information is when one party to an exchange has more or better information than the other party.

information, the less informed party may profit less from a trade than they expect. If the less informed party recognizes this problem in advance, they may withdraw from the market and decide that trade is too risky or not in their interest. In extreme cases, asymmetric information can mean that markets fail to exist.

In Chapter 10 we saw that markets may not be ideal when there are significant effects on bystanders. In one sense, asymmetric information is a more severe challenge to markets than externalities because problems of asymmetric information mean that markets may not work well even for buyers and sellers! In another way, the problem is less severe. Buyers and sellers don't have an incentive to solve externality problems but buyers and sellers do have an incentive to solve problems of asymmetric information so they can complete mutually profitable trades. As we will see, market institutions, as well as laws and regulations, have evolved to deal with problems of asymmetric information. To understand the solutions, however, we must first understand the problem.

Let's begin with the problem of moral hazard.

Moral Hazard

Parties with better information may be tempted to exploit their information advantage at the expense of their trading partners; this possibility is called **moral hazard**. The auto mechanic or the dentist who recommends unnecessary services—these are examples of moral hazard.

Moral hazard is when an agent tries to exploit an information advantage in a dishonest or undesirable way.

No one wants to be ripped off but the problem of moral hazard runs deeper than a transfer of wealth from buyer to seller. Let's focus on the example of the mechanic. Suppose the mechanic tells you that you need an engine overhaul when all your car really needs is a minor new part. Overhauling the engine isn't just a ripoff, it's a waste of time and resources—the economy is producing a good that no one actually wants or needs.

A second problem occurs when buyers, knowing that the mechanic might rip them off, decide not to buy any service at all. Frankly, we don't always listen to our dentist, especially when our dentist recommends expensive treatments. Sometimes that is the right thing to do but some services really are needed even when they are expensive. Refusing service means there's no possibility of a rip-off but also no possibility of mutual gain through trade.

The bottom line is that if we lived in a world of symmetric information, sometimes we would get less treatment and sometimes we would get more. Both of these deviations represent a cost of asymmetric information.

For most goods, asymmetric information isn't a big deal. You may not know how the new item on the restaurant menu tastes but you buy it once, and if you like it, you buy it again, and if not, well, the cost of trying and sampling was low. In the case of auto mechanics, dentists, and surgeons—not to mention marriage partners (see later in this chapter)—the decisions we must make are more expensive, longer-lasting, and more difficult to reverse, so we need to think carefully about asymmetric information.

There are two solutions to asymmetric information and moral hazard problems: either provide more information, thereby reducing the asymmetry, or reduce the incentive for the knowledgeable party to exploit their information advantage. Let's examine each of these solutions.

Overcoming Moral Hazard by Providing More Information

The Internet has played a big role in helping overcome asymmetric information problems by making it easier for buyers to pool their knowledge. On Angi, for example, buyers can find reviews of local auto mechanics and plumbers. Yelp provides similar reviews for restaurants. Reviews of sellers on Amazon Marketplace help potential buyers judge which sellers are most likely to deliver on their promises. Reviews have two advantages. First, they make it easier to avoid shady mechanics. Second, they raise the cost to mechanics of exploiting their information advantage.

The shady mechanic always faces a risk: If buyers think that they have been ripped off, they won't return with repeat business. Before the Internet, an upset buyer might have warned away a few friends and family. But with the Internet, an upset buyer can warn the world and that decreases the incentive for sellers to attempt a moral hazard rip-off.

More generally, the Internet has increased the value of having a good reputation. Two economists, Daniel Houser and John Wooders, found that sellers with good reputations on eBay were able to sell their goods for higher prices.[3] The Internet has also increased the cost of having a bad reputation, as students who post compromising pictures on Instagram may discover to their chagrin.

For all of their virtues, however, consumer review sites like Yelp overcome asymmetric information problems only imperfectly. We know some authors who ask their friends to post friendly and presumably nonobjective reviews on Amazon. Some stores have hired fake reviewers to praise their product, or condemn the product of a rival. In response to these problems, Yelp even set up a sting operation to catch fakers. In other words, a new kind of asymmetric information problem is introduced into the market, namely assessing the honesty and accuracy of the reviews themselves.

The general problem is that the more important a rating becomes, the greater the incentive to fake or manipulate that rating. *U.S. News & World Report* reviews and rates U.S. colleges and universities, and these ratings have a big influence on where students want to study. But where does *U.S. News & World Report* get the data to rate universities? Often from the universities themselves! We won't mention names (don't worry, we're sure *your* institution wouldn't do anything wrong), but colleges have engaged in such practices as lying about the class rank and SAT scores of admitted freshmen, lying about student retention rates, lying about fund-raising success, and misrepresenting student–faculty ratios. Other times, the college does not lie but rather manipulates admission practices to achieve higher scores. One university offered financial incentives for *admitted* students to retake the SAT, so that the university could report a higher average SAT score among its students.[4] Other colleges have delayed the admission of students with lower SAT scores so that these lower scores would not be counted when average SAT data were collected. Many universities encourage students to apply who they know are unlikely to be accepted just so they can report a lower acceptance rate and thus appear to be more "selective."

When we can't rely on seller or buyer reviews, third-party organizations can sometimes be trusted to provide independent advice. The magazine and website *Consumer Reports* (*CR*) tests and rates a wide variety of products, from washing machines to cars to computers, not to mention bassinets and blood glucose meters—all to help their subscribers and paid-up users of their website make better-informed decisions. To demonstrate its credibility, *CR* does all of its own tests (it doesn't rely on what the sellers claim) and it will not accept advertisements or other forms of payment from the companies whose products are being rated.

Organizations like *CR*, however, are probably underprovided relative to their social usefulness. Many forms of information are a *public good*, which means that it is difficult to exclude nonpayers (and also that consumption is nonrival; see Chapter 19). Nonexcludability makes it hard to sell information even when the information is valuable. Let's say, for instance, that an individual can either pay for *CR* or they can go to Google and try to get that same information for free. Most people opt for the cheaper option, and indeed if you Google "best new cars" you will come across plenty of free information, some of it even drawn from *CR*. Once the underlying research has been produced, it tends to make its way into the world, whether in someone else's article, blog post, or tweet, and Google will bring us much of that information, again for free. The result is that many people **free ride** on all the testing and research that *CR* does to produce its product ratings. Since not everyone who benefits from *CR*'s research pays for it, the market for such information is smaller than ideal.

By the way, did you know that *CR* forbids its ratings from being used in any product advertisements? *CR* argues that this prevents even the hint of impropriety. Notice that this policy also makes it harder to find *CR* ratings, except by buying *CR* magazine. Thus, the no-advertising policy also helps *CR* to prevent free riders.

A **free rider** consumes but does not pay.

Since buyers are reluctant to pay for information, independent third-party reviewers often aren't as independent as we would like. The bond-rating companies Standard and Poor's and Moody's evaluate the creditworthiness of companies and also of financial securities, including mortgage securities. The rating companies are supposed to help buyers pick safe securities on the basis of objective data. The recent track record of these companies, however, isn't good. Right up until the financial crash of 2007–2008, for example, the credit rating companies were rating many mortgage-backed securities as very safe. A short time later, the largest wave of real estate defaults in the United States since the Great Depression made quite a few of these securities very bad investments. If you are wondering who paid for these ratings, it was the firms whose securities were being rated, not potential buyers. If credit rating companies are too critical, they may lose business from their true customers, the finance firms who want favorable reports about the securities that they are selling. Arguably, the rating companies were biased because they were trying to please those who paid them.

The ratings companies would have better incentives if they were paid directly by buyers, but again the buyers won't pay because of free rider problems, as there are many buyers for any potential security but typically only one main issuer. In general, information problems are difficult to solve completely because damping down one problem often inflates another.

CHECK YOURSELF

• *Consumer Reports* is a non-profit. How does this help to limit problems of moral hazard?

Overcoming Moral Hazard by Creating Better Incentives

Better-informed buyers are one solution to asymmetric information problems. Another solution is to give sellers less of an incentive to exploit their information advantage. We have already seen how reputation can make sellers less willing to exploit their information advantage. Splitting the selling of a service from the diagnosis of how much service is needed can also help to reduce moral hazard. Before signing the deed, for example, most house buyers will hire a house inspector, and indeed often a mortgage lender will require this. Since the house inspector is paid by the buyer, the inspector has no incentive to underreport bad news. In addition, it's illegal for house inspectors to profit from any repairs that they recommend, so inspectors also do not have an incentive to overreport bad news.

Recall our opening story of auto mechanics and dentists. When the buyer came to the mechanic with a problem, such as intermittent starting, the problem usually was fixed, albeit sometimes involving unnecessarily expensive repairs. But mechanics and dentists also recommended unnecessary repairs, and that's when you ought to take special care. The general lesson is to trust experts more when you have a problem and when you can verify whether the expert fixed the problem. But if your mechanic is recommending an expensive repair for something you didn't even know was wrong, get a second opinion.

Similarly, for major medical decisions, it makes sense to seek a second opinion. Not only will you get more information, but if you tell the second doctor that they will not be performing the service regardless, you are likely to get an opinion stripped of moral hazard.

Part of the original Hippocratic Oath, which physicians swear, reads, "Whatever houses I may visit, I will come for the benefit of the sick, remaining free of all intentional injustice [and] of all mischief." The oath and the professional ethics and training that come with it probably do limit moral hazard. But as always, economics is about thinking on the margin, and even physicians appear to make choices that on the margin are shaded to their benefit.

Obstetricians are typically paid more when a baby is delivered via caesarean section, a surgical procedure, than by vaginal delivery. Are you surprised that when the fee for c-sections increases, so does the number of c-sections? Incentives matter. Interestingly, when the patient is herself a physician, and thus better informed than the average patient, we do not see this relationship, and that further indicates the importance of more symmetric information. A further test of the theory of moral hazard as applied to obstetricians comes from HMOs, or health maintenance organizations, which are one form of health care provider. HMOs pay their obstetricians a salary that is *not* dependent on the delivery method. As expected, patients in HMOs have lower c-section rates (relative to similar non-HMO patients). Don't assume, however, that we can remove incentives completely. C-sections are also more common on Fridays, probably because physicians (and some patients!) would like to free up their weekends.[5]

Instead of trying to eliminate a seller's incentives, another method of reducing moral hazard is to better align the buyer's and seller's incentives. How do you know your lawyer is working hard on your case and not being lazy? Without a lot of expert knowledge and monitoring, it's hard to know. To overcome the potential moral hazard problem, plaintiffs often pay their lawyers with a contingent fee—the lawyer is paid, typically a third of any judgment, *only* if the case is won. Real estate agents are also paid only if the house sells but in this case the contingent fee, typically 3% of the price of the house, is much smaller than a lawyer's fee. As a result, real estate agents are more eager to sell houses quickly than are homeowners. If waiting an additional week raises the price by $1,000, that's an extra $970 for the homeowner and only $30 more for the agent. Interestingly, when agents sell their own homes, they use their information advantage and keep their houses on the market about 10 days longer than similar houses sold by owners with agents.[6]

Finally, don't think that moral hazard is limited to markets. Politicians typically have more information than voters and bureaucrats often have more information than politicians. A deep-seated problem of political science is how to incentivize politicians and bureaucrats to act in the public interest and not to use their information advantage for their own interest. Competitive elections, checks and balances, a free and independent press, and other institutions all can be understood as ways to limit moral hazard in politics (we take up more of these issues in Chapter 20).

Let's be honest: Moral hazard is everywhere because self-interest is everywhere (even if you don't think that self-interest is the only motivation). Recall Big Idea Two from Chapter 1: Good Institutions Align Self-Interest with the Social Interest. When it comes to moral hazard, reputation, ratings, and contract design, such as contingent fees, are some of the institutions that align self-interest with the social interest. Most importantly, note that these institutions are continually evolving in response to new challenges.

Let's turn now to another problem of asymmetric information.

Adverse Selection

Groucho Marx, the famous comedian, once said that he didn't want to belong to any club that would have him as a member. Believe it or not, the economist George Akerlof won a Nobel Prize for analyzing when Groucho-type reasoning makes sense and what the consequences are for market equilibrium and efficiency! Groucho was using the fact that a club was offering him membership to infer something about the quality of the club, namely that the club couldn't be very exclusive. Akerlof analyzed the more general situation of **adverse selection**, when an offer conveys negative information about what is being offered.

Adverse selection occurs when an offer conveys negative information about the product being offered.

Quick: Who is most likely to want health insurance? Answer: the sick. That's adverse selection. The offer, in this case the offer to buy health insurance, conveys the negative information that the buyer is likely to have above-average health care costs. Notice that Groucho didn't want to join a club that most wanted him as a member, and insurance companies don't want to sell insurance to the people who most want to buy—this is the basic problem of adverse selection.

Let's give another example that was first analyzed by Akerlof. Suppose that there are two types of used cars: lemons (used cars with a lot of problems) and plums (used cars in excellent mechanical shape). Lemons are worth $8,000; plums are worth $12,000. Suppose also that among the currently owned cars there are equal numbers of lemons and plums. Now, here is the key assumption of asymmetric information: Assume that only sellers know the true quality of their car and that there is no cheap way for buyers to distinguish lemons from plums. The market structure is simple but the assumption of asymmetric information has surprising consequences.

MRU

mru.org/asymmetric-info

Asymmetric Information and Used Cars

Suppose that you were a buyer in this market. How much would you be willing to pay for a used car? You might reason that since there are equal numbers of lemons and plums, the probability is $\frac{1}{2}$ that you will be purchasing a lemon and $\frac{1}{2}$ that you will be purchasing a plum. Thus, you would be willing to pay the expected or average value, namely $(\frac{1}{2} \times \$8,000) + (\frac{1}{2} \times \$12,000) = \$10,000$.

This reasoning is incomplete. To see why, now put yourself in the shoes of a seller with a plum, a high-quality used car. Buyers are willing to pay only $10,000 for a used car, but your car is worth $12,000. Do you sell? No.

Type of car	Lemons (low quality)	Plums (high quality)
Value	$8,000	$12,000

Now put yourself back in the shoes of the buyer and think like Groucho. Even if half of the existing cars are plums, does it make sense to assume that half of the cars *for sale* are plums? No. In fact, no owner of a plum will want to sell, so the mere fact that a car is offered for sale suggests that it's a lemon. How much are you willing to pay for a used car now?

Since buyers know that every used car for sale is a lemon, the most they will be willing to pay for a used car is $8,000.

Notice what is wrong with this outcome. Even if lots of people would like to buy a plum at $12,000 and lots of people would like to sell a plum at $12,000, there is no market for plums. Plums—the high-quality used cars—don't trade. That is a market failure.

We assumed that there were only two types of used cars, but the outcome gets even more disturbing when there are many qualities of used car from low to high. The general logic is that of the vicious circle, or "death spiral." Buyers can't easily tell the quality of a used car so they play the averages. An average price, however, means that the owners of higher-quality autos aren't getting a good price. The owners of high-quality used cars drop out of the market, thereby reducing the average quality of the cars for sale and, in turn, reducing how much buyers are willing to pay. The process continues until only the worst lemons are for sale.

Of course, in the real world not every used car for sale is a lemon. The reality is that about 40 million used cars (and small trucks) are bought and sold in an average year in the United States, as compared with about 13 million new cars.[7] It hardly seems that the used car market has shut down, nor are used vehicle sales in the United States overwhelmingly dominated by low-quality lemons.

How does the used car market manage to work as well as it does? Let's turn to some of the market institutions, laws, and regulations that have evolved to deal with adverse selection.

First, potential buyers can have an experienced mechanic look over the car. Similarly, used cars are also often accompanied by what are called "CARFAX" reports, which detail the repair history of the car. Both of these techniques help to overcome information asymmetry and increase trade.

Second, millions of used cars today are certified, which means they are bought by a dealer, inspected, repaired and refurbished, and then sold with an extended warranty. The warranty reduces consumer

In the market for used cars . . . The lemons are the only used cars that will be bought and sold.

A **credible** promise is one that the promisor has an incentive to keep.

fears about getting a lemon. A warranty also makes the dealer's promise to sell a plum **credible** because if a dealer sells a lemon, the dealer ends up paying. Warranties are best when they are never used! The firm selling the warranty is often the original manufacturer of the car. For example, Mercedes offers warranties for certified preowned Mercedes vehicles. Thus, Mercedes' reputation for high-quality new cars is also on the line when they sell certified preowned cars. That also reassures consumers and communicates the message that the car is really a good one.

Similarly, notice that many used cars are bought and sold between friends and family. If your brother tells you that his car is a plum, you may be more likely to believe him—because he's your brother and also because if the car isn't a plum, you can punish him in ways that you could not punish a stranger! In essence, reputation outside the market for used cars helps to sell used cars.

Third, suppose that some sellers of used cars will sell even when the price is low. Perhaps some owners of used cars simply love that new car smell and want to replace their used car regardless. Other owners have leased their cars and want a new car every two years, or perhaps they simply need the cash. If some used car owners sell even if they have a plum, that action raises the expected value of used cars and makes buyers more willing to buy and (other) sellers more willing to sell. Thus, the presence of some sellers who sell regardless of price keeps the price high enough so that other owners of plums want to sell.

Adverse selection hasn't shut down the market for used cars because market institutions have developed to reduce information asymmetry and its consequences. It's not that everyone has a great experience buying a used car (or a new car, for that matter), but the used car market is an active and well-functioning market that gives many people the chance to buy (or sell) personal transportation at a discounted price.[8] Still, the adverse selection model helps us to understand the real-world institutions that have evolved to overcome adverse selection.

CHECK YOURSELF
• Go to eBay and search for Picassos. What do you infer about these Picassos?

Adverse Selection in Health Insurance

Let's look in more detail at the challenge of selling health insurance. When a health insurance company offers a policy, it worries that perhaps the sickest individuals, or those with the greatest potential future problems, are the ones most likely to buy. After all, a perfectly healthy person doesn't benefit much from health insurance, unless, of course, some sudden accident befalls them. But if only the sick buy insurance, the insurance company has to raise its rates to reflect the higher costs. The higher rates in turn make health insurance an even worse deal for healthy individuals, pushing them out of the market. As rates rise and healthy individuals drop out of the market, the composition of customers becomes even more costly for the health insurance company, which in turn pushes rates yet higher. Figure 24.1 illustrates this process, which is sometimes called the "adverse selection death spiral," with some specific numbers and assumptions.

As in the market for used cars, some market features help limit this adverse selection problem:

Inspections or Checkups An insurance company can inspect the health of potential insurance customers to overcome asymmetric information and adjust rates accordingly. If insurance companies can charge people different rates depending on their expected costs, the adverse selection "death spiral" will be avoided.

Group Plans An insurance company can emphasize sales to groups, such as through the workplace, to increase the chances of signing up both healthy and

FIGURE 24.1

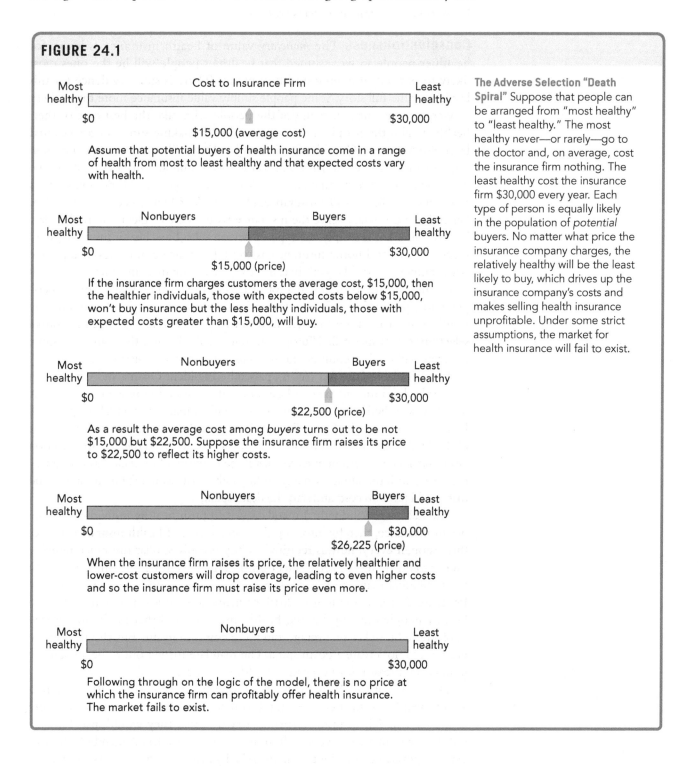

The Adverse Selection "Death Spiral" Suppose that people can be arranged from "most healthy" to "least healthy." The most healthy never—or rarely—go to the doctor and, on average, cost the insurance firm nothing. The least healthy cost the insurance firm $30,000 every year. Each type of person is equally likely in the population of *potential* buyers. No matter what price the insurance company charges, the relatively healthy will be the least likely to buy, which drives up the insurance company's costs and makes selling health insurance unprofitable. Under some strict assumptions, the market for health insurance will fail to exist.

unhealthy customers. In fact, most health insurance in the United States is not bought by individuals but by firms that purchase insurance for their employees as a group. Since healthier individuals typically cannot opt out of their employer's group health insurance plan, this limits adverse selection problems. In addition, in the United States, as a matter of law, employer-supplied group health insurance plans have only a limited legal ability to kick out or raise rates for individuals who come down with financially costly health problems. That also helps to keep insurance markets working.

Conscientiousness The *monetary* value of health insurance is lower for healthier people so we assumed that healthier people will be the ones most likely to opt out of buying health insurance. There is some evidence for this but it's not the full story. Some people simply value insurance more than others. In fact, it turns out that many of the people who take the best care of their health are also the people most concerned with making sure they are covered by health insurance. Consider Devin and Jan. Devin likes to drive fast and often forgets to wear a seatbelt. Jan keeps to the speed limit and makes sure everyone is buckled up before starting any trip. If you had to guess, who do you think is more likely to have health insurance, Devin or Jan? Devin needs it more than Jan and in a monetary sense the insurance would benefit Devin more than Jan, but we think Jan is simply the type of person who buys health insurance (and probably auto and home insurance as well). Insurance companies love people with temperaments like Jan's because they buy insurance and they are careful about their health. If there are a lot of Jans in the world—that is, lots of people whose personality trait of conscientiousness correlates with demand to buy health insurance—then this will lead not to adverse selection but to positive selection (sometimes called "propitious selection"). Even if there are only some Jans, this will tend to counter and moderate the adverse selection death spiral.[9]

The Affordable Care Act (ACA), passed by President Obama and Congress in 2010, subsidized the purchase of health insurance for poorer individuals and families. The so-called individual mandate compelled many individuals to purchase health care insurance by force of law, and was one of the most controversial aspects of the ACA. One motivation for the mandate was to avoid the adverse selection death spiral. The government feared that if the purchase of insurance was voluntary, then, even with the subsidies, many healthy individuals wouldn't buy insurance and that would push up costs and start the death spiral.

The idea of the individual mandate was to push healthy individuals to buy health insurance, thereby lowering the average cost of health insurance. Under this vision, if everyone was required to buy broadly similar insurance policies, there would be less adverse selection. The penalty for noncompliance with the individual mandate was controversial, however, and it was eliminated by President Trump beginning in 2019. As many economists had predicted, some healthy people did stop buying health insurance and that made the insured pool a little bit sicker on average and more costly to insure. But eliminating the penalty did not create a death spiral. The mandate turned out to be a relatively unimportant reason for purchasing health insurance.

The critics of the ACA focus on a moral hazard problem with insurance. When people are insured, they tend to behave differently—people with fire insurance may fail to install a sprinkler system that they would install if they didn't have insurance, drivers with insurance may drive less diligently, banks that expect a government bailout if things go badly may take on more risk. In the case

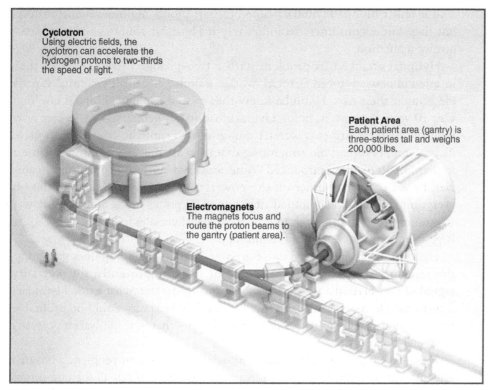

Cyclotron
Using electric fields, the cyclotron can accelerate the hydrogen protons to two-thirds the speed of light.

Patient Area
Each patient area (gantry) is three-stories tall and weighs 200,000 lbs.

Electromagnets
The magnets focus and route the proton beams to the gantry (patient area).

Proton Therapy High-tech science or moral hazard?

of health insurance, we aren't so much worried about a person taking on more risk but of demanding more services. When patients, doctors, and hospitals know an insurance company is paying the final bill, the patients tend to demand more procedures and treatments. Doctors and hospitals, in turn, supply those procedures and treatments, knowing they will be paid for them, and that is a form of moral hazard at the expense of the insurance companies.

Hospitals around the country, for example, have been building nuclear particle accelerators—which were once used only by physicists looking to understand the universe!—to treat cancer. The accelerators cost hundreds of millions of dollars and involve massive magnets and giant buildings. Unfortunately, there is very little evidence that so-called proton therapy improves health and even less that we need dozens of these facilities in the United States. If patients had to pay for these treatments out of pocket, they would be unlikely to want them but when insurance companies and taxpayers are the ones paying the bills, patients will demand them and hospitals will supply them.

Health care in the United States already consumes about 18% of GDP. Critics of the ACA worry that by reducing price signals and market incentives in favor of greater reliance on government guarantees, health care costs may rise even further, creating longer-run harms.

Signaling as a Response to Asymmetric Information

Hyundai Motor Company was founded in South Korea in 1967 and began selling cars in the United States in 1986. Hyundai cars were inexpensive and sold reasonably well but Hyundai was perceived as a low-quality brand with a poor repair history. Hyundai wanted to start producing more luxurious cars but they knew consumers wouldn't buy if Hyundai couldn't shake its low-quality reputation.

Hyundai attacked its problem with a two-pronged strategy. First, they invested in new, advanced factories, worker training, and quality control. If people bought their cars, Hyundai knew they would last but Hyundai couldn't wait 10 years to prove its point. Hyundai had to get people to buy its cars now if all the new investments weren't going to bankrupt the company. To solve its problem, Hyundai did something dramatic for the second prong of their strategy. In 1998, they introduced "America's Best Warranty" on all their vehicles, 10 years/100,000 miles on the powertrain and 5 years/60,000 miles on everything else. Hyundai immediately gained 28 points in the annual JD Power Customer Satisfaction survey and the next year their sales increased by 82%, the largest jump in the history of the industry.

Hyundai's warranty served two purposes. First, if something does go wrong, the warranty has value as insurance. But more importantly, the warranty **signaled** that Hyundai was serious about quality. In fact, what made Hyundai's signal credible was that the only way Hyundai's warranty could be profitable for the company is if its cars didn't break down—that is, if the warranty wasn't used very often!

Hyundai's signal overcame an asymmetric information problem. Hyundai knew that it had greatly improved its production process but all the consumers had to go on was Hyundai's less than stellar history. The signal worked because offering a warranty is cheap for a company that produces high-quality cars but expensive for a company that produces low-quality cars.

> A **signal** is an expensive action that is taken to reveal information.

Signaling in the Job Market

You are an aspiring software programmer and you see the perfect job being advertised in Silicon Valley at a starting salary of $125,000 a year. Awesome! You really want the job and, remembering your economics lesson that incentives matter, you tell the interviewer that you would be willing to take the job for just $100,000. You are confident that you have underbid the other applicants and so will get the job. You don't get the job. What happened? Your reasoning about the power of underbidding is correct if the interviewer can easily evaluate the quality of all the job candidates. Who wouldn't want high quality at a low price? But evaluating job candidates is notoriously difficult. Some candidates who look good on paper are disasters in practice, and vice versa. The interviewer doesn't know your true quality. As a result, when the interviewer hears your offer to work for much less, the interviewer may infer that you are desperate—a low-quality candidate who can't get a job elsewhere—not someone the company wants to hire. Once again, this is a problem of adverse selection: The interviewer is worried that the people who most want the job are not the people the firm most wants to hire. This is one reason why unemployed people often find it harder to get hired than do similar employed workers looking for a new job.

Offering to work for low pay sends a signal that you might be a low-quality worker. How could you signal a potential employer about your high quality? Here's a hint: You might be signaling right now. We hope that you are learning something from this textbook that will be useful to you in your future career. One theory of education, however, says that education pays not because it offers any practical advice but only because a degree is a signal of IQ and conscientiousness, including grit and determination.

As professional academics, we have in fact noticed that not every degree prepares people for the real world. A lot of study seems to consist of academic exercises with few practical applications. Some degrees do pay more, including chemical engineering and economics! But if you graduate with a degree in art or ancient Greek history, don't despair. Most degrees pay even if your eventual job has nothing to do with your degree. Signaling helps explain why. It's easier for someone with a high IQ and good work habits to get a degree—almost any degree—than it is for someone with a low IQ and a lack of determination. Thus, completing a degree signals to employers that you are likely to have the kinds of qualities that employers are willing to pay for.

Consider the following thought experiment. Which do you think would pay more, a diploma from Harvard without a Harvard education or a Harvard education without the diploma? There is some evidence for the former. If education were only about learning and not at all about signaling, you would expect that people who took all the courses except *one* would receive almost as big a boost in their wages as a person who took all the courses and graduated with a diploma. After all, the two individuals have nearly the same education. And yet people with a degree earn much more than people with nearly the same education but without the degree. In the literature, this is called the "sheepskin effect" (degrees were made of sheepskin a long time ago) because it says that the sheepskin you hang on the wall is worth a large fraction of the value of the education.[10] The lesson here is to finish your degree!

MRU

mru.org/duel-education

ECON DUEL

Econ Duel: Is Education Signaling or Skill Building?

Signaling in Dating, Marriage, and the Animal Kingdom

Signaling pervades our lives, and it is not restricted to narrowly economic transactions. Criminals, for example, often need to signal to each other their propensities to break the law, yet without incriminating themselves should they be dealing with an undercover police officer. Facial tattoos are one way to do this because the tattoo shows that the person has given up on any chance of achieving a normal, mainstream life. In South African prisons, for instance, such tattoos are a common way for true criminals to identify each other and verify that they really are disreputable lawbreakers. One South African prisoner had the phrase "Spit on my grave" tattooed across his forehead and "I hate you, Mum" imprinted on his left cheek. That's a pretty good sign that person is not looking to go straight or to reform and enter mainstream life.[11]

Employers interview potential employees extensively because it's much cheaper to avoid hiring a bad employee than it is to fire one. It's also much cheaper to avoid marrying a bad partner than it is to divorce one. Thus, you can think of dating as a series of marriage interviews! As with a job interview, marriage interviews contain a lot of signaling.

Recall the aspiring programmer who offers to work for less money. The programmer's offer is rejected because employers fear that someone who is so desperate for work that they offer to work for less is actually worth less. In this respect, getting a job and getting a date are not so different. Dating experts—not just economists—recommend, for example, that for both men and women, it's important not to look too eager.

Richard I'Anson/Getty Images

Tiina Tuomaala/Alamy Stock Photo

If I weren't such a stud, could I afford this?

Engagement rings are a signal of our commitment to our partners or potential partners but to work they have to be expensive. An expensive ring is a signal because expensive rings are cheaper if you truly expect to remain married! If you think that rings are bought because they are beautiful rather than for signaling, consider the following thought experiment. How long would the tradition of giving a diamond engagement ring last if a new technology made diamonds cheap?

Many women, when they marry, face the choice of whether to take the last name of their husband or perhaps to adopt a joint, hyphenated last name. If the woman takes the last name of her husband, it is a signal that a future divorce will be especially costly to her. She would then either be stuck with the last name of a man she has fallen out of love with, or she would have to change her name once again, which could make it harder to establish or keep a reputation and create costs for her professional life. On the other hand, if a woman keeps her maiden name, she is signaling a strong attachment to building or maintaining a career reputation. Some women try to have it both ways by using two names (one at the workplace, the other at home) or by using hyphenated names, while many other people wonder why this burden of adjustment is distributed so fully on women and not on men.

Signaling even pervades the animal kingdom. Charles Darwin was perplexed by the peacock's tail. Why would a peacock use so many of its resources on a tail that not only didn't help it survive but that actually hindered survival by making it more difficult for the peacock to escape predators? The theory of signaling and sexual selection offers an answer. Since only the healthiest and most robust peacocks can grow large and beautiful tails, the peacock's tail signals to peahens that the peacock is healthy, has good genes, and would make a good partner for procreation.

Is Signaling Good?

Signaling creates benefits by generating information, but in most signaling models there is some inefficiency. It typically takes at least four years to get a degree, and if education doesn't add much to future productivity, then that's four years of effort just to signal IQ and perseverance. Maybe you have fun during the university years but university can't be too much fun or everyone would do it, even those without high IQs and perseverance. Ideally, there might be a cheaper way to communicate this information to potential employers. We see the same issues with diamond rings. If there were a cheaper way to signal commitment, you could get your partner a much cheaper cubic zirconia ring and use the savings to buy a nice Viking refrigerator. Solving these problems isn't easy, however. We are both professors of economics and believe us when we say that we didn't even try to eliminate the costs of signaling with diamond rings.

Finally, note that while signaling eases some problems of asymmetric information, it creates others. In particular, when signaling is rife, some moral hazard problems may become worse. Let's go back to education as a signal of worker productivity. If finishing an education gets you higher wages whether or not you learn anything useful, that sad reality removes some of the pressure on colleges and universities to teach you something useful. Students might prefer to learn something practical rather than just jumping through hoops, but professors will find it easier to teach what interests them and many administrators will tolerate this. After all, conscientious students will still attend and finish college simply to get the higher wages, whether or not they learn very much. We return again to a key theme of this chapter: Many asymmetric information problems can be eased or traded in for easier-to-handle information problems, but asymmetric information will continue as a general market phenomenon.

Takeaway

Markets work best when both buyers and sellers know exactly what is being exchanged. When one party to an exchange has more or better information than the other party, we get problems of asymmetric information, such as moral hazard and adverse selection.

Moral hazard is when an agent tries to exploit an information advantage in a dishonest or undesirable way. Not all people try to exploit their information advantage but incentives do matter. When moral hazard is possible, the less informed party may be exploited and resources may be consumed without generating value (remember the mechanic who replaces the part that doesn't need replacing). Or, fearing moral hazard, parties with less information may simply decide not to trade, thereby reducing the gains from trade.

Adverse selection occurs when an offer conveys negative information about the product being offered. When buyers can't easily evaluate the quality of a good, they may assume that any good offered for sale will be of low quality and they will be willing to pay only accordingly. Sellers, seeing that the price is low, will choose to sell only the low-quality good. Buyers and sellers both get what they paid for (unlike with moral hazard) but both would be better off if they could also buy and sell high-quality goods.

Moral hazard and adverse selection problems challenge markets, but market institutions, laws, and regulations have evolved to deal with these problems. Ratings, reviews, and inspections all work to generate more information and to reduce asymmetry. Reputation and certification, second opinions (separating the provider of information from the provider of the service), and contingent fees all help to align buyer and seller interests. Even when the relevant information cannot be shown directly (only the heart knows its secrets), sometimes it can be signaled by an investment in something else.

The solutions to asymmetric information problems are never without cost and they are rarely perfect or complete. Ratings and reviews can be faked, reputations are sometimes undeserved, contracts rarely fully align incentives, and signals are noisy. Nevertheless, we think that understanding the problems of asymmetric information and their (partial) solutions can help you to understand and navigate your world.

CHAPTER REVIEW

Go online to practice with more examples of these types of problems, including live links to videos, data sources, and feedback.

KEY CONCEPTS

asymmetric information, p. 473

principal–agent problem, p. 473

moral hazard, p. 474

free rider, p. 476

adverse selection, p. 478

credible, p. 480

signal, p. 484

FACTS AND TOOLS

1. Determine whether the following situations represent problems caused by asymmetric information. If so, determine whether they represent problems of moral hazard or adverse selection.

    a. Unrest in the Middle East causes oil speculators to buy up oil futures, driving gasoline prices higher.

    b. Karol is halfway to work before he realizes that he forgot to lock the back door. Because he has renter's insurance, he decides it is not worth being late just to go home to lock the door.

    c. Joanne applies for a job as a part-time manager at a fast-food restaurant. Her MBA makes her overqualified for the job, yet the position goes to someone else who doesn't have a college degree.

    d. Frances lives in an apartment above a restaurant, and her apartment always smells like burgers and fries. She has tried unsuccessfully to get the restaurant owner to remedy the problem.

    e. The potential costs of long-term care (such as a nursing home stay) can be very high and also very uncertain. Despite this, the private market for long-term care in the United States has remained fairly small.

    f. Reggie is the pitcher for his baseball team, but he's frequently worried about being injured by quick line drives back up the middle. However, after buying a chest protector to bear the impact, he begins to relax and adopts a riskier play style.

    g. Chantelle has a long-standing knee injury but has yet to see a doctor about it. When her annual health insurance enrollment period opens at work, she decides to enroll in the premium plan with the intention of getting her knee treated in the coming year.

2. Describe how the following facts represent solutions to problems of asymmetric information.

    a. Auto insurance rates are higher for teenagers than for non-teenagers.

    b. Your car insurance coverage probably includes a deductible—an amount that you have to pay out of pocket before your insurance coverage kicks in.

    c. Many states have laws like Virginia's that give customers the right to keep or inspect parts that are removed by an auto mechanic.

    d. For many couples, weddings are lavish affairs that cost tens of thousands of dollars and are attended by hundreds of guests.

3. George Akerlof's model of the used car market results in a market in which only lemons are sold and there is no market for high-quality used cars. But, in fact, we observe that the used car market is a robust market in which millions of used cars of varying quality are sold. Does that mean Akerlof's model is wrong? Why or why not?

4. In March of 2023, the Federal Reserve announced a "bailout" for the depositors of the Silicon Valley Bank, which had run into trouble when the market value of its assets dipped below the value of its deposits, leading to a bank run. Can you think of an argument against such a bailout that is related to the material in this chapter? Where's the information asymmetry?

5. Explain the difference between moral hazard and adverse selection. In general, which problem is more likely to arise prior to making a transaction, and which problem is more likely to arise after the transaction has been made?

THINKING AND PROBLEM SOLVING

6. Insurance markets are often plagued by problems of asymmetric information. In part, this is because insurance markets themselves exist only because of incomplete information—nobody knows what the future holds, so households pay insurance companies to bear the risk of an uncertain future. Both households and insurance companies have incomplete information, but problems arise because the information is asymmetrically incomplete.

    Consider the market for medical insurance. What information might buyers in this market have that insurance companies don't have? Here's a harder question: What information might sellers of medical insurance have that buyers don't have?

7. Health economists use the phrase "supplier-induced demand" to describe the ability that physicians have to influence their patients' demand for medical care. One of the reasons that this ability exists is asymmetric information.

    a. What do physicians know more about than patients?

    b. If physicians can influence their patients' demand, then what would prevent them from always providing diagnoses of severe conditions that require expensive (profitable) treatments?

    c. Health economists point out that third-party payment schemes (such as medical insurance that pays your medical bills for you) also contribute to supplier-induced demand. How would third-party payment exacerbate the problems of asymmetric information?

8. Suppose used cars come in two varieties—plums (cars that run well) and lemons (cars with many problems). The sellers of used cars know perfectly well which type of car they have, whereas buyers cannot tell the difference between them. The buyers know, however, that their maximum willingness to pay for a plum is $8,000 and for a lemon is $4,000. The buyers also know that the probability of any given car being a plum or lemon is 30% and 70%, respectively.

    a. What is a buyer's maximum willingness to pay for a car of unknown quality, assuming they are risk neutral?

    b. If most consumers are risk averse instead of risk neutral, would that increase or decrease their maximum willingness to pay for a used car?

    c. If sellers of plums have a minimum willingness to sell of $7,000 and sellers of lemons have a minimum willingness to sell of $3,000, which cars will get traded in this market?

9. Suppose your band is about to take off, so you go out and buy a brand-new Marshall Tube Head and Cabinet amplifier for the list price of about $4,500. But your band breaks up after you've used the amplifier only once. You hang on to it for a year or so in case your drummer and bass player can work out their differences, but it never happens. You finally decide to sell it on Craigslist. Since you know it's been used only once, and it's been properly stored for a year, you reason that it's still worth close to what you paid for it, so you list it for $4,000—over 10% off the new price. How is this likely going to turn out?

10. Kaplan Test Prep offers courses and private tutoring arrangements that prepare students for standardized tests, such as the GRE, GMAT, or LSAT (tests that you may take soon). Kaplan offers students a "Higher Score Guarantee," which essentially promises that your score when you take the test after completing a Kaplan course will be higher than your prior test score (or your "diagnostic" score if it's your first time taking the test). If it's not, you can take the course again or get your money back.

    a. Discuss how this guarantee functions as insurance.

    b. Discuss how this guarantee functions as a signal.

11. Consider the following unusual insurance products. For each one, determine whether you think this insurance product could exist in the marketplace, or whether it would be subject to moral hazard or adverse selection (or both). (And for some interesting examples of unusual insurance products that actually exist in the marketplace, try a Google search for "weird insurance policies.")

    a. GPA insurance for people with 4.0 GPAs after two years of college that pays out if you ever have a semester with a GPA lower than 3.50.

b. GPA insurance for anyone that pays out if you ever have a semester with a GPA lower than 3.50.

c. Loneliness insurance that pays out if you reach a certain age and still have not married.

d. Toe-stubbing insurance that pays out any time you stub your toe.

e. Insurance that pays out if and only if you get hit and killed by a school bus.

12. When the cause of death is suicide, life insurance policies typically pay out only when the suicide occurred after an exclusionary period has passed, usually around a year after purchasing the life insurance. Why do life insurance companies insist on an exclusionary period? If you compared suicide rates in the year before and the year after the exclusionary period, what do you predict you would find?

13. You are driving on a trip and have two choices on the highway to stop for a snack: a well-known chain or a local restaurant that you have never heard of but that looks okay. What lessons from this chapter might lead you to choose the chain even if you think that their food is just average? How have smartphones changed this decision-making process over the last decade and a half? And how might you choose differently if these two choices were in your neighborhood?

14. Lawyers will often work for a contingent fee—they only get paid if they win and are typically paid a share of the proceeds. In the text, this was explained as a way of incentivizing the lawyer to work hard, even when the client can't see how much they are working. Can you offer another explanation for why a lawyer might offer a contingent fee based on another theory discussed in this chapter?

CHALLENGES

15. Consider a restaurant that wants to avoid kitchen fires. The restaurant could make many investments both to avoid the fires in the first place and to quickly and safely put them out if they do occur. Suppose that the marginal cost (*MC*) and marginal benefit (*MB*) of these investments in fire control technologies is illustrated in the following figure.

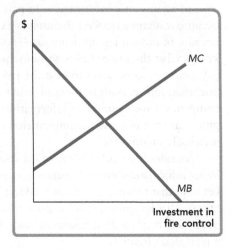

a. If no fire insurance is available, how much investment in fire control would the restaurant purchase? Illustrate the quantity on the graph.

b. If *full* insurance is available, how much investment in fire control would the restaurant purchase?

c. The moral hazard incentivized by full insurance creates a deadweight loss. Show the deadweight loss in the diagram.

d. Suppose that the insurance policy would only cover 50% of the losses from fire; that is, the restaurant has a 50% copay. How much fire control would the restaurant purchase? Illustrate this example on the graph. (*Hint:* One curve will shift, so you need to determine which curve, which direction, and the size of the shift.)

e. Suppose that the insurance policy would cover only 50% of the losses but the insurance company also offered a discount on insurance to restaurants that installed water sprinklers or other fire suppression technologies. How would the curves shift? What quantity of fire investment would be purchased? Comment on the role of copays and discounts.

16. As we saw in Facts and Tools #1f, safety improvements in the world of sports may accidentally cause the rate of athlete injury to increase. Another example can be seen in boxing. Prior to the development of boxing gloves, striking an opponent in the head

was very dangerous not only to the recipient but to the striker as well. The striker could easily crack or break one of the many small bones located in the fingers. Therefore, most strikes in bare-knuckle boxing are aimed at the torso, which is much more fleshy and less likely to cause serious injury to either boxer. With the development of boxing gloves, this "problem" was solved, allowing boxers to strike each other in the head with a low chance of finger injury. As a result, head injuries for boxers have become more frequent. What type of asymmetric information problem does this represent? Can you think of any similar examples in other sports? Do you think that *removing* safety equipment could potentially make these sports *safer*?

17. Usage-based insurance is a new type of auto insurance that requires that the buyer install a device in their car that monitors speed, distance traveled, acceleration, time of day, and other factors. (Alternatively, the insurance company may tap directly into the vehicle's telematics system [e.g., OnStar] or may require the driver to use a smartphone app to track their driving habits.) Discuss the effects of this type of insurance on different drivers and their behavior. The terms "adverse selection," "moral hazard," and "signaling" should all be relevant.

18. Home cleaning services and general contractors often advertise that they are bonded. What this means is that the seller of the service has put up money with a third party that is available to the buyer if, for example, the cleaners damage or steal property or the general contractor fails to complete the project or completes it in a substandard way. Using the concepts of moral hazard and signaling, explain the purpose of bonding. As a bonus, why is bonding used for these services in particular?

19. The following demand and supply diagram represents the market for routine outpatient appointments with a primary care physician. D_1 shows the annual demand for a typical patient when they have no insurance and must pay the entire price of the appointment out of pocket. D_2 shows how the typical patient responds to the price when they have to pay only 50% out of pocket, with the rest covered by medical insurance.

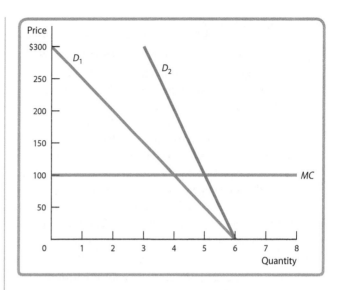

a. Can you explain the shape/position of demand curve D_2?

Suppose the marginal cost of an appointment is $100 and the market is perfectly competitive. Answer all of the following questions twice: once considering a market *without* medical insurance and once considering a market *with* medical insurance.

b. How many physician appointments will the typical patient have each year without and with insurance?

c. How much will the patient pay for physician appointments each year? How much will be paid by the insurance company?

d. What is the total annual value to the patient of the appointments?

e. Comparing your answers to parts c and d, what is the amount of net total surplus generated by the market for these physician appointments?

f. How does this relate to the chapter?

20. Grade inflation is the process by which instructors gradually lower the standards in their classes to allow more students to earn higher grades. How does this process impact the signaling value of a college degree? What are some strategies that good students might pursue to overcome this?

21. Human-made diamonds, which are just as beautiful and essentially indistinguishable from mined diamonds, are becoming much cheaper to produce. Diamond engagement rings, therefore, could soon become much less expensive. Great news for people who plan to get married, right? Or wrong? Explain.

WORK IT OUT

For interactive, step-by-step help in solving this problem, go online.

A private equity firm is considering whether to take over another firm, called the "target." The target has several projects in the pipeline so no one is certain exactly what the target is worth but estimates are that it is worth anywhere between 0 and 100, with each value equally likely. Although the value of the target is uncertain, the private equity firm knows that the target is currently ill managed and that in their hands they could increase the target's value by 50%, that is, multiply the target's value by a factor of 3/2. If the firm is currently worth 60, for example, it would be worth $60 \times (3/2) = 90$ after new management is installed.

a. Find a mutually profitable price for the acquisition, that is, a price such that, on average or in expectation, the owners of both the target and the private equity firm expect to profit. (*Hint:* It helps to know that, when any outcome between a and b is equally likely, the expected or average outcome is $a + (b - a)/2$, as illustrated in the diagram. FYI, if you have taken statistics, this is a property of the uniform distribution.)

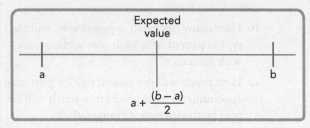

b. Now assume that the current owners of the target know whether the projects in the pipeline are going well or not and so they know the current value of the firm. Only the outsider buyer, the private equity firm, is uncertain about the value of the target, which they continue to estimate is worth between 0 and 100, with each value equally likely. Until the target is bought, information about its true value cannot be credibly communicated to the potential buyer. Naturally, the current owners will sell only if the private equity firm offers them at least as much or more than the current value.

Notice that we have transformed a problem of uncertain but symmetric information into a problem of asymmetric information.

Consider the mutually profitable price that you arrived at in part a. Is the price still mutually profitable? Why or why not? If not, find a new mutually profitable price for the acquisition (if you can). Remember that it is still the case that the firm will be worth 50% more if it is acquired by the buyer.

c. Comment on asymmetric information and trade.

25

Consumer Choice

In this chapter, we take a deeper look at how rational consumers choose. In previous chapters, we analyzed a fairly simple choice. What should a consumer do when the price of a good falls? Buy more! That was easy. In this chapter, we look at more complicated choices such as whether a consumer should shop at Costco. Costco, like Sam's Club or BJ's, offers lower prices, but to shop there, you have to pay a membership fee. How much will consumers be willing to pay to shop at Costco? As you might imagine, this is a key question for Costco executives!

We will also be looking at how much labor a worker should supply in response to a lower wage. In our chapter on labor supply, we pointed out that a worker might respond to a lower wage by working less (called the substitution effect) or the worker might choose to work more to make up for the shortfall in income at the lower wage (the income effect). In this chapter, we introduce two new tools—budget constraints and indifference curves—that will help us understand in greater detail the substitution and income effects, and how consumers and workers choose when faced with complicated decisions.

How to Compare Apples and Oranges

Despite being warned not to, consumers do compare apples and oranges. In fact, consumers have to compare apples, oranges, and every other good if they are to spend their limited budget wisely.

Apples and oranges both produce value or, in economic terms, "utility" for the consumer. We call the increase in utility generated by an additional apple the **marginal utility** of an apple and denote it MU_A. We will assume that marginal utility is diminishing. **Diminishing marginal utility** means that the first apple is great, the second good, the third not bad, and so on. Figure 25.1, for example, shows a marginal utility curve for apples on the left and a marginal utility curve for oranges on the right. In the figure, the marginal utility of the first apple is 70 "utils," the second is 60 utils, the third is 58 utils, and so forth.

But apples and oranges aren't free. There is a price for apples, which we write as P_A, and there is a price for oranges, which we write as P_O. A consumer might love oranges more than any other fruit, but if the price of oranges is high, that consumer may buy apples. The real problem a consumer faces, therefore, is

Marginal utility is the change in utility from consuming an additional unit.

Diminishing marginal utility means that each additional unit of a good adds less to utility than the previous unit.

FIGURE 25.1

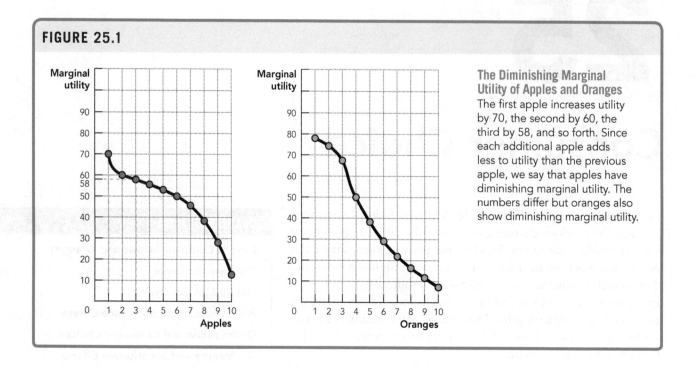

The Diminishing Marginal Utility of Apples and Oranges
The first apple increases utility by 70, the second by 60, the third by 58, and so forth. Since each additional apple adds less to utility than the previous apple, we say that apples have diminishing marginal utility. The numbers differ but oranges also show diminishing marginal utility.

not to choose apples and oranges directly, but to choose how many dollars to spend on apples and how many dollars to spend on oranges. Apples and oranges are two alternative ways of generating utility from dollars. So how should a consumer allocate their dollars between apples and oranges?

As usual, the way to solve this problem is to think on the margin. Each additional dollar allocated to apples generates a certain amount of utility. For example, if the marginal utility of an apple is 70 and the price of apples is $2 per apple, then the marginal utility per dollar spent on apples is 35. More generally, the marginal utility per dollar spent on apples is $\frac{MU_A}{P_A}$. To simplify, if we suppose that $P_A = P_O = \$1$, then we can use the same figure as before, except now the axis is in terms of marginal utilities per dollar.

So which combination of apples and oranges maximizes utility? It's easiest to begin with a bundle that doesn't maximize utility. Once we understand why such a bundle doesn't maximize utility, the solution to the problem will become clear.

Consider Figure 25.2 and suppose that the consumer has $10 in income and they buy 10 oranges and no apples. From the right panel, we can see that the 10th orange is generating 9 utils per dollar. Now consider how much utility would be generated by consuming one dollar less of oranges and one dollar more of apples. From the left panel, we can see that the first dollar spent on apples will generate 70 utils. Thus, by consuming one fewer orange (−9 utils) and one more apple (+70 utils), the consumer can get an increase of 61 utils in total utility.

Keep following this logic. Should the consumer consume 9 oranges and 1 apple? No. Notice that the marginal utility per dollar of the second apple exceeds the marginal utility per dollar of the ninth orange, so the consumer

FIGURE 25.2

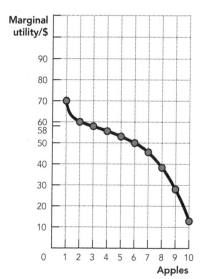

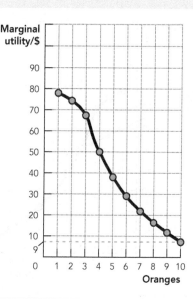

Diminishing Marginal Utility
Imagine that apples and oranges are $1 each. The curves now show the marginal utility per dollar of spending on apples and oranges. Suppose the consumer spends their entire budget of $10 on oranges. The 10th dollar of spending on oranges increases utility by 9. If the consumer spent one dollar less on oranges (−9 utils) and one dollar more on apples (+70 utils), the consumer's total utility would increase by 61.

can increase total utility by shifting another dollar of consumption away from oranges and toward apples.

In other words, if the marginal utility per dollar of apples is higher than the marginal utility per dollar of oranges, then the consumer gets more "bang from a buck" spent on apples than on oranges. Thus, they should buy more apples and fewer oranges:

If $\frac{MU_A}{P_A} > \frac{MU_O}{P_O}$, then buy more apples and fewer oranges.

By exactly the same logic, if the marginal utility per dollar of apples is less than that of oranges, then the consumer gets more bang from a buck spent on oranges. Thus, they should buy fewer apples and more oranges, that is,

If $\frac{MU_A}{P_A} < \frac{MU_O}{P_O}$, then buy fewer apples and more oranges.

Putting these two conditions together, we find that there is only one condition when the consumer cannot increase utility by adjusting their spending, that is, only one condition when the consumer is maximizing utility:

If $\frac{MU_A}{P_A} = \frac{MU_O}{P_O}$, then utility is maximized.

Figure 25.3 shows that if one follows this logic, the point of maximum utility for the consumer is to consume 6 apples and 4 oranges.

We have derived our rule for just two goods, but the idea is perfectly general. Thus, to maximize utility, the **optimal consumption rule** says that a consumer should allocate their spending so that the marginal utility per dollar is equal for all purchases:

$$\frac{MU_A}{P_A} = \frac{MU_O}{P_O} = \frac{MU_i}{P_i} = \cdots = \frac{MU_z}{P_z}$$

Even if you don't consciously think of the "marginal utility per dollar of an apple" as a specific number, the rule tells us that to maximize utility, we should spend our bucks until the bang from a buck is the same for all purchases.

The **optimal consumption rule** says that to maximize utility, a consumer should allocate spending so that the marginal utility per dollar is equal for all purchases.

FIGURE 25.3

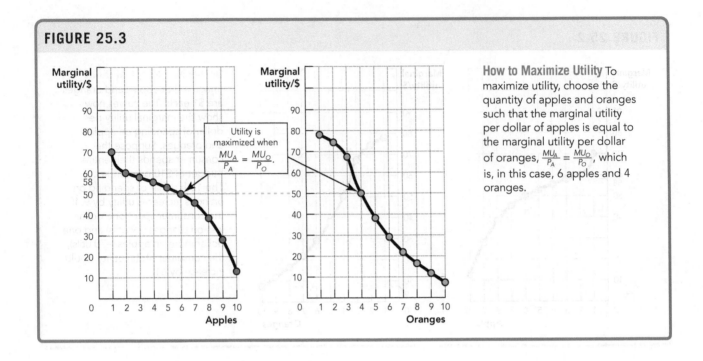

How to Maximize Utility To maximize utility, choose the quantity of apples and oranges such that the marginal utility per dollar of apples is equal to the marginal utility per dollar of oranges, $\frac{MU_A}{P_A} = \frac{MU_O}{P_O}$, which is, in this case, 6 apples and 4 oranges.

The Demand Curve

The optimal consumption rule also gives us an informal explanation for why a consumer's demand curve slopes downward. Suppose that the consumer is currently maximizing utility, so the two-goods version of the optimal consumption rule says:

$$\frac{MU_A}{P_A} = \frac{MU_O}{P_O}$$

Now imagine that the price of apples P_A increases. An increase in P_A means that apples now provide less utility per dollar, so we have $\frac{MU_A}{P_A} < \frac{MU_O}{P_O}$. But recall our previous rule:

If $\frac{MU_A}{P_A} < \frac{MU_O}{P_O}$, then buy fewer apples and more oranges.

We can see that an increase in the price of apples leads to the consumer buying fewer apples. The optimal consumption rule therefore gives us a foundation for demand curves based on individual choice.

The optimal consumption rule is an intuitive and useful way of thinking about how consumers choose to allocate their dollars, but we have derived the rule informally and in a form that makes it difficult to make specific predictions. It's not obvious from the optimal consumption rule, for example, how changes in income affect choices. We also showed how an increase in P_A means that a consumer should buy fewer apples and more oranges, but we didn't say much about when the dominant effect is fewer apples and when the dominant effect is more oranges. The theory, as we presented it, also puts this strange idea of "utils" front and center even though no one has ever seen a util. We can fix all of these problems and produce a richer, more complete theory by developing consumer choice theory a bit more formally. Fortunately, the optimal consumption rule will continue to hold true even in our richer model.

The Budget Constraint

Imagine that there are only two goods as before, but just for variety, we will switch to gasoline and pizza. Gasoline is $2 per gallon and pizzas are $10 apiece. Let's suppose that the consumer has $100 of income. Figure 25.4 shows the consumer's **budget constraint**, namely all of the bundles of gasoline and pizza that the consumer can afford given their income and prices. For example, the consumer could buy 50 gallons of gas and 0 pizzas, or 10 pizzas and 0 gallons of gas, or any consumption bundle along the line connecting these two points. The consumer cannot afford bundles that are "outside" the budget constraint. For example, the consumer cannot afford the red bundle of 40 gallons and 6 pizzas. (How much income would the consumer need to afford this bundle?)

In addition to the points along the budget constraint, the consumer can also afford any point that is "inside" the budget constraint, such as the green point of 10 gallons and 4 pizzas. If the consumer bought this bundle of goods, however, they would spend $60 ($2 × 10 + $10 × 4), leaving them with $40 in income. Note, however, that in this model, there are only two goods and no future periods, so saving doesn't have any benefits. Thus, a consumer will always want to purchase a consumption bundle that lies on the budget constraint.

The budget constraint depends on the consumer's income and also on the prices of gasoline and pizza. Let's look at income first. Imagine, for example, that the consumer had $140 of income. Now the consumer could purchase any of the consumption bundles shown in Figure 25.5.

> A **budget constraint** shows all the consumption bundles that a consumer can afford given their income and prices.

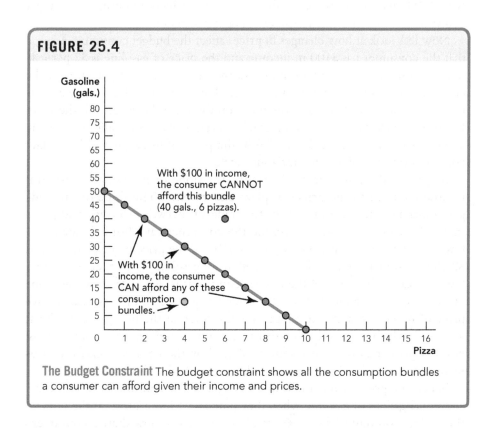

FIGURE 25.4

The Budget Constraint The budget constraint shows all the consumption bundles a consumer can afford given their income and prices.

FIGURE 25.5

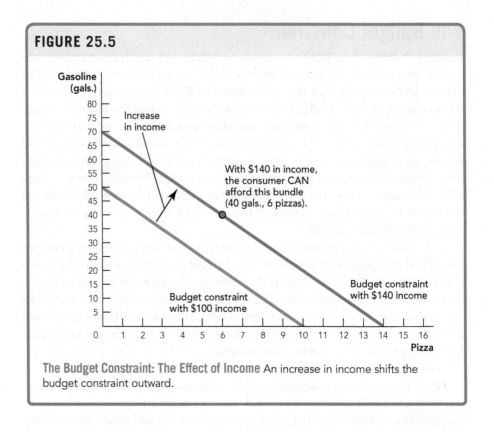

The Budget Constraint: The Effect of Income An increase in income shifts the budget constraint outward.

mru.org/budget-constraint

The Budget Constraint

Notice that with $140 in income, the consumer can now afford the red consumption bundle (40 gallons of gasoline, 6 pizzas) that they could not afford with $100 income. More generally, an increase in income pushes the budget constraint outward, parallel to the old budget constraint.

Now let's look at how changes in prices affect the budget constraint. Assume that the consumer has $100 in income and the price of gasoline is $2 per gallon, but now there is a sale on pizzas so the price falls to $5 per pizza. If the consumer spends all of their money on gasoline, they can still purchase 50 gallons of gasoline and 0 pizzas so the point on the vertical axis remains the same. If they spend all their money on pizza, however, they can now afford 20 pizzas. Thus, as shown in Figure 25.6, a fall in the price of pizzas *rotates* the budget constraint outward along the horizontal axis.

As you might expect from the figure, the slope of the budget constraint is closely related to the prices of pizza and gasoline. The slope of the budget constraint, the rise/run, tells us the trade-off between gasoline and pizza, that is, how many gallons of gasoline the consumer can afford if they buy 1 fewer pizza. When the price of a pizza is $10 and the price of a gallon of gas is $2, the consumer can afford 5 more gallons of gasoline when they purchase 1 fewer pizza, so the slope of the budget constraint is $\frac{P_{\text{Pizza}}}{P_{\text{Gas}}} = \frac{\$10}{\$2} = 5$. The slope of the budget constraint is also called the relative price. In this case, the relative price of pizza to gas is 5. To be precise, the slope of the budget constraint is *negative* 5, which reflects the fact that to get more gasoline, the consumer must purchase *fewer* pizzas, but economists often drop the negative sign for convenience (mathematicians, however, would be horrified at this practice).

When the price of pizza falls to $5 per pizza, the consumer can afford 2.5 additional gallons of gasoline when they purchase 1 fewer pizza, so the slope of the budget constraint falls to $\frac{P_{\text{Pizza}}}{P_{\text{Gas}}} = \frac{\$5}{\$2} = 2.5$. We can now draw a consumer's

FIGURE 25.6

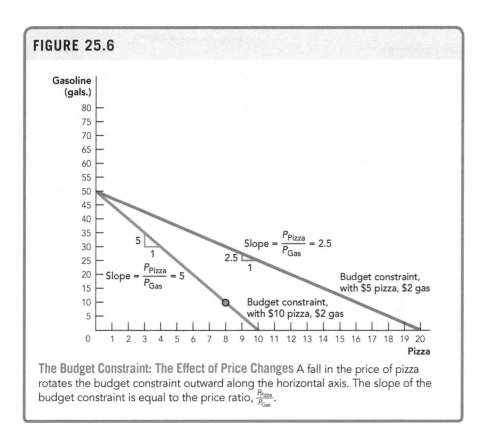

The Budget Constraint: The Effect of Price Changes A fall in the price of pizza rotates the budget constraint outward along the horizontal axis. The slope of the budget constraint is equal to the price ratio, $\frac{P_{Pizza}}{P_{Gas}}$.

budget constraint for any income and set of prices. We know that the consumer will choose a consumption bundle somewhere along the budget constraint, but to say more about the exact consumption bundle, we need to say more about preferences.

Preferences and Indifference Curves

Consider a particular consumption bundle, say, bundle A in Figure 25.7. Now let's find all the bundles that the consumer regards as *just as good as* bundle A. If bundle A is just as good as bundle B, we say the consumer is indifferent between bundle A and bundle B, or equivalently, we say that bundle A and bundle B give the consumer an equal amount of utility. An indifference curve connects all the bundles that give the consumer an equal amount of utility and so we have drawn an indifference curve in Figure 25.7 showing all the consumption bundles that give an equal amount of utility to bundle A.

The indifference curve in Figure 25.7 is curved inward. Let's explain why this is a plausible shape for indifference curves. Notice that bundle A has 10 pizzas and 0 gallons of gas—that's an awful lot of pizza and not so much gas, or at least not so much gasoline. Since the consumer has a lot of pizza at bundle A, they probably would be willing to give up a pizza to get just a few gallons of gasoline—say, 2.5 gallons for 1 pizza—which would place the consumer at bundle B. The number of gallons per pizza that the consumer requires to remain indifferent is called the **marginal rate of substitution (MRS)** and is given by the slope of the indifference curve (noting, once again, that we have dropped the negative sign).

CHECK YOURSELF

• Draw a consumer's budget constraint when the consumer has an income of $100, P_{Gas} = $2, and P_{Pizza} = $10. Now draw the new budget constraint when income = $80.

• Draw a consumer's budget constraint when the consumer has an income of $100, P_{Gas} = $2, and P_{Pizza} = $10. Now draw the new budget constraint when P_{Gas} = $4.

• In 1970, the price of pizza was $2.50 and the price of a gallon of gas was $0.50. Suppose today the price of pizza is $10 and the price of a gallon of gas is $2. Has the relative price of pizza changed?

The **marginal rate of substitution (MRS)** is the rate at which the consumer is willing to trade one good for another and remain indifferent. The MRS is equal to the slope of the indifference curve at that point.

FIGURE 25.7

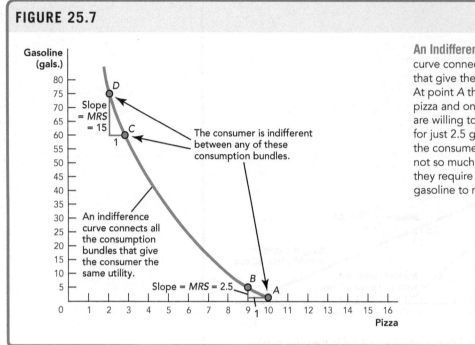

An Indifference Curve An indifference curve connects all consumption bundles that give the consumer the same utility. At point A the consumer has lots of pizza and only a little gasoline so they are willing to give up 1 pizza in return for just 2.5 gallons of gas. At point C the consumer has lots of gasoline and not so much pizza so to give up 1 pizza they require an additional 15 gallons of gasoline to remain indifferent.

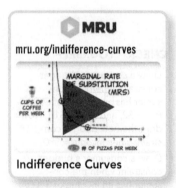

mru.org/indifference-curves

Indifference Curves

CHECK YOURSELF

• Use an argument similar to the one we used in the last paragraph to show that (1) indifference curves can never cross and (2) indifference curves must have a negative slope.

But now consider bundle C. At bundle C, the consumer has fewer pizzas and more gas than at bundle A, so to remain indifferent, the consumer now requires 15 additional gallons of gasoline to give up 1 pizza. As the consumer gives up more pizza and gets more gasoline, pizza becomes more valuable and gasoline less valuable, so the consumer requires more and more gasoline in return for the same number of pizzas. Graphically, what this behavior implies is an indifference curve that is curved inward.

In Figure 25.8, we illustrate a second indifference curve showing all the consumption bundles that have the same utility as consumption bundle Y. What is the relationship between the ABCD indifference curve and the XYZ indifference curve? Compare consumption bundles C and Y. Consumption bundle Y has more gasoline and more pizza than consumption bundle C, so we can say for sure that consumption bundle Y has higher utility or is more preferred than consumption bundle C. But how does consumption bundle C compare with consumption bundle Z (which has more gasoline but fewer pizzas) or consumption bundle X (which has more pizzas but less gasoline)? We know that bundle Y is preferred to C but we also know that the consumer is indifferent between X, Y, and Z, so it follows that bundles X and Z are also preferred to bundle C. In fact, through a similar argument, we can say that any consumption bundle on XYZ is preferred to any consumption bundle on ABCD. This means that indifference curves toward the northeast of the diagram give the consumer more utility, so the consumer wants to be as far to the northeast as possible.

Optimization and Consumer Choices

Now that we understand budget constraints and preferences, we can find the consumer's optimal consumption bundle. We know that the consumer must be on (or inside) the budget constraint and the consumer wants to be on the

FIGURE 25.8

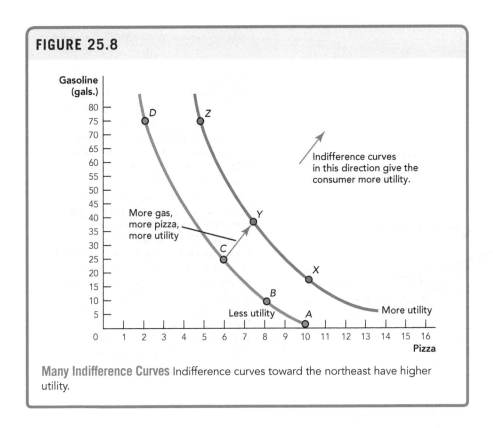

Many Indifference Curves Indifference curves toward the northeast have higher utility.

indifference curve that is the farthest to the northeast. Thus, to find the optimal consumption bundle, we look for the consumption bundle that is on the highest indifference curve but still on the budget constraint (shown in Figure 25.9).

Notice from Figure 25.9 that at the optimal bundle, the slope of the indifference curve is equal to the slope of the budget constraint. This is not an accident but a requirement. To see why, try to "push" an indifference curve as far as you can toward the northeast while still keeping at least one point on the budget constraint. The point of maximum utility is found where the indifference curve has been pushed just far enough to touch the budget constraint at a single point—the optimal point.

More formally, consider the point labeled "Possible but not optimal." This point is on the consumer's budget constraint, which explains why it is possible. Why isn't this point optimal? At "Possible but not optimal," the slope of the indifference curve is 2, which means that the consumer needs just 2 additional gallons of gas to be indifferent to giving up 1 pizza. The slope of the budget constraint is 5, which means that the consumer can get 5 gallons of gas if they give up 1 pizza—that's more gas than they require to be indifferent! Thus at "Possible but not optimal," the consumer can increase their utility by buying more gas and fewer pizzas and therefore this point cannot be optimal. What we have just shown is that the consumer can always do better if the slope of the indifference curve is different from the slope of the budget constraint.

Thus, remembering that the slope of the indifference curve is the *MRS* and the slope of the budget constraint is the price ratio, we can write that the optimal consumption bundle is found where

Slope of indifference curve $\equiv MRS = \frac{P_{\text{Pizza}}}{P_{\text{Gas}}} \equiv$ Slope of budget constraint

FIGURE 25.9

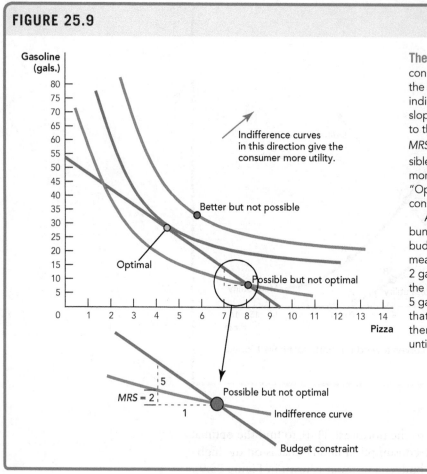

The Consumer's Optimum The optimal consumption bundle is found where the budget constraint is tangent to an indifference curve. At this point the slope of the indifference curve is equal to the slope of the budget constraint, $MRS = \frac{P_{Pizza}}{P_{Gas}}$. The "Better but not possible" bundle has more gasoline and more pizza than the bundle labeled "Optimal" but it is not on the budget constraint and thus not affordable.

At the "Possible but not optimal" bundle the $MRS = 2$ and the slope of the budget constraint, $\frac{P_{Pizza}}{P_{Gas}} = 5$. What this means is that the consumer will accept 2 gallons of gas to give up 1 pizza but the market is willing to give the consumer 5 gallons of gas if they give up 1 pizza—that is a good deal! The consumer, therefore, will trade pizza for gas until the $MRS = \frac{P_{Pizza}}{P_{Gas}}$.

Perhaps you are wondering how $MRS = \frac{P_{Pizza}}{P_{Gas}}$ relates to the optimal consumption rule stated earlier:

$$\frac{MU_{Pizza}}{P_{Pizza}} = \frac{MU_{Gas}}{P_{Gas}}$$

This can be rearranged algebraically as:

$$\frac{MU_{Pizza}}{MU_{Gas}} = \frac{P_{Pizza}}{P_{Gas}}$$

Can you guess what we are going to say next? Correct, it turns out that $MRS = \frac{MU_{Pizza}}{MU_{Gas}}$, so fortunately our two conditions for optimal consumption, $\frac{MU_{Pizza}}{P_{Pizza}} = \frac{MU_{Gas}}{P_{Gas}}$ and $MRS = \frac{P_{Pizza}}{P_{Gas}}$, are really just two ways of writing the same thing.*

$\star$ The proof is slightly involved but not difficult. Suppose that we take away from a consumer a small amount of pizza, Δ_{Pizza}, and we give them in return a small amount of gas, Δ_{Gas}; then the change in total utility, ΔU, from this exchange is $\Delta U = -\Delta_{Pizza} \times MU_{Pizza} + \Delta_{Gas} \times MU_{Gas}$. Along an indifference curve, total utility is constant, so $\Delta U = 0$ and thus $-\Delta_{Pizza} \times MU_{Pizza} + \Delta_{Gas} \times MU_{Gas} = 0$. Then rearrange to find $\Delta_{Gas}/\Delta_{Pizza} = MU_{Pizza}/MU_{Gas}$. But $\Delta_{Gas}/\Delta_{Pizza}$ is the MRS, the slope of the indifference curve, so we have shown that $MRS = MU_{Pizza}/MU_{Gas}$.

FIGURE 25.10

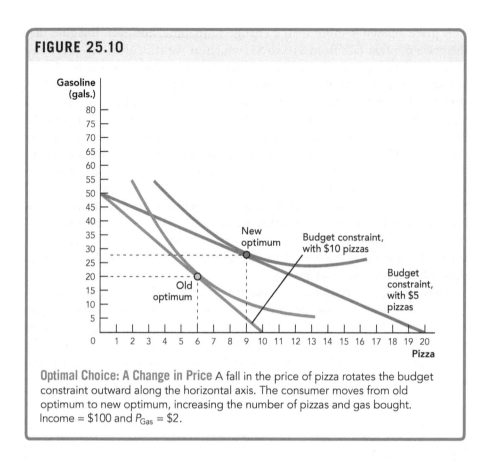

Optimal Choice: A Change in Price A fall in the price of pizza rotates the budget constraint outward along the horizontal axis. The consumer moves from old optimum to new optimum, increasing the number of pizzas and gas bought. Income = $100 and P_{Gas} = $2.

Now that we know how to find the consumer's optimal consumption bundle, we can show how the optimal bundle changes as income and prices change. Figure 25.10, for example, shows how a consumer responds to a decrease in the price of pizzas from $10 to $5. When P_{Pizza} = $10 and P_{Gas} = $2, the consumer maximizes utility by choosing 6 pizzas and 20 gallons of gas at the point labeled "Old optimum." As we showed in Figure 25.6, a decrease in the price of pizzas rotates the budget constraint along the horizontal axis. With the new budget constraint, the consumer chooses 9 pizzas and 27.5 gallons of gas at the point labeled "New optimum."

Notice that a fall in the price of pizza increases the number of pizzas purchased, but in this example it also increases the number of gallons of gasoline consumed. At first, this result may seem confusing: Why should a fall in the price of pizza increase the consumption of gasoline? The reason is that a fall in the price of pizza has two effects, the income effect and the substitution effect. Let's now explain these two effects.

The Income and Substitution Effects

When the price of pizza was $10, the consumer bought 6 pizzas for a total pizza spending of $60. When the price of pizza falls to $5, the consumer can buy 6 pizzas for $30, so the drop in the price of pizza gives the consumer an additional $30 to spend. With greater income, the consumer may choose to spend more money on pizza *and* more money on gas. More generally, a fall in the price of a good means the consumer's income goes further than before, so a fall in price is in some ways similar to an increase in income.

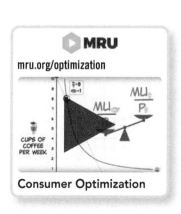

MRU

mru.org/optimization

Consumer Optimization

A price change is more than a change in income, however. Imagine that the price of pizza falls from $10 to $5, which, as we said, gives the consumer an extra $30 to spend. Feeling richer, the consumer heads to the market to buy more pizza and gasoline, but on the way a pickpocket takes the extra $30. Without the extra income, should the consumer still change their consumption bundle? Yes. The price of pizza has fallen relative to the price of gas and the consumer should take advantage of this change in relative prices by consuming more pizza. Of course, if the consumer has been pickpocketed on the way to market, the only way they can consume more pizza is by consuming less gasoline. Even so, the consumer will be better off by substituting pizza for gasoline in response to the change in relative prices. Remember, the optimal consumption rule says that to maximize utility, we need $\frac{MU_{Pizza}}{P_{Pizza}} = \frac{MU_{Gas}}{P_{Gas}}$, but if the consumer was maximizing utility before the price change, then after the P_{Pizza} falls, it must be that $\frac{MU_{Pizza}}{P_{Pizza}} > \frac{MU_{Gas}}{P_{Gas}}$. This tells us that after P_{Pizza} falls, the consumer should buy more pizza and less gas.

Thus, a change in price causes consumers to change their consumption bundle for two reasons, *the income effect* and the relative price, or *substitution effect*. In Figure 25.11, we show how to decompose the total effect of a price change into the income and substitution effects. The fall in the price of pizza causes the consumer to shift from buying 6 pizzas at the old optimum to buying 9 pizzas at the new optimum. This is the total effect of the price change. To decompose

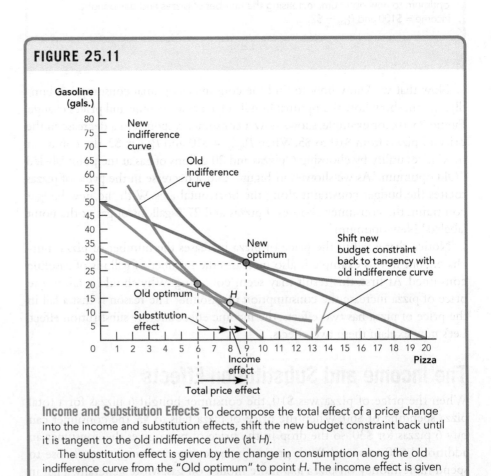

FIGURE 25.11

Income and Substitution Effects To decompose the total effect of a price change into the income and substitution effects, shift the new budget constraint back until it is tangent to the old indifference curve (at *H*).

The substitution effect is given by the change in consumption along the old indifference curve from the "Old optimum" to point *H*. The income effect is given by the change in consumption from point *H* to the "New optimum."

the total effect, we take the new budget constraint, which reflects the new relative prices, and we shift it back toward the origin until it is tangent to the old indifference curve at point *H*. The shifting back of the budget constraint is like the pickpocket we described earlier—we reduce the consumer's income until the consumer has the same utility level (is on the same indifference curve) as before the price change.[*]

We can now define the substitution and income effects more precisely. The **substitution effect** is the change in consumption caused by a change in relative prices holding the consumer's utility level constant. Thus, in Figure 25.11, the substitution effect is the change in consumption from "Old optimum" to point *H*. The **income effect** is the change in consumption caused by the change in purchasing power from a price change. Thus, in Figure 25.11, the income effect is given by the movement from *H* to "New optimum."

Applications of Income and Substitution Effects

We have now developed the key tools that we need to better understand consumer and worker choice. Let's look at some applications of income and substitution effects.

How Much Should Costco Charge for Membership?

Costco, one of the largest retailers in the world, offers low prices on many consumer goods. But to shop at Costco, you have to join the Costco "club" and pay a yearly membership fee. How much should Costco charge for membership?

To answer this question, let's create a budget constraint and indifference curve diagram with income on the vertical axis and goods you can buy at Costco on the horizontal axis. Without Costco membership, the consumer faces the blue budget constraint in Figure 25.12, labeled "Without Costco Membership," and consumes the No Costco bundle. Costco members pay lower prices, so if there were no membership fee, Costco members would face the red budget constraint, labeled "With Costco membership," and consume the "Costco without fee" bundle.

Costco, however, wants to charge as high a membership fee as possible. How much can the retailer charge? The membership fee is equivalent to a decrease in the consumer's income, so another way of asking this question is to ask how much can we decrease the consumer's income and still leave the consumer at least as well-off with Costco membership as without it? If we shift the green budget line, which reflects the lower prices at Costco, back toward the origin, we can shift the line until it is tangent to the old indifference curve at the point labeled "Costco with fee." At "Costco with fee," the consumer is indifferent between joining Costco, paying the fee, and enjoying the lower prices, and not joining Costco, saving on the fee, but paying higher prices. Since income is on the vertical axis, we can easily read the ideal membership fee off the graph.

Costco charges $60 for membership. This may not seem like a lot, but in 2022 membership fees earned Costco revenues of $4.2 billion, a large fraction

The **substitution effect** is the change in consumption caused by a change in relative prices holding the consumer's utility level constant.

The **income effect** is the change in consumption caused by the change in purchasing power from a price change.

---

[*] If you are following very closely, you may notice that our pickpocket leaves the consumer with just enough income to purchase the old bundle at the point labeled "Old optimum" but our graphical pickpocket takes a little bit more. The first version of the income effect is called the *Slutsky income effect*, while the second is called the *Hicks income effect*, after their originators. For a small price change, the difference between these two versions of the income effect is slight and can be ignored, which is what we do here.

FIGURE 25.12

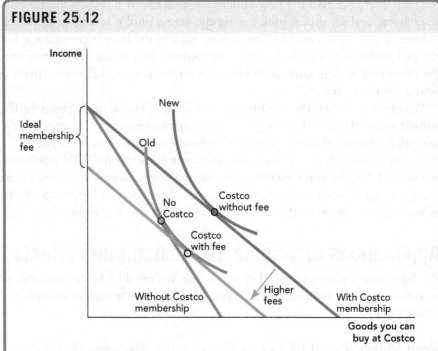

How Much Should Costco Charge for Membership? Without Costco membership the price ratio is given by the slope of the "Without Costco membership" budget constraint and the consumer chooses the bundle at "No Costco." If the consumer joins Costco they can buy the goods that Costco sells at lower prices so the budget constraint rotates out. With no membership fee the consumer would consume the bundle at "Costco without fee."

Costco would like to charge as high a membership fee as possible. The membership price is a decrease in the consumer's income so we can ask how much income we can take from the consumer and still leave the consumer at least as well-off as without membership.

The ideal membership fee (from Costco's point of view!) is the reduction in income that keeps the consumer on their old indifference curve. With the ideal membership fee the consumer consumes the bundle at "Costco with fee."

of its profits of $5.8 billion. Costco, therefore, is very concerned with setting the ideal membership fee.

Labor Supply

In Chapter 18, we discussed how a worker's labor supply curve can be backward-bending; that is, a decrease in the wage could cause a worker to work more. At first, this might seem surprising. Why would a worker work more hours when the payoff to working is going down? To see the intuition, imagine a janitor, perhaps an immigrant from a developing country, whose wage falls. The janitor may choose to work more hours in response to the lower wage, because at a lower wage, they need to work more hours to make enough money to put their children through college. Similarly, when the Beatles were young and unknown, they were paid low wages but they played 4 to 5 sets a day, 7 days a week in German strip clubs, just to make ends meet. As their fame grew, so did their wages and the Beatles responded by playing fewer hours.

Eventually, they stopped touring altogether, and a few years after that, they split up completely.

More generally, remember that a lower wage has two effects: the substitution effect and the income effect. When the wage decreases, that's the same as a decrease in the price of leisure so the substitution effect says you should "buy" more leisure by working fewer hours. When the wage decreases, however, that also makes you poorer. The income effect says that when your income falls, you should buy fewer (normal) goods including leisure.

Notice that the substitution and income effects work in opposite directions in this case. If the substitution effect dominates, the worker works fewer hours when the wage rate falls. If the income effect dominates, the worker works more hours when the wage rate falls.

In Figure 25.13, we explain the basics of the income–leisure model of labor supply. We put income on the vertical axis and leisure on the horizontal axis. We will think about daily labor supply so the maximum number of hours of leisure is 24. Imagine that the wage is $20 an hour. If the worker chooses 24 hours of leisure (0 hours of work), they earn $0. If the worker chooses 0 hours of leisure (24 hours of work), they earn $480 a day. The budget constraint labeled $w = \$20$, therefore, shows all the income–leisure possibilities open to

FIGURE 25.13

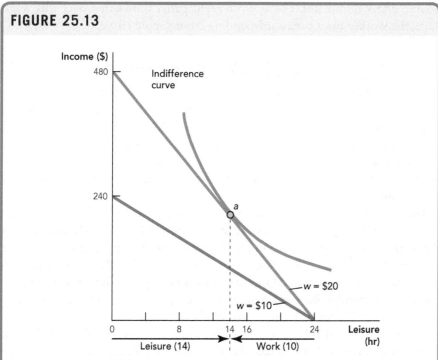

The Income–Leisure Model of Labor Supply Leisure is measured on the horizontal axis moving toward the right, so work hours are measured toward the left. Suppose the wage is $20 an hour. By choosing 24 hours of leisure, the worker earns $0. By choosing 0 hours of leisure (24 hours of work), the worker earns $480. The blue budget constraint thus shows all the income–leisure possibilities open to the worker when the wage is $20 an hour. At the optimal choice the worker chooses 14 hours of leisure (10 hours of work).

The red budget constraint shows all the income–leisure possibilities open to the worker when the wage is $10 an hour.

the worker when the wage is $20 an hour. As usual, the optimum is found where the budget constraint is tangent to the indifference curve. At point *a*, the worker chooses 14 hours of leisure (10 hours of work).

Suppose the wage is cut to $10 an hour. If the worker chooses 24 hours of leisure, they still earn $0, but if the worker chooses 0 hours of leisure (24 hours of work), their take-home pay falls to $240. The budget constraint labeled *w* = $10, therefore, shows all the income–leisure possibilities open to the worker when the wage is $10 an hour. The worker will choose a new point (not shown) on the new budget constraint.

In Figure 25.14, we use this model to show how a decrease in the wage can decrease or increase labor supply. In the top left panel, the worker chooses 14 hours of leisure (10 hours of work) when the wage is $20 an hour. A decrease in the wage causes the worker to increase leisure to 16 hours (8 hours of work). We haven't drawn the substitution and income effects in the diagram (we leave that as an exercise), but since the total effect of the decrease in wages is a decrease in labor supply, we know that in this case the substitution effect dominates. The top right panel translates the same information into a labor supply diagram.

In the bottom left panel, the worker chooses 14 hours of leisure (10 hours of work) when the wage is $20 an hour. A decrease in the wage causes the worker to decrease leisure to 12 hours (12 hours of work). Since the total effect of the decrease in wage is an increase in labor supply, we know that in this case the income effect dominates. The bottom right panel shows that over this wage range, the worker has a backward-bending labor supply curve.

Labor Supply and Welfare Programs

Let's use the income–leisure model to examine the labor supply effects of welfare programs. The traditional model of welfare works like a guaranteed minimum income under which the government subsidizes or "tops up" the income of any worker who earns less than the guaranteed amount. For example, suppose the guaranteed minimum income for an individual is $10,000 a year; in that case, an individual with yearly earnings of $6,000 would receive $4,000 in welfare payments.

The economics of this program are shown in Figure 25.15. We use the same setup as before, only now we measure leisure and work on a yearly basis in days rather than on a daily basis in hours. Before the welfare program, the worker faces the No welfare budget constraint and chooses 125 days of leisure (240 days of work.) The guaranteed minimum income expands the worker's opportunities. In particular, the worker now has the option of taking the guaranteed income and 365 days of leisure. The worker pictured earns more utility by taking the option of the guaranteed minimum income and the 365 days of leisure. Not every worker will take the guaranteed minimum income, but every worker who does take the option will reduce work effort.

We can explain why the guaranteed minimum income reduces work effort in a second way. Consider again how a guaranteed minimum income of $10,000 works. If a worker earns $2,000, they receive $8,000 in welfare for a total of $10,000. If a worker earns $4,000, they receive $6,000 in welfare for a total of $10,000. If a worker earns $7,000, they receive $3,000 in welfare for a total of $10,000. Do you see a pattern? Under the guaranteed minimum income, for

FIGURE 25.14

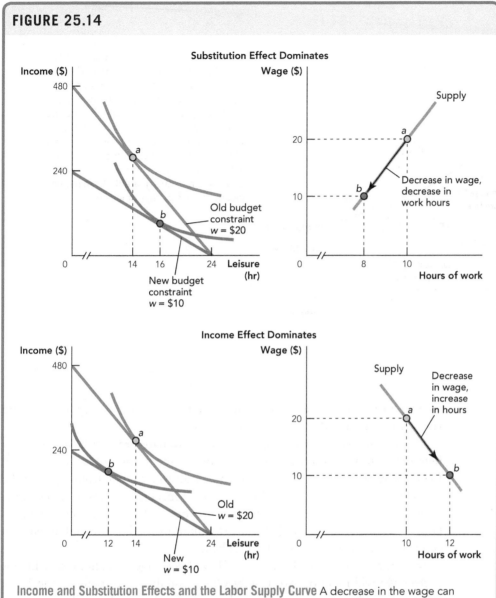

Income and Substitution Effects and the Labor Supply Curve A decrease in the wage can cause a worker to work fewer or more hours depending on the balance of the substitution and income effects. In the top left panel the substitution effect (not shown) dominates, so a decrease in the wage from $20 to $10 increases leisure from 14 hours a day to 16 (i.e., a decrease in work from 10 to 8 hours). The same information is shown in the top right panel but translated into a labor supply diagram. When the substitution effect dominates we get a positively sloped supply curve.

In the bottom left panel a decrease in the wage from $20 to $10 causes the worker to decrease leisure hours from 14 hours a day to 12 (i.e., an increase in work hours from 10 to 12 hours). The same information is translated into a labor supply diagram in the bottom right panel. When the income effect dominates we get a negatively sloped, or "backward-bending," supply curve.

every $1 in income that the worker earns, the government subtracts $1 in welfare so the worker's take-home pay doesn't change. Thus, under the guaranteed minimum income, a worker faces a 100% tax rate until they are earning more than $10,000 a year (the break-even point). Thus, under a guaranteed minimum

FIGURE 25.15

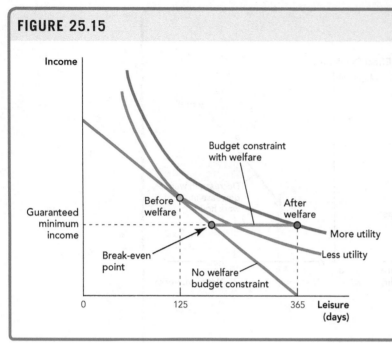

Labor Supply Effects of the Guaranteed Minimum Income The guaranteed minimum income is a welfare program that tops up income so that everyone receives at least the guaranteed amount. Before the program the worker chooses "Before welfare" with 125 days of leisure (240 days of work). With the guaranteed minimum income the worker chooses "After welfare" and consumes the guaranteed minimum income and 365 days of leisure.

income, many workers will choose to work 0 hours. How many hours would you work if you faced a 100% marginal tax rate?

On the one hand, most people feel that a welfare program is necessary to help those in need. On the other, we don't want to discourage work effort. Even a low-paying job, for example, may lead to a higher-paying job in the future. The trade-off between ethics and the disincentive effects of welfare programs have bedeviled policymakers for decades. In fact, economists dating as far back as Adam Smith and John Stuart Mill in the eighteenth and nineteenth centuries have worried about this problem.[1]

Several resolutions to this trade-off have been suggested, none of which is perfect. We will mention two briefly. One possibility is to focus on the 100% tax rate faced by people on welfare. Instead of reducing the welfare payment by $1 for every $1 of earnings, how about reducing payments by, say, $0.50 for every dollar of earnings? This is called a negative income tax (NIT) program. Under a negative income tax, for example, a worker who works 0 hours would receive $10,000 in welfare for a total of $10,000. But a worker who earned $4,000 would receive $8,000 in welfare (not $6,000 as before) for a total of $12,000. In this way, some of the incentives to work are restored for those receiving welfare.

Unfortunately—precisely because the program is more generous—the negative income can encourage more people to reduce labor supply at least somewhat and to take at least some welfare, even if they are able to work. Under the traditional guaranteed income program, for example, a worker who was earning, say, $14,000 a year might refuse the option of $10,000 a year and 365 days of leisure, but under a negative income tax, that same individual might be happy to accept $12,000 a year with 200 days of leisure.

Even though the negative income tax can encourage some people to partially reduce their hours of work, it encourages everyone to have at least some kind of job. If having a job, even a part-time job, is what matters for gaining experience, learning skills, moving up the work ladder, and so forth, then the NIT may work acceptably well.

Another approach is to limit how much welfare a person can accept or put various requirements on welfare recipients. If a person knows in advance that welfare is available only for a limited time, for example, they will treat welfare as more of an insurance program to be used only in bad times rather than as a guaranteed minimum income to be used as an alternative to work.

In practice, the United States has pursued both of these approaches to various degrees. The Earned Income Tax Credit (EITC), for example, supplements the wages of low-wage workers. For instance, depending on your income and other factors, if you earn $100 at work, the government tops it off, through the tax system, to make it worth $120. Unlike a negative income tax, the EITC is available only to workers. The EITC, however, helps offset the incentive to quit work, as contained in some of the other welfare programs, and makes the total package more like a negative income tax. From another direction, the Personal Responsibility and Work Opportunity Reconciliation Act (PRWORA) of 1996 put limits on welfare. Under PRWORA, a person can receive only 5 years of welfare benefits over their lifetime, and after 2 years on welfare, recipients must work at least 30 hours a week.

Both of these programs appear to have been relatively successful at encouraging welfare recipients to enter the job force. Analyzing the incentive and disincentive effects of welfare programs continues to be an active area of research for economists.

Takeaway

Economists use the language of prices and marginal utilities to analyze consumer decisions and, in general, consumers choose to allocate their dollars so the marginal utility per dollar of all purchases is equalized. To maximize utility, allocate dollars such that

$$\frac{MU_A}{P_A} = \frac{MU_O}{P_O} = \frac{MU_i}{P_i} = \cdots = \frac{MU_z}{P_z}$$

This equation may look tough, but it simply reflects what happens when consumers allocate their money wisely.

The budget constraint represents how much money a consumer has to spend and the prices that the consumer faces. If we put together a budget constraint and information about consumer preferences—as expressed in the form of indifference curves—we can solve for a consumer's optimal consumption bundle. This is a standard economic story, namely that preferences and constraints come together to shape an outcome.

The concepts of income and substitution effects, and more generally preferences and constraints, are useful for analyzing many economic problems. This includes how labor supply responds to welfare programs and how much Costco should charge for membership.

CHAPTER REVIEW

Go online to practice with more examples of these types of problems, including live links to videos, data sources, and feedback.

KEY CONCEPTS

marginal utility, p. 493

diminishing marginal utility, p. 493

optimal consumption rule, p. 495

budget constraint, p. 497

marginal rate of substitution (MRS), p. 499

substitution effect, p. 505

income effect, p. 505

FACTS AND TOOLS

1. The table that follows shows the marginal utility a consumer receives from the weekly consumption of streaming movie rentals and Thai takeout meals. One streaming movie rental costs $5, and Thai takeout costs $10 per meal. Suppose this consumer is currently (for some reason) eating Thai takeout 10 times per week and is spending all of their $100 income, so that they have no money left over for movie rentals. Is the consumer maximizing utility?

Streaming Movies	Marginal Utility	Thai Takeout Meals	Marginal Utility
1	50	1	50
2	30	2	45
3	20	3	40
4	15	4	35
5	10	5	30
6	8	6	25
7	6	7	20
8	4	8	15
9	2	9	10
10	1	10	5

2. Imagine that for the past two years, you've consumed only two goods: lattes and scones. As you're probably aware, prices tend to go up over time. If the price of your latte increased from $3 to $4.50 over the last two years, and the price of scones increased from $2.50 to $3.75, what impact would this have on your budget constraint if your $240 weekly take-home pay didn't change at all over the same two-year period? Draw both budget constraints on the same set of axes. What if you were able to negotiate a raise to $360 per week? Draw this final budget constraint on the same set of axes as the first two. How does your final budget constraint compare with your original budget constraint from two years ago?

3. You learned in the chapter that the process of utility maximization involves a comparison of marginal utilities per dollar, which are calculated as marginal utility divided by price. Consider two goods that most people consume at least some of during their lives: apples and cars.

   a. If utility maximization was only about marginal utility (not marginal utility per dollar), which good (apples or cars) would consumers want to consume? Would they ever consume the other good?

   b. If utility maximization was only about price (as opposed to marginal utility divided by price), which good (apples or cars) would consumers want to consume? Would they ever consume the other good?

   c. Given your answers to parts a and b, and given the observation that some people eat apples *and* drive cars, explain why utility maximization involves a comparison of marginal utility *divided* by price, and not just one or the other.

4. Fill in the blanks with either "good X" or "good Y," where good X is measured on the x-axis and good Y is measured on the y-axis.

a. If the price of _____ is $8 and the price of _____ is $12, then the price ratio (also the slope of the budget constraint) is 1.5.

b. A price ratio of 1.5 means that the consumer is able to trade 1 unit of _____ for 1.5 units of _____.

c. If another unit of _____ would give a consumer 20 extra units of utility, and another unit of _____ would give a consumer 10 extra units of utility, then the marginal rate of substitution for this consumer is equal to 2.

d. A marginal rate of substitution of 2 means that, from the consumer's point of view, 1 more unit of _____ is as good as 2 more units of _____.

e. If the price ratio is 1.5 and the marginal rate of substitution is 2, then the market values _____ more than the consumer does, and the consumer values _____ more than the market does. In this case, the consumer ought to buy less of _____ and more of _____.

5. Suppose Haya has $120 of income left each week after she pays her bills and puts some money away in a savings account, and she has two ways to spend this extra money: go to the movies, which costs $18 including popcorn and a soda, or go out to a club with several friends, which costs $33 including the cover charge and drinks. Assuming these are her only two choices to spend the extra money, what can you say about the following bundles of going to the movies and clubbing? Which of these could possibly be the utility-maximizing bundle?

a. 3 movies and 2 nights out at the club

b. 2 movies and 3 nights out at the club

c. 2 movies and 2 nights out at the club

6. The utility-maximizing bundle of goods is found at the point of tangency between the budget constraint and an indifference curve. In the following diagram, the utility-maximizing bundle is the one labeled point K. There are two different, but equally important, ways to interpret this point.

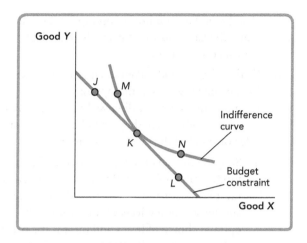

a. Of the three points on the consumer's budget constraint (J, K, and L), what makes K special?

b. Of the three points on the consumer's indifference curve (M, K, and N), what makes K special?

7. Is marginal utility always diminishing? Consider playing cards. If playing cards were purchased one at a time, what would be true about the marginal utility of the 51st playing card compared with the marginal utility of the 52nd playing card? Why do you think it's okay for economists to assume that marginal utility diminishes? How does the concept of marginal utility explain why playing cards are not sold individually, but only as entire 52-card decks?

THINKING AND PROBLEM SOLVING

8. In Major League Baseball, teams in the American League have used a designated hitter (DH) to bat in place of the pitcher since 1978, while until 2022, teams in the National League required their pitchers to bat. Sports economists have noted that in the National League, prior to the adoption of the designated hitter in 2022, batters were hit by pitches 15% less often than in the American League. Can you use the concepts from this chapter to explain this behavior from the point of view of the pitcher's utility-maximizing decision about whether to throw pitches high and inside (where they are more likely to hit the batter)?

9. Consider Facts and Tools question 2. Explain the income and substitution effects of the price changes on your optimal consumption bundle when the latte and scone prices increased, but your income did not.

10. With inferior goods (like ramen noodles), the income effect works in the opposite direction from the income effect discussed in the text. If a consumer feels richer, they would buy less of an inferior good. If they feel poorer, more.

   a. Suppose that a consumer eats two different foods: beans and meat. Beans are inferior, and meat is a luxury. Describe both the income and substitution effects on the consumer's optimal choice of beans and meat if the price of beans were to rise. Put the two effects together. What can you conclude?

   b. What if you knew for sure that the substitution effect dominated the income effect? What would happen to the consumer's optimal choices for beans and meat?

   c. What if instead you knew that the income effect dominated the substitution effect? What would happen in this case? Why is this result a bit unusual?

11. In early 2020, Panera Bread introduced a drink subscription program: For about $12 per month, subscribers can enjoy unlimited cups of hot or iced coffee, hot tea, fountain drinks, and Charged Lemonades at any Panera location. Imagine a consumer with $50 to spend each month at bakeries and cafés. Without a drink subscription, the consumer can buy cups of coffee (or other drinks) for $2 each. Panera also sells baked goods that have a price equal to $2 per unit.

   a. What does the budget constraint look like for someone who does not purchase a Panera drink subscription? Draw it.

   b. What does the budget constraint look like for someone who purchases a Panera drink subscription? This one's easy to draw, but a little tricky to figure out. Take your time.

   c. Which type of consumer is likely to buy the drink subscription? Which type of consumer is likely not going to pay for the subscription? You can use indifference curves to help illustrate and explain your answer.

12. In this chapter, we focused a lot on budget constraints, but time is an additional constraint that consumers face. Marcus has $40 per week to spend on leisure activities. He likes to bowl and

to play basketball. Bowling costs $4 per game, and a day pass to the local rec center costs $8. Marcus only has 7 hours of leisure time per week, and both bowling and basketball each take 1 hour per game. Construct Marcus budget constraint and his time constraint on the same diagram. Consider each of the consumption bundles that follow. How does each of these bundles relate to Marcus two constraints?

   a. Bowling twice per week and playing basketball four times per week

   b. Bowling four times per week and playing basketball three times per week

   c. Bowling six times per week and playing basketball once per week

CHALLENGES

13. This chapter argues that the ideal membership fee from Costco's point of view would leave consumers indifferent between shopping at Costco and shopping elsewhere. Do you think most of the shoppers at Costco are indifferent? What prevents Costco from setting its ideal fee?

14. Assume a consumer earns $50 in period 1 and $150 in period 2, and that saving and borrowing are both interest-free. Draw a budget constraint where consumption in period 1 is represented on the x-axis and consumption in period 2 is represented on the y-axis. Now let's see if we can add some more real-life detail.

   a. Draw a new budget constraint for the consumer if the period 1 income remains at $50, but the period 2 income falls to $100. Use the ideas of income and substitution effects to describe how this change would affect the optimal choice of the consumer.

   b. Now let's add another wrinkle: an interest rate. Assume as before that the consumer earns $50 in period 1 and $150 in period 2. Construct a budget constraint for a consumer that can earn 20% interest by saving money in period 1 for use in period 2, but also has to pay 20% interest to borrow money from period 2 for use in period 1. (These interest rates are high so that the impact is obvious on your graph; the results will still hold—although less dramatically—with lower interest rates.)

What is the substitution effect of the addition of the interest rate? The income effect is more complicated, because it depends on the consumer's preferences, which could be revealed by the pre-interest-rate behavior.

c. In October 2022, the average interest rate on money market and savings accounts was around 0.2%, but the average rate on a variable-rate credit card was around 15%. Obviously, the previous assumption that the interest rate is the same for borrowers and savers is not very realistic. Again, using more dramatic interest rates, can you construct a budget constraint for a consumer with the same initial endowment as previously who faces a 1% interest rate for saving and a 50% interest rate for borrowing? What do you notice about this budget constraint?

15. For people who haven't converted fully to streaming (Disney+) or who simply like having physical copies of the media they own, Disney has a movie club that, by joining, allows you to purchase four Disney movies on Blu-ray (which also generally includes a cloud-based copy) or DVD for $1 each (4K is also available but at a higher price), but you have to commit to buying at least five more movies at $20 each over the next two years. Suppose the normal market price of a Disney Blu-ray or DVD is $16.

a. Construct two budget constraints: one for a consumer who joins Disney's movie club and another for a consumer who doesn't. Assume that both consumers have $160 worth of income. Place income on the vertical axis just as in Figure 25.12.

b. What kind of consumer is likely to get more utility from joining Disney's movie club? What kind of consumer would not?

c. If Disney's movie club wanted to charge an additional membership fee to generate more revenue, what would be the maximum it could charge for membership and still attract some members?

16. Two special cases might result in indifference curves that look a little different from the ones discussed in the text.

a. If two goods are perfect substitutes, that means the consumer would always be willing to trade one for the other in a certain, fixed proportion. In this case, the MRS would be constant, which means that indifference curves would be straight lines. Suppose a consumer's MRS between two goods X and Y is a constant 2.5, which means that the consumer is always willing to give up 1 unit of good X for 2.5 units of good Y. If the consumer has $180 in income to spend, the price of good X is $20 per unit, and the price of good Y is $10 per unit, what is this consumer's utility-maximizing bundle of X and Y? Answer the question by thinking it through and then show with a diagram (including a budget constraint and an indifference curve) why your answer works.

b. If two goods are perfect complements, indifference curves have a very unusual shape. Let's see if you can reason through this one. Consider left and right shoes. For most people, having left shoes alone (or right shoes alone) does not really provide any utility; rather, people get utility from having a pair of shoes that they can wear. In this case, left and right shoes are perfect 1:1 complements. Can you figure out what indifference curves would look like in such a case? To do this, it might be helpful to think about questions like the following: If someone has 4 right shoes and 4 (matching) left shoes, what's the marginal utility of an extra right shoe? If a consumer had to compare the bundles (4 left shoes, 4 right shoes), (4 left shoes, 5 right shoes), and (7 left shoes, 4 right shoes), how would these bundles rank? Would any of these bundles be better than the others?

WORK IT OUT

For interactive, step-by-step help in solving this problem, go online.

Suppose we wanted to investigate the saving and borrowing behavior of consumers. It's not that difficult to extend our basic model. We can use the same framework as before, but define our two goods as "consumption in period 1" (horizontal axis) and "consumption in period 2" (vertical axis).

a. Construct a budget constraint for a consumer who earns $100 in income in period 1 and $300 of income in period 2. Label this point E for the "Endowment" point. Assume that they can choose to save some income in period 1 to be used in period 2, or to borrow some income from period 2 to use in period 1. (Let's imagine the consumer saves the money by putting it in a piggy bank and can borrow money from their parents, who don't charge interest.)

b. For the consumer in the situation just described, do you think they would consume at their endowment point or would they borrow or save?

A

Reading Graphs and Making Graphs

Economists use graphs to illustrate both ideas and data. In this appendix, we review commonly used graphs, explain how to read them, and give you a few tips on how you can make graphs using Microsoft Excel or similar software.

Graphs Express Ideas

In economics, graphs are used to express ideas. The most common graphs we use throughout this book plot two variables on a coordinate system. One variable is plotted on the vertical or y-axis, while the other variable is plotted on the horizontal or x-axis.

In Figure A.1, for example, we plot a very generic graph of variable Y against variable X. Starting on the vertical axis at $Y = 100$, you read across to the point at which you hit the graph and then down to find $X = 800$. Thus, when $Y = 100$, $X = 800$. In this case, you can also see that when $X = 800$, then $Y = 100$. Similarly, when $Y = 60$, you can read from the graph that $X = 400$, and vice versa. As you may recall, the slope of a straight line is defined as the rise over the run or rise/run. In this case, when Y rises from 60 to 100, a rise of 40, then X runs from 400 to 800, a run of 400, so the slope of the line is $40/400 = 0.1$. The slope is positive, indicating that when Y increases so does X.

Let's now apply the idea of a graph to some economic concepts. In Chapter 3, we show how a demand curve can be constructed from hypothetical data on the price and quantity demanded of oil. We show this here as Figure A.2.

The table on the left of the figure shows that at a price of $55 per barrel buyers are willing and able to buy 5 million barrels of oil a day (MBD), or more simply at a price of $55, the quantity demanded is 5 MBD. You can read this information off the graph in the following way. Starting on the vertical axis, locate the price of $55. Then look to the right for the point where the $55 price hits the demand curve: Looking down from this point, you see that the quantity demanded is 5 million barrels of oil per day. How about at a lower price of $20 per day? Start at $20 on the vertical axis and read to the right until the price hits the demand curve, then read down. Can you see that the quantity demanded at this price of $20 per barrel is 25 million barrels of oil per day?

We said that graphs express ideas, so what is the idea being expressed here? The most important fact about a demand curve is that it has a negative slope; that is, it slopes downward. This tells us the important but simple idea that as the price of a good falls, the quantity demanded increases. This is key: As the price of a good such as oil falls, people demand more of it.

FIGURE A.1

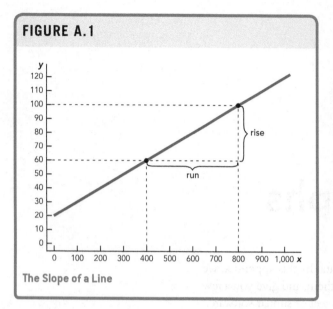

The Slope of a Line

FIGURE A.2

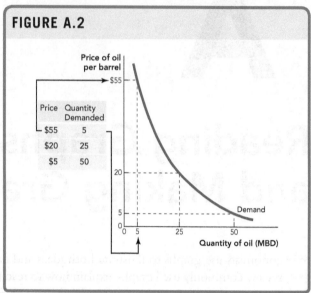

A demand curve is a description of what *would happen* to the quantity demanded as the price of a good changed, *holding fixed all other influences on the quantity of oil demanded.* (In this sense, demand curves are hypothetical and we rarely observe them directly.)

The quantity of oil demanded, for example, depends not just on the price of oil but on many other factors such as income or the price of other goods like automobiles and population, to name just a few of many influences. Today's demand curve for oil, for example, depends on today's income, price of automobiles and population. Imagine, for example, that average income today is $10,000, the price of an average automobile is $25,000 and world population is 7 billion. The blue curve in Figure A.3 shows the demand curve for oil under these conditions. Note that there are also many other influences on the demand for oil that we don't list but that are also being held fixed. Most importantly, if any of these conditions changes then the demand curve for oil will shift.

FIGURE A.3

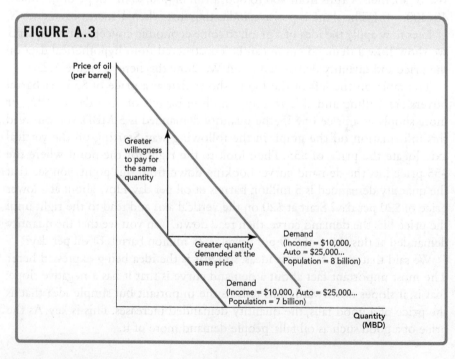

If world population increases to 8 billion, for example, there will be a new demand curve for oil. With a greater population, there will be more barrels of oil demanded at every specific price so the demand curve will shift to the right. Equivalently, as the population increases, there will be a greater willingness to pay for any given quantity of oil, so the demand curve will shift up. Thus, we say that an increase in demand is a shift in the curve up and to the right shown by the red curve in Figure A.3. Chapter 3 explains in greater detail how a demand curve shifts in response to changes in factors other than price.

What is important to emphasize here is that a demand curve is drawn holding fixed every influence on the quantity demanded other than price. Changes in any factor that influences the demand for oil other than price will produce a new demand curve.

One more important feature of two variables graphed in a coordinate system is that these figures can be read in two different ways. For example, as we mention in Chapter 3, demand curves can be read both horizontally and vertically. Read "horizontally," you can see from Figure A.4 that at a price of $20 per barrel demanders are willing and able to buy 25 million barrels of oil per day. Read "vertically," you can see that the maximum price that demanders are willing to pay for 25 million barrels of oil a day is $20 per barrel. Thus, demand curves show the quantity demanded at any price or the maximum willingness to pay (per unit) for any quantity.

FIGURE A.4

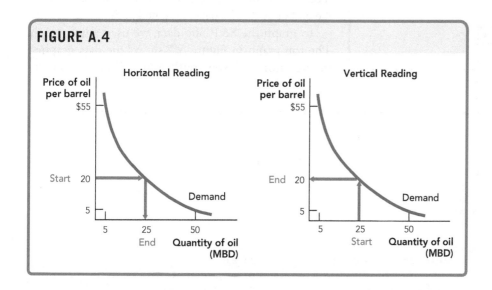

It may seem difficult at first to interpret these graphs, but as you will see, graphs are amazingly useful for thinking about difficult economic problems. It's like learning to drive a car—at first it's not easy and you will make some mistakes but once you learn how to drive, your ability to do things and go places increases enormously. The same thing is true with graphs!

Data Graphs

As well as expressing ideas, graphs can also be used to illustrate data. For example, GDP can be broken down according to the national spending identity into these components: Consumption, Investment, Government Purchases, and Net Exports (Exports minus Imports), that is, $GDP = Y = C + I + G + NX$. U.S. GDP for 2007 is shown in Table A.1.

TABLE A.1 U.S. GDP 2007 (in billions of dollars)

Category	GDP
Consumption	9,710.2
Investment	2,130.4
Government	2,674.8
Net Exports	−707.8
GDP (Total)	13,807.6

Data from: U.S. Bureau of Economic Analysis.

FIGURE A.5

	B7			f_x	=SUM(B2:B5)
	A	B	C	D	
1	Category	GDP			
2	Cons	9710.2			
3	Inv	2130.4			
4	Govt	2674.8			
5	NX	-707.8			
6					
7	GDP (Total)	13807.6			
8					

If you type the components into Excel, as shown in Figure A.5, you can use the sum function to check that the components do add up to GDP.

Highlighting the data in columns A and B and clicking Insert > Column > Clustered Column and (with a few modifications to add axis titles and to make the graph look pretty), we have the graph on the left side of Figure A.6.

The graph on the right side of Figure A.6 shows exactly the same data only on the right side we chose Stacked Column (and we switched the rows and columns). Sometimes one visualization of the data is more revealing than another so it's a good idea to experiment a little bit with alternative ways of presenting the same data. But please don't get carried away with adding 3-D effects or other chart junk. Always keep the focus on the data, not on the special effects.

In this book, we explain the economics of stocks, bonds, and other investments. A lot of financial data is available for free on the web. We used Yahoo! Finance, for example, to download data for the value of the S&P 500 Index on the first trading day of the month from 1950 to the end of 2000. The data is graphed in Figure A.7.

To graph the S&P 500 data, we used a line graph. The top graph in Figure A.7 shows the data graphed in the "normal" way, with equal distances on the

FIGURE A.6

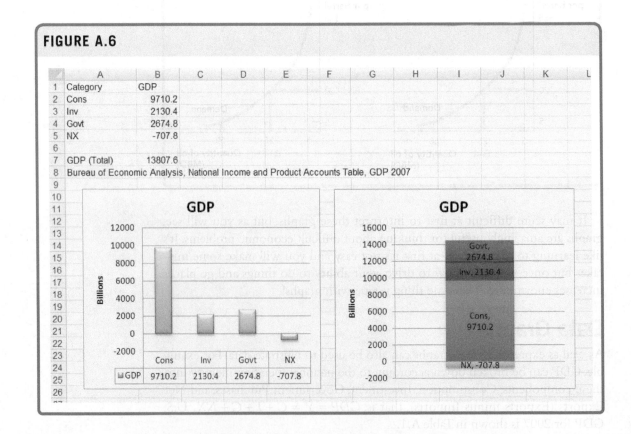

FIGURE A.7

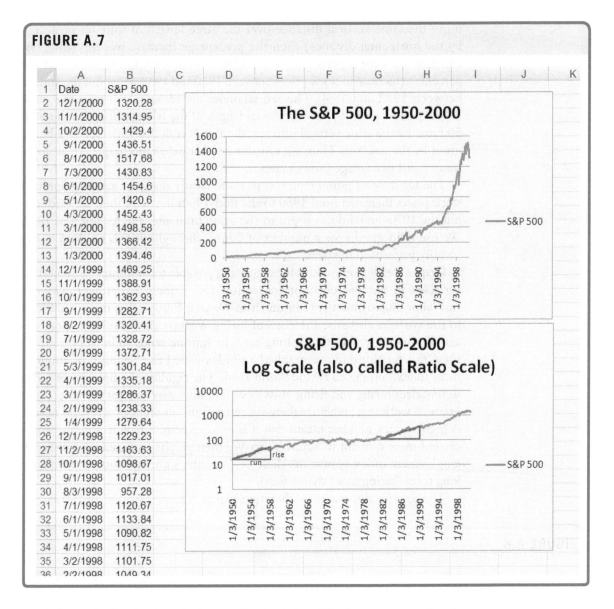

	A	B
1	Date	S&P 500
2	12/1/2000	1320.28
3	11/1/2000	1314.95
4	10/2/2000	1429.4
5	9/1/2000	1436.51
6	8/1/2000	1517.68
7	7/3/2000	1430.83
8	6/1/2000	1454.6
9	5/1/2000	1420.6
10	4/3/2000	1452.43
11	3/1/2000	1498.58
12	2/1/2000	1366.42
13	1/3/2000	1394.46
14	12/1/1999	1469.25
15	11/1/1999	1388.91
16	10/1/1999	1362.93
17	9/1/1999	1282.71
18	8/2/1999	1320.41
19	7/1/1999	1328.72
20	6/1/1999	1372.71
21	5/3/1999	1301.84
22	4/1/1999	1335.18
23	3/1/1999	1286.37
24	2/1/1999	1238.33
25	1/4/1999	1279.64
26	12/1/1998	1229.23
27	11/2/1998	1163.63
28	10/1/1998	1098.67
29	9/1/1998	1017.01
30	8/3/1998	957.28
31	7/1/1998	1120.67
32	6/1/1998	1133.84
33	5/1/1998	1090.82
34	4/1/1998	1111.75
35	3/2/1998	1101.75
36	2/2/1998	1049.34

vertical axis indicating equal changes in the index. That's not necessarily the best way to graph the data, however, because a quick look at the top figure suggests that stock prices were rising faster over time. In other words, the graph looks pretty flat between 1950 and approximately 1980, after which it shoots up. The appearance of faster growth, however, is mostly an illusion. The problem is that when the S&P 500 was at the level of 100, as it was around 1968, a 10% increase moves the index to 110, or an increase of 10 points. But when the index is at the level of 1,000, as it was around 1998, a 10% increase moves the index to 1,100, or an increase of 100 points. Thus, the same percentage increase looks much larger in 1998 than in 1968.

To get a different view of the data, right-click on the vertical axis of the top figure, choose "Format Axis," and click the box labeled "Logarithmic Scale," which produces the graph in the bottom of Figure A.7 (without the red triangles, which we will explain shortly).

Notice on the bottom figure that equal distances on the vertical axis now indicate equal percentage increases or ratios. The ratio 100/10, for example, is the same as the ratio 1,000/100. You can now see at a glance that if stock prices move the same vertical distance over the same length of time (as measured by the horizontal distance) then the percentage increase was the same. For example, we have superimposed two identical red triangles to show that the percentage increase in stock prices between 1950 and 1958 was about the same as between 1982 and 1990. The red triangles are identical, so over the same 8-year period, given by the horizontal length of the triangle, the run, the S&P 500 rose by the same vertical distance, the rise. Recall that the slope of a line is given by the rise/run. Thus, we can also say that on a ratio graph, equal slopes mean equal percentage growth rates.

The log scale or ratio graph reveals more clearly than our earlier graph that stock prices increased from 1950 to the mid-1960s but were then flat throughout the 1970s and did not begin to rise again until after the recession in 1982. We use ratio graphs for a number of figures throughout this book to better identify patterns in the data.

Graphs are also very useful for suggesting possible relationships between two variables. In the macroeconomics section, for example, we present evidence that labor employment laws in much of Western Europe that make it difficult to fire workers also raise the costs of hiring workers. As a result, the percentage of unemployment that is long term in Europe tends to be very high. To show this relationship, we graphed an index called the "rigidity of employment index," produced by the World Bank. The rigidity of employment index summarizes hiring and firing costs as well as how easy it is for firms to adjust hours of work (e.g., whether there are restrictions on night or weekend hours). A higher index number means that it is more expensive to hire and fire workers and more difficult to adjust hours. We then graphed a country's rigidity of employment index against the share of a country's unemployment rate that is long term (lasting more than a year).

The data for this graph are shown in Figure A.8.

FIGURE A.8

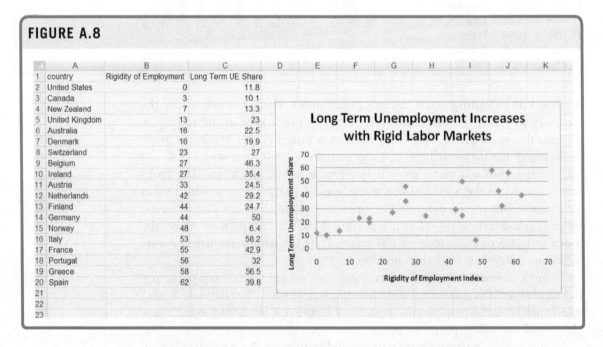

We can do something else of interest with this data. If you right-click on any of the data points in the figure, you will get the option to "Add Trend Line." Clicking on this and then clicking the two boxes "Linear" and "Display Equation on Chart" produces Figure A.9 (absent the red arrow, which we added for clarity).

FIGURE A.9

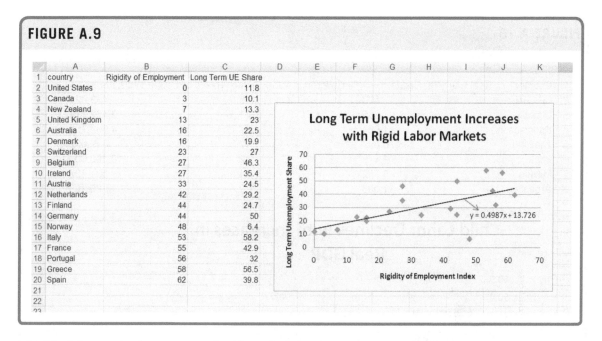

	A	B	C
1	country	Rigidity of Employment	Long Term UE Share
2	United States	0	11.8
3	Canada	3	10.1
4	New Zealand	7	13.3
5	United Kingdom	13	23
6	Australia	16	22.5
7	Denmark	16	19.9
8	Switzerland	23	27
9	Belgium	27	46.3
10	Ireland	27	35.4
11	Austria	33	24.5
12	Netherlands	42	29.2
13	Finland	44	24.7
14	Germany	44	50
15	Norway	48	6.4
16	Italy	53	58.2
17	France	55	42.9
18	Portugal	56	32
19	Greece	58	56.5
20	Spain	62	39.8

The black line is the linear curve that "best fits" the data. (Best fit in this context is defined statistically; we won't go into the details here but if you take a statistics class you will learn about ordinary least squares.) Excel also produces for us the equation for the best-fit line, $Y = 0.4987 \times X + 13.726$.

Do you remember from high school the formula for a straight line, $Y = m \times X + b$? In this case m, the slope of the line or the rise/run, is 0.4987, and b, the intercept, is 13.726. The slope tells us that a 1-unit increase in the rigidity of employment index (a run of 1) increases the share of unemployment that is long term by, on average, 0.4987 percentage points (a rise of 0.4987). Using the equation, you can substitute any value for the index to find a predicted value for the share of long-term unemployment. If the rigidity of employment index is 15, for example, then our prediction for the long-term unemployment share is $21.2065 = 0.4987 \times 15 + 13.726$ If the index is 55, our prediction for the long-term unemployment share is $41.1545 = 0.4987 \times 55 + 13.726$.

Graphing Three Variables

In our international trade chapter, we present evidence that child labor decreases with increases in GDP per capita. Figure A.10 shows some data on child labor and GDP per capita circa 2000. We put our X variable, real GDP per capita, in column B and our Y variable, the percentage of children ages 10–14 in the labor force, in column C. In column D, we have the total number of children in the labor force. In Burundi, a larger fraction (48.5%) of the children are in the labor force than in India (12.1%), but since Burundi is a small country, the total number of children in the labor force is larger in India. To understand the problem of child labor, it's important to understand both types of information so we put both types of information on a graph.

Excel's bubble chart will take data arrayed in three columns and use the third column to set the area of the bubble or data point. In Figure A.10, for example, India has the largest number of children in the labor force and so has the bubble with the largest area. The area of the other bubbles is in relative proportion, so Mexico's bubble is 1/25th the size of India's bubble because there are 1/25th as many children in the labor force in Mexico as in India. (Unfortunately, Excel doesn't label the bubbles automatically so we added these by hand.)

FIGURE A.10

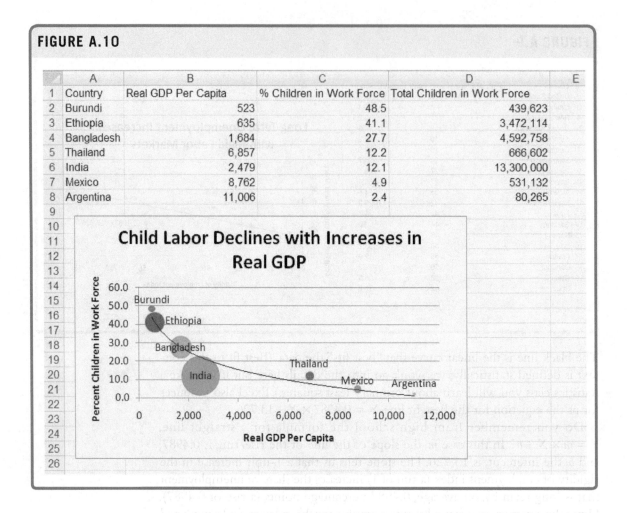

	A	B	C	D	E
1	Country	Real GDP Per Capita	% Children in Work Force	Total Children in Work Force	
2	Burundi	523	48.5	439,623	
3	Ethiopia	635	41.1	3,472,114	
4	Bangladesh	1,684	27.7	4,592,758	
5	Thailand	6,857	12.2	666,602	
6	India	2,479	12.1	13,300,000	
7	Mexico	8,762	4.9	531,132	
8	Argentina	11,006	2.4	80,265	

Child Labor Declines with Increases in Real GDP

Cause and Effect

Do police reduce crime? If so, by how much? That's a key question that economists and criminologists are interested in understanding because local governments (and taxpayers) spend billions of dollars on police every year and would like to know whether they are getting their money's worth. Should they spend less on police or more? Unfortunately, it's surprisingly difficult to answer this question. To illustrate why, Figure A.11 shows the relationship between crime per capita and police per capita from across a large number of U.S. cities.

Figure A.11 shows that cities with more police per capita have more crime per capita. Should we conclude that police cause crime? Probably not. More likely is "reverse causality," crime causes police—that is, greater crime rates lead to more hiring of police. We thus have two chains of potential cause and effect: More police reduce crime, and more crime increases police. Unfortunately, you can't tell much about either of these two potential cause-and-effect relationships by looking at Figure A.11, which shows the correlation between police and crime but not the causation. But if you want to estimate the value of police, you need to know causation not just correlation. So what should you do?

The best way to estimate how much police reduce crime would be to take say 1,000 roughly similar cities and randomly flip a coin dividing the cities into two groups. In the first group of cities, double the police force and in the second group do nothing. Then compare crime rates over say the next year

FIGURE A.11

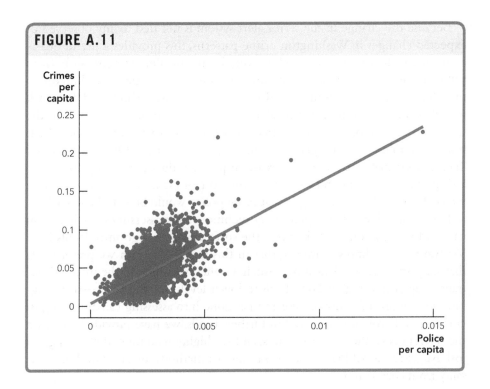

in cities with and without an increase in police. If the cities with an increase in police have lower rates of crime, then you can safely ascribe this difference to the effect of police on crime. What makes the correlation evidence in Figure A.11 difficult to interpret is that increases in crime sometimes cause increases in police. But if you increase the number of police randomly, you eliminate the possibility of this "reverse causality." Thus, if crime falls in the cities that have random increases in police, the cause is most plausibly the increase in police. Similarly, if crime were to increase in cities that have random decreases in police, the cause is most plausibly the decrease in police.

Unfortunately, randomized experiments have at least one big problem—they are very expensive. Occasionally, large randomized experiments are done in criminology and other social sciences but because they are so expensive we must usually look for alternative methods for assessing causality.

If you can't afford a randomized experiment, what else can you do? One possibility is to look for what economists call quasi-experiments or natural experiments. In 1969, for example, police in Montreal, Canada, went on strike and there were 50 times more bank robberies than normal.[1] If you can think of the strike as a random event, not tied in any direct way to increases or decreases in crime, then you can be reasonably certain that the increase in bank robberies was caused by the decrease in police.

The Montreal experiment tells you it's probably not a good idea to eliminate all police, but it doesn't tell you whether governments should increase or decrease police on the street by a more reasonable amount, say 10% to 20%. Jonathan Klick and Alex Tabarrok use another natural experiment to address this question.[2] Since shortly after 9/11, the United States has had a terror alert system run by the Department of Homeland Security. When the terror alert level rises from "elevated" (yellow) to "high" (orange) due to intelligence reports regarding the current threat posed by terrorist organizations, the Washington, D.C., Metropolitan Police Department reacts by increasing the number of hours each officer must work.

Because the change in the terror alert system is not tied to any observed or expected changes in Washington crime patterns, this provides a useful quasi-experiment. In other words, whenever the terror alert system shifts from yellow to orange—a random decision with respect to crime in Washington—the effective police presence in Washington increases. Klick and Tabarrok find that during the high terror alert periods when more police are on the street, the amount of crime falls. Street crime such as stolen automobiles, thefts from automobiles, and burglaries decline especially sharply. Overall, Klick and Tabarrok estimate that a 10% increase in police reduces crime by about 3%. Using these numbers and figures on the cost of crime and of hiring more police, Klick and Tabarrok argue that more police would be very beneficial.

Economists have developed many techniques for assessing causality from data and we have only just brushed the surface. We can't go into details here. We want you to know, however, that in this textbook when we present data that suggests a causal relationship—such as when we argue in the international trade chapter that higher GDP leads to lower levels of child labor—that a significant amount of statistical research has gone into assessing causality, not just correlation. If you are interested in further details, we have provided you with the references to the original papers, and we highly recommend checking out Josh Angrist's Nobel Prize lecture on modern methods for distinguishing causality from correlation.

MRU

mru.org/courses/mastering
-econometrics/joshua-angrist
-nobel-prize-lecture-2021

Alex Brandon/AP Photo

Joshua Angrist, Nobel Prize Lecture, 2021

APPENDIX A QUESTIONS

1. We start with a simple idea from algebra: Which of the graphs at the top of the next page have a positive slope, and which have a negative slope?

2. When social scientists talk about social and economic facts, they usually talk about a "positive relationship" or a "negative relationship" instead of "positive slope" or "negative slope." Based on your knowledge, which of the following pairs of variables tend to have a "positive relationship" (a positive slope when graphed), and which have a negative relationship? (*Note:* "Negative relationship" and "inverse relationship" mean the same thing. Also, in this question, we're only talking about correlation, not causation.)

   a. A professional baseball player's batting average and their annual salary.

   b. A professional golfer's average score and their average salary.

   c. The number of cigarettes a person smokes and their life expectancy.

   d. The size of the car you drive and your probability of surviving a serious accident.

   e. A country's distance from the equator and how rich its citizens tend to be. (For the answer, see Hall, Robert, and Charles Jones. 1999. Why do some countries produce so much more output per worker than others? *Quarterly Journal of Economics* 114: 83–116.)

3. Let's convert Klick and Tabarrok's research on crime into a simple algebra equation. We reported the result as the effect of a 10% increase in police on the crime rate in Washington, D.C. In the equation below, fill in the effect of a 1% increase in the police on the crime rate:

   The percent change in crime = _____ ×
   The percent change in police officers

4. Let's read the child labor graph (Figure A.10) horizontally and then vertically:

   a. According to the trend line, in a typical country with 10% of the children in the labor force, what's the real GDP per person?

   b. According to the trend line, when a country's GDP per person is $2,000, roughly what percentage of children are in the labor force?

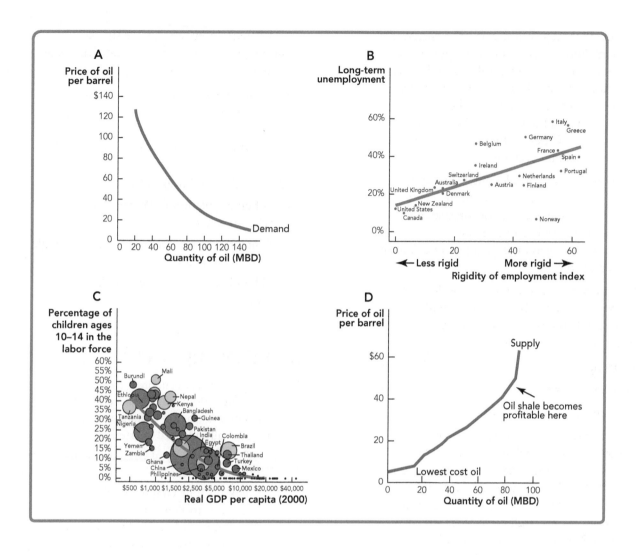

5. Let's take another look at the ratio scale, and compare it to a normal scale.

   a. In Figure A.7, which one is presented in ratio scale and which in normal scale?

   b. In the top graph, every time the S&P 500 crosses a horizontal line, how many points did the S&P rise?

   c. In the bottom graph, every time the S&P 500 crosses a horizontal line, how many *times* higher is the S&P?

6. As a scientist, you have to plot the following data: The number of bacteria you have in a large petri dish, measured every hour over the course of a week. (*Note:* E. coli bacteria populations can double every 20 minutes.) Should this data be plotted on a ratio scale and why?

7. People who are educated are supposed to point out (correctly) that "correlation isn't proof of causation." This is an important fact—which explains why economists, medical doctors, and other researchers spend a lot of time trying to look for proof of causation. But sometimes, correlation is good enough. In the following examples, take the correlation as a true fact, and explain why the correlation is, all by itself, useful for the task presented in each question.

   a. Your task is to decide what brand of car to buy. You know that Brand H usually gets higher quality ratings than Brand C. You don't know what causes Brand H to get higher ratings—maybe Brand H hires better workers, maybe Brand H buys better raw materials. All you have is the correlation.

   b. Your task is to hire the job applicant who appears to be the smartest. Applicant M has a degree from MIT, and applicant S has a degree from a typical state university. You don't know what causes MIT graduates to be smarter than typical state university graduates—maybe they start off smarter before they get to MIT, maybe their professors teach them a lot, maybe having smart classmates for four years gives them constant brain exercise.

  c. Your task is to decide which city to move to, and you want to move to the city that is probably the safest. For some strange reason, the only fact you have to help you with your decision is the number of police per person.

8. If you haven't practiced in a while, let's calculate some slopes. In each case, we give two points, and you can use the "rise over run" formula to get the right answer.

  a. Point 1: $x = 0$, $y = 0$. Point 2: $x = 3$, $y = 6$

  b. Point 1: $x = 6$, $y = -9$. Point 2: $x = 3$, $y = 6$

  c. Point 1: $x = 4$, $y = 8$. Point 2: $x = 1$, $y = 12$

9. We mentioned that a demand curve is a hypothetical relationship: It answers a "what if" question: "What if today's price of oil rose (or fell), but the average consumer's income, beliefs about future oil prices, and the prices of everything else in the economy stayed the same?" When some of those other features change, then the demand curve isn't fixed any more: It shifts up (and right) or left

(and down). In Figure A.3, we showed one shift graphically: Let's make some changes in algebra:

The economy of Perovia has the following demand for oil:

$$\text{Price} = B - M \times \text{Quantity}$$

When will B tend to be a larger number:

  a. When population in Perovia is high or when it is low?

  b. When the price of autos in Perovia is high or when it is low?

  c. When Perovian income is high or when it is low?

Discovering DATA

10. Using the FRED economic database (http://fred.stlouisfed.org) search for U.S. Real Gross Domestic Product and graph the seasonally adjusted quarterly series.

  a. What was U.S. Real GDP in the first quarter of 1980?

  b. Click on Edit Graph and change the Units to Percent Change from Year Ago and Modify Frequency to Annual. By how much did the U.S. economy shrink in 2009?

APPENDIX
B

Solutions to Check Yourself Questions

Here are suggested answers to the Check Yourself questions found within the chapters.

Chapter 2
Page 21

1. Specialization increases productivity because it increases knowledge.

2. If people can't trade for other goods, they won't specialize in producing just one good. Thus, trade is necessary if people are to benefit from specialization.

3. Usain Bolt has a comparative advantage in running, but Harry has a comparative advantage in mowing Usain's lawn because Harry faces a much lower opportunity cost in mowing lawns than Usain Bolt does.

Chapter 3
Page 33

The operating system for smartphones is a complement to Google's search and advertising business. Free smartphone software, therefore, increases the demand for Google's primary product, advertising.

Page 34

1. A rise in the income of Indian workers will lead to an increase in the demand for automobiles. At first as income rises, workers may demand more charcoal bricks for heating, but charcoal bricks are a dangerous and unpleasant way to heat a home, so as income increases beyond a certain level, workers will demand fewer charcoal bricks. Thus, a good can be a normal good over some levels of

income and an inferior good over other (usually higher) levels of income.

2. As the price of oil rises, some people will substitute mopeds for automobiles, so the demand for mopeds will increase.

Page 42

1. Improvements in chip-making technology have driven down the costs of this input, so the supply of computers increases, meaning that the supply curve for computers shifts to the right and down.

2. The ethanol subsidy lowers the cost of producing ethanol, therefore increasing the supply of ethanol (the supply curve for ethanol shifts to the right and down).

Chapter 4
Page 51

1. If the demand for large trucks and SUVs falls unexpectedly, auto companies will find that at the current price they have a surplus of trucks and SUVs. The quantity supplied is greater than the quantity demanded, so they will lower prices in order to sell already manufactured trucks and SUVs.

2. Sellers have produced too many clothes if they have them available at outlet malls where price discounts are the norm. Sellers are cutting their prices to reduce the surplus and move the clothes out the door.

Page 54

1. As the price of cars goes up, the least-valued wants will be the first to stop being satisfied. For example,

parents may be more reluctant to buy their teenage sons and daughters a new automobile.

2. If telecommunication firms overinvest in fiber-optic cable, for example, they will have to lower the price of using fiber-optic lines. For example, a company such as Verizon will offer fiber-optic Internet and phone connections at discount prices. The ensuing losses from price cutting will dampen future investment in fiber-optic cable. More generally, firms invest in order to make a profit. If firms overinvest, they will take losses, which give them an incentive to invest carefully.

3. Kiran values the good at $50, and in a free market will buy it from store B for $35, earning a total consumer surplus of $15 ($50 − $35). If store B is prevented from selling, say by a regulation or a tax, then Kiran will buy from store A for $45, but total consumer surplus will fall to $5 ($50 − $45).

Page 58

1. If flooding destroys some of the corn and soybean crops, these crops will have a decrease in supply. This decrease in supply will lower the equilibrium quantity and increase the equilibrium price.

2. If resveratrol (from Japanese knotweed) increases life expectancy in fish, people might think it will have the same effect in humans, and so more people will demand it, increasing demand. This will increase the price of Japanese knotweed and lead to an increase in the quantity grown.

3. The demand for hybrid cars will increase as the price of gas increases; that is, the demand curve shifts to the right/up. We show this in Figure 4.7: Think of the New demand as the demand for hybrids when the price of gas is high, and the Old demand as the demand for hybrids when the price of gas is low. The price of hybrids will rise with an increase in demand, especially in the short run.

Page 62

1. The price of oil rose in 1991 primarily because of a supply shock, the Persian Gulf War. (It would also be okay to label this as a demand shock because the demand for oil increased when people expected that the war would reduce the future supply of oil.) Bonus points if you recognized both possibilities.

2. From 1981 to 1986, the price of oil fell steadily. The higher price in the preceding years encouraged exploration, which several years later led

to increased supply, especially from non-OPEC sources.

Chapter 5
Page 79

1. There are more substitutes for a brand than for a general product category, so there are more substitutes for Dell computers than for computers. When there are more substitutes, demand is more elastic, so demand is more elastic for Dell computers than for computers.

2. An elasticity of demand of 0.1 is an inelastic demand. With inelastic demand, revenue and price move together. Thus, if the price of eggs increases, total revenue will increase. Bonus points if you said that with an elasticity of 0.1, when price goes up by 10%, quantity goes down by 1%, so revenues (= $P \times Q$) increase by approximately 9%.

3. A fashionable clothing store might raise its prices by 25% if it thought there was inelastic demand for its products: The increase in price on everything would more than make up for the decrease in sales (quantity).

Page 86

1. Supply is usually not very elastic in the short run. In the case of computer chips, a factory can run 24 hours per day and pay overtime, but it takes years to build a new factory. In the long run, supply is more elastic because over time a computer chip firm can respond to increased demand by building new factories.

2. Manhattan is an island with very little land available for development, so the supply of housing in Manhattan is very inelastic. In contrast, a lot of unbuilt land is available in the Des Moines area, so the supply is more elastic. The same increase in demand will increase the price more when the supply is inelastic than elastic; thus, the same increase in demand will increase prices more in Manhattan than in Des Moines.

Chapter 6
Page 106

1. Because demand for insulin is highly inelastic, the users of insulin are likely ultimately to pay a government insulin tax. Producers of insulin have

some ability to produce other products and so can escape the tax more readily.

2. The government would rather tax items that have relatively inelastic demands and supplies rather than elastic demands and supplies because the deadweight loss from taxation is lower when supply and demand are inelastic.

3. The easiest way to show this is to go back to Figure 6.5. In the right panel, draw in an almost inelastic supply curve. Now draw in an almost elastic supply curve. Visually examine the relative differences in consumer surplus and producer surplus. Remember that elasticity = escape, so the relatively elastic side escapes and loses less surplus while the relatively inelastic side can't escape and so loses more surplus.

Page 109

The supply of coal miners is likely to be much more inelastic than the supply of restaurant workers, so a subsidy will benefit current coal miners (and current coal mine owners) more than it will benefit current restaurant workers (and owners). Thus, coal miners are more likely to lobby for subsidies than restaurant workers.

Page 112

1. Because of the ethanol subsidy, the quantity supplied of ethanol increases. The subsidy increases the price received by the ethanol producers (corn growers) and lowers the price paid by ethanol users. The relative amount received by producers versus that paid by buyers depends on the relative elasticities of demand and supply.

2. Government subsidies for college education increase the demand for education. The supply of education, however, is relatively inelastic, especially at elite colleges. Thus, the benefits of the subsidy flow to suppliers; that is, the price paid to suppliers increases by more than the price paid by buyers falls. Much of the subsidy ends up raising the incomes of professors! Perhaps this is one reason that many professors argue for subsidies to education.

Chapter 7
Page 121

1. If farmers receive a higher price for turning corn into ethanol, they will supply more of their corn for ethanol production. Thus, the (opportunity) cost

of supplying corn for cornbread will increase and there will be a decrease in the supply of corn for cornbread. As a result, the price of cornbread will increase and customers will consume less, perhaps substituting cheaper items such as regular bread.

2. During the housing boom, the use of lumber skyrocketed, as did the supply of a lumber by-product, sawdust. The increase in the supply of sawdust caused a fall in the price of sawdust. Since a lot of sawdust is used in bedding milk cows, this reduced the cost of producing milk. When the housing boom collapsed, less lumber was produced, so less sawdust was produced and the price of sawdust rose, which increased the cost of producing milk and thus the price of milk. Markets are linked in nonobvious ways. Who would have thought the housing and milk markets were linked so closely?

Page 124

1. We aren't peanut experts either, but the highest value of peanuts is probably in its use as a food; furthermore, there are fewer substitutes for peanuts in paint, varnish, and furniture polish, where the peanut has some unique properties, than in insecticides or soap or finally bird feed. So let's rank the uses of peanuts from highest to least valued as follows: food, paint, varnish, furniture polish, insecticides, soap, and bird feed. Any ranking you have is fine—the point is that there is a ranking.

2. If there is a peanut crop failure in a large producer such as China, the price of peanuts and peanut products will rise and people will substitute away from peanuts in their least-valued uses. Thus, we would expect fewer peanuts used in bird feed, soap, and insecticides, which will free up more peanuts for use in the higher-valued categories. Thus, as the price of peanuts rises, there is a reallocation of peanuts from lower- to higher-valued uses. It's important to recognize that the best way of figuring out which uses are higher valued is to see what happens when the price rises.

Page 125

1. No central planner could possibly know or understand all of the links between products, so the messaging system is unlikely to send the right information. But let's suppose that the *information problem* was solved. Even if the government sent the right messages, there would still be an *incentive problem*. What incentives would producers and

consumers have to obey the messages? In contrast, the price system sums up all of the links between products in one number, the price, and it provides an incentive to pay attention to the price. Thus, the price system solves the information problem and the incentive problem, which is why we say that a price is a signal wrapped up in an incentive.

2. If firms do not have to face bankruptcy, they can continue with poor products, practices, and efforts. The fear of bankruptcy is a spur to innovate and grow, but the fear has to be backed up by the reality.

Page 128

In hindsight, it is clear that Lehman Brothers was engaged in wishful thinking. Speculators, with their money on the line, did not believe the Lehman forecasts. Companies can have a tendency to look at things in the best possible way and to ignore reality, and speculators provide a market vote (a reality check).

Chapter 8

Page 147

1. Price ceilings set below equilibrium prices cause shortages. Price ceilings set above equilibrium prices have no effects.

2. A price control reduces the incentive to respond to shifts in demand; thus, resources become misallocated according to essentially random factors. For example, it costs much more to ship oil from Alaskan oil fields to refineries on the East Coast than to those on the West Coast. Price ceilings did not let that difference become factored in the price, and therefore reduced the incentive to ship oil to where it was most needed, so shortages could be worse in some areas than in others.

Page 151

1. If landlords under rent control have an incentive to do only minimum upkeep, deteriorating buildings inevitably accompany rent control. Only major repairs are made. Tenants with dripping faucets may never get a response from landlords, and have to fix it themselves. At a minimum, they will have to wait, maybe until the drip becomes something larger and so has an effect on the landlord's water bill.

2. Vested interests will fight any attempt at rolling back rent control, and these vested interests become powerful over time. It's especially difficult

to eliminate rent controls because tenants (people who already have an apartment) don't care much about the shortage—they do not have to find a new apartment every week. In contrast, buyers of gasoline have to deal with the shortage every time they need a fill-up, so it may be easier to get rid of price controls on oil than on apartments.

Page 152

1. Price ceilings cause shortages. Universal price controls cause shortages across the economy, with no obvious pattern. Sometimes one product is in abundance, at other times there are shortages. A rational response when there are products that face inexplicable shortages is to buy as much as possible when possible: buy as much toilet paper now because who knows when it will come available again? In other words, hoarding is a standard response to universal price controls. Hoarding is wasteful because it implies a misallocation of resources. Some people, for reasons of luck (or influence), may have a lot of toilet paper while others have none. If trade were allowed, people would experience gains from trade and products would gravitate to their highest-value uses.

2. The Soviet Union also faced surpluses of goods as well as shortages because under universal price controls there was no incentive to get products to the places at the times that they had the highest-value uses. As a result, goods would be misallocated and production and consumption would be chaotic. One week a farm might get enough oil to deliver its chickens to the city and in that week the city shops would get a lot of chickens as the farm dumped its accumulated stock. A few weeks later there might be no oil available and chickens would disappear from the shops.

Page 157

1. A price floor set above the equilibrium price leads to surpluses. Because the European Union price floor for butter is above the equilibrium price, the EU has created a surplus of butter, which the government must buy. The surplus has been so large that it has been called a butter mountain.

2. The U.S. price floor for milk, set above the equilibrium price, has led to a surplus of milk. The government has dealt with the surplus by buying the surplus and giving away milk and dairy products produced from milk (such as cheese) to schools. This accounts for the low or zero price you paid for milk at most schools.

Chapter 9
Page 176

1. Domestic producers gain from a tariff and domestic consumers lose.

2. Trade protectionism leads to wasted resources because it shifts production from the lowest-cost producers to higher-cost producers.

3. You hear more often about people who gain from trade restrictions than people who lose because the gains from trade restrictions are concentrated on a few winners, while the losses are diffused over many losers. Even though the total gains are smaller than the total losses, the concentrated benefits mean that the winners have a greater incentive to argue for trade restriction than the losers do to argue against it.

4. In Figure 9.3, area C is the lost gains from trade; demanders are willing to pay more than suppliers require, but these trades do not occur because the demanders must also pay the tariff.

Page 180

1. The movement of the garment trade overseas has been a net benefit for the United States because clothing is now much cheaper for U.S. consumers and U.S. workers specialize in the fields in which they are most productive.

2. If the U.S. government subsidized the Silicon Valley computer industry, it would encourage more computer chip manufacturing, but at a higher cost (production would not be as efficient). This would be a waste of resources. Foreign competitors would be pushed out of the industry. Consumers of computer chips would benefit from the subsidy, but they would benefit by less than the cost to U.S. taxpayers.

Chapter 10
Page 193

1. If the government overshoots and sets a Pigouvian tax that is too high, it will result in an equilibrium quantity that is lower than the efficient equilibrium. A tax that is too high will create a deadweight loss from too few trades. If the tax is much too high, it can be worse than leaving the externality alone.

2. If the government undershoots and provides a subsidy that is too low, the equilibrium quantity will be lower than the efficient equilibrium. In this case, there will be an undersupply.

Page 195

1. Using the Coase theorem, a solution to the prospect of elderly neighbors complaining about your party is to buy the elderly couple tickets to a movie or to a night away at a hotel. Transaction costs are low in this case: You can easily contact your neighbors and you might even pay for the gift by collecting contributions from the partygoers.

2. A solution to the polluting factory problem depends on the transactions costs. Are there many neighbors or only a few? Are the victims of the pollution located nearby or are they spread out? Is it clear whether the factory has the right to pollute, say, because it was there first and everyone moved into the area knowing about the pollution? Transaction costs are key here, because even if the factory has the right to pollute, if you and your neighbors can negotiate, you may be able to pay off the factory if it has certain property rights.

Page 202

1. A falling price for tradable pollution allowances tells us that the value of the allowance has fallen. This means that the costs of eliminating pollution have fallen—perhaps because of technological developments in clean energy.

2. If a local government sets tradable allowances for pollution in the neighborhood, some groups that would press for a large total quantity of allowances would be the big polluters: chemical factories, meat-processing plants, sometimes automobile repair shops. Some groups that would press for a smaller total quantity of allowances would be homeowners, parents sending their children to local schools but who live outside of the immediate vicinity, and the elderly. Unfortunately, there is no theorem that says the rough-and-tumble of the political process will result in an efficient equilibrium. If the political process gets it approximately right and the externality is serious, the tradable allowance system will improve social welfare, but this is not guaranteed.

Chapter 11
Page 211

1. In a competitive market, if a firm prices its product above the market price, no one will buy the firm's product. Why should anyone pay more for the same product? In a competitive market, if a

firm prices its product below the market price, it will sell everything it produces, but why should it set price below the market price when it can sell the same amount at the market price?

2. Demand for a competitive firm's product is perfectly elastic, portrayed as a horizontal demand curve for the firm's product. It can sell all it wants at the competitive price.

3. If there is more than one firm in the industry, then the demand for a particular firm's product is always more elastic than the demand for the product itself. The demand for each stripper well's oil is very elastic even though the demand for oil is inelastic because there are very good substitutes for the oil from a particular firm, namely the oil from any other firm.

Page 216

1. When the firm in Figure 11.2 produces 4 barrels rather than 3, $33 in additional profit is made. Going from 7 to 8 barrels, no additional profit is made. Going from 8 to 9 barrels, profit falls to −$40. Looking at the figure, $MR = MC$ when the quantity produced is 8 barrels. At this quantity, marginal profit is $0.

2. The fixed cost is the total cost when $Q = 0$, 30.

3. The profit-maximizing quantity is 8, the same as before. Changes in fixed cost do not change the profit-maximizing quantity.

Page 218

1. Profit equals (price minus average cost) times quantity, $\pi = (P − AC) \times Q$. Another way of saying this is that profit per unit is price minus average cost (the cost for each unit), and profit per unit times the number of units sold gives you total profits.

2. Assuming that the firm produces the optimal quantity (found where $P = MC$), then at *any* price greater than average cost, the firm is making a profit, and at *any* price less than average cost, the firm is taking a loss.

Page 227

1. In the early stages, an automobile manufacturing industry is a decreasing cost industry because as the industry expands, it can draw on economies of scale both in auto manufacturing and in steel, plastic, and other input industries. Economies of scale,

however, don't increase forever, so once the industry matures, it becomes an increasing cost industry. Today, for example, the automobile industry is an increasing cost industry because greater demand for autos means an increased demand for steel and plastic, which will drive up the price of steel and plastic, thus increasing costs in the auto industry.

2. The U.S. film industry is clustered around Hollywood because the central location leads to lower costs. Perhaps only in Hollywood could a movie director easily arrange to interview four movie stars in a single afternoon.

Chapter 12
Page 242

If Sandy's MC is higher than Pat's MC, total costs can be reduced by producing a little bit less on Sandy's farm and a little bit more on Pat's farm.

Page 244

1. In competitive markets, profits are a signal for new firms to enter. It is as if entrepreneurs see a sign flashing "Profits, Profits, Profits."

2. In competitive markets, because a firm has no control over price, its best opportunity for profits is to keep its costs low.

   Alternatively, firms can innovate and enter (even create new) markets where the price is high. However, this is an ongoing process, as subsequent entry of other firms will eventually drive prices down in this market.

Chapter 13
Page 255

1. As a firm with market power moves down its demand curve, the price it can charge on all units moves down as well.

2. A firm with market power prefers to face an inelastic demand curve because the more inelastic the demand curve, the more the firm with market power can raise its price above marginal cost. See Figure 13.4 for a display of this.

Page 256

1. A monopolist always prices its product above the price of an equal cost-competitive firm.

2. A monopolist always produces less than an equal cost-competitive firm because this way it produces more profit than a competitive firm.

Page 259

1. Apple has market power and plausibly it encourages innovation. Pharmaceutical companies have an incentive by the patent system to use market power to innovate. One can argue that many utilities have market power but do not seem to be great innovators. The U.S. Postal Service has market power but does not seem to innovate much.

2. The prize for a new cancer drug should be calculated by taking the number of people expected to die of cancer over a long period, then multiplying this by the presumed willingness of people with cancer to pay for a cure, discounted for payments received over a long period, minus the probable cost of research and the low marginal cost of producing the drug. The size of the prize is likely to be enormous.

Page 264

Telephones used to be a natural monopoly because it was much cheaper for one firm to lay one set of lines and serve everyone than to have competing phone companies. Today, cell phones have broken the natural landline monopoly because cell towers cost much less to create than telephone poles and wires, so it makes sense to have multiple, competing operators. In this way, technology can quickly abolish what was once a natural monopoly.

Page 266

1. Major league baseball and professional football restrict the entry of competitors in local areas, thus supporting the market power of these local teams. With market power, teams raise prices, without the fear that competitors will see the higher prices as opportunities to enter. In this case, prospective teams face more than just barriers to entry in the form of high entry costs: The leagues prohibit the teams' entry.

2. Barriers to entry are strong when they are mandated and enforced: The U.S. Postal Service still has a monopoly on delivering first-class mail, because by law other firms must charge three times as much as the Postal Service if they wish

to deliver a letter. Of course, the prevalence of e-mail has made this monopoly less valuable. In contrast to this, when Congress took away the U.S. Postal Service's monopoly on the delivery of parcels, competitors such as UPS and FedEx jumped in and took over much of the market. People still send parcels through the Postal Service, but often not when delivery needs to be fast and guaranteed. NBA basketball restricts entry just as major league baseball does, and that looks to be fairly permanent for the near term, though the league may let additional teams enter over time.

Chapter 14
Page 278

1. If a monopolist segments a market, it can price-discriminate between the different segments and so raise its profits.

2. When demand is more inelastic, the price-discriminating firm would set higher prices. Remember that elasticity = escape. People with inelastic demand find it harder to escape and so will pay more.

3. Arbitrage is taking advantage of price differences for the same good in different markets by buying low in one market and selling high in another market. When the monopolist price-discriminates by setting a low price in one market and a high price in another, it creates a potential arbitrage opportunity. In order to profitably price-discriminate, the monopolist must prevent this arbitrage.

Page 282

1. The early bird special is a form of price discrimination if people who want to eat at a later time have a more inelastic demand curve. This could be true, for example, if people who want to eat at a later hour are wealthier (perhaps because they are working long hours!). An alternative explanation is that the restaurant's marginal costs increase as the restaurant becomes more crowded—thus, restaurants charge more during peak hours. In the first case, the markup of price over marginal cost increases in the later evening; in the second the firm's costs and price both increase in the later evening. It's not obvious which explanation is correct!

2. People who want to see movies right after the movies are released have a more inelastic demand for them than people who are willing to wait for the movies to be released on demand. Movie theaters know this and set their prices relatively high for those who cannot wait (have an inelastic demand). For the same reason, books are more expensive when they are first released in hardback than later when they are released in paperback. The increased costs of producing a hardback are trivial compared with the difference in price.

Page 283

1. Price discrimination is likely to increase total surplus if output increases.

2. Price discrimination helps industries with high fixed costs because profits increase with market size. Simply, having more market segments means that the price-discriminating firm can extract more consumer surplus. This leads to higher revenues, which fund the high fixed costs. Universities have high fixed costs. The ability for a university to price-discriminate means it can attract more paying students to its campus and so pay for its high fixed costs.

Page 286

1. Tying cell phones to service plans is a type of price discrimination whereby high demanders (long talkers) are charged more. If cell phone companies were not allowed to tie cell phones with service plans, the price of cell phones likely would rise and the price of phone calls likely would fall. This would be good for people who want to talk a lot but bad for people who want to use their cell phone only occasionally. Profits for the cell phone companies would also fall, so there would be fewer funds to pay for the fixed costs of building cell phone towers and infrastructure.

2. Bundling is likely to increase total surplus in high-fixed-cost, low-marginal-cost industries because without some form of price discrimination, it's difficult to provide these goods at optimal levels.

Chapter 15
Page 302

1. When Great Britain found oil in the North Sea, it could obtain the benefits of OPEC

(the cartel price) without any of the disadvantages of joining the cartel, such as limiting production. Why join?

2. The surprising conclusion of the prisoner's dilemma is that there are situations when the pursuit of individual interest leads to a group outcome that is in the interest of no one. Think of three cases. First, the invisible hand is a metaphor for the idea that under the right circumstances the pursuit of self-interest can lead to the social interest. Second, theft is an intermediate case where the pursuit of self-interest benefits one's self but not the social interest. Third, the prisoner's dilemma reminds us that in some circumstances when everyone pursues their self-interest, the result can be against the interest of everyone!

Page 306

1. Though individual auto firms try to act as if they are monopolies, they do not band together in an attempt to raise prices and cut back on quantities. Such banding together is illegal in the United States. It is not illegal in various other places in the world.

2. When a firm in an oligopoly reduces output, it shares equally in the gains from the reduction with the other firms.

Chapter 16
Page 327

1. Your old cell phone provider makes it difficult for you to take your address list to a new cell phone from a new cell phone provider as a way of setting up high switching costs in an attempt to prevent you from changing your service.

2. Google is in a contestable market because it would be fairly easy for a competitor to enter the search market, as Microsoft has done with its Bing search engine.

Page 328

A firm with an established network good such as Microsoft Office faces competition or potential competition for the market. Network monopolies can last for a long time but then evaporate very quickly.

Chapter 17

Page 345

1. Monopolistic competitors earn zero economic profits in the long run and they produce above-minimum average cost. This categorization tells us that McDonald's, Burger King, and Wendy's over the long term will earn zero economic profits, with costs higher than the minimum of average costs.

2. Monopolistic competitors produce differentiated products. In the eyes of the consumer, a hamburger is not the same at all of these firms.

Page 348

1. Wood is practically the same everywhere as far as building houses is concerned. Windows are a differentiated product. Thick and double-paned windows with various cold-stopping features are manufactured for northern climates. There may be a benefit for an individual firm to advertise differentiated products, unlike similar products such as wood.

2. Famous athletes' endorsement of sports products that they use informs us that the product is of superior quality. Even if the product has nothing to do with sports, the endorsement signals quality rather than providing information.

Chapter 18

Page 355

The marginal product of labor falls as more workers are hired because the first worker will focus on the most important tasks and so the marginal product of labor will be high. The next worker will focus on the next important tasks, but these tasks will not be as important as those the first worker tackled, so the marginal product of labor will not be as high as for the first worker. As more workers are hired, they do progressively less important tasks, so their marginal product falls relative to the first workers.

Page 357

An individual's labor supply curve might be backward-bending because at some point, individuals might prefer more leisure to working more, even at a higher wage. In other words, one of the things that people may buy more of when their wage goes up is leisure.

Page 364

1. An increase in mine safety would lower the wages of miners because mine workers are paid extra money to undertake their risky jobs. Making the job less risky would increase the number of people willing to be miners and thus would drive down wages.

2. Firms will pay for human capital improvements if the firm can reap the benefit. Training on a firm's specific inventory techniques will help the firm, but this is a skill that it is difficult for a worker to take to other firms, so the firm need not pay a higher wage to individuals with specific training. In this sense, the firm reaps the benefit of this training exclusively. In contrast, an MBA provides skills that can be used by many firms, so an individual with an MBA can earn a higher wage at other firms. In order to benefit from training an individual with general skills, the firm must keep the individual around at the lower wage long enough to recover its costs. Thus, the time requirement helps the firm recover a large portion of its investment in the worker.

Page 371

1. Employer discrimination is dumb or at least costly from a profit-making perspective because hiring equally good workers at a lower wage increases profit.

2. Market economies have had the most effect on eliminating discrimination by employers because the profit motive is a powerful incentive—notice that the more employers discriminate against minorities, the greater the profit from hiring a minority worker. Market economies have had some success in mitigating customer discrimination because market transactions bring different groups into regular contact with each other and thereby break down barriers. Market economies have had the toughest time eliminating employee discrimination because this type of discrimination can be self-reinforcing.

Chapter 19

Page 382

If government provides more of national defense than is efficient, it is pulling resources away from other, more valuable goods and having taxpayers bear the burden. People with a very strong preference for national defense would perhaps benefit as well as those involved in providing national defense.

Page 383

Advertising could be used to pay for the upkeep of public parks. Advertising could be seen in obvious places such as signs by entryways to the park, on garbage cans, or on the sides of refreshment stands. If there is a music bandshell or a stage (in larger parks), advertising could be seen on the sides of these structures. Notice that under the Adopt-a-Highway program, advertising on roads supports road cleanup.

Page 387

1. Small communities find it easier to deal with common resource problems than states or nations because they have an easier time enforcing norms (standards of behavior) that reduce free riding. Even so, the more unrelated people that have access to a common good, the harder it is to deal with common resource problems.

2. The establishment of property rights can help solve the tragedy of the commons because people who have property rights have no incentive to overuse a resource. The tragedy of the commons occurs because people have an incentive to overuse common resources: to get theirs before someone else takes it.

Chapter 20
Page 400

National voters have a smaller chance of influencing the election than do local voters, which suggests that people have a greater incentive to be informed about local issues. On the other hand, local issues are less important than national issues and there is less free information (e.g., from online news sources like BuzzFeed or news satire like *The Daily Show*) about local issues than about national issues, which suggests local voters would be even more rationally ignorant than national voters.

Page 403

1. Because of the benefits that special interests receive from current programs, they would fight against the establishment of a commission to examine federal waste. If the commission was set up, these special interests would then try to

"capture" the commission: argue that their specific programs were needed, and exert political pressure to keep these programs. The bearers of the costs of these programs—the taxpayers—are too large and diverse a group to zero in on any particular program. The commission idea might be popular, but the chance of its success is low.

2. The beneficiaries of the local history collection at the library are the users of the collection. Ultimately, the taxpayers of the state pay for it. Benefits are concentrated on a small group, while the costs are spread over a large body of people (the taxpayers). Don't be surprised if the reading room is named after the state senator!

Page 406

If voters are myopic, politicians could prefer a policy with small gains now and big costs later (let's get reelected and maybe someone else will have to deal with the large costs down the road) than a policy with small costs now and large gains later (why jeopardize my chance to get reelected?). For these reasons, dealing with a large potential problem, such as the fiscal sustainability of Medicare, is often put off until the last minute when the solutions are much more difficult and costly.

Page 413

The free flow of ideas helps democracies function by getting alternatives out and on the table. Voters will always be rationally ignorant to some extent, but the more information that is out there and available at low cost, the more voters will be informed, at least about the big issues. Debate and dissent can improve the quality of ideas. The free flow of information reduces the possibility of corruption. New ideas help democracies adapt to changing conditions.

Chapter 21
Page 430

It is plausible that total utility would go up with kidney redistribution because the receiver gains more utility from a kidney that gives them life than the giver loses. Kidney redistribution would also tend to make the worst off better off, at least if we count dying of kidney disease as putting one in the worst off category. There is, however, lots of room for debate on these issues.

Page 431

Surprisingly, all of the theories tend to support immigration. The libertarian theory places strong value on an individual's right to move and engage in peaceful trade, which is what most immigrants want to do. As we argue in the text, immigrants gain much more from immigration than current citizens lose, so utilitarianism also supports immigrants. Finally, being under the veil of ignorance, you don't know whether you are the immigrant or not. If you didn't know which side of the border you were born on, wouldn't you favor immigration?

Philosophers debate these issues but those are the basic considerations.

Chapter 22

Page 441

1. Workers sometimes fear that if they work harder under a piece rate system, they will work themselves out of a job. Lincoln's policy of guaranteed employment reassures workers that productivity will always work to their advantage, not to their detriment.

2. It is sometimes said that the word "tips" stands for "To Insure Prompt Service." Certainly, the idea is that restaurant customers will give bigger tips the better the service, thus giving waiters an incentive to be attentive. Thus, we would predict that waiters would be less attentive in Europe where the tip is typically automatic than in America where it usually is not.

Page 446

1. Professors have an incentive to be known as hard graders because this reputation will keep away all but the serious students and maybe also all but the brightest students. Grading on a curve would encourage the usual diverse spectrum of students, from serious to indifferent and from smart to struggling.

2. In a tournament, one worker's gain is another's loss. Sometimes tournaments can encourage too much competition by discouraging cooperation. If a firm wants its sales staff to work together to land sales, for example, then it would not want a strong tournament scheme. Professors who want their students to work together on projects should not grade on a curve.

Page 449

1. A famous paper in economics calculated that, on average, $10 spent on gifts was worth only $8 to the gift recipients. In other words, when your Uncle gives you $10 in cash, you get $10 worth of utility, but when your Uncle gives you a $10 pair of socks, on average, you get only $8 worth of utility. Thus, according to the author of the study, Joel Waldfogel, Christmas wastes billions of dollars. Even though most people understand this idea when it is explained to them, we don't see a big shift to giving cash. Why not? Perhaps gift giving is valuable precisely because it is challenging. If you spend $10 giving something to someone that they value for $50, this shows how much you must really understand and care for them. Or perhaps we want the gift giver to buy something for us that we would not have bought for ourselves. Or perhaps people give gifts to signal something about themselves. Giving someone a CD of Bach sonatas says something about you that a gift of $15 does not. Understanding the answer to this question may tell us a lot about social life. See Waldfogel, Joel. 1993. The deadweight loss of Christmas. *The American Economic Review* 83(5): 1328–1336.

2. Maybe. Maybe not. If we pay for grades, some people worry that this will stifle the love of learning and perhaps send the message that getting good grades is like a job that the student is free to quit at any time. A number of experiments are currently under way testing these ideas.

Chapter 23

Page 461

According to the efficient markets hypothesis, one cannot consistently beat the market. Therefore, past performance is not a good guide to future success. On average, mutual funds that have performed well in the past are no more likely to perform well in the future than mutual funds that have performed poorly in the past.

Page 467

1. Investing in the stocks of other countries helps to diversify your investments because the economies of other countries do not always rise and fall at the same time as the U.S. economy. If all economies tended to rise and fall together, there would

not be any large benefits in diversifying across countries.

2. If many people dream of owning a football or baseball team, it is likely that the rewards to owning one go beyond monetary rewards. Thus, the monetary return on these assets is likely to be relatively low.

Page 469

This question is being hotly debated by many economists. It can be said that identifying and bursting bubbles is more difficult than it looks. How does the Federal Reserve know when there is a bubble? Increases in prices do not necessarily signify a bubble. Even if it can be said to be fairly certain that a bubble is present, how does the Federal Reserve burst the bubble while avoiding widespread collateral damage?

Chapter 24
Page 476

Consumer Reports has no vested interest in any of the products it evaluates, so this minimizes moral hazard.

Page 480

Real Picassos are rare and valuable, meaning that they don't need to be put on eBay to foster high prices. The Picassos listed on eBay are probably fakes.

Chapter 25
Page 499

1.

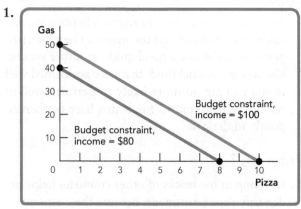

2.

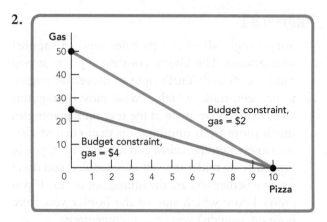

3. No, the relative price of pizza has not changed.

Page 500

Indifference curves can never cross because each consumption bundle must correspond to a unique total utility level. Indifference curves must have a negative slope because more is better.

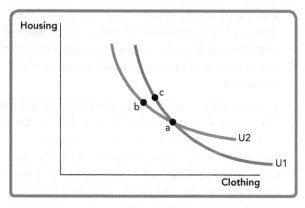

The figure shows indifference curves crossing but notice that this creates a contradiction with our assumptions. Utility is the same on indifference curve U1 and U2 at point a. But since an indifference curve shows points of equal utility, it's also true that utility is the same at points b and c. But point c has more Housing and more Clothing than point b, which violates the assumption that more is better.

A positively sloped indifference curve would also violate the more is better assumption.

GLOSSARY

absolute advantage the ability to produce the same good using fewer inputs than another producer

accounting profit total revenue minus explicit costs

adverse selection when an offer conveys negative information about the product being offered

antitrust laws laws that give the federal government legal authority to prosecute monopolies or attempts to monopolize

arbitrage the practice of taking advantage of price differences for the same good in different markets by buying low in one market and selling high in another market

asymmetric information when one party to an exchange has more or better information than the other party

average cost the cost per unit; the total cost of producing a given quantity divided by that quantity, $AC = TC / Q$

barriers to entry factors that increase the cost to new firms of entering an industry

budget constraint all the consumption bundles that a consumer can afford given his or her income and their prices

bundling the requirement that products be bought together in a bundle or package

buy and hold the practice of buying stocks and then holding them for the long run, regardless of what prices do in the short run

cartel a group of suppliers that tries to act *as if* they were a monopoly

club goods goods that are excludable but nonrival

Coase theorem the principle that if transactions costs are low and property rights are clearly defined, private bargains will ensure that the market equilibrium is efficient even when there are externalities

common resources goods that are nonexcludable but rival

comparative advantage the ability to produce a good or service at a lower opportunity cost than another producer

compensating differential a difference in wages that offsets differences in working conditions for otherwise similar jobs

complements two goods for which a decrease in the price of one leads to an increase in the demand for the other, for example hamburgers and hamburger buns

constant cost industry an industry in which costs of production do not change with greater industry output; shown with a flat supply curve

consumer surplus the consumer's gain from exchange, or the difference between the maximum price a consumer is willing to pay for a certain quantity and the market price

consumer surplus (total) quantity measured by the area beneath the demand curve and above the price

contestable market condition in which a competitor could credibly enter and take away business from the incumbent

coordination game game in which the players are better off if they choose the same strategies than if they choose different strategies, and there is more than one strategy on which to potentially coordinate

corporate culture the shared collection of values and norms that govern how people interact in an organization or firm

credible promise a strategy or promise is credible if it is in an agent's interest to follow through on that strategy or keep the promise

deadweight loss the reduction in total surplus caused by a market distortion or inefficiency

decreasing cost industry an industry in which the costs of production decrease with an increase in industry output; shown with a downward-sloped supply curve

demand curve a function that shows the quantity demanded at different prices

diminishing marginal utility each additional unit of a good adds less to utility than the previous unit

direct network effect when more side-one users increase the value of the good to other side-one users

discount rate the interest rate banks pay when they borrow directly from the Fed at the discount window

dominant strategy a strategy that has a higher payoff than any other strategy no matter the strategies of other players

economic profit total revenue minus total costs including implicit opportunity costs

economies of scale the advantages of large-scale production that reduce average cost as quantity increases

efficient equilibrium the price and quantity that maximizes social surplus

efficient markets hypothesis the claim that the prices of traded assets reflect all publicly available information

efficient quantity the quantity that maximizes social surplus

elastic when the absolute value of the elasticity is greater than 1

elasticity of demand = $\dfrac{\%\Delta Q_D}{\%\Delta P}$

a measure of how responsive the quantity demanded is to a change in price

elasticity of supply = $\dfrac{\%\Delta Q_S}{\%\Delta P}$

a measure of how responsive the quantity supplied is to a change in price

elimination principle the principle that in a competitive market, above-normal profits are eliminated by entry and below-normal profits are eliminated by exit

equilibrium price the price at which the quantity demanded is equal to the quantity supplied

equilibrium quantity the quantity at which the quantity demanded is equal to the quantity supplied

explicit cost a cost that requires a money outlay

external benefit a benefit received by people other than the consumers or producers trading in the market

external cost a cost borne by people other than the consumer or the producer trading in the market

externalities external costs or external benefits

fixed costs costs that do not vary with the quantity produced

forced rider someone who pays a share of the costs of a public good but who does not enjoy the benefits

free rider consuming the benefits of a public good without paying a share of the costs

futures a standardized contract to buy or sell specified quantities of a commodity or financial instrument at a specified price with delivery set at a specified time in the future

great economic problem how to arrange our scarce resources to satisfy as many of our wants as possible

human capital tools of the mind; the productive knowledge and skills that workers acquire through education, training, and experience

implicit cost a cost that does not require an outlay of money

incentives rewards and penalties that motivate behavior

income effect the change in consumption caused by the change in purchasing power from a price change

increasing cost industry an industry in which the costs of production increase with greater output; shown with an upward-sloped supply curve

indirect network effect when more side-one users increase the value of the good to side-two users and more side-two users increase the value to side-one users

inelastic when the absolute value of the elasticity is less than 1

inferior good a good for which demand decreases when income increases

inflation an increase in the general or average level of prices

internalizing an externality adjusting incentives so that decision makers take into account all the benefits and costs of their actions, private and social

investment expenditures private spending on tools, plant, and equipment used to produce future output; that is the purchase of new capital goods

long run the time it takes for substantial new investment and entry to occur

marginal cost (MC) the change in total cost from producing an additional unit

marginal product of labor (MPL) the increase in a firm's revenues created by hiring an additional laborer

marginal rate of substitution (MRS) the rate at which the consumer is willing to trade one good for another and remain indifferent; the MRS is equal to the slope of the indifference curve at that point

marginal revenue (MR) = $\dfrac{\Delta TR}{\Delta Q}$

the change in total revenue from selling an additional unit; for a firm in a competitive industry, MR = Price

marginal utility the change in total utility from consuming an additional unit

market power the power to raise prices above marginal cost without fear that other firms will enter the market

median voter theorem the principle that when voters vote for the policy that is closest to their ideal point on a line, then the ideal point of the median voter will beat any other policy in a majority rule election

monopolistic competition a market with a large number of firms selling similar but not identical products

monopoly a firm with market power

moral hazard when an agent tries to exploit an information advantage in a dishonest or undesirable way

Nash equilibrium a situation in which no player has an incentive to change strategy unilaterally

natural monopoly a situation when a single firm can supply the entire market at a lower cost than two or more firms

network good a good that increases in value to a given person the more other people use the good

nonexcludable when people who don't pay cannot easily be prevented from using the good, the good is nonexcludable

nonrival (or nonrivalrous) goods when one person's consumption of the good does not limit another person's consumption

normal good a good for which demand increases when income increases

normative economics recommendations or arguments about what economic policy should be

Nozick's entitlement theory of justice principle that the distribution of income in a society is just if property is justly acquired and voluntarily exchanged

oligopoly a market dominated by a small number of firms

opportunity cost the value of possibilities lost when a choice is made

optimal consumption rule principle that to maximize utility, a consumer should allocate spending so that the marginal utility per dollar is equal for all purchases

perfect price discrimination (PPD) the situation that exists when each customer is charged his or her maximum willingness to pay

piece rate any payment system that pays workers directly for their output

Pigouvian subsidy a subsidy on a good with external benefits

Pigouvian tax a tax on a good with external costs

platform firm a firm that helps two (or more) sides of a market to connect with one another for mutual gain

positive economics describing, explaining, or predicting without making recommendations

prediction market a speculative market designed so that prices can be interpreted as probabilities and used to make predictions

price ceiling a maximum price allowed by law

price discrimination the selling of the same product at different prices to different customers

price floor a minimum price allowed by law

principal-agent problem how can a principal incentivize an agent to work in the principal's interest even when the agent has information that the principal does not?

prisoner's dilemma situations in which the pursuit of individual interest leads to a group outcome that is in the interest of no one

private cost a cost paid by the consumer or the producer (as opposed to external cost)

private goods goods that are excludable and rival

producer surplus the producer's gain from exchange, or the difference between the market price and the minimum price at which a producer would be willing to sell a particular quantity

producer surplus (total) an amount measured by the area above the supply curve and below the price up to the quantity traded

production possibilities frontier all the combinations of goods that a country can produce given its productivity and supply of inputs

protectionism the economic policy of restraining trade through quotas, tariffs, or other regulations that burden foreign producers but not domestic producers

public choice the study of political behavior using the tools of economics

public goods goods that are nonexcludable and nonrival

quantity demanded the quantity that buyers are willing and able to buy at a particular price

quantity supplied the quantity that sellers are willing and able to sell at a particular price

rational ignorance when the benefits of being informed are less than the costs of becoming informed, a person may be rationally ignorant

Rawls's maximin principle principle that justice requires maximizing the benefits going to society's most disadvantaged group

rent control a price ceiling on rental housing

risk-return trade-off higher returns come at the price of higher risk

saving income that is not spent on consumption goods

scarce when there isn't enough of a specific resource to satisfy all of our wants

shortage a situation in which the quantity demanded is greater than the quantity supplied

short run the period before entry occurs

short-run aggregate supply curve (SRAS) curve that shows the positive relationship between the inflation rate and real growth during the period when prices and wages are sticky

signal an expensive action that is taken to reveal information

social cost the cost to everyone; the private cost plus the external cost

social surplus consumer surplus plus producer surplus plus everyone else's surplus

speculation the attempt to profit from future price changes

statistical discrimination discrimination using information about group averages to make conclusions about individuals

strategic decision making decision making in situations that are interactive

substitutes two goods for which a decrease in the price of one leads to a decrease in demand for the other

substitution effect the change in consumption caused by a change in relative prices holding the consumer's utility level constant

sunk cost a cost that once incurred cannot be recovered

supply curve a function that shows the quantity supplied at different prices

surplus a situation in which the quantity supplied is greater than the quantity demanded

tacit collusion when firms limit competition with one another but they do so without explicit agreement or communication

tariff a tax on imports

total consumer surplus *see* consumer surplus (total)

total costs the costs of producing a given quantity of output

total producer surplus *see* producer surplus (total)

total revenue price times quantity sold: $TR = P \times Q$

tournament a compensation scheme in which payment is based on relative performance

trade quota a restriction on the quantity of goods that can be imported: imports greater than the quota amount are forbidden or heavily taxed

tragedy of the commons the tendency of any resource that is unowned, and hence nonexcludable, to be overused and undermaintained

transaction costs the costs necessary to reach an agreement

tying a form of price discrimination in which one good, called the base good, is tied to a second good called the variable good, for example printer and ink

unit elastic when the absolute value of the elasticity is exactly equal to 1

utilitarianism the idea that the best society maximizes the sum of utility

variable costs costs that vary with output

zero profits (or **normal profits**) the condition when $P = AC$; at this price the firm is covering all of its costs including enough to pay labor and capital their ordinary opportunity costs

REFERENCES

Chapter 1 Notes

1. Quoted in **Christopher, Emma.** 2007. "The slave trade is merciful compared to [this]": Slave traders, convict transportation and the abolitionists. In **Christopher, E., C. Pybus, and M. Rediker** (eds.), *Many Middle Passages*, Chap. 6, pp. 109–128. Berkeley, CA: University of California Press.

2. **Chadwick, Edwin.** 1862. Opening address of the British Association for the Advancement of Science. *Journal of the Statistical Society of London* **25**(4): 502–524.

3. *Ibid.*, Opening address.

4. On the impact of new drugs, see **Lichtenberg, Frank.** 2007. The impact of new drugs on U.S. longevity and medical expenditure, 1990–2003. *American Economic Review* **97**(2): 438–443.

5. **Celis III, William.** December 28, 1991. Study finds enrollment is up at colleges despite recession. *New York Times.*

Chapter 2 Notes

1. On this point, see **Sowell, Thomas.** 1980. *Knowledge and Decisions.* New York: Basic Books. See also Chapter 4 of **Reisman, George.** 1996. *Capitalism: A Treatise on Economics.* Ottawa, IL: Jameson.

2. **Smith, Adam.** August 2, 2006. *An Inquiry into the Nature and Causes of the Wealth of Nations.* Edited by Edwin Cannan, Book IV, II. 2.11. Indianapolis, IN: Library of Economics and Liberty. http://www.econlib.org/library/Smith/smWN13.html. Originally published London: Methuen, 1904 [1776].

3. **Boudreaux, Donald J.** 2008. *Globalization.* Westport, CT: Greenwood Press.

Chapter 3 Notes

1. On changing U.S. demographics and their impact on the economy, see **Kotlikoff, Laurence J., and Scott Burns.** 2004. *The Coming Generational Storm.* Cambridge, MA: MIT Press.

2. **Stigler, George J.** 1971. The theory of economic regulation. *Bell Journal of Economics* Spring: 137–146.

3. https://www.texasalmanac.com/articles/oil-and-texas-a-cultural-history.

4. See information available at the **U.S. Energy Information Administration** website. http://www.eia.gov/.

5. Production costs vary by year and by country and even by well within a country. The figures in the text give an idea of the relative costs by region. For more precise figures, see **Asker, John, Allan Collard-Wexler, and Jan De Loecker.** 2017. Market power, production (mis)allocation and OPEC. Working Paper, Working Paper Series, National Bureau of Economic Research. https://doi.org/10.3386/w23801.

Chapter 4 Notes

1. **Smith, Vernon.** 1991. Experimental economics at Purdue. In **Smith, V.** (ed.), *Papers in Experimental Economics.* Cambridge, UK: Cambridge University Press. Originally appeared in **Horwich, G., and J. P. Quirk** (eds.), *Essays in Contemporary Fields of Economics.* Lafayette, IN: Purdue University Press, 1981.

2. **Conover, Ted.** July 2, 2006. Capitalist roaders. *New York Times Magazine,* pp. 31–37, 50.

Chapter 5 Notes

1. See **International Monetary Fund.** 2005. *World Economic Outlook—2005.* Washington, DC: IMF. See, in particular, Chapter 4.

2. On the elasticity of demand for oil, see **Cooper, John C. B.** 2003. Price elasticity of demand for crude oil: Estimates for 23 countries. *OPEC Review* **27**(1): 1–8. On the elasticity of demand for Minute Maid orange juice, see **Capps, Oral Jr., and H. Alan Love.** 2002. Econometric considerations in the use of electronic scanner data to conduct consumer demand analysis. *American Journal of Agricultural Economics* **84**(3): 807–816.

3. On the elasticity of demand for illegal drugs, see **Cicala, Steve J.** 2005. The demand for illicit drugs: A meta-analysis of price elasticities. Working paper, University of Chicago. On the elasticity of demand for cigarettes, see **Keeler T. E., T. W. Hu, P. G. Barnett, and W. G. Manning.** 1993. Taxation, regulation, and addiction: A demand function for cigarettes based on time-series evidence. *Journal of Health Economics* **12**(1): 1–18.

4. Colorado Department of Revenue. 2014. *Market Size and Demand for Marijuana in Colorado.*

5. On the elasticity of supply for cocoa, see **Burger, K.** 1996. *The European Chocolate Market and the Effects of the Proposed EU Directive.* Amsterdam: Economic and Social Institute, Free University. For the elasticity of supply of coffee, see **Akiyama, T., and P. Varangis.** 1990. The impact of the international coffee agreement on producing countries. *World Bank Economic Review* **4**(2): 157–173.

6. **Callahan, C., F. Rivara, and T. Koepsell.** 1994. Money for guns: Evaluation of the Seattle gun buy-back program. *Public Health Reports* **109**: 472–477.

7. **Welch, William M.** March 17, 2008. Critics take aim at gun buybacks. *USA Today.*

8. See **Mullin, Wallace P.** 2001. Will gun buyback programs increase the quantity of guns? *International Review of Law and Economics* 21: 87–102.

9. For a review of some of the evidence on a variety of crime fighting policies, see **Levitt, Steven D.** 2004. Understanding why crime fell in the 1990s: Four factors that explain the decline and six that do not. *Journal of Economic Perspectives* **18**(1): 163–190.

10. **Glaeser, Edward, and Joseph Gyourko.** 2018. The economic implications of housing supply. *Journal of Economic Perspectives* **32**(1): 3–30. https://doi.org/10.1257/jep.32.1.3.

11. **Green, Richard K., Stephen Malpezzi, and Stephen K. Mayo.** 2005. Metropolitan-specific estimates of the price

elasticity of supply of housing, and their sources. *American Economic Review* **95**(2): 334–339.

12. Compare the zoning map with the U.S. Geological Survey's Soil Type and Shaking Hazard map for the Bay Area that shows that significant portions of the least-restricting buildings areas are on the worst soil type for earthquake hazards. See https://earthquake.usgs.gov/hazards/urban/sfbay/soiltype.

13. It is also possible to make predictions about quantities using two similar formulas.

14. The proof of these formulas is not difficult, but a bit more advanced than is necessary for this textbook. For a proof, see **McAfee, Preston.** 2006. *Introduction to Economic Analysis.* https://authors.library.caltech.edu/25025/2/MCAiea200.pdf.

15. **The White House: George W. Bush.** https://georgewbush-whitehouse.archives.gov/news/releases/2005/11/20051103-10.html.

16. The Klick and Tabarrok and Gruber articles use advanced statistical techniques to argue that the increase in police causes the decrease in crime and the increase in giving causes the decrease in attendance. For more details, see **Klick, J., and A. Tabarrok.** 2005. Using terror alert levels to estimate the effect of police on crime. *Journal of Law and Economics* **48**(1): 267–280. Also, **Gruber, Jonathan.** 2004. Pay or pray? The impact of charitable subsidies on religious attendance. *Journal of Public Economics* **88**(12): 2635–2655.

Chapter 6 Notes

1. On Tepper's move to Florida, see **Frank, Robert**. 2016. One top taxpayer moved, and New Jersey shuddered. *New York Times*, April 30. http://www.nytimes.com/2016/05/01/business/one-top-taxpayer-moved-and-new-jersey-shuddered.html. And on how the elderly wealthy move to low-estate tax states, see **Bakija, Jon and Joel Slemrod**. 2004. Do the rich flee from high state taxes? Evidence from federal estate tax returns. Working Paper 10645. National Bureau of Economic Research, Washington, DC. http://www.nber.org/papers/w10645.

2. On estate taxes in Australia, see **Gans, Joshua S., and Andrew Leigh.** 2009. Did the death of Australian inheritance taxes affect deaths? *Topics in Economic Analysis & Policy* **6**(1), http://works.bepress.com/andrewleigh/4; in the United States, see **Wojciech, Kopczuk, and Joel Slemrod.** 2003. Dying to save taxes: Evidence from estate-tax returns on the death elasticity. *Review of Economics and Statistics* **85**(2): 256–265. The influence of the tax system on births is discussed in **Leonhardt, David.** December 20, 2006. To-do list: Wrap gifts. Have baby. *New York Times*. Also, **Dickert-Conlin, Stacy, and Chandra Amitabh.** 1999. Taxes and the timing of births. *Journal of Political Economy* **107**(1): 161–177.

3. Estimates of the Massachusetts mandate on wages can be found in **Kolstad, Jonathan T., and Amanda E. Kowalski.** 2012. Mandate-based health reform and the labor market: Evidence from the Massachusetts reform. Working Paper 17933. National Bureau of Economic Research, Washington, DC. http://www.nber.org/papers/w17933.

4. Congressional Budget Office. 2014. Labor market effects of the Affordable Care Act: Updated estimates. http://www.cbo.gov/sites/default/files/cbofiles/attachments/45010-breakout-AppendixC.pdf.

Chapter 7 Notes

1. http://www.aboutflowers.com/.

2. Ecuador and Colombia also export millions of roses to the United States.

3. See **Hennock, Mary.** 2002. Kenya's flower farms flourish. *BBC News Online.* http://news.bbc.co.uk/2/hi/business/1820515.stm. For more on Kenya and the Dutch flower market, refer to **McMillan, John.** 2002. *Reinventing the Bazaar.* New York: W. W. Norton. Also **Wijnands, Jo.** 2005. *Sustainable International Networks in the Flower Industry: Bridging Empirical Findings and Theoretical Issues.* The Hague: International Society for Horticultural Science. Also https://mambo.hypotheses.org/1808.

4. For more information, see **Wikipedia.** Ethanol fuel in Brazil. http://en.wikipedia.org/wiki/Ethanol_fuel_in_Brazil.

5. See the *New York Times.* July 8, 2006. Ethanol is the new real estate. Page B5.

6. **American Petrochemical Institute.** How much lubricant in a barrel of crude oil? www.petronomics.com/pdf/crude_oil.pdf.

7. https://rustonpaving.com/asphalt-producers-and-contractors-are-dealing-with-fluctuating-oil-prices/.

8. **Smith, Vernon.** 1982. Microeconomic systems as an experimental science. *American Economic Review* **72**: 923–955.

9. **Federal Highway Administration.** 1993. *A Study of the Use of Recycled Paving Material.* Document no. FHWA-1993-RD-93-147. Washington, DC: FHWA.

10. **Roll, Richard.** 1984. Orange juice and weather. *American Economic Review* **74**(5): 861–880.

11. For much more on prediction markets and how they can be used to make decisions, see **Hanson, Robin D.** 2002. Decision markets. In **Tabarrok, Alexander** (ed.), *Entrepreneurial Economics: Bright Ideas from the Dismal Science,* pp. 79–85. Oxford: Oxford University Press. Also **Hanson, Robin.** 2007. Shall we vote on values, but bet on beliefs? *Journal of Political Philosophy* **21**(2): 151–178.

Chapter 8 Notes

1. A $2'' \times 4''$ refers to the preplaned dimensions, which after planing are typically $1\frac{3}{4}'' \times 3\frac{3}{4}''$; with price controls, the average size fell to $1\frac{5}{8}'' \times 3\frac{5}{8}''$. See **Hall, Thomas.** 2003. *The Rotten Fruits of Economic Controls and the Rise from the Ashes: 1965–1989.* New York: University Press of America.

2. *Business Week.* February 16, 1974. Page 122. Quoted in **Bradley, Robert Jr.** 1996. *Oil, Gas and Government: The U.S. Experience,* Vol. 2, p. 1635. Lanham, MD: Rowman & Littlefield.

3. Prices were frozen at levels no higher than the May 25, 1970, price or a price at which 10% or more of transactions took place in the 30 days prior to August 14, 1971. Some adjustments for seasonal differences were allowed for some products, such as fashion items, but not for oil. See **Bradley**, Vol. 2, especially pp. 1607–1608.

4. See **Hall, Thomas E.** 2003. *The Rotten Fruits of Economic Controls and the Rise from the Ashes, 1965–1989.* New York: University Press of America.

5. **Bradley, Robert Jr.** 1996. *Oil, Gas and Government: The U.S. Experience.* Vol. 1. Lanham, MD: Rowman & Littlefield.

6. See the *Washington Post*. November 26, 1973. Steps ordered by Nixon to meet energy crisis. Page A12.

7. *Time*. December 10, 1973. The shortage's losers and winners.

8. **Grayson, Jackson C.** February 6, 1974. Let's end controls—completely. *Wall Street Journal*, p. 14.

9. See **Bradley,** Vol. 1, pp. 477, 515.

10. **Hall, Jonathan, Cory Hendrick, and Chris Nosko.** 2015. The effects of Uber's surge pricing: A case study. Working Paper.

11. **Brodeur, Abel, and Kerry Nield.** 2018. An empirical analysis of taxi, Lyft and Uber rides: Evidence from weather shocks in NYC, with K. Nield. *Journal of Economic Behavior & Organization* **152**: 1–16.

12. **Cohen, Peter, Robert Hahn, Jonathan Hall, Steven Levitt, and Robert Metcalfe.** 2016. Using big data to estimate consumer surplus: The case of Uber. Working paper.

13. **Diamond, Rebecca, Timothy McQuade, and Franklin Qian.** 2018. The effects of rent control expansion on tenants, landlords, and inequality: Evidence from San Francisco. Working Paper 24181. National Bureau of Economic Research. https://doi.org/10.3386/w24181.

14. **Lindbeck, Assar.** 1972. *The Political Economy of the New Left*. New York: Harper & Row. See especially p. 39.

15. Quoted in **Block, Walter.** August 29, 2006. Rent control. In **Henderson, David R.** (ed.), *The Concise Encyclopedia of Economics*. Indianapolis, IN: Liberty Fund, Library of Economics and Liberty. http://enonlib.org/library/Enc1/RentControl.html.

16. **Oust, Are.** 2018. The removal of rent control and its impact on search and mismatching costs: Evidence from Oslo. *International Journal of Housing Policy*. **18**(3): 433–453. https://doi.org/10.1080/19491247.2017.1336876.

17. **Glaeser, Edward L., and Erzo F. P. Luttmer.** 2003. The misallocation of housing under rent control. *American Economic Review* **93**(4): 1027–1046.

18. For a discussion, see **Arnott, Richard.** 1995. Time for revisionism on rent control? *Journal of Economic Perspectives* **9**(1): 99–120.

19. On housing vouchers, see **Olsen, Edgar.** 2003. Housing programs for low-income households. In **Moffitt, Robert** (ed.), *Means-Tested Transfer Programs in the U.S.* Chicago: University of Chicago Press.

20. Drawn from **Smith, Hedrick.** 1976. Consumers: The art of queuing. In *The Russians*. New York: Ballantine Books.

21. **Bureau of Labor Statistics.** 2013. Characteristics of Minimum Wage Workers 2012. Washington, DC: BLS. http://www.bls.gov/opub/reports/minimum-wage/archive/minimumwageworkers_2012.pdf.

22. For a listing and abstract of many studies on the minimum wage, see **U.S. Congress Joint Economic Committee.** *50 Years of Research on the Minimum Wage*. Recent studies include **Neumark, D., and W. Wascher.** 1992. Employment effects of minimum and subminimum wages: Panel data on state minimum wage laws. *Industrial and Labor Relations Review* **46**(1): 55–81. **Deere, D., K. M. Murphy, and F. Welch.** 1995. Employment and the 1990–1991 minimum-wage hike. *American Economic Review* **85**(2): 232–237. Not all studies find a significant reduction in employment. For a well-designed study that challenges the conventional wisdom, see **Card, David, and Alan B. Krueger.** September 1994. Minimum wages and employment: A case study of the fast-food industry in New Jersey and Pennsylvania. *American Economic Review* **84**: 772–793.

23. **Bureau of Labor Statistics,** *op. cit.*

24. In fact, it's already happening: https://www.today.com/food/restaurants/white-castle-hire-100-robots-flip-burgers-rcna16770.

25. On deregulation, see **Peltzman, Sam.** 1989. The economic theory of regulation after a decade of deregulation. Brookings Papers on Economic Activity. *Microeconomics*: 1–59.

26. On deregulation, see **Morrison, Steven A., and Clifford Winston.** 1986. *The Economic Effects of Airline Deregulation*. Washington, DC: Brookings Institution.

Chapter 9 Notes

1. **Fajgelbaum, Pablo D., Pinelopi K. Goldberg, Patrick J. Kennedy, and Amit K. Khandelwal.** 2019. The return to protectionism. Working Paper 25638. National Bureau of Economic Research. https://doi.org/10.3386/w25638.

2. On the environmental cost of sugar production, see **Schwabach, Aaron.** 2002. How protectionism is destroying the Everglades. *National Wetlands Newsletter* **24**(1): 7–14.

3. https://www.vox.com/new-money/2017/3/29/15035498/autor-trump-china-trade-election.

4. **Fajgelbaum et al.** 2019.

5. **Pitt, David.** 2018. U.S. farmers store record soybean crop as China dispute slashes exports. November 27, 2018. https://www.chicagotribune.com/business/ct-biz-soybean-crop-china-trade-war-20181127-story.html.

6. On the $20 increase in Whirlpool's price, see **Tankersley, Jim.** January 25, 2019. How tariffs stained the washing machine market. *New York Times*, https://www.nytimes.com/2019/01/25/business/economy/how-tariffs-stained-the-washing-machine-market.html? At the time, there were about 63.3 million Whirlpool shares outstanding.

7. On the different reasons why more educated workers and their political representatives tend to be more supportive of free trade, see **Galantucci** (2013) and **Hainmueller and Hiscox** (2006).

8. See **Bellamy, Carol.** 1997. *The State of the World's Children—1997*. New York: Oxford University Press, and UNICEF. https://www.jstor.org/stable/4227511?seq=13#metadata_info_tab_contents.

9. See **Edmonds, Eric V., and Nina Pavcnik.** January 2006. International trade and child labor: Cross-country evidence. *Journal of International Economics*: 115–140.

10. **Bharadwaj, Prashant, Leah K. Lakdawala, and Nicholas Li.** 2013. Perverse consequences of well intentioned regulation: Evidence from India's child labor ban. Working Paper 19602. National Bureau of Economic Research. https://doi.org/10.3386/w19602.

11. Quoted in **Norberg, Johan.** 2003. *In Defense of Global Capitalism*. Washington, DC: Cato Institute.

12. On the 1918 flu, see **Barry, John M.** 2005. *The Great Influenza: The Epic Story of the Deadliest Plague in History*. New York: Penguin. On policy for a future pandemic, see **Cowen, Tyler.** 2005. Avian flu: What should be done. Working paper, Mercatus Center, George Mason University, Arlington, VA.

https://ppe.mercatus.org/system/files/PDF_WP_Avian_Flu_20060726.pdf.

13. To simplify the diagram we also assume that that there are no domestic suppliers.

Chapter 10 Notes

1. On the external cost of antibiotic use, see **Elbasha, Elamin H.** 2003. Deadweight loss of bacterial resistance due to over-treatment. *Health Economics* **12**: 125–138.

2. See the estimate of 18.2 million excess deaths up to December 31, 2021. **Wang, Haidong, Katherine R. Paulson, Spencer A. Pease, Stefanie Watson, Haley Comfort, Peng Zheng, Aleksandr Y. Aravkin, et al.** 2022. Estimating excess mortality due to the COVID-19 pandemic: A systematic analysis of COVID-19-related mortality, 2020–21. *The Lancet* **399**(10334). https://doi.org/10.1016/S0140-6736(21)02796-3.

3. See **Castillo, Juan Camilo, Amrita Ahuja, Susan Athey, Arthur Baker, Eric Budish, Tasneem Chipty, Rachel Glennerster, Alex Tabarrok, et al.** 2021. Market design to accelerate COVID-19 vaccine supply. *Science* **371**(6534): 1107–1109. https://doi.org/10.1126/science.abg0889. See also **Barro, Robert J.** 2022. Vaccination rates and COVID outcomes across U.S. States. Working Paper 29884, Working Paper Series, National Bureau of Economic Research. https://doi.org/10.3386/w29884.

4. **Meade, J. E.** 1952. External economies and diseconomies in a competitive situation. *Economic Journal* **62**: 54–67. On the market for pollination, see **Cheung, Steven N. S.** 1973. The fable of the bees: An economic investigation. *Journal of Law and Economics* **16**: 11–33. Also for a description of the market in the United States, see **Sumner, Daniel A., and Hayley Boriss.** 2006. Bee-conomics and the leap in pollination fees. *Agricultural and Resource Economics Update* **3**(9): 9–11.

5. *Consumer Reports.* June 2007. Washers and dryers: Dirty laundry.

6. The elasticity of demand for electricity is about –0.5, so a 2% increase in the price would reduce consumption by about 1%.

7. For a good overview of the acid rain program, see the EPA's *Acid Rain and Related Programs 2007 Progress Report.* https://www.epa.gov/sites/production/files/2015-08/documents/2007arpreport.pdf.

8. See **Currie, Janet, and Reed Walker.** 2011. Traffic congestion and infant health: Evidence from E-ZPass. *American Economic Journal: Applied Economics* **3**(1): 65–90. https://doi.org/10.1257/app.3.1.65; **Kunn, Steffen, Juan Palacios, and Nico Pestel.** 2019. The impact of indoor climate on human cognition: Evidence from chess tournaments. Working paper, Maastricht University; **Heissel, Jennifer A., Claudia Persico, and David Simon.** 2022. Does pollution drive achievement? The effect of traffic pollution on academic performance. *Journal of Human Resources* **57**(3): 747–776.

Chapter 11 Notes

1. For information on stripper wells, see **U.S. Department of Energy.** *Stripper Well Consortium Looks Back on Fifteen Years of Innovative Technology and Partnership.* https://nswa.us/stripper-wells.

2. **Bernstein, William J.** *A Splendid Exchange: How Trade Shaped the World.* New York: Atlantic Monthly Press, 2008. See p. 62.

Chapter 12 Notes

1. **Schumpeter, Joseph.** 1975/1942. *Capitalism, Socialism and Democracy.* New York: Harper. See, in particular, pp. 82–85.

2. Based on data from 1972 to 1992 in **Adams, William J.** 1993. TV program scheduling strategies and their relationship to new program renewal rates and rating changes. *Journal of Broadcasting and Electronic Media* **37**: 465–475. The renewal rate is probably lower today, as there are more television stations and viewers are more difficult to keep.

Chapter 13 Notes

1. On deaths due to AIDS, see https://www.cdc.gov/nchs/fastats/aids-hiv.htm. On the efficacy of antiretrovirals, see **Weller, I. V., and I. G. Williams.** 2001. ABC of AIDS: Antiretroviral drugs. *British Medical Journal* **322**(7299): 1410–1412. And, on developing countries, **Severe, P., et al.** 2005. Antiretroviral therapy in a thousand patients with AIDS in Haiti. *New England Journal of Medicine* **353**(22): 2325–2334. Also **Lichtenberg, Frank.** 2003. The effect of new drugs on HIV mortality in the U.S., 1987–1998. *Economics and Human Biology* **1**: 259–266.

2. On the cost of AIDS drugs in the United States, see https://www.healthline.com/health/hiv-aids/cost-of-treatment#2.

3. On the number of people worldwide with AIDS, see **Global AIDS Overview**, http://aids.gov/federal-resources/around-the-world/global-aids-overview/.

4. On the cost of Combivir, see http://www.money.cnn.com/magazines/fortune/fortune_archive/2006/09/18/8386170/index.htm?postversion=2006090806 and http://news.bbc.co.uk/2/hi/business/2981015.stm, and further below on patents and differential pricing.

5. See **Pepper, Daniel.** September 18, 2006. Patently unfair. *Fortune.* http://money.cnn.com/magazines/fortune/fortune_archive/2006/09/18/8386170/index.htm?postversion=2006090806.

6. It's possible to prove why the *MR* shortcut is true using calculus. Let the demand curve be written in the form $P = a - bQ$, so the slope is b. Total revenue is $P \times q = TR = aQ - bQ^2$. Marginal revenue is the derivative of total revenue with respect to quantity or $MR = \frac{dTR}{dQ} = a - 2bQ$. Notice that the slope of the *MR* curve is $2b$, twice the slope of the demand curve.

7. American Airlines reservation website.

8. https://jamanetwork.com/journals/jama/fullarticle/2762311; https://www.forbes.com/sites/matthewherper/2013/08/11/how-the-staggering-cost-of-inventing-new-drugs-is-shaping-the-future-of-medicine/?sh=39dcde2b13c3.

9. One study suggests that a 10% decline in price will lead to at least a 5% decline in the number of new drugs. See also **Vernon, John.** 2005. Examining the link between price regulation and pharmaceutical R&D investment. *Health Economics* **14**(1): 1–17.

10. **North, Douglass C.** 1981. *Structure and Change in Economic History.* New York: W. W. Norton. See p. 164.

11. **Kremer, M.** 1998. Patent buyouts: A mechanism for encouraging innovation. *Quarterly Journal of Economics* **113**: 1137–1167.

12. https://www.ppic.org/wp-content/uploads/content/pubs/report/R_103CWR.pdf.

Chapter 14 Notes

1. Information on the Combivir smuggling operation can be found at https://www.cbc.ca/news/world/cheap-aids-drugs -meant-for-africa-sold-in-europe-1.339043 and https://khn .org/morning-breakout/dr00014285/.

2. See **McAfee, R. Preston.** 2002. *Competitive Solutions: The Strategist's Toolkit.* Princeton, NJ: Princeton University Press.

Chapter 15 Note

1. **Barris, David, and Frank Scott.** 2020. Single bidders and tacit collusion in highway procurement auctions. *The Journal of Industrial Economics* **68**(3): 483–522.

Chapter 16 Notes

1. **Watts, Duncan J., M. J. Salganik, and P. S. Dodds.** 2006. Experimental study of inequality and unpredictability in an artificial cultural market. *Science* **311**: 854–856.

2. **Brown, Anne Elizabeth.** 2018. Ridehail revolution: Ride-hail travel and equity in Los Angeles. UCLA. https://eschol-arship.org/uc/item/4r22m57k.

3. **Cui, Ruomeng, Jun Li, and Dennis Zhang.** 2016. Reducing discrimination with reviews in the sharing economy: Evidence from field experiments on Airbnb. SSRN Scholarly Paper ID 2882982. Rochester, NY: Social Science Research Network. https://papers.ssrn.com/sol3 /papers.cfm?abstract_id=2882982.

Chapter 17 Notes

1. See **Bagwell, Kyle.** 2007. The economic analysis of advertising. In **Armstrong, Mark and Robert H. Porter** (eds.), *The Handbook of Industrial Organization,* Vol. III, p. 1745. Amsterdam: Elsevier and North Holland.

2. **Ippolito, Pauline M., and Alan D. Mathios.** Autumn 1990. Advertising and health choices: A study of the cereal market. *RAND Journal of Economics* **21**(3): 459–480.

3. http://www.youtube.com/watch?v=R1NnyE6DDnQ.

4. http://www.beautifullife.info/advertisment/history-of-coca -cola-in-ads/.

5. http://en.wikipedia.org/wiki/Coca-Cola.

6. **McClure, Samuel M., Jian Li, Damon Tomlin, Kim S. Cypert, Latane M. Montague, and P. Read Montague.** October 14, 2004. Neural correlates of behavioral preference for culturally familiar drinks. *Neuron* **44**: 379–387.

7. **Becker, Gary S., and Kevin M. Murphy.** 1993. A simple theory of advertising as a good or bad. *Quarterly Journal of Economics* **108**(4): 941–964.

Chapter 18 Notes

1. On dangerous professions, see, for instance, http://www .forbes.com/2007/08/13/dangerous-jobs-fishing-lead -careers-cx_tvr_0813danger.html.

2. Here is one estimate of coal miner earnings: https://mint .intuit.com/salary/coal-miner#:~:text=the%20United%20 States%3F-,The%20average%20salary%20for%20a%20coal %20miner%20in%20the%20United,bonuses%2C%20tips %2C%20and%20more.

3. **Viscusi, Kip.** 2016. Economic incentives for job safety. *The Environmental Forum.* September/October, p. 51.

4. For one estimate of the union wage premium, see https:// onlinelibrary.wiley.com/doi/full/10.1111/j.1468-0335 .2008.00726.x.

5. **Pencavel, John H.** 2004. The surprising retreat of union Britain. In *Seeking a Premier Economy: The Economic Effects of British Economic Reforms, 1980–2000,* 181–232. University of Chicago Press.

6. **Agan, Amanda, and Sonja Starr.** 2018. Ban the Box, criminal records, and racial discrimination: A field experiment. *Quarterly Journal of Economics* **133**(1): 191–235. https://doi.org/10.1093/qje /qjx028.

7. **Doleac, Jennifer L., and Luke C. D. Stein.** 2013. The visible hand: Race and online market outcomes. *Economic Journal* **123**(572): F469–F492. https://doi.org/10.1111 /ecoj.12082.

Chapter 19 Notes

1. **Preston, Douglas.** March 29, 2019. The day the dinosaurs died. https://www.newyorker.com/magazine/2019/04/08 /the-day-the-dinosaurs-died.

2. From Aristotle, *Politics,* Book II, Chap. III, 1261b. **Jowett, Benjamin** (trans.). 1885. *The Politics of Aristotle.* With Introduction, Marginal Analysis, Essays, Notes, and Indices. Oxford: Clarendon Press. See Vol. 2.

3. The system was later modified so the ITQs gave rights to a certain share of the total allowable catch.

4. https://www.unep.org/news-and-stories/press-release /ozone-layer-recovery-track-helping-avoid-global-warming -05degc.

5. https://www.discovermagazine.com/environment/the -demise-of-easter-islands-eco-collapse-parable.

6. **Demsetz, Harold.** 1967. Towards a theory of property rights. *AER* **57**: 2.

Chapter 20 Notes

1. **House of Commons.** November 11, 1947. Official Report, 5th Series, Vol. 444, cc. 206–207.

2. **Kaiser/Harvard Program on the Public and Health/ Social Policy Survey.** January 1995.

3. https://www.nytimes.com/2017/12/27/business/economy /tax-loopholes.html.

4. See, for instance, **DeLorme, Charles D., Stacey Isom, and David R. Kamerschen.** April 2005. Rent seeking and taxation in the ancient Roman Empire. *Applied Economics* **37**: 705–711. http://ideas.repec.org/a/taf/applec/v37y2005i6p 705-711.html.

5. **Einstein, Katherine Levine, David M. Glick, and Maxwell B. Palmer.** 2019. *Neighborhood Defenders: Participatory Politics and America's Housing Crisis.* New York: Cambridge University Press.

6. See **Fair, Ray.** 2012. *Predicting Presidential Elections and Other Things.* 2nd ed. Redwood City, CA: Stanford University Press.

7. See https://www.jstor.org/stable/2951346?seq=2.

8. **Leeson, Peter T.** 2008. Media freedom, political knowl-edge, and participation. *Journal of Economic Perspectives* **22**(2): 155–169.

9. State Media Monitor Database, https://statemediamonitor.com/. See also **Djankov, Simeon, Caralee McLiesh, Tatiana Nenova, and Andrei Shleifer.** 2003. Who owns the media? *Journal of Law and Economics* **46**(2): 341–381.

10. **Djankov, S., C. McLiesh, T. Nenova, and A. Shleifer.** 2003. Who owns the media? *Journal of Law and Economics* **46**(2): 341–381.

11. See **Conquest, Robert.** 1987. *Harvest of Sorrow.* New York: Oxford University Press.

12. **Sen, Amartya.** August 2, 1990. *Public Action to Remedy Hunger.* Arturo Tanco Memorial Lecture.

13. **Besley, T., and R. Burgess.** 2002. The political economy of government responsiveness: Theory and evidence from India. *Quarterly Journal of Economics* **117**(4): 1415–1452.

14. https://www.natso.com/governmentaffairs.

Chapter 21 Notes

1. https://econjwatch.org/File+download/9/ejw_derc_sep09_whaples.pdf?mimetype=pdf.

2. **Meckler, Laura.** November 13, 2007. Kidney shortage inspires a radical idea: Organ sales. *Wall Street Journal.* Page A1.

3. The commercial logging mortality rate derives from https://www.bls.gov/news.release/pdf/cfoi.pdf. The kidney donation mortality rate derives from https://www.ncbi.nlm.nih.gov/pmc/articles/PMC4447489/.

4. See https://www.euronews.com/culture/2021/09/22/france-announces-2022-culture-budget-exceeds-4-billion-euros and https://www.aft.gouv.fr/en/state-budget.

Chapter 22 Notes

1. **Jacob, Brian A., and Steven D. Levitt.** 2003. Rotten apples: An investigation of the prevalence and predictors of teacher cheating. *Quarterly Journal of Economics* **118**: 843–878.

2. **Figlio, D. N., and L. S. Getzler.** 2006. Accountability, ability and disability: Gaming the system? In **Gronberg, T., and D. Jansen** (eds.), *Improving School Accountability Check-Ups or Choice*, pp. 35–49. *Advances in Applied Microeconomics*, Vol. 14, https://doi.org/10.1016/S0278-0984(06)14002-X.

3. For a calculation along these lines, see **Kane, T., and D. O. Staiger.** 2002. The promise and pitfalls of using imprecise school accountability measures. *Journal of Economic Perspectives* **16**(4): 91–114.

4. For more on private prisons, see **Tabarrok, Alexander** (ed). 2003. *Changing the Guard: Private Prisons and the Control of Crime.* Oakland, CA: The Independent Institute.

5. **Lazear, Edward P.** 2000. Performance pay and productivity. *AER* **90**(5): 1346–1361.

6. **Billikopf, Gregory, and Maxwell Norton.** 1992. Pay method affects vineyard pruner performance. *California Agriculture* **46** (September): 12–13. https://doi.org/10.3733/ca.v046n05p12.

7. **Lemieux, T. W., Bentley MacLeod, and Daniel Parent.** 2007. Performance pay and wage inequality. Working Paper 13128. National Bureau of Economic Research, Washington, DC.

8. **Bertrand, Marianne, and Sendhil Mullainathan.** 2001. Are CEOs rewarded for luck? The ones without principals are. *Quarterly Journal of Economics* **116**: 901–932.

9. *Ibid.*

10. **Bebchuk, Lucian A., Alma Cohen, and Holger Spamann.** November 24, 2009. The wages of failure: Executive compensation at Bear Stearns and Lehman 2000–2008. *Yale Journal on Regulation* **27**: 257–282.

11. **Brown, Jennifer.** 2011. Quitters never win: The (adverse) incentive effects of competing with superstars. *Journal of Political Economy* **119**(5): 982–1013. https://doi.org/10.1086/663306.

12. *Business Week.* January 9, 2006. The struggle to measure performance.

13. On employee ownership of stock, see **National Center for Employee Ownership.**

14. **Thaler, Richard H., and Cass R. Sunstein.** 2008. *Nudge: Improving Decisions about Health, Wealth, and Happiness.* New Haven, CT: Yale University Press.

15. http://www.nytimes.com/2009/09/27/business/economy/27view.html.

Chapter 23 Notes

1. **Malkiel, Burton.** 1996. *A Random Walk Down Wall Street.* 6th ed. New York: W. W. Norton. See, in particular, p. 24.

2. For a comprehensive review of efficient markets and the performance of mutual fund managers, see **Hebner, Mark T.** 2007. *Index Funds: The 12 Step Program for Active Investors.* Irvine, CA: IFA.

3. See **Marshall, Ben, Rochester Cahan, and Jared Cahan.** March 2008. Does intraday technical analysis in the U.S. equity market have value? *Journal of Empirical Finance*: 199–210.

4. On the relatively safe nature of Walmart, see, for instance, this analysis: http://www.slate.com/articles/business/moneybox/2008/02/the_walmart_puzzle.html.

5. **Siegel, Jeremy.** 2022. *Stocks for the Long Run: The Definitive Guide to Financial Market Returns & Long-Term Investment Strategies.* 6th ed. New York: McGraw-Hill.

6. **Smith, Vernon L., Gerry L. Suchanek, and Arlington W. Williams.** 1988. Bubbles, crashes, and endogenous expectations in experimental spot asset markets. *Econometrica* **56**(5): 1119–1151; and **Hussam, Reshmaan N., David Porter, and Vernon L. Smith.** 2008. Thar she blows: Can bubbles be rekindled with experienced subjects? *American Economic Review* **98**(3): 924–937.

7. **Barber, Brad M., Xing Huang, Terrance Odean, and Christopher Schwarz.** 2021. Attention induced trading and returns: Evidence from Robinhood users. SSRN scholarly paper. Rochester, NY. http://dx.doi.org/10.2139/ssrn.3715077.

Chapter 24 Notes

1. **Schneider, Henry S.** 2012. Agency problems and reputation in expert services: Evidence from auto repair. *The Journal of Industrial Economics* **60**(3): 406–433.

2. **Gottschalk, Felix, Wanda Mimra, and Christian Waibel.** 2020. Health services as credence goods: A field experiment. *The Economic Journal* **130**(629): 1346–1383. https://doi.org/10.1093/ej/ueaa024.

3. **Houser, Daniel, and John Wooders.** 2006. Reputation in auctions: Theory, and evidence from eBay. *Journal of Economics & Management Strategy* **15**(2): 353–369, doi:10.1111/j.1530-9134.2006.00103.x.

4. Gaming the college rankings, http://www.nytimes.com/2012/02/01/education/gaming-the-college-rankings.html?pagewanted=all.

5. **Johnson, Erin M., and M. Marit Rehavi.** 2016. Physicians treating physicians: Information and incentives in childbirth. *American Economic Journal: Economic Policy* **8**(1): 115–141.

6. On the incentives of real estate agents, see **Levitt, Steven D., and Chad Syverson.** 2008. Market distortions when agents are better informed: The value of information in real estate transactions. *Review of Economics and Statistics* **90**(4): 599–611, doi:10.1162/rest.90.4.599.

7. **Goolsbee, Austan, Steven Levitt, and Chad Syverson.** *Microeconomics.* New York: Worth, 2012, beginning of Chapter 15, drawn from U.S. Department of Transportation, National Transportation Statistics 2012. For recent data, see https://www.bts.gov/content/new-and-used-passenger-car-sales-and-leases-thousands-vehicles.

8. **Genesove, David.** 1993. Adverse selection in the wholesale used car market. *Journal of Political Economy* **101**(4): 644–665.

9. See **David Hemenway,** 1990. Propitious selection. *Quarterly Journal of Economics* **105**(4): 1063–1069, and, more generally, search for the term "propitious selection."

10. http://econlog.econlib.org/archives/2013/02/sheepskin_effec.html.

11. **Gambetta, Diego.** 2009. *Codes of the Underworld: How Criminals Communicate.* Princeton, NJ: Princeton University Press.

Chapter 25 Note

1. For a good discussion, see **Persky, Joseph.** 1997. Retrospectives: Classical family values: Ending the poor laws as they knew them. *Journal of Economic Perspectives* **11**(1): 179–189.

Appendix A Notes

1. **Clark, Gerald.** 1969. What happens when the police go on strike. *New York Times Magazine*, November 16, Sec. 6, pp. 45, 176–185, 187, 194–195.

2. **Klick, Jonathan, and Alexander Tabarrok.** 2005. Using terror alert levels to estimate the effect of police on crime. *Journal of Law & Economics* **48**(1): 267–280.

INDEX

Note: Page numbers in **boldface** indicate where terms are defined. Page numbers followed by *f* indicate figures, those followed by *n* indicate footnotes, and those followed by *t* indicate tables.

Supply and Demand

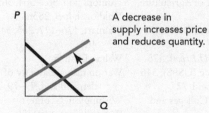

A decrease in supply increases price and reduces quantity.

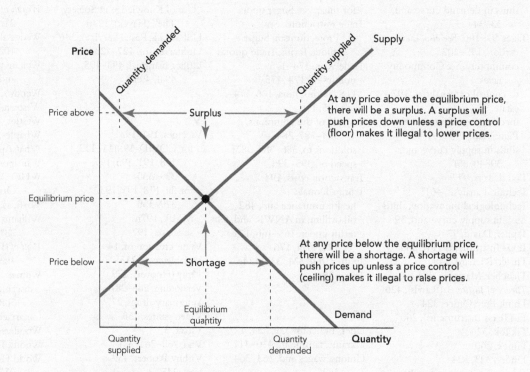

At any price above the equilibrium price, there will be a surplus. A surplus will push prices down unless a price control (floor) makes it illegal to lower prices.

At any price below the equilibrium price, there will be a shortage. A shortage will push prices up unless a price control (ceiling) makes it illegal to raise prices.

An increase in demand increases price and quantity.

A decrease in demand decreases price and quantity.

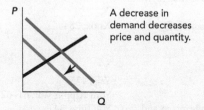

An increase in supply decreases price and increases quantity.

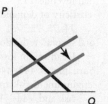

Elasticity

The elasticity of demand is a measure of how responsive the quantity demanded is to a change in price.

$$E_d = \frac{\text{Percentage change in quantity demanded}}{\text{Percentage change in price}} = \frac{\%\Delta Q_{\text{Demanded}}}{\%\Delta \text{Price}} = \frac{\dfrac{Q_{\text{Before}} - Q_{\text{After}}}{(Q_{\text{Before}} + Q_{\text{After}})/2}}{\dfrac{P_{\text{Before}} - P_{\text{After}}}{(P_{\text{Before}} + P_{\text{After}})/2}}$$

Inelastic Demand

$|E_d| \geq 1$

Quantity is not very Responsive to Price

Revenue and price move in same direction.

$R = P \times Q$

Elastic Demand

$|E_d| > 1$

Quantity is very Responsive to Price

Revenue and price move in opposite directions.

$R = P \times Q$

Monopoly

Marginal Revenue, *MR*, is the change in total revenue from selling an additional unit.

Marginal Cost, *MC*, is the change in total cost from producing an additional unit.

To maximize profit, a firm produces until $MR = MC$.

The more inelastic the demand, the greater the monopoly markup of *P* over *MC*.

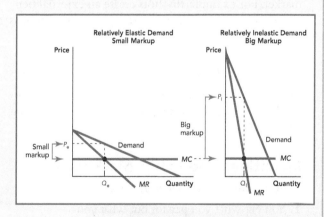

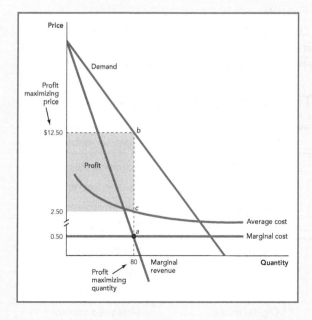

The Principles of Price Discrimination

1a. If the demand curves are different, it is more profitable to set different prices in different markets than a single price that covers all markets.

1b. To maximize profit, the firm should set a higher price in markets with more inelastic demand.

2. Arbitrage makes it difficult for a firm to set different prices in different markets, thereby reducing the profit from price discrimination.

Externalities

An **external cost** is a cost paid by people other than the consumer or the producer trading in the market. For example, pollution creates an external cost. When external costs are significant, output is too high.

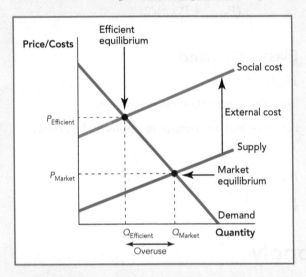

An **external benefit** is a benefit received by people other than the consumers or producers trading in the market. For example, flu shots create an external benefit. When external benefits are significant, output is too low.

Labor Markets

In a competitive market, firms will hire workers until the marginal product of labor equals the wage, $MPL = W$.

Incentives and Labor Markets

Four lessons of good incentive design:

1. You get what you pay for but what you pay for is not always what you want.
2. Tie pay to performance to reduce risk.
3. Money isn't everything.
4. Nudges can work.

A **compensating differential** is a difference in wages that offsets differences in working conditions.

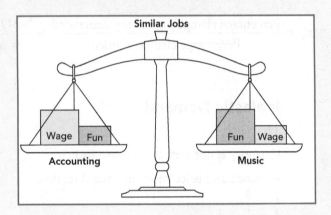

Public Goods and Tragedy of the Commons

A **good is nonexcludable** if people who don't pay cannot be easily prevented from using the good.

A **good is nonrival** if one person's use of the good does not reduce the ability of another person to use the same good.

A **free rider** enjoys the benefits of a public good without paying a share of the costs.

A **forced rider** is someone who pays a share of the costs of a public good but who does not enjoy the benefits.

The **tragedy of the commons** is the tendency of any resource that is unowned and hence nonexcludable to be overused and undermaintained.

The Four Types of Goods

	Excludable	Nonexcludable
Rival	**Private Goods** Jeans Hamburgers Contact lenses	**Common Resources** Tuna in the ocean The environment Public roads
Nonrival	**Club Goods** Streaming TV Wi-Fi Digital music	**Public Goods** Asteroid deflection National defense Mosquito control